ETHICAL THEORY AND BUSINESS

Second Edition

Edited by

TOM L. BEAUCHAMP
Georgetown University

NORMAN E. BOWIE
University of Delaware

Prentice-Hall, Inc., Englewood Cliffs, New Jersey 07632

Library of Congress Cataloging in Publication Data
Main entry under title:

Ethical theory and business.

  Includes bibliographies.
  1. Business ethics—Addresses, essays, lectures.
2. Business ethics—Case studies—Addresses, essays,
lectures.   3. Industry—Social aspects—United States—
Addresses, essays, lectures.   4. Industry—Social
aspects—United States—Case studies—Addresses,
essays, lectures.   5. Corporation law—United States.
I. Beauchamp, Tom L.   II. Bowie, Norman E., 1942–
HF5387.E82 1983   174'.4   82–21585
ISBN   0-13-290452-7

Printed in the United States of America

10   9   8   7   6   5   4   3

Editorial/production supervision by Virginia Cavanagh Neri
Interior design by Fred Bernardi
Cover design by Karolina Harris
Manufacturing buyer: Harry Baisley

ISBN 0-13-290452-7

Prentice-Hall International, Inc., *London*
Prentice-Hall of Australia Pty. Limited, *Sydney*
Prentice-Hall of Canada, Ltd., *Toronto*
Prentice-Hall of India Private Limited, *New Delhi*
Prentice-Hall of Japan, Inc., *Tokyo*
Prentice-Hall of Southeast Asia Pte. Ltd., *Singapore*
Whitehall Books Limited, *Wellington, New Zealand*

CONTENTS

Theories of Corporate Social Responsibility

Legal Perspectives

Cases

3   EMPLOYEE RIGHTS   128

INTRODUCTION   128

The Status of Employee Rights

Free Speech and Trade Secrets

Worker Safety

**5   ADVERTISING AND INFORMATION
DISCLOSURE   310**

INTRODUCTION   310

9   THEORIES OF ECONOMIC JUSTICE   590

PREFACE

When the first edition of *Ethical Theory and Business* went to the press in late 1977, business ethics had received very little attention by philosophers, and was hidden under other labels in business schools. Although there were signs of increased pressure for business schools to emphasize ethics in the curriculum, there was little agreement about what needed to be done. Much has changed since 1977. The American Assembly of Collegiate Schools of Business has insisted that ethics be a part of the business student's education, and a host of philosophers have contributed to an increasingly sophisticated literature in business ethics. Collaboration between philosophers and business professors is increasingly common, and the field of so-called "applied ethics" has flourished in the intervening years.

Faculty familiar with the first edition of *Ethical Theory and Business* will see that the second edition is not just a cosmetically changed edition of the first, hastily fashioned to counter the competing forces. This edition is radically reorganized. An entirely new and greatly expanded Chapter 1 appears, and a chapter on employee rights has been added. Over half the articles, case studies, and legal perspectives are new. The case studies have been expanded not only in number, but in detail as well. New subsections have been added to several chapters. We have also made every effort to have this edition reflect topics currently emphasized in the literature and to make available the best current articles. We have retained our emphasis on controversy and sophisticated analysis consistent with a style accessible to students. Minimal technical jargon and maximal teachability have been important criteria.

We have received many helpful suggestions for improving the anthology. It is impossible to recognize them all, but special thanks should be given to R. Jay Wallace, Jr., John Atwell, Joseph Des Jardins, Herbert J. Nelson, Lisa Newton, Raymond Pfeiffer, Janice Schultz, and the unidentified Prentice-Hall Reviewers. Both Sandy Manno and Mary Ellen Timbol, assisted by Tim Hodges, shepherded draft after draft of this new edition through the press—always with patience and good humor.

T.L.B.
N.E.B.

CHAPTER 1

ETHICAL THEORY AND ITS APPLICATION TO BUSINESS

The problems and issues discussed in this book have emerged from professional practice in various fields of business and include problems related to law, economics, engineering, and international relations. In order to understand how special moral problems arise in business, some acquaintance with philosophical ethics and the nature of moral problems in general is advisable. Many essays in this volume are not written by philosophers, however, and a basic grasp of legal theories, economic theories, tax policy, marketing and management practices, and the like can often enhance the understanding of an author's orientation and purposes. Nonetheless, the unifying theme in the volume is that of moral reflection, and ethical theory is the dominant field that promotes such reflection.

The goal of this first chapter is to provide a foundation in ethical theory sufficient for reading and criticizing essays in the ensuing chapters. The first half of this chapter is entitled "Fundamental Concepts and Problems" because it introduces certain basic and recurring distinctions, definitions, and issues. The second half examines the most influential and relevant normative theories.

PART ONE: FUNDAMENTAL CONCEPTS AND PROBLEMS

MORALITY AND ETHICAL THEORY

"Ethical theory," as used in the title of this book, refers to the philosophical study of the nature and justification of ethical principles, decisions, and problems. The term "morality," by contrast, refers to traditions of belief about right and wrong conduct. Morality, unlike ethical theory, is a social institution with a history and a code of learnable rules. Like political constitutions and natural languages, morality exists before persons are instructed in its rules, and its requirements are learned as part of the acculturation process.

Morality and Prudence

The first step in this process is learning how to distinguish moral rules from rules of prudence (self-interest). This task is sometimes difficult, because the two kinds of rules are often learned together. For example, we are constantly reminded in our early years that we must observe such rules as "Don't touch the hot stove," "Don't cross the street without looking both ways," "Brush your teeth after meals," and "Eat your vegetables." Most of these oughts and ought nots are instructions in our self-interest. They are instructions in *prudence.* However, we are later given oughts or ought nots of a different kind. We are told either by our parents, teachers, or peers that there are certain things we ought or ought not to do because these actions affect the interests of other people. "Don't pull your sister's hair." "Don't take money from your mother's pocketbook." "Share your toys." "Write a thank-you note to Grandma." As we grow up, we learn what society expects of us in terms of taking the interests of other people into account. We thus learn what society expects in the way of *moral* behavior.

Unfortunately it is not quite as easy to distinguish between morality and prudence in business judgments. Very often morality and prudence are bound together in a single statement. A simple but not insignificant example of both moral and prudential reasoning at work in business is found in the decision by Procter and Gamble to take off the market, within two weeks, its Rely brand tampons, which had been causally linked to toxic shock syndrome.[1] Procter and Gamble had invested twenty years of research and approximately $75 million in the product's preparation. But it became convinced, after its own thorough investigation, that there was a possible causal connection to the toxic shock condition. At first, when scientific research seemed to indicate that the material in the tampons did not encourage bacterial growth, Edward G. Harness, chairman of the board and chief executive of Procter and Gamble, said he was "determined to fight for a brand, to keep an important brand from being hurt by insufficient data in the hands of a bureaucracy."[2] However, by September 18, 1980, Procter and Gamble stopped production of the Rely tampon, probably because of negative publicity and a report from the Center for Disease Control that linked Rely statistically to toxic shock syndrome—a report Procter and Gamble's own physicians, microbiologists, and epidemiologists were unable to refute. "That was the turning point," Mr. Harness said. The company subsequently pledged their research expertise to the Center for Disease Control to investigate toxic shock syndrome, and agreed to finance and direct a large educational program about the disease, as well as issue a warning to women not to use Rely. Referring to the Rely case, Mr. Harness later made the following public announcement:

> Company management must consistently demonstrate a superior talent for keeping profit and growth objectives as first priorities. However, it also must have enough breadth to recognize that enlightened self-interest requires the

company to fill any reasonable expectation placed upon it by the community and the various concerned publics. Keeping priorities straight and maintaining the sense of civic responsibility will achieve important secondary objectives of the firm. Profitability and growth go hand in hand with fair treatment of employees, of direct customers, of consumers, and of the community.[3]

The extent to which prudence and morality are intertwined and the extent to which they ought to be distinguished, are subjects to which we shall return in the section on the Problem of Egoism (pp. 15–21).

Moral Reflection

Many people go through life with an understanding of morality largely given to them by their culture. Other persons, however, are not satisfied simply to conform to the morality of society. Such individuals want difficult questions answered: Is what our society forbids really wrong? Is what our society values really good? What is the purpose of morality? Do the moral rules of society fit together in a unified whole, or are there conflicts and inconsistencies in society's moral rules? If there are conflicts and inconsistencies, how should they be resolved? What should we do when we face a moral problem for which society has, as yet, provided no instruction?

One who raises such questions and works at answering them is engaged in rudimentary ethical inquiry. Philosophical ethics is inquiry into theories of what is good and evil and into what is right and wrong, and thus is inquiry into what we ought and ought not to do. Persons actively engaged in normative ethics examine the theoretical basis of a society's morality and, where appropriate, make suggestions for improvement. Their reflection eventuates in systematic ethical theories. Ethical theory is often critical of conventional moral beliefs, and hence the two can easily conflict. (Despite these terminological distinctions, the terms "ethical" and "moral" will be subsequently employed as identical in meaning, and "ethics" will be used as a very general term referring both to moral beliefs and to ethical theory. "Ethical theory" and "philosophical ethics," however, will be reserved for philosophical theories, including philosophical reflection on social morality.)

It is common to hear people say that both morality and ethical theory are of little concern to businesspersons. They say that ethics is ethics and business is business, and that executives like Mr. Harness only appeal to moral notions because the appeal is good for business. The implication is either that ethical issues do not matter much to people in business, or that business presents no distinctive ethical problems. Such views seem odd, for the existence of business can depend on the moral behavior of the vast majority of citizens. Imagine trying to practice business in a society where lying, stealing, and other immoral actions are routine. Business could not be practiced in such a society, for business often requires a society where contracts are honored and where property is respected. Moreover, bribery, kickbacks, fraud, and certain monopolistic activities in the restraint of trade have all been judged inappropriate, precisely because they involve immoral practices. There also exist special moral norms for business activity, norms usually devised by businesspersons themselves.

There are, for example, standards of good business practice, some of which are written into special business codes of ethics—as we shall witness many times in this volume.

Nonetheless, the morality of many business practices has recently been questioned. Even actions long accepted in the business community are now widely condemned as immoral—e.g., the discharge of waste into the air and water, business relocation on economic grounds alone, large political contributions to those who support business interests, and employment practices that result from mergers. Many persons in society are claiming that these business practices are no longer acceptable. Because business activity takes place within a larger social framework, businesspersons are forced to reflect on these moral judgments of their activities. But what does it mean to reflect on morality and to make moral judgments?

TAKING MORAL POSITIONS

This text contains selections by people who take moral positions on issues. While we now have some understanding of the nature of morality, virtually nothing has been said thus far about the distinction between taking a moral position and taking some other kind of position on, for example, a prominent controversy over acceptable business practices. We all have some familiarity with this problem, for people often act as if they had the weight of morality behind their pronouncements, while others wonder whether the proclaimed "moral position" has anything to do with morality. For example, in the summer of 1980, a United States senator accused France of "immorally" providing nuclear capabilities to certain Arab countries in the Middle East in return for rights to oil. The senator clearly held a position on an issue, but was it a moral one, or was it entirely rooted in some political, personal, or even prejudiced conception of foreign policy?

Many critics of the moral views of others accuse them of reacting emotionally and thereby confusing their *personal* views with a sober, properly distanced *moral* position. Can such a distinction be sustained, and if so, how? These questions lead us to reflect more generally on how a moral position is properly contrasted with prejudiced, personal, or political positions, as well as with positions rooted in emotion or rationalization.

The "weight of morality" is generally decided through a process of history and social consensus, a context which business, of course, cannot escape. In professional contexts, one important way of defending a view as morally proper is by appeal to professional obligations, requirements, or rules that are so basic and broadly presupposed that they scarcely need to be made explicit. It is validly assumed, for example, that the executive has an obligation to promote the interests of his or her corporation. These professional obligations may be understood as examples of the class of duties which sociologists characterize as "role norms": persons behave in conformity to the rules of institutions and organizations to which they belong, and their professional obligations are among a set of duties and responsibilities established in such institutional settings. The moral urgency of some professional duties and responsibilities is often reflected in professional codes of ethics, where it is common to discover basic role obligations developed in detail. Such codes of ethics are occasionally discussed in this volume, especially in Chapter 8. One important question about such codes is how the particular moral positions delineated in such codes are to be *justified,* for codes too take a moral position.

Moral philosophers have formed a loose consensus (1) that only a restricted range of general ethical theories counts as providing "very general standards" and "ultimate grounds" for more particular moral judgments and (2) that our everyday moral judgments need justification and refinement through *some* more general moral principles or theory. Let us, then, look further at how morality and ethical theory can be examined and defended.

APPROACHES TO THE STUDY OF MORALITY

Morality and ethical theory can be studied and developed by a variety of methods, but four general approaches have dominated the literature. Two of these approaches presumably describe and analyze morality without taking moral positions; two other approaches do involve taking moral positions and involve some appeal to ethical theory. These four approaches can be outlined as follows:

Descriptive approaches
    Scientific studies
    Conceptual studies
Prescriptive approaches
    General normative ethics
    Applied normative ethics

These categories do not express rigid and always clearly distinguishable approaches. Indeed, they often overlap. Nonetheless, when understood as broad polar contrasts exemplifying models of inquiry, these distinctions are valuable.

First among the two descriptive fields of inquiry is the *scientific study* of ethics. The factual description and explanation of moral behavior and beliefs as performed by anthropologists, sociologists, and historians is typical of this approach. Here moral attitudes, codes, and beliefs are described. These include sexual practices, codes of honor, and rules governing permissible killing in a society. An example can be found in certain *Harvard Business Review* articles that report what business executives think is morally acceptable and morally unacceptable.

The second descriptive field involves the *conceptual study* of ethics. Here the meanings of central terms in ethics such as "right," "obligation," "good," "virtue," and "responsibility" are analyzed, and forms of moral reasoning are studied. The proper analysis of the term "morality" and the distinction between the moral and the nonmoral is a typical example of a conceptual problem. (Descriptive ethics and conceptual studies may not be the only forms of nonnormative inquiry. For example, there may be biological bases of moral behavior that deserve inquiry.)

One matter of conceptual interest for business ethics is that persons in business often seem to mean something rather different in their use of the term "ethics" than do philosophers. "Ethics" is sometimes implicitly understood in the business community as a code word for a set of rules of correct conduct, in the sense of things one must do in order to avoid trouble with the law or with one's associates. Ethics is implicitly thought of as something that should not be a public matter; it should stay "in-house" or "in the profession." For example, the principles of confidentiality of information adopted at a computer center may be thought of as only a private list of principles for the employees of that computing center, and not something company officials would wish to make public. Of course, not all codes or sets of ethical principles in business can be understood in this way, for companies are often eager to make their principles and practices public. The conceptual point of importance is that the idea of a private code or one not meant to apply to all persons in a group is very foreign to what philosophers mean when they use the terms "morality" and "ethics."[4]

General normative ethics, as noted above, is a prescriptive study that attempts to formulate and defend basic moral norms governing moral life. Normative moral philosophy thus aims at determining what *ought* to be done, as distinguished from what *is* in fact practiced. Ideally, an ethical theory will provide reasons for adopting a whole system of moral principles or virtues. The most prominent and general of these theories are utilitarianism and deontology. Utilitarians argue that there is one and only one fundamental principle determining right action, which can be roughly stated as "An action is morally right if and only if it produces at least as great a balance of value over disvalue as any available alternative action." Deontologists, by contrast, have argued that one or more fundamental principles of ethics differ from the principle of utility. These are usually principles of strict duty, such as "Never treat another person merely as a means to your own goals." We shall examine both forms of these theories in Part Two, together with other dimensions of ethical theory.

The principles of general normative ethics are commonly applied to such specific moral problems as abortion, widespread hunger, corporate responsibility, and racial and sexual discrimination. This use of ethical theory is therefore referred to as *applied ethics.* Philosophical treatments of medical ethics, engineering ethics, journalistic ethics, jurisprudence, and business ethics involve distinct areas of the application of general ethical principles to moral problems that arise in these professions. Substantially the same general ethical principles apply to the problems across these professional fields and in areas beyond professional ethics as well. One might appeal to principles of justice, for example, in order to illuminate and resolve issues of taxation, health care distribution, environmental responsibility, criminal punishment, and reverse discrimination (see Chapters 7, 8, and 9). Similarly, principles of veracity (truthfulness) apply to debates about secrecy and deception in international politics, misleading advertisements in business ethics; balanced reporting in journalistic ethics, and the disclosure of the nature and extent of an illness to a patient in medical ethics. Presumably, greater clarity about the conditions in general under which truth must be told and when it may be withheld would enhance understanding of what is required in all of these areas. (See portions of Chapters 3 and 5.)

Applied ethics is the focus of most essays in this volume. It has been frequently employed in recent years in contexts of public policy and business ethics, where an interdisciplinary approach is required. Practitioners bring experience and technical information to the discussion, while moral philosophers contribute familiarity with traditions of ethical reflection, insights into various distinctions and categories that can illuminate moral issues, and skill in probing the presuppositions and implications of positions.

JUSTIFICATION IN ETHICS

Many problems in applied ethics are best illustrated by particularly graphic cases. The following case is an example: In January of 1971, the Equal Employment Opportunity Commission (EEOC) brought charges of discrimination in hiring and promotion against American Telephone and Telegraph Company (AT&T), the largest private employer in the United States. The EEOC filed a petition to block a rate increase of $385 million per year until the company ended its discriminatory practices. The petition alleged that job bias at AT&T kept rates from declining. AT&T denied the charges, claiming that its record demonstrated equality of treatment for minorities and women. The company adduced statistics showing that it was in no respect guilty of the alleged injustices. AT&T produced 100,000 pages of documents and statistics to justify its contentions, and the EEOC filed 30,000 pages of counterargument. The EEOC claimed that customers would pay lower phone rates if AT&T ended its discriminatory practices, and that if AT&T had operated to minimize labor costs (i.e., if it had employed workers at the lowest possible wage regardless of sex), the company would have employed more women in all job categories, for a total reduction in rates of 2 to 4 percent. (For further detail and documentation, see Case 4 at the end of Chapter 9.)

Moral arguments about this and most cases focus on whether certain judgments or practices are justified. In the AT&T case, a central question is whether minorities and women were justifiably treated in the distribution of positions and promotions. Almost everyone interested in moral problems at some point asks the more general question, Can answers about what is morally good and right be justified at all? If so, what counts as an adequate justification? An easy answer to this question is to say that moral judgments are justified by giving *reasons* for them. However, not all reasons are *good* reasons, and not all good reasons are *sufficient* for justification. For example, as we shall see in Chapter 8, a good reason for regulating various business practices—such as those of industries involved in the use of radioactive products—is that they present a clear and present

danger to other persons. Many have believed that this reason is also sufficient to justify a broad set of regulatory practices, e.g., the EEOC protections against employer "discrimination" as found in the AT&T case. By
contrast, a reason sometimes offered as a good reason for regulation but
which many people consider a bad reason (because it involves a deprivation of liberty), is that persons in business simply cannot be trusted to
police themselves. If someone holds that past failures of self-regulatory
mechanisms constitute a good and sufficient reason to justify federal
regulation, we expect that person to give us some further account as to *why
this reason is both good and sufficient.* That is, we expect the person to give further justifying reasons for his or her belief that the reason offered is good
and sufficient. We expect the person to refer, for example, to the dire consequences for the public interest if government fails to intervene. We expect the person to invoke certain principles about the importance of protecting against inadvertent disasters such as the near disaster at Three Mile
Island. In short, we expect the person to give a set of reasons that amounts
to an argued defense of his or her perspective on the issues.

Every belief we hold is subject to challenge of this sort and therefore to
justification by reasoned argument. No matter what we believe about the
justifiability of certain business practices, our views are subject to criticism
and require defense. But what is an argued defense, and what role do
arguments play in attempts at justification? An argument is a group of
related statements where one statement in the group, the conclusion, is
claimed to be either the consequence of or justified by the others, called
variously evidence, reasons, grounds, and premises. In general, every
argument can be put into the following form: *X* is correct; therefore, *Y* is
correct. However, arguments are rarely presented in this simplified form.
More often they are submerged in complex patterns of discourse; they are
disguised by rhetoric, irrelevancies, redundancies, and subtle connections
with other arguments.

Moreover, an argument in which conclusions correctly follow from
premises does not necessarily constitute a proof. The term "proof" refers
to a sound argument or one which establishes the correctness of its conclusion. Just as there are good and bad reasons, so there are good and bad
arguments. Logic alone, however, cannot determine whether the *premises*
in an argument are correct or incorrect. Some form of evidence or insight
must determine whether the premises used are acceptable, and we must
know whether the premises are acceptable in order to know whether an
argument proves anything. It is the business of *logic* to tell us whether conclusions follow from premises; it is the business of a substantive inquiry
such as *ethics* to tell us whether the premises should be accepted in the first
place. For example, only ethics, not logic, can tell us if it is ever morally
permissible to bluff or deceive in business deals (a subject discussed in
Chapter 5).

However, different kinds of premises are found in moral reasoning and
argument. A moral *judgment,* for example, expresses a decision or verdict
about a particular action or character trait. Moral *rules* are general guides
governing actions of a certain kind; they assert what ought (or ought not) to

be done in a range of particular cases. Moral *principles* are more general and in some respects more fundamental than such rules, and serve (at least in some systems of ethics) as the justifying reasons for accepting rules. A simple example of a moral rule is, "It is wrong to deceive clients"; but moral principles of autonomy and privacy (as discussed below), may be the basis of several moral rules of the deception-is-wrong variety. Finally, ethical *theories* are bodies of principles and rules, more or less systematically related.

These different kinds of moral discourse are often at work in moral justification. Judgments about what morally ought to be done can be viewed as justified (i.e., good and sufficient independent reasons for the judgments are given) by rules, which in turn are justified by principles, which then are justified by ethical theories. Many justifications found in this volume either conform to or can be reconstructed to conform to this model. How we are to determine the best justifying reasons and theories—and thus the best premises to use in moral arguments—is, however, an open question. As we shall see in Part Two of this Introduction, it is unreasonable to expect certainty in ethical theory, but defense of a point of view by principled reflection, criticism, and justification is imperative.

THE CONCEPT OF CONSCIENCE

The slogan "Let your conscience be your guide" has long been for many the bottom line in moral justification, and this slogan remains an influential one in popular ethical writings. It also frequently receives attention in articles on business ethics. In a society where considerable latitude of autonomous choice is allowed in circumstances of open social disagreement, it is easy to see why autonomous agents would appeal to their own heartfelt reasons as a justification for various forms of resistance to social pressures and arrangements. There is a distinguished literature on conscientious objection that helpfully points to the importance of preserving autonomous disagreement in such contexts; in light of this literature, appeals to conscience cannot be set aside as merely an unjustifiable form of relativism or subjectivism. We shall encounter several instances of "conscientious objection" in the section on whistle blowing (Chapter 4).

An interesting case of conscience occurred in 1965 when a physical plant superintendent at Eastern Illinois University repeatedly protested what he believed to be faulty construction plans for a new campus building expansion program. Against the advice of a close friend, he did not simply report his evaluation; he objected again and again. His complaints, however, fell on unsympathetic ears in the university administration, and soon his pay was cut $100 a month, his responsibilities were diminished, and a psychiatric examination was recommended for him by the president of the University. Subsequently his contract was not renewed, and he resigned. After some public furor, the governor of Illinois appointed a committee of engineering experts to investigate the alleged construction irregularities. The plant superintendent, Gerald Cravey, offered the following reason for his dogged insistence on revisions in the construction plans: "I sometimes think that my friend's advice would have been the best course. But I still had to live with myself. Today I can look myself in the mirror when I shave. I couldn't if I had kept quiet about what I saw."[5]

Despite our admiration for the "person of conscience," philosophers have generally judged appeals to conscience *alone* as insufficient and untrustworthy. Consciences vary radically from person to person and time to time, and are often altered by circumstance and training. For example, views about the right to publish pornography and rights of the press are matters of hot debate and deep conviction, but these convictions alone hardly seem to advance or resolve the issues. Consciences seem subject to impulse and whim, and are rather more acute when, for instance, a police officer is sighted than when there are no enforcers nearby. Recent psychological theories have also been used by some writers to undermine the claim that there is a rational and impartial basis to appeals to conscience. Moreover, many appeals to the rightness of an action on the ground that "my conscience was my guide" seem to external observers to be rationalizations for an immoral act. Political assassins and terrorists, for example, commonly appeal to conscience as a source of justification for their actions.

The reliability of conscience is thus not self-certifying and is always in doubt; support is needed from some source external to conscience itself. But can there be such a source? Is morality in the end reducible to mere individual rules and nothing more? This problem takes us straight to the issue of moral relativism.

RELATIVISM

Many important questions have been raised about the whole idea of "justifying a moral position," and one of the most important problems is generally referred to as relativism. Cultural variations relative to moral judgment have led many people to doubt that there are correct and objective justifications in morals and that there could be a neutral standpoint from which to view our many moral disagreements. Thus, some have contended that moral views are simply based on how one feels or how a culture accommodates the desires of its peoples, not on some deeper set of objectively justifiable principles. Tension between the belief that morality is purely subjective and the belief that it has an objective basis leads to issues of relativism and disagreement in morals, as we shall see in this and succeeding sections. Each of these problems raises questions about whether an objective morality is possible and about whether reason has any substantial role to play in ethics.

Moral relativists contend that all moral beliefs and principles are relative to individual cultures or individual persons. One person's or one culture's values, they maintain, do not or need not govern the conduct of others. This position is defended by appeal to data indicating that moral rightness and wrongness vary from place to place and that there are no absolute or universal moral standards that could apply to all persons at all times. Proponents of relativism add that rightness is contingent on individual or cultural beliefs and that the concepts of rightness and wrongness are therefore meaningless apart from the specific contexts in which they arise.

Anthropologists have often asserted that patterns of culture can only be understood as unique wholes. Moral beliefs are thus connected in a culture to other cultural characteristics such as language and political institutions. Studies show, they maintain, that what is deemed worthy of moral approval or disapproval in one society differs, both in detail and as a whole pattern, from moral standards in other societies. So far as uniformity is concerned, these anthropologists believe that their data show that, at most, in all societies persons possess a moral conscience, i.e., a general sense of right and wrong. Their reasoning is that in every culture some actions and intentions are approved as right or good, and others are disapproved as wrong or bad. On the other hand, the particular actions, motives, and rules that are praised and blamed vary greatly from culture to culture—practices of business payoffs, employee treatment and loyalty, and corporate taxation being but a few among thousands of possible examples.

From this perspective a moral standard is simply an historical product sanctioned by custom—nothing more, nothing less. Psychological and historical versions of this same thesis hold that the moral beliefs of individuals vary according to historical, environmental, and familial differences. Moreover, the evolution and transformation over time of these beliefs either in cultures or in individuals can often be reconstructed by historians. The weight of anthropological, psychological, and historical evidence thus conspires to suggest, according to relativists, that moral beliefs are relative to groups or individuals and that there are no universal norms, let alone universally *valid* ones.

These problems of apparent moral diversity—evident, for example, in the differences between Anglo-American culture and the customs prevalent in Iran, China, and India—offer a serious challenge to moral philosophy. Although it has at times been a fashionable view in the social sciences that relativism is a correct and highly significant doctrine, moral philosophers have generally tended to reject relativism. Among the best known arguments advanced against it is that there is a universal structure of human nature or at least a universal set of human needs which leads to the adoption of similar, or even identical, basic moral principles in all cultures. This line of argument may rest partially on empirical claims about what actually is believed across different cultures. More important than a survey of beliefs, however, is the claim that although cultural or individual practices and beliefs vary, people do not necessarily *ultimately* disagree about moral standards. For example, if personal payments for special services are common in one culture and punishable as bribery in another, it follows that these customs are different, but it does not follow that moral principles are relative. The two cultures may agree about basic principles of morality, yet disagree about how to apply these principles in particular situations. For example, one culture may believe such practices produce a social good by eliminating government interference, while another culture believes a social good is introduced by eliminating special favors. Both beliefs look to the overall social good.

This possibility indicates that a basic conflict between cultural values could only occur if apparent cultural disagreements about proper principles or rules occurred at a sufficiently fundamental level and so could not be arbitrated by appeal to higher rules. Otherwise, the apparent disagreements can be understood in terms of, and perhaps be arbitrated by, appeal to higher rules. If a moral conflict were truly fundamental, then the conflict could not be removed even if there were perfect agreement about the facts of a case, about the concepts involved, and about background beliefs.

Moreover, even if individuals in the same culture or persons from different cultures do not actually agree on the same ultimate norm or set of norms, it does not follow that there is no ultimate norm or set of norms in which everyone *ought* to believe. Consider an analogy to religious disagreement: From the fact that people have incompatible religious and atheistic beliefs, it does not follow that there is no single correct set of religious or atheistic propositions. Given anthropological data, one might be skeptical that there could be a compelling argument in favor of one system of religion or morality. But nothing more than skepticism seems justified by the facts adduced by anthropology, and this would hold even if *fundamental* conflicts of belief were discovered. Skepticism of course presents serious philosophical issues, but alone it does not support relativism, for it is left open for ethical theory to try to determine which is the best set of moral beliefs.

When two parties argue about some moral issue—killing animals or withholding information from contracting parties, for example—we tend to think that at least one party is mistaken, or that some genuinely fair compromise may be reached, or perhaps we remain uncertain while on the lookout for a best argument to emerge. But we do not infer from the mere fact of a conflict between beliefs that there is no way to establish one view as correct, or at least as better argued than the other. The more absurd the position advanced by one party, the more convinced we become that some views being defended are mistaken or require supplementation. We are seldom tempted to conclude that there could not be any correct ethical theory that might resolve such a dispute among reasonable persons.

We shall turn to ethical theories in Part Two of this Introduction, but moral disagreements need further discussion now.

MORAL DISAGREEMENTS

As we have seen already, many situations that arise in business practice present moral dilemmas. Such dilemmas occur whenever good reasons for mutually exclusive alternatives can be cited; if any one set of reasons is acted upon, outcomes desirable in some respects but undesirable in others will result. Thus, parties on different sides of dilemmatic controversies can correctly marshal moral principles in support of their substantially different conclusions. Yet the parties may not be able to show that their preferred position is the lone correct position. Moral dilemmas generally present a need to balance competing ideal claims in nonideal situations. The reasons on each side of many moral problems are weighty, and there is a sense in which all the reasons ought to be acted on.

In any pluralistic culture there are many sources of moral value, and consequently a pluralism of moral points of view on many issues involving conflict: not disclosing pertinent information in business deals, whistle blowing in the military, advertising on children's television, preferential hiring policies, and the like. On the other hand, there may be ways to resolve or at least reduce the level of some disagreements. Several methods for dealing constructively with moral disagreements have been employed in the past, and each deserves recognition as a method of easing and perhaps even settling conflicts.

1. Obtaining Information

Many moral disagreements can be at least partially resolved by obtaining factual information on which points of moral controversy turn. It has often been uncritically assumed that moral disputes are (by definition) produced solely by differences over moral judgments or principles, and not by a lack of information. This assumption is overly simplistic, however, for moral disputes—that is, disputes over what morally ought or ought not to be done—often have nonmoral elements as central ingredients. For example, debates about the allocation of tax dollars to prevent accidents or disease in the workplace have often bogged down over factual issues of whether particular measures such as masks or lower levels of toxic chemicals actually function to prevent death and disease. (See Chapter 3, under "Worker Safety.")

In a publicized controversy over the morality of "exaggerated claims" in advertising, the Federal Trade Commission (FTC) alleged that the Standard Oil Company of California (SOCAL) was guilty of intentionally misleading the public with its commercials for Chevron gasoline containing the additive F-310. Among the most damaging of the FTC's charges was the claim that SOCAL was falsely representing its F-310 additive as a unique product. Preliminary conferences and investigations, however, substantiated the factual validity of SOCAL's claims about its product's uniqueness, and the FTC thereupon withdrew its now demonstrably unfounded charges. While the dispute regarding other aspects of the F-310 advertising campaign was to continue, the appeal to the factual record had narrowed and focused the ground of disagreement and therefore advanced the moral and legal controversy toward a resolution.

Controversies like those about the use of saccharin in diet sodas, toxic substances in the workplace, fluoridation of public waters, and the manufacture, dissemination, and advertisement of swine-flu vaccine are laced with issues of both values and facts. The arguments used by disagreeing parties may turn on some dispute about liberty or justice, and therefore may be primarily moral; but they may also rest on factual disagreements over, for example, the efficacy of a product. New information may have only a limited bearing on the resolution of some of these controversies, while in others it may have a direct and almost overpowering influence. The problem is that rarely, if ever, is all the information obtained that would be sufficient to settle even the factual matters.

2. Definitional Clarity

Controversies have been settled by reaching conceptual or definitional agreement over the language used by disputing parties. In some cases stipulation of a definition or a clear explanation of what is meant by a term may prove sufficient, but in other cases agreement cannot be so conveniently achieved. Controversies over the morality of "affirmative action" and "reverse discrimination," for example, are often needlessly complicated because different senses of the expression are employed, yet disputing parties have much invested in their particular definitions (see Chapter 7). There is no common point of contention in such cases, for the parties are addressing entirely separate issues through their conceptual assumptions. Of course, conceptual agreement provides no guarantee that a dispute will be settled, but it should at least facilitate direct discussion of the outstanding issues. For this reason, many essays in this volume dwell at some length on problems of conceptual clarity.

3. Adopting a Code

Resolution of moral problems can also be facilitated if disputing parties can come to an agreement on a common set of moral principles or adopt a common code to govern their behavior. If this requires a complete shift from one starkly different moral point of view to another, agreement will rarely if ever be achieved. Differences that divide persons at the level of their most cherished principles are deep divisions, and conversions are infrequent. Various forms of discussion and negotiation can, however, lead to the adoption of a new or changed moral framework that can serve as a common basis for discussion.

As we shall see repeatedly in this volume, problems of moral controversy are often handled in professional communities by drafting and agreeing to codes of professional ethics, which are usually composed of quite specific rather than highly general moral rules. Questions about the adequacy and comprehensiveness of such codes are addressed in several chapters.

4. Example-Counterexample

Resolution of moral controversies can be aided by a method of example and opposed counterexample. Here cases or examples favorable to one point of view are brought forward and counterexamples to these cases are thrown up by a second person against the examples and claims of the first. In the AT&T case described earlier, for instance, the dispute between the company and the EEOC was initially advanced by the citation of statistics and examples that allegedly documented the claims made by each side. AT&T showed, for example, that 55 percent of the people on its payroll were women and that 33 percent of management positions were held by women. To sharpen its allegation of discriminatory practices in the face of this evidence, the EEOC countered by citing a government study which demonstrated that 99 percent of all operators were female, while only 1 percent of craft workers were female. Such use of example and counterexample serves as a format for weighing the strength of conflicting considerations.

5. Analysis of Arguments

Finally, one of the most important methods of philosophical inquiry is that of exposing the inadequacies and unexpected consequences of an argument. This method of inquiry can be brought to bear on moral disagreements. If an argument is invalid, then pointing out its invalidity will change the argument and shift the focus of discussion. However, there are many more subtle ways of attacking an argument. If a moral argument leads to conclusions which a proponent is not prepared to defend and did not previously anticipate, then part of the argument will have to be changed, and the distance between those who disagree will perhaps be reduced by this process. This style of argument can be supplemented by one or more of the previously mentioned four ways of reducing moral disagreement. Work published in philosophical journals often takes precisely these forms of attacking arguments, using counterexamples (as in #4), and proposing alternative frameworks (as, for example, in #3).

Many moral disagreements may not be resolvable by any of the above five methods. No contention is made here that moral disagreements can always be resolved, or even that every rational person must accept the same method for approaching such problems. We may never have a single ethical theory or a single method adequate to resolve all our disagreements. There is thus always a possibility of ultimate disagreement, and the resolution of cross-cultural conflicts such as those faced by multinational corporations may prove especially elusive. However, *if* something is to be done about these problems of justification in contexts of disagreement, a resolution seems most likely to occur if methods like those outlined in this section are used. Similar strategies are found in numerous articles included in this anthology.

THE PROBLEM OF EGOISM

Many businesspersons' attitudes have been analyzed as fundamentally "egoistic." The claim is that each business acts from *prudence,* as we earlier defined it—that is, each is out to promote its own interest, and indeed has no other real interest. Business practice is also said by some to be egoistic because businesspersons believe that individuals should strive to be as successful in competition as possible. This problem of egoism extends well beyond the business community, of course, and, like relativism, egoism presents a significant problem for ethical theory.

The theory behind egoism has familiar origins. Each of us has been confronted with occasions on which a choice must be made between spending money on ourselves or on some worthy charitable enterprise. For example, when one elects to purchase new clothes for oneself rather than contribute to a university scholarship fund for poor students, self-interest is given priority over the interests of those students. Egoism generalizes beyond such familiar occasions of choice to all human choices. The egoist contends that all choices either do involve or should involve self-promotion as their sole objective. Thus, a person's only goal and perhaps only moral duty is self-promotion; one owes no sacrifices and no obligations to others.

We can begin the task of examining egoism by distinguishing its two main varieties—psychological egoism and ethical egoism.

Psychological Egoism

Psychological egoism is the view that everyone is always motivated to act in his or her own perceived self-interest. This theory concerns human motivation and offers an *explanation* of human conduct, as contrasted with a *justification* of human conduct. It says that people always do what pleases them or what is in their own interest. Typical popular ways of expressing this viewpoint include: "People are at heart selfish, even if they appear to be unselfish"; "People always look out for Number One first"; "In the long run, everybody always does what he or she wants to do or whatever is least painful"; and "No matter what a person says, everybody always acts for the sake of personal satisfaction."

Psychological egoism presents a serious challenge to moral philosophy, for, if correct, there could be no purely altruistic or moral motivation (as we commonly use the term "morality"). Normative ethics presupposes that one *ought* to behave in accordance with certain moral principles, whether or not such behavior promotes one's own interest. If people are so constituted that they must always act in their own interest, then it would be absurd ever to ask them to act contrary to this self-interest. Ethics is based on a postulate put somewhat misleadingly as "Ought implies can." This expression in effect asserts that it is pointless to tell someone that he or she ought to do something when he or she cannot do it. Thus, if psychological egoism is true, the whole enterprise of ethics seems either futile or redundant.

Those who tend toward acceptance of psychological egoism do so because they are convinced by their observation of themselves and others that people are thoroughly self-centered. Conversely, those who reject the theory are likely to do so because they see such obvious examples of altruistic behavior in the lives of saints, heroes, and public servants, and because contemporary psychology offers many compelling studies of sacrificial behavior. Even if it is conceded that people are basically selfish, it seems undeniable that there are at least *some* outstanding examples of preeminently unselfish actions. Those who take this view point to employees who blow the whistle on unsafe or otherwise improper business practices, when they stand to lose their jobs and suffer social ostracism on account of their actions.

The defender of psychological egoism, of course, is not impressed by the exemplary lives of saints and heroes or by social practices of sacrifice. The psychological egoist does not contend that people always behave in an *out-*

wardly selfish manner. No matter how self-sacrificing a person's behavior may be at times, these egoists maintain, the desire behind the action is always selfish; one is ultimately out for oneself—whether in the long or the short run. In their view, an egoistic action is perfectly compatible with behavior that we standardly refer to as altruistic. The clever person who is self-interested can appear to be the most unselfish person around, for whether the person is really acting egoistically depends on the motivation behind the appearance of the behavior. Any apparently altruistic person may simply believe that an unselfish appearance best promotes his or her own long-range interests. The fact that some ''sacrifices'' (pseudo-sacrifices) may be necessary in the short run thus fails to count against egoism.

The psychological egoist tries to show that all persons who spend a great deal of effort to help others, to promote the general welfare, or even to risk their lives for the welfare of others are really acting to promote themselves. In loving others, for example, we strengthen their love for us. By sacrificing for our children, we take satisfaction in their achievements. By following society's moral codes, we avoid both the police and social ostracism. The egoist thus claims that the ultimate motive for any act is self-interest. You may protest that people often act contrary to their self-interest and that some people seem to act contrary to their self-interest most of the time. The psychological egoist concedes this. People do make mistakes about what is in their self-interest, and a few people stupidly overlook their own best interest. The psychological egoist is not saying that people are motivated to act in terms of their *real* self-interest. The egoist is only committed to the view that everyone always is motivated to act in accordance with *perceived* self-interest.

As an account of the motivation of human behavior, psychological egoism has found a sympathetic response both in student quarters and in the world of business. To determine whether psychological egoism is true as a matter of psychological fact is a task too complicated for this introductory chapter. Nonetheless, since there do seem to be cases of genuinely altruistic acts that are clearly not in the interest of the individual performing them—for example, giving up one's life to save another—it is tempting for the psychological egoist to make the theory true by definition. This point can be clarified by an illustration. Suppose a biologist makes the claim that all swans are white. While traveling in Australia you discover a bird that has all the characteristics of a swan except one: it is black instead of white. Does this discovery refute the biologist? It is tempting for the biologist to claim that by definition something cannot be a swan unless it is white. If the biologist makes this move, he or she has given up his claim about the world and has proposed in its place a thesis about how he or she will use words. A new *name* will be created for your new bird, rather than revise his scientific claim.

Psychological egoists often seem to succumb to similar temptations. When confronted with what looks like genuinely altruistic acts, they appeal to unconscious motives of self-interest or claim that every act is based on some desire of the person performing the act and that acting on that desire is what is meant by "self-interest." But this latter move may be only a verbal trick; for they may only have changed their definition of self-interest. At first, "self-interest" meant acting exclusively on behalf of one's own self-interest. Now "self-interest" has been redefined to mean acting on any interest one has. But of course the main question still remains. Are there two different kinds of human motives? Do we sometimes have an interest in acting for ourselves and sometimes on behalf of others, or do we simply act for ourselves? We often do act in terms of our own self-interest, and often our interests and the interests of others coincide, but philosophy and psychology have yet to establish that we never act contrary to our perceived self-interest.

Ethical Egoism

The second type of egoistic theory may be roughly defined as the theory that the only valid standard of conduct is the obligation to promote one's own well-being above everyone else's. Whereas psychological egoism is a psychological theory about human motivation, ethical egoism purports to be a general theory about what we *ought* to do. According to psychological egoism we always *do* act on the basis of what we believe to be our own interest. According to ethical egoism, one *ought* always to act on the basis of one's own best interest.

Everyone has heard the advice that one should always try to maximize one's own personal good in any given circumstance. This counsel is generally put in somewhat looser terms by saying, "You're a sucker if you don't always look out for yourself first and others second." Such a proposal is clearly unacceptable in light of virtually all culturally shared moral requirements. Morality requires that we return a lost puppy to its owner even if we become quite enamored of it, and that we correct bank statements containing errors in our favor. Yet, why should we look out for the interests of others on such occasions? This question has troubled many reflective persons, some of whom have concluded that acting against one's own interest is actually contrary to *reason*. These thinkers have seen conventional morality as tinged with irrational sentiment and indefensible constraints on the individual. They are the supporters of ethical egoism.

It is tempting to dismiss ethical egoism as silly, because it is committed to the view that we ought never to take the interests of others into account. Such a characterization of ethical egoism is incorrect, however. An ethical egoist does consider the interests of others when it suits his or her own interest, and usually it *is* in our interest to treat others well because it is to our advantage to do so. It is important, therefore, to consider what society would be like if ethical egoism were the conventional, prevailing theory of proper conduct. Some philosophers and political theorists have argued that anarchism and chaos would prevail unless certain preventive measures were adopted. A classic statement of this position was made by the philosopher Thomas Hobbes: Imagine a world with limited resources, where persons are approximately equal in their ability to harm one another, and yet everyone acts exclusively in his or her own interest. Hobbes argued that in such a world everyone would be at everyone else's throat; such a "state of nature" would be plagued by anxiety, violence, and constant danger. As Hobbes put it, life would be "solitary, poor, nasty, brutish, and short." However, Hobbes also assumed that human beings were sufficiently rational to recognize their own interests. To avoid the war of all against all he urged that they form a powerful state to protect themselves.

Hobbes's argument might be recast in the following form: Any clever person will realize that he or she has no moral obligations to others besides those he or she voluntarily assumes. One should accept moral rules and assume specific obligations only when doing so promotes one's self-interest. One may take the offensive and bring some benefit or liberty to oneself, or one may adopt a more defensive strategy by avoiding the enmity and limited sympathies of others; but any intelligent person will see that it is personally advantageous to make all such decisions using egoistic standards. Even if one agrees to live under a set of laws of the state that are binding on everyone, any obligation should be assumed only as a part of this general offensive and defensive strategy. Moreover, one should obey rules and laws only in order to protect oneself and to bring about a situation of communal living that is personally advantageous. One should also back down on an "obligation" whenever it becomes clear that it is to one's long-range disadvantage to fulfill the obligation. Thus, when confronted by a social revolution, the questionable trustworthiness of a colleague, or an incompetent administration at one's place of employment, one is under no obligation to obey the law, fulfill one's contracts, or tell the truth. These obligations exist only because one assumes them, and one ought to assume them only as long as doing so promotes one's own interest.

What now can be said by way of criticism of this Hobbesian form of universal ethical egoism? One popular contention is that the theory gives incompatible directives in circumstances of moral conflict. If everyone acted egoistically, it seems reasonably certain that signficant and protracted conflicts would occur, just as many international conflicts now arise among nations primarily pursuing their own interests. According to universal egoism, both parties in a circumstance of conflict ought to pursue their own best interests exclusively, and it is morally permissible for both to do so. For example, suppose it is in the interest of a consumer activist to stop production and distribution of an automobile of allegedly hazardous design. It is no less in the interest of the automobile manufacturer to prevent the consumer activist from stopping production and distribution of the model. Egoism urges both parties to pursue their interests exclusively and holds both pursuits to be morally permissible.

The oddity of this situation can be brought out by imagining that the consumer activist is an egoist. In order to be a consistent egoist, the activist must hold to a theory that the automobile manufacturer ought to pursue its interest, which would involve thwarting his or her own consumer objectives (for *all* ought to pursue their interests and thwart others if necessary). Yet, in thus striving for consistency, the egoist supports a theory that works against his or her own interest, and so seems to fall into inconsistency in the attempt. Another way of looking at this example is to see the egoist as having incompatible objectives. The egoist says that everyone ought to seek his or her own maximal satisfaction, even though the pursuit by everyone of their interests would negatively affect the egoist's pursuit of maximal satisfaction.

Perhaps the most plausible egoistic reply to this objection is that it springs from a misunderstanding of the rules and policies that an ethical egoist would actually promote. If everyone were to act on more or less fixed rules such as those found in conventional moral and legal systems, this arrangement would produce the most desirable state of affairs from an egoistic point of view. The reason is that such rules arbitrate conflicts and make social life more agreeable. These rules would include, for example, familiar moral and legal principles of justice that are intended to make everyone's situation more secure and stable. Only an unduly narrow conception of *genuine* self-interest, the egoist might argue, leads critics to think that the egoist would not willingly observe such rules of justice, for it is clearly in one's self-interest to do so. If society can be structured to resolve personal conflicts through courts and other peaceful means, the egoist will see it as in his or her interest to accept those binding social arrangements—just as the egoist will see it as prudent to treat other individuals well in his or her personal contacts with them. Notice that the egoist is saying not that his or her best interests are served by promoting the good of others—but rather, that one's personal interests are served by observing impartial rules irrespective of the outcome for others. The egoist does not care about the welfare of others except insofar as it affects her or his own welfare.

Egoistic Business Practices and Utilitarian Results

A different view from that of Hobbes, one which has been extremely influential in the personal philosophy of the business community, is that of Adam Smith. Smith believed that the public good evolves out of a suitably restrained clash of competing individual interests. As each person pursues his or her own self-interest, the interactive process is guided by an "invisible hand," so that the public interest is achieved. It is ironic that, according to Smith, individual egoism leads not to the war of all against all, but rather to utilitarianism, i.e., to the greatest good of the greatest number. The existence of the invisible hand is, Smith thought, a far better method of achieving the public good than the highly visible and authoritarian hand of Hobbes's all-powerful sovereign state. To protect individual freedom, government should be fairly limited. Of course, Smith recognized that concern with our own self-interest could get out of control, and hence that a minimal state is required to provide and enforce the rules of the competitive game.

Adam Smith's picture of an egoistic world has captivated many in the business community. They do not picture themselves as selfish and indifferent to the interests of others, and they recognize that a certain element of cooperation is necessary if their own interests are to flourish. At the same time, they recognize that when their interests *do* conflict with the interests of others *within the established rules of the competitive game,* they should pursue their own interests. Within the rules of business practice, they see business ethics as the ethics of a suitably restrained egoist. It is egoistic because it is an ethic based on the active pursuit of one's own interest. It is restrained because self-interest is subservient to the rules of business practice.

Many in the business community also believe that a suitably restrained egoism leads to utilitarian outcomes (even if not to the utilitarian moral philosophy). Individual competition advances the good of the corporation, and competition among individual firms advances the good of society as a whole. Hence, a popular view of business ethics might be captured by the phrase, "individual egoism leads to utilitarian outcomes." Or, as Adam Smith put it, as people pursue their individual interests, they are led by an invisible hand to promote the public good. This kind of confident optimism has been severely challenged, however. We can best see why by turning at this point to the study of ethical theory, and to utilitarian ethical theories in particular.

PART TWO: NORMATIVE ETHICAL THEORY

In contemporary philosophy, ethical theories are commonly divided into two fundamental types, teleological and deontological. We therefore begin our treatment of ethical theory with these two types. Presumably the two approaches provide radically different perspectives on the moral life and entail different conclusions about what ought to be done. However, the two types have never been demonstrated to be inconsistent, and their exact similarities and differences deserve close study.

UTILITARIAN THEORIES

Teleological theories hold that the moral worth of actions or practices is determined solely by the consequences of the actions or practices. The most widely studied teleological theory is utilitarianism. This theory is rooted in the thesis that an action or practice is right (when compared to any alternative action or practice) if it leads to the greatest possible balance of good consequences or to the least possible balance of bad consequences in the world as a whole. In taking this perspective, utilitarians invite consideration of the overall purpose or function of morality as a social institution, where "morality" is understood to include shared rules of justice and other principles of the moral life. The purpose of the institution of morality, utilitarians insist, is to promote human welfare by minimizing harms and maximizing benefits. A good example of this approach to the moral life is found in Chapter 8 of this volume, where certain authors see the purpose of government regulation and the use of cost/benefit analysis to be utilitarian and utilitarian alone.

Mill's Utilitarianism

The first developed utilitarian philosophical writings were those of David Hume (1711-1776), Jeremy Bentham (1748-1832), and John Stuart Mill (1806-1873). It is generally conceded that the major theoretical exposition of utilitarianism is Mill's *Utilitarianism* (1863). In this work Mill discusses two foundations or sources of utilitarian thinking: (1) a *normative* foundation in the principle of utility and (2) a *psychological* foundation in human nature. The principle of utility, or the "greatest happiness principle," he proposes as the foundation of normative ethical theory: Actions are right, he says, in proportion to their tendency to promote happiness or absence of pain, and wrong insofar as they tend to produce pain or displeasure. Pleasure and freedom from pain, Mill argues, are alone desirable as ends; all desirable things (which are numerous) are therefore desirable either for the pleasure inherent in them, or as means to the promotion of pleasure and the prevention of pain.

Mill's second foundation of utilitarianism derives from his belief that most, and perhaps all, persons have a basic desire for unity and harmony with their fellow human beings. Whereas Bentham had argued for utilitarianism by claiming that it is in our own self-interest to promote everyone's interest, Mill appeals to the importance of social feelings. Just as we feel horror at crimes, he says, so we have a basic moral sensitiveness to the needs of others. In the end, his view seems to be that the purpose of morality is at once to tap natural human sympathies so as to benefit others, while at the same time controlling unsympathetic attitudes that cause harm to others. The principle of utility is conceived as the best means to these basic human goals.

Essential Features of Utilitarianism

Several essential features of utilitarianism may be extracted from the reasoning of Mill and other utilitarians. First, utilitarianism is committed to the maximization of the good, for it asserts that we ought always to produce the greatest possible balance of value for all persons affected. The obvious means to maximization is efficiency, a goal with which business executives are certainly sympathetic, since efficiency is highly prized in the entire economic sector. Efficiency is a means to higher profits and to lower prices, and the struggle to be maximally profitable seeks to obtain maximum production from limited economic resources. These produced goods and services are presumably intended to promote the greatest good of the greatest number. The utilitarian commitment to the principle of optimal productivity through efficiency is thus an essential part of the traditional business conception of society and a standard part of business practice. We could correctly say that the enterprise of business harbors a fundamentally utilitarian conception of the good society.

There is more to utilitarianism than efficiency, however, and hence a second essential feature must be considered. This feature is the utilitarians' theory of intrinsic value. Efficiency itself is simply an instrumental good, that is, it is valuable strictly as a means to something else. In the corporation, efficiency is valuable as a means to maximizing profit. Within the free enterprise system of competing firms, efficiency is valuable as a means toward maximizing the production of goods and services. Within utilitarian moral theory, efficiency is the means for maximizing the good. But what is "good" according to the utilitarian? And what does it mean to assert that some things are good in themselves and not merely good as a means to something else? We can begin to frame an answer to this question by considering, as an illustration, the working of the stock market. Daily activities on Wall Street are not usually considered to be intrinsically good, but are extrinsically good as a means to another end, such as financial security and happiness. Utilitarians believe that what we really ought to seek in life are certain experiences and conditions that are good in themselves without reference to their further consequences, and that all values are ultimately to be gauged in terms of these intrinsic goods. Health, friendship, and freedom from pain would be included among such values. An intrinsic value, then, is a value in life that we wish to possess and enjoy just for its own sake and not for something else that it brings.

However, utilitarians are in disagreement as to what constitutes the complete range of things or states that are good. Bentham and Mill are hedonists; i.e., they believe that only pleasure or happiness (which are synonymous terms in this context) can be good in itself. Everything besides pleasure is merely instrumentally good, i.e., good as a means to the end of pleasure. *Hedonistic* utilitarianism, then, believes that any act or practice which maximizes pleasure (when compared with any alternative act or practice) is right. Hedonistic utilitarians insist that "pleasure" covers a broad range of experiences and states of affairs, including most satisfactions we find in life. Nonetheless, later utilitarian philosophers have argued that other values besides pleasure possess intrinsic worth—e.g., friendship, knowledge, courage, health, and beauty. Those utilitarians who believe in many intrinsic values are referred to as *pluralistic* utilitarians.

In recent philosophy, economics, and psychology, neither the approach of the hedonists nor that of the pluralists has prevailed. Both approaches have seemed relatively useless for purposes of objectively aggregating widely different interests in order to determine maximal value and therefore right action. The contemporary approach is to appeal to individual *preferences*. The concept of utility is understood from this perspective not in terms of states of affairs such as happiness, but rather in terms of the satisfaction of individual preferences, as determined by a person's behavior. In the language of business, utility is measured by what a person purchases or otherwise pursues. Accordingly, to maximize a person's utility is to provide that which he or she has chosen or would choose from among the available alternatives. To maximize the utility of all persons affected by an action or policy is to maximize the utility of the aggregate group. This approach has been extensively used in attempts to formulate public policy, including government policies that regulate business in the public interest (see Chapters 6–8).

While this preference-based utilitarian approach to value has been viewed by many as superior to its predecessors, it has not proved to be trouble-free as a general theory of morals. A major theoretical problem arises when individuals have morally unacceptable preferences. For example, a person's strong sexual preference may be to rape young children, or an employment officer may prefer to discriminate against women, yet such preferences are morally intolerable. We reject such preferences as harmful and without any positive value. Utilitarianism based purely on subjective preferences is satisfactory, then, only if a range of *acceptable* preferences can be formulated. This latter task has proved difficult in theory, and it may even be inconsistent with a pure preference approach.

Nonetheless, some plausible replies to this objection are open to utilitarians. First, since most people are not perverse and do have morally acceptable (albeit sometimes odd) values, utilitarians believe they are justified in proceeding under the assumption that the preference approach is not fatally marred by a speculative problem. As Mill noted, any moral theory may lead to unsatisfactory outcomes if one assumes universal idiocy. Second, because "perverse" desires have been seen (on the basis of past experience) to work against the larger objectives of utilitarianism (maximal public welfare) by creating unhappiness, the utilitarian could argue that such desires (preferences) could never even be permitted to count in the calculus of preferences. We discount preferences to rape children and to discriminate against women not only because they obstruct the preferences of children and women, but because, more generally, such preferences eventuate in a great deal of unhappiness and conflict in society. Preferences that serve merely to frustrate the preferences of others are thus ruled out by the goal of utilitarianism (though experience may be needed to know this). As Mill argued, the cultivation of certain kinds of desires is built into the "ideal" of utilitarianism.

Still, even if most people are not perverse and the ideals of utilitarianism are well entrenched in society, some rational agents may have preferences that are immoral or unjust; and a major problem for utilitarian theory is that it may need a supplementary criterion of value beside mere preference. (Many critics have suggested that at least a principle of justice must supplement the principle of utility.)

A third essential feature of utilitarianism is its commitment to the measurement and comparison of goods. On the hedonistic view, we must be able to measure pleasurable and painful states and be able to compare one person's pleasures with another's in order to decide which is greater. Bentham, for example, worked out a measurement device which he called the *hedonic calculus.* He thought he could add the quantitative units of individual happiness, subtract the units of individual unhappiness, and thereby arrive at a measure of total happiness. By the use of this hedonic calculus we allegedly can measure and compare individual happiness and can ultimately determine the act or practice that will provide the greatest happiness to the greatest number.

The idea that pleasurable experiences, or at least subjective preferences, can be measured and compared has had great appeal to economists and to the framers of public policy. Indeed, economic analysis was for some time expressed in utilitarian language. Many readers of this text may recall with some dismay their struggles in economics with "the law of diminishing marginal utility." This is not the place to rekindle unpleasant memories. However, a few examples will reveal how utilitarian analysis can be incorporated within economic thought. Historically, some economists have maintained that the maximum amount of goods and services can be squeezed from scarce resources through a free market, competitive economy. These economists further believed that in maximizing the production of valued goods and services, happiness was maximized as well. Utilitarian analysis provided the bridge for that conclusion.

Here is a simplified example: Suppose a man goes to the grocery store for a six-pack of beer. While there, he meets a friend who is also buying a six-pack. Since both pay $3.50 for the beer, economists assume that, other things being equal, both men receive the same satisfaction from the beer. Suppose, however, the price of beer goes up to $3.75 and one man shifts to wine while the other stays with the six-pack. It is then assumed that one obtains more satisfaction from the $3.75 six-pack than the other who is unwilling to pay this price. By replacing Bentham's hedonic calculus with the measuring stick of *price,* economists have argued that an economy constructed along the lines of the postulates of free competition maximizes utility. Economic theory was thus utilitarian at its core, and business theory borrowed and built upon that utilitarian base.

Act and Rule Utilitarianism

Utilitarian moral philosophers are conventionally divided into two types, act utilitarians and rule utilitarians. An act utilitarian argues that in all situations one ought to perform that act which leads to the greatest good for the greatest number. This approach seems natural, because utilitarianism aims at maximizing value, and the most direct means to this goal would seem to be that of maximizing value on every single occasion. This position does not demand, however, that every time we act, we determine what should be done without any reference to general guidelines. We clearly learn from past experience, and the act utilitarian does permit summary rules of thumb. The act utilitarian thus regards rules such as "You ought to tell the truth in making contracts" as useful guidelines, but not as valid for all circumstances. An act utilitarian would not hesitate to break such rules if a violation were actually to lead to the greatest good for the greatest number in a particular case.

Consider the following case, in which American business practices and standards run up against the quite different practices of the Italian business community.[6] The case turns on the tax problems encountered by the Italian subsidiary of a major American bank. It seems that in Italy, the practices of corporate taxation typically involve elaborate negotiations between hired company representatives and the Italian tax service, and that the tax statement initially submitted by a corporation is always regarded as a dramatically understated bid intended only as a starting point for the negotiating process. In the case in question, the American manager of the Italian banking subsidiary decided, against the advice of locally experienced lawyers and tax consultants, to ignore the native Italian practices and file a conventional American-style tax statement (i.e., one in which the subsidiary's profits for the year were *not* dramatically understated). Among his reasons for this decision was, apparently, the belief that to conform to the local customs would be to violate the important moral rule of truth telling, and that such a violation could not be justified in the circumstances.

An act utilitarian, however, might well take exception to this conclusion. Admittedly, to file an Italian-style tax statement *would* be to violate a moral rule of truth telling; but the act utilitarian would argue that such a rule is only a rule of thumb which can justifiably be violated whenever such violation would produce the greatest good. In the present case, the argument would go, the greatest good would evidently be done by following the local consultants' advice and conforming to the Italian practices. Only by following those practices will the appropriate amount of tax be paid. This conclusion is confirmed by the ultimate outcome of the present case: the Italian authorities forced the bank to enter into the customary negotiations, a process in which the original, truthful tax statement was treated as an understated opening bid, and a dramatically excessive tax payment was consequently required.

In contrast to the position of act utilitarians, rule utilitarians hold that rules have a central position in morality which cannot be compromised by the demands of particular situations. Such compromise would threaten the general effectiveness of the rules, the observance of which would in theory maximize social utility further than would any possible substitute rule (or no rule). An example of this problem is found in a case involving Listerine "antiseptic" mouthwash.[7] Its manufacturer, The Warner-Lambert Co., advertised for over forty years that Listerine cures colds and fights sore throats. The United States government claimed recently to have proof that this boast was false, and the advertisements therefore deceptive. The rule utilitarian position is that even in the arena of advertising, fraught with exaggerated and questionable claims as it is, rules against deception cannot be compromised simply because certain practices might be in the best interests of business (as clearly was the case for Listerine). The reason is that the overall interests of most members of society ("the public interest") is best protected by continual observation of a set of basic moral rules which govern everyone's conduct.

For the rule utilitarian, then, actions are justified by appeal to rules such as "Don't deceive," "Don't bribe," and "Don't break promises." These rules, in turn, are justified by an appeal to the principle of utility. The rule utilitarian believes this position can escape the objections to act utilitarianism, precisely because rules are not subject to change by the demands of individual circumstances. Utilitarian rules are in theory firm and protective of all classes of individuals—just as human rights (as we shall see below) are rigidly protective of all individuals regardless of social convenience and momentary need.

Act utilitarians, however, have a reply to the criticisms advanced by rule utilitarians. Act utilitarians regard rule utilitarians as unfaithful to the fundamental demand of utilitarianism, which requires that we *maximize* happiness (or at least that we maximize intrinsic value). There are many cases in which abiding by a generally beneficial rule will not prove most beneficial to the persons actually affected in the circumstances, *even in the long run.* Act utilitarians argue that there is a third possibility that lies between never obeying a rule and always obeying it—that it should be only sometimes obeyed. An example of this act utilitarian form of reasoning is found in the defense offered by A. Carl Kotchian, former president of Lockheed Corporation, of $12 million in "grease payments" made to high Japanese officials in order to facilitate sales of his TriStar plane. Kotchian recognized that "extortion," as he called it, was involved, and that American rules of business ethics forbid such payments. Mr. Kotchian advanced two arguments in defense of his payments: (1) "such disbursements did not [at the time] violate American laws," and (2) the TriStar payments . . . would provide Lockheed workers with jobs and thus redounded to the benefit of their dependents, their communities, and stockholders of the corporation." Kotchian went on to argue that the financial consequences of "commercial success" and the public interest in both Japan and the United States were sufficient to override "a purely ethical and moral standpoint."[8] This is precisely the form of reasoning that rule utilitarians have generally rejected, but which act utilitarians have defended as at least meriting serious consideration.

In the end the act-utilitarian view seems to involve a prediction that we will be better off in the moral life if we sometimes obey and sometimes disobey rules, because this kind of conduct will not fundamentally erode either moral rules or our general respect for morality. The rule utilitarian would, of course, challenge the part of this argument that claims that less rather than more damage will be done to the institution of morality by adopting an act-utilitarian position. Much current debate within utilitarianism focuses on this issue.

It is also appropriate to ask whether rule utilitarians can escape the very criticisms they level at act utilitarians. There are often conflicts between moral rules—e.g., rules of confidentiality conflict with rules protecting individual welfare. We shall see in Chapter 4 that many people believe an employer's rights can conflict with the rights of employees—cases of whistle blowing raising some of the most difficult issues. If the moral life were so ordered that we always knew which rules and rights should receive priority, there would be no serious problem for moral theory. Yet such a ranking of rules seems clearly impossible, and in a pluralistic society there are many rules that some persons accept and others reject. But even if everyone agreed on the same rules and on their interpretation, it might be better in one situation to blow the whistle in order to protect someone else or one's own integrity, while in another circumstance it might be better to leave the matter undisclosed.

Mill briefly considered this problem. He held that the principle of utility should itself decide in any given circumstance which rule is to take priority. However, if this solution is accepted by rule utilitarians, then their theory must rely directly on some occasions on the principle of utility to decide *in particular situations* which *action* is preferable to which alternative action in the absence of a governing rule.

The rule utilitarian can reply to this criticism that a sense of relative weight and importance should, insofar as is possible, be built directly into moral rules. For example, the rule utilitarian might argue that rules which prohibit false and misleading advertising of products are of such vital social significance (i.e., have such paramount social utility) that they can never be overridden by an appeal to rules that allow manufacturers the freedom to advertise and market their product. Rule utilitarians may acknowledge that weights cannot be so definitely formulated and built into principles that irresolvable conflicts among rules will *never* arise. What they need not concede is that this problem is unique to rule utilitarianism. Every moral theory, after all, has certain practical limitations in cases of conflict. It will nonetheless be possible to distinguish theories which require strict observance of rules from those, such as act utilitarianism, that do not.

The Problem of Quantifying Goodness

One major criticism of all utilitarian theories centers on the commitment to quantify and measure goodness. The question is "can units of happiness or some other utilitarian value be measured and compared so as to determine the best among alternatives?" How is Congress to compare, for example, the value of a financial support program for the automobile industry with the value of regular inspections of plants in order to prevent occupational disease? This criticism might be called the comparison problem, or the apples-and-oranges problem. This difficulty in comparing different experiences clearly extends in practical ways to business firms. For example, one device suggested for measuring corporate responsibility is the corporate social audit. In addition to providing a financial picture of the company, the social audit is supposed to provide a picture of the company's sense of social responsibility. However, problems have arisen in the measurement and comparison of a corporation's ethical assets and liabilities that have left the corporate social audit in a relatively primitive state. (We will examine the corporate social audit in Chapter 8.)

Bentham's theory that pleasure alone is good and that it can be quantified has been a special object of attack. Even Mill charged that, on Bentham's account, it would be better to be a satisfied pig than a dissatisfied Socrates. Human experience, Mill argued, is such that some pleasures seem to be *qualitatively* better than others. Mill was convinced that it is better, all things considered, to be a dissatisfied Socrates than a satisfied pig; Socratic pleasures of the mind are qualitatively better than purely bodily pleasures. Mill thus had to grapple with a new problem of measuring value: "qualitative betterness" must be weighed and compared, and yet it has struck many as impossible to do so.

Moreover, although Mill thought this strategy preserves hedonism, it appears to many modern philosophers that it does not. After all, what special quality does a somewhat *less* pleasurable experience have that makes it better? It cannot be the pleasure itself. But if it is not pleasure alone, then hedonism must be given up, because it is theoretically committed to the view that pleasure is the sole good.

Utilitarians who were not hedonists encountered other serious problems with quantification. Economists, for example, either simply appropriated the word "utility" to denote that experience of satisfaction in which economists were interested, or they abandoned the word "utility" and talked about "preference orderings" instead. But many still doubt that construing utility in these ways will resolve the measurability problem. Suppose Jim prefers to spend his 97 cents on milk and Sally prefers to spend her 97 cents on bread. Suppose neither Sally nor Jim has any money and we have only $1.30 to distribute. What can utilitarianism advise when utility is limited to preference orderings? It seems that no advice is possible unless some inferences are made that enable us to go from revealed preferences to considerations of welfare and happiness. The difficulty in justifying such inferences is perhaps a weakness in the utilitarian method.

The utilitarian reply to these criticisms is that we make crude, rough and ready comparisons of values every day, including pleasures and dislikes. For example, we decide to go as a group to a bar rather than have an office party, because we think the bar function will satisfy more members of the group. It is easy to overestimate the demands of utilitarianism and the precision with which its exponents have employed it. Accurate measurements of others' goods or preferences can seldom be provided because of limited knowledge and time. In everyday affairs such as purchasing supplies, administering business, or making legislative decisions, severely limited knowledge regarding the consequences of our actions is often all that is available. What is important, from the utilitarian moral perspective, is that one conscientiously attempts to determine the most desirable action and then with equal seriousness attempts to perform that action.

One further problem in measurement focuses on what to measure, and even most utilitarians would agree that this slippery problem remains unresolved. Utilitarianism stipulates that in matters of ethics only consequences count. Suppose we accept this claim for the moment. What counts as a consequence of an act, and how far into the future must consequences be considered? Utilitarians argue among themselves about this, and these debates are not unrelated to problems of business ethics. For most of our country's history, the so-called "externalities" of business practice were not taken into account in calculating the cost of doing business. Examples of these include air, water, and noise pollution. As noted in Chapter 6, environmental deterioration has now reached a point where such consequences must be counted as part of the *social cost* of doing business.

This changing perception of the costs and consequences of business has had unsettling effects. The rules of the game are changing, and as a result ethical dilemmas multiply. The issues which result from redefining the consequences of doing business are discussed in several chapters of this text.

The Problem of Unjust Consequences

Utilitarianism has also been challenged on the grounds that it can lead to injustice. It can be argued that the action that produces the greatest balance of value for the *greatest number* of people may bring about unjustified harm or disvalue to a minority. An ethical theory requiring that the rights of individuals be surrendered in the interests of the majority seems plainly deficient.

Consider an extreme example. Suppose a slave society produced the greatest happiness for the greatest number. Would a rule utilitarian have to say that the practice of slavery in that particular society is morally obligatory? One standard response of a utilitarian is to deny that the world of human relations would ever be such that slavery would *in fact* lead to the greatest happiness for the greatest number. Such a response is unsettling, however. Many political philosophers and legal theorists have argued that documents such as the Bill of Rights in the United States Constitution contain rules that prohibit or constrain utilitarian calculations rather than serve as examples of utilitarian policy decisions. The Bill of Rights, they say, is inserted into the Constitution because those rights protect individuals against slavery and other practices even if they are *not* rules that lead to the greatest good for the greatest number. Their justification thus seems nonutilitarian, for their purpose is to protect the individual rights of citizens from being sacrificed in the name of the public good.

Some critics chastise utilitarian practices of business on the same basis. Take the following case involving a conflict between efficiency and the rights of consumers.[9] The case arises from the decision by the Giant Corporation to introduce a computerized checkout system in its Washington, D.C. area supermarket outlets in the mid-1970s. The company argued that this technological innovation would bring about a reduction in food prices, caused by the elimination of the need for individual product pricing. Consumer advocates contended, however, that the loss of individual pricing would be a blow to consumers' rights, arguing that the change would leave customers in ignorance if the computer makes a mistake, would make comparative shopping difficult, and would promote generally passive and unreflective consumer behavior. Giant's market surveys soon revealed that an overwhelming percentage of its customers favored the new system for its convenience, precision, and lowered costs, and that only about a quarter of all customers desired a return to individual item pricing. This data suggests a conflict between utilitarian reasoning and the claims of justice. On straightforward, preference-utilitarian grounds, the new checkout system would seem to be justified as maximizing the values (convenience, precision, cost containment) that are important to most interested parties. But consumer advocates would argue that such utilitarian reasoning needs to be constrained by recognition of the fundamental right of grocery store customers to be informed, cost-conscious consumers—even if only a minority of the customers feel strongly about exercising that right (see Chapter 5).

The doctrine of individual rights within business institutions has not traditionally been a major part of business ethics, though this situation may now be changing. Employees were and often still are fired for what superiors consider disloyal conduct, and employees traditionally have had no internal right to "blow the whistle" on corporate misconduct. Many alleged abuses of management privileges and authority have also been cataloged, and at present protections against unjust business practices are being demanded, sometimes within companies and sometimes in court. The development of theories of employee rights, consumer rights, and stockholder rights, the clashes among rights claims, and the alleged clash between utilitarianism and nonutilitarian rights theories provide the framework for major contemporary debates within business ethics. (See especially Chapter 4.)

In evaluating possible utilitarian replies to these criticisms, it is important to remember that utilitarians insist that *all* entailed costs and benefits of an action or practice must be considered in evaluating its merit. In the case of employee and consumer rights, for example, costs include protests from labor and consumer groups, impairment to social ideals, further alienation of employees from executives, the loss of customers to competitors, etc. Second, rule-utilitarian analyses emphatically deny that single cost/benefit determinations ought always to be accepted. Such utilitarian analyses propose that general rules of justice (justified by broad considerations of utility) ought to constrain particular actions or uses of cost/benefit calculations in all cases. They also claim that the criticisms discussed above are short-sighted, for they focus on injustices that might be done through a too superficial or short-term application of the principle of utility. If one takes a long-range view, utilitarians argue, one will see that utility never eventuates in overall unjust outcomes. We shall encounter this problem again when we come to the subject of justice, and again in Chapter 9.

DEONTOLOGICAL THEORIES

An underlying assumption of the above criticisms of utilitarianism is that an adequate ethical theory must be deontological or duty-based rather than consequential. A deontological theory denies what teleological (and therefore what utilitarian) theories assert—namely, that in ethics only the consequences of actions and rules count. Deontologism (derived from the Greek for "duty") maintains that the concept of duty is independent of the concept of good, and that actions are not justified by their consequences. Factors other than good outcomes determine the rightness of actions—for example the fairness of distribution, a personal promise, a debt to another person, or a contractual relationship.

Deontologists therefore argue that a variety of relationships between persons have significance independent of the *consequences* of these relationships. Some examples:

1. Businesspersons tend to treat each customer according to the history of their relationship. If the person is an old customer and the merchandise being sold is in scarce supply, the customer will be given preferential treatment, for a relationship of commitment and trust has already been established.
2. The consequences of an attempted murder are usually less severe than the real thing, but in terms of motive, the one who attempts murder is often as wicked, sometimes more so, than an actual murderer.

3. Being a parent is said to place a person in a special relation of obligation. In the event of a burning apartment house, a father presumably ought to save his child first, even if the world would be better off if he saved someone else in the building who was more valuable to society.
4. The fact that one has made a promise often obligates one to keep the promise even if it becomes obvious that keeping the promise will not lead to the greatest good.

For the deontologist, in short, there are many special, nonconsequential relations such as friendships, parent-child relations, and business affiliations that intrinsically enrich the moral life.

It is likely that deontological motives play as important a part in some aspects of business ethics as utilitarian ones, though this fact is often overlooked. After all, one tenet of business ethics is the sanctity of contracts. The contractual relationship is a form of promise keeping and the obligatoriness of promises, independent of consequences, is a standard deontological notion. (The role of promise keeping and the contractual nature of business relationships will be discussed further in Chapters 2, 3, and 8.) Moreover, it is often argued that employers stand in special relationships to employees or to their customers and that, as a result, corporations have special moral obligations to their employees or customers, independent of the general good. Deontological "duties" are, from this perspective, an undeniable feature of business ethics.

Another important difference between utilitarians and deontologists arises from the characteristic means/end reasoning used by utilitarians. We have seen that utilitarians focus on goals and on the most efficient means to these ends—a conception of the moral life that both empirical scientists and businesspersons may find congenial. Deontologists, however, think it is fundamentally wrong to conceptualize the moral life—even that of the business community—in such terms. It is wrong because we seldom can be certain of our ultimate goals, and even less do we have the capacity to predict and control the consequences of our actions. Deontologists insist that we abruptly encounter the claims, rights, and moral problems of others, and we are called upon by morality to observe the rights of others and to help them through difficult times.

Consider the following example.[10] In his great novel of big business in Hong Kong, *Noble House,* James Clavell tells the story of a decision made in 1894 by the most powerful business leader in the colony. The city was at that time threatened by bubonic plague, and tens of thousands were dying. The elimination of the rat population was thought essential to the elimination of the plague bacillus; yet in the poverty-ridden hillside village of Tai-ping Shan the superstitions of the inhabitants led them to do nothing to assist in the effort to drive out the rats. In the face of this monumental ignorance and the continued spread of the plague, the business leader acted as follows:

> In the stench of late summer when it seemed the colony was once more doomed, with deaths mounting daily, I had Tai-ping Shan put to the torch by night, the whole monstrous stenching mountainside. That some inhabitants were consumed is on my conscience, but without the cleansing fire the Colony was doomed and hundreds of thousands more doomed.

Whereas such consequential reasoning seems characteristic of (act) utilitarian reasoning, deontologists urge that the rights and claims of villagers in Tai-ping Shan should never even be conceived in terms of social utility. Their rights and person *transcend* utilitarian calculations.

The Importance of Motives

Deontologists commonly insist on the importance of the motives and character of the agent, quite apart from the consequences actually produced by the agent. (A utilitarian will agree that motives are critical, but will always insist that right motives are determined by the intention to produce the best possible consequences.) To understand the deontologist's point about motives, consider the example of three different people making personal sacrifices for a sick relative. Fred makes the sacrifices only because he fears the social criticisms that would result if he didn't. He hates making the sacrifices and secretly resents having to be involved. Bill, however, is naturally a kind-hearted soul. He does not view the "sacrifice" as a genuine sacrifice at all. His deepest satisfaction comes from helping others, especially this relative who suffers the misfortunes of illness. Sam, by contrast, derives no personal satisfaction from taking care of his sick relative. He would rather be doing other things, and he takes care of his sick relative purely from a sense of personal duty.

Let us assume that in the cases of these three differently motivated persons, the consequences are equally good, because the sick aunt is adequately cared for. Suppose we ask, however, which person is behaving in a morally praiseworthy manner. On a utilitarian theory such a question might be hard to answer, especially if act utilitarianism were in question. Most of us would focus on the different motives of the three persons. The deontologist takes this conventional reaction as confirmation of the view that in ordinary moral evaluation motives count substantially. But which motive is morally superior? Nearly everyone would agree that Fred's motive is not a moral motive at all. It is a motive of prudence, and perhaps springs from fear. This is not to say that Fred's action does not have good consequences. It does. However, Fred does not deserve any special moral credit for his act.

This distinction between the motive for an act and the consequences of an act is important for business ethics. Those who argue for a broad notion of corporate responsibility sometimes give arguments analogous to Fred's: acts of social responsibility avoid charges of irresponsibility and thus are in the long run in the self-interest of the business community (see Chapter 2). To recognize the prudential basis of the beneficial consequences does not of course detract from the goodness of the consequences. Indeed, given the purpose or function of the business enterprise, the motive of self-interest may be the most appropriate motive to ensure good consequences. The only point a deontologist would make is that a business derives no special *moral* credit for acting in its own interest, even if society is benefited by and pleased by the action.

If Fred's motive is not moral, what about Bill's and Sam's? Here deontologists disagree about an appropriate answer. Some identify morally correct motivation with altruistic motivation. Bill's behavior is morally right because his action is motivated by a concern for others. This altruistic attitude is absent in Sam's case, and hence Sam's action is morally inferior. However, the eighteenth-century philosopher Immanuel Kant (1734–1804)—without doubt the most influential of all deontological writers—argues on behalf of the moral superiority of Sam's motive. Kant thinks that Bill hardly deserves any more moral credit than Fred. Bill is *naturally* motivated to do the right thing. That he is so motivated merits no moral praise. Kant is saying that you only deserve moral credit when your act is done neither for self-interested reasons nor as the result of a natural psychological impulse. Let us now look further at his rather complicated views in the context of his general ethical theory.

Kantian Ethics

Kant emphasizes performing one's duty for the sake of duty and not for any other reason—one indication that he espouses a pure form of deontology. He insists that all persons act not only *in accordance with duty* but *for the sake of duty*. That is, the person's *motive* for acting must be a recognition of the act as resting on duty. It is not good enough, in Kant's view, that one merely performs the morally correct action, for one could perform one's duty for self-interested reasons having nothing to do with morality. For example—to take up a subject found in Chapter 3—if an employer discloses a health hazard to an employee only because he or she fears a lawsuit, and not because of a belief in the importance of truth telling, then such an employer acts rightly but deserves no moral credit for doing so.

Kant tries to establish the ultimate basis for the validity of moral rules of duty in pure (practical) reason, not in intuition, conscience, or the production of utility. Morality, he contends, provides a rational framework of principles and rules that constrain and guide everyone, independent of their own personal goals and preferences. He thought all considerations of utility and self-interest secondary, because the moral worth of an agent's action depends exclusively on the moral acceptability of the rule according to which the person is acting—or, as Kant prefers to say, moral acceptability depends on the rule that determines the agent's *will*. An action, therefore, has moral worth only when performed by an agent who possesses what Kant calls a good will; and a person has a good will only if moral duty based on a valid rule is the sole motive for the action.

When a person behaves according to binding moral rules valid for everyone, Kant considers that person to have an *autonomous* will. Kant contrasts autonomy with what he calls heteronomy—the determination of the will by persons or conditions other than oneself. Autonomy of the will is present when one knowingly accepts and governs oneself in accordance with universally valid moral principles. To say that an agent "accepts" a moral principle does not mean either that the principle is merely subjective or that each individual must wholly create (author or originate) his or her own moral principles. Kant holds only that each individual must *will the acceptance* of the moral principles to be acted upon. A person's autonomy consists in the ability to govern himself or herself through these moral principles. Kant develops this notion into a fundamental moral law which he characterizes as a categorical demand that persons be treated as ends in themselves and never solely as means to the ends of others. In other words, one must treat persons as having their own autonomously established goals and never treat them purely as the means to one's own personal goals.

In what appears to be his favored formulation, the principle is stated as follows: "I ought never to act except in such a way that I can also will *that my maxim should become a universal law.*" Kant calls this principle the "categorical imperative." It is *categorical,* he argues, because it admits of no exceptions and is absolutely binding. It is *imperative* because it gives instruction about how one must act. He gives several examples of moral maxims that are made imperative by this fundamental principle: "Help others in distress," "Do not commit suicide," and "Work to develop your abilities."

As the above formulation suggests, Kant emphasizes the notion of "rule as universal law." Duty is the proper motive for genuinely moral action, but duty as a motive for moral action has a special characteristic which Kant calls "universality." This odd sounding thesis may be explained as follows: Acts done from moral duty alone have moral worth, and there is a definite source of their worth. That source is found in a principle or rule that determines how we ought to act. Kant is here returning to the importance of motives. Praise or blame depends on what our motives or intentions are, and these are spelled out by the rule or principle on which we act. And what makes these rules that determine duty correct is their universality, i.e., the fact that they consistently apply to everyone.

This Kantian criterion of universality offers some worthwhile lessons. Some of the clearest cases of immoral behavior involve a person trying to make an exception of himself or herself. Sometimes this consistency requirement is captured by the notion of justice, as in these cases: One should not push ahead in a line while attempting to buy tickets to a popular movie; a student should not cheat on exams; a businessperson should not engage in the practices of giving kickbacks and bribes. These practices involve making exceptions of oneself, or exempting oneself from the rules without being willing to grant similar privileges to others.

An example of this Kantian form of reasoning was found in 1969 when some self-announced "entrepreneurs" took pictures from the air of a new E.I. DuPont de Nemours methanol plant in Beaumont, Texas. (Methanol is a chemical used in making antifreeze and was then secret and unpatented.) DuPont sued, alleging wrongful obtaining of trade secrets. Those who took the pictures claimed that there had been no wrongdoing. The pictures had been taken in public airspace, they reasoned, and so were in the public domain. The court upheld DuPont's position. Its argument was that society cannot "accept the law of the jungle as the standard of morality expected in our commercial relations." The court contended that moral standards apply universally in these transactions, and then issued the following universal rule: "To obtain knowledge of a process without spending the time and money to discover it independently is *improper* unless the holder voluntarily discloses it or fails to take reasonable precautions to ensure its secrecy."[11]

But suppose someone is willing to sanction invasion of privacy, theft, line cutting, cheating, kickbacks, and bribes. What would Kant then say? Such practices, he argues, are "contradictory." They are not consistent with the larger social practices of which they are a part. Consider cases of promising, information disclosure, and lying—as found in Chapters 3–5. If one were consistently to recommend that anyone should lie when it worked to his or her advantage, our conventional practices of truth-telling would be undermined. The universalization of rules that allow lying would entitle everyone to lie to you, just as you can lie to them. In this event, one could never tell if a person were telling the truth or lying. Such a rule would thus be self-defeating. Similarly, cheating undermines the practice of examinations. Kickbacks and bribes undermine business practices. All such practices are self-defeating or inconsistent because they undermine a rule or practice that they presuppose.

A dilemma may be constructed that captures Kant's point. Suppose a student were to reflect on whether it is permissible to cheat on an exam. If the student is consistent, he or she must agree to allow any student to cheat. If he or she does not allow cheating for others, he or she seems guilty of a contradiction. On the other hand, if the student is consistent and recommends universal cheating, then the purpose of the exam is undermined and he or she cannot gain the advantage of cheating. Kant's point is implicitly recognized by the business community when corporate officials despair of the immoral practices of corporations and denounce executives engaging in shady practices as undermining the business enterprise itself. (See the discussions in Chapter 2.)

However, the plausibility of Kant's criterion of universalizability will depend on how tightly or loosely it is formulated. In some weak formulations the criterion seems uncontroversially to capture a necessary condition of morality. For example, consistency requires that whenever we judge an act of a certain description to be right (or wrong), we are logically committed to judging *all relevantly similar* acts right (or wrong), whether or not we are interested in specifically *moral* rightness or wrongness. If a person holds that one act is right and another act wrong, but cannot point to any relevant differences between them, the judgment seems both arbitrary and without rational foundation.

However, if formulated differently, it is less plausible to hold that the criterion of universalizability is a necessary condition of morality. If we understand the criterion to hold that all moral principles apply universally to everyone and never apply simply to restricted groups or to individuals, then many more controversial questions arise. Some moral judgments seem tailored to particular cultures and particular times (consider, e.g., the Italian tax case discussed above). Some would also argue that many moral positions involve a significant measure of personal choice that even the individual making the choice would not wish to generalize for others. For example, the statements "An employee ought to comply with the requests of superiors" or "Private property must be respected" are not easily generalizable for all circumstances.

Respect for Persons

Our examination of Kant's philosophy is not yet complete. It has been widely stated in contemporary textbooks that Kant holds categorically that we can never treat another as a means to our ends. This interpretation, however, seems to misrepresent his views. He argues only that we must not treat another *exclusively* as a means to our own ends. When employees are ordered to perform odious tasks, they are treated as a means to an employer's or supervisor's ends, but they are not exclusively used for others' purposes, because they do not necessarily become mere servants or objects. Kant does not prohibit this use of persons categorically and without qualification. His imperative demands only that such persons be treated with the respect and moral dignity to which every person is entitled at all times, including those times when they are used primarily as means to the ends of others. To treat persons merely as means, strictly speaking, is to disregard their personhood by exploiting or otherwise using them without regard to their own interests, needs, and conscientious concerns.

Kant's claim that people must always treat each other as ends in themselves and never as means has in subsequent times been developed as a principle of respect for persons. To treat persons according to Kant's rule is to treat their decisions and values with respect. To fail to respect persons is to treat them as mere means in accordance with our own ends, and thus as if they were not independent agents. To exhibit a lack of respect for persons is either to reject a person's considered judgments or to deny the person the liberty to act on those judgments. For example, an intentional suppression of information to someone, on the basis of which they might have decided not to purchase a house or an automobile, is taken by many to involve just such disrespect. Of course the liberty implied by this principle is not unlimited. Actions that harm others can rightfully be restrained. Nor does the principle prevent us from appreciating that some persons may not be capable of autonomous action. But to the extent that a competent person's unconstrained actions affect only the actor, this principle requires that the reasons for the actions be respected and the actions themselves not be prevented or otherwise interfered with. The most obvious and immediate application of this principle in this volume comes in certain requirements that adequate, nondeceptive disclosure be made to customers, government agencies, employees, clients, and stockholders, prior to the development, marketing, or advertisement of a product or service. (See Chapters 3–5, 8.)

Respect for the human being is often said by deontologists in the Kantian tradition to be demanded for no other reason than that human beings possess a moral *dignity,* and therefore are rightfully the determiners of their own destinies. If it is asked further *why* humans have a moral dignity that entitles them to such respect or *which* properties of the person lead us to respect them, differing answers are available. One view, advanced by many writers in both moral philosophy and the behavioral sciences, is based on a contrast between the human species and other species. Here the argument is that only human beings intentionally perform actions that are motivated by moral rules. Animals may perform quite ably in a laboratory experiment, and such performance might even lead us to say that they act on reasons; but even so, their reasons would not be *moral* reasons. From these premises it is but a short step to the conclusion that because humans act morally and have rational wills, they posses value independently of any special circumstances conferring value; and because all human beings and only human beings have such unconditional value, it is always inappropriate to treat them as if they had the merely conditional value possessed by animals and natural objects.

Respect for persons, thus construed, may easily seem to come into conflict with the constraints of economic interactions. Many people would, for instance, see this Kantian principle at issue in an interesting case involving the Plasma International Company.[12] The case developed in the wake of a disaster in Nicaragua that produced a sudden need for fresh blood to be used in transfusions. Plasma International had obtained the blood in underdeveloped West African countries (often paying as little as 15 cents per pint), and the transaction ultimately yielded the firm nearly a quarter of a million dollars in profits. Because they gave vulnerable West Africans just pennies for a substance whose importance to the situation in Nicaragua was then exploited for tremendous economic gain, Plasma International was accused of treating human beings as though they possessed the merely conditional value of lower animals or natural objects. (This distinction is further explored in Chapter 7.) The company seemed to deny people the respect appropriate to their special dignity. (However, it should once again be emphasized that because people are sometimes treated as having a conditional value in the economic marketplace, it does not automatically follow that they are not also being accorded the respect which is their due.)

Prima Facie Duties

An important deontological theory developed by W.D. Ross is based on his account of *prima facie duties*. He argues that there are several types of moral duties, and that they do not derive from either the principle of utility or Kant's categorical imperative. For example, our promises create duties of fidelity, wrongful actions create duties of reparation, and the generous gifts of our friends create duties of gratitude. Ross defends several additional duties, such as duties of self-improvement, nonmaleficence, beneficence, and justice.

Unlike Kant's system, Ross's list of duties is not based on any overarching principle. He defends it simply as a reflection of our ordinary moral beliefs and judgments. He argues that we must find "the greatest duty" in any given circumstance by finding "the greatest balance" of right over wrong in that particular context. In order to determine this balance, Ross introduces the distinction between *prima facie* duties and *actual* duties. *Prima facie* indicates a duty that is always to be acted upon unless it conflicts on a particular occasion with an equal or stronger duty. Such a duty is always right and binding, all other things being equal. A *prima facie* duty in this sense is "conditional on not being overridden or outweighed by competing moral demands." One's actual duty is determined by an examination of the respective weights of the competing *prima facie* duties. *Prima facie* duties are thus not absolute, since they can be overridden under some conditions; but at the same time they have far greater moral significance than mere rules of thumb.

For example, Ross considers promise keeping a *prima facie* duty. Does this mean that one must always, under all circumstances, keep one's promise? No, for there certainly are situations in which breaking a promise is justified. Minor defaults on a promise are justified whenever disastrous harms would be inflicted on another if one were to keep the promise. To call promise breaking *prima facie* wrong means simply that insofar as an act involves promise breaking it is wrong, unless some more weighty moral consideration is overriding in the circumstances. Should the duty to keep promises come into conflict with the duty to protect innocent persons—as when one breaks a promise in order to protect someone from harm that would occur if the promise were kept—then the actual duty may be to protect innocent persons (thus overriding the *prima facie* duty of promise keeping). We shall return to this problem of *prima facie* claims later while discussing the notion of *prima facie* rights.

Criticisms of Deontological Theories

In conclusion, let us investigate an important criticism of deontological theories that has been expressed by utilitarians, together with a response that deontologists might offer. A widespread utilitarian criticism is that deontologists *covertly* appeal to consequences in order to demonstrate the rightness of actions. John Stuart Mill, for example, argues that even Kant's theory does not avoid appeal to the consequences of an action in determining whether it is right or wrong. On Mill's interpretation of Kant, the categorical imperative demands that an action be morally prohibited if "the *consequences* of (its) universal adoption would be such as no one would choose to incur." Kant fails "almost grotesquely," as Mill puts it, to show that any form of certification of a moral rule appears purely by universalizing rules of conduct. Mill argues that Kant's theory relies on a covert appeal to the utilitarian principle that if the consequences of the universal performance of a certain type of action can be shown to be undesirable overall, then that sort of action is wrong.

One possible defense of Kant against such charges is the following: It is not entirely accurate to say that Kant urges us to disregard consequences, or even that he believes an action is morally right (or wrong) without regard to its consequences. Kant holds only that the features of an action that make it right are not dependent upon any particular outcome. He never advises that we disregard consequences entirely. The consequences of an action often cannot be separated from the nature of the action itself, and so they too must be considered when an agent universalizes the action in order to determine whether it is permissible.

On the other hand, almost no moral philosopher finds Kant's system fully satisfactory. Even his contemporary defenders tend to argue nothing stronger than that Kant provides elements essential for a sound moral position when joined with some contemporary elaborations. For example, by using Kantian elements as a basis, some have attempted to construct a more encompassing deontological theory. Some philosophers are using the Kantian notion of respect for persons as a ground for providing moral theories of justice and rights. If people do have intrinsic unconditional worth, they reason that social and economic institutions should be arranged to protect and sustain individual human worth. Philosophers subscribing to this orientation argue that social and economic institutions, including business enterprises, should promote justice and sustain and enrich rights rather than, as is often the case, subvert them. There is still considerable controversy, however, as to whether deontological theories are adequate to this task and better than utilitarian theories. Let us turn, then, specifically to theories of justice and rights.

THEORIES OF JUSTICE

Human society is to a great extent a cooperative enterprise structured by various moral, legal, and cultural rules and principles. These rules and principles form what may be called the terms of cooperation in society, the implicit and explicit terms under which individuals are obligated to cooperate with others. Sociology, history, cultural anthropology, and social philosophy are all concerned in their different ways, with how rules and principles defining cooperation evolve, are adapted to new situations, and acquire legitimacy for those whom they govern. Philosophers, however, have typically been less interested in questions of history and social science than in questions concerning the justice of the terms of cooperation: what gives one person or group of people a right to expect cooperation from another person or group of people in some societal interchange (especially an economic one) where the former benefit from it and the latter do not? Is it just for some to have more than others? Is it right for one person to gain an economic advantage over another, even if both are abiding by existing societal rules?

Some deontologists have held that principles of justice have a moral priority over all other moral principles, or at least that major moral issues must be framed within a theory of distributive justice. But what is justice, and wherein does its uniqueness lie? Basic notions of justice can be explicated in terms of fairness and "what is deserved." A person has been treated justly when he or she has been given what is due or owed, what he or she deserves or can legitimately claim. What is deserved may, however, be either a benefit or a burden. If a person is morally entitled to confidentiality of information, for example, justice has been done when that information is kept confidential, even if discharging the duty of nondisclosure is inconvenient and difficult. Naturally, any denial of something to which a person has a right or entitlement is an injustice.

The more restricted expression "distributive justice" refers to the proper distribution of social benefits and burdens. Usually it refers to the distribution of social goods—e.g., economic goods and fundamental political rights. But social burdens must also be considered. Paying taxes and being drafted into the armed services to fight a war are distributed burdens, while Medicare checks and grants to do research are distributed benefits. As we shall see in Chapter 9, recent literature on distributive justice has tended to focus on considerations of fair *economic* distribution, especially unjust distributions in the form of inequalities of income between different classes of persons and unfair tax burdens on certain classes. But there are many problems of distributive justice besides strictly economic ones, including the issues raised in prominent contemporary debates over preferential hiring and reverse discrimination, as discussed in Chapter 7.

The notion of justice has been analyzed differently in rival theories (again, see Chapter 9). But common to all theories of justice is this principle: like cases should be treated alike—i.e., equals ought to be treated equally and unequals unequally. This principle is referred to as the formal principle of justice, sometimes the formal principle of equality. It merely asserts that whatever particulars are under consideration, *if* persons are equal in those respects, they should be treated alike. Thus, the formal principle of justice does not tell us how to *determine* equality or proportion in these matters, and it therefore lacks substance as a specific guide to conduct. In any group of persons there will be many ways in which they are both similar and different, and therefore this account of equality must be understood as "equality in relevant respects."

This formal principle leaves space for differences in the interpretation of how justice applies to particular situations, and philosophers have developed many diverse theories of justice that are compatible with it. Again, however, one theme common to most of these theories is that programs or services designed to assist people of a certain class must as a matter of justice be made available to *all* members of that class. To provide some with access to such programs, while denying access to others who are equally qualified (and so entitled) is declared unfair. The principle of justice thus understood is particularly applicable to problems of inequality and unfairness—such as those involved in "unfair hiring practices" and "unfair exploitation of workers." (See Chapters 4, 7, and 9.)

General Theories

Systematic theories of justice attempt to be more specific than the formal principle by precisely elaborating some notion of equality or proportion in distribution, specifying in detail how people are to be compared and what it means to give people their due. Philosophers achieve this specificity by developing *material* principles of justice, so called because they put material content into a theory of justice. Each material principle of justice identifies a relevant property on the basis of which burdens and benefits should be distributed. The following is a sample list of major candidates for the position of valid principles of distributive justice (though longer lists have been proposed):

1. To each person an equal share;
2. To each person according to individual need;
3. To each person according to that person's rights;
4. To each person according to individual effort;
5. To each person according to societal contribution;
6. To each person according to merit.

There is no reason not to accept more than one of these principles, and some theories of justice accept all six as valid. Most societies use several in the belief that different rules are appropriate to different situations.

A particular case from business practice may help to make clearer the variety and interrelation of material principles of justice. The case involves one Mark Dalton, a histology technician in the employ of a large chemical company.[13] Dalton was an excellent worker, but a week-long sick leave led a company nurse to discover that he had a chronic kidney disease. Furthermore, it was discovered that the permissible chemical vapor exposure levels of Dalton's job might exacerbate his kidney condition. The company management found another job at the same rate of pay for which Dalton was qualified, but it turned out that two other employees eligible for promotion were also interested in the job. Both employees had more seniority and better training than Dalton, and one was a woman. In this situation, each of the three employees can appeal to a different material principle of justice to substantiate his or her claim to the available position. Dalton can cite the material principle of need, arguing that his medical condition requires that he be offered the new position. With their superior experience and training, each of the other two employees can invoke material principles of merit, societal contribution, and perhaps individual effort on behalf of their claims to the position. Additionally, considerations of equal opportunity might give the woman valid grounds for claiming that justice should take account of her special individual rights, introducing yet another material principle.

While this case is meant to illustrate the possible complexity of appeals to justice, most general *theories* of justice attempt to systematize and simplify moral intuitions by selecting and emphasizing one or more of the available material principles. As we shall see in detail in Chapter 9 of this volume, *egalitarian* theories of justice emphasize equal access to primary goods; *Marxist* theories emphasize need; *libertarian* theories emphasize rights to social and economic liberty; and *utilitarian* theories emphasize a mixed use of such criteria so that public and private utility are maximized.

Just Procedures and Just Results

In the literature on justice there also exists an important distinction between just procedures and just results. The term "distribution" may refer to the procedure of distributing, or it may refer to the result of some system of distribution. Ideally it is preferable to have both just procedures and just results, but it is not always possible to have both. For example, one might achieve a just result in distributing wealth, but one might use an unjust procedure, such as undeserved taxation of certain groups, in order to achieve it. By contrast, a just procedure such as a fair trial reaches unjust results when the innocent are found guilty. In discussions of justice it is often the system which is in question, although those who are criticizing the system may be pointing to unjust results. It is important to be clear on whether it is the procedures or the results or both which are under consideration.

Let us examine the notion of procedural justice by supposing that three friends order a pizza. When the pizza arrives, how should it be divided? Barring special circumstances, the result or outcome which seems most just is that each person receives an equal share. But what procedure should be used to ensure that result? An appropriate procedure for this purpose is to make the person cutting the pizza take the last piece. The pizza example provides an illustration of fairness in both procedures and results. In some cases, however, just procedures alone must be relied upon to determine just results. Consider a lottery as an example. It makes perfect sense to speak of the conditions of a fair lottery. But what makes it fair? Suppose that most entrants are poor, but the winner is an extremely rich man. Can we say that the lottery is unjust? Certainly not. As with horse races, we condemn a lottery which is fixed, but we do not condemn one where the rich are winners. In situations like these, as long as the procedures are just, the results too are just. Many problems of justice that we must handle as a cooperative society are ones of designing a system or set of procedures that provides as much justice as possible. Once we agree on appropriate procedures, then as long as a person is treated according to those procedures, the procedure is just—even if it turns out to produce inequalities that seem by other standards unjust. Naturally, in situations where procedural justice is the best we can do, we should accept the results of our procedural system with a certain amount of humility, and where possible we should perhaps make allowances for inevitable inequalities.

Because unfortunate (but not necessarily unfair) outcomes are inevitable in purely procedural systems, shifting the issue from results to procedures will not avoid all ethical controversy. The various traditional theories of ethics will provide competing theories of criteria of just procedures as well as of just outcomes. Resolution of all debate would require a common set of procedures (or a metaprocedure). Within the American system, of course, representative democracy acts as something of a final procedure, but agreement on this procedure will clearly not suffice to quiet all controversy about just treatment.

In Chapter 9 we will study rival theories of justice and the controversies they generate over both just procedures and just results. It would be unfortunate if the discussion here (or there) led the reader to the conclusion that theories of justice are in perpetual warfare and in the end yield no insights into real life circumstances of injustice. One perspective from which to judge competing conceptions of justice is by using the method John Rawls calls *reflective equilibrium*. Rawls agrees with many moral philosophers that there are paradigm cases of unjust behavior, such as punishing the innocent, and of just behavior, such as an impartial and thorough court of appeals. He assumes, then, that no moral principle can be adequate which would permit such cases of immoral behavior as punishing the innocent or which would not praise a court that found an innocent person not guilty. If all moral issues had such paradigm-case resolutions, there would be no need for moral principles. However, many moral issues have no clear parallel solution; for example, the problems of "deceptive" advertising and environmental responsibility present numerous dilemmas (see Chapters 5 and 7). The purpose of moral principles such as principles of justice is to assist persons in making difficult decisions about these dilemmas. As we actively engage in making moral judgments, there is an interplay between the principles we use and the cases to which we apply our principles. We start with paradigm cases about certain acts that are either obviously morally right or morally wrong. We then search for principles which are consistent with these paradigm cases, are consistent with each other, and assist us in resolving difficult moral problems. These principles are then tested to see if they yield results which are counterintuitive. If so, they are readjusted or are given up and new principles are developed. Moral inquiry and moral practice in virtually every prominent theory of justice reflect this mutual testing of cases against principles and principles against cases. These theories thus may be viewed as general attempts to put all our moral judgments into as consistent a framework as possible.

The situation in business ethics is similar. The competitive free enterprise system is viewed by businesspersons as a justified procedure for organizing economic institutions, although the competitive free enterprise system can lead to unjust results and is a good example of procedural justice that can lead to very unfortunate outcomes. When criticized, some economists and business leaders admit that free enterprise distribution can lead to unfortunate results, but they argue that no other scheme is procedurally more satisfactory. Like most systems of criminal punishment (retributive justice), they argue, the free enterprise system of distributive justice is hardly perfect; but in structure it may be the best possible. Periodically, however, the general public itself comes to doubt the justice of the free enterprise system and to search for alternatives or modifications to it. In such times, discussions in business ethics are particularly appropriate and useful, for business practices may be examined in a way that behooves both the business community and its critics to enter into a dialogue and to attempt to build a new consensus about morally acceptable business practices. This book is designed to present the student with some of the major issues that must be discussed in any such dialogue.

THEORIES OF RIGHTS

Much of the modern ethical discussion that we shall encounter throughout this volume turns on ideas about rights. Many public policy issues are said to be matters of justice in that they concern rights or attempts to secure rights. Indeed, our political tradition has itself developed from a conception of "natural rights." However, until the seventeenth and eighteenth centuries, problems of political philosophy were rarely discussed in terms of rights, perhaps because duties to lord, king, state, church, and God had been the dominant focus of political and ethical theory. New political views were introduced at this point in history, including the notion of universal "natural rights." These rights were thought to consist primarily of rights not to be interfered with, or liberty rights. Proclamations of such rights as those to life, liberty, property, a speedy trial, and the pursuit of happiness subsequently formed the core of major political and legal documents.

Thus, historically, the notion of "natural" (or "human") rights may be seen to arise out of a need to check the sovereign power of states. In this sense, rights are opposed to mere "edicts of toleration." To say that a person or persons have a *right* to X is to say more than that the sovereign power tolerates their having something or exercising some power; it says that it would be wrong for them not to have X. When someone appeals to rights, a response is demanded and we must either accept the person's claim as valid, discredit the claim by countervailing considerations, or acknowledge the right but show how it can be overridden by competing moral claims.

The idea that certain moral rights exist prior to and independent of social conventions and laws has led philosophers to speculate about the nature and source of rights. They ask questions such as the following: Are there rights independent of laws and conventions, or are rights merely cultural fictions? If they exist, are they grounded purely in the obligations of others? Do moral rights exist prior to and independently of what governments recognize as rights? What are the limits on the scope of such rights? What does it mean to say "X has a right," and how did X acquire such a right?

Rights have various origins. If I swear to you that I will tell the whole truth and nothing but the truth, you acquire a right to be told the truth. Still other rights are transmitted by family ties. But do all rights rest on such contingent relations? Many philosophers have maintained that we have *fundamental* rights, irrespective of merit, just because we are human. This brings to mind the classical idea that humanity is a quality possessed by all people. This humanity is said to confer rights to impartial treatment in matters of justice, freedom, equality of opportunity, and so on. Thus, when members of minority groups complain about discriminatory hiring practices that destroy their human dignity and self-respect, one plausible interpretation of these complaints is that those who register them believe that their fundamental moral rights are being violated.

Everyone agrees that legal rights exist and are commonly violated, but the status of moral rights is more puzzling, and the language of moral rights is still greeted by some with scepticism. Many also find absurd both the proliferation of and the conflict among diverse rights claims (especially in recent political debates). For example, it has been claimed by some parties that one has a right to have an abortion, while others claim that there is a right to life that precludes the right to have an abortion. As we shall see repeatedly throughout this volume, rights language has been extended to include such controversial rights as the right to privacy, the rights of children, the rights of animals, the rights of the elderly, rights to confidential information, and the rights of special interest groups.

One such extension of rights language is found in recent discussions of the decisions made by female employees of chemical companies to undergo voluntary sterilization in order to retain their jobs. This practice raises a number of interesting moral issues, many of which turn on questions of moral and legal rights. Spokesmen for the chemical companies have argued that unborn fetuses have moral and legal rights that the companies, as employers of fertile women, are obliged to protect—the implication being that these obligations justify company decisions to remove nonsterilized women from high paying but potentially dangerous positions.[14] Opponents of such policies argue that the fertile female employees themselves have countervailing moral and economic rights that need to be taken into account. The intractability of such appeals to rights highlights the importance of analyzing the moral and legal foundations of rights claims, and it will therefore prove useful to examine some of the carefully drawn distinctions regarding the nature and types of rights that have emerged in ethical theory.

Prima Facie and Absolute Rights

Prima facie duties were discussed in the earlier section on deontological theories. Such duties are not absolute, for they are simply strong moral demands that may be overridden by more stringent competing moral demands. Such competition occurs in the case of rights as well—as we just noticed in discussing the rights of unborn fetuses and of fertile female employees. Here the problem of competing rights undercuts the assumption, owing perhaps to political statements about fundamental human rights, that rights are absolute. For this reason most writers in ethics agree that a person can only exercise a right to something if *sufficient justification* exists—i.e., when a right has an overriding status. Rights such as a right to equal economic opportunity, a fetus's right to physical well-being, and a right to be saved from starvation thus must compete with other rights in many situations—producing protracted controversy and a need to balance with great discretion the competing rights claims.

Moral and Legal Rights

There are substantial differences between moral and legal rights, for legal systems do not formally require reference to moral systems for their understanding or grounding, nor do moral systems formally require reference to legal systems. One may have a legal right to do something patently immoral, or have a moral right without any corresponding legal guarantee. Legal rights are derived from political constitutions, legislative enactments, case law, and the executive orders of the highest state official. Moral rights, by contrast, exist independently of and form a basis for criticizing or justifying legal rights. Finally, legal rights can be eliminated simply by lawful amendments to political constitutions, or even by a coup d'etat, but moral rights cannot be eroded or banished by political votes, powers, or amendments.

Some rights are neither moral nor legal. Official organizations create institutional rights, i.e. claims supportable by reference to the basic rules of an institution. For example, by joining a club, one may, according to the rules governing the club, acquire the right to use their tennis courts; one's claim to the use of the tennis courts is justified by reference to the rules. Arrangements that define institutional roles and responsibilities often confer rights, as in the case of the physician-patient relationship. These conventional rights contrast with moral rights in that they do not exist independently of the set of conventions or rules governing the enterprise. They differ from legal rights in that they are not always recognized as rights in the law.

The Correlativity of Rights and Obligations

We have thus far not determined how precisely we are to understand the language and basis of rights in moral discourse, and in what respect (if any) there is a relationship between one person's rights and another's obligations. A plausible beginning is to say that any right entails an obligation on the part of others either to provide something or not to interfere with one's liberty. Thus, if a state promises or otherwise incurs an obligation to provide such goods as food stamps or certain forms of consumer protection, then citizens can claim an entitlement—a *positive* right—to the stamps or the protections when they meet the relevant criteria of need. The right to die, the right to privacy, the right to a healthy environment, and all so-called *negative* rights entail that someone is obligated to abstain from interfering with one's intended course in life. This analysis accords with the widely accepted idea that the language of rights is translatable into the language of obligations—that is, that rights and obligations are logically correlative.

An illustration of this correlativity of rights and obligations is provided by the issues surrounding a recent strike at the Adolph Coors brewery in Golden, Colorado.[15] In April of 1977, 1,400 workers at the brewery left their jobs in what was to become a prolonged and bitter walkout. At first, the industrial action appeared to turn on technical questions involving seniority, the nature of the work week, etc., but more general issues of employee rights and employer obligations gradually came to the fore as the dispute wore on. Citing such practices as the use of lie detector tests in screening job applicants and the tendency of company interviewers to ask non-job related questions, union spokesmen claimed that Coors' management was not fulfilling its moral obligation to respect employee rights to privacy. Such negative rights, an argument on behalf of the striking workers might go, carve out a sphere of protected activity with which the employer is morally obliged not to interfere. The argument in effect is that employee rights to privacy entail (by correlativity) an obligation on employers not to invade privacy (see Chapter 3).

If the general correlativity thesis illustrated by this case is correct, there is perhaps little that is distinctive about rights as a moral category. The moral basis for their assertion rests in the obligations of others (though it is controversial whether rights are generated from obligations or obligations generated from rights). This analysis of rights suggests—but does not prove—that rights are grounded in obligations. If so, a theory of rights would require a theory of obligations for its justification. The issue of whether there are rights to privacy, equal employment opportunity, or whatever would thus turn on whether there are certain moral obligations to provide these benefits or to ensure these liberties. The basis of the required obligations—if there are such obligations—could in theory plausibly be justice, social utility, contractual agreement, or any of the ethical principles and theories studied previously.

CONCLUSION

In this chapter several central concepts and issues in ethical theory have been examined. The objective has been to explore major options and distinctions so as to promote critical reflection on the cases and articles in subsequent chapters. Many authors whose writings are found in later chapters would not subscribe without further qualification to theories such as utilitarianism or deontology presented in this chapter. Yet many appeals found in their work conform to these theories in some form, and in this respect the broad characterizations found here should prove useful for understanding the orientation of these authors.

On the other hand, ethical theory will not alone suffice as a tool of analysis in the case of many essays, for some controversies found in this volume are largely factual and some are more conceptual than moral. Ethical theory also has promoted rival answers to important moral problems, which present obvious difficulties for the corporate executive, labor leader, or employee who is called upon to make actual decisions that cannot wait for the perfect ethical theory. Nonetheless, the unifying thread throughout this volume is critical and constructive reflection on moral problems, and ethical theory provides an indispensable means to this end.

T.L.B.

Notes

1. Our discussion of this case is indebted to Richard Wokutch's write-up found in the cases at the end of Chapter 2 in this volume; also to Elizabeth Gatewood and Archie B. Carroll, ''Anatomy of a Corporate Social Response: The Procter & Gamble Rely Case,'' *Business Horizons* (September 1981). For later developments see the book mentioned in footnote 6.
2. Dean Rotbard and John A. Prestbo, ''Killing a Product,'' *Wall Street Journal* (November 3, 1980), p. 21.
3. Edward G. Harness, ''Views on Corporate Responsibility,'' *Corporate Ethics Digest,* 1 (September-October 1980).
4. We are indebted to John Cronquist for some of the observations in this paragraph.
5. This case is reprinted in Robert J. Baum, ed., *Ethical Problems in Engineering,*

2nd ed., Vol. 2: Cases (Troy, N.Y.: Rensselear Polytechnic Institute, 1980), pp. 58–62; quotation p. 58.

6. Tom L. Beauchamp, ed., *Case Studies in Business, Society, and Ethics* (Englewood Cliffs, N.J.: Prentice-Hall, 1983).

7. *Ibid.*

8. See Mr. Kotchian's defense in his article in the *Saturday Review* (July 9, 1977).

9. See both Beauchamp, *op. cit.*, and Earl A. Molander, *Responsive Capitalism: Case Studies in Corporate Social Conduct* (New York: McGraw-Hill, 1980), pp. 100–112.

10. James Clavell, *Noble House* (New York: Delacorte Press, 1981), p. 857.

11. Quoted from George A. Steiner and John F. Steiner, *Casebook for Business, Government, and Society*, 2nd ed. (New York: Random House, 1980), p. 151.

12. T. W. Zimmerer and P. L. Preston, "Plasma International," in Beauchamp, *op. cit.*, and in R. D. Hay, *et al.*, eds., *Business and Society* (Cincinnati: South-Western Publishing Co., 1976).

13. This case report by Robert E. Stevenson is found in *Hastings Center Report*, 10 (December 1980), p. 25.

14. See, e.g., Philip Shabecoff, "Industry and Women Clash Over Hazards in the Workplace," *The New York Times* (January 3, 1981), and the DuPont case in Beauchamp, *op. cit.*

15. This case is taken from Vincent Barry, *Moral Issues in Business* (Belmont, Calif.: Wadsworth Publishing Company, Inc., 1979), p. 149.

SUGGESTED SUPPLEMENTARY READINGS

Business Ethics and Ethical Theory

VELASQUEZ, MANUEL. *Business Ethics: Concepts and Cases.* Englewood Cliffs, N.J.: Prentice-Hall, 1982.

Morality and Ethical Theory

BEAUCHAMP, TOM L. *Philosophical Ethics.* New York: McGraw-Hill, 1982.

FRANKENA, WILLIAM K. *Ethics.* 2nd edition. Englewood Cliffs, N.J.: Prentice-Hall, 1973.

MACINTYRE, ALASDAIR. *A Short History of Ethics.* New York: The Macmillan Company, 1966.

MACKIE, JOHN. *Ethics: Inventing Right and Wrong.* Harmondsworth, Eng.: Penguin Books Ltd., 1977.

NIELSEN, KAI. "Problems of Ethics," in Edwards, Paul, ed., *Encyclopedia of Philosophy.* New York: Macmillan and Free Press, 1967. Vol. 3, pp. 117-134.

TAYLOR, PAUL W., ed. *Problems of Moral Philosophy,* 3rd edition. Belmont, Calif.: Wadsworth Publishing Company, Inc., 1978. Chapter 1.

Justification

GRIFFITHS, A. PHILLIPS. "Ultimate Moral Principles: Their Justification," in Edwards, Paul, ed., *Encyclopedia of Philosophy.* New York: Macmillan and Free Press, 1967. Vol. 8, pp. 177-182.

HELD, VIRGINIA. "Justification: Legal and Political." *Ethics,* 86 (October, 1975), 1-16.

Relativism and Moral Disagreement

BEAUCHAMP, TOM L. *Philosophical Ethics.* New York: McGraw-Hill, 1982. Chapter 2.

BRANDT, RICHARD B. "Ethical Relativism," in Edwards, Paul, ed., *Encyclopedia of Philosophy.* New York: Macmillan and Free Press, 1967. Vol. 3, pp. 75-78.

LADD, JOHN, ed. *Ethical Relativism.* Belmont, Calif.: Wadsworth Publishing Company, Inc., 1973.

RACHELS, JAMES. "Can Ethics Provide Answers?" *Hastings Center Report,* 10 (June, 1980), 32-40.

Egoism

BRANDT, RICHARD B. *Ethical Theory.* Englewood Cliffs, N.J.: Prentice-Hall, 1959. Chapter 14.

KALIN, JESSE. "On Ethical Egoism," *American Philosophical Quarterly Monograph Series* No. 1: *Studies in Moral Philosophy* (1968), pp. 26-41.

MACINTYRE, ALASDAIR. "Egoism and Altruism," *Encyclopedia of Philosophy,* Edwards, Paul, ed. New York: Macmillan and Free Press, 1967. Vol. 2, pp. 462-466.

MILO, RONALD D., ed. *Egoism and Altruism.* Belmont, Cal.: Wadsworth Publishing Co., Inc., 1973.

RACHELS, JAMES. "Two Arguments Against Ethical Egoism," *Philosophia*, 4 (1974): 297–314.

Utilitarianism

BAYLES, MICHAEL D., ed. *Contemporary Utilitarianism*. Garden City, N.Y.: Doubleday & Co., Inc., 1968.

BENTHAM, JEREMY. *Introduction to the Principles of Morals and Legislation* (1789), ed. W. Harrison, with *A Fragment on Government*. Oxford: Hafner Press, 1948.

GOROVITZ, SAMUEL, ed. *Mill: Utilitarianism, with Critical Essays*. New York: Bobbs-Merrill, 1971.

MILL, JOHN STUART. *On Liberty*. London: J. W. Parker, 1859. (Widely reprinted.)

Deontology

KANT, IMMANUEL. *Foundations of the Metaphysics of Morals*. Trans. by Lewis White Beck. Indianapolis: Bobbs-Merrill, 1959.

NELL, ONORA. *Acting on Principle, An Essay on Kantian Ethics*. New York and London: Columbia University Press, 1975.

RAWLS, JOHN. *A Theory of Justice*. Cambridge, Mass.: Harvard University Press, 1971.

ROSS, WILLIAM D. *The Right and the Good*. Oxford: Oxford University Press, 1930.

WOLFE, ROBERT P. *Kant: A Collection of Critical Essays*. Garden City, New York: Doubleday, 1967. Part Two.

Justice

BENN, STANLEY I. "Justice," in Edwards, Paul, ed., *Encyclopedia of Philosophy*. New York: Macmillan and Free Press, 1967. Vol. 4.

FEINBERG, JOEL. *Social Philosophy*. Englewood Cliffs, N.J.: Prentice-Hall, 1973. Chapter 7.

[See Chapter 9 for more advanced reading on topics of justice.]

Moral and Legal Rights

DWORKIN, RONALD. *Taking Rights Seriously*. Cambridge, Mass.: Harvard University Press, 1977.

FEINBERG, JOEL. *Social Philosophy*. Englewood Cliffs, N.J.: Prentice-Hall, 1973. Chapters 4–6.

GOLDING, MARTIN P. "The Concept of Rights: A Historical Sketch," in Bandman, Elsie, and Bandman, Bertram, eds., *Bioethics and Human Rights*. Boston: Little, Brown & Co., 1978. Chapter 4.

LYONS, DAVID, ed. *Rights*. Belmont, Calif.: Wadsworth Publishing Company, 1979.

SHUE, HENRY. *Basic Rights: Subsistence, Affluence, and U.S. Foreign Policy*. Princeton: Princeton University Press, 1980.

CHAPTER 2

CORPORATE SOCIAL RESPONSIBILITY

INTRODUCTION

LOCATING THE MORAL AGENT

To some, the question "What is the social responsibility of a corporation?" is meaningless. You can't talk about corporations as moral agents. After all, "moral responsibility" is a term we apply to fully autonomous persons. We don't apply the term to mental defectives or small children, and we certainly don't apply it to nonhuman entities like coyotes and mountains. Since a corporation is an artificial creation and hence more like a poem than a poet, how can society view it as morally responsible?

As Walter Wriston has said:

> On current values: Values are topsy-turvy. It boggles the mind—the transfer of personal integrity to institutional integrity. Now college students have a mixed dormitory, men live on one floor and women on the next, and they all sit around worrying about whether or not General Motors is being honest. When I was in college, it was different. We were concerned about personal values. I believe that there are no institutional values, only personal ones.[1]

Wriston's words can be interpreted in two different ways. On the one hand, he could be interpreted to mean that since corporations are not persons, they cannot be held morally responsible. Any talk of corporate responsibility or corporate values must ultimately be a shorthand device for talk about the responsibility of corporate officials. A second, more radical interpretation is that one cannot speak meaningfully of the social responsibility of corporations or of the social responsibility of corporate officials. On this interpretation, Wriston would be saying that there are moral questions about coeds living together, but there are no moral questions that can arise about the behavior of General Motors.

This second interpretation is not without its defenders. In his article

"Can Corporations Have Moral Responsibility?" Richard De George refers to those holding this position as subscribers to the "Organizational View." On this view, a corporation was *created* with an end toward profit. The organization's goal is profit. As an artificial creation, it is not an autonomous rational agent and hence is not an object we can morally evaluate. Moreover, each employee has a specific role (function) which he or she is to carry out in accordance with organizational goals. With respect to these organizational goals, they do not act autonomously. Hence, the actions of corporate employees cannot be morally evaluated. Neither the corporation itself nor corporate employees can be held morally responsible.

This argument certainly seems questionable. We often talk and act as if either corporations or corporate employees could be considered morally responsible. Moreover, if we changed our habits of acting and talking, then both corporations and corporate employees would be given moral immunity. Any corporate action would be morally legitimate if it contributed to the corporate goal of profit making. However, if individual lying or stealing on behalf of individual interests are wrong, aren't lying or stealing on behalf of the interest of corporate profit equally wrong? Historically there is no warrant for saying that society created corporations with the intention that they be exempt from moral constraints. Moreover, there is currently considerable debate as to whether or not the only goal—or even the primary goal—of a corporation is profit making. Corporations may have explicit moral goals as well. For these reasons and others, researchers in business ethics are in virtually unanimous agreement that the organizational view is mistaken.

In holding a corporation morally accountable, are we simply holding individuals in the corporation morally accountable, or is there a sense in which we can hold the corporation itself morally responsible as well? De George emphasizes the moral responsibility of individuals within the corporation. He concludes his essay by delineating five models for assigning, within the corporation, responsibility for corporate acts, and by considering which model, if any, is most appropriate for the task.

In their article, "Can a Corporation Have A Conscience?" Goodpaster and Matthews argue that you can speak of holding both corporate employees and the corporation itself morally responsible. Just as you can describe corporate decisions as impulsive or nonimpulsive, long-term or short-term, rational or nonrational, you can speak of corporate decisions as embodying or not embodying the moral point of view.

GOOD BUSINESS PRACTICE AND THE PURPOSE OF BUSINESS

It is one thing to show that a corporation can be held morally responsible. It is quite another to show what its moral responsibilities are. As a businessperson considers some of the objectives and criticisms of traditional business practices, sooner or later he or she will undoubtedly ask, "What constitutes a good business practice?" What does it mean to be a *good* thing, whether the thing in question is a toy, a business, a parade, or whatever? Over two thousand years ago, Greek moral philosophers posed this question by asking what the purpose or function of something is. Suppose, for example, we want to know what a good racehorse is. On the first level, a good racehorse is a horse that wins races. By studying the horses to learn what characteristics contribute to the winning of races—speed, agility, discipline, etc.—we learn the characteristics of a good racehorse. And so it is with tools, works of art, and methods of accounting. The question "What is a good painting, or a good accountant, or a good house?" is answered by enumerating those characteristics essential to the purpose or function of a painting, an accountant, or a house. This way of looking at the world of objects, events, and practices represents a common bond between our way of thinking and the thinking of these early Greek moral philosophers.

Using this same functional analysis, Plato (427–347 B.C.) and Aristotle (384–322 B.C.) attempted to give an account of the good state. To reach his conclusions, Plato considered the various groups or classes within the state and asked what the appropriate function of each class is. So long as each class within the state is performing its proper function, he argued, then the state is good. However, should members of one class aspire to perform the activities of another class, the state becomes disordered and is no longer a good state. Plato focused on three classes: the business and labor community (as we shall call it here), the armed forces or soldiers, and the rulers or top agents of national policy. The rulers he took to be analogous to reason in the human soul, the soldiers analogous to will, and the labor and business community analogous to appetite.

Businesspersons and workers might be annoyed at being compared with the "lower" aspect of the human soul. However, one powerful and influential view held by some businesspersons is distinctly Platonic. These businesspersons would agree with Plato that the appropriate function of the business community is *to provide for the material needs of the citizens of the state in an efficient manner.* This is Plato's larger thesis. Many would also agree with Plato that the making of policies that promote the general good of the state is the proper function of government, and that when members of the business community try to bring about the public good without legitimate authorization, such action will only lead to a confusion of functions and to general disorder. On such matters, Plato and the contemporary economist Milton Friedman are in agreement. On Friedman's view, the statement "The business of business is business" is not an empty definition but is a Platonic moral program for the good or well-ordered state.

Friedman defends a "classical" or "narrow" view of corporate social responsibility, which limits corporate responsibility to making profits for its shareholders. Defenders of the narrow view indicate that business has its appropriate function, which is making a profit, and that in a free and good society, each group within society should simply work at performing its own particular function well. The notion that various groups within society have discrete functions supports a commitment to pluralism. According to this theory, the key feature of pluralism is the advocacy of multiple centers of power, and the chief danger to democracy and to individual freedom is the centralization of power, especially government power.

Many concerned businesspersons fear that calls for increased social responsibility on the part of businesspersons will only increase government control. An argument on behalf of the limitation of increased government control presupposes the functional analysis, for it is generally recognized that the function of government is to look after the public interest. If business were to expand its function from making profits to looking after the public interest, it would be exercising prerogatives appropriate to government, and hence would put itself under government control. Other businesspeople fear that calls for increased corporate responsibility will put too much power in the hands of corporate officials, who, unlike government officials, are not elected representatives charged with determining the public good. In a democratic society, corporate executives have neither the expertise nor the right to implement their own views of the public good. Both of these concerns about excess centralized power are discussed in the article by Theodore Levitt, "The Dangers of Social Responsibility."

The classical view that a corporation's primary responsibility is to maximize the profit of stockholders is embodied in *Dodge* v. *Ford Motor Company*. The Court ruled that the benefits of higher salaries for Ford workers and the benefits of lower Ford auto prices to consumers could not take priority over the interests of the stockholders. It was not until 1953 in the case of *A.P. Smith Manufacturing Company* v. *Barlow, et al.*, that corporate officials had something approaching legal permission to undertake acts designed to promote the public good. This case, and the subsequent appeal decision, which is partially reprinted in this chapter, mark a watershed in the history of the development of corporate responsibility. Judges Stein and Jacobs recognize that the corporate good and the good of society are bound together: To twist a saying, "What is good for America is good for General Motors." Legal recognition of the interrelation of public good and corporate good permits a broader view of corporate social responsibility.

But if business has moral obligations exceeding the obligation to make a profit, what are those obligations? Perhaps profit maximization should be constrained by some specifiable moral minimum. John Simon, Charles Powers, and Jon Gunnemann argue that the concept of the moral minimum draws on a distinction between negative injunctions and affirmative duties. Their distinction is based on the distinction between not causing harm and doing everything one can to promote the good. They argue that although society cannot legitimately impose affirmative duties on corporations, society certainly can legitimately impose negative injunctions on corporations, i.e., society can legitimately insist that corporate activities not cause harm. These authors recognize that many of our actions indirectly cause harm and hence that some criteria are needed for determining what harms fall under a person's or corporation's area of responsibility.

By contrast, a much broader set of social responsibilities for business is envisioned in the selection by Keith Davis, who provides a rationale for some of the broader demands society is currently making on corporations.

THE BUSINESS CONTRACT WITH SOCIETY

Another way to approach the question of the specific obligations and duties of corporations is through the notion of a contract. Contract arguments are both familiar to and well accepted by the business community. Any incorporated business has a charter which is a kind of contract in which society permits the corporation to do business. It is presumed that business practices will lead to the public good. Original charters were based on the assumption that the pursuit of profit yielded utilitarian results. In other words, the narrow view of corporate responsibility represented by Friedman and Levitt was assumed to be in the best interest of the public at large. If that assumption were successfully challenged, one would have grounds for justifying a broader conception of social responsibility. The current interest in business ethics reflects the concern of many members of society who are challenging this traditional view. The idea of changing the social contract with business is the focal point of Melvin Anshen's provocative article.

Any fundamental change in our society's understanding of the function of business or of the basis on which society charters corporations (enters into contracts with business) raises fundamental moral issues of its own. Those like Friedman and Levitt who take the so-called narrow view of corporate responsibility could raise a legitimate moral point in the face of society's demands that the social contract with business be changed. The making of a contract is a type of promise making. Just as one party cannot simply break a promise when the keeping of the promise would be inconvenient, so society cannot change the rules under which business operates whenever it would be convenient for society to do so. Would society not be treating business unjustly when it demands changes in the rules? The selection by Norman Bowie not only addresses this issue, but considers some of the moral principles which should govern any attempt to rewrite the social contract with business.

If business and society are to develop a new social contract, then new principles or rules will have to be added to supplement the principle of profit maximization. The injuction to follow the moral minimum may be sufficient as a general principle, but it needs to be carefully analyzed in particular situations. After all, a business which cannot make a profit cannot, in the long run, stay in business. A nonexistent business cannot contribute to the public good. Businesspersons argue with some force that those who demand that business assist in alleviating every social ill overlook the competitive realities and the necessity of being profitable. On the other hand, the pursuit of profit, like the winning of an athletic contest, is not everything. In that regard, Vince Lombardi was wrong. There is a notion of dirty football, and the desire to win does not justify playing dirty football. Similarly, there are notions of unacceptable business practice and the desire to make a profit does not justify engaging in those unacceptable practices.

The difficult problems in business ethics occur when some balancing of profit and the broader social good must be accomplished. One such problem is considered by John Kavanagh. If profit were the main concern, many plants would be closed or relocated. But plant closings cause real harm to the communities in which they are located, and in a one company town, the harm is catastrophic. The principle, "maximize profit no matter what the impact," appears to violate morality. Yet the opposing principle, "Never close a plant on economic grounds," is unrealistic and, if followed, would frustrate one of the legitimate purposes of a corporation—the pursuit of profit. Kavanagh sets for himself the task of finding acceptable moral principles which would enable businesspersons considering a plant closing to balance the company's duty to pursue profit against the company's obligation to the community in which the plant exists.

Kavanagh's analysis suggests that corporations have multiple obligations. The classical theory of a sole obligation to shareholders would be replaced by a contemporary theory of obligation to stakeholders, where stakeholders include shareholders, employees, customers, suppliers, and lenders. The task of the corporate manager would be to harmonize these varied and often conflicting obligations. Many businesspersons agree that the modern manager is not being socially responsible if his or her only concern is the interest of the shareholders.[2]

N.E.B.

Notes

1. *New Yorker,* Vol. 56, Jan-Feb 16, 1981.
2. For the most advanced work aimed at providing a mechanism for harmonizing stakeholder interests, see R. Edward Freeman and David L. Reed, "Stockholders and Stakeholders: A New Perspective on Corporate Governance." Wharton ARC Publication No. 2168. Philadelphia, Pa., 1981.

CAN CORPORATIONS HAVE MORAL RESPONSIBILITY?

Richard T. De George

The notion of collective moral responsibility has received relatively little treatment in the Anglo-American philosophical literature.[1] This is surprising, given the increasingly widespread practice of ascribing moral respon-

Richard T. De George, "Can Corporations Have Moral Responsibility?", in "Collective Responsibility in the Professions," ed. Michael A. Payne, *University of Dayton Review,* Vol. 5, 2 (Winter 1981-82), 3-15. Reprinted by permission.

sibility to groups, peoples, and other collections of individuals. After World War II it was common for people to speak of the moral responsibility of the German people for Nazi atrocities; during the Vietnam War many people accused America of immorality in carrying on an immoral war and using immoral tactics such as defoliation and napalm bombings; the whites in the United States have been said to be morally responsible for the plight of the blacks and responsible for making due reparation; and so on. There are many issues involved in the ascription of collective moral responsibility. In this paper I shall focus on collective responsibility as it pertains to corporations.

Corporations make for a special case of discussion of collective responsibility because they are a special kind of entity. Chief Justice Marshall, in *Dartmouth College* v. *Woodward* in 1819 gave the corporation its classical formulation: "A corporation is an artificial being, invisible, intangible, and existing only in contemplation of law. Being the mere creature of law, it possesses only those properties which the character of creation confers upon it, either expressly, or as incidental to its very existence. These are such as are supposed best calculated to effect the object for which it was created."[2] Corporations are not natural persons, they do not have the properties of natural persons, and they have neither all the liberties nor all the liabilities of natural persons. These are the minimum legal facts which every theory concerning a corporation must acknowledge and take into account.

Now there are two views of the moral responsibility of the corporation with which I shall begin my analysis. Each is deficient in some respects. But each raises issues which it is important to be clear about. The first I shall call the Organizational View; the second the Moralistic View.

The Organizational View starts from the legal definition of the corporation and draws out some of its implications. The literature on organizations is immense, and the Organizational View of corporations has been developed by sociologists and organizational theorists.[3] The view of the corporation developed by them has not been universally accepted, though it has been accepted by a large number of businessmen and workers, as well as by theoreticians.

According to the Organizational View, a corporation is a legal entity established for certain limited purposes—profit, production, the provision of services, and similar restricted ends. It is organized to fulfill these specific tasks. As Chief Justice Marshall noted, it has only those properties which its charter confers upon it. It is not a natural person, and is a person at all only for legal purposes. Since a corporation is not a natural person it needs human agents if it is to function. The human agents, however, when they act as parts of the corporation do not act for themselves, as natural individuals in their private capacity. They act as impersonal agents of the corporation in order to fulfill the corporation's ends. Each person working within the corporation has a function which he is to carry out in accordance with the stated ends of the organization. Each person is replaceable by other people. The corporation has "the blessings of potentially perpetual life and limited liability,"[4] which its individual employees in their personal lives do not have. In acting for the corporation an individual person does not act for himself but for the corporation. As long as his actions are part of the proper task assigned him and in accordance with the proper ends of the corporation, the actions are corporate actions, and the liability incurred are the corporation's liabilities. To the extent that an individual cheats the corporation, manipulates it, or in other ways acts contrary to its ends and his function, he incurs personal liability. But these are actions he performs as a person in his own right and not as an agent of the corporation.

Now on this view a corporation is a legal person only. It is not a moral person. To speak of it in moral terms, therefore, is to make a category mistake.[5] It is to take a corporation for a kind of entity which it is not. Since, moreover, its employees, when acting in their official capacity as impersonal agents of the corporation, are not acting in their own right, it is also a mistake to try to impute moral responsibility to them for their actions. This confuses their status as natural and hence moral persons, with their impersonal, legal functions. Individuals in a corporation should not let their personal moral notions supercede the ends of the corporation. If a corporation is established to produce goods and profits, and some members of the corporation feel that more good could be done by giving the profits to charity than distributing dividends to shareholders, as agents of the corporation they are not empowered to follow their own moral bent. To do so would be to make them legally liable as individuals for improper use of corporate assets. The Organizational View maintains, therefore, that moral responsibility cannot properly be assigned either to a corporation for its actions, nor to the agents of a corporation when they act as corporate agents. As legal entities corporations can be legally restrained and can have legal responsibility. But they cannot logically be held morally responsible or have moral responsibility. For they are not moral agents or entities.

Now some organizational theorists conclude from this description that morality is not part of a corporation's concern. Laws must be complied with. But moral concerns have no place in its structure. This is true both in the external dealings of the corporation, when it acts to achieve its ends, and also in the internal structuring of the organization. If people are hired by managers to work for the organization, moral notions which the manager may have about wages and rights should not color his official actions. Workers are free to accept a job with the corporation or not. No one should be forced to work for a corporation. But if someone does agree to work for a corporation, then he agrees to the conditions the corporation attaches to his position. Both the freedom of the worker to enter a contract and the freedom of the corporation to hire individuals is guaranteed by law. As long as all parties abide by the law, personal moral judgments are irrelevant.

This view is accepted, I have indicated, by many workers as well as by many managers and owners of corporations. And holding this view they are understandably annoyed by those outside the corporation who wish to evaluate it from a moral point of view, who wish to impose their moral views on its activities. If producing napalm bombs is legal, and if in fact the government is the prime purchaser, then those who from some moral point of view claim that producing napalm bombs is immoral, that Dow Chemical is immoral to produce them, and that any employees of that company who continue to work for it are immoral because they are taking part in an immoral activity, are simply mistaken. Those who make such charges may be moral people. But they are confused. They fail to understand that a corporation is a legal, not a moral person, and that the persons who work for a corporation work not as persons exercising their own moral views but as impersonal agents restrained by the ends and structures of the corporation.

For those who hold this Organizational View it is proper to discuss the legal responsibility of corporations and of persons within a corporation, but it is improper to speak of either's moral responsibility, individual or collective.

For those who hold what I have called the Moralistic View, these conclusions are simply morally outrageous. If it is a category mistake to apply moral language to corporations, then corporations in effect have moral immunity. Thus, while murder by an individual can be morally condemned, Murders, Inc., cannot be faulted from a moral point of view for pursuing its goal, nor can its agents for doing what is necessary to achieve the corporation's ends. To pick a case in which the end is not illegal, Hitler's SS, if incorporated, could not be morally faulted for exterminating Jews. Nor can Advertisers, Inc., be morally faulted for its ads, providing they are within the letter of the law, nor Shoddy, Inc., if it produces dangerous tools not prohibited by law. All of them may be legally restrained; but they are morally immune. This is so preposterous, the advocates of the Moralistic View claim, that the Organizational View is obviously fundamentally and dangerously mistaken. Individuals do not cease to be moral persons simply because they are employed by corporations; nor are corporations or other organizations or legal entities, such as nations, immune from moral evaluation and criticism. To hold such a view is to fail to understand the nature of morality, and to fail to understand that all human activities are subject to moral evaluation. Incorporation does not render one morally immune.

Now in favor of the Moralistic View is the fact that people do morally evaluate corporations and other similar organizations and collective entities. If it is immoral to do *x*, then it is immoral whether it is done by an individual or by a corporation. To hold otherwise might be a legal nicety, but it fails to take account of a widespread moral practice. A widespread moral practice may be an erroneous practice. But in this case the practice is held to be erroneous only because of a theory of organizations. And the defense of that theory, the reason why we should adopt that one rather than some other one, is by no means compelling. Given a choice between holding the Organizational View with the implication that all moral judgments of corporations are mistaken, and holding an alternative view which better accounts for the fact that people do morally judge the actions of corporations, it seems to me the latter is to get preference. We should admit that the Organizational View is at least in part deficient and see whether it can be remedied, though to say it is deficient is not to say that it is completely mistaken. Moreover, if the Moralistic View claims that corporations are moral agents in the same way and in the same sense that natural persons are, it also is mistaken. In claiming that a corporation which makes napalm bombs is acting immorally, or that a corporation which exploits its workers is acting immorally we seem to be saying something quite appropriate, and the claim that we are making a category mistake seems arbitrary. But if we speak of the moral feelings of the corporation, or of its pangs of conscience, or of its moral shame, we would obviously be speaking metaphorically at best. Though individuals within a company may express shame or pangs of conscience, corporations cannot; nor is it clear that the individuals within the corporation, if they do express shame for the company's actions, do so as agents of the corporation. . . . Corporations are simply not moral agents with feelings, emotions, conscience, and so on. . . .

But all this does not answer the question of whether corporations can be morally responsible for actions, and if so in what sense. . . . A corporation has a public face and its public face is corporate. Its responsibility when looked at in this way is also corporate. In dealing with other firms, in dealing with customers, in dealing with government, it always deals in its corporate mode. The corporation acts, commits itself, delivers and produces goods, abides by or breaks the law, and so on. When, from a moral point of view, we judge the actions of the corporation, we hold the corporation responsible and accountable. We are not, in most cases, either knowledgeable or particularly concerned with the individuals within the corporation.

We can take a clue here from legal responsibility. In many instances, the corporation is legally responsible for its actions. It can be sued, fined, forced to make reparations, desist from certain activities, undertake others, and so on. If the corporation is to take affirmative action, then the corporation as a whole is evaluated as to whether such action has been taken. All this views the corporations as an entity from the outside. The actions can be viewed from a moral point of view as well. If a clothing company practices discrimination or is guilty of gross exploitation, consumers might boycott its goods, bringing moral pressure on the company as a whole. Such action need not be concerned with how the corporation is structured internally. It is concerned with the external face of the corporation and the actions of that face. Where an action is considered immoral, moral sanctions, such as boycotting, might be imposed by those who feel the injustice of the practice in question. In expressing one's moral indignation in this way, one takes moral sanctions against the corporation. The aim is to affect the corporation as such, not particular individuals within it, though of course the aim is to impel those with the power to do so in a corporation to change the corporation's practices. But if a boycott leads to reduced production and to the laying off of particular workers, though they may be seen as the one's most affected by the boycott, they are not its object. The object as such is the corporation.

By those outside the corporation moral responsibility is ascribed to the corporation as such. If moral responsibility is so defined that it must be able to be assumed as well as ascribed, and if the latter requires moral feelings, then it might be argued that moral responsibility cannot correctly be appropriately ascribed to corporations. However, as the above example shows, it seems perfectly plausible to ascribe more responsibility to corporations even if they do not have moral feelings. This is because it is proper and useful to speak of the actions of corporations, and since they affect society and its members, to evaluate those actions from a moral point of view. To ascribe moral responsibility for those actions to the corporation as a whole means that if the assignment is properly made, it is appropriate to apply moral sanctions to the corporation for those actions. To condemn its actions as immoral might motivate some of those within it to resign; it might encourage those outside the corporation not to buy its products or otherwise deal with it, and so on. Hence moral responsibility should not be defined so narrowly as to require that moral feelings be possible on the part of those to whom it is ascribed.

We should be clear, however, that in ascribing moral responsibility to a corporation we are ascribing it to an entity, and so we are involved with the ascription of individual, not collective, responsibility. . . .

Though a corporation acts, it only acts insofar as individuals within it act. It cannot act independently of the individuals within it. But to say that the corporation acts or that it incurs responsibilities is not the same as saying that one can always reduce these to specific individuals within the corporation. If a corporation is to meet its responsibilities, then someone within the corporation must do something. Those within the corporation know this. Internally there may be organizational structures which assign responsibilities and functions. It is possible that everyone within a small corporation is authorized to do everything, and that the corporation can incur obligations by any one of them committing the corporation. It is then the responsibility of all of them to take the appropriate action, which perhaps can be discharged by only one of them taking certain action.

One difference between the moral responsibility of a natural person and of a corporation is that in the case of the natural person the one who incurs the responsibility, the one to whom responsibility is assigned by others, and the one who can and should assume the responsibility can all be, and typically are, the same individual. This is not the situation in the case of corporate responsibility. Moral responsibility can be assigned to the corporation by others who look at it from the outside as an individual agent. But from the inside the corporation does not have the unity of a natural person, and for it to act individuals within it must act.

From within, how is moral responsibility assigned, imputed, and assumed? The first reply is that it may not be. A corporation can be forced by the power of the state to obey its laws. Those within the corporation know this and react accordingly. But from within, those who work for a corporation know that they are not legally bound to be moral, providing the corporation's immoral behavior is not illegal. This is the position of the Organizational View, which rejects the moral ascription from outside and so consistently does not bother with it from inside.

But this situation is no different from individual moral responsibility. For if others ascribe moral responsibility to a natural person, the individual himself need not acknowledge or assume such responsibility. He may differ with them about the appropriateness of the ascription, or he may simply be amoral. Those who agree with the imputation can impose moral sanctions. But these may not be able to force compliance, much less internal assumption of the imputed moral responsibility. In the case of corporations, the fact that those within it may not acknowledge or assume the moral responsibility imputed to it by others proves little. However, if members of the moral community admit that *x*, e.g., theft, is immoral, and if they wish to be consistent, they should admit that it is immoral for corporate as well as for natural persons.

But who within the corporation is responsible for assuming the moral responsibility of a corporation correctly ascribed to it from outside? To answer this question we should look more closely at how moral responsibility can be ascribed from without and assumed from within. A corporation is a single entity for purposes of external action. That is its external face. But from within it is a collection of individuals, each of whom fills certain positions within an organizational structure, and each of whom has certain functions related to the corporation's internal activity. Those outside can sometimes appropriately pierce the external shield of a corporation to ascribe responsibility to those within it, though most frequently they do not. Those within the corporation can assume the responsibility of the corporation jointly or can themselves divide it up. . . .

Now consider five different ways of internally assigning responsibility for corporate actions. We can consider them five models. We can first consider two models of the corporation in which moral responsibility is not internally assigned to the corporation as such but the moral responsibility externally imputed is assigned to or assumed by individuals within the corporation. . . . The actions of a corporation are here reduced to the individual actions of the members of the corporation. On the first model, each individual is assigned and/or assumes the full responsibility assigned to the corporation from without. This model may be modified to produce a variant in which full responsibility is internally assigned to or assumed by only those who play an active role in the action in question. Thus, if a corporation decides to move out of a town paying no attention to what such an action will do to its workers and to the town, the corporation's action might be judged to be immoral. Internally that decision may be one for which each member of the board of directors, for instance, is held fully responsible, though each cast only one vote out of many. Even if a member voted against the action, if it was taken by the board and implemented, and if he did not dissociate himself by resigning, then he bears full responsibility for the action. If the action is immoral, each bears full moral responsibility for it. The responsibility here is collectively held fully by each individual.

The second model is similar to the first, but it assigns only partial responsibility either to all the members of the corporation or, as a variant, only to those involved in any decision or action taken by a corporation. Thus if a board decides on the issue above, and each person casts only one vote, and if ten votes were required for a motion to pass, each person who voted for it would bear a proportional amount of responsibility, the proportion being divided by the number of affirmative votes. This view wishes to take into account that no one individual acting alone took the decision and that no one individual acting alone could have passed the motion. It was truly a joint action, and must be treated as such. To call it a joint action is to acknowledge joint and partial responsibility, which in this case means dividing it among all those who took part. Those who voted against the measure but did not resign when it was passed may or may not be assigned responsibility on this model. Both variants are possible. If responsibility is internally assigned to them (and/or assumed by them), it may be less than the responsibility assigned to (and/or assumed by) those who voted affirmatively. There are thus several variants of the second model.

The above two models break down all corporate responsibility into individual responsibility. In the third model, the corporation is held fully responsible for its actions as well as all the individuals involved in it, with individual responsibility assigned as in model one above. Thus, for instance, a worker in a corporation who had no part in making a decision which leads to the immoral action on the part of a corporation judges the corporation to have acted immorally as well as imputing responsibility to those who made the decision. Does he have, he may ask, the moral obligation to leave a corporation which acts in this manner? Should he assume some responsibility for the corporation's action simply because he works for it and thus helps enable it to act immorally? This way of looking at the moral responsibility of those within a corporation is different from considering the immorality of a corporation's actions to be reducible to those making the decision.

The fourth model is full corporate responsibility with individual responsibility assigned as in model two.

The fifth model assigns responsibility for corporate actions only to the corporation as such, not to any of the members in it individually. This model concedes that corporate actions are not simply the sum of individual actions but that they are actions attributable to the corporation, a separate entity which exists over and above its individual members. The individual members are mortal and replaceable. The corporation is not a fiction, but an organization and a continuing legal person, with a history, traditions, typical ways of acting, rules that govern its behavior, standards which may not be the making of any of the individuals presently employed by the company or by any of its present owners, and so on. If moral responsibility had to be accepted, this would be the model the Organizational View suggests. It is held only collectively and not distributively.

There are obviously other models. One would hold, for instance, that moral responsibility is to be only partially imputed to a corporation, though fully to its members. Another might hold a corporation morally responsible for its actions only if the persons in the corporation who caused them were still employed in the same positions. But neither of these nor other possible models seem particularly plausible or have any defenders I know of.

There are also mixes of the models within the corporation. All the actions of the company might be considered the responsibility, moral as well as legal, of the board of directors. If they do not have knowledge of and control over all that the company does, they are nonetheless responsible for all of its actions. Another view would put the onus on management rather than on the board. If the full responsibility is held by these people either from an external or an internal point of view, they could still hold those below them either fully or partially responsible in certain areas. Another view would put, perhaps naively, ultimate responsibility on neither managers nor the board but on the owners of the corporation, on the shareholders, who in fact are the ones penalized if the corporation, for instance, is fined and the corporation cannot pass on the fine either to the public in higher prices or to the workers in lower wages.

If my argument thus far has been correct, then it is appropriate to judge the actions of corporations from a moral point of view and to ascribe moral responsibility to a corporation. If correctly imputed, it should be morally assumed. Since the corporation acts only through its members, it can be assumed by them, and I have indicated various ways this can be done. Once the responsibility of the corporation and for the corporation is assumed, this can generate responsibilities internally for certain individuals to act in certain ways. Those responsibilities may also be variously distributed. Corporate responsibility can be seen, therefore, as a type of collective responsibility when viewed from within, and it may operate in a variety of ways.

I take these conclusions to be important ones in answer to the question of whether collective responsibility makes sense, and to the question, if it does make sense, of what it means in the case of corporations.

There are a group of other problems which remain. Which of these models is correct, it may be asked? How are we to decide among the models of collective responsibility as applied to corporations? Who *really* has moral responsibility for corporate actions?

Once again we can turn to law for a clue. In some recent cases the courts have come to feel that fines against corporations, even if the fines are large, are not as effective a way of policing corporate activities as the courts would like. For the fines can in some instances be passed off onto consumers. If this is not possible, then frequently the shareholders, who may have had no knowledge of the activity in question, suffer the consequences. Judges, courts, and legislatures have therefore found it advisable in some instances to hold members of the board legally liable for the actions of the corporation. The theory is that if those who make the decisions are held liable for them personally, if they will go to jail for illegal actions, they will be more careful not to engage in illegal practices than if the penalty for such action is simply a fine paid by the corporation from its assets. What the company gains from its illegal actions might even be worth the price of the fine. It is less likely to be viewed by a board member as being worth a personal term in prison.

Even if legal responsibility were assigned only in these ways, it is clear that once a company is fined or found guilty of some illegal action it is possible for some companies in at least some instances to internally pinpoint responsibility and perhaps fire the person in question, or remove him from his position. If a company finds that it cannot pinpoint responsibility, it may, if it wishes to be able to do so, take measures to reorganize the lines of responsibility so that responsibility can be assigned. This is likely to happen, for instance, in those cases in which board members or managers are held responsible for the actions of all those under them.

Now the point to which I wish to draw attention is that in answer to the question of who really has legal responsibility, we must go to the laws and to specific interpretations, and we learn that legal responsibility can be and is assigned in a variety of ways. It can be assigned to the corporation as well as to members within it or only to members within it. The assigning of responsibility in each of these ways carries with it appropriate penalties for violation of the responsibility, penalties which fall either on the corporation or both on the corporation and on individuals within it, or only on individuals within it. In answer to the question, but which one of these is proper, the response is that all of them are, if they fulfill the function they are intended to fulfill. Laws have certain purposes, and if they are to control in certain ways the actions of corporations and of people within corporations, then they are effective insofar as they fulfill their aims. There is no one correct way of legally assigning responsibility with respect to corporate activity . . . . This itself, since it is an act of law, might be modified and changed, so that the corporation might be given more or fewer legally recognized attributes. The question of how many of the freedoms of natural persons corporations should enjoy is a question that many recent court decisions have been concerned with. But the answer is in part one that must be decided—decided for good reasons, to be sure—but decided. It is not a matter of somehow seeing, in some arcane sense of seeing, which freedom the corporation really has.

Now I suggest that the situation is similar with respect to the moral responsibility of corporations. That a part-time janitor working for a corporation should be held fully morally responsible for the immoral actions done by that corporation may sound extreme. In most cases it undoubtedly would be an extreme view. But in others, if the actions of a corporation are truly morally heinous, and if working for the company in any way is to condone its actions, then the janitor might be held morally responsible for the company's actions. But obviously we would like to know what it means to hold someone morally responsible, and what it means to hold a company morally responsible, and what it means to hold both the company and its employees responsible, and so on; and we would want to know what difference it makes if we hold the company but not the employees responsible, and vice versa, and so on through the list of possibilities. Those within the corporation can raise parallel questions. If the janitor is morally responsible we might expect him, on realizing this, to quit. If the manager is morally responsible we might expect him, on realizing this, to change the corporation's policies, assuming it is possible for him to do so. Ascribing responsibility and assuming it might imply responsibility to act in differing ways, depending on one's position. . . .

The thrust of my paper on this point by now, however, should be clear. There is no one sense of moral responsibility which we must discover and in discovering it find whether there is collective moral responsibility and where and how it applies. Morality is a social institution. This does not mean that it is arbitrary, nor necessarily that it is conventional in some narrow meaning of that term. But moral responsibility, just as other moral terms, can be clarified. The clarification should start with some basis in common moral experience. But the concept may well have to be reformulated, more accurately stated for certain purposes, its implications spelled out and evaluated. This is, in fact, the approach that I think should be taken with the notion of collective moral responsibility. . . .

Society, in my view, should not accept the thesis of the Organizational View that the agents of the corporation and the corporation cannot be morally evaluated. They can and should be, since they affect the lives of the members of society and the society as a whole.

Where corporations are so structured that it is difficult for anyone to know whether he is responsible for any particular action or where it is difficult to pinpoint responsibility, I believe that it should be reorganized so that individuals can know what they are responsible for and so that others can hold them responsible for it. Within the organization I would expect that the moral level of corporate activity would probably rise, if this were the case. If the individual moral responsibility of those within the corporation were clear and if their moral decisions were respected, then the overall result would be that there would be moral pressure brought to bear within a corporation so that each of these involved in decisions concerning the corporation would consider the actions of the corporation and their own participation in those actions from a moral point of view. . . .

Notes

1. See D. E. Cooper, "Collective Responsibility," *Philosophy,* XLIII (1968), pp. 258–268; Joel Feinberg, "Collective Responsibility," *The Journal of Philosophy,* LXV (1968), pp. 674–688; Virginia Held, "Can a Random Collection of Individuals Be Morally Responsible", *The Journal of Philosophy,* LXVII (1970), pp. 471–481; H. E. Lewis, "Collective Responsibility,"*Philosophy,* XXIII (1948), pp. 3–18; and W. H. Walsh, "Pride, Shame and Responsibility," *The Philosophical Quarterly,* XX (1970), pp. 1–13. See also Peter French (ed.), *Individual and Collective Responsibility: The Massacre at My Lai* (Cambridge, Mass.: Schenkman Publishing Co., 1972) which contains some of the above mentioned essays in reworked form, as well as some other essays.
2. Chief Justice Marshall, Dartmouth College v. Woodward, 4 Wheat. 518.636 (1819).
3. See, among others, Herbert A. Simon, *Administrative Behavior,* 2nd ed., (New York: Free Press, 1965); Peter M. Blau and W. Richard Scott, *Formal Organizations,* (San Francisco: Chandler Publishing Co., 1962); and David Silverman, *The Theory of Organizations.* (New York: Basic Books, 1971).
4. Mr. Justice Rehnquist, dissenting, First National Bank of Boston vs. Francis X. Belloti, No. Us 76–1172 (1978).
5. See John Ladd, "Morality and the Ideal of Rationality in Formal Organizations," *The Monist,* LIV (1970), p. 500.

CAN A CORPORATION
HAVE A CONSCIENCE?

Kenneth E. Goodpaster and John B. Matthews, Jr.

If people are going to adopt the terminology of "responsibility" (with its allied concepts of corporate conscience) to suggest new, improved ways of dealing with corporations, then they ought to go back and examine in detail what "being responsible" entails—in the ordinary case of the responsible human being. Only after we have considered what being responsible calls for in general does it make sense to develop the notion of a corporation being responsible.*

Christopher Stone

During the severe racial tensions of the 1960s, Southern Steel Company (actual case, disguised name) faced considerable pressure from government and the press to explain and modify its policies regarding discrimination both within its plants and in the major city where it was located. SSC was the largest employer in the area (it had nearly 15,000 workers, one-third of whom were black) and had made great strides toward removing barriers to equal job opportunity in its several plants. In addition, its top executives (especially its chief executive officer, James Weston) had distinguished themselves as private citizens for years in community programs for black housing, education, and small business as well as in attempts at desegregating all-white police and local government organizations.

SSC drew the line, however, at using its substantial economic influence in the local area to advance the cause of the civil rights movement by pressuring banks, suppliers, and the local government:

> As individuals we can exercise what influence we may have as citizens, but for a corporation to attempt to exert any kind of economic compulsion to achieve a particular end in a social area seems to me to be quite beyond what a corporation should do and quite beyond what a corporation can do. I believe that while government may seek to compel social reforms, any attempt by a private organization like SSC to impose its views, its beliefs, and its will upon the community would be repugnant to our American constitutional concepts and that appropriate steps to correct this abuse of corporate power would be universally demanded by public opinion.

Weston could have been speaking in the early 1980s on any issue that corporations around the United States now face. Instead of social justice, his theme might be environmental protection, product safety, marketing practice, or international bribery. His statement for SSC raises the important issue of corporate responsibility. Can a corporation have a conscience?

*From *Where the Law Ends* © 1975 by Christopher D. Stone. Reprinted with permission of Harper & Row, Publishers, Inc.

Weston apparently felt comfortable saying it need not. The responsibilities of ordinary persons and of "artificial persons" like corporations are, in his view, separate. Persons' responsibilities go beyond those of corporations. Persons, he seems to have believed, ought to care not only about themselves but also about the dignity and well-being of those around them—ought not only to care but also to act. Organizations, he evidently thought, are creatures of, and to a degree prisoners of, the systems of economic incentive and political sanction that give them reality and therefore should not be expected to display the same moral attributes that we expect of persons.

Others inside business as well as outside share Weston's perception. One influential philosopher—John Ladd—carries Weston's view a step further:

> It is improper to expect organizational conduct to conform to the ordinary principles of morality. We cannot and must not expect formal organizations, or their representatives acting in their official capacities, to be honest, courageous, considerate, sympathetic, or to have any kind of moral integrity. Such concepts are not in the vocabulary, so to speak, of the organizational language game.[1]

In our opinion, this line of thought represents a tremendous barrier to the development of business ethics both as a field of inquiry and as a practical force in managerial decision making. This is a matter about which executives must be philosophical and philosophers must be practical. A corporation can and should have a conscience. The language of ethics does have a place in the vocabulary of an organization. There need not be and there should not be a disjunction of the sort attributed to SSC's James Weston. Organizational agents such as corporations should be no more and no less morally responsible (rational, self-interested, altruistic) than ordinary persons.

We take this position because we think an analogy holds between the individual and the corporation. If we analyze the concept of moral responsibility as it applies to persons, we find that projecting it to corporations as agents in society is possible.

DEFINING THE RESPONSIBILITY OF PERSONS

When we speak of the responsibility of individuals, philosophers say that we mean three things: someone is to blame, something has to be done, or some kind of trustworthiness can be expected. (See the *Exhibit* on page 70.)

Holding Accountable

We apply the first meaning, what we shall call the *causal* sense, primarily to legal and moral contexts where what is at issue is praise or blame for a past action. We say of a person that he or she was responsible for what happened, is to blame for it, should be held accountable. In this sense of the word, *responsibility* has to do with tracing the causes of actions and events, of

THREE USES OF THE TERM RESPONSIBLE

The causal sense	"He is responsible for this." Emphasis on holding to account for past actions, causality.
The rule-following sense	"As a lawyer, he is responsible for defending that client." Emphasis on following social and legal norms.
The decision-making sense	"He is a responsible person." Emphasis on an individual's independent judgment.

finding out who is answerable in a given situation. Our aim is to determine someone's intention, free will, degree of participation, and appropriate reward or punishment.

Rule Following

We apply the second meaning of *responsibility* to rule following, to contexts where individuals are subject to externally imposed norms often associated with some social role that people play. We speak of the responsibilities of parents to children, of doctors to patients, of lawyers to clients, of citizens to the law. What is socially expected and what the party involved is to answer for are at issue here.

Decision Making

We use the third meaning of *responsibility* for decision making. With this meaning of the term, we say that individuals are responsible if they are trustworthy and reliable, if they allow appropriate factors to affect their judgment; we refer primarily to a person's independent thought processes and decision making, processes that justify an attitude of trust from those who interact with him or her as a responsible individual.

The distinguishing characteristic of moral responsibility, it seems to us, lies in this third sense of the term. Here the focus is on the intellectual and emotional processes in the individual's moral reasoning. Philosophers call this "taking a moral point of view" and contrast it with such other processes as being financially prudent and attending to legal obligations.

To be sure, characterizing a person as "morally responsible" may seem rather vague. But vagueness is a contextual notion. Everything depends on how we fill in the blank in "vague for _____ purposes."

In some contexts the term "six o'clockish" is vague, while in others it is useful and informative. As a response to a space-shuttle pilot who wants to know when to fire the reentry rockets, it will not do, but it might do in response to a spouse who wants to know when one will arrive home at the end of the workday.

We maintain that the processes underlying moral responsibility can be defined and are not themselves vague, even though gaining consensus on specific moral norms and decisions is not always easy.

What, then, characterizes the processes underlying the judgment of a person we call morally responsible? Philosopher William K. Frankena offers the following answer:

> "A morality is a normative system in which judgments are made, more or less consciously, [out of a] consideration of the effects of actions . . . on the lives of persons . . . including the lives of others besides the person acting. . . . David Hume took a similar position when he argued that what speaks in a moral judgment is a kind of sympathy. . . . A little later, . . . Kant put the matter somewhat better by characterizing morality as the business of respecting persons as ends and not as means or as things. . . ."[2]

Frankena is pointing to two traits, both rooted in a long and diverse philosophical tradition:

1. **Rationality.** Taking a moral point of view includes the features we usually attribute to rational decision making, that is, lack of impulsiveness, care in mapping out alternatives and consequences, clarity about goals and purposes, attention to details of implementation.

2. **Respect.** The moral point of view also includes a special awareness of and concern for the effects of one's decisions and policies on others, special in the sense that it goes beyond the kind of awareness and concern that would ordinarily be part of rationality, that is, beyond seeing others merely as instrumental to accomplishing one's own purposes. This is respect for the lives of others and involves taking their needs and interests seriously, not simply as resources in one's own decision making but as limiting conditions which change the very definition of one's habitat from a self-centered to a shared environment. It is what philosopher Immanuel Kant meant by the "categorical imperative" to treat others as valuable in and for themselves.

It is this feature that permits us to trust the morally responsible person. We know that such a person takes our point of view into account not merely as a useful precaution (as in "honesty is the best policy") but as important in its own right.

These components of moral responsibility are not too vague to be useful. Rationality and respect affect the manner in which a person approaches practical decision making: they affect the way in which the individual processes information and makes choices. A rational but not respectful Bill Jones will not lie to his friends *unless* he is reasonably sure he will not be found out. A rational but not respectful Mary Smith will defend an unjustly treated party *unless* she thinks it may be too costly to herself. A rational *and* respectful decision maker, however, notices—and cares—whether the consequences of his or her conduct lead to injuries or indignities to others.

Two individuals who take "the moral point of view" will not of course always agree on ethical matters, but they do at least have a basis for dialogue.

Now that we have removed some of the vagueness from the notion of moral responsibility as it applies to persons, we can search for a frame of reference in which, by analogy with Bill Jones and Mary Smith, we can meaningfully and appropriately say that corporations are morally responsible. This is the issue reflected in the SSC case.

To deal with it, we must ask two questions: Is it meaningful to apply moral concepts to actors who are not persons but who are instead made up of persons? And even if meaningful, is it advisable to do so?

If a group can act like a person in some ways, then we can expect it to behave like a person in other ways. For one thing, we know that people organized into a group can act as a unit. As business people well know, legally a corporation is considered a unit. To approach unity, a group usually has some sort of internal decision structure, a system of rules that spell out authority relationships and specify the conditions under which certain individuals' actions become official actions of the group.[3]

If we can say that persons act responsibly only if they gather information about the impact of their actions on others and use it in making decisions, we can reasonably do the same for organizations. Our proposed frame of reference for thinking about and implementing corporate responsibility aims at spelling out the processes associated with the moral responsibility of individuals and projecting them to the level of organizations. This is similar to, though an inversion of, Plato's famous method in the *Republic*, in which justice in the community is used as a model for justice in the individual.

Hence, corporations that monitor their employment practices and the effects of their production processes and products on the environment and human health show the same kind of rationality and respect that morally responsible individuals do. Thus, attributing actions, strategies, decisions, and moral responsibilities to corporations as entities distinguishable from those who hold offices in them poses no problem.

And when we look about us, we can readily see differences in moral responsibility among corporations in much the same way that we see differences among persons. Some corporations have built features into their management incentive systems, board structures, internal control systems, and research agendas that in a person we would call self-control, integrity, and conscientiousness. Some have institutionalized awareness and concern for consumers, employees, and the rest of the public in ways that others clearly have not.

As a matter of course, some corporations attend to the human impact of their operations and policies and reject operations and policies that are questionable. Whether the issue be the health effects of sugared cereal or cigarettes, the safety of tires or tampons, civil liberties in the corporation or the community, an organization reveals its character as surely as a person does.

Indeed, the parallel may be even more dramatic. For just as the moral responsibility displayed by an individual develops over time from infancy to adulthood,[4] so too we may expect to find stages of development in organizational character that show significant patterns.

EVALUATING THE IDEA OF MORAL PROJECTION

Concepts like moral responsibility not only make sense when applied to organizations but also provide touchstones for designing more effective models than we now have for guiding corporate policy.

Now we can understand what it means to invite SSC as a corporation to be morally responsible both in-house and in its community, but *should* we issue the invitation? Here we turn to the question of advisability. Should we require the organizational agents in our society to have the same moral attributes we require of ourselves?

Our proposal to spell out the processes associated with moral responsibility for individuals and then to project them to their organizational counterparts takes on added meaning when we examine alternative frames of reference for corporate responsibility.

Two frames of reference that compete for the allegiance of people who ponder the question of corporate responsibility are emphatically opposed to this principle of moral projection—what we might refer to as the "invisible hand" view and the "hand of government" view.

The Invisible Hand

The most eloquent spokesman of the first view is Milton Friedman (echoing many philosophers and economists since Adam Smith). According to this pattern of thought, the true and only social responsibilities of business organizations are to make profits and obey the laws. The workings of the free and competitive marketplace will "moralize" corporate behavior quite independently of any attempts to expand or transform decision making via moral projection.

A deliberate amorality in the executive suite is encouraged in the name of systemic morality: the common good is best served when each of us and our economic institutions pursue not the common good or moral purpose, advocates say, but competitive advantage. Morality, responsibility, and conscience reside in the invisible hand of the free market system, not in the hands of the organizations within the system, much less the managers within the organizations.

To be sure, people of this opinion admit, there is a sense in which social or ethical issues can and should enter the corporate mind, but the filtering of such issues is thorough: they go through the screens of custom, public opinion, public relations, and the law. And, in any case, self-interest maintains primacy as an objective and a guiding star.

The reaction from this frame of reference to the suggestion that moral judgment be integrated with corporate strategy is clearly negative. Such an integration is seen as inefficient and arrogant, and in the end both an illegitimate use of corporate power and an abuse of the manager's fiduciary role. With respect to our SSC case, advocates of the invisible hand model would vigorously resist efforts, beyond legal requirements, to make SSC right the wrongs of racial injustice. SSC's responsibility would be to make steel of high quality at least cost, to deliver it on time, and to satisfy its customers and stockholders. Justice would not be part of SSC's corporate mandate.

The Hand of Government

Advocates of the second dissenting frame of reference abound, but John Kenneth Galbraith's work has counterpointed Milton Friedman's with insight and style. Under this view of corporate responsibility, corporations are to pursue objectives that are rational and purely economic. The regulatory hands of the law and the political process rather than the invisible hand of the marketplace turns these objectives to the common good.

Again, in this view, it is a system that provides the moral direction for corporate decision making—a system, though, that is guided by political managers, the custodians of the public purpose. In the case of SSC, proponents of this view would look to the state for moral direction and responsible management, both within SSC and in the community. The corporation would have no moral responsibility beyond political and legal obedience.

What is striking is not so much the radical difference between the economic and social philosophies that underlie these two views of the source of corporate responsibility but the conceptual similarities. Both views locate morality, ethics, responsibility, and conscience in the systems of rules and incentives in which the modern corporation finds itself embedded. Both views reject the exercise of independent moral judgment by corporations as actors in society.

Neither view trusts corporate leaders with stewardship over what are often called noneconomic values. Both require corporate responsibility to march to the beat of drums outside. In the jargon of moral philosophy, both views press for a rule-centered or a system-centered ethics instead of an agent-centered ethics. In terms of the *Exhibit,* these frames of reference countenance corporate rule-following responsibility for corporations but not corporate decision-making responsibility.

The Hand of Management

To be sure, the two views under discussion differ in that one looks to an invisible moral force in the market while the other looks to a visible moral force in government. But both would advise against a principle of moral projection that permits or encourages corporations to exercise independent, noneconomic judgment over matters that face them in their short- and long-term plans and operations.

Accordingly, both would reject a third view of corporate responsibility that seeks to affect the thought processes of the organization itself—a sort of "hand of management" view—since neither seems willing or able to see the engines of profit regulate themselves to the degree that would be implied by taking the principle of moral projection seriously. Cries of inefficiency and moral imperialism from the right would be matched by cries of insensitivity and illegitimacy from the left, all in the name of preserving us from corporations and managers run morally amok.

Better, critics would say, that moral philosophy be left to philosophers, philanthropists, and politicians than to business leaders. Better that corporate morality be kept to glossy annual reports, where it is safely insulated from policy and performance.

The two conventional frames of reference locate moral restraint in forces external to the person and the corporation. They deny moral reasoning and intent to the corporation in the name of either market competition or society's system of explicit legal constraints and presume that these have a better moral effect than that of rationality and respect.

Although the principle of moral projection, which underwrites the idea of a corporate conscience and patterns it on the thought and feeling processes of the person, is in our view compelling, we must acknowledge that it is neither part of the received wisdom, nor is its advisability beyond question or objection. Indeed, attributing the role of conscience to the corporation seems to carry with it new and disturbing implications for our usual ways of thinking about ethics and business.

Perhaps the best way to clarify and defend this frame of reference is to address the objections to the principle found in the ruled insert on pages 76–80. There we see a summary of the criticisms and counterarguments we have heard during hours of discussion with business executives and business school students. We believe that the replies to the objections about a corporation having a conscience are convincing.

LEAVING THE DOUBLE STANDARD BEHIND

We have come some distance from our opening reflection on Southern Steel Company and its role in its community. Our proposal—clarified, we hope, through these objections and replies—suggests that it is not sufficient to draw a sharp line between individuals' private ideas and efforts and a corporation's institutional efforts, but that the latter can and should be built upon the former.

Does this frame of reference give us an unequivocal prescription for the behavior of SSC in its circumstances? No, it does not. Persuasive arguments might be made now and might have been made then that SSC should not have used its considerable economic clout to threaten the community into desegregation. A careful analysis of the realities of the environment might have disclosed that such a course would have been counterproductive, leading to more injustice than it would have alleviated.

The point is that some of the arguments and some of the analyses are or would have been moral arguments, and thereby the ultimate decision that of an ethically responsible organization. The significance of this point can hardly be overstated, for it represents the adoption of a new perspective on corporate policy and a new way of thinking about business ethics. We agree with one authority, who writes that "the business firm, as an organic entity intricately affected by and affecting its environment, is as appropriately adaptive . . . to demands for responsible behavior as for economic service."[5]

The frame of reference here developed does not offer a decision procedure for corporate managers. That has not been our purpose. It does, however, shed light on the conceptual foundations of business ethics by training attention on the corporation as a moral agent in society. Legal systems of rules and incentives are insufficient, even though they may be necessary, as frameworks for corporate responsibility. Taking conceptual cues from the features of moral responsibility normally expected of the person in our opinion deserves practicing managers' serious consideration.

The lack of congruence that James Weston saw between individual and corporate moral responsibility can be, and we think should be, overcome. In the process, what a number of writers have characterized as a double standard—a discrepancy between our personal lives and our lives in organizational settings—might be dampened. The principle of moral projection not only helps us to conceptualize the kinds of demands that we might make of corporations and other organizations but also offers the prospect of harmonizing those demands with the demands that we make of ourselves.

Is a Corporation a Morally Responsible 'Person'?

Objection 1 to the Analogy:

Corporations are not persons. They are artificial legal constructions, machines for mobilizing economic investments toward the efficient production of goods and services. We cannot hold a corporation responsible. We can only hold individuals responsible.

Reply:

Our frame of reference does not imply that corporations are persons in a literal sense. It simply means that in certain respects concepts and functions normally attributed to persons can also be attributed to organizations made up of persons. Goals, economic values, strategies, and other such personal attributes are often usefully projected to the corporate level by managers and researchers. Why should we not project the functions of conscience in the same way? As for holding corporations responsible, recent criminal prosecutions such as the case of Ford Motor Company and its Pinto gas tanks suggest that society finds the idea both intelligible and useful.

Objection 2:

A corporation cannot be held responsible at the sacrifice of profit. Profitability and financial health have always been and should continue to be the "categorical imperatives" of a business operation.

Reply:

We must of course acknowledge the imperatives of survival, stability, and growth when we discuss corporations, as indeed we must acknowledge them when we discuss the life of an individual. Self-sacrifice has been identified with moral responsibility in only the most extreme cases. The pursuit of profit and self-interest need not be pitted against the demands of moral responsibility. Moral demands are best viewed as containments—not replacements—for self-interest.

This is not to say that profit maximization never conflicts with morality. But profit maximization conflicts with other managerial values as well. The point is to coordinate imperatives, not deny their validity.

Objection 3:

Corporate executives are not elected representatives of the people, nor are they anointed or appointed as social guardians. They therefore lack the social mandate that a democratic society rightly demands of those who would pursue ethically or socially motivated policies. By keeping corporate policies confined to economic motivations, we keep the power of corporate executives in its proper place.

Reply:

The objection betrays an oversimplified view of the relationship between the public and the private sector. Neither private individuals nor private corporations that guide their conduct by ethical or social values beyond the demands of law should be constrained merely because they are not elected to do so. The demands of moral responsibility are independent of the demands of political legitimacy and are in fact presupposed by them.

To be sure, the state and the political process will and must remain the primary mechanisms for protecting the public interest, but one might be forgiven the hope that the political process will not substitute for the moral judgment of the citizenry or other components of society such as corporations.

Objection 4:

Our system of law carefully defines the role of agent or fiduciary and makes corporate managers accountable to shareholders and investors for the use of their assets. Management cannot, in the name of corporate moral responsibility, arrogate to itself the right to manage those assets by partially noneconomic criteria.

Reply:

First, it is not so clear that investors insist on purely economic criteria in the management of their assets, especially if some of the shareholders' resolutions and board reforms of the last decade are any indication. For instance, companies doing business in South Africa have had stockholders question their activities, other companies have instituted audit committees for their boards before such auditing was mandated, and mutual funds for which ''socially responsible behavior'' is a major investment criterion now exists.

Second, the categories of ''shareholder'' and ''investor'' connote wider time spans than do immediate or short-term returns. As a practical matter, considerations of stability and long-term return on investment enlarge the class of principals to which managers bear a fiduciary relationship.

Third, the trust that managers hold does not and never has extended to "any means available" to advance the interests of the principals. Both legal and moral constraints must be understood to qualify that trust—even, perhaps, in the name of a larger trust and a more basic fiduciary relationship to the members of society at large.

Objection 5:

The power, size, and scale of the modern corporation—domestic as well as international—are awesome. To unleash, even partially, such power from the discipline of the marketplace and the narrow or possibly nonexistent moral purpose implicit in that discipline would be socially dangerous. Had SSC acted in the community to further racial justice, its purposes might have been admirable, but those purposes could have led to a kind of moral imperialism or worse. Suppose SSC had thrown its power behind the Ku Klux Klan.

Reply:

This is a very real and important objection. What seems not to be appreciated is the fact that power affects when it is used as well as when it is not used. A decision by SSC not to exercise its economic influence according to "non-economic" criteria is inevitably a moral decision and just as inevitably affects the community. The issue in the end is not whether corporations (and other organizations) should be "unleashed" to exert moral force in our society but rather how critically and self-consciously they should choose to do so.

The degree of influence enjoyed by an agent, whether a person or an organization, is not so much a factor recommending moral disengagement as a factor demanding a high level of moral awareness. Imperialism is more to be feared when moral reasoning is absent than when it is present. Nor do we suggest that the "discipline of the marketplace" be diluted; rather, we call for it to be supplemented with the discipline of moral reflection.

Objection 6:

The idea of moral projection is a useful device for structuring corporate responsibility only if our understanding of moral responsibility at the level of the person is in some sense richer than our understanding of moral responsibility on the level of the organization as a whole. If we are not clear about individual responsibility, the projection is fruitless.

Reply:

The objection is well taken. The challenge offered by the idea of moral projection lies in our capacity to articulate criteria or frameworks of reasoning for the morally responsible person. And though such a challenge is formidable, it is not clear that it cannot be met, at least with sufficient consensus to be useful.

For centuries, the study and criticism of frameworks have gone on, carried forward by many disciplines, including psychology, the social sciences, and philosophy. And though it would be a mistake to suggest that any single framework (much less a decision mechanism) has emerged as the right one, it is true that recurrent patterns are discernible and well enough defined to structure moral discussion.

In the body of the article, we spoke of rationality and respect as components of individual responsibility. Further analysis of these components would translate them into social costs and benefits, justice in the distribution of goods and services, basic rights and duties, and fidelity to contracts. The view that pluralism in our society has undercut all possibility of moral agreement is anything but self-evident. Sincere moral disagreement is, of course, inevitable and not clearly lamentable. But a process and a vocabulary for articulating such values as we share is no small step forward when compared with the alternatives. Perhaps in our exploration of the moral projection we might make some surprising and even reassuring discoveries about ourselves.

Objection 7:

Why is it necessary to project moral responsibility to the level of the organization? Isn't the task of defining corporate responsibility and business ethics sufficiently discharged if we clarify the responsibilities of men and women in business as individuals? Doesn't ethics finally rest on the honesty and integrity of the individual in the business world?

Reply:

Yes and no. Yes, in the sense that the control of large organizations does finally rest in the hands of managers, of men and women. No, in the sense that what is being controlled is a cooperative system for a cooperative purpose. The projection of responsibility to the organization is simply an acknowledgement of the fact that the whole is more than the sum of its parts. Many intelligent people do not an intelligent organization make. Intelligence needs to be structured, organized, divided, and recombined in complex processes for complex purposes.

Studies of management have long shown that the attributes, successes, and failures of organizations are phenomena that emerge from the coordination of persons' attributes and that explanations of such phenomena require categories of analysis and description beyond the level of the individual. Moral responsibility is an attribute that can manifest itself in organizations as surely as competence or efficiency.

Objection 8:

Is the frame of reference here proposed intended to replace or undercut the relevance of the ''invisible hand'' and the ''government hand'' views, which depend on external controls?

Reply:

No. Just as regulation and economic competition are not substitutes for corporate responsibility, so corporate responsibility is not a substitute for law and the market. The imperatives of ethics cannot be relied on—nor have they ever been relied on—without a context of external sanctions. And this is true as much for individuals as for organizations.

This frame of reference takes us beneath, but not beyond, the realm of external systems of rules and incentives and into the thought processes that interpret and respond to the corporation's environment. Morality is more than merely part of that environment. It aims at the projection of conscience, not the enthronement of it in either the state or the competitive process.

The rise of the modern large corporation and the concomitant rise of the professional manager demand a conceptual framework in which these phenomena can be accommodated to moral thought. The principle of moral projection furthers such accommodation by recognizing a new level of agency in society and thus a new level of responsibility.

Objection 9:

Corporations have always taken the interests of those outside the corporation into account in the sense that customer relations and public relations generally are an integral part of rational economic decision making. Market signals and social signals that filter through the market mechanism inevitably represent the interests of parties affected by the behavior of the company. What, then, is the point of adding respect to rationality?

Reply:

Representing the affected parties solely as economic variables in the environment of the company is treating them as means or resources and not as ends in themselves. It implies that the only voice which affected parties should have in organizational decision making is that of potential buyers, sellers, regulators, or boycotters. Besides, many affected parties may not occupy such roles, and those who do may not be able to signal the organization with messages that effectively represent their stakes in its actions.

To be sure, classical economic theory would have us believe that perfect competition in free markets (with modest adjustments from the state) will result in all relevant signals being "heard," but the abstractions from reality implicit in such theory make it insufficient as a frame of reference for moral responsibility. In a world in which strict self-interest was congruent with the common good, moral responsibility might be unnecessary. We do not, alas, live in such a world.

The element of respect in our analysis of responsibility plays an essential role in ensuring the recognition of unrepresented or under-represented voices in the decision making of organizations as agents. Showing respect for persons as ends and not mere means to organizational purposes is central to the concept of corporate moral responsibility.

Notes

1. See John Ladd, "Morality and the Ideal of Rationality in Formal Organizations," *The Monist,* October 1970, p. 499.
2. See William K. Frankena, *Thinking About Morality* (Ann Arbor, University of Michigan Press, 1980), p. 26.

3. See Peter French, "The Corporation as a Moral Person," *American Philosophical Quarterly,* July 1979, p. 207.
4. A process that psychological researchers from Jean Piaget to Lawrence Kohlberg have examined carefully; see Jean Piaget, *The Moral Judgment of the Child* (New York, Free Press, 1965) and Lawrence Kohlberg, *The Philosophy of Moral Development* (New York, Harper & Row, 1981).
5. See Kenneth R. Andrews, *The Concept of Corporate Strategy,* revised edition (Homewood, Ill., Dow Jones-Irwin, 1980), p. 99.

THE SOCIAL RESPONSIBILITY OF BUSINESS

Milton Friedman

The view has been gaining widespread acceptance that corporate officials and labor leaders have a "social responsibility" that goes beyond serving the interest of their stockholders or their members. This view shows a fundamental misconception of the character and nature of a free economy. In such an economy, there is one and only one social responsibility of business—to use its resources and engage in activities designed to increase its profits so long as it stays within the rules of the game, which is to say, engages in open and free competition, without deception or fraud. Similarly, the "social responsiblity" of labor leaders is to serve the interests of the members of their unions. It is the responsibility of the rest of us to establish a framework of law such that an individual in pursuing his own interest is, to quote Adam Smith again, "led by an invisible hand to promote an end which was no part of his intention. Nor is it always the worse for the society that it was no part of it. By pursuing his own interest, he frequently promotes that of the society more effectually than when he really intends to promote it. I have never known much good done by those who affected to trade for the public good."[1]

Few trends could so thoroughly undermine the very foundations of our free society as the acceptance by corporate officials of a social responsibility other than to make as much money for their stockholders as possible. This is a fundamentally subversive doctrine. If businessmen do have a social responsibility other than making maximum profits for stockholders, how are they to know what it is? Can self-selected private individuals decide what the social interest is? Can they decide how great a burden they are justified in placing on themselves or their stockholders to serve that social interest? Is it tolerable that these public functions of taxation, expenditure, and control be exercised by the people who happen at the moment to be in charge of particular enterprises, chosen for those posts by strictly private

From *Capitalism and Freedom* by Milton Friedman, pp. 133–136. Copyright © 1962 by the University of Chicago Press. Reprinted by permission of the publisher.

groups? If businessmen are civil servants rather than the employees of their stockholders then in a democracy they will, sooner or later, be chosen by the public techniques of election and appointment.

And long before this occurs, their decision-making power will have been taken away from them. A dramatic illustration was the cancellation of a steel price increase by U.S. Steel in April 1962 through the medium of a public display of anger by President Kennedy and threats of reprisals on levels ranging from anti-trust suits to examination of the tax reports of steel executives. This was a striking episode because of the public display of the vast powers concentrated in Washington. We were all made aware of how much of the power needed for a police state was already available. It illustrates the present point as well. If the price of steel is a public decision, as the doctrine of social responsibility declares, then it cannot be permitted to be made privately.

The particular aspect of the doctrine which this example illustrates, and which has been most prominent recently, is an alleged social responsibility of business and labor to keep prices and wage rates down in order to avoid price inflation. Suppose that at a time when there was upward pressure on prices . . . every businessman and labor leader were to accept this responsibility and suppose all could succeed in keeping any price from rising, so we had voluntary price and wage control without open inflation. What would be the result? Clearly product shortages, labor shortages, gray markets, black markets. If prices are not allowed to ration goods and workers, there must be some other means to do so. Can the alternative rationing schemes be private? Perhaps for a time in a small and unimportant area. But if the goods involved are many and important, there will necessarily be pressure, and probably irresistible pressure, for governmental rationing of goods, a governmental wage policy, and governmental measures for allocating and distributing labor.

Price controls, whether legal or voluntary, if effectively enforced would eventually lead to the destruction of the free-enterprise system and its replacement by a centrally controlled system. And it would not even be effective in preventing inflation. History offers ample evidence that what determines the average level of prices and wages is the amount of money in the economy and not the greediness of businessmen or of workers. Governments ask for the self-restraint of business and labor because of their inability to manage their own affairs—which includes the control of money—and the natural human tendency to pass the buck.

One topic in the area of social responsibility that I feel duty-bound to touch on, because it affects my own personal interests, has been the claim that business should contribute to the support of charitable activities and especially to universities. Such giving by corporations is an inappropriate use of corporate funds in a free-enterprise society.

The corporation is an instrument of the stockholders who own it. If the corporation makes a contribution, it prevents the individual stockholder from himself deciding how he should dispose of his funds. With the corporation tax and the deductibility of contributions, stockholders may of course want the corporation to make a gift on their behalf, since this would enable them to make a larger gift. The best solution would be the abolition of the corporate tax. But so long as there is a corporate tax, there is no justification for permitting deductions for contributions to charitable and educational institutions. Such contributions should be made by the individuals who are the ultimate owners of property in our society.

People who urge extension of the deductibility of this kind of corporate contribution in the name of free enterprise are fundamentally working against their own interest. A major complaint made frequently against modern business is that it involves the separation of ownership and control—that the corporation has become a social institution that is a law unto itself, with irresponsible executives who do not serve the interests of their stockholders. This charge is not true. But the direction in which policy is now moving, of permitting corporations to make contributions for charitable purposes and allowing deductions for income tax, is a step in the direction of creating a true divorce between ownership and control and of undermining the basic nature and character of our society. It is a step away from an individualistic society and toward the corporate state.

Note

1. Adam Smith, *The Wealth of Nations* (1776) Bk. IV, Chapter ii, (Cannon ed., London, 1930) p. 421.

THE DANGERS OF SOCIAL RESPONSIBILITY

Theodore Levitt

The function of business is to produce sustained high-level profits. The essence of free enterprise is to go after profit in any way that is consistent with its own survival as an economic system. The catch, someone will quickly say, is "consistent with." This is true. In addition, lack of profits is not the only thing that can destroy business. Bureaucratic ossification, hostile legislation, and revolution can do it much better. Let me examine the matter further. Capitalism as we like it can thrive only in an environment of political democracy and personal freedom. These require a pluralistic society—where there is division, not centralization, of power; variety, not unanimity, of opinion; and separation, not unification, of workaday economic, political, social, and spiritual functions.

We all fear an omnipotent state because it creates a dull and frightening conformity—a monolithic society. We do not want a society with one locus

From *Harvard Business Review,* September-October 1958. Copyright © 1958 by the President and Fellows of Harvard College; all rights reserved.

of power, one authority, one arbiter of propriety. We want and need variety, diversity, spontaneity, competition—in short, pluralism. We do not want our lives shaped by a single viewpoint or by a single way of doing things, even if the material consequences are bountiful and the intentions are honorable. . . .

Now there is nothing wrong as such with the corporation's narrow ambitions or needs. Indeed, if there is anything wrong today, it is that the corporation conceives its ambitions and needs much too broadly. The trouble is not that it is too narrowly profit-oriented, but that it is not narrowly profit-oriented *enough*. In its guilt-driven urge to transcend the narrow limits of derived standards, the modern corporation is reshaping not simply the economic but also the institutional, social, cultural, and political topography of society.

And there's the rub. For while the corporation also transforms itself in the process, at bottom its outlook will always remain narrowly materialistic. What we have, then, is the frightening spectacle of a powerful economic functional group whose future and perception are shaped in a tight materialistic context of money and things but which imposes its narrow ideas about a broad spectrum of unrelated noneconomic subjects on the mass of man and society.

Even if its outlook were the purest kind of good will, that would not recommend the corporation as an arbiter of our lives. What is bad for this or any other country is for society to be consciously and aggressively shaped by a single functional group or a single ideology, whatever it may be.

If the corporation believes its long-run profitability to be strengthened by these peripheral involvements—if it believes that they are not charity but self-interest—then that much the worse. For, if this is so, it puts much more apparent justification and impulse behind activities which are essentially bad for man, bad for society, and ultimately bad for the corporation itself. . . .

Business wants to survive. It wants security from attack and restriction; it wants to minimize what it believes is its greatest potential enemy—the state. So it takes the steam out of the state's lumbering engines by employing numerous schemes to win its employees and the general public to its side. It is felt that these are the best possible investments it can make for its own survival. And that is precisely where the reasoning has gone wrong. These investments are only superficially *easy* solutions, not the best.

Welfare and society are not the corporation's business. Its business is making money, not sweet music. The same goes for unions. Their business is "bread and butter" and job rights. In a free enterprise system, welfare is supposed to be automatic; and where it is not, it becomes government's job. This is the concept of pluralism. Government's job is not business, and business's job is not government. And unless these functions are resolutely separated in all respects, they are eventually combined in every respect. In the end the danger is not that government will run business, or that business will run government, but rather that the two of them will coalesce, as we saw, into a single power, unopposed and unopposable.

rights movement of the early 1960's, the slogan, "You can't leg[islate] morality," was a popular cry on many fronts. Obviously, we have not [suc]ceeded in devising laws that create within our citizens a predispositio[n] love and kindness; but we can devise laws which will minimize the inju[ry] that one citizen must suffer at the hands of another. Although the virtue [of] love may be the possession of a few, justice—in the minimal sense of not in[-] juring others—can be required of all.

The distinction between negative injunctions and affirmative duties is old, having roots in common law and equity jurisprudence.[3] Here it is based on the premise that it is easier to specify and enjoin a civil wrong than to state what should be done. In the Ten Commandments, affirmative duties are spelled out only for one's relations with God and parents; for the more public relationships, we are given only the negative injunction: "Thou shalt not. . . ." Similarly, the Bill of Rights contains only negative injunctions.

Avoidance and Correction of Social Injury as a "Moral Minimum"

We do not mean to distinguish between negative injunctions and affirmative duties solely in the interests of analytical precision. The negative injunction to avoid and correct social injury threads its way through all morality. We call it a "moral minimum," implying that however one may choose to limit the concept of social responsibility, one cannot exclude this negative injunction. Although reasons may exist why certain persons or institutions cannot or should not be required to pursue moral or social good in all situations, there are many fewer reasons why one should be excused from the injunction against injuring others. Any citizen, individual or institutional, may have competing obligations which could, under some circumstances, override this negative injunction. But these special circumstances do not wipe away the prima facie obligation to avoid harming others.

In emphasizing the central role of the negative injunction, we do not suggest that affirmative duties are never important. A society where citizens go well beyond the requirement to avoid damage to others will surely be a better community. But we do recognize that individuals exhibit varying degrees of commitment to promote affirmatively the public welfare, whereas we expect everyone equally to refrain from injuring others.

The view that all citizens are equally obligated to avoid or correct any social injury which is self-caused finds support in our legal as well as our moral tradition. H. L. A. Hart and A. M. Honoré have written:

> In the moral judgments of ordinary life, we have occasion to blame people because they have caused harm to others, and also, if less frequently, to insist that morally they are bound to compensate those to whom they have caused harm. These are the moral analogues of more precise legal conceptions: for, in all legal systems liability to be punished or to make compensation frequently depends on whether actions (or omissions) have caused harm. Moral blame is not of course confined to such cases of causing harm.[4]

The only political function of business, labor, and agriculture is to fight each other so that none becomes or remains dominant for long. When one does reach overwhelming power and control, at the very best the state will eventually take over on the pretense of protecting everybody else. At that point the big business executives, claiming possession of the tools of large-scale management, will come in, as they do in war, to become the bureaucrats who run the state.

The final victor then is neither government, as the representative of the people, nor the people, as represented by government. The new leviathan will be the professional corporate bureaucrat operating at a more engrossing and exalted level than the architects of capitalism ever dreamed possible.

The functions of the four main groups in our economy—government, business, labor, agriculture—must be kept separate and separable. As soon as they become amalgamated and indistinguishable, they likewise become monstrous and restrictive. . . .

Business will have a much better chance of surviving if there is no nonsense about its goals—that is, if long-run profit maximization is the one dominant objective in practice as well as in theory. Business should recognize what government's functions are and let it go at that, stopping only to fight government where government directly intrudes itself into business. It should let government take care of the general welfare so that business can take care of the more material aspects of welfare.

The results of any such single-minded devotion to profit should be invigorating. With none of the corrosive distractions and costly bureaucracies that now serve the pious cause of welfare, politics, society, and putting up a pleasant front, with none of these draining its vitality, management can shoot for the economic moon. It will be able to thrust ahead in whatever way seems consistent with its money-making goals. If laws and threats stand in its way, it should test and fight them, relenting only if the courts have ruled against it, and then probing again to test the limits of the rules. And when business fights, it should fight with uncompromising relish and self-assertiveness, instead of using all the rhetorical dodges and pious embellishments that are now so often its stock in trade.

Practicing self-restraint behind the cloak of the insipid dictum that "an ounce of prevention is worth a pound of cure" has only limited justification. Certainly it often pays not to squeeze the last dollar out of a market—especially when good will is a factor in the long-term outlook. But too often self-restraint masquerades for capitulation. Businessmen complain about legislative and other attacks on aggressive profit seeking but then lamely go forth to slay the dragon with speeches that simply concede business's function to be service. The critic quickly pounces on this admission with unconcealed relish—"Then why *don't* you serve?" But the fact is, no matter how much business "serves," it will never be enough for its critics. . . .

If the all-out competitive prescription sounds austere or harsh, that is only because we persist in judging things in terms of utopian standards. Altruism, self-denial, charity, and similar values are vital in certain walks of our life—areas which, because of that fact, are more important to the long-run future than business. But for the most part those virtues are alien to competitive economics.

If it sounds callous to hold such a view, and suicidal to publicize it, that is only because business has done nothing to prepare the community to agree with it. There is only one way to do that: to perform at top ability and to speak vigorously *for* (not in defense of) what business does. . . . But it is only a beginning.

In the end business has only two responsibilities—to obey the elementary canons of everyday face-to-face civility (honesty, good faith, and so on) and to seek material gain. The fact that it is the butt of demagogical critics is no reason for management to lose its nerve—to buckle under to reformers—lest more severe restrictions emerge to throttle business completely. Few people will man the barricades against capitalism if it is a good provider, minds its own business, and supports government in the things which are properly government's. Even today, most American critics want only to curb capitalism, not to destroy it. And curbing efforts will not destroy it if there is free and open discussion about its singular function.

To the extent that there is conflict, can it not be a good thing? Every book, every piece of history, even every religion testifies to the fact that conflict is and always has been the subject, origin, and life blood of society. Struggle helps to keep us alive, to give élan to life. We should try to make the most of it, not avoid it.

Lord Acton has said of the past that people sacrificed freedom by grasping at impossible justice. The contemporary school of business morality seems intent on adding its own caveat to that unhappy consequence. The gospel of tranquility is a soporific. Instead of fighting for its survival by means of a series of strategic retreats masquerading as industrial statesmanship, business must fight as if it were at war. And, like a good war, it should be fought gallantly, daringly, and, above all, *not* morally.

THE RESPONSIBILITIES OF CORPORATIONS AND THEIR OWNERS

John G. Simon, Charles W. Powers, Jon P. Gunnemann

For better or worse, the modern American business corporation is increasingly being asked to assume more responsibility for social problems and the public welfare. How corporate responsibility is understood, and whether it is perceived to be for better or worse, may depend in the last analysis on the beholder's emotional reaction to the corporation itself: one either extols the corporation as part of the creative process or condemns it

as the work of the Devil. Thus, almost four centuries ago the English ju Sir Edward Coke wrote of corporations that "they cannot commit treas nor be outlawed nor excommunicated for they have no souls," while mo recently Justice Louis D. Brandeis characterized the corporation as t "master instrument of civilized life. . . ."[1]

Our analysis of the controversies surrounding the notion of corpora responsibility—and the suggestion that the university as an invest should be concerned with corporate responsibility—proceeds in large pa from our approach to certain issues in the area of social responsibility ar public morals. In particular, we (1) make a distinction between negativ injunctions and affirmative duties; (2) assert that all men have the "mora minimum" obligation not to impose social injury; (3) delineate those cor ditions under which one is held responsible for social injury, even where is not clear that the injury was self-caused; and (4) take a position in th argument between those who strive for moral purity and those who striv for moral effectiveness.

NEGATIVE INJUNCTIONS AND AFFIRMATIVE DUTIES

A distinction which informs much of our discussion differentiates between injunctions against activities that injure others and duties which require the affirmative pursuit of some good. The failure to make this distinction in debate on public ethics often results in false dichotomies, a point illustrated by an article which appeared just over a decade ago in the *Harvard Business Review*. In that article, which provoked considerable debate in the business community, Theodore Levitt argued against corporate social responsibility both because it was dangerous for society and because it detracted from the primary goal of business, the making of profit. We deal with the merits of these arguments later; what is important for our immediate purpose, however, is Levitt's designation of those activities and concerns which constitute social responsibility. He notes that the corporation has become "more concerned about the needs of its employees, about schools, hospitals, welfare agencies and even aesthetics," and that it is "fashionable . . . for the corporation to show that it is a great innovator; more specifically, a great public benefactor; and, very particularly, that it exists 'to serve the public.'"[2] Having so delimited the notion of corporate responsibility, Levitt presents the reader with a choice between, on the one hand, getting involved in the management of society, "creating munificence for one and all," and, on the other hand, fulfilling the profit-making function. But such a choice excludes another meaning of corporate responsibility: the making of profits in such a way as to minimize social injury. Levitt at no point considers the possibility that business activity may at times injure others and that it may be necessary to regulate the social consequences of one's business activities accordingly. . . .

Our public discourse abounds with similar failures to distinguish between positive and perhaps lofty ideals and minimal requirements of social organization. During the election campaigns of the 1950's and the civil

We know of no societies, from the literature of anthropology or comparative ethics, whose moral codes do not contain some injunction against harming others. The specific notion of *harm* or *social injury* may vary, as well as the mode of correction and restitution, but the injunctions are present.

In using the term *moral minimum* to describe this obligation, we mean to avoid any suggestion that the injunction against doing injury to others can serve as the basis for deriving the full content of morality. Moreover, we have used an expression which does not imply that the injunction is in any way dependent upon a natural law point of view. A person who subscribed to some form of natural law theory might indeed agree with our position, but so could someone who maintained that all morality is based on convention, agreement, or contract. Social contract theorists have generally maintained that the granting of rights to individuals by mutual consent involves some limitation on the actions of all individuals in the contract: to guarantee the liberty of all members, it is essential that each be enjoined against violating the rights of others.[5]

We asserted earlier that it is easier to enjoin and correct a wrong than it is to prescribe affirmatively what is good for society and what ought to be done. Notions of the public good and the values that men actively seek to implement are subjects of intense disagreement. In this realm, pluralism is almost inevitable, and some would argue that it is healthy. Yet there can also be disagreement about what constitutes social injury or harm. What some people think are affirmative duties may be seen by others as correction of social injury. For example, the notion that business corporations should make special effort to train and employ members of minority groups could be understood by some to fulfill an affirmative duty on the part of corporations to meet society's problems; but it could be interpreted by others as the correction of a social injury caused by years of institutional racism. As a more extreme example, a Marxist would in all probability contend that *all* corporate activity is socially injurious and that therefore all social pursuits by corporations are corrective responses rather than affirmative actions.[6]

Although the notion of *social injury* is imprecise and although many hard cases will be encountered in applying it, we think that it is a helpful designation and that cases can be decided on the basis of it. In the law, many notions (such as *negligence* in the law of torts or *consideration* in the law of contracts) are equally vague but have received content from repeated decision making over time. We would hope that under our proposed Guidelines similar "case law" would develop. Moreover, our Guidelines attempt to give some content to the notion of *social injury* by referring to external norms: *social injury* is defined as "particularly including activities which violate, or frustrate the enforcement of, rules of domestic or international law intended to protect individuals against deprivation of health, safety or basic freedoms."[7]

In sum, we would affirm the prima facie obligation of all citizens, both individual and institutional, to avoid and correct self-caused social injury. Much more in the way of affirmative acts may be expected of certain kinds of citizens, but none is exempt from this "moral minimum."

In some cases it may not be true—or at least it may not be clear—that one has caused or helped to cause social injury, and yet one may bear responsibility for correcting or averting the injury. We consider next the circumstances under which this responsibility may arise.

NEED, PROXIMITY, CAPABILITY, AND LAST RESORT (THE KEW GARDENS PRINCIPLE)

Several years ago the public was shocked by the news accounts of the stabbing and agonizingly slow death of Kitty Genovese in the Kew Gardens section of New York City while thirty-eight people watched or heard and did nothing.[8] What so deeply disturbed the public's moral sensibility was that in the face of a critical human need, people who were close to that need and had the power to do something about it failed to act.

The public's reaction suggests that, no matter how narrowly one may conceive of social responsibility, there are some situations in which a combination of circumstances thrusts upon us an obligation to respond. Life is fraught with emergency situations in which a failure to respond is a special form of violation of the negative injunction against causing social injury: a sin of omission becomes a sin of commission.

Legal responsibility for aiding someone in cases of grave distress or injury, even when caused by another, is recognized by many European civil codes and by the criminal laws of one of our states:

> (A) A person who knows that another is exposed to grave physical harm shall, to the extent that the same can be rendered without danger or peril to himself or without interference with important duties owed to others, give reasonable assistance to the exposed person unless that assistance or care is being provided by others. . . .
>
> (C) A person who wilfully violates subsection (A) of this section shall be fined not more than $100.00.[9]

This Vermont statute recognizes that it is not reasonable in all cases to require a person to give assistance to someone who is endangered. If such aid imperils himself, or interferes with duties owed to others, or if there are others providing the aid, the person is excepted from the obligation. These conditions of responsibility give some shape to difficult cases and are in striking parallel with the conditions which existed at Kew Gardens. The salient features of the Kitty Genovese case are (1) critical need; (2) the proximity of the thirty-eight spectators; (3) the capability of the spectators to act helpfully (at least to telephone the police); and (4) the absence of other (including official) help; i.e., the thirty-eight were the last resort. There would, we believe, be widespread agreement that a moral obligation to aid another arises when these four features are present. What we have called the "moral minimum" (the duty to avoid and correct self-caused social injury) is an obvious and easy example of fulfillment of these criteria—so obvious that there is little need to go through step-by-step analysis of these factors. Where the injury is not clearly self-caused, the application of these criteria aids in deciding responsibility. We have called this combination of features governing difficult cases the "Kew Gardens Principle." There follows a more detailed examination of each of the features:

Need. In cases where the other three criteria are constant, increased need increases responsibility. Just as there is no precise definition of social injury (one kind of need), there is no precise definition of need or way of measuring its extent.

Proximity. The thirty-eight witnesses of the Genovese slaying were geographically close to the deed. But proximity to a situation of need is not necessarily spatial. Proximity is largely a function of notice: we hold a person blameworthy if he knows of imperilment and does not do what he reasonably can do to remedy the situation. Thus, the thirty-eight at Kew Gardens were delinquent not because they were near but because nearness enabled them to know that someone was in need. A deaf person who could not hear the cries for help would not be considered blameworthy even if he were closer than those who could hear. So also, a man in Afghanistan is uniquely responsible for the serious illness of a man in Peoria, Illinois, if he has knowledge of the man's illness, if he can telephone a doctor about it, and if he alone has that notice. When we become aware of a wrongdoing or a social injury, we take on obligations that we did not have while ignorant.

Notice does not exhaust the meaning of proximity, however. It is reasonable to maintain that the sick man's neighbors in Peoria were to some extent blameworthy if they made no effort to inquire into the man's welfare. Ignorance cannot always be helped, but we do expect certain persons and perhaps institutions to look harder for information about critical need.[10] In this sense, proximity has to do with the network of social expectations that flow from notions of civic duty, duties to one's family, and so on. Thus, we expect a man to be more alert to the plight of his next-door neighbor than to the needs of a child in East Pakistan, just as we expect a man to be more alert to the situation of his own children than to the problems of the family down the block. The failure of the man to act in conformance with this expectation does not give him actual notice of need, but it creates what the law would call *constructive notice*. Both factors—actual notice and constructive notice growing out of social expectation—enter into the determination of responsibility and blame.

Capability. Even if there is a need to which a person has proximity, that person is not usually held responsible unless there is something he can reasonably be expected to do to meet the need. To follow Immanuel Kant, *ought* assumes *can*. What one is reasonably capable of doing, of course, admits to some variety of interpretation. In the Kew Gardens incident, it might not have been reasonable to expect someone to place his body between the girl and the knife. It was surely reasonable to expect someone to call the police. So also it would not seem to be within the canons of reasonability for a university to sacrifice education for charity. . . . But if the university is able, by non-self-sacrificial means, to mitigate injury caused by a company of which it is an owner, it would not seem unreasonable to ask it to do so.

Last Resort. In the emergency situations we have been describing, one becomes more responsible the less likely it is that someone else will be able to aid. Physical proximity is a factor here, as is time. If the knife is drawn, one cannot wait for the policeman. It is important to note here that determination of last resort becomes more difficult the more complex the social situation or organization. The man on the road to Jericho, in spite of the presence of a few other travelers, probably had a fairly good notion that he was the only person who could help the man attacked by thieves. But on a street in New York City, there is always the hope that someone else will step forward to give aid. Surely this rationalization entered into the silence of each of the thirty-eight: there were, after all, thirty-seven others. Similarly, within large corporations it is difficult to know not only whether one alone has notice of a wrongdoing, but also whether there is anyone else who is able to respond. Because of this diffusion of responsibility in complex organizations and societies, the notion of last resort is less useful than the other Kew Gardens criteria in determining whether one ought to act in aid of someone in need or to avert or correct social injury. Failure to act because one hopes someone else will act—or because one is trying to find out who is the last resort—may frequently lead to a situation in which no one acts at all.[11] This fact, we think, places more weight on the first three features of the Kew Gardens Principle in determining responsibility, and it creates a presumption in favor of taking action when those three conditions are present.[12]

Notes

1. We are indebted for the juxtaposition of these two quotes to Harris Wofford, president of Bryn Mawr College. From some points of view, of course, being the "master instrument of civilized life" is to be convicted of soullessness.

   Debate about the corporation in American society and about its desirability in a democratic nation goes back at least to the writers of the American Constitution: Hamilton wanted to give the federal government the power to issue corporate charters for the purpose of promoting trade and industry; Madison felt that corporations would prevent men from participating in public action and were thus a threat to freedom. The debate was resolved in Madison's favor—although in later years some federal charters were issued.

   For a brief discussion of the early debates between the Jeffersonians and the Hamiltonians, see Harvey C. Bunke, *A Primer on American Economic History* (New York, 1969), Ch. 3, and Edwin M. Epstein, *The Corporation in American Politics* (Englewood Cliffs, N.J., 1969). For fuller discussion, see Oscar and Mary Handlin, "Origins of the American Business Corporation," *Journal of Economic History* 5 (May 1945), and Joseph S. David, *Essays in the Earlier History of American Corporations* vol. 2 (Cambridge, Mass., 1917).

2. Theodore Levitt, "The Dangers of Social Responsibility," in Marshall, ed., *Business and Government,* pp. 22–23.

3. We are grateful to President Edward Bl\oustein of Rutgers University for suggesting this terminology and for inviting our attention to its historical antecedents. Further analysis of the distinction between *negative injunctions* and *affirmative duties* is given in the following sections of this chapter.

4. H. L. A. Hart and A. M. Honoré, *Causation in the Law* (Oxford, 1959), p. 59.

5. Jeremy Bentham wrote that " . . . [A]ll rights are made at the expense of liberty. . . . [There is] no right without a correspondent obligation. . . . All

coercive law, therefore . . . and in particular all laws creative of liberty, are, as far as they go, abrogative of liberty." "Anarchical Fallacies," in *Society, Law and Morality,* ed. F. A. Olafsson (Englewood Cliffs, N.J., 1961), p. 350. Clearly, Bentham understood that any creation of rights or liberties under the law entailed recognition of an injunction against violating the rights of others.

6. The notion of social injury may also change over time. External norms in the form of government regulations now provide that failure to actively recruit minority group members constitutes discrimination, i.e., is a matter of social injury. See the "affirmative action" requirements, including recruiting measures, imposed on all federal contractors by the federal "contract compliance" regulations, 41 *Code of Federal Regulations,* Section 60-62. At one time, such recruitment was not subject to a negative injunction.

7. We do not suggest that social injury is identical to violation of the legal norms to which we are referring. (In other words, we recognize that some laws themselves cause social injury in the eyes of many persons, and also that not all social injury is prohibited by law.) We are only saying that reference to legal norms will help individuals and institutions to make their own judgments about social injury.

8. See A.M. Rosenthal, *Thirty-Eight Witnesses* (New York, 1964).

9. "Duty to Aid the Endangered Act," *Vt. Stat. Ann.,* Ch. 12, § 519 (Supp. 1968). See G. Hughes, "Criminal Omissions," 67 *Yale L. J.* 590 (1958).

10. See, for example, Albert Speer's reflection on his role during the Hitler regime: "For being in a position to know and nevertheless shunning knowledge creates direct responsibility for the consequences—from the very beginning." *Inside the Third Reich* (New York, 1970), p. 19.

11. Failure to respond to need in social situations may also have another effect, equally detrimental to public morality: it suggests to others who might have stepped forward that the situation is really not serious. Thus, two psychologists, John M. Darley and Bibb Latané, after conducting experiments on social reaction to simulated emergencies, concluded that "it is possible for a state of 'pluralistic ignorance' to develop, in which each bystander is led by the apparent lack of concern of the others to interpret the situation as being less serious than he would if alone. To the extent that he does not feel the situation is an emergency, he will be unlikely to take any helpful action." Darley and Latané, *The Unresponsive Bystander: Why Doesn't He Help?* (New York, 1970), cited by Israel Shenker, *New York Times,* 10 April 1971, p. 25. The latter article was based on a separate experiment conducted by Prof. Darley and Dr. C. Daniel Batson at Princeton Theological Seminary designed to determine why people do not help. A group of students were given biblical texts to record, then given individual directions to the recording studio that required them to pass a writhing, gasping student lying in a doorway. It was found that the only significant differentiating factor in determining whether a student stopped to aid was the amount of time he thought he had; those who were told they were late for the recording session stopped to help much less often (10 per cent) than those who were told that they had sufficient time (63 per cent). It made no statistical difference that half of the seminary students had been given the Parable of the Good Samaritan to record.

12. We do not invoke the Kew Gardens Principle to establish corporate responsibility for clearly self-caused social harm, but rather to demonstrate how shareholders—who may not appear to be directly involved in corporate-caused injury—are obligated to attempt to avert or avoid such injury.

AN EXPANDED VIEW OF THE
SOCIAL RESPONSIBILITY OF BUSINESS

Keith Davis

Business's need for social response and social responsibility has been discussed loudly and at length. What does it all mean? One way to understand the issues is to examine the basic propositions offered in the social responsibility debate.

Modern society presents business with immensely complicated problems. Technology has advanced to a level that tests intellectual capacities, markets have become more complex and international in scope, and difficult new problems of social issues and social responsibility have arisen. In earlier periods, the mission of business was clear. It was strictly an economic one—to produce the best quality of goods and services at the lowest possible price and to distribute them effectively. The accomplishment of this mission was remarkably effective, so effective that large numbers of the population found their minimum economic needs reasonably satisfied and began to turn their thoughts toward other needs.

Beginning in the 1950s, the public's mood shifted sharply toward social concerns, and this mood was reflected in extensive social demands made on institutions. Since business interacts extensively with all of society, perhaps more of these demands were made on business than any other institution. By sticking strictly to its economic role in the past, business had left the social side of its activities largely untended and was unprepared to deal effectively with social issues. However, the public also was unprepared for its new role as social protagonist, and, as a result, churning and ferment have marked discussion of social priorities, how they are to be accomplished, and what role business should play in this accomplishment.

After more than twenty years of controversy, the debate over business and social issues has now reached some maturity. Out of this maturity a degree of uniform support is developing for certain social propositions to guide the conduct of business as well as of other institutions. These guidelines apply to a greater or lesser degree according to individual circumstances, but the important point is that they do apply. Intelligent businessmen will take heed of these guidelines if they wish to avoid unnecessary confrontations with society. This article examines [two] of these guidelines which are supported by a degree of consensus.

SOCIAL RESPONSIBILITY AND POWER

One basic proposition is that *social responsibility arises from social power*. Modern business has immense social power in such areas as minority

From *Business Horizons*, Vol. XVIII, no. 3, June 1975. Copyright © 1975 by the Foundation for the School of Business at Indiana University. Reprinted by permission.

employment and environmental pollution. If business has the power, then a just relationship demands that business also bear responsibility for its actions in these areas. Social responsibility arises from concern about the consequences of business's acts as they affect the interests of others. Business decisions do have social consequences. Businessmen cannot make decisions that are solely economic decisions, because they are interrelated with the whole social system. This situation requires that businessmen's thinking be broadened beyond the company gate to the whole social system. Systems thinking is required.

Social responsibility implies that a business decision maker in the process of serving his own business interests is obliged to take actions that also protect and enhance society's interests. The net effect is to improve the quality of life in the broadest possible way, however quality of life is defined by society. In this manner, harmony is achieved between business's actions and the larger social system. The businessman becomes concerned with social as well as economic outputs and with the total effect of his institutional actions on society.

Business institutions that ignore responsibility for their social power are threatened by what Keith Davis and Robert L. Blomstrom call the Iron Law of Responsibility: "In the long run, those who do not use power in a manner which society considers responsible will tend to lose it."[1] The record of history has supported operation of this law as one institution after another has found its power either eroded or overthrown when it fails to use power responsibly. The implication for business is that, if it wishes to retain its viability and significance as a major social institution, then it must give responsible attention to social issues.

The fundamental assumption of this model is that society has entrusted to business large amounts of society's resources to accomplish its mission, and business is expected to manage these resources as a wise trustee for society. In addition to the traditional role of economic entrepreneurship, business now has a new social role of trusteeship. As trustee for society's resources, it serves the interests of all claimants on the organization, rather than only those of owners, or consumers, or labor. . . .

SOCIAL RESPONSIBILITIES AS CITIZENS

. . . [Another] basic proposition is that *beyond social costs business institutions as citizens have responsibilities for social involvement in areas of their competence where major social needs exist.* [This] proposition is based essentially on the reasoning that business is a major social institution that should bear the same kinds of citizenship costs for society that an individual citizen bears. Business will benefit from a better society just as any citizen will benefit; therefore, business has a responsibility to recognize social problems and actively contribute its talents to help solve them.

Such involvement is expected of any citizen, and business should fulfill a citizenship role. Business will not have primary responsibility for solving problems, but it should provide significant assistance. For example, business did not directly cause educational problems, but it does stand to gain some benefit from their solution; therefore, it has some responsibility to help develop and apply solutions.

A Matter of Harmony

The thrust of the foregoing propositions is that business, like any individual, needs to act responsibly regarding the consequences of its actions. The socially responsible organization behaves in such a way that it protects and improves the social quality of life along with its own quality of life. In essence, quality of life refers to the degree to which people live in harmony with their inner spirit, their fellow man, and nature's physical environment. Business has a significant effect on each of these, particularly the last two. It can support harmony among people as well as in the environment if it will take the larger system's view.

Although quality of life embraces harmony, it is not a static concept that seeks to preserve a utopian status quo. Rather, it is a dynamic concept in which people live harmoniously with the changes occurring in nature and in themselves. It is, however, a utopian concept in the sense that most people use it as an ultimate goal that they realize probably will never be obtained absolutely. It is essentially a set of criteria by which judgments may be made about social progress. The social responsibility model seeks to improve the quality of life through its five propositions.

Certain observations can be made concerning the implementation of the social responsibility model.

First, it applies to all organizations. Although this discussion has been presented in the context of business, the social responsibility model does not single out business for special treatment. All organizations have equal responsibilities for the consequences of their actions.

Similarly, social responsibility applies to all persons in all of their life roles, whether employee, camper, renter, or automobile driver. An individual who tosses his rubbish along a roadside is just as irresponsible as a business that pours pollutants into a river. The individual may argue that his offense is less in magnitude, but when his rubbish is added to all the rest, it becomes a massive offense against the public interest.

As a matter of fact, quality of life will be improved less than people expect if only business is socially responsible. Substantial improvement will be achieved only when most organizations and persons act in socially responsible ways.

Second, the movement toward greater social responsibility is not a fad but a fundamental change in social directions. Business executives will do their organizations grievous damage if they assume social responsibility is merely something to be assigned to a third assistant with action to be taken only when absolutely necessary and when the organization is backed into a corner.

Social responsibility is here to stay despite its intangibles and imponderables. As stated earlier, business probably has been a significant cause of the rise of social responsibility ideas because it did its economic job so well that it released people from economic want, freeing them to pursue new social goals.

Third, social response by business will increase business's economic costs. Social responsibility is not a free ride or a matter of simple goodwill. Actions such as the reduction of pollution take large amounts of economic resources. The costs are there. It is true that some of these costs are transferred from other segments of society, so society as a whole may not bear higher costs for some actions; however, these costs are brought into the business system and, in most instances, will flow through in the form of higher prices.

This situation is likely to put further strain on business-consumer relations. It may even lead to consumer demands for less social involvement in the short run, but the long-run secular trend toward more social involvement is likely to remain.

Note

1. Keith Davis and Robert L. Blomstrom, *Business and Society: Environment and Responsibility,* 3rd ed. (New York: McGraw-Hill Book Company, 1975), p. 50. Italics in original. A number of analysts believe that the desirable course of events is for business to lose a substantial part of its power. That is a separate issue not treated in this article, but for details the reader is referred to the review of Richard Barnet and Ronald Muller's *Global Reach: The Power of the Multinational Corporation,* in William G. Ryan, "The Runaway Global Corporation," *Business Horizons* (February 1975), pp. 91–95.

CHANGING THE SOCIAL CONTRACT: A ROLE FOR BUSINESS

Melvin Anshen

Among the problems confronting top corporate officers, none is more disturbing than the demand that they modify or abandon their traditional responsibility to devote their best talent and energy to the management of resources with the goal of maximizing the return on the owners' investment.

This demand takes many forms. It may appear as pressure:

to withhold price increases to cover rising costs;

to give special financial support to black ghetto properties and businesses;

to provide special training and jobs for the hard-core unemployed;

to invest in equipment designed to minimize environmental contamination by controlling, scrubbing or eliminating industrial process discharges into air or water;

From *The Columbia Journal of World Business,* V, no. 6, November-December 1970. Reprinted by permission.

to contribute generously to the support of charitable, educational and artistic organizations and activities;

to refuse to solicit or accept defense and defense-related contracts;

to avoid or dispose of investments in countries where racial or political policies and practices offend elements of the citizenry;

to provide for "public" or "consumer" representation on boards of directors;

to make executives available to serve without compensation on public boards or other non-business assignments.

The common element in all these pressures is their departure from, even contradiction of, the economic considerations which have been regarded as appropriate criteria for determining the allocation and use of private resources. They challenge the thesis that decisions taken with a view to maximizing private profit also maximize public benefits. They deny the working of Adam Smith's "invisible hand."

This cluster of pressures is not limited to alleged deficiencies in the traditional elements of management decision making. It also raises fundamental questions about the intellectual ability of business managers—reflecting their education, experience and norms of behavior—to respond adaptively and creatively to new goals, new criteria for administering resources, new measures of performance. . . .

One way of comprehending the whole development is to view it as an emerging demand for a new set of relationships among business, government, non-economic organizations and individuals. Some such set of relationships, of changing character and composition, has existed throughout recorded history. Without some implicit and broadly accepted design for living together, man's existence with his fellow men would be chaotic beyond endurance.

Philosophers and political theorists have observed the persistence and the necessity of this organizing concept. They have even coined a useful descriptive phrase for it: "the social contract." . . .

The ultimate determinant of the structure and performance of any society is a set of reciprocal, institutionalized duties and obligations which are broadly accepted by its citizens. The acceptance may be described as an implicit social contract. Without such a contract, not less real or powerful for being implicit, a society would lack cohesiveness, order and continuity. Individuals would be confused about their own behavior and commitments as well as about their appropriate expectations with respect to the behavior and commitments of the private and public institutions which employ them, service them and govern them. . . .

The concept of the implied social contract is an old one in Western civilization. It found early expression in the writings of the Greek philosopher Epictetus. It was central to the intellectual system developed by Thomas Hobbes in the first half of the seventeenth century. Without such an implicit contract, he observed, man faces the terror of anarchy, for the natural condition of man is "solitary, short, brutish and nasty." Hobbes used his concept to rationalize the power of the state to compel obedience to the terms of the implied contract. A few decades later, John

Locke converted this view of compulsion as the lever to the view of consent as the lever—the consent of the citizens to a relationship of reciprocal duties and obligations.

In the next century, Jean Jacques Rousseau expanded the idea into an intellectual system in which each member of society entered into an implicit contract with every other member, a contract that defined the norms of human behavior and the terms of exchanges and trade-offs among individuals and organizations, private and public. His view even provided for handling disagreements about ends and means. The implied social contract, he wrote, stipulated that the minority would accept the decisions of the majority, would express its opposition through legitimate channels of dissent, and would yield before proceeding to rebellion. To Rousseau, therefore, the act of rebellion signified not what it appeared to be on the surface—a rebellion against the ends and means favored by the majority—but rather a rejection of the very terms of the contract itself.

Most recently, the fundamental thrust of such a book as John Kenneth Galbraith's *The New Industrial State* challenges the terms of the implicit social contract that defines, among other things, the function and role of private enterprise in today's society, the popular view of the responsibilities and performance of private corporations and the network of reciprocal relationships among corporations, government, and citizens. Galbraith's description of the enterprise system is distorted and incomplete, but his perception of the fundamental contract and its pervasive influence is accurate.

The terms of the historic social contract for private business, now coming under critical attack, are brilliantly clear. They existed for more than a hundred years with only minor modifications. Indeed, they acquired a popular, almost mythic, concept which purported to define a set of institutional arrangements uniquely advantageous for the national well-being, superior to all alternatives. . . .

These contractual terms were an outgrowth of interlaced economic, social and technological considerations in which the economic issues were overwhelmingly dominant. Economic growth, summed in the grand measure of gross national product, was viewed as the source of all progress. The clear assumption was that social progress (including those benefits associated with ideas about the quality of life) was a by-product of economic progress and impossible to achieve without it. Technological advance both fueled economic progress and was fueled by it in a closed, self-generating system.

The engine of economic growth was identified as the drive for profits by unfettered, competitive, private enterprise. Natural and human resources were bought in an open market and were administered in the interest of profit maximization. Constraints were applied only at the margins and were designed either to assure the continuance of the system (as in antitrust legislation and administration) or to protect those who could not protect themselves in the open market (as in legislation prohibiting child labor, assuring labor's right to organize or restraining deliberate injury to consumers). These and similar constraints were "the rules of the game," a suggestive term. The rules protected the game and assured its continuance as a constructive activity.

The implicit social contract stipulated that business could operate freely within the rules. Subject only to the constraints on conduct imposed by the rules, the responsibility of business was to search for and produce profits. In doing this competitively, business yielded benefits for society in the form of products and services wanted by consumers who earned the purchasing power to supply their wants by working at jobs created by business. . . .

The most dramatic element for business in the emerging new contract is a shift in the conceptual relation between economic progress and social progress. Until recently, the primacy of economic growth as the chief engine of civilization was generally not seriously questioned. Some of its unpleasant or wounding by-products were, to be sure, superficially deplored from time to time. But they were accepted by most people as fundamentally inevitable and were appraised as a reasonable price to pay for the benefits of a steadily rising gross national product. As a result, the by-products were rarely studied in depth, their economic and social costs were not measured—indeed, little was done even to develop accounting techniques for tooling such measurement.

Michael Harrington's book, *The Other America,* with its quantitative documentation of the existence of an unacknowledged poor nation within a rich nation, could strike with genuine shock on the mind and conscience of many professional and managerial leaders in public and private organizations. The facts of urban decay and the implications of trends projected into the future were not analyzed and reported in terms that would permit a realistic assessment of their present and future costs. Nor, certainly until the outbreak of mass riots in minority ghettos, was there penetrating consideration of the relation of social disturbance to continued economic progress.

While much remains to be done in scientific research and analysis of the side effects of economic progress, the accumulating formal and informal documentation has begun to influence the set of general ideas that constitute the terms of the contract for business. The clause in the contract that stipulated the primacy of economic growth, and thereby gave a charter to free enterprise within broad rules of competitive economic behavior, is now widely challenged. It is becoming clear that in the emerging new contract, social progress (the quality of life) will weigh equally in the balance with economic progress. . . .

Such equality foreshadows some drastic revisions in the rules of the game. As one example, it will no longer be acceptable for corporations to manage their affairs solely in terms of the traditional internal costs of doing business, while thrusting external costs on the public. Since the 1930s, of course, some external costs have been partially returned to business firms, as in the case of unemployment compensation. But most have not, and this situation is on the edge of revision. This means, as is even now beginning to occur, that the costs associated with environmental contamination will be transferred from the public sector to the business firms which generate the contamination. It also means that corporations whose economic activities are judged to create safety hazards (from automobiles to atomic power plants) will be compelled to internalize the costs of minimizing these hazards by conforming with stipulated levels of acceptable risk or of mandatory manufacturing and performance specifications.

To be rigorously correct, it should be noted that industry's new cost structure will be reflected in its prices. Purchasers of goods and services will be the ultimate underwriters of the increased expenses. But a moment's reflection on the supply-demand charts that sprinkle the pages of economics texts will demonstrate that a new schedule of supply prices will intersect demand curves at different points than formerly. This may lead to a changed set of customer purchase preferences among the total assortment of goods and services. What is implied is not a simple pass-through of newly internalized social costs. The ultimate results will alter relative market positions among whole industries and, within industries, among firms. Choices from available options in short-term technological adjustments to the new contamination and safety requirements and in long-term pricing strategies to reflect higher costs will, in the familiar competitive way, determine success or failure for a number of companies. Some interesting management decisions lie ahead.

The internalization of traditional social costs of private operations is the most obvious of the changes that will follow on striking a new balance between economic and social progress. More subtle, and eventually more radical, relocations of responsibility can be foreseen. The complex cluster of socio-economic problems associated with urbanization, population shifts and the needs of disadvantaged minorities are already overwhelming the administrative capacities, probably also the resources, of city, county and state governments. Evidence is accumulating that the public expects private business to contribute brains and resources to the amelioration and resolution of these massive strains. History suggests that such expectations will be transformed into demands. . . .

If the thrust of this analysis is generally on target, the principal lesson for private management is clear. It must participate actively in the redesign of the social contract. There can be no greater danger than to permit the new rules to be formulated by either the small group of critics armed only with malevolence toward the existing system or the much larger group sincerely motivated by concern for ameliorating social ills but grossly handicapped by their ignorance of the techniques and dynamism of private enterprise. . . .

A good place to begin would be the uncharted jungle of cost estimates. We need concepts and techniques for measuring and accounting for the real costs of environmental contamination. We need to build a body of reliable information about what the costs are in all their complexity, where they originate, where they impact. We also need to evaluate present and potential technologies for suppressing or removing contaminants, along both engineering and economic parameters. Using history, experimentation and game theory, we need to study the relative effectiveness of all types of cost transfer instruments, both inducements and penalties. One might speculate that the conclusion will be in favor of applying a variety of

devices, each fitted to a specific set of technical and economic circumstances, rather than a single instrument. But this is a foresighted
guess, not a basis for public policy determination.

A second area where business competence can make a contribution is
the cluster of problems associated with poverty in the midst of plenty,
unemployed or underemployed minorities, and urban decay. Less clearly
defined than the contamination issue, this area possesses much greater
potential for violent disruption that could mortally shred the fabric of our
society. If this occurs (and there are too many recent examples of limited
local disruptions to be comfortably skeptical about the possibilities ahead),
many of the environmental conditions essential for the private enterprise
system will disappear. There can be little doubt that what would follow
would be an authoritarian, social-service, rigid society in which the conditions of production and distribution would be severely controlled. In such a
setting, the dynamism, creativeness and flexibility of the economy would
disappear, together with all the incentives for individual achievement in
any arena other than, possibly, the political.

It is not easy to project with confidence how private business might
move effectively into this area while retaining its fundamental profit orientation. One interesting possibility is to transfer the concept of the defense
contractor to the non-defense sector. The brute economics of low-cost urban housing, for example, may rule out unsubsidized, business-initiated
investment. Not ruled out, however, is business as contractor, remodeler
and operator under negotiated or competitive-bid contracts. There has
been limited experimentation in arrangements of this type, in housing,
education, urban systems analysis and planning, and other fields. Freer
exploration in diverse circumstances and in public-private relationships
might discover an attractive potential for alleviating and removing major
causes of gross social discontent while retaining a large degree of private initiative and the familiar web of revenue-cost relationships. The true social
costs remaining, representing the layer of subsidies that may be found
necessary to absorb the remaining expenses of an acceptable ground level
of general welfare, could then be allocated through the tax system.

This is obviously not the only possibility in sight. Business has made
only a few limited experiments in the application of incentives. More extensive analysis and trial might suggest at least the special circumstances in
which this tool could effectively supplement or supplant the public contractor device. A third possibility is suggested by the concept embodied in
Comsat—the mixed public-private corporation. Other options, including
combinations of the foregoing, await imaginative creation.

The incentive for business management to enroll as a participant in the
general exploration of ways and means for removing the cancerous growth
in the vitals of society is classically selfish. Somehow, this cancer will be
removed. The recognition is spreading rapidly that its continuance is intolerable. Some of the proposed or still-to-be-proposed lines of attack may
be destructive of other elements in society, including the private enterprise
system. Management is in a position to contribute rational analysis,
technical competence and imaginative innovations. The interests served

by continuing the enterprise system coincide here with other social interests.

These and comparable innovations imply for private managers a willingness to think about new economic roles and social relationships that many will see as dangerous cracks in the wall of custom. It is not unreasonable, however, to suggest that we are considering nothing more adventurous than the explorations and commitments that managers have long been accustomed to underwrite in administering resources. The only significant difference is that the stakes are higher. In place of the marginal calculus of profit and loss, what may be involved is the preservation of the civilization that has created such an unparalleled record of wealth and growth.

CHANGING THE RULES

Norman E. Bowie

It is not merely the introductory philosophy students who ask, "Why be moral?" An examination of much of the contemporary literature in business ethics indicates that the "Why be moral" question is very much on the mind of businesspersons as well.

One possibility for providing an answer to the "why be moral" question is to indicate the contractual basis on which business rests. The operation of a business, particularly when the business is a corporation, is not a matter of right. Rather the individuals enter into a contract with society. In return for the permission to do business, the society places certain obligations and duties on the business. The corporation is created by society for a specific purpose or purposes. Robert A. Dahl has put the point this way:

> Today it is absurd to regard the corporation simply as an enterprise established for the sole purpose of allowing profit making. We the citizens give them special rights, powers, and privileges, protection, and benefits on the understanding that their activities will fulfill purposes. Corporations exist only as they continue to benefit us. . . . Every corporation should be thought of as a social enterprise whose existence and decisions can be justified only insofar as they serve public or social purposes.[1]

Actually not only does Dahl's quotation indicate that the relation between business and society is contractual, but Dahl spells out the nature of that contract. The corporation must not only benefit those who create it, it must benefit those who permit it (namely society as a whole).

In many discussions of business ethics no one defines terms like "moral" or "corporate responsibility." This inadequacy can be corrected by adopting the perspective of the contract analysis. The morality of business or corporate responsibility is determined by the terms of the contract with society. The corporation has those obligations which the society imposes on it in its charter of incorporation. In accepting its charter, the corporation accepts those moral constraints. Failure to be moral is a violation of the principle of fairness. The corporation which violates the moral rules contained in or implied by its charter is in the position of agreeing to the rules and then violating them. It is in the positon of one who makes a promise and then breaks it. Such unfairness is often considered a paradigm case of injustice and immorality. The corporation which finds itself in the position of breaking the agreements it has made is in a particularly vulnerable position, since the corporate enterprise depends for its survival on the integrity of contractual relations. Understanding business as a contractual relation between the corporation and the society as a whole provides a preliminary answer to our ''why be moral'' question. The corporation should be moral because it has agreed to be. However, what a corporation's moral obligations are is contained in the contract itself.

Although this analysis does provide the framework for showing that certain corporate activities are immoral and provides a moral *reason* for indicating why a corporation should not engage in them, many complicated questions remain to be answered.

The first focuses on the content of the contract. Many corporate executives could accept the contract analysis as outlined thus far and argue that current demands on corporations to be more socially responsible are themselves violations of the contract. After all, corporate charters do not contain an open-ended moral requirement that the corporation promote the public interest. Rather, corporations are founded primarily to promote the financial interests of the investors (the stockholders). Society had believed that by furthering the interests of the stockholders, society as a whole benefited. Now society has changed its mind, and frustrated corporation executives rightly argue that it is the corporate responsibility zealots and not the corporate executives who are changing the terms of the contract.

In several respects the corporate response is appropriate. Society is changing the rules of the game and it is appropriate to ask why corporations should acquiesce in these unilateral changes. Before considering these issues, however, I should like to point out one respect in which the corporate officials' charge that the rules are being changed is incorrect. In addition to the obligations spelled out in the contract itself, there are certain moral requirements, moral background conditions, if you will, which are assumed. Certain moral rules are rules that are required if contracts are to be made at all. These moral requirements are as obligatory as the obligations spelled out in the contract itself. After all, when I agree to pay my bills in order to get a Master Charge card, I do not also sign a meta-agreement that I keep my agreements . The whole market exchange mechanism rests on conditions of trust which can be embodied in moral principles. What is shocking about some of the current corporate scandals—bribery, falsification of records, theft, and corporate espionage—is that these acts violate the conditions for making contracts and market exchanges, conditions which are at the very heart of the free enterprise system. Such violations cannot be excused by saying that they do not appear in the contract. Such excuses are almost as absurd as someone defending the murder of a creditor by saying: I only promised to pay him back; I didn't promise not to murder him. Hence we can conclude that a company has moral obligations in the contract it makes with society and it has obligations to those moral rules which make contracts possible. Its agreement in the former is explicit; its agreement in the latter, implicit. Violation of either is a violation of fairness—a failure to keep one's promises.

We can now return to the charge that it is society which is changing the terms of the contract. Fortunately, not all the charges of immorality and irresponsibility leveled at corporations are directed at violations of contractual morality. Corporations are charged with neglecting to solve such social problems as pollution, racism, sexism, and urban blight. They are charged with sins of omission. At this point the corporation can argue that they have no obligation to resolve all of society's problems. Such a broad-based moral obligation is not a part of their contract with society. That corporations do not have such general contractual obligations is conceded by most experts in the field.

We now face a more complicated form of the "why be moral" question. Why should the corporation agree to a rewriting of its contract with society—a rewriting which will impose greatly expanded social responsibilities on it?

One answer is prudential. It is in the interests of the corporation to do so. This idea has been expressed in the form of a law called the Iron Law of Responsibility: In the long run those who do not use power in a manner which society considers socially responsible will tend to lose it.[2] If society demands a rewriting of the contract, society has the *power* to rewrite it unilaterally. However, can we go beyond prudence to offer any moral reasons for business to revise its agreements? I believe there are several.

One might be called the principle of contribution: If one contributes to a social harm, then one has a proportional obligation to contribute to its alleviation. Since business clearly does contribute to social problems, it has at least some obligation to correct them. In saying that business has some responsibility, I do not wish to imply that it has the only responsibility. Government, labor, and all of us as consumers contribute our part to the problems and hence have some responsibility to work toward solutions. It is neither fair nor prudent to expect one segment of society to shoulder the entire burden. Hence only a *contribution* is required.

Another moral reason for business to accept a new contract might be based on the notion of power. Those constituents of society which have the most in the way of resources should contribute the most to resolving social ills. Since business is either the most powerful force or second only to the federal government, its superior resources impose special obligations upon it. There is an analogy here to arguments made on behalf of progressive taxation.

If the moral arguments are sound, there are moral reasons as well as a very strong prudential reason for corporations to revise their contractual relations with society. However, the corporation can reciprocally require certain agreements on the part of society. First, since a contract should be mutually acceptable, the contract cannot be rewritten unilaterally. Representatives from the corporate sector have a right to participate in the redrafting. Second, grounds of consistency require that other contributors to society's problems also contribute to their solution and that the requirements for the more powerful constituencies be stronger. So long as these conditions are met, corporations should agree to a revised contract and our original fairness arguments can be used to show why individual corporations should follow it.

Notes

1. Robert A. Dahl, ''A Prelude to Corporate Reform.'' In *Corporate Social Policy,* ed. Robert L. Heilbroner and Paul London (Reading, Mass.: Addison-Wesley Publishing Company, 1975), pp. 18–19.
2. Keith Davis and Robert L. Blomstrom, *Business and Society: Environment and Responsibility,* 3rd ed. (New York: McGraw-Hill Book Company, 1975), p. 50.

ETHICAL ISSUES IN PLANT RELOCATION

John P. Kavanagh

The location of a major new manufacturing plant in a community is often the occasion of great rejoicing. City fathers welcome the enterprise as a vital addition to the town's economy. Visions of augmented tax base to support municipal services, jobs for the unemployed and for entrants into the work force, opportunities for local entrepreneurs to expand markets for goods and services, additional sources of support for civic and charitable endeavors, new challenges for educators to provide education and training—all these contribute to the euphoria of a new plant in the community.

Contrast this picture with that of a community experiencing the shutdown or relocation of a major plant, particularly one which has operated in the community for many years. Many people are hurt. For some it means actual hardship; others find their future expectations diminished to the point of despair. The community as a whole feels a shock to its economic vitality and perhaps to its fiscal stability as well.[1]

Yet economists assure us that changes in business locations are merely ''adjustments to economic forces and are to be expected in any large and dynamic economy.''[2] Even the severest critics of plant relocations who advocate laws to regulate such movements agree that prudent use of scarce resources ''often calls for the removal of resources from some activities to

The author gratefully acknowledges support from the Rockefeller Foundation and the Center for the Study of Values, University of Delaware.

more productive functions elsewhere''; they only want ''to assure that the transfer of capital from one use in one location to another elsewhere will not ride roughshod over the needs of the people and the communities involved.''[3]

The thesis which I would like to establish is simple, but it has relatively far-reaching implications. In its basic form it may be stated:

> In deciding whether or not to relocate a manufacturing operation, a company has moral obligations to its employees and to the community in which the operation is located which require that the company
> (1) take into account the impact of the proposed move on employees and the community;
> (2) avoid the move if reasonably possible;
> (3) notify the affected parties as soon as possible if the decision is to make the move; and
> (4) take positive measures to ameliorate the effects of the move.[4]

In making a decision whether or not to move, companies often do not take into account the impact on employees and the community. The management weighs economic reasons very carefully. It considers the effect on production, sales, public relations and, ultimately, profit. On the basis of reasonable assumptions, it projects the outcomes expected to result from each of the options under consideration. Too often, however, there is no place in the economic calculus for any recognition of the effect the move will have on the work force or the community. Our thesis asserts that the company is not morally free to ignore this impact, since employees and members of the community are not mere things but people, whom the company has an obligation not to harm.[5] This moral fact not only deserves consideration along with economic facts but should be the overriding consideration unless there are countervailing moral reasons.

If the company takes this obligation seriously, it ought to start with a strong presumption that the move should be avoided if at all reasonably possible. It should consider every reasonable alternative: rehabilitation of the existing facility, construction of a new plant within the same community, renegotiation of the labor contract, financial assistance from civic or governmental sources, negotiation of special tax incentives, even acceptance of less than maximum profit return. Only after ruling out other available options should the company decide in favor of the move.[6]

After giving serious consideration to other alternatives, the company may still decide it has no reasonable choice but to move. In that case, two obligations remain: the company should notify the affected parties as soon as possible, and it should do whatever is necessary to ameliorate the effects of the move.

Timely notification is important. If given before the final decision is taken, it might provide the opportunity for labor organizations, civic groups, or government agencies to offer options which would enable the company to continue operations. In any event, notification is essential to permit planning for an orderly transition and preparation of programs to accommodate the change.

Ameliorating the effects of the move is not likely to be easy. Companies often offer employees the opportunity to transfer to the new location; for some this might be acceptable, but for others it would be a real hardship. Alternatively, the company might provide effective out-placement efforts as well as income maintenance for displaced workers, at least during a transition period.

To offset adverse effects on the community, the company should make a serious attempt to find a new employer to replace the lost job opportunities. A large corporation might be able to find a replacement within its own organization. Another approach would be to seek another employer among customers, vendors, competitors, or other companies who could utilize the facilities and work force being abandoned. The departing company might donate its plant, if still usable, to the community or local development organization. In some cases the better offer might be to demolish existing facilities and make the improved site available, along with financial help to the local agency concerned with promoting the location of new industries.[7]

These steps may help to make the community whole again, but some situations may require additional effort. In close consultation and cooperation with municipal officials, the company may have to work out a plan to relieve the community of financial burdens of infrastructure improvements, for instance, which were made to serve the company's special needs.

ARGUMENT IN SUPPORT OF THESIS

It should be a little clearer now what the proposed thesis means. Before proceeding to argue directly in favor of this position, however, I would like first to establish the following "Externalities Lemma":

> By locating and operating a manufacturing plant (or similar job-creating operation) in a community, a company produces certain externalities, affecting both workers and the community, which are pertinent to the relocation issue.

The term "externalities" is common enough in the literature of economics. It refers to unintended side effects—good or bad—which an operation produces along with its intended product. In recent years environmentalists have emphasized externalities which affect the quality of the air or water in the vicinity of manufacturing plants. A firm really interested in producing paper, for example, also produces physical and chemical waste products which may affect the surrounding environment adversely if not properly controlled. The company has no interest in producing these products nor any direct intention of doing so, but in doing what it does intend—making paper—it also perforce produces these unwanted products.[8]

Environmentalists have successfully urged that companies should "internalize" these externalities by recognizing them as real even though unintended products and making them part of the economic system. In some cases the companies have been able to eliminate or minimize the externalities by modifying processes. In other instances, they have been able to convert them into useful products, for example, by recycling spent pulp liquor to provide purified chemicals usable a second time in the process or by converting them to products which could be sold for some other purpose. When conversions of this kind have proved to be impractical, companies have internalized the externalities by findings ways to treat or dispose of the effluent safely and including costs incurred as production expenses reflected in price and profit computations.

The "Externalities Lemma" asserts that the operation of a plant results in certain externalities pertinent to the issue of plant relocation. Although the company's intention is simply to manufacture and distribute its product, the act of doing so produces unintended results which seriously affect its workers and the community in which the company operates.

When a person agrees to work for a company, her pay is a return for effort expended to produce the product. These wages, however, do not take into account the myriad relationships which the employee builds up as a result of accepting the job. In addition to providing labor for the company, the worker adopts a life style which contributes to the work. Many people move their place of residence, enroll children in school, join local churches, become members of clubs, take interest in civic affairs—in short, make a total commitment of their lives to the community and the company. They build up a whole network of relationships based on their association with the company.

These life style commitments are advantageous to the worker, to be sure. They enable him to live a fully rounded life. But the advantage is not one-sided. The company benefits from having an employee involved in these relationships. The situation enhances the worker's ability to do his job, encourages loyalty to the company, and facilitates the employee's continuing progress in learning to do his job effectively.

The stable relationships developed benefit the community as well, but the company's presence also affects the community in other ways. City engineers adjust traffic patterns to accommodate traffic generated by workers going to or leaving the plant as well as incoming and outgoing freight movements. The municipality may have to plan, build, and maintain water and sewerage facilities on a much larger scale to serve the company's needs. Police and fire departments may require more personnel and equipment because of the plant's presence.

Assuming an equitable tax structure, the company will pay its fair share for services provided. Other taxpayers are usually willing to contribute as well because of the indirect benefits they receive. The whole system can work smoothly because of the symbiotic relationship between the plant, its workers, and the community. Merchants, purveyors of services, schools, and private support agencies of all kinds prosper so long as the relationship continues.

When a major plant discontinues operations, however, it becomes evident that an unintended situation has been created. Not only are employees out of work, deprived of their livelihood or dependent on others for it, but the community itself suffers. Businesses dependent on the company or its employees feel the impact. The municipality and its taxpayers are left with more employees and infrastructure than they need, with continuing cost burdens far out of proportion with revenue. Schools, churches, and private associations all find themselves overbuilt as people leave or are unable to contribute to their support.

Results of the kind described are especially obvious in a small community with a single major employer. In such circumstances it is easy to isolate the phenomenon. The same effects occur, however, in larger communities with more complex economies, only they tend to be less easily observed. In the larger setting the impact on the total community may be somewhat less, but it is no less real on those affected. What remains in any case is the whole web of relationships built up which would not exist if the company had not started the operation and particularly if it had not continued over a relatively long period. The company did not intend to create this web, but it is there nevertheless because of the plant—and the operation could not have survived without it.

In light of what we can observe, the "Externalities Lemma" seems to be inescapably true. If that is indeed the case, it is not difficult to establish our thesis. One of the accepted dicta in the law of property, clearly grounded in basic ethical principles of fairness and justice, is the maxim *sic utere tuo ut alienum non laedas*—use that which is yours in such a way that you do not injure another. A company which has established a plant in a community, particularly when it had continued the operation over a long period, would clearly be injuring others if it closed or moved that operation without taking into account—in a significant way—the impact of that move on its workers and the community. By its presence the plant has created the externalities described. It is the company's moral obligation to internalize them—to replace its divot, so to speak. It can move toward meeting this obligation by undertaking the kind of actions discussed above.

One might object that the injury or harm done the workers is not really the kind of harm which the *sic utere* principle proscribes. Certainly the harm is not intentional; the company intends merely to use its capital to the best advantage in making a profit. Even unintentional harm, however, may be morally wrong; in any event, it is reasonable to ask for moral justification of the harmful actions.

The employer might invoke the Common Law concept that the employment relationship is strictly "at-will"—that an employer is free to discharge an employee whenever she chooses, for any reason or no reason at all. Even the Common Law, however, has come to recognize that rigid application of this doctrine cannot withstand the moral criticism arising out of contemporary social and economic circumstances. At the very least, our sense of equity demands that the employer justify the discharge by showing that race, gender or age discrimination, or retaliation for lawful exercise of rights, did not motivate the harmful action.

Almost any moral system recognizes that every moral agent has an obligation to treat human beings as persons rather than as things. Hiring a person creates a special kind of relationship. For the employer it is not like buying a piece of material or a machine: these are things, which the buyer is free to use as a means of achieving an end, with no moral responsibility owed to the purchased objects. But the employer is not free, morally speaking, to use an employee as a thing, as simply a means to an end. Since the employee is a person, the employer has an obligation to respect her integrity as a person: her feelings, values, goals, emotional relationships, cultural attachments, self-regard. As an autonomous living entity the employee is the center of a complex web of relationships and it is this whole composite with which the employer becomes involved. Obviously, the employer is not responsible for everything which happens to or within this web; but he is responsible for whatever his actions change or otherwise affect. The relationships mentioned in discussing the ''Externalities Lemma'' are ones which the employer's actions affect adversely in (unmitigated) plant closure decisions. Even though the company no longer needs its workers as a means to its end of profitable production, it may not with moral impunity treat them like excess material or machines, but has an obligation to protect them from the adverse consequences brought about by the company's use of them.

A company which closes or relocates a plant without ameliorating actions is acting unfairly toward its employees and the community. The general idea of fairness is that anyone who chooses to get involved with others in a cooperative activity has to do his share and is entitled to expect others involved to do likewise.[9]

In the kind of situation we are concerned with there is a reasonably just cooperative arrangement under which a person agrees to work for a company; the primary *quid pro quo* is the employer's fair day's pay for the employee's fair day's work. But each party to the agreement has additional legitimate expectations about the other. The employer expects the worker to make a commitment to the job; one of the largest corporations has this to say:

> . . . The challenges of the workplace impose strong mutual responsibilities upon General Motors and its employees. . . .
>
> An employee's most basic responsibility is to work consistently to the best of his or her ability—not just to follow instructions, but to ask questions, think independently, and make constructive suggestions for improvement.
>
> A first-rate job requires employees to maintain their good health and mental alertness, to be prompt and present on the job, to cooperate with fellow workers, and to be loyal to the Corporation—its people and products. Because GM people *are* General Motors—in the eyes of their friends and neighbors—employees also are encouraged to take interest in the basic goals, problems, and public positions of the Corporation.
>
> . . . General Motors encourages employees as individual citizens to involve themselves in community service and politics. . . .[10]

The employee, in turn, expects the company to do somewhat more than simply pay agreed-on wages. For example, no one would question that being provided a safe and at least tolerably pleasant workplace is within the worker's legitimate expectations. Beyond that, if it is fair for the company to expect that employees will take all the actions and have all the attitudes which a company like General Motors encourages and considers requisite to ''a first-rate job'' it also seems reasonable for workers to expect that the employer will not suddenly shut up shop and leave them high and dry with unpaid mortgages (on houses bought so they could be "prompt and present on the job" and involved in "community service and politics"), children in school, and commitments to various people or organizations; all this is part of a lifestyle to which they committed themselves when they entered into their agreement to work for the company—the kind of agreement which the GM statement calls a "partnership which can help assure the Corporation's success in the years to come, as well as contribute to an improved quality of life for the men and women of General Motors."[11]

There is nothing extraordinary in all this. In most social relationships the parties involved in an agreement have legitimate expectations which are often not expressed in the agreement itself. Fairness requires that a company either avoid a move which would cause grave hardship to workers or at least take action which would render the action harmless, since this is a legitimate expectation of the implicit "partnership" agreement between employer and employee.

OBJECTIONS TO THE THESIS

Having defended the "Externalities Lemma," I now turn to a defense of the larger thesis. Advocates of pure *laissez faire* capitalism would reject categorically any notion that a company has a moral obligation in the circumstances described. Milton Friedman insists that a company has no "social responsibilities" other than "to use its resources and engage in activities designed to increase its profits so long as it stays within the rules of the game, which is to say, engages in open and free competition, without deception or fraud."[12] Another writer expresses essentially the same thought in slightly less provocative language: "In the end business has only two responsibilities—to obey the elementary canons of everyday face-to-face civility (honesty, good faith, and so on) and to seek material gain."[13]

On the face of it, positions of this kind would seem to exclude the possibility that companies have the kind of obligation referred to in our thesis. Their authors would undoubtedly agree. Even admitting for the sake of argument the validity of these positions, however, one could argue that the proposed obligations still hold. No one would maintain that a company has no obligation to pay its debts, for instance, even if its "exclusive" duty is to make as much money as possible. The statements quoted above explicitly admit an obligation to "stay within the rules of the game," to avoid violations of open and free competition, to refrain from deception or fraud, to "obey the elementary canons of everyday face-to-face civility." The rules of the game comprise not only specific positive laws but, as another writer puts it, the moral constraints included in an implied "contract with society."[14]

Just as individuals or companies do not enter into explicit meta-agreements to keep their agreements when they sign contracts so also people may not advert to the implicit obligations they incur in performing acts—or in discharging obligations which are explicit. One of the implicit moral rules in any use of property is the obligation captured in the *sic utere* maxim, which requires the avoidance of harm to others. Even if the only explicit obligation of business firms were to make a profit, they could not avoid the implicit obligation to avoid harm to others in the use of their property and to restore a just order of things if even unintentionally their actions should disrupt it.

Another possible objection rests on the notion of the risks inherent in the capitalistic system. It is essential to "free enterprise" that entrepreneurs freely undertake the risk of losing the time and money they invest in a venture in return for the opportunity of gain. In the nature of things there are inherent risks in establishing a manufacturing operation and everybody knows they don't last forever. These employees didn't have to go to work for us, the company may argue. They know, or should have known, the risk involved. It was their free choice when they agreed to accept the job.

All this is true so far as it goes, but it doesn't wipe out the company's moral obligations. The workers are not free to the same extent as the employer; the way the system works, they have to accept some job just to stay alive and support their families and in most instances their choice of employment is extremely limited. The entrepreneur's reward for undertaking risk is the profit generated by the enterprise, a reward shared to some extent by higher salaried management employees but not by the ordinary worker. Wages are compensation for work performed, not for assumption of risk. They are carried on the company's books as a cost item which the company has an obligation to pay whether or not it makes a profit. What our thesis asserts is that the company has certain unacknowledged structural costs consequent on the fact that it is operating the plant, over and above the operational obligation of wage payments.

Like the workers, the community is not a partner in the company's entrepreneurial risk, nor does it expect to share in the venture's profit. The company presumably pays its fair share of operational expenses through taxes (and perhaps to some extent through charitable contributions to civic causes). When the plant moves or shuts down, the community is left with significant structural changes brought about by company operations; it is the problem brought about by these changes which the company has a moral obligation to help solve.

One additional objection to the proposed thesis is that a company accepting it would be unable to compete with others which do not. The expense to the company, this arguments holds, would make its costs higher than others producing the same product; others could then establish lower prices and gain a clear market advantage.

This is a powerful objection and gets to the heart of the question. Against it, one could urge that there are certain countervailing advantages in terms of worker morale, community cooperation and public relations, but in the end I would have to concede the economic soundness of the argument. What I would not concede is that the objection is a persuasive refutation of our thesis. To act in accordance with a moral obligation not infrequently entails acceptance of personal disadvantage in terms of nonmoral goods. Personal and economic advantage or disadvantage doesn't count as an argument against the existence of a moral obligation.

The thesis asserts the existence of an obligation, on the part of a company, to give appropriate moral weight to the adverse consequences of its action in moving or discontinuing an operation and to take appropriate action to avoid those consequences even in the face of an economic disadvantage. If all companies similarly situated were to recognize this obligation, of course, the competitive disadvantage would disappear. Assuming the costs were internalized—anticipated and treated like other expense items—they would be reflected in the pricing mechanism and only market factors would determine the effect on profits.

But isn't this an unlikely outcome? Is it not more probable that those companies which recognize their moral obligations will suffer for it and lose the competitive edge to those which do not? If corporate management attempts to act morally in this regard and ends up with lower profits, will not stockholders replace them with less conscientious management or invest their money elsewhere? Will not consumers refuse to pay a price for a product which is higher simply because it reflects true costs previously borne by workers and the community?

An affirmative answer to those questions might well be appropriate in a purely descriptive account of the existing economic system. In considering the proposed thesis, however, we are concerned with normative rather than descriptive issues. The question is what should be done, not how does in fact the present system work. This thesis asserts a moral obligation to be concerned about certain human consequences of a company's action: it does not assert that other consequences should be disregarded. Certainly company management should consider what effect its decision will have on profits. Certainly stockholders will consider whether managers are acting in their best interest and whether their money could be invested more profitably elsewhere. Certainly consumers will express their preference in the market and decide whether the price asked for a product is a fair one which they are willing to pay. But the proposed thesis insists that there are moral questions which must be asked, along with economic questions; important as the economic issues may be, they should be considered relevant only within a context of morally permissible actions: the moral issues are overriding.

Notes

1. These initial observations, as well as several others throughout the paper, are based on the author's direct involvement in plant relocation situations in the course of more than twenty-five years of work as a senior official in Michigan state government agencies concerned with economic development programs. There is also a wealth of empirical literature on the subject referenced in the publications cited below by McKenzie; Bluestone and Harrison; and Stern *et al.*

2. Richard B. McKenzie, *Restrictions on Business Mobility* (Washington: American Enterprise Institute for Public Policy Research, 1979), p. 1.

3. Barry Bluestone and Bennett Harrison, *Capital and Communities* (Washington: The Progressive Alliance, 1980), p. ii.

4. For brevity's sake I will generally speak of "relocation," although I mean also to include discontinuation of operations in the community without removal to another location.
5. The question of whether a company, a corporation or any collective can be the subject of moral acts is much controverted, but it is not the point at issue here. For those who reject the collective responsibility position, substitute the phrase "those persons morally responsible for the actions of the company" for the "company." In support of collective responsibility, see Peter A. French, "The Corporation as a Moral Person," *American Philosophical Quarterly*, 16 (1979), p. 207.
6. See John M. Clark, *Economic Institutions and Human Welfare* (New York: Alfred A. Knopf, 1957), pp. 195–197, for an interesting discussion from an economist's view point of social obligations of a company in a relocation situation.
7. One plan which has received considerable attention calls for the company to transfer ownership to former workers or the community or a joint community-employee corporation. This has worked well in particularly favorable circumstances but has failed in other cases. See Robert N. Stern, K. Haydn Wood, and Tove Helland Hammer, *Employee Ownership in Plant Shutdowns* (Kalamazoo, Michigan: The W. E. Upjohn Institute for Employment Research, 1979). A current (November, 1981) instance is a planned purchase of the New Departure-Hyatt Bearing Division of General Motors Corp. at Clark, N.J. by former employees after GM announced its intention to close the plant.
8. Externalities can be beneficial. A paper operation may require management of forest resources to assure an adequate supply of timber. This may open previously inaccessible land for recreational use. Although the company may only intend to improve its timber holdings, it may also enhance the wildlife capabilities of the forest. The paper plant itself may become a tourist attraction, providing an unintended benefit to the community.
9. See John Rawls, *A Theory of Justice* (Cambridge, Mass.: Harvard University Press, 1971), p. 343.
10. *1980 General Motors Public Interest Report*, p. 83.
11. Citing of General Motors' statement should not be interpreted as critical of that company; the Corporation has a policy of replacing obsolete plants with new facilities in the same area "whenever it is economically feasible" and also, under its union contracts and salaried worker policies, pays substantial compensation to laid-off employees. GM has currently committed $10 billion to the rehabilitation and replacement of production facilities in Michigan alone.
12. Milton Friedman, "The Social Responsibility of Business," in *Ethical Theory and Business*, second edition, edited by Tom L. Beauchamp and Norman E. Bowie (Englewood Cliffs, N.J.: Prentice-Hall, Inc., 1979), p. 81.
13. Theodore Levitt, "The Dangers of Social Responsibility," *Harvard Business Review*, Sept.-Oct., 1958, p. 49. By 1973, Prof. Levitt had modified his position somewhat, arguing in his book *The Third Sector* (New York: AMACOM, a division of American Management Associations, 1973) the necessity for corporate "responsiveness" to demands for social improvements.
14. Norman E. Bowie, "Changing the Rules," Beauchamp and Bowie, pp. 103–104. See also Melvin Anshen, "The Socially Responsible Corporation: From Concept to Implementation," in Melvin Anshen, ed., *Managing the Socially Responsible Corporation* (New York: Macmillan Publishing Co., Inc., 1974), pp. 3ff.

DODGE v. FORD MOTOR CO.

. . . When plaintiffs made their complaint and demand for further dividends, the Ford Motor Company had concluded its most prosperous year of business. The demand for its cars at the price of the preceding year continued. It could make and could market in the year beginning August 1, 1916, more than 500,000 cars. Sales of parts and repairs would necessarily increase. The cost of materials was likely to advance, and perhaps the price of labor; but it reasonably might have expected a profit for the year of upwards of $60,000,000. . . . Considering only these facts, a refusal to declare and pay further dividends appears to be not an exercise of discretion on the part of the directors, but an arbitrary refusal to do what the circumstances required to be done. These facts and others call upon the directors to justify their action, or failure or refusal to act. In justification, the defendants have offered testimony tending to prove and which does prove, the following facts: It had been the policy of the corporation for a considerable time to annually reduce the selling price of cars, while keeping up, or improving, their quality. As early as in June, 1915, a general plan for the expansion of the productive capacity of the concern by a practical duplication of its plant had been talked over by the executive officers and directors and agreed upon; not all of the details having been settled, and no formal action of directors having been taken. The erection of a smelter was considered, and engineering and other data in connection therewith secured. In consequence, it was determined not to reduce the selling price of cars for the year beginning August 1, 1915, but to maintain the price to accumulate a large surplus to pay for the proposed expansion of plant and equipment, and perhaps to build a plant for smelting ore. It is hoped, by Mr. Ford, that eventually 1,000,000 cars will be annually produced. The contemplated changes will permit the increased output.

The plan, as affecting the profits of the business for the year beginning August 1, 1916, and thereafter, calls for a reduction in the selling price of the cars. . . . In short, the plan does not call for and is not intended to produce immediately a more profitable business, but a less profitable one; not only less profitable than formerly, but less profitable than it is admitted it might be made. The apparent immediate effect will be to diminish the value of shares and the returns to shareholders.

It is the contention of plaintiffs that the apparent effect of the plan is intended to be the continued and continuing effect of it, and that it is deliberately proposed, not of record and not by official corporate declaration, but nevertheless proposed, to continue the corporation henceforth as a semi-eleemosynary institution and not as a business institution. In support of this contention, they point to the attitude and to the expressions of Mr. Henry Ford. . . .

"My ambition," said Mr. Ford, "is to employ still more men, to spread the benefits of this industrial system to the greatest possible number, to help them

204 Mich. 459, 170 N.W. 668 3 A.L.R. 413. Majority opinion by Justice J. Ostrander, Supreme Court of Michigan.

build up their lives and their homes. To do this we are putting the greatest share of our profits back in the business.''

"With regard to dividends, the company paid sixty per cent, on its capitalization of two million dollars, or $1,200,000, leaving $58,000,000 to reinvest for the growth of the company. This is Mr. Ford's policy at present, and it is understood that the other stockholders cheerfully accede to this plan.''

He had made up his mind in the summer of 1916 that no dividends other than the regular dividends should be paid, ''for the present.''

"Q. For how long? Had you fixed in your mind any time in the future, when you were going to pay— A. No.
"Q. That was indefinite in the future? A. That was indefinite; yes, sir.''

The record, and especially the testimony of Mr. Ford, convinces that he has to some extent the attitude towards shareholders of one who has dispensed and distributed to them large gains and that they should be content to take what he chooses to give. His testimony creates the impression, also, that he thinks the Ford Motor Company has made too much money, has had too large profits, and that, although large profits might be still earned, a sharing of them with the public, by reducing the price of the output of the company, ought to be undertaken. We have no doubt that certain sentiments, philanthropic and altruistic, creditable to Mr. Ford, had large influence in determining the policy to be pursued by the Ford Motor Company—the policy which as been herein referred to.

It is said by his counsel that—

"Although a manufacturing corporation cannot engage in humanitarian works as its principal business, the fact that it is organized for profit does not prevent the existence of implied powers to carry on with humanitarian motives such charitable works as are incidental to the main business of the corporation.'' . . .

In discussing this proposition counsel have referred to decisions [citations omitted]. These cases, after all, like all others in which the subject is treated, turn finally upon the point, the question, whether it appears that the directors were not acting for the best interests of the corporation. We do not draw in question, nor do counsel for the plaintiffs do so, the validity of the general proposition stated by counsel nor the soundness of the opinions delivered in the cases cited. The case presented here is not like any of them. The difference between an incidental humanitarian expenditure of corporate funds for the benefit of the employees, like the building of a hospital for their use and the employment of agencies for the betterment of their condition, and a general purpose and plan to benefit mankind at the expense of others, is obvious. There should be no confusion (of which there is evidence) of the duties which Mr. Ford conceives that he and the stockholders owe to the general public and the duties which in law he and his codirectors owe to protesting, minority stockholders. A business corporation is organized and carried on primarily for the profit of the stockholders. The powers of the directors are to be employed for that end. The discretion of directors is to be exercised in the choice of means to attain that end, and does not extend to a change in the end itself, to the reduction of profits, or to the nondistribution of profits among stockholders in order to devote them to other purposes. . . . As we have pointed out, and the proposition does not require argument to sustain it, it is not within the lawful powers of a board of directors to shape and conduct the affairs of a corporation for the merely incidental benefit of shareholders and for the primary purpose of benefiting others, and no one will contend that, if the avowed purpose of the defendant directors was to sacrifice the interests of shareholders, it would not be the duty of the courts to interfere. . . . It is obvious that an annual dividend of 60 per cent, upon $2,000,000, or $1,200,000, is the equivalent of a very small dividend upon $100,000,000, or more.

The decree of the court below fixing and determining the specific amount to be distributed to stockholders is affirmed. . . .

A. P. SMITH MANUFACTURING CO. v. BARLOW

The Chancery Division, in a well-reasoned opinion by Judge Stein, determined that a donation by the plaintiff The A. P. Smith Manufacturing Company to Princeton University was *intra vires.* Because of the public importance of the issues presented, the appeal duly taken to the Appellate Division has been certified directly to this court under Rule 1:5-1(a).

The company was incorporated in 1896 and is engaged in the manufacture and sale of valves, fire hydrants and special equipment, mainly for water and gas industries. Its plant is located in East Orange and Bloomfield and it has approximately 300 employees. Over the years the company has contributed regularly to the local community chest and on occasions to Upsala College in East Orange and Newark University, now part of Rutgers, the State University. On July 24, 1951 the board of directors adopted a resolution which set forth that it was in the corporation's best interests to join with others in the 1951 Annual Giving to Princeton University, and appropriated the sum of $1,500 to be transferred by the corporation's treasurer to the university as a contribution towards its maintenance. When this action was questioned by stockholders the corporation instituted a declaratory judgment action in the Chancery Division and trial was had in due course.

Mr. Hubert F. O'Brien, the president of the company, testified that he considered the contribution to be a sound investment, that the public expects corporations to aid philanthropic and benevolent institutions, that they obtain good will in the community by so doing, and that their charitable donations create favorable environment for their business operations. In addition, he expressed the thought that in contributing to liberal arts institutions, corporations were furthering their self-interest in

Atlantic Reporter 98 A 2d 581. Opinion by Judge J. Jacobs, Supreme Court of New Jersey.

assuring the free flow of properly trained personnel for administrative and other corporate employment. Mr. Frank W. Abrams, chairman of the board of the Standard Oil Company of New Jersey, testified that corporations are expected to acknowledge their public responsibilities in support of the essential elements of our free enterprise system. He indicated that it was not "good business" to disappoint "this reasonable and justified public expectation," nor was it good business for corporations "to take substantial benefits from their membership in the economic community while avoiding the normally accepted obligations of citizenship in the social community." Mr. Irving S. Olds, former chairman of the board of the United States Steel Corporation, pointed out that corporations have a self-interest in the maintenance of liberal education as the bulwark of good government. He stated that "Capitalism and free enterprise owe their survival in no small degree to the existence of our private, independent universities" and that if American business does not aid in their maintenance it is not "properly protecting the long-range interest of its stockholders, its employees and its customers." Similarly, Dr. Harold W. Dodds, President of Princeton University, suggested that if private institutions of higher learning were replaced by governmental institutions our society would be vastly different and private enterprise in other fields would fade out rather promptly. Further on he stated that "democratic society will not long endure if it does not nourish within itself strong centers of non-governmental fountains of knowledge, opinions of all sorts not governmentally or politically originated. If the time comes when all these centers are absorbed into government, then freedom as we know it, I submit, is at an end." . . .

When the wealth of the nation was primarily in the hands of individuals they discharged their responsibilities as citizens by donating freely for charitable purposes. With the transfer of most of the wealth to corporate hands and the imposition of heavy burdens of individual taxation, they have been unable to keep pace with increased philanthropic needs. They have therefore, with justification, turned to corporations to assume the modern obligations of good citizenship in the same manner as humans do. Congress and state legislatures have enacted laws which encourage corporate contributions, and much has recently been written to indicate the crying need and adequate legal basis therefor. . . . In actual practice corporate giving has correspondingly increased. Thus, it is estimated that annual corporate contributions throughout the nation aggregate over 300 million dollars, with over 60 million dollars thereof going to universities and other educational institutions. Similarly, it is estimated that local community chests receive well over 40% of their contributions from corporations; these contributions and those made by corporations to the American Red Cross, to Boy Scouts and Girl Scouts, to 4-H Clubs and similar organizations have almost invariably been unquestioned.

During the first world war corporations loaned their personnel and contributed substantial corporate funds in order to insure survival; during the depression of the '30s they made contributions to alleviate the desperate hardships of the millions of unemployed; and during the second world war they again contributed to insure survival. They now recognize that we are faced with other, though nonetheless vicious, threats from abroad which must be withstood without impairing the vigor of our democratic institutions at home and that otherwise victory will be pyrrhic indeed. More and more they have come to recognize that their salvation rests upon sound economic and social environment which in turn rests in no insignificant part upon free and vigorous nongovernmental institutions of learning. It seems to us that just as the conditions prevailing when corporations were originally created required that they serve public as well as private interests, modern conditions require that corporations acknowledge and discharge social as well as private responsibilities as members of the communities within which they operate. Within this broad concept there is no difficulty in sustaining, as incidental to their proper objects and in aid of the public welfare, the power of corporations to contribute corporate funds within reasonable limits in support of academic institutions. But even if we confine ourselves to the terms of the common-law rule in its application to current conditions, such expenditures may likewise readily be justified as being for the benefit of the corporation; indeed, if need be the matter may be viewed strictly in terms of actual survival of the corporation in a free enterprise system. The genius of our common law has been its capacity for growth and its adaptability to the needs of the times. Generally courts have accomplished the desired result indirectly through the molding of old forms. Occasionally they have done it directly through frank rejection of the old and recognition of the new. But whichever path the common law has taken it has not been found wanting as the proper tool for the advancement of the general good. . . .

In the light of all of the foregoing we have no hesitancy in sustaining the validity of the donation by the plaintiff. There is no suggestion that it was made indiscriminately or to a pet charity of the corporate directors in furtherance of personal rather than corporate ends. On the contrary, it was made to a preeminent institution of higher learning, was modest in amount and well within the limitations imposed by the statutory enactments, and was voluntarily made in the reasonable belief that it would aid the public welfare and advance the interests of the plaintiff as a private corporation and as part of the community in which it operates. We find that it was a lawful exercise of the corporation's implied and incidental powers under common-law principles and that it came within the express authority of the pertinent state legislation. As has been indicated, there is now widespread belief throughout the nation that free and vigorous non-governmental institutions of learning are vital to our democracy and the system of free enterprise and that withdrawal of corporate authority to make such contributions within reasonable limits would seriously threaten their continuance. Corporations have come to recognize this and with their enlightenment have sought in varying measures, as has the plaintiff by its contribution, to insure and strengthen the society which gives them existence and the means of aiding themselves and their fellow citizens. Clearly then, the appellants, as individual stockholders whose private interests rest entirely upon the well-being of the plaintiff corporation, ought not be permitted to close their eyes to present-day realities and thwart the long-visioned corporate action in recognizing and voluntarily discharging its high obligations as a constituent of our modern social structure.

The judgment entered in the Chancery Division is in all respects Affirmed.

case 1:   The Sloane Products Case

Sloane Products is a regional manufacturer of metal dispensers for paper products used in restaurants, hotels, and passenger terminals. The products bear the Sloane brand and are advertised in trade journals. Sloane sells its products through wholesalers. There is no information on the amount of output eventually sold in minority-operated establishments. Sloane assumes the amount is relatively small. The manufacturing plant, however, is in an older metropolitan area with a large black population, though the plant itself is far from the center of the black neighborhoods and the firm has only a few black employees.

In response to pleas from the metropolitan chapter of the National Alliance of Business, Sloane's board adopted the following policy on minority purchasing:

> Sloane managers are expected to make extra efforts to find minority suppliers and even to help minority enterprises adjust to Sloane's purchasing requirements. The board's instructions also made it clear that the effort was not expected to impose any serious disruption on Sloane's operations.

Right after the procurement directive was issued, Frank Gambetta, head of purchasing, had found a local firm, Diamond Carton Company, a black owned and managed producer of corrugated boxes for shipping merchandise. For quotation purposes, Gambetta's office had given Diamond information on quantity, quality, sizes, and delivery requirements.

Diamond had admitted being new to the business but assured the people at Sloane that Diamond could meet the product and delivery specifications.

Diamond had sent quotations to Gambetta's office. After some negotiation, Diamond was awarded a contract by Sloane, who then reduced quantities purchased from other sources.

However, Diamond did not provide samples for pre-production approval at the time specified in the original agreement. When samples eventually appeared, they proved to be below standard. Gambetta and production chief Sam Fritzel then spent time helping the managers at Diamond work out the defects, and eventually Diamond did produce samples that could be approved.

First production deliveries were satisfactory, but since then every delivery has been either late or substandard. This has been going on for four months.

Fritzel is ready to end the agreement on the grounds that the relationship with Diamond is disrupting Sloane's operations.

Adapted from a case by Lawrence G. Lavengood, Professor of Business History, Graduate School of Management, Northwestern University. Reprinted by permission.

Questions

1. Has Sloane done enough for Diamond to justify ending the agreement at the present time?
2. Is the fact that the relationship with Diamond is disrupting Sloane's operation good enough reason by itself for ending the agreement?
3. If Sloane does end the agreement with Diamond, does it have any obligation to find another minority supplier?
4. Given Sloane's geographical location, does it have any special moral obligation to the black community at all?

case 2: Shutdown at Eastland

When Speedy Motors Company closed its assembly plant in Eastland, Michigan, lobbyists for organized labor cited the case as one more reason why the Federal government should pass a law regulating plant closings. With less than a month's notice, the company laid off nearly 2,000 workers and permanently shut down the facility, which had been in operation more than 20 years. The local union president called the action "a callous and heartless treatment of the workers and of the community."

Company executives defended the decision as inevitable in view of the harsh competitive realities of the automotive industry. "Purchases of the Speedy model produced at Eastland have fallen to almost nothing and there is nothing we can do about changes in consumer preferences," a company spokesman said.

Labor lobbyists insist that instances such as this show the need for a Federal law which would require companies to give as much as two years' notice before closing a major factory, unless they can demonstrate that an emergency exists. The proposed legislation would also require the employer to provide special benefits to workers and the community affected by the shutdown.

"Closing plants needlessly and without warning is an antisocial, criminal act," a union leader said. "Giant corporations don't give a thought to the hardships they are imposing on long-time employees and communities that depend on their jobs. The only thing they consider is their profit."

Opponents of the legislation maintain that the proposed law would strike at the heart of the free enterprise system. "Companies must be free to do business wherever they choose without being penalized," a corporate spokesman argued. "Plant closing legislation would constitute unjustified interference in private decision making. Laws which restrict the ability of management to operate a business in the most efficient manner is counterproductive and in direct conflict with the theory of free enterprise."

Adapted from a case by John P. Kavanagh, Assistant Professor of Philosophy, Center for the Study of Values, University of Delaware. Reprinted by permission.

1. Does the closing of a plant when it ceases to be profitable violate the "moral minimum"?
2. Should one of the rules of the game in a new social contract between society and business stipulate procedures for a morally justified plant closing?
3. Who should take primary responsibility for those laid off or terminated due to a plant closing?

case 3:   Procter and Gamble and Toxic Shock Syndrome

In September 1980, Procter and Gamble reached a consent agreement with the Food and Drug Administration (FDA) to "demarket" its new super absorbent Rely tampon which had been twenty years in development. This agreement was reached one week after Procter and Gamble representatives were confronted by the FDA with results of a Center for Disease Control (CDC) study which found a strong correlation between the use of Rely tampons and Toxic Shock Syndrome (TSS). By then, TSS, a disease characterized by vomiting, high fever, diarrhea, and a rapid drop in blood pressure resulting in shock, had been blamed as the cause of death for 25 women since 1975.

Procter and Gamble was initially made aware of evidence linking tampon usage with TSS in June 1980 when it, along with other tampon manufacturers, received the results of a preliminary CDC study. Shortly thereafter, Procter and Gamble conducted its own studies of Rely, and found no significant link between TSS and this particular brand of tampons. Given a week to respond to the September CDC study, Procter and Gamble quickly assembled a previously selected independent panel of health and scientific experts to review the CDC findings. This panel reported that they did not find convincing evidence linking Rely in particular to TSS (as opposed to tampons in general). On the other hand, they reported that they could not refute the claims of the CDC study either.

As a result of this panel's findings, Procter and Gamble immediately discontinued sales of Rely. When its representatives next met with the representatives of the FDA, Procter and Gamble signed the consent agreement calling for the "withdrawal" of Rely from the market. Under this agreement Procter and Gamble attempted to buy back all of the product which was still in the hands of consumers or retailers through a concentrated campaign consisting of 340,000 letters and telegrams sent to retailers, and radio, television, and print advertisements directed at consumers.

According to the consent agreement, Procter and Gamble did not have to declare the product unsafe or defective and in fact they stated they had no evidence that it was. The motivation for reaching this agreement was at least partly the fear of being forced by the FDA into a "product recall" in which they

This case was prepared by Richard Wokutch, Assistant Professor of Management, Virginia Polytechnic Institute and State University. Reprinted by permission.

would have to admit the product was unsafe—an admission that would certainly be used in product liability litigation. Procter and Gamble is also particularly sensitive to adverse publicity and this product withdrawal was viewed as a way to cut its losses on this dimension.

Toxic shock syndrome remains a mystery. Scientists believe it is caused by a virulent strain of bacteria, and evidence persists that contraction of the disease is linked to certain forms of tampon usage, but the precise connection is unclear. Both men and nonmenstruating women have contracted the disease.

For Procter and Gamble the withdrawal of Rely from the market was estimated to have cost $75 million after taxes (compared with total corporate profits of $640 million in the preceding year). Procter and Gamble was also left with no product in the $1 billion per year menstrual market, although they were considering new entries. The company's reputation, which suffered during the controversy, seems to have largely been redeemed. A public opinion survey conducted after the withdrawal found that the public gave Procter and Gamble high marks for its quick action. Lawsuits against the company remain to be settled however. At the time of this writing, a number of product liability claims are slowly making their way through the courts, and some have resulted in the award of damages to plaintiffs.

Questions

1. When confronted with the September CDC study, what were Procter and Gamble's response options?
2. Was the selected response strategy the most "socially responsible"? Was it the most profitable?
3. If Procter and Gamble had not been faced with the prospect of a government-mandated "product recall" do you think they would have responded any differently? What do you think they should have done in such a circumstance?
4. Discuss the factors you would consider in marketing a product where there is uncertainty about the risks involved.

case 4: The Case of the Leaking Valve

The Hawley Corporation, which ranks among the nation's 100 largest manufacturing firms, had a persistent problem with a leaking valve assembly on the hydraulic presses they make and distribute. Unable to remedy the defect on their own, Hawley engineers called in several vendors of this type of assembly and described the problem to them. The Hawley group explained that

This case was prepared by the Committee for Education in Business Ethics under a grant from the National Endowment for the Humanities.

they hoped the vendors would be willing to find a solution to the problem but that corporate policy did not permit paying for this sort of developmental work done outside the company.

Only one of the vendor firms, Allbright, Inc., decided to proceed on this basis with developing something that could answer Hawley's difficulty. Allbright reasoned that if they produced the remedy they were in an excellent position to get the contract for supplying Hawley with the improved assembly.

The engineering departments of the two firms worked together and after a fairly lengthy effort a modification of the Hawley assembly was perfected that eliminated the leaking.

The Hawley purchasing department then sent out requests for bids on the new assembly to a number of vendors, Allbright included. Reston Corporation underbid Allbright and was awarded the order by Hawley.

Questions

1. Did the fact that Allbright agreed to assist Hawley without compensation morally justify Hawley's acceptance of Reston's bid?
2. Does Hawley have any duty based on gratitude to compensate Allbright in some way?
3. Is Hawley's corporate policy which does not permit paying for the type of development work Allbright did unfair?
4. Should low bid always be the only consideration in the awarding of a contract?

SUGGESTED SUPPLEMENTARY READINGS

ANSHEN, MELVIN, ed., *Managing the Socially Responsible Corporation.* New York: Macmillan Publishing Co., 1974.

BLUMBERG, PHILLIP I. "Selected Materials on Corporate Social Responsibility." *Business Lawyer,* July 1972.

BOWIE, NORMAN E. *Business Ethics.* Englewood Cliffs, N.J.: Prentice-Hall, 1982.

CHAMBERLAIN, NEIL W. *The Limits of Corporate Responsibility.* New York: Basic Books, 1973.

COMMITTEE FOR ECONOMIC DEVELOPMENT (CED). *Social Responsibilities of Business Corporations.* New York: CED, 1971.

DAHL, ROBERT. "A Prelude to Corporate Reform." *Business and Society Review,* 1 (Spring 1972).

DAVIS, KEITH and ROBERT L. BLOMSTROM. *Business and Society: Environment and Responsibility* (3rd ed.). New York: McGraw Hill Book Company, 1975.

DeGEORGE, RICHARD T. *Business Ethics.* New York: Macmillan Publishing Co., Inc., 1982. Chpt. 8.

DONALDSON, THOMAS. *Corporations and Morality.* Englewood Cliffs, N.J.: Prentice-Hall, 1982.

FRENCH, PETER A. "The Corporation as a Moral Person." *American Philosophical Quarterly,* July 1979.

FRENCH, PETER A. "What is Hamlet to McDonnell-Douglas or McDonnell-Douglas to Hamlet: DC-10." *Business and Professional Ethics Journal,* Vol. 1, No. 2, Winter 1982.

GILLESPIE, NORMAN C. "The Business of Ethics." *Business Review,* XXVII (November 1975).

HODGES, LUTHER H., and MILTON FRIEDMAN. "Does Business Have a Social Responsibility?" *Magazine of Bank Administration,* 47 (April 1971).

HOFFMAN, W. MICHAEL. *Proceedings of the First National Conference on Business Ethics.* Business Values and Social Justice: Compatibility or Contradiction? Waltham, Mass.: Center for Business Ethics at Bentley College, 1977.

JACOBY, NEIL H. *Corporate Power and Social Responsibility.* New York: Macmillan Publishing Co., 1973.

JOHNSON, BRUCE M., ed., *The Attack on Corporate America.* New York: McGraw Hill Book Company, 1978.

KAPP, K. WILLIAM. *The Social Costs of Private Enterprise.* New York: Schocken Books, 1971.

PURCELL, THEODORE V., S. J. "A Practical Guide to Ethics in Business." *Business and Society Review,* V 13 (Spring 1975) pp. 43–50.

REPRINTS FROM HARVARD BUSINESS REVIEW. *Ethics for Executives Series.* Cambridge, Mass.: Harvard University Press, contents copyrighted 1955–61, 1966–68.

SETHI, PRAKASH S. *Up Against the Corporate Wall: Modern Corporations and Social Issues of the Eighties* (4th ed.). Englewood Cliffs, N.J.: Prentice-Hall, 1982.

STEINER, GEORGE A. *Business and Society* (2nd ed.). New York: Random House, 1975.

VELASQUEZ, MANUEL G. *Business Ethics Concepts and Cases.* Englewood Cliffs, N.J.: Prentice-Hall, 1982.

WALTON, CLARENCE C. *Corporate Social Responsibilities.* Belmont, Calif.: Wadsworth Publishing Company, 1967.

CHAPTER 3

EMPLOYEE RIGHTS

INTRODUCTION

The introduction to the previous chapter concluded by raising the possibility that the task of the socially responsible manager is to harmonize the legitimate interests of various corporate stakeholders. Traditionally, the shareholder has been considered the primary stakeholder. Recently, more attention has been directed toward the employee. There are good economic reasons for this shift of attention. The declining productivity rate of American labor in the face of stiff international competition is a matter of great concern. This decline in productivity cannot be explained entirely by government regulation or inadequate research and development expenditures. Some commentators have argued that the organization of American business and employer attitudes toward employees have hurt productivity. Traditionally, business firms are organized hierarchically. Production line employees are at the bottom of the hierarchy. In classical economic theory, labor is treated in the same way that land, capital, and machinery are treated—as means toward profit. The employees in many business organizations feel like replaceable cogs in a wheel. Management will employ them only until a better machine comes along. Yet what employees primarily want is to be treated with dignity and respect. As one labor leader said, ''Why shouldn't parking spaces be assigned on a first-come, first-serve basis? Why should white collar workers automatically have spaces near the plant?'' If employees were recognized as making unique and important contributions to the business firm and if they were treated as autonomous responsible agents, productivity would improve.

THE STATUS OF EMPLOYEE RIGHTS

Many employees believe that they are being treated unfairly and that their rights are not being honored. In considering employee rights, we should ask what rights employees have now. More importantly, we should ask what rights employees should have. In answering these questions, we must keep in mind the distinction introduced in Chapter 1 between legal rights and moral rights. As both Phillip Blumberg and David Ewing indicate, employees have very few legal rights other than those specified by the contract. According to common law tradition, an employee is to obey all orders of the employer unless they are immoral or illegal. The employee is to be loyal to his employer and is bound by "the duty of confidentiality" not to disclose information that would harm the economic interests of the employer. Although an employee is not bound to carry out an illegal or immoral order, he or she can easily be dismissed for noncompliance. Moreover, there are other ways besides dismissal to punish recalcitrant employees.

Of particular concern is the dilemma created when an employee's obligations to the general public conflict with an employee's obligation to be loyal to his or her employer. For example, in a well-publicized case, an Eastern Airlines pilot refused to jettison three gallons of excess fuel in the atmosphere. He was discharged for disobeying company policy and reinstated only after public pressure and pressure from the Airline Pilots Association were applied. Even though the pilot argued he was protecting the public by cutting down on pollution, he had no protection in law. Leaving aside the issue of the constitutional rights of the employee, this case indicates that the common law tradition fails to adequately protect the public interest. This chapter focuses attention both on arguments on behalf of employee rights and the public interest and on behalf of mechanisms for achieving this protection.

This absence of legal rights does not settle the matter, however. If an employee has no legal right against arbitrary dismissal, he or she may nonetheless have moral rights against arbitrary dismissal. In fact, Blumberg, Ewing, and Clyde Summers all argue that workers should have certain rights against unjust dismissal. Summers's approach is to correct the gap in the law. He argues that there should be a statute that protects all employees against unjust dismissal. However, he also recognizes that both employers and employees have legitimate rights that should be protected in dismissal cases and that some mechanism should be found for adjudicating disputes. His own proposal is a statute requiring, under some conditions, compulsory arbitration.

MORAL RIGHTS, FREE SPEECH, AND TRADE SECRETS

A discussion of employee rights extends beyond the right to protection against unjust dismissal. Up to this point, our discussion has focused on legal rights—rights which are conferred on employees either by statute or by a collective bargaining agreement. However, many philosophers, as we saw in Chapter 1, maintain that there are certain fundamental rights that everyone has just because they are persons. These include rights to impartial treatment in matters of justice, freedom, equality of opportunity, and respect. By appealing to these fundamental rights, we have an argument to show why it is wrong that workers are not protected against arbitrary dismissal. If a society permits arbitrary dismissal, it permits the violation of an employee's right to impartial treatment on matters of justice as well as the right to respect. Since violations of rights are moral wrongs, society is permitting a moral wrong. Moreover, since society has as one of its essential purposes the protection of the moral and legal rights of its citizens, it has the obligation to provide the mechanism for protection. If traditional philosophers are correct in arguing that all persons have a right to impartial treatment, then society has the correlative obligation to make sure that such rights are protected.

But suppose someone denies that employees have rights or denies that employees have a specific right such as the right to freedom of speech. Against the former claim, Norman Bowie argues that the typical employment contract presupposes that each party to the contract is a bearer of rights—specifically the right to freedom. The thrust of Bowie's argument is to ground employee rights in the actual practices of business. His argument also provides a ground for employer rights. Although he provides a few principles for resolving rights conflicts between employers and employees, he admits that most conflicts will have to be settled either in court or in the collective bargaining process.

One of the more likely places for conflicts to appear between employee rights and employer rights is in the area of free speech. Even the constitutional guarantee of free speech is limited, and so it is no surprise that employees have no absolute right to free speech. However, should the workplace operate under more restrictions on speech (and assembly, etc.) than would be permitted in the political arena?

Robert Ladenson distinguishes two different types of arguments on behalf of freedom of expression in the workplace: The *utilitarian* argument identifies the good consequences that arise from the practice of free expression, and the *rights* approach argues that free expression is "an inherent right grounded in basic principles of social morality." Ladenson argues that the rights approach is more defensible because a utilitarian justification renders employee freedom subject to cost benefit considerations. The chief task of an adherent of the rights approach, he holds, is to show how the priority given to freedom of expression in the political context can be transferred to the market place. Ladenson even argues that when free expression limits profit, then profit rather than free speech must be sacrificed.

Among the legal obligations of an employee under common law is the duty of confidentiality. When an employee has information which could damage the economic interests of his employer, he or she is under an obligation to keep that information confidential. This duty remains in force even when the employee leaves the firm and takes employment elsewhere. Of course, the employee leaves with a wealth of experience at a *type* of job and often with considerable knowledge about a manufacturing process, a product, a computer program, research priorities, or detailed financial information. Some of this information can legitimately be described as a trade secret or the intellectual property of the company. For example, the formula for Coca-Cola is the property of the Coca-Cola Company. If an employee gave the formula to Pepsi, he or she would be giving away a trade secret. Other knowledge cannot be so constituted, for example, the general knowledge a researcher on computer technology at Bell Labs obtains in the process of doing her job.

Given the nature of a trade secret as *intellectual* property, a conflict of rights between the employer and the employee seems inevitable. The employer (corporation) has a right to its intellectual property; the employee has a right to seek gainful employment which uses his or her abilities. Moreover, the conflict between the right to the protection of property and the right to seek gainful employment does not exhaust the relevant issues. Trade secrets are necessary to protect American industry from foreign competitors and to improve productivity. They are also necessary if American firms are to undertake heavy expenditures for basic research. Yet the protection of trade secrets can have adverse consequences for the public good. What if the trade secrets involve dangerous research processes or the illegal dumping of chemical byproducts? Although extensive government regulation can threaten trade secrets, the public interest must be protected.

How are such conflicts to be resolved? In his article, Michael Baram argues that the common law in this matter has been unsuccessful in resolving the conflict. Traditionally, business has been given the benefit of the doubt. Sissela Bok challenges the traditional wisdom in this regard. She finds the traditional argument on behalf of trade secrets to be inconclusive. Hence, she thinks the burden of proof in a trade secret case should be shifted to the company. Baram is more sympathetic to the traditional business position. He attempts to sketch a management policy which both protects a corporation's intellectual property yet is sensitive to the ethical problems which arise as a result of that protection.

WORKER SAFETY

The advent of OSHA (Occupational Safety and Health Administration) placed the issue of worker safety in the headlines and on the agendas of chief executive officers. The critics of business and government have argued that workers were knowingly exposed to dangerous situations and never informed of that fact. American GIs have been exposed to agent orange. Asbestos workers have not been told of the dangers of contracting cancer. Construction workers have been killed when flimsy rigging collapsed. Miners have perished from mine explosions. The categories of injuries can be continued indefinitely.

To discuss adequately the issue of worker safety and the "consent" of workers to risk, some conceptual analysis of what it means to have a safe workplace is required. William Lowrance contends that the workplace cannot be made absolutely safe. He would judge the workplace safe if the risks are judged to be acceptable. But what counts as acceptable risk? In making these judgments, one must consider a number of factors. One complicated factor is the question of probabilities in measuring risk, and another is how to devise questions in a test of the reasonableness of assum-

ing certain risks. What is "reasonableness"? Can we measure it? Can we
define it? Should everyone be held to the same standard of reasonableness?

In any decision concerning product safety, someone must be held
responsible. But who? Lowrance asks, "Should technically trained people
be expected to bear any social responsibilities different from those borne by
others?" Of particular concern to Ruth Faden and Tom Beauchamp is the
employer's responsibility to inform his or her employees about risks in the
workplace and the employee's right to refuse hazardous job assignments.
Faden and Beauchamp appeal to the moral principle of individual
autonomy to support an appropriate standard of information disclosure.
They also consider three possible standards for determining whether a
refusal to work or a safety walkout is justified. They note that all the proposed standards justifying a safety walkout are similar to the standard
which requires that workers be informed of hazards in the workplace.

This chapter unfolds in a way similar to the last. In both, a traditional
point of view is widely seen as inadequate in confronting contemporary
issues of business. Just as the classical theory of corporate responsibility
seems inadequate for addressing the legitimate interests of the multiple
corporate stakeholders, the common-law tradition of employer prerogatives seems inadequate for addressing the legitimate rights of employees.
Employees are demanding management recognition of a new set of employee rights of which the right to free speech and information on safety
hazards are good examples. Yet management has rights as well, including
rights to employee loyalty and protection of trade secrets. Just as the task of
the modern manager is to harmonize the interests of corporate stakeholders, the task of those concerned with ethical issues in employee/em-
ployer relations is to resolve the legitimate conflicting rights claims of the
two parties.

N.E.B.

CORPORATE RESPONSIBILITY AND THE EMPLOYEE'S DUTY OF LOYALTY AND OBEDIENCE

Phillip I. Blumberg

This article constitutes a preliminary inquiry into aspects of a problem
that the author believes will become an area of dynamic change in the corporate organization and in time will produce significant change in estab-

From "Corporate Responsibility and the Employee's Duty of Loyalty and Obedience:
A Preliminary Inquiry," Phillip Blumberg, in *Oklahoma Law Review* vol 24. no. 3. August
1971. Reprinted by permission of *Oklahoma Law Review*.

lished legal concepts. It is concerned with the impact of the new view of the corporation upon traditional concepts of the duties of loyalty and obedience of the employee to his employer, firmly recognized in the law of agency. This impact has been illustrated by a number of recent developments, which have a common core: the right of the employee of the large public corporation to take action adverse to the interests of his employer in response to the employee's view as to the proper social responsibility of his corporate employer. . . .

THE RESTATEMENT OF AGENCY

A review of the relevant provisions of the *Restatement of Agency* provides an obvious starting point for consideration of the new view of the role and duties of the employee.[1]

A. *The Duty of Obedience*

Section 383 and *Section 385* state the agent's duty to obey the principal. Section 385(1) imposes upon the agent "a duty to obey all reasonable directions" of the principal.[2] Comment *a* points out:

> In determining whether or not the orders of the principal to the agent are reasonable . . . *business or professional ethics* . . . are considered. [Emphasis added.]

Comment *a* continues:

> In no event would it be implied that an agent has a duty to perform acts which . . . are *illegal or unethical* . . . [Emphasis added.]

Thus, Comment *a* expressly excludes matters contrary to "business or professional ethics" or "illegal or unethical" acts from those which an agent would be required to perform. This frees the agent from participation in such behavior and authorizes him to withdraw from the agency relation if the principal persists. It in no way authorizes him to disclose such directions of the principal, or not to comply with an instruction of the principal not to disclose any information about the principal's affairs, even in those cases where he is privileged not to perform in accordance with the principal's instructions. The duty exists not only so long as the agent remains an agent but continues after the agency has been terminated as well.

Section 385 (2) provides:

> (2) Unless he is privileged to protect his own or another's interests, an agent is subject to a duty not to act in matters entrusted to him on account of the principal contrary to the directions of the principal. . . .

The Comments make it clear that "an interest" which the agent is privileged to protect refers only to an economic interest, such as a lien or his business reputation. There is no suggestion that an interest which "he is privileged to protect" includes the public interest.

B. *The Duty of Loyalty*

Section 387 expresses the general principle that:

an agent is subject to a duty to his principal to act solely for the benefit of the principal in all matters connected with his agency.

Comment *b* emphasizes the high degree of the duties of loyalty of the agent by stating that they "are the same as those of a trustee to his beneficiaries." It provides, however, that:

> The agent is also under a duty not to act or speak disloyally . . . except in the protection of his own interests or those of others. He is not, however, necessarily prevented from acting in good faith outside his employment in a manner which injuriously affects his principal's business.

and provides the following illustration:

> 3. A, employed by P, a life insurance company, in good faith advocates legislation which would require a change in the policies issued by the company. A has violated no duty to P.

Thus, the agent is free to act "in good faith outside his employment," even in a manner which injures his principal's business, but is subject to a duty identical with that of a trustee with respect to "all matters connected with his agency." Under the comment and illustration, the General Motors employee may campaign in good faith for legislation imposing costly antipollution or product safety controls on automobile manufacturers, but he occupies a position equivalent to a trustee with respect to information about General Motors operations which he has acquired in the course, or on account, of his employment.

Section 394 prohibits the agent from acting:

> for persons whose interests conflict with those of the principal in matters in which the agent is employed.

The numerous examples in the comments relate to competitors or adverse parties in commercial transactions or parties with adverse claims and make it plain that the reference to conflicting "interests" means economic interests.

C. The Duty of Confidentiality

Section 395 imposes a duty upon the agent:

> not to use or to communicate information confidentially given him by the principal or acquired by him during the course of or on account of his agency . . . to the injury of the principal, on his own account or on behalf of another . . . unless the information is a matter of general knowledge.

Comment *a* emphasizes that the agency relation "permits and requires great freedom of communication between the principal and the agent." It expands the agent's duty by stating that the agent:

> also has a duty not to use information acquired by him as agent . . . for any purpose likely to cause his principal harm or to interfere with his business, although it is information not connected with the subject matter of his agency.

Comment *b* extends the duty beyond "confidential" communications to "information which the agent should know his principal would not care to have revealed to others." Both Comments *a* and *b* refer to protection of the principal against competition, but it is clear that this is merely one of the interests of the principal protected by the section.

Comment *f* creates a privilege, significantly enough for a public, not an economic, interest:

> An agent is privileged to reveal information confidentially acquired . . . in the protection of a superior interest of himself or of a third person. Thus, if the confidential information is to the effect that the principal is committing or is about to commit a crime, the agent is under no duty not to reveal it.

This is the only illustration in the *Restatement* that the term "interest" may embrace something of a noneconomic nature. The public interest in law enforcement is deemed a "superior interest" giving rise to a privilege to reveal otherwise confidential information.

If construed to include disclosure to any person, and not solely to law enforcement agencies, Comment *f* would support the "public interest disclosure" proposal to the extent it relates to "illegal" matters, without regard to the nature or seriousness of the offense. *Section 395,* Comment *f*, however, refers only to commission of a "crime." This contrasts with *Section 385(1)* relating to the duty of obedience which refers not only to "illegal" but also to "unethical" acts and to "business or professional ethics." The inclusion of these latter elements in *Section 385(1)* and their omission in *Section 395* would indicate that the release of confidential information privileged under *Section 395* does not extend beyond criminal acts.

Although *Section 395* refers only to the agent's use or communication of information "on his own account or on behalf of another" and does not literally prohibit use or communication of such information for the benefit of the public, Comment *a* prohibits such use "for any purpose likely to cause his principal harm or to interfere with his business." Comment *a* thus would appear to expand the duty of the agent beyond acts "on his own account or on behalf of another" to include disclosures made to advance the "public interest," which were not related to commission of a "crime" privileged under Comment *f*. . . .

In summary, except in the single area of "crime," the *Restatement* provides no support for the view that the employee may disclose nonpublic information about his employer acquired as a result of the employment relationship in order to promote the superior interest of society. . . . The reference in *Section 395,* Comment *f* permitting the agent to disclose confidential information concerning a criminal act committed or planned by the principal is the sole exception to a system of analysis that is otherwise exclusively concerned with matters relating to the economic position of the parties. Thus, the question may fairly be asked to what extent the *Restatement* and the common-law decisions are useful in the analysis of a proposal that rests on the concept of an agent's primary obligation as a citizen to the society, transcending his economic duty to the principal.

Are doctrines resting on a policy of protecting the economic position of the principal against impairment by reason of an agent's effort to achieve economic gain properly applicable to the employee who releases nonpublic information about his employer without intent to obtain economic advantage for himself—and motivated by a desire to promote the public good rather than to injure the principal (although such injury may in fact result)?

The duties of loyalty and obedience on the part of the agent are unquestionably central to the agency relationship, irrespective of economic considerations. But these duties, as the *Restatement* itself recognizes, have limitations. To paraphrase Mr. Justice Frankfurter's well-known admonition:[3] To say that an agent has duties of loyalty and obedience only begins analysis; it gives direction to further inquiry. It is thus not enough to say that the agent has duties of loyalty and obedience which will be impaired. One must inquire more deeply and ascertain the outer perimeter of the agent's obligations by balancing the conflicting considerations. On this critical question of how far the duties of loyalty and obedience extend, the *Restatement* enunciating the traditional rules in their economic setting provides limited guidance. . . .

The Changing Role of the Corporate Employee

. . . In the balance of the conflicting rights of the government employee as citizen and the objective of government for efficient administration, the courts have placed a lesser value on the traditional duties of loyalty and obedience and have subordinated these duties to the employee's right of free speech in order to enable the employee to play a role as a citizen in matters of public controversy. Similarly, one may inquire whether, in time, erosion of the traditional employer-employee relation and the traditional concepts of loyalty and obedience will not also occur within the major American corporation. . . .

In an illuminating article,[4] Dean Blades has reexamined the traditional concept of employment at will and the employer's traditional power to discharge the employee at any time for any reason (or indeed for no reason) and has suggested that in time the doctrine—already hedged in by statute and collective bargaining agreements—will be modified, possibly by the legislatures, perhaps by the courts, to protect the employee against discharge for exercise of those personal rights which have no legitimate connection with the employment relationship. . . .

As one moves from the theoretical level to the practical level, one may inquire whether the employer's right of discharge has not already been impaired at least in those cases where public sympathy is squarely behind the employee, as in the case of the Eastern Airlines pilot who placed his concern with air pollution above obedience to company regulations. The rules of law may condemn such activity as a clear breach of the duty of loyalty and obedience. The corporation may be tempted to exercise its right of discharge, but its freedom of action (without regard to obligations under any union contract) will be severely restricted by the climate of public opinion which may well have been significantly influenced by the publicity attending the affair.

In the arena of public opinion, the issue will involve the merits of the conduct of the employee, not whether the conduct was contrary to instructions. In the Eastern Airlines case, the intentional violation of regulations and the impracticability of allowing each of the 3,700 Eastern Airlines pilots to ''make his own rules'' were not the issues before the public. The subject of the public debate was the impact of the Eastern Airlines practice on air pollution. Unless the corporation can prevail in the battle for public opinion on the merits of the conduct in issue, it must yield to public clamor or face the consequences of unfavorable public reaction. Moreover, if the employer is unionized, it is unlikely that the union efforts on behalf of the employee will be limited to the legal question of whether the conduct constitutes ''just cause'' for discharge under the collective agreement.

At this stage, whatever the traditional legal doctrines, the corporation's right of discharge may be illusory. The major corporation must recognize that it has become a public institution and must respond to the public climate of opinion. Thus, whether or not the major corporation in the law of the future comes to be regarded as a quasi-governmental body for some purpose, it operates today as a political as well as economic institution, subject to political behavior by those affected by it and to public debate over those of its actions which attain public visibility.

The pervasive public concern with corporate social responsibility will unquestionably lead to employee response to an appeal for disclosures of confidential information tending to show corporate participation in the creation of social or environmental problems. It is only realistic, therefore, to anticipate the appearance of the government-type ''leak'' in the major corporation. Whether or not it violates traditional agency concepts, a ''public interest clearing house'' may be expected to transact considerable business. Aggrieved employers are hardly going to feel free to resort to theoretically available legal or equitable remedies for redress so long as the unauthorized disclosures relate to ''antisocial'' conduct and do not reflect economic motivation. The corporation that is guilty of environmental abuse reported to the ''clearing house'' will not be well-advised to compound its conduct by instituting action against the ''clearing house'' or the employee (if it can identify him) and thereby assure even greater adverse publicity with respect to its objectionable environmental activities. . . .

Another aspect of the proposal for a ''public interest clearing house'' has considerable merit. This is the objective to provide protection through exposure to public opinion for corporate employees discharged for refusal to participate in illegal, immoral, or unprofessional acts. Involving no breach of confidentiality, this is a laudable effort to translate into reality the theoretical legal rights of the employee recognized at common law and in the *Restatement of Agency* in the face of the grave economic inequality between the individual employee and the giant corporate employer. Such an effort should receive the support of all interested in raising the standards of industrial morality. . . .

Statutory relief is another possible method to achieve appropriate protection for the rights of employees covering unionized and nonunionized employees alike. Antidiscrimination employment statutes already prohibit discrimination on the basis of ''race, color, religion, sex, or national origin," age, or union membership. They might well be extended to make unlawful discrimination for political, social or economic views even when publicly expressed in opposition to an employer's policy. Similarly, statutory prohibition of discharge for refusal to participate in acts that are illegal or contrary to established canons of professional ethics, or for cooperation with governmental law-enforcement, legislative or executive agencies, deserves serious consideration.

CONCLUSION

The duties of loyalty and obedience are essential in the conduct of any enterprise—public or private. Yet, they do not serve as a basis to deprive government employees of their rights as citizens to participate in public debate and criticism of their governmental employer and should not be utilized to deprive corporate employees of similar rights.

As employee attitudes and actions reflect the increased public concern with social and environmental problems and the proper role of the corporation in participating in their solution, traditional doctrines of the employee's duties of loyalty and obedience and the employer's right of discharge will undergo increasing change. The pressure of "public interest" stockholder groups for increased corporate social responsibility will also be reflected by employees. At some point in the process, disagreement with management policies is inevitable. When the employees persist in their disagreement and the disagreement becomes public, an erosion of the traditional view of the duties of loyalty and obedience will have occurred. Yet, this hardly seems a fundamental problem for the corporation or undesirable from the point of view of the larger society. The real question is to establish civilized perimeters of permissible conduct that will not silence employees from expressing themselves on the public implications of their employers' activities in the social and environmental arena and at the same time will not introduce elements of breach of confidentiality and impairment of loyalty that will materially impair the functioning of the corporation itself. A balancing of interests, not a blind reiteration of traditional doctrines, is required. It is hoped that this preliminary review will suggest some possible solutions to the problem.

Notes

1. For the purposes of this paper, "agent" should be regarded as interchangeable with "employee."
2. *Restatement (Second) of Agency* (1958), § 385(1) (hereinafter cited as *Restatement*).
3. See Mr. Justice Frankfurter in SEC v. Chenery Corp., 318 U.S. 80, 85–86, 63 S.Ct. 454, 458, 87 L.Ed. 626, 632 (1943).
4. See Blades, "Employment At Will v. Individual Freedom: or Limiting the Allusive Exercise of Employer Power," 67, *Columbia Law Review*, 1404 (1967).

CIVIL LIBERTIES IN THE CORPORATION

David W. Ewing

"In our country," Mark Twain once observed, "we have those three unspeakably precious things: freedom of speech, freedom of conscience, and the prudence never to practice either." He must have been thinking of our corporations and government agencies. In most of these organizations, during working hours, civil liberties are a will-o'-the-wisp. The Constitutional rights that employees have grown accustomed to in family, school, and church life generally must be left outdoors, like cars in the parking space. As in totalitarian countries, from time to time a benevolent chief executive or department head may encourage speech, conscience, and privacy, but these scarcely can be called rights, for management can take them away at will. As former Attorney General Ramsey Clark once noted, "A right is not what someone gives you; it is what no one can take away."

This situation is the curious, anomolous, and accidental product of two parallel trends, one legal, the other commercial.

Since the Code of Hammurabi, Western law has given the employer a fairly free hand in hiring and firing employees. Until a century or so ago there were good reasons for this. Businesses were small, the employer-employee relationship was close, commercial life, like personal life, was tenuous, and labor tended to be manual, simple, and interchangeable. But then came the era of the large organization, corporate power, and the so-called "knowledge worker."

The intimacy of the employer-employee relationship vanished; size made the corporation more stable, more long-lived than any employee or management group; technology and specialization produced employees who were not interchangeable among companies, employees who, though extremely valuable for *some* companies, might be of no value whatsoever to most. However, only in a few respects, such as collective bargaining, did the law change to accommodate this momentous change.

In the meantime a revolution was occurring in the operation and direction of business. The large corporation appeared and, with it, professional management. "In the past, the man has been first," said Frederick Winslow Taylor, often called the father of scientific management; "in the future, the system must be first." Taylor and the legions of industrial engineers and management experts who followed him looked at the organization as a system whose main function was to be efficient and effective. Individualism was something that, while appropriate in private life, was atavistic in worklife, relevant only if its suffocation might conflict with the prosperity of the system.

The consequence of these two trends, neither planned or nurtured in relationship to the other, was a loss of civil liberties and a rise of authoritarianism that none of the Founding Fathers could have anticipated. It would not be fair to say that their dream of Constitutionalism was eviscerated, for American political and social liberties expanded steadily in the next two centuries. Further, the American public can, acting through Congress and the state legislatures, alter or abolish the laws that nurture the corporation at any time and in any way that it chooses to do so. On the other hand, it is fair to say that an enormous corporate archipelago has grown which, in terms of civil liberties, is as different from the rest of America as day is from night. In this archipelago, as Taylor mandated, the system comes first, the individual second (except where collective bargaining, equal employment opportunity, safety and health, and similar regulations provide otherwise). Externally, the system operates at the sufferance of the consumer—no corporation survives unless it pleases a constituency in the marketplace. Internally, however, the employee works and behaves at the sufferance of the system as represented by his or her supervisors and managers.

This staggering sacrifice of civil liberties is defended on the basis of efficiency. Now, it is indisputable that organizations have to be productive or they cannot serve the public. To be productive, good management is necessary. Does this mean civil liberties must be sacrificed? There is no evidence that civil liberties (unlike the methods of "industrial democracy") conflict with the exercise of management's right to manage. Nor need they conflict with the rights of ownership. Indeed, as we shall see, experience suggests they may enhance, rather than diminish, the bottom line.

Awareness of this relationship seems to be growing among jurists, businessmen, employees, and legislators. Let us take the three most controversial civil liberties—speech, conscience, and privacy—and, beginning with the traditional legal viewpoint toward dissidents as a benchmark, see how a few courts and corporations are leading industry in a new direction.

Speech: The Gag Loosens

Nearly a century ago a Tennessee court made a memorable statement about employer prerogatives. Employers, said the court, in a decision that was later overruled but on other grounds, "may dismiss their employees at will . . . for good cause, for no cause, or even for cause morally wrong, without thereby being guilty of legal wrong."[1] A quarter of a century later a California court made a similarly strong statement, observing that the "arbitrary right of the employer to employ or discharge labor, with or without regard to actuating motives," is a proposition "settled beyond peradvanture."[2] Shortly after World War II a Minnesota court put the same idea a little more cautiously, this time in terms of the venerable master-servant relationship:

> "The relation of master and servant . . . casts certain duties upon . . . the servant, which he was bound to fulfill and discharge; and the principal one was that of obedience to all reasonable orders of . . . the master, not inconsistent with the contract. Disobedience of reasonable orders is a violation of the law which justifies . . . the peremptory discharge of the servant."[3]

Finally, to bring us to the present decade, a U.S. district court in Missouri recognized the traditional rule in ruling against a whistle-blowing engineer of General Motors.[4] . . .

Adding reinforcement to the concept of obedience, common law requires that an agent must be loyal to an employer or boss, acting solely for their benefit in all matters connected with the working relationship. The employee is also duty-bound ''not to act or speak disloyally'' except in the pursuit of his own interests outside work.

What some observers consider the high-water mark of the traditional rule is the recent case of Louis V. McIntire. A chemical engineer, McIntire had worked for the DuPont Company in Orange, Texas from 1956 until 1972. During this period he was promoted several times and was paid very respectable salaries. In 1972, however, his supervisors became acquainted with a novel he and his wife published in 1971 under the title, *Scientists and Engineers: The Professionals Who Are Not*. The novel was published by an unincorporated company set up by the author; about 2,000 copies were sold or distributed.

In the novel, a doleful character named J. Marmaduke Glumm argues that technical employees should form a national federation to push legislation favoring its members. ''It is a peculiar paradox,'' says Glumm, ''That workingmen with little bargaining leverage have more actual job security than we do.'' Other characters in the novel inveigh against management for favoritism, screwing inventors out of bonuses they deserve for their discoveries, and taking unfair advantage of professionals in employment contracts. In superficial respects the fictional employer, Logan Chemical Company, is not too different from McIntire's real-life employer, DuPont—the authors' criticisms are thinly veiled. It is not hard to see why some of his supervisors were displeased, especially since professional unions, opposed by management, were winning favor among American scientists and engineers.

After his summary discharge, McIntire sued DuPont for $20 million. Late in 1974 a Texas district court threw out his claim that his Constitutional right of free speech had been violated.[5] (However, other claims he made—that he had been blackballed among prospective employers after his discharge, not been paid adequately for his inventions, and been denied due process—are still being litigated as this is written.) . . .

Recent Decisions:

In view of the foregoing, it might seem that the ancient law of master and servant were alive and well and living par excellence. In actuality, however, its health may be failing.

In 1974 the U.S. District Court of Connecticut heard the case of a skilled worker named Michael Holodnak, who had been employed in Stratford, Connecticut by the Avco-Lycoming Division of Avco Corporation. Holodnak had had the temerity to write an article for a bi-weekly newsletter in New Haven (its circulation was about 750 readers) accusing Avco-Lycoming of sabotaging the grievance procedure. Holodnak may have had a subconscious desire to be hung for a goose rather than an egg, for he also criticized the local United Auto Workers union leadership for being passive. When the article was read by his bosses, they called him in, declared the article violated a rule of conduct for employees ("making false, vicious, or malicious statements concerning . . . the employee's relationship" to the company), asked for his badge, and showed him to the door. Holodnak had worked in the plant for nine years.

First he went to arbitration. But the union attorney made only half-hearted attempts to defend him (in the opinion of the District Court), and the arbitrator's decision went in favor of the company.

The District Court was impressed by the fact that Holodnak's article was "less vituperative and critical" of company practices than some of the union's own leaflets. It also felt he had not been given a fair shake in the grievance procedure. But most of all the court was impressed by Avco-Lycoming's relationship to the government. About 80% of production was military hardware—nose cones for missiles, helicopter engines, and so forth. While agreeing that the First Amendment does not apply to a private employer, the Court noted that it did apply to public employees (it cited the *Pickering* case, to be described presently). Therefore, workers at Avco-Lycoming were protected because of the "governmental presence" at the plant. The fact that Holodnak was speaking out on labor-management relations also helped his case. The District Court ordered the company to make modest payments to Holodnak for wages lost and damages.[6]

A great many companies do a substantial amount of business for the government and therefore could be said to have a "governmental presence," as at Avco. It will be interesting to see if this reasoning rides again in other jurisdictions in the future.

On the opposite coast, the following year, the Santa Clara Superior Court heard the case of *Murray* v. *Microform Data Systems, Inc.*[7] In this case, Marvin Murray, an engineer (employed "at will") became worried about the safety of a computer-controlled console being produced and marketed by his company. Checking with a state agency, he learned that his fears were justified. He went to his superiors and urged changes in the console to make it safe. He was sacked. Relying on the case of *Petermann* v. *International Brotherhood of Teamsters*, 344 P.2d 25 (1959) a 1959 case in California holding that a terminable-at-will employee (in this case, a union official) cannot be discharged in violation of public policy. Murray's attorney, Matthew F. Quint, argued that the firing was in retaliation for an effort to comply with the engineering profession's code of ethics and to correct unsafe working conditions, and therefore in violation of public policy. The trial court judge accepted this argument and included it in his instructions to the jury, which returned a verdict for the plaintiff. The decision was widely reported in the engineering profession. Since the company did not appeal, the case lacks precedential value in California law. Nevertheless, the decision is a sign of a change in judicial thinking. . . .

In the public sector, the U.S. Supreme Court's rescue of a whistle-blowing schoolteacher in the *Pickering* case[8] has become a well known precedent.[9] In view of the close relationship between public sector and private sector organizations, the logic of protecting dissidents in the one sector but not in the other is likely to elude many judges.

Company Actions:

Although under no legal compulsion to do so, a small but important number of companies are encouraging employee speech—not arguments with boss over judgments on operating matters, but questions and criticisms concerning policies affecting employee welfare, the community, ethical norms, and the law.

For example, at a New England plant of Corning Glass, executives encourage two-way communication with employees at regular "coffee rap" meetings and through bulletin boards and the plant newspaper. When the effort was started, employees were suspicious and only questioned trite matters. But when management's sincerity became clear, the questioning became less guarded and more expansive. Searching questions about the company's long-range planning and other important policies were asked.

Donnelly Mirrors, Inc., the major supplier of mirrors used in U.S. automobiles, organizes employees into work teams that tackle such questions as cost reduction, capital investment, compensation, and other matters. At meetings of the teams, discussion is free and open, and there seems to be a no-holds-barred attitude on criticism of any function or of personalities in management.

One big division of General Electric operates a "hot line" for employees who have questions, worries, or wrongdoing to report. More than a hundred thousand calls were received and answered last year. New England Telephone operates a similar kind of system cabled "Private Lines." The employee can remain anonymous, he or she can challenge management in highly sensitive areas like discrimination and dishonesty, and all questions are answered promptly, either by the "Private Lines" staff or company officials.

Dow Chemical and American Airlines open pages of their company publications to employee criticisms and questions. Embarrassing letters are published—accusations of management featherbedding, sham in labor relations, stupid supervisory practices. The official responses don't always satisfy the critics but there is no doubt that the criticisms are heard, sometimes loud and clear. I know of no evidence that critics, when they give their names, have been penalized.

Delta Airlines holds regular meetings with its 28,000 employees in different locations where top officials ask workers, after supervisors and foremen are excused, "What's bothering you?" Questions can be submitted anonymously by card. All queries are answered on the spot or as soon as possible after the meeting, sometimes on bulletin boards.

CONSCIENCE: CURBS ON THE UNETHICAL BOSS

Developments in employee speech serve as a kind of paradigm for developments in the area of conscience. The right to object to an immoral or unethical order or request is particularly important to employees. Indeed, this form of rightlessness probably troubles more employees more often than does lack of free speech, judging from surveys by the *Harvard Business Review.*[10]

However, there are not as many cherries to pluck from this legal cake—good, representative cases are few. One example of the traditional rule is the case of Shirley Zinman, a secretary in a Philadelphia employment agency, who had to resign when she refused to follow her boss's directive to monitor telephone conversations with outsiders without their knowledge. When she sought unemployment compensation from the local board, she was denied on the ground that her resignation was not "compelling and necessitous." She appealed to the Pennsylvania Commonwealth Court and, in a 1973 decision hailed by civil rights leaders, the state board's decision was reversed.[11] This case is significant for what it does *not* say. The liberally-inclined court does not suggest that Zinman should be reinstated in the company.

In business circles, "grapevine cases" like the following are well known: A factory was making plans for expansion. The new general manager went over the details with the facilities engineer, an older man who was a few years away from comfortable retirement (assuming he kept his pension). An eager-beaver type who wanted to make a good profit showing, the general manager insisted that the engineer specify footings and structural steel specifications that were below the standards of good practice. When the engineer balked, he was told to choose between doing as told and losing his job.

Suppose the engineer had balked, been fired, and gone to court to get his job back? Presumably, if the judges were traditionalists, they would have decided against him.

Recent Decisions:

However, at least a few courts are unwilling to ride with tradition. Olga Monge was hired to work in the Beebe Rubber Company. She did well on her first job but, on applying for a higher-paying job, was told by her foreman she would have to be "nice." Not sure what "nice" meant, she took the job. The foreman defined "nice" by insisting that she go out with him. She refused, mentioning that she was married and had three children. The foreman then harassed her, demoted her, and finally got her fired. She went to court and a jury awarded her damages. The company appealed. The Supreme Court of New Hampshire decided in her favor (though remanding the case on the ground she was not entitled to recover damages for mental suffering). A malicious discharge, it said, was "not in the best interests of the economic system or the public good."[12]

That such an opinion may reflect the mood of a growing number of judges is suggested by a public sector case. Paulette Barnes took a job in the Environmental Protection Agency. Her boss sought an "after-hours affair" with her, suggesting that it would improve her chances of promotion and a pay increase. When she rebuffed him, he had her job abolished, and she was reassigned to another workplace. The U.S. District Court held against her claim for redress under Title VII of the Civil Rights Act of 1964, but the Court of Appeals for the District of Columbia ruled in her favor.[13]

In a different type of case, a veteran truck driver refused to drive a truck that was overloaded. The overload was in violation of Ohio state law and the Teamsters union contract with the company. The driver was fired. Both the arbitrator and the National Labor Relations Board confirmed his dismissal. Appealing to the U.S. Circuit Court of Appeals, he won.[14] The court based its decision on the public interest and used language broad enough for the case to serve as a precedent in a wide variety of illegal work assignment cases and perhaps even in cases involving potentially harmful work assignments.

Company Actions:

Thanks to the unions, women's rights activists, and, more generally, a growing, ubiquitous disenchantment with the philosophy of *le droit du seigneur,* business seems to have growing sympathy with the conscientious objector.

In a 1971 survey which drew extensive answers from 3,453 managers, I found that a strong majority took the side of an accountant who (in a case described to respondents) refused to doctor the figures to change a loss into a profit. More than nine-tenths of managers at all levels felt that such a person should be reinstated, if fired; three-fourths of them believed that their organization would reinstate the employee if the case came to light. (Many more respondents would go along with firing an employee who blabbered about such an incident to an important outsider, causing harm to the organization. Only about two-fifths said they would reinstate the employee in that case.)[15]

In another questionnaire survey that I sent out early in 1977, a strong majority of business executives again took the side of the employee in cases where a person was fired for refusing to obey unethical directives. A great many managers expressed willingness to "rock the boat," if necessary, to get the victim back in the job.[16]

Perhaps the main question is how to organize, how to institutionalize defenses for the conscientious objector. Assuming a prevailing sentiment in favor of moral actions, probably the most effective procedure is a prompt hearing in the organization. Union-supported grievance procedures may qualify quite well. In nonunionized companies, or for nonunion employees of unionized companies, a management-supported hearing procedure may meet the need. The best example I know of is Polaroid Corporation, with about 12,000 non-unionized employees and a well-institutionalized committee whose job it is to represent an employee with a grievance. This is done in a hearing before representatives of management. The committee members are elected from the ranks. Reportedly a fair number of management decisions are overruled in the hearings. If the decision goes against the aggrieved employee, he or she is entitled by company rules to submit the case to an outside arbitrator.

A hearing procedure like this is the corporate equivalent of due process.

It is itself one of the rights needed in order to constitutionalize the corporation.

PRIVACY: RESISTANCE TO BIG BROTHER?

When employees are in their homes, before and after working hours, they enjoy well-established rights to privacy and to protection from arbitrary search and seizure of their papers and possessions. But no such rights protect them in the company, government agency, or other organization; their superiors need only the flimsiest pretext to search their lockers, desks, and files. Because employees are supposed to be loyal myrmidons, regardless of what the organization is doing, the boss can rummage through their letters, memoranda, and tapes looking for evidence they are about to "rat" on the company. "Ratting" includes such possibilities as reporting a violation of safety standards to the Occupational Safety and Health Administration, or telling Ralph Nader about a product defect, or giving the mayor's office requested information about a violation of energy-use regulations.

It doesn't matter that employees may be right about the facts, or that it may be the superiors, not the employees, who are disloyal to the stockholders. In one of his verses for "The Watergate Mother Goose," published in the *Chicago Tribune,* Bob Cromie expressed the management rationale as follows:

> I do not like thee, Dr. Fell,
> But why this is I cannot tell;
> Meanwhile, to erase those smiles,
> We plan to rummage thru your files.[17]

The personnel records of employees are not confidential. Even when an employer misuses personal information about an employee and the employee is fortunate enough to find out, the way to a remedy can be very difficult. "Claims by an employee who has been injured by misuse of his personal information may fall between the effective privacy and defamation causes of action," states Mordechai Mironi, an attorney and researcher at the University of Minnesota.[18]

An employee's privacy is invaded in still other ways in organizations that exercise the full freedom given them by the traditional law. It is invaded when the employer collects data about the worker. Exhaustive questionnaires about the person's life and habits, psychological tests, and electronic tests—even their enthusiastic supporters in personnel departments admit that they raise a legitimate question of unfair invasion. But they insist that the benefit to management and society outweighs the invasion. The employee's privacy is invaded again when the information collected is put to use. Managers make decisions on the basis of information the employee may not know about, including hearsay comments and off-the-cuff opinions gleaned from quick interviews. The organization uses the same information to answer inquiries from social workers, credit bureaus, union officials, insurance companies, lawyers, government agencies, and other sources.

Another form of invasion is eavesdropping. For instance, in all but two states, company managers are free to monitor employees' conversations on company telephones without telling the employees. The two exceptions are California, which requires a beeper to be used on monitored phones, and Georgia, where the Public Service Commission requires that monitored phones be marked with a bright orange lable and that monitoring supervisors obtain licenses.

If the personal impressions and "common knowledge" of many employees mean anything, quite a few companies monitor secretly. Electronic equipment for monitoring has become quite sophisticated, and an employee cannot know whether, to what extent, or for what purpose he or she is unwittingly sharing telephone calls with a supervisor or higher-up.

Incidentally, there is no legal restriction on a supervisor's putting any notes thus gathered in the personnel folder of the individual monitored, locked up from that person's view but available to senior management people and, if organization policy allows, outside groups.

Company Action:

Some observers feel that many courts might curtail the Big Brother freedoms of employers if employees sued. Thus far, however, no such opportunities appear to have been given state or federal judges. This has left it up to corporations themselves to take remedial action voluntarily. Quite a few have followed the lead of government agencies, universities, and other organizations that allow employees to examine their personnel files. Under the Privacy Act of 1974, federal agencies are required to do this.

But the real leadership comes from IBM. This company has enacted for its nearly 300,000 employees a privacy code which may be the most advanced code of any organization in the world. In addition to ruling out surreptitious monitoring of employee conversations and snooping on employee's home lives, IBM insists on such principles as the following:[19]

1. Management can collect and keep in its personnel files only those facts about employees that are required by law or that are necessary to manage operations. Thus, IBM's job application forms no longer ask for previous addresses, or whether the employee has relatives working for IBM, or about prior mental problems, or about convictions more than five years back, or about more recent criminal charges that did not result in conviction.
2. Performance evaluations more than three years old must be weeded out from an employee's file.
3. Employees are entitled to know how filed information about them is being used. As IBM chairman Frank T. Cary notes, employees should understand that "there's no great mystery about it."
4. An employee is entitled to see *most* of the information on file about him (or her). Only in this way can he share in the responsibility for accuracy. Of course, there may be some information that management is justified in withholding. An example is a confidential discussion of an opportunity for

promotion that was never given, or a boss's personal reactions to an unusual request made by an employee.

5. Personality and general intelligence tests are not permissible. However, aptitude and skill tests may be legitimate, for they give an employer relevant knowledge about an applicant's ability. For example, typing tests may be given at IBM.

The IBM approach is becoming the corporate sermon on the mount in the privacy field. Companies large and small have espoused it or are considering espousing it. But an old problem in the business world is already in evidence: The companies that need improvement the most are the ones that are paying the least attention to it. Obviously there is an important role to play for the courts, legislators, and unions.

CONCLUSION

"Let me add," Thomas Jefferson wrote to James Madison in 1787, when the two men were pondering the need for a Constitutional bill of rights, "that a bill of rights is what the people are entitled to against every government on earth, general or particular."

Although Jefferson didn't know it, the state governments of that day were to be surpassed in size by corporate governments. The "population" of AT&T is 939,000 employees, nearly twice the size of the population of Virginia when the revolution started. To be sure, Ma Bell's population is mostly daytime, whereas the people of Virginia were governed night and day. On the other hand, the telephone company controls its employees far more carefully than the Virginia statehouse ever dreamed of controlling its tradesmen and farmers.

The time-honored rebuttal to the suggestion that corporations should be "constitutionalized" is that, without strict economic discipline, our economic system would come apart at the seams. Any form of dissidence, any type of criticism of management prerogatives, however well motivated, is greeted as the most contemptible of crimes. Management has an unmanageable fear of the dissident, regarding him as such a hideous threat that even the purest of motives cannot excuse him.

The reality, of course, is that civil liberties are far less of a threat to the requirements of effective management than are collective bargaining, labor-management committees, job enrichment, work participation, and a number of other schemes that industry takes for granted. Moreover, the companies that lead in encouraging rights—organizations such as Polaroid, IBM, Donnelly Mirrors, and Delta Airlines—have healthier-looking bottom lines than the average corporation does.

The law is marked like a road map from head to toe with solicitousness for the employer; you can travel the length and breadth of the legal body over superhighways of concern for the rights of owners, managers, creditors, and agents. This preoccupation is not wholly materialistic. Indeed, it is not completely inconsistent with humanistic concern for life, liberty, and individualism. For unless organizations survive and prosper, people cannot rise much above the subsistence level.

On the other hand, little is gained if organizations prosper while the souls within them vie (in John Donne's phrase) "to watch one another out of fear." In the long run no organization can achieve much at the expense of the quality of life in its offices, factories, and stores.

Notes

1. Payne v. Western & A.R.R., 81 Tenn. 507, 519–520 (1884).
2. Union Labor Hospital Association v. Vance Redwood Lumber Co., 158 Cal. 551, 555 (1910).
3. Mair v. Southern Minnesota Broadcasting Co., 226 Minn. 137, (1948).
4. Percival v. General Motors Corporation, 400 F. Supp. 1322 (1975).
5. McIntire v. E.I. DuPont de Nemours and Co., 165th Judicial District Court, Harris County, Texas, No. 954,904.
6. Holodnak v. Avco Corporation, 514 F. 2d 285 (1975).
7. Murray v. Microform Data Systems, Inc., Superior Court, Santa Clara, Calif., No. 337237 (1975).
8. Pickering v. Board of Education, 391 U.S. 563 (1968).
9. See Rafferty v. Philadelphia Psychiatric Center, 346 F. Supp. 500 (1973), Muller v. Conlisk, 429 F.2d 900 (1970), Tepedino v. Dumpson, 249 N.E.2d 751 (1969), Dendor v. Board of Fire and Police Commissioner, 197 N.E.2d 316 (1973), and Mt. Healthy City School Dist. v. Doyle, 691 Gov. Emp. Relations Rep. 24 (U.S. Jan 11, 1977). Also see my book, *Freedom Inside the Organization: Bringing Civil Liberties to the Workplace* (E.P. Dutton & Co., New York, 1977).
10. See Raymond C. Baumhart, "How Ethical Are Businessmen?" *Harvard Business Review* (July-August, 1961), p. 6; and Steven Brenner and Earl Molander, "Is the Ethics of Business Changing?" *Harvard Business Review* (January-February, 1977), p. 57.
11. *8 Pa. Comm. Ct. Reports* 649, 304 A.2d 380 (1973).
12. Monge v. Beebe Rubber Company, 316 A. 2d 549 (1974).
13. Barnes v. Costle, U.S. Court of Appeals, D.C. No. 74–2026 (1977).
14. Banyard, v. NLRB, 505 F.2d 342 (1974)
15. David Ewing, "Who Wants Employee Rights?" *Harvard Business Review* (November-December, 1971), p.22.
16. David Ewing, "What Business Thinks About Employee Rights," *Harvard Business Review* (September-October, 1977), p. 81.
17. *Chicago Tribune*, November 4, 1973.
18. Mordechai Mironi, "The Confidentiality of Personnel Records: A Legal and Ethical View," *Labor Law Journal*, May, 1974, p. 286.
19. For a more complete discussion of the IBM code, see Frank Cary's interview "IBM's Guidelines to Employee Privacy," *Harvard Business Review* (September-October, 1976), p. 82.

THE MORAL CONTRACT BETWEEN EMPLOYER AND EMPLOYEE

Norman E. Bowie

. . . My central thesis is that if a corporation or business is to treat its employees with dignity, it must recognize that these employees have certain rights that must be respected. In arguing for this thesis, I will contend that the "factors-of-production view of labor" is ethically unacceptable. Although I support David Ewing's strategy of extending constitutional rights to the workplace, I will argue on moral and conceptual rather than legal grounds. Specifically, I will claim that the very practice of business presupposes a recognition of employee rights on the part of the corporation. Hence I will conclude that the central issues are the identification and implementation of employee rights rather than the defense of them.

THE ARGUMENT

The Contractual Context

One of the most useful devices in the practice of business is the notion of a business contract. The contract device is used in the hiring of employees, in the establishment of credit, in the ordering and supplying of goods, and in the issuing of a warranty. Now a contract is a kind of promise and, hence, is a moral device. In other words, since the use of contracts is central to business, the morality of promise keeping is central to business. Persons who are engaged in the making of contracts are essentially engaged in moral activity.

We can use the contract notion to establish the central thesis that business firms must admit that employees have certain rights which must be respected. The structure of the argument is as follows:

1. One person can enter a valid business contract only if the parties to the contract are responsible, autonomous adults.
2. If a person is a responsible, autonomous adult, then that person must view himself and be viewed by others as a moral agent.
3. A person can be a moral agent only if he has rights which he or she can press as claims against others.
4. Therefore, a person who enters a valid business contract is a person who has rights.
5. To recognize that a person has rights is to recognize that other persons entering the business contract have rights as well.
6. Therefore, a person entering a valid business contract must recognize the rights claims of the other contractees.

Adapted from Norman E. Bowie, "The Moral Contract between Employer and Employee," in *The Work Ethic in Business,* W. M. Hoffman and T. J. Wyly (Cambridge, Mass.: Oelgeschlager, Gunn, & Hair, 1981), pp. 195–202. Reprinted by permission.

Let us examine this argument in some detail. Premise 1 asks who the promisers and promisees are. They are persons who must be considered to be responsible, autonomous agents. In other words, such persons are free adults who can be held accountable for their actions. Generally speaking, contracts with children, mental defectives, and criminals are not binding. The ideal contract maker is a responsible, autonomous adult.

Premise 2 exploits the conceptual relationship between being an autonomous responsible individual and being a moral individual. In considering yourself as a responsible autonomous being, you must consider yourself to be a moral being—an agent who can make moral claims against others. After all, what must a person be like to be capable of being a moral agent? He or she must be a rational person capable of making his or her own choices and willing to live by the consequences of the choices. In other words, a moral being is a rational, autonomous agent—just the kind of being who is capable of entering into contracts. When you enter into a contract with another person, you are treating that person as a responsible, autonomous contract maker. From the perspective of morality, parties to a contract are equals. Hence, arguing from a Kantian perspective, you must treat other contract makers in a similar way. You must recognize them as moral agents as well.

Premise 3 is the key to the argument. It asserts that one can be a moral agent only if he or she has rights which can be pressed as claims against others. The essential concepts in a defense of this premise are responsibility, dignity, and rights. A responsible being is one who can make choices according to his or her own insights. He or she is not under the control of others. He or she does not live simply for another. In other words, a responsible person is a person who has dignity and self-respect. But a person has dignity and self-respect when asserting himself or herself in the world. He can only have dignity and self-respect if he can say such things as "I may be wrong, but I am entitled to my opinion," "I will not change the research results because such behavior would violate the code of professional ethics which I have voluntarily adopted," or "What I do on my free time is none of the company's business." In uttering these remarks, he is asserting rights claims since rights are moral entitlements. What I have been arguing is that rights must be presupposed to account for our use of moral language and moral concepts. The following quotation captures my point exactly:

> Rights, we are suggesting, are fundamental moral commodities because they enable us to stand up on our own two feet, "to look others in the eye," and to feel in some fundamental way the equal of anyone. To think of oneself as the holder of rights is not to be unduly but properly proud, to have that minimal self-respect that is necessary to be worthy of the love and esteem of others. Conversely, to lack the concept of oneself as a rights bearer is to be bereft of a significant element of human dignity. Without such a concept, we could not view ourselves as beings entitled to be treated as not simply means but ends as well.[1]

Let me review the argument thus far. A person can enter a valid business contract only if he or she is a responsible, autonomous adult. But a responsible, autonomous adult is the paradigm case of a moral agent. He can be a moral agent, however, only if he has rights that can be pressed against others. Therefore, a person who enters a valid business contract is a person who has rights.

The remainder of the argument is rather simple. Premise 5 represents nothing more than the straightforward application of the moral principle of universalizability. What counts as a reason in one case must count as a reason in relevantly similar cases. The argument for our conclusion that persons entering a business contract must recognize the rights claims of others is now established as both valid and sound. Since the relation between an employer and an employee is essentially a contractual one, the thesis of this paper that an employer must recognize that his employees have certain rights has been established. Our analysis has shown that a focal point for any discussion of worker dignity in the corporation must be employee rights.

What Rights Do Employees Have?

To establish the conclusion that contractees must recognize the rights of other contractees is one thing. To argue what such recognition would amount to is something else. In this section I shall propose one analysis of what would constitute appropriate recognition. Our focus on contracts will continue to serve us well. Contract makers must look upon each other as rights bearers. What human right is closely associated with contract making? Surely it is the right to liberty. One cannot conclude a valid contract unless one is free to do so. That the market economy presupposes at least a negative right to liberty is accepted by almost the entire spectrum of political opinion from libertarians to welfare democrats.

To move from the claim that every human has a right to liberty to a list of specifications as to what the right to liberty entails is a difficult enterprise. On the most general formulation the right to liberty is a right to noninterference. But obviously that right to noninterference is not open-ended. We are not free to do whatever we want. The classic specification of a right to liberty is provided by John Stuart Mill:

> . . . the sole end for which mankind are warranted individually or collectively in interfering with the liberty of action of any of their number is self protection. That the only purpose for which power can be rightfully exercised over any member of a civilized community, against his will, is to prevent harm to others. His own good, either physical or mental is not a sufficient warrant.[2]

The concept of harm provides a wide escape clause, however. Corporations could and, indeed, have argued that apparent violations of individual liberty are necessary to prevent harm to the corporation. On the basis of that argument companies have regulated the dress, social life, family life, and political opinions of employees. Any employee action which adversely affects profit "harms" the corporation and could be restricted. The problems are not just theoretical. Let me amplify this analysis with some practical questions raised by the senior vice president of a major life insurance company as we discussed the issue of employee rights. . . . Consider freedom of religious conscience. Suppose a life insurance company acquires a health insurance company. This health insurance company pays medical bills for abortions. The claims processor from the parent company is a member of a church which holds abortion to be a deadly sin. On grounds of religious conscience, he or she refuses to process claims for medical expense to cover abortion. Does the company have a right to fire this person, and if the company did, would it violate the employee's freedom of religious conscience? Specifically, the company must balance the harm caused if it denies an employee an opportunity to exercise one of his liberties against the harm done if it doesn't deny the employee that opportunity. Such balancing must often be done if the employee's exercise of his or her liberty would not violate Mill's condition. Does this mean that companies have unlimited justification for limiting employee freedom of action whenever profits are adversely affected? Certainly not.

Business activity takes place within a social framework. Society permits business to seek profits only insofar as business plays by the rules society establishes. Hence, business activity should conform to the laws and basic moral norms of society. Once this background condition is understood, a business cannot restrict the freedom of an employee when that restriction requires the employee to perform some act which violates either the law or a basic moral norm of society. An employee cannot be ordered to falsify experimental data relating to product safety or to discriminate against a fellow employee on the basis of race. The fact that the falsification of the data or the discrimination would improve profits is irrelevant.

But what about restrictions on individual liberty that do not violate fundamental moral norms or statutes of law? Some further specification of the extent of a person's right to liberty is provided by the Constitution. It is here that the work of such writers as David Ewing is so important. Introducing constitutional rights shows how additional constraints can be placed on business. Since business activity takes place within American society, presumably business activity should be conducted consistently with the Bill of Rights which specifies our right to liberty. For example, free speech and freedom of religious conviction are specific examples of the right to liberty embodied in the Constitution. As such, these rights should be honored by business practice.

But what about those difficult cases where the rights of employees clash with the rights of management? After all, the employer is a party to the contract between employer and employee and the contract argument works just as well in establishing employer rights as it does in establishing employee rights. For example, it is already an established point at law that an employer has a legal right to loyalty. . . .

Both the interpretation of rights claims and the adjudication among competing rights claims rest with the courts or with other appropriate procedural mechanisms—e.g., the collective bargaining process. Moral philosophers cannot provide correct solutions to conflicting rights claims—neither can anyone else for that matter. As employees begin to press these rights claims, management has only two viable responses. It can allow the court to resolve such matters or it can provide the mechanism for resolving the conflicts within the corporate decision-making process itself. . . .

Notes

1. Norman E. Bowie and Robert L. Simon *The Individual and the Political Order* (Englewood Cliffs, New Jersey: Prentice-Hall, 1977), p. 78.
2. John Stuart Mill, *On Liberty,* Currin V. Shield (ed.), (Indianapolis: Bobbs-Merrill, Library of Liberal Arts Edition, 1956), p. 13.

PROTECTING ALL EMPLOYEES AGAINST UNJUST DISMISSAL

Clyde W. Summers

Do Rights Need Protection?

The justification for legal protection should need no argument. Beyond the claim to equal treatment is the demand for simple justice and due process when an employee's valuable right is at stake—his right to his job. These are values to which management should be particularly sensitive when employee rights are involved. Guaranteeing individual rights and providing fair procedures to employees is a social obligation of management and it produces social values in which the employer shares.

Such legal protection is not just a hair shirt; it can contribute to effective management of the enterprise. The fact that an employee has legal recourse puts pressure on all levels of management to police their procedures, examine their decisions, and correct their mistakes. Hierarchical ratification cannot conceal or condone arbitrary actions at lower levels because the employee can demand justification of the discipline in an open hearing before an impartial tribunal. Of course, life is made more difficult for those lower-level supervisors who impose ill-considered or arbitrary discipline and also for those upper-level managers who cannot or will not control their subordinates.

But where management's policy is to treat employees fairly, the presence of legal protection reinforces that policy of fairness. In the long run, this presence reassures employees that they will be treated fairly and softens the image of management they may have as arbitrary or autocratic.

Corporate executives may argue that a law is unnecessary because they recognize and protect the right against arbitrary termination through their own internal procedures. The simple fact is that most companies have not recognized and protected that right.

To be sure, most employers try to be fair and believe that they are fair. But their employees often do not share that belief, for they understandably doubt that the facts will be fully developed and their interests fairly weighed in any process other than a full hearing before an impartial tribunal. In the absence of a collective agreement, few employers have been willing to allow their disciplinary actions to be tested before a neutral arbitrator; the usual "last resort" is the company personnel director. To my knowledge, only three employers provide outside arbitration as the final step in their complaint procedures—Lockheed, Trans World Airlines, and Michael Reese Hospital in Chicago.

From the viewpoint of management, the fairer its procedures and decisions, the more it gains from the availability of legal recourse to subordinates who claim they have been treated unfairly. A worker's failure to make use of an available legal remedy reveals the emptiness of his complaint; and an adjudication in favor of the company dispels doubts as to management's fairness.

Moreover, those companies that treat their employees fairly share some of the stigma created by those that do not, because employees and the public tend to put all of business in a single stereotype. Corporate management, by supporting protective legislation, would publicly affirm its unqualified commitment to fairness. By opposing such legislation, however, management would put in question its confidence in the fairness of its own procedures and the genuineness of its concern for employee rights.

The method of providing legal protection against unjust discipline can be quite simple and can avoid, or at least reduce, most of the problems that might be feared in such legislation. My proposal, in brief, is to create a statutory arbitration structure parallel to that provided by collective agreements. Employees unprotected by such agreements could appeal disciplinary action to this statutory system. . . .

WHAT IS THE LAW?

According to common law, in the absence of explicit contract provisions to the contrary, every employment is an employment "at will" and either the employer or the worker is free to terminate it at any time without notice or reason. As one court decision said, an employer may discharge an employee at any time "for good cause, for no cause, or even for cause morally wrong."[1] . . .

Statutory Repudiation

Whatever may have been the premises and reasoning used to justify the common law rule, Congress and some state legislatures have repudiated them in principle. The major legislative break with the common law came, of course, with the passage of the Wagner Act of 1935. It prohibited employers from discharging workers because of union membership or union activities and gave employees dismissed in violation of the statute the right to reinstatement with back pay. (Supervisors, however, were left unprotected.)

Since the passage of civil rights legislation, discrimination because of race, creed, nationality, sex, or age has been illegal. Although their primary focus is on hiring, promotion, and seniority practices, these laws apply equally to dismissals. In fact nearly one-third of all charges filed with the Equal Employment Opportunity Commission allege discriminatory dismissals.

Because these statutes create exceptions to the common law rule, they are being stretched to reach as many cases as possible. Employees who believe that their discharges are unjust attempt to characterize them as a form of discrimination. Thus charges of discrimination have been filed by long-haired and/or bearded male workers and by females who allegedly were fired for rejecting their male supervisors' sexual advances, gaining weight, getting married, getting pregnant, or refusing to shave their legs. Discharged workers over 45 years of age often claim discrimination because of age.

Federal and state laws protect war veterans and public employees in civil service against unjust dismissal. Many local government bodies, of course, provide job security under local charters or ordinances, and teachers are specially protected under tenure laws.

These statutes are important because they articulate a legal principle diametrically opposed to the common law rule. They also demonstrate that a cohesive interest group, such as unions or veterans, can influence the legislative negation of the common law rule. But random individuals who are unjustly terminated are isolated and without organizational or political voice. For them the harsh common law rule remains.

The Arbitration Law

Overshadowing these statutes is the body of law created by arbitration under collective agreements. In enforcing provisions of these agreements, arbitrators have established standards for what constitutes just cause for discipline, developed fair and efficient procedures for determining the guilt or innocence of accused employees, exercised responsibility for reviewing the appropriateness of penalties, and established effective remedies of reinstatement and back pay.

Four characteristics of the body of law should be noted here.

First, it has been built without elaborate or detailed definitions. Collective agreement language is typically terse, simply prohibiting discipline "without cause" or "without just cause." Even where these words are missing, an arbitrator will read them into the contract as implied by seniority clauses or grievance and arbitration provisions. As one arbitrator has said, "It is the part of the 'common law' of industrial relations—one of the tacit assumptions underlying all collective agreements—that an employer shall not arbitrarily exercise his power to discipline workers."

Second, arbitrators have built a comprehensive, integrated, and stable body of both substantive and procedural principles. The thousands of reported cases are not merely a mass of random decisions. Although what constitutes just cause inevitably depends on the industrial setting and the circumstances, arbitrators have achieved substantial consensus about underlying principles and many rules.

Although arbitrators do not consider other cases as binding precedents, they do feel bound by the general principles that have gained acceptability in the last five decades. Arbitration of discipline cases now consists largely of applying established principles to new problems and special-fact situations. The results are quite predictable, perhaps more predictable than most cases in the courts.

Third, protection against unjust discipline through arbitration has demonstrated its acceptability and workability in the eyes of management and employees. Collective agreements barring discipline except for just cause cover nearly 25 million workers from professional engineers to bank clerks to truck drivers. More telling, in negotiating new agreements the parties retain the "just cause" language with few or no elaborations or limitations; the parties continue to rely on arbitrators to develop general principles and apply them to particular cases.

Fourth, arbitration of discipline cases does provide needed security. A study by the American Arbitration Association shows that in more than half the discharge cases the employee was reinstated, either with or without back pay.[2] Where the penalty was less than discharge, it was reversed or modified in 44% of the cases.

This, however, is but a small portion of the actual protection obtained because of the availability of arbitration. Employers who know that their actions are subject to review will avoid unjustified discipline in the first instance. They articulate reasonable rules of conduct, establish fair procedures, make careful investigations, and develop other controls to increase fairness. After an employee is disciplined, the availability of arbitration gives the employer an occasion and incentive to reconsider whether the discipline was for just cause. For every injustice remedied by arbitration, many are circumvented or corrected without it.

The most important contribution of arbitration discipline is the life and meaning it has given to the principle that an employee has a legally protected right to his job—a right he cannot be deprived of without just cause. Furthermore, the value of this asset to the employee increases with length of service. In a discharge case, the offense must be serious, or often repeated, and the proof of guilt must be clear. The burden is on the employer to justify depriving the worker of his "property" right to his job.

A Practical Proposal

But the common law rule remains. No one can now seriously contend that it is either necessary or appropriate to the efficient and orderly functioning of modern business. The protection that 30% of our work force is now given has earned acceptance as an essential element of a tolerable and humane employment relationship.

The solution is readily apparent: establish by statute the right of employees not to be disciplined, except for just cause, and channel the adjudication of cases arising under the law into the arbitration process. The statute need not—indeed ought not—attempt to define "just cause," for the existing body of arbitration cases has given these words a workably defined content while allowing flexibility to fit special circumstances and meet changed conditions.

Channeling the cases into the arbitration process would not be difficult, particularly if legislation is at the state level, as it should be to maintain simplicity and permit variety and experimentation. The statute need only provide for claims arising under the statute to be submitted to arbitration; and if the parties are unable to agree on an arbitrator, one would be selected from a list maintained by the state mediation service or some other state agency. A number of state mediation services, such as in Connecticut and New York, already maintain panels from which parties to a dispute can select an arbitrator or from which the mediation service can appoint one.

There are, however, some subsidiary questions to be answered. None goes to the core of the proposal, and for each there is a range of acceptable solutions in the framework of the proposal. Here are the most difficult questions.

Who will bear the costs? The administrative costs and arbitrators' fees should be paid by the state, just as the costs of maintaining courts and paying judges' salaries are borne by the state. Connecticut and some other states provide arbitration at public expense, and in Pennsylvania panels of lawyers for arbitrating small claims are paid by the state. Because discharged employees are out of work, they have a strong claim to be free of the costs of providing tribunals to vindicate their rights.

However, the procedure might be burdened with frivolous claims when the discipline is clearly justified or the penalty is insubstantial. For this reason, the costs of using the procedure should be enough to discourage such claims. A possible solution would be to assess each party a flat fee, such as $100, or to adjust the fee to the employee's earnings, such as one week's take-home pay, not to exceed $250.

Who will represent the employee? He should be free to choose whomever he wants to represent him in the arbitration, and the proceedings should be kept informal so that a lawyer is not necessary. The employee should pay for his own representative, but an indigent employee should have access to legal assistance on the same basis as in any other civil proceeding.

What employees will be covered? While all employees should be protected, there are three limitations:

1. An employer needs a probationary period for judging the suitability of a worker, and the worker has limited claim to protection until he has been employed long enough to gain a sense of permanence in the job. Different probationary periods for different kinds of jobs might be appropriate and desirable, but defining the jobs would probably be so difficult that it would be more practical to fix a uniform probationary period, such as six months.

2. Small companies could be exempted at the outset for administrative reasons. While there is no reason in principle for this, social legislation is

frequently applicable only to businesses with a minimum number of employees. Administrative considerations might justify limiting this statute to employers of 10 persons or more, with the expectation that the number would shortly be reduced.

3. Top-level employees should probably be exempted, but any exceptions must be narrowly defined. Exclusion of all those defined as supervisors under the labor relations acts would be inappropriate inasmuch as that exclusion is based on a potential conflict of interest in union-management relations which is irrelevant to an unjust dismissal statute.

More important, foremen, lower- and middle-management, and professional and administrative personnel are most in need of statutory protection. They are seldom covered by collective agreements, usually prefer not to unionize, and are often prohibited from organizing. The German and Swedish statutes protect all employees up to the level of top management; the British statute has no cutoff but excludes employees who have fixed-term contracts of two years or more. Both of these approaches have proved satisfactory and workable.

The cutoff line could be drawn in a number of ways. The excluded group could be defined as those officers with general management responsibility, the approach used in the German and Swedish statutes. The excluded group could be defined as those having fixed-term contracts of two years or more, as under the British statute. Or the company could designate those exempt but must limit the number to 1% of all employees (with special provision for smaller companies). Where and how the cutoff line is drawn are not crucial to the proposal so long as it excludes only top management.

What will constitute discipline or dismissal? The statute should not, of course, prevent an employer from ordering layoffs, transfers, or demotions to meet economic and production needs. But the selection of a particular employee to bear the brunt of such a change might be based on his conduct and be punitive in character. (Collective agreements largely avoid this problem by use of seniority provisions.)

One consequence of the new legislation will be the obligation of companies to establish some objective standard for selecting the employees affected by economic adjustments. It need not be a strict seniority standard; it might include such factors as training, breadth of skill, productivity, or family responsibilities.

But the factors must be relevant, capable of objective measurement, and systematically applied. Otherwise, those laid off might accuse the employer of acting on hidden motives, and if the arbitrator were unable to find a rational basis for the selection, he would likely find that the selection amounted to dismissal without just cause.

Objections to a Statute

Opponents of this statutory proposal argue that just cause is difficult to define and almost impossible to prove; that employers would be required to retain marginal or unproductive employees, or employees who are personally incompatible; that employers would be hobbled in maintaining discipline and managing the enterprise; and that arbitrators with no experience in industry would be second-guessing management decisions. These arguments could be raised with equal force against just cause clauses in collective agreements, and just cause clauses have been generally accepted by management for more than 40 years.

Four objections, however, do warrant discussion. First is the objection that statutory protection would require creation of yet another government agency with its costs and encumbrances. This plan, however, requires little administrative machinery. In most states the functions of maintaining a panel of arbitrators and naming arbitrators from it could be added to existing mediation and arbitration agencies.

The second objection is that a statute would produce a flood of cases that the machinery could not handle. There will, of course, be a substantial number of cases because three times as many people will be protected as at present. Also, there will be no grievance procedure to screen and settle cases prior to arbitration.

But whether the frequency of cases taken to arbitration under the statute will be greater or less than under collective agreements is unclear. Most employees will be slower to appeal minor penalties because of both the cost and the lack of union reinforcement. Unlike the union, they will not go to arbitration to establish a principle or to satisfy political pressures.

Even when substantial penalties are involved, an individual who is guilty may be less ready to pursue the case at his own expense (the $100 plus any lawyer's fee) than to press the union to demand arbitration. Although unions can settle discharge cases in the grievance procedure, many unions feel a moral or political obligation to carry all discharge cases to arbitration.

An indication of the potential number of cases may be the number that have occurred under the unemployment insurance laws. An employee who is discharged for misconduct is disqualified from benefits. He can appeal to a state board on the grounds that he was not guilty of misconduct or that the discharge was for other reasons. On the basis of the limited data available, I estimate that there is about one such appeal each year for every 2,000 employees.

A third objection, sometimes voiced by management, is that arbitrators unduly favor the employees at the company's expense. Some decisions will, of course, go against management; but this would be true regardless of what tribunal makes the decision. Management may feel that arbitrators tend to give too much weight to the employee's rights and too little weight to management's needs; but arbitrators have more knowledge of the competing interests and more experience in judging them than any other tribunal.

The most telling evidence in favor of arbitration is the fact that employers with 25 million employees covered by collective agreements have entrusted these decisions to arbitrators. Even those employers who, from time to time, complain about the "softness" of arbitrators in discipline cases do not propose that these cases should be submitted to some other tribunal such as the courts or the National Labor Relations Board.

The fourth objection, one raised by unions, is that a statute will discourage labor organization because workers would be less inclined to join unions if they were provided with the same protection that unions offer. Security against dismissal, however, is not the only clause in the labor agreement, and not necessarily the most important one for many employees.

The fact that public employees have statutory protection against unjust dismissal has not visibly impeded organization; on the contrary, it has made them less fearful of reprisals for joining unions. Even if the objection were sound, however, the right of a worker to his job and the right not to be unjustly disciplined are so basic that an individual ought not to be required to join a union to obtain protection of those rights.

Is Voluntary Action Sufficient?

There remains the question whether companies could eliminate the need for legislation by improving their internal complaint procedures. Two points are important here:

1. No solution short of a full hearing before a neutral tribunal will give employees adequate assurance that their appeals would be fairly decided. Moreover, the tribunal must be perceived by the worker as being genuinely neutral and independent. The arbitrator selected by the employer will be viewed as management's man. If the company can veto the worker's selection, the veto will be seen as a denial of a fair hearing. The employer must delegate ultimate authority for selection of an arbitrator to some outside neutral agency.

2. Although some employers may be prepared to establish such an appeals procedure, the great majority have not. Even those companies that do establish adequate procedures still bear the social obligation to support legislation that will require standards of due process and fairness for all workers.

There is no reason to continue this painful paradox in our industrial life. A simple solution is at hand by which we can give to all employees the same protection now enjoyed by those covered by collective agreements. We do not need to define just cause; we already have an established body of law and accepted principles. We do not need to devise a special procedure; we already have the tested procedure of arbitration. We do not need to establish a system of courts or to appoint judges; we already have a cadre of trained arbitrators on call with procedures for assigning them to cases.

The problems to be solved are peripheral and readily susceptible to solution. The objections, on close examination, are based on an unwillingness to give up a small portion of autonomy in return for delivering justice.

Notes

1. H. G. Wood, *Master and Servant,* § 134 (1877).
2. American Arbitration Association, *Procedural and Substantive Aspects of Labor-Management* (New York, 1954), p. 23.

FREEDOM OF EXPRESSION IN THE CORPORATE WORKPLACE

Robert F. Ladenson

In a novel entitled *Scientists and Engineers: The Professionals Who Are Not,* the author, Louis V. McIntire, presents a highly negative picture of life as an employee in a large private business corporation.[1] Characters in the novel inveigh against management favoritism, cheating inventors out of bonuses, and taking unfair advantage of employees in employment contracts. The fictional employer bears a striking resemblance to DuPont, the company for which McIntire worked as a chemical engineer from 1956 through 1971, the year the book was published. In 1972 McIntire was fired.[2]

Should employees of large private business corporations be free to speak out on any subject without fear of dismissal or other sanctions even when they level harsh criticism at their corporate employers? In this paper I will argue that they should for reasons that closely parallel one of the fundamental bases for the principle of freedom of expression pertaining to the relation between individuals and the state. An important and controversial consequence of this view is that corporate employees should be free to speak without fear of sanctions even when they make false allegations that lead to a decline in either productivity or profits.

One can begin such an analysis by contrasting two basically different ways of making out the case for freedom of expression in corporations, which I will refer to respectively as the volunteer public guardian and the fundamental value of liberty approaches. The first mode of argument, the volunteer public guardian approach, sees the case for free expression of corporate employees as having to do primarily with associated potential benefits to society from increased exposure of corporate corruption, waste, and negligence. The following quotation from *Where the Law Ends* by Christopher Stone exemplifies this approach.

> . . . anyone concerned with improving the exchange of information between the corporation and the outside world must pay serious regard to the so called whistleblower. The corporate work force in America, in the aggregate, will always know more than the best planned government inspection system we are likely to finance. Traditionally workers have kept their mouths shut about ''sensitive'' matters that come to their attention. There are any number of reasons for this, ranging from peer group expectations, to the employee's more solid fears of being fired . . .
>
> This means that if ethical whistleblowing is to be encouraged some special protections and perhaps even incentives will have to be afforded the whistleblower.[3]

From Robert Ladenson, ''Freedom of Expression in the Corporate Workplace,'' in *Business and Professional Ethics,* eds., J. Ellin, W. Robison, and M. Pritchard (Crescent Manor, N.J.: Humana Press, 1982), pp. 146–152. Reprinted by permission.

The second mode of argument for freedom of expression of corporate employees, the fundamental value of liberty approach, does not focus upon the immediate social benefits to be gained as a result of a more open atmosphere in corporations. Instead, it suggests that we should look upon the value of freedom of expression in the corporate workplace as grounded in basic considerations of social morality. Such an outlook is reflected in the quotation below from David Ewing's book *Freedom Inside The Organization*.

> A classic formulation of the philosophy of the First Amendment was given decades ago by Supreme Court Justice Louis D. Brandeis. Although he was commenting upon free speech in the political area, his observations would seem to be equally valid for the governance of corporations . . . Brandeis, wrote: "Those who won our independence knew that . . . it is hazardous to discourage thought, hope, and imagination . . . They eschewed silence coerced by law—the argument of force in its worst form . . .
> . . . many executives in business and government find (the above view) . . . "unrealistic" when it comes to employee speech. In the name of discipline, they feel that free thinking about an organization's policies should be suppressed. In this respect, if no other, they are in league with radical left philosopher Herbert Marcuse who argues that free speech cannot be justified when it becomes too distracting.[4]

We have then two kinds of arguments in support of freedom of expression in corporations. The volunteer public guardian approach stresses immediate benefits to society that will flow presumably from making the climate in corporations more conducive to free speech. The fundamental value of liberty approach, on the other hand, looks to basic principles of social morality akin to those that underlie the First Amendment in its most familiar applications. These two kinds of arguments differ in an important way brought out sharply by considering the question "What should happen to whistleblowers who turn out to be wrong?"

Following the volunteer public guardian approach one would treat this question by performing a comparative analysis of the social benefits and costs associated with corporate whistleblowing. As mentioned above, on the benefit side one can cite the increased exposure of corporate waste, corruption, and negligence. On the cost side, however, one must include the possibility of a general decline in productivity stemming from decreased efficiency as a result of disruptions in the corporate decision making and administrative routines. In addition, where whistleblowers are mistaken in their allegations about the safety or quality of a product the affected corporations may unfairly suffer a decline in profits.

A social cost-benefit analysis of corporate dissent not only requires attaching weights to the above factors, but also necessitates an assessment of both the prevalence of anti-social corporate behavior and the nature of its consequences. A person who regards such behavior not only as commonplace but also as gravely harmful would advocate extensive protection for corporate dissenters, holding that the costs associated with mistaken allegations they might make count for relatively little in the balance. On the other hand, if serious corporate misbehavior is looked upon as the exception rather than the rule, then a different view of the matter becomes appropriate. Indeed, depending upon how exceptional one regards it, and upon how heavily one weighs the costs associated with corporate dissent, it might be reasonable to suggest that such dissent should be thought of on analogy with the common law rules in regard to citizen's arrests. Specifically, a person making a citizen's arrest avoids tort liability for unlawful detention only if the person he or she arrested *actually* committed a felony. Reasonable belief is not a defense.[5] By analogy, someone who regards corporate misconduct as exceptional might say that freedom of expression in corporations should only extend to dissenters who turn out to be right.

The prevalence of serious corporate misbehavior, and the nature of its social consequences, are empirical issues lying beyond the scope of this paper.[6] The point to be noted here, however, is that when one makes the case for freedom of expression in corporations by way of the volunteer public guardian approach, the question of *how much* freedom corporate employees should have involves a weighing of costs and benefits which essentially depends upon one's beliefs about these empirical matters.

By contrast, the fundamental value of liberty approach eschews appeal to any such considerations. If freedom of expression, conceived of as a fundamental value, extends to the employee-employer relationship in a corporation, then questions about its nature and scope cannot be settled through balancing immediate social benefits and costs. Moreover, if a coherent philosophical account of the principle of freedom of expression pertaining to citizens and the state can be extended reasonably to cover the relationship between employers and employees then we have a short answer to our question about the whistleblower who turns out to be wrong. Such an individual can no more justifiably be made subject to sanctions by his or her employer than a citizen can justifiably be punished at the hands of the government simply for expressing incorrect views.

A crucial question for the fundamental value of liberty approach then is whether such an extension can be made. This question, in turn, requires a brief review of some important points about freedom of expression. To begin, the primary task for a philosophical defense of it can be stated in the following way. Acts of expression can, at times, lead to very undesirable consequences, consequences which when caused in any other way would be regarded as so grave that behavior causing them ought to be legally prevented. Nonetheless, for those who regard the right to freedom of expression as fundamental, even when its exercise leads to certain of these undesirable consequences, limitations upon freedom of expression are still considered unjustifiable. How one can defend such an outlook must be explained.

The search for such an explanation inevitably leads to the arguments advanced respectively in chapters two and three of John Stuart Mill's classic essay *On Liberty*. Boiled down to essentials, Mill contends in chapter two that countenancing routine governmental interference with the expression of beliefs and attitudes by citizens would only make sense if we believed it possible to identify infallible, perfectly benevolent human beings and to put them into positions of political power. Since, of course, this cannot be done it follows that if governmental authorities routinely prevent the expression of beliefs and attitudes on the basis of their content the result will be inevitably a widespread acceptance of seriously erroneous viewpoints. What is worse, this benighted condition of society will persist in all likelihood over many generations because the most obvious means of overcoming it, free discussion, will not be available. The value attached to freedom of expression may thus be treated as fundamental in view of the extraordinary social interest its acknowledgement serves—namely, the avoidance of social action predicated upon mistaken beliefs over the long run.

The foregoing argument constitutes a formidable case for freedom of citizens from governmental interference to express their beliefs and attitudes. It does not, however, apply in an obvious way to the relations between corporate employees and their employers. The argument calls attention to the grave long run social harm that stems from giving a *single* individual or group power to regulate expression and hence to control thought. Now while corporate employers can, and undoubtedly often do, exercise substantial coercive force to discourage their employees from freely expressing themselves it would seem that no one corporation could exercise the kind of centralized power to control thought of which a strong government would be capable. Accordingly, Mill's argument in chapter two of *On Liberty* does not go to establish that freedom of expression should exist in private business corporations.

The situation is quite different, however, with regard to Mill's line of reasoning in chapter three entitled "Of Individuality As One Of The Elements Of Well Being." To grasp the essentials of this argument one must first concentrate upon the passage below.

> . . . to conform to custom merely *as* custom does not educate or develop in (a person) any of the qualities which are the distinctive endowment of a human being. The human faculties of perception, judgment, discriminative feeling, mental activity, and even moral preference are exercised only in making a choice. He who does anything because it is the custom makes no choice. He gains no practice in discerning or in desiring what is best . . .
>
> He who lets the world, or his own portion of it choose his plan of life for him has no need of any faculty other than the ape-like one of imitation. He who chooses his plan for himself employs all his faculties. He must use observation to see, reasoning and judgment to foresee, activity to gather materials for decision, and when he has decided, firmness and self-control to hold to his deliberate decision. And these qualities he requires and exercises exactly in proportion as the part of his conduct which he determines according to his own judgment and feelings is a large one.[7]

In chapter three of *On Liberty* Mill can thus be thought of as arguing in the following way. Certain abilities and capacities, such as observation, judgment, discrimination, firmness of will, and so forth are the distinctive endowment of a human being. These abilities and capacities, which Mill takes to be the elements of what he terms "individuality," make it possible to discern and desire what is best. Thus, in the proportion to which people have them they become both more valuable to themselves and potentially more valuable to others.[8] According to any reasonable conception of the good for society it should be a primary function of social arrangements to facilitate everyone's cultivating his or her individuality, as understood above, to the greatest possible degree. Individuality, so understood, however, consists in the possession of a variety of different abilities and capacities all of which can only be developed by exercising them. Without freedom of expression, however, the likelihood for such development on a large scale is extremely low. Accordingly, even if freedom of expression sometimes leads to serious harm, this must be borne as a cost of making it possible for a society to develop in which large numbers of people cultivate their individuality.[9]

Unlike the line of reasoning in chapter two of *On Liberty,* the foregoing argument directly applies to the situation of employees in a large private business corporation. Mill contends here that without freedom of expression a person's individuality remains uncultivated; and from both an individual and a social perspective the development of this trait should be accorded primary importance. The undesirable condition associated with a denial of free expression to which Mill calls our attention in chapter three—that is, the stifling of individuality—can obtain when coercive interference with the expression of beliefs and attitudes stems from a multitude of independent sources. Accordingly, that restrictions upon expression in the corporate workplace tend to have precisely the above effect would appear to be a compelling ground for holding they should not exist.[10]

It is important to note that Mill's arguments in *On Liberty* do not purport to establish the unjustifiability of any kind of governmental restriction upon expression. Mill's conclusion should be understood as the claim that it is never justifiable for authorities to interfere with the expression of a given thought simply on the ground that such interference is necessary to prevent either (a) harm to certain individuals which consists in their coming to have false beliefs as a result of the expression of that thought, or (b) harm that is the consequence of certain acts which people perform because the thought in question caused them to believe those acts are worth performing. Looked at in the above way Mill's arguments pertain solely to governmental interference with the expression of beliefs and attitudes based upon their content.

Holding that freedom of expression should exist in the corporate workplace thus commits one to the view that content-based restrictions upon employee speech are never justifiable. Even if what an employee says disrupts the normal corporate decision making and administrative routines, this price should be paid in order to foster the development of individuality. By the same token, even though an employee's words can harm the reputation of a product unfairly, this no more justifies prior restraints upon employee speech than the possibility that what someone says may result in unfair rejection by the public of a particular governmental policy justifies imposing prior restraints upon individual citizens or the press. To be sure, declines in productivity and unfair losses of profits are serious matters. But what makes the principle of freedom of expression significant is precisely that it requires important considerations such as these to be subordinated to the interest in maintaining an open atmosphere for the expression of beliefs and attitudes.

To argue against content restrictions upon expression by corporate employees, however, does not rule out regarding other kinds of restrictions as justified. Indeed, it seems to me that most of the situations in which governmental interferences with expression are generally considered justifiable, and hence not violations of the principle of freedom of expression, have analogues in the corporate employer-employee situation. For example, consider the case of an employee who voices his dissent continuously during working hours, haranguing other employees so as to make it impossible for them to carry on their work. Sanctions of some kind or other seem reasonable here. This case, however, appears to fall under a rubric similar to the well entrenched principle of First Amendment case law, that governmental restrictions which go to time, place, and manner, rather than content, will be upheld so long as they are reasonable.[11] That is, employees should be able to say anything they want, but not necessarily at any time or place or in any manner they choose. Just as in the realm of First Amendment adjudication, however, restrictions in these regards must not be so arbitrary or vague as to be nothing more than thinly veiled subterfuges for regulating the content of employee speech.[12]

To consider another case, what about the disclosure of trade secrets? The issues here appear to be similar to those that arise in connection with officially classified information. The extensive and complicated governmental system for classifying information that has emerged since World War Two has increasingly come to be viewed as incompatible with the basic principles of a free society.[13] Insofar as the rationale for such a system is simply to "prevent sensitive information from falling into the wrong hands," one can justify classifying virtually anything. The classification of information by governmental bodies may not be completely unjustified from the standpoint of the principle of freedom of expression. Nonetheless, it would seem that a legitimate standard for designating material as classified, at the very least, must impose strict limitations as to scope and duration.[14] An analogous proposition appears to hold in the corporate realm. Perhaps some restrictions upon employees from disclosing corporate secrets are consistent with the principle of freedom of expression. The only credible examples I can conceive of, however, would pertain to such matters as the particular figure to be bid on a government contract, the precise formula for a chemical product about to be submitted for a patent, and so forth. In these cases it seems possible to frame relatively narrow restrictions upon expression that would protect the interests of corporate employers without by implication according these employers an unlimited authority to control the content of employee speech subject to no scope or duration restrictions.

Some restrictions upon employee speech thus can be justified. The important point to emphasize, however, is that if the foregoing analysis has merit then employees should not be prevented or deterred from expressing themselves for reasons having to do with the content of their beliefs and attitudes. The cultivation of individuality fostered by freedom of expression counts for more than almost anything else over the long run. It thus counts for more than the interests that may be compromised by opening up the atmosphere in corporations.

Notes

1. Louis V. McIntire and Marion B. McIntire, *Scientists and Engineers: The Professionals Who Are Not* (Lafayette, La.: Arcola Pub. Co., 1971).
2. Nicholas Wade, "Protection Sought for Satirists and Whistleblowers," *Science,* Vol. 182. (Dec. 7, 1973), pp. 1002-3.
3. Christopher Stone, *Where The Law Ends* (New York: Harper and Row, 1975), p. 213.
4. David Ewing, *Freedom Inside The Organization* (New York: Dutton, 1977), pp. 97-98.
5. For a general discussion of citizen's arrests see William F. Prosser, *Law of Torts,* St. Paul: West Pub. Co. (1971), pp. 42-49.
6. In this regard the following study is interesting—James Olson, "Engineer Attitudes Toward Professionalism, Employment, and Social Responsibility," *Professional Engineer,* Vol. 42 (August, 1972), pp. 30-32.
7. *On Liberty* (Currin V. Shields, ed) Library of Liberal Arts Edition, pp. 71-72.
8. *On Liberty,* pp. 76-77.
9. The foregoing interpretation of Mill's argument in chapter three of *On Liberty* departs admittedly from the received view. I have defended this interpretation in my article entitled "Mill's Conception of Individuality" *Social Theory and Practice,* Vol. 4 (1977), pp. 167-82. I also suggested in an article entitled "A Theory of Personal Autonomy" *Ethics,* Vol. 86 (1975), pp. 30-48 that Dewey defends the principle of freedom of expression in a manner similar to Mill's approach in chapter three.
10. William H. Whyte's classic portrait of corporate employees in *The Organization Man* (New York: Simon and Shuster, 1956) provides a compelling illustration of the diverse ways in which corporate life dampens the individual spirit.
11. A good review of the pertinent cases in this regard can be found in Gerald Gunther, *Individual Rights in Constitutional Law,* (Mineola, N.Y.: The Foundation Press, 1976), pp. 740-804.
12. In this regard see Lovell v. Griffin 303 U.S. 444 (1938), Schneider v. State 308 U.S. 147 (1938), Hague v. C.I.O. 307 U.S 496 (1939), Cox v. New Hampshire 312 U.S. 569 (1941), Saia v. New York 334 U.S. 558 (1948), Kunz v. New York 340 U.S. 290 (1951), and Cohen v. California 403 U.S. 15 (1971).
13. See Benedict Karl Zobrist II, "Reform in the Classification and Declassification of National Security Information: Nixon Executive Privilege Order 11652," Vol. 59 No. 1 *Iowa Law Review* (1973), pp. 110-143.
14. See Executive Order 11652: Classification of National Security Information and Material (*Federal Register,* Vol. 37 No. 4 March 10, 1972).

TRADE AND CORPORATE SECRECY

Sissela Bok

PROTECTION AGAINST BETRAYAL AND THEFT

I believe I undertook amongst other things
not to disclose any trade secrets. Well,
I am not going to.

Joseph Conrad, *Heart of Darkness*

The evils exposed in *Heart of Darkness* were indeed no trade secrets, though they had been kept secret and did concern trade, and though their disclosure might well destroy that trade. Except in an extended and sinister sense, they were far from the most widely cited legal definition of "trade secret":[1]

> any formula, pattern, device, or compilation of information which is used in one's business and which gives him an opportunity to obtain an advantage over competitors who do not know or use it.

Trade secrecy is the most frequent claim by those who want to protect secrets in business—legitimate secrets as well as many forms of abuse and exploitation. To call something a trade secret is to invoke for it the protections due property, in particular that of keeping it hidden from others. I shall consider the exercise of trade secrecy, its rationale, and the limits to the protection this rationale supports against the background of corporate secrecy more generally; and weigh the claims to secrecy against those of government agencies, competitors, employees, or others for disclosure of certain kinds of information.

Like property, trade secrets can be bought and sold, stolen and recaptured, even lost for good if their owner dies without passing them on. But unlike most property, trade secrets can also be betrayed. The great clandestine wars over trade secrecy have been fought with every means of seduction, bribery, and threat precisely in order to induce or prevent betrayal. . . .

BORROWED FINERY

Those who argue for trade secrecy usually appeal, at least implicitly, to one or more of five premises: personal autonomy, property, confidentiality, incentives to invest, and national security. How persuasive are these arguments? And what are their limitations?

The appeal to *personal autonomy* is fundamental for the support of individual claims to control over trade secrets. It invokes the individual's

Adapted from Sissela Bok, *Secrets: On the Ethics of Concealment and Revelation*. (New York: Random House, Inc., 1983).

legitimate claim to control over secrecy and openness about thoughts, ideas, inventions, and plans. Without such control, I have argued, personal identity might itself be threatened. Someone who cherishes a secret recipe or who is working in secret on a scientific formula or a new design for a machine may see its secrecy as of the highest personal importance, and efforts to discover the secret as invasive in the extreme. The invasiveness of such action is especially blatant when the secret exists in thought only. To try to wrench it loose by force or trickery is then an inroad, not only on secrecy, but on basic liberty; and a society that condoned such inroads in pursuit of trade secrets—as of all others—would be intolerable.

The presumption is therefore strong against overriding such personal autonomy over secrets. But it is not absolute: with trade secrets as with others, concealment may present such dangers that outside pressure to reveal them becomes necessary. If, for instance, someone is known to keep secret the composition of a desperately needed drug that could save the lives of many, the presumption shifts, and the claim to personal autonomy over the secret loses its force.

The claim to personal autonomy over trade secrets, moreover, cannot simply be extrapolated to collective autonomy. Yet the two are often linked in arguments concerning trade secrecy. Thus Warren and Brandeis urged, in their 1890 article on privacy, that "the right to be let alone" should apply to trade secrets as well as to more personal matters.[2] The authors may have been thinking primarily of the individual entrepreneur or inventor, rather than of large firms; and they could perhaps not have foreseen trade secrecy on the scale now practiced by the multi-national corporations. Other writers have suggested extending privacy law to cover even such conglomerates, but have, so far, failed to convince courts to take such a step.[3] Neither the concept of privacy nor that of personal autonomy can, by themselves, easily be expanded to fit both the individual entrepreneur and the large corporation.*

Does the second appeal, to *property,* provide the necessary further support for extensive trade secrecy? This argument asserts the right to guard one's property as one sees fit, and through secrecy if need be. Many take the right to property to be so fundamental as to need no justification. Yet here again, the legitimacy of extrapolating from individual to collective ownership of trade secrets requires scrutiny. And no matter what one concludes in that regard, the connection of trade secrecy and property raises two further questions: should secret knowledge necessarily count as property? And does owning something entail the legitimacy of keeping it secret? Consider the relationship of secrecy, knowledge, and property in the following two cases, one hypothetical, the other recently decided in an American court:[5]

---

*This is not to say that there are no arguments for group autonomy; merely that they cannot be extrapolated from individual autonomy in the context of trade secrecy. To be sure, no firm or government agency could function if every new idea, every tentative plan or draft, were under constant outside scrutiny. I discuss this problem in Chapter XIII.[4]

Suppose that, in a ''state of nature'' a group of people live near a river and subsist on fish, which they catch by hand, and berries. There is great difficulty in catching fish by hand. Berries are however fairly plentiful. There are bits of metal lying around and I discover how to make one of them into a fishhook. With this invention I quadruple my catch of fish. My neighbours cannot discover the knack and I decline to tell them. They press me to lend them the fishhook or to give them lessons in acquiring the technique. I have however acquired Western notions of property law. . . . I point out that I have a just title to the fishhook . . . .

A chemical company had developed a new process for making methanol, after extensive secret research. Expecting the new product to be highly profitable, company executives decided to build a plant for its manufacture. At one point during the construction, an unfinished roof exposed the interior design of the plant in such a way that a trained eye could detect the nature of the secret process. Spokesmen for the company later brought suit, claiming that a competitor had arranged to photograph the plant from an airplane at the time when the process was discernable. The spokesmen alleged wrongful discovery of a trade secret. The court held the competitor culpable, and the company entitled to relief.

If asked, both the inventor of the fishhook and the guardians of the manufacturing process might argue that they are entitled to keep others from benefiting from their knowledge; that they have a property right in it, and therefore the right to refuse handing it over to them, teaching them its use, even a right, in the case of the chemical company, to prevent competitors from flying across the plant under construction. Their arguments exhibit both the seeming naturalness of the trade secrecy rationale's appeal to property and its weaknesses. . . .

Whatever one's view of property, the two examples raise a further question: should knowledge about how to make fishhooks and how to plan industrial processes count as property in the first place? Is there not a difference, in this respect, between saying, No, you can't use my fishhook, and saying, No, I won't let you find out how to make one to use for yourself? Trade secrets are often odd aspirants to the status of property. They may or may not remain out of reach of the knowledge of others; but one cannot always claim, on grounds of ownership, to have some entitlement to keep them thus unknown. I have argued . . . that the claim to ownership for secrets is often spurious, no matter how legitimate one may be in guarding them. Certainly company records of trade secrets or machinery embodying them constitute property. To purloin them is theft; but was it theft in the same way to fly over and photograph the chemical plant?

Still another question remains, even for those who would regard all such efforts at discovery as theft, and all trade secrets as property: do the rights that come with property go so far as to justify secrecy? Some have argued that the Lockian view of property establishes a moral right to exclude others from its use or benefit therefrom, that this right is transmissible from one person to another, and from one generation to the next. This view of property rights as exclusive, permanent, and transmissible is by no means self-evident. Those who believe it ubiquitous or "natural" betray as limited and naive a perspective as that of the many nineteenth-century thinkers who believed that all cultures once exhibited "primitive communism."[6]

Few practices of property guarantee exclusivity under all circumstances. Someone who turns out to have the only uncontaminated well in an epidemic will not be able to claim the right to exclude others from its use. But even if exclusivity were the rule, it would not automatically entail the right to secrecy for what one owns. For some kinds of property, secrecy would require intolerably high fences, or physical restraints on bypassers, or deceit of various kinds.

Why might secrecy be allowed as an extension of such exclusivity more often for trade secrets than for other kinds of property? The argument for doing so stems from the peculiar nature of trade secrets. Unlike most forms of property, trade secrets are of an ephemeral nature. They may be lost merely from being photographed or even seen; they may evaporate as a result of a glance at a facial expression at the moment a formula is guessed at. Control over exclusivity, permanence, and transmissibility is more fragile for trade secrets than for other property; unusual secrecy is therefore needed to guard them.

The special need for secrecy in such cases is clear; but the property argument does not suffice to justify it. This argument cannot easily accommodate both individual and collective trade secrecy; nor does it establish all trade secrets *as* property; nor, finally, does it always legitimate the use of secrecy in the protection of trade secrets.

A third argument, that of *confidentiality,* is often brought in to shore up or even to replace the limited and indirect supports that claims to liberty and property offer. It holds that trade secrets, once shared, should be kept by those who have promised to do so, simply because of the promise itself. The word "confidentiality" in this context can be confusing, for it refers both to promises about trade secrets and to the confidentiality owed employees concerning their personal files. In the first of these two uses, unlike the second, confidentiality has no extra binding force apart from that of promises in general. It is not premised on the personal nature of the information conveyed (except through some vast and sentimentalized identification between persons and their property). One does not confess to trade secrets as one might to personal ones; and the promise of secrecy about a formula or a design is different from that about illness or family rifts.

Confidentiality about trade secrets may bring into play loyalty of a different kind from that in professional relationships: loyalty to the company. Such loyalty may be entirely appropriate; but like all practices of secrecy it becomes morally problematic when it brings individuals into the secret who are thereby hampered, injured, or rendered less free. This can happen when employees, sometimes even without prior knowledge or consent, learn facts which make it more difficult for them to leave their place of employment; or when a condition of employment is that any inventions or innovations by the employee will be the property of the employer. . . .

A great many companies in Europe and the United States and elsewhere now ask employees to sign some agreement to protect patent and trade secret rights. Employees may be asked not to accept work with competitors for a specified time after they leave the company, or not to use certain kinds of "know-how" they have acquired in the company, or not to disclose company secrets of a wide variety. And their mobility will be affected from the outset whenever potential employers fear that hiring persons who have signed such a contract may invite a lawsuit.

Confidentiality concerning trade secrets may also conceal dangerous aspects of a product. Under its shield, the side effects of certain drugs have been kept secret, as has the uselessness of others. For a number of years the United States Department of the Interior consented to protect as trade secrets all information received from industries about the amount and kinds of pollutants discharged into rivers and lakes from industrial plants.[7] In such cases, trade secrecy is a means of shielding and covering up, much as medical confidentiality can conceal malpractice.

Even when confidentiality regarding trade secrets is not actually dangerous to the public, it may extend far beyond what is ordinarily regarded as trade secrets. Consider the following recommendations by a specialist in trade secrecy. He suggests that a company should post a statement on bulletin boards as part of its "trade secret program" that should include this provision:[8]

> Second, our trade secrets are Company assets. They were developed at great expense and only after long periods of experimentation. . . .if one of the Company's trade secrets is disclosed to a competitor or to the public, an asset of the Company will be destroyed and rendered useless to the Company.

Basic List of Company Trade Secrets

The following information, although certainly not all-inclusive, is certainly to be considered *at all times* to be confidential:

a. Formulas for all products sold by this Company.
b. Research and development material.
c. Current sales data.
d. Advertising data.
e. Marketing data.
f. Customer information.
g. Purchasing, pricing, and profit data.
h. Personnel files.

In such statements—and parallels are to be found in a growing number of companies—vast amounts of information that are not, strictly speaking, trade secrets are grouped with it for protection. If taken literally, such injunctions would prohibit most work-related conversations. Because they are not taken literally, and because their excesses could never be enforced in court, they are routinely disregarded; as a result, the boundaries surrounding those few trade secrets that companies regard as indispensable grow even more confused.

Trade secrecy vis-a-vis competitors is, in its strict sense, only one aspect of corporate secrecy, though many other aspects may be brought under its umbrella for protection. In addition, corporations conceal their activities and especially their plans from many others; from shareholders who might question investments and links to other companies; from the government in order to avoid interference and the publicity that may surround information once it is given over into the government's hands; from consumers in order not to lose business; and from employees about such matters as hidden dangers at the workplace, imminent relocation plans, and risks of bankruptcy.

In support of such general business secrecy as well as of trade secrecy we encounter a fourth and a fifth argument. Because they invoke no rights such as autonomy and property, they do not raise the same problems of extrapolation and application as the first three. They concern, rather, the benefits to companies, and indirectly to society, that secrecy brings: the protection of incentives to innovate and to invest, and the need to guard against foreign competition and industrial espionage.

THE SCOPE OF CORPORATE SECRECY

The fourth defense of secrecy in business concerns *incentives*. If corporate secrecy did not exist, this argument holds, it would have to be invented. No matter what our views about the inherent right to hold property or to keep secrets, societies need to allow a measure of commercial secrecy in order to preserve the incentive to make changes, and to invest resources without such incentives, the argument holds, social stability and progress will be endangered.[9] Thus Richard Posner argues that "some measure of privacy is necessary [. . .] to enable people, by concealing their ideas from other people, to appropriate the social benefits of their discoveries and inventions."[10]

Up to a point, this argument is surely persuasive. To develop new processes and achieve new knowledge in industry takes time and often great resources; to copy them very little. Why should a company use its stockholders' money and its own manpower and resources to develop, say, a new fertilizer, if other firms can wipe out its future profits by merely copying its final results? Without protection from competing firms, it would have no incentive to make the necessary outlays. In order to avoid the resulting stagnation and failure to innovate, a society must therefore protect some corporate secrecy as a matter of policy.

Arguments pointing to such benefits from secrecy nevertheless have two kinds of limit: the benefits may be overridden by moral considerations, or disputed on empirical grounds. First, the knowledge that secrecy allows may concern practices so harmful or invasive that they ought to be revealed, no matter how much secrecy would increase business incentives. Certain kinds of knowledge are owed to the persons who might be adversely affected by what a firm does—to employees, for example, stockholders, customers, or persons living near its factories. Thus a newspaper conglomerate may claim the need for secrecy regarding its administrative decisions: but such a claim rings hollow when it is used to defend the failure to notify employees of one of its papers of an imminent bankruptcy, so that they find a notice pinned to the entrance door one morning, announcing the bankruptcy, effective immediately. Likewise research processes that present high risks to experimental subjects, or the dumping of toxic chemical byproducts of manufacture in woods and waterways might well help firms compete and stimulate investment; but that is hardly a sufficient argument for allowing such secrecy.

Second, even when the information is not such that it is owed to persons who stand to be hurt by it, or to the public at large, the argument defending corporate secrecy on grounds of incentives has practical bounds. Because it posits benefits of secrecy and costs of openness, it becomes vulnerable as soon as these costs and benefits are in doubt—when secrecy appears counterproductive, so that it not only fails to foster competition and new ideas, but helps to stifle them.

A current debate weighs precisely such costs and benefits of corporate secrecy. Some argue that the economy would benefit from greatly reduced secrecy. True, they admit, individual firms might suffer; but society would gain, as the market came closer to the "perfect information" that encourages innovation and growth.[11] Others hold, on the contrary, that businesses are now suffering from too much openness and probing into company affairs. They argue that the decline in productivity in the United States is in part traceable to the Federal Government's role in first demanding vast quantities of information from firms through innumerable regulations and then failing to keep it confidential, because of the requirements of the Freedom of Information Act. The Act, these critics suggest, is increasingly used by business as a vehicle for mutual surveillance at the public's expense, to the disadvantage of all.[12] . . .

Both sides agree that neither "perfect information," with all that it implies of disclosure and surveillance, nor pervasive corporate secrecy are desirable. Their disagreement stems from different evaluations of the costs of the various practices of secrecy and openness.

Some of the differences in view stem from the misapprehension that there are *no* costs associated either with secrecy or with openness. I have discussed the drawbacks of secrecy in business and the disadvantages of full openness. But other costs, sometimes quite specific, are often overlooked, such as those of gathering and reproducing the data required for fiscal or other purposes, and the corresponding costs of storing, indexing, protecting, and retrieving the data thus gathered. For an example of the scope and intricacy of the conflicts generated by requirements of openness and secrecy, consider the prolonged controversy over trade secrecy between drug manufacturers and scientists working for the Food and Drug Administration (FDA).

In 1974, fourteen current and former employees of the FDA went before the United States Senate to denounce a number of abuses—among them what they held to be trade secrecy detrimental to the public interest.[13] They charged that their efforts to investigate new drugs met with resistance and harassment, and that the drug industry applied inappropriate pressures to the drug review process.

A panel set up to consider the various allegations found little evidence of inappropriate pressures from drug companies; but it held that the secrecy shrouding drug information posed serious problems.[14] The public, kept in ignorance about matters of the highest importance, had no way to know about possible mistakes or fraud that might have grave consequences for the public health. The secret practices forced the public to take the decisions of the FDA on faith. No one other than chosen outsiders could question the data or compare alternative choices.

Equally serious was the danger to human subjects. The secrecy shrouding drug development meant that different drug companies, working to develop similar drugs, engaged in duplicating experimentation on human beings—placing many more at risk than if the information could have been shared.

Spokesmen for the drug industry replied that trade secrecy was needed in the testing and licensing of new drugs. Competition in the drug industry is fierce. Between two and seven million dollars are expended over several years in the development of the average new drug, and in proving it, to the FDA's satisfaction, sufficiently safe and efficacious to be put on the market. How can the FDA both demand to see the data and refuse the companies confidentiality, these spokesmen asked. How can there be sufficient incentive for the companies to invest in the production of new drugs if "me-too" drugs can quickly be remarketed by competitors having acquired all the necessary information? Without trade secrecy protection, they argued, there would be no profit in being first, to compensate for the great preliminary investments.

The controversy opposed the drug industry, with its immense investments and resources, to those who fear that secrecy conceals abuses, duplication, and risks to human subjects, and thus renders the public powerless to control the safety and efficacy of new drugs. To resolve the conflict and diminish the risks of secrecy while protecting the drug companies' competitive advantage, it has been suggested that all files be opened, but that no company be allowed to "copy" another one's processes for some period of time. In this way, both property and protection would be granted, without need for the secrecy that, in this case, carries so many disadvantages.[15]

I find such methods of enforcing disclosure while ensuring incentives to invest and to innovate preferable. They may increasingly be required, as the effects of corporate secrecy on employees, customers, stockholders, and others come to be better known. It is likely that these solutions, combining accountability and protection, will be aided by the greater difficulty of permanent concealment, in industry as elsewhere; and by the growing realization that much secrecy, often unthinkingly applied, is counterproductive. While some freedom from oversight is obviously necessary to preserve initiative, alternatives to secrecy are preferable whenever they can serve that purpose. For the same reason, patents are thought preferable to trade secrecy.

Corporate secrecy differs in this respect from individual secrecy, where the burden of proof is on those who see reason to limit autonomy over personal information. Because all collective secrecy magnifies risks of harm and increases imitation and retaliation, the burden of proof must be on those who advocate more than a minimum to show why additional secrecy is needed and legitimate. Corporate secrecy differs, too, from those practices of professional confidentiality which *concern* such personal information (rather than, say, insurance fraud or medical malpractice).

This conclusion, however, is disputed by a last defense of business secrecy—one that is voiced ever more urgently in the 1980s. It is the cost-benefit argument writ large. Translated from national to international terms, it warns of possible catastrophe for societies which do not expand commercial secrecy in the name of *national security*. The costs of industrial openness, or even slackness about security regulation, according to this argument, threaten not only individual firms but entire nations and defense alliances.

Thus a spokesman for a company specializing in "security services" argued in 1981 that the United States "has become a soft target for industrial espionage that is costing the nation its technological superiority." The prime weakness, he held, is that the government has no consistent policies "to protect trade secrets and stop the flow of technology out of the country."[16] He proposed tightening up the Freedom of Information Act, placing a total embargo "on information relating to research, technology, manufacturing, and marketing of all American products, military and consumer," and extension of security checks to all persons receiving "information of a quasi-classified or highly classified type."

Underlying this argument are two assumptions. The first links economic well-being and strategic security. When societies fall behind economically, they are seen as more vulnerable militarily. According to the second, societies must, in order not to fall behind in such a way, protect their industry, commerce, and scientific research from foreign surveillance and theft of secrets; conversely, they must do all that is in their power to keep up with technological development abroad.

In evaluating these assumptions, the disadvantages of secrecy are often forgotten. It is easy to think of commercial secrecy in the interests of national security as inherently neutral—much like a blanket one can put on and remove at will. But the dangers of complacency, inefficiency, corruption, and mismanagement would be unusually great if such a vast system of secrecy were implemented.

In the light of these risks, one must further ask just how much information the practices of secrecy will succeed in safeguarding. Such practices of secrecy hardly guarantee *actual* secrecy—least of all in a world in which the technology of detection and surveillance has been so assiduously pursued. Even from a strictly military point of view, then, extensive industrial secrecy may be unwise. If implemented, it may offer yet another version of the Maginot Line: a set of fortifications erected at great human and commercial cost that gives a false sense of security while newer practices of intelligence gathering continue unabated, and satellites glide across it with ease.

Notes

1. American Law Institute, *Restatement of Torts* (1939), p. 757, comment b. See further, for works on trade secrecy:

   Rudolf Callman, *Unfair Competition, Trademarks, and Monopolies* (Wilmette, Ill.: Callaghan and Co., Third edition, 5 volumes, 1976), pars. 51–54.

   Comment, "The Scott Amendment to the Patent Revision Act: *Should Trade Secrets Receive Federal Protection?*" *Wisconsin Law Review,* 1971, pp. 900–921.

   R. M. Cummings, "Some Aspects of Trade Secrets and Their Protection," *Kentucky Law Journal,* 54, 1966, pp. 190–205.

   Gordon L. Doerfer, "The Limits of Trade Secret Law Imposed by Federal Patent and Antitrust Supremacy," *Harvard Law Review,* 80, 1967, pp. 1432–1462.

   Ridsale Ellis, *Trade Secrets* (New York: Baker, Voorhis & Co., Inc., 1953).

   Roger M. Milgrim, *Trade Secrets* (New York: Matthew Bender, 1978, first publ. 1967).

   Roger M. Milgrim, *Protecting and Profiting from Trade Secrets,* Practicing Law Institute, 1979, New York.

   "Note, Protection and Use of Trade Secrets," *Harvard Law Review,* 64, 1951, pp. 976–986.

   Brian J. O'Connell, "Secrecy in Business," *Society,* 16, May-June 1979, pp. 40–45.

   John K. Stedman, "Trade Secrets," *Ohio State Law Journal,* 23, 1962, pp. 4–34.

   "Trade Secrets: How Long Shall an Injunction Last?" *UCLA Law Review,* 26, October 1978, pp. 203–233.
2. Samuel Warren and Louis Brandeis, "The Right to Privacy," *Harvard Law Review,* Vol. 4, 1890, p. 212.
3. Cym H. Lowell, "Corporate Privacy: A Remedy for the Victim of Industrial Espionage," *Patent Law Review* (Renamed *Intellectual Property Law Review*), 1972, 4, pp. 407–449.
4. For a discussion of the role of administrative secrecy in business, see Mark V. Nadel, "Corporate Secrecy and Political Accountability," *Public Administration Review,* 1975, Vol. 35, pp. 14–23; and Brian J. O'Connell, "Secrecy in Business: A Sociological View," in Tefft, ed., *Secrecy: A Cross-Cultural Perspective,* pp. 229–244.
5. The first case is taken from A. M. Honoré, "Property, Title, and Redistribution," in Virginia Held, ed., *Property, Profit, and Economic Justice* (Belmont, California: Wadsworth Publishing Company, 1980), pp. 84–92, at p. 88; the second is discussed in Stevenson, *Supra,* p. 16, and refers to E.I. duPont de Nemours & Co., Inc. v. Christopher, 431 F 2nd 1012 (5th Cir. 1970).
6. See Melville J. Herskovits, *Economic Anthropology* (New York: Alfred A. Knopf, 1952), Ch. 14.
7. Ralph Nader, Peter Petkas, and Kate Blackwell, *Whistle Blowing* (New York: Grossman Publishers, 1972), p. 211.
8. Roger M. Milgrim, *Protecting and Profiting From Trade Secrets* (New York: Practicing Law Institute, 1979) pp. 303–364.
9. Compare Hume's view, dismissing claims holding that property exists in a state of nature, that it is a right emanating from men's joining their labor to objects or to nature, and that men have property in their own persons. Prop-

erty, rather, is a convention established by men to "bestow stability on the possession of those external goods, and leave every one in the peaceable enjoyment of what he may acquire by his fortune and industry." *A Treatise of Human Nature,* Book III, Section II, in L. A. Selby-Bigge, ed. (Oxford: Clarendon Press, 1978).

10. Richard A. Posner, *The Economics of Justice* (Cambridge, Ma.: Harvard University Press, 1981), p. 148.

11. See Russell B. Stevenson, Jr., *Corporations and Information—Secrecy, Access, and Disclosure* (Baltimore: Johns Hopkins University, 1980).

12. See, for example, John E. Marthinsen and Laurence S. Moss, "Businesses Move to Get Low-Cost Government Information About Competitors," *The Collegiate Forum,* Fall 1980, p. 3.

13. *Review Panel on New Drug Regulation,* Department of Health, Education, and Welfare. Final Report, 1976 May.

14. Norman Dorsen and Jeffrey M. Miller, "The Drug Regulation Process and the Challenge of Regulatory Reform," *Annals of Internal Medicine,* Vol. 91, No. 6, Dec. 1979, pp. 908–913.

15. See Thomas O. McGarity and Sidney A. Shapiro, "The Trade Secret Status of Health and Safety Testing Information: Reforming Agency Disclosure Policies," *Harvard Law Review,* Vol. 93, 1980, pp. 837–888.

16. Herschell Britton, "The Industrial-Spy Peril," *The New York Times,* June 30, 1981.

TRADE SECRETS: WHAT PRICE LOYALTY?

Michael S. Baram

In 1963, the Court of Appeals of Ohio heard an appeal of a lower court decision from The B.F. Goodrich Company. The lower court had denied Goodrich's request for an injunction, or court order, to restrain a former employee, Donald Wohlgemuth, from disclosing its trade secrets and from working in the space suit field for any other company.

This case, as it was presented in the Court of Appeals, is a fascinating display of management issues, legal concepts, and ethical dilemmas of concern to research and development organizations and their scientist and engineer employees. The case also represents an employer-employee crisis of increasing incidence in the young and vigorous R&D sector of U.S. industry. Tales of departing employees and threatened losses of trade secrets or proprietary information are now common.

Such crises are not surprising when one considers the causes of mobility. The highly educated employees of R&D organizations place primary emphasis on their own development, interests, and satisfaction. Graduates of major scientific and technological institutions readily admit that they accept their first jobs primarily for money and for the early and brief experience they feel is a prerequisite for seeking more satisfying futures with smaller companies which are often their own. Employee mobility and high personnel turnover rates are also due to the placement of new large federal contracts and the termination of others. One need only look to the Sunday newspaper employment advertisements for evidence as to the manner in which such programs are used to attract highly educated R&D personnel.

This phenomenon of the mobile employee seeking fulfillment reflects a sudden change in societal and personal values. It also threatens industrial reliance on trade secrets for the protection of certain forms of intellectual property. There are no union solutions, and the legal framework in which it occurs is an ancient structure representing values of an earlier America. The formulation of management responses—with cognizance of legal, practical, and ethical considerations—is admittedly a difficult task, but one which must be undertaken.

In this article I shall examine the basic question of industrial loyalty regarding trade secrets, using the Goodrich-Wohlgemuth case as the focal point of the challenge to the preservation of certain forms of intellectual property posed by the mobile employee, and then offer some suggestions for the development of sound management policies.

The Appeals Case

Donald Wohlgemuth joined The B.F. Goodrich Company as a chemical engineer in 1954, following his graduation from the University of Michigan, and by 1962 he had become manager of the space suit division. As the repository of Goodrich know-how and secret data in space suit technology, he was indeed a key man in a rapidly developing technology of interest to several government agencies. Nevertheless, he was dissatisfied with his salary ($10,644) and the denial of his requests for certain additional facilities for his department.

A Goodrich rival, International Latex, had recently been awarded the major space suit subcontract for the Apollo program. Following up a contact from an employment agency hired by Latex, Wohlgemuth negotiated a position with Latex, at a substantial salary increase. In his new assignment he would be manager of engineering for industrial products, which included space suits. He then notified Goodrich of his resignation, and was met with a reaction he apparently did not expect. Goodrich management raised the moral and ethical aspects of his decision, since the company executives felt his resignation would result in the transfer of Goodrich trade secrets to Latex.

After several heated exchanges, Wohlgemuth stated that "loyalty and ethics have their price and International Latex has paid this price. . . ." Even though Goodrich threatened legal action, Wohlgemuth left Goodrich for Latex. Goodrich thereupon requested a restraining order in the Ohio courts.

At the appeals court level, the Goodrich brief sought an injunction that would prevent Wohlgemuth from working in the space suit field for *any* other company, prevent his disclosure of *any* information on space suit technology to *anyone,* prevent his consulting or conferring with *anyone* on Goodrich trade secrets, and finally, prevent *any* future contact he might seek with Goodrich employees.

These four broad measures were rejected by the Ohio Court of Appeals. All were too wide in scope, and all would have protected much more than Goodrich's legitimate concern of safeguarding its trade secrets. In addition, the measures were speculative, since no clear danger seemed imminent. In sum, they represented a form of "overkill" that would have placed undue restraints on Wohlgemuth.

The court did provide an injunction restraining Wohlgemuth from disclosure of Goodrich trade secrets. In passing, the court noted that in the absence of any Goodrich employment contract restraining his employment with a competitor, Wohlgemuth could commence work with Latex. With ample legal precedent, the court therefore came down on both sides of the fence. Following the decision, Wohlgemuth commenced his career with Latex and is now manager of the company's Research and Engineering Department.

COMMON-LAW CONCEPTS

The two basic issues in crises such as the Goodrich-Wohlgemuth case appear irreconcilable: (1) the right of the corporation to its intellectual property—its proprietary data or trade secrets; and (2) the right of the individual to seek gainful employment and utilize his abilities—to be free from a master-servant relationship.

There are no federal and but a few state statutes dealing with employment restraints and trade secrets. The U.S. courts, when faced with such issues, have sought to apply the various common-law doctrines of trade secrets and unfair competition at hand to attain an equitable solution. Many of these common-law doctrines were born in pre-industrial England and later adopted by English and U.S. courts to meet employment crises of this nature through ensuing centuries of changing industrial and social patterns. In fact, some of the early cases of blacksmiths and barbers seeking to restrain departing apprentices are still cited today.

To the courts, the common legal solution, as in *Goodrich* v. *Wohlgemuth,* is pleasing because it theoretically preserves the rights of both parties. However, it is sadly lacking in practicality, since neither secrets nor individual liberty are truly preserved.

The trade secrets which companies seek to protect have usually become an integral portion of the departing employee's total capabilities. He cannot divest himself of his intellectual capacity, which is a compound of information acquired from his employer, his co-workers, and his own self-generated experiential information. Nevertheless, all such information, if kept secret by the company from its competition, may legitimately be claimed as corporate property. This is because the employer-employee relationship embodied in the normal employment contract or other terms of employment provides for corporate ownership of all employee-generated data, including inventions. As a result, a departing employee's, intellectual capacity may be, in large measure, corporate property.

Once the new position with a competitor has been taken, the trade secrets embodied in the departing employee may manifest themselves quite clearly and consciously. This is what court injunctions seek to prohibit. But, far more likely, the trade secrets will manifest themselves subconsciously and in various forms—for example, as in the daily decisions by the employee at his new post, or in the many small contributions he makes to a large team effort—often in the form of an intuitive sense of what or what not to do, as he seeks to utilize his overall intellectual capacity. Theoretically, a legal injunction also serves to prohibit such "leakage." However, the former employer faces the practical problem of securing evidence of such leakage, for little will be apparent from the public activities and goods of the new employer. And if the new employer's public activities or goods appear suspicious, there is also the further problem of distinguishing one's trade secrets from what may be legitimately asserted as the self-generated technological skills or state of the art of the new employer and competitor which were utilized.

This is a major stumbling block in the attempt to protect one's trade secrets, since the possessor has no recourse against others who independently generate the same information. It is therefore unlikely that an injunction against disclosure of trade secrets to future employers prevents any "unintentional" transfer (or even intentional transfer) of information, except for the passage of documents and other physical embodiments of the secrets. In fact, only a lobotomy, as yet not requested nor likely to be sanctioned by the courts, would afford security against the transfer of most trade secrets.

Conversely, the departing employee bears the terrible burden of sensitivity. At his new post, subconscious disclosure and mental and physical utilization of what he feels to be no more than his own intellectual capacity may result in heated exchanges between companies, adverse publicity, and litigation. He is marked, insecure, and unlikely to contribute effectively in his new position. In fact, new co-workers may consider him to be a man with a price, and thus without integrity. Frequently, caution on the part of his new employer will result in transfer to a nonsensitive post where he is unlikely to contribute his full skills, unless he has overall capability and adaptability.

The fact that neither secrets nor individual liberty will be truly preserved rarely influences the course of litigation. Similarly, these practical considerations are usually negligible factors in the out-of-court settlements which frequently terminate such litigation, because the settlements primarily reflect the relative bargaining strengths of disputing parties.

Finally, there is the full cost of litigation to be considered. In addition to the obvious court costs and attorney's fees, there is the potentially great cost to the company's image. Although the drama enacted in court reflects legitimate corporate concerns, the public may easily fail to see more than an unequal struggle between the powerful corporate machine and a lonely individual harassed beyond his employment tenure. Prospective employees, particularly new and recent graduates whose early positions are stepping stones, may be reluctant to accept employment with what appears to be a vindictive and authoritarian organization.

Practical & Legal Aspects

Trade secrets are, of course, a common form of intellectual property. Secrecy is the most natural and the earliest known method of protecting the fruits of one's intellectual labors. Rulers of antiquity frequently had architects and engineers murdered, after completion of their works, to maintain secrecy and security. The medieval guilds and later the craftsmen of pre-industrial Europe and America imposed severe restraints on apprentices and their future activities.

Recognition and acceptance of the practice of protecting intellectual property by secrecy is found throughout Anglo-American common or judge-made law, but statutory protection has not been legislated. Perhaps the failure to do so is because of the recognition by the elected officials of industrial societies that secrecy is not in the public interest and that the widest dissemination of new works and advances in technology and culture is necessary for optimal public welfare. . . .

To summarize this common law briefly, virtually all information—ranging from full descriptions of inventions to plant layouts, shop know-how, methods of quality control, customer and source lists, and marketing data—is eligible for protection as trade secrets. No standard of invention or originality are required. If such information is not known to the public or to the trade (or it is known but its utility is not recognized), and if such information is of value to its possessor, it is eligible for protection by the courts.

Further, and of greatest importance in terms of favorably impressing the courts, there must be evidence that the possessor recognized the value of his information and treated it accordingly. In the context of confidential relationships, "treatment" normally means that the possessor provided for limited or no disclosure of trade secrets. This means many things: for example, total prohibition of disclosure except to key company people on a need-to-know basis; provision of the information to licensees, joint ventures, or employees having contractual restraints against their unauthorized disclosure or use; division of employee responsibilities so that no employee is aware of more than a small segment of a particular process; and use in labs of unmarked chemicals and materials.

There must also be evidence that particular efforts were expended for the purpose of preserving secrecy for the specific data claimed as trade secrets. General company policies indiscriminately applied to data and employees or licensees will not suffice in the legal sense to convince the courts of the presence of trade secrets.

When the possessor and his information do fulfill such criteria, court recognition and the award of compensation to damaged parties, or injunctive restraints to protect parties in danger of imminent or further damage, will follow. If there is evidence of (a) breach of confidential relationships (contracts or licenses) which were established to preserve the secrecy of company information, (b) unauthorized copying and sale of secrets, or (c) conspiracy to damage the possessor, the courts will act with greater certitude. But in many cases, such as in the Goodrich-Wohlgemuth litigation, no such evidence is present.

Finally, the courts will not move to protect trade secrets when an action is brought by one party against another who independently generated similar information, or who "reverse-engineered" the publicly sold products of the party petitioning the court, unless there is some contractual, fiduciary, or other relationship based on trust connecting the parties in court.

Other Considerations

In addition to the foregoing practical and legal aspects, basic questions of industrial ethics and the equitable allocation of rights and risks should be examined to provide management with intelligent and humane responses to employer-employee crises that involved intellectual property. The patent and copyright systems for the stimulation and protection of such property are premised on dissemination of information and subsequent public welfare. These systems reflect public concern with the proper use of intellectual property, which the common law of trade secrets lacks.

Will the courts continue to utilize common-law concepts for the protection of trade secrets, when such concepts are based solely on the rights of the possessors of secret information, and when the application of such concepts has a detrimental effect on both the rights of employees and the public welfare? Since current court practice places the burden of industrial loyalty solely on the employee, the skilled individual has to pay the price. In other words, the law restricts the fullest utilization of his abilities. And the detrimental effect on public welfare can be inferred from recent federal studies of technology transfer, which indicate that employee mobility and the promotion of entrepreneurial activities are primary factors in the transfer of technology and the growth of new industries.

The continuation of trade secret concepts for the preservation of property rights in secret information at the expense of certain basic individual freedoms is unlikely. The law eventually reflects changing societal values, and the mobile R&D employee who seeks career fulfillment through a succession of jobs, frequently in sensitive trade secret areas, is now a reality—one not likely to disappear. Thus it is probable that the courts will eventually adopt the position that those who rely on trade secrets assume the realities or risks in the present context of public concern with technological progress and its relationship to the public good, and with the rights of the individual. Resulting unintentional leakage of secret information through the memory of a departing employee is now generally accepted as a reasonable price to pay for the preservation of these societal values. However, the courts will never condone the theft or other physical appropriation of secret information, nor are the courts likely to condone fraud, conspiracy, and other inequitable practices resulting in some form of unfair competition.

The failings of the statutory systems serve, not as justification for the inequitable application of medieval trade secret concepts, but as the basis for legislative reform. Injunctive restraints against the unintentional leakage of secrets and the harassment of departing employees through litigation should not be part of our legal system. This is especially true when there is a growing body of evidence that management can respond, and has intelligently done so, to such crises without detriment to the individual employee, the public good, or the company itself.

MANAGEMENT RESPONSE

How then shall managers of research and development organizations respond to the reality of the mobile employee and his potential for damage to corporate trade secrets?

Contractual Restraints

Initial response is invariably consideration of the use of relevant contractual prohibitions on employees with such potential. For a minority of companies, this means the institution of employment contracts or other agreements concerning terms of employment. For most, a review of existing company contracts, which at a minimum provide for employee disclosure of inventions and company ownership of subsequent patents, will be called for to determine the need for relevant restraints.

Contractual prohibitions vary somewhat, but they are clearly of two general types: (1) restraints against unauthorized disclosure and use of company trade secrets or proprietary information by employees during their employment tenure or at any time thereafter; (2) restraints against certain future activities of employees following their employment tenure.

A restraint against unauthorized disclosure or use is normally upheld in the courts, provided it is limited to a legitimate company concern—trade secrets. But it is usually ineffective, due to the unintentional leakage and subconscious utilization of trade secrets, and the difficulties of "policing" and proving violation, as discussed earlier. In fact, several authorities feel that this type of restraint is ineffective unless coupled with a valid restraint against future employment with competitors. . . .

Courts have been naturally reluctant to extend protection to trade secrets when the freedom of an individual to use his overall capability is at stake. In addition, the former employer faces the practical difficulty of convincing almost any court that a prohibition of future employment is necessary, since the court will look for clear and convincing evidence that the ex-employee has, or inevitably will, exercise more than the ordinary skill a man of his competence possesses. A few states—such as California by statute and others by consistent court action—now prohibit future employment restraints.

It therefore appears that a contractual prohibition of future employment in a broad area, which prevents an ex-employee from using his overall capability, is invalid in most states. . . .

Internal Policies

Another response of R&D management to the mobile employee and his potential for damage to corporate trade secrets is the formulation of internal company policies for the handling of intellectual property of trade secret potential. Such policies may call for the prior review of publications and addresses of key employees, prohibition of consulting and other "moon-lighting," dissemination of trade secrets on a strict "need to know" basis to designated employees, and prohibitions on the copying of trade secret data. More "physical" policies may restrict research and other operational areas to access for designated or "badge" employees only and divide up operations to prevent the accumulation of extensive knowledge by any individual—including safety and other general plant personnel. Several companies I know of distribute unmarked materials—particularly chemicals—to employees.

Although internal policies do not necessarily prevent future employment with competitors, they can serve to prevent undue disclosures and lessen the criticality of the departure of key personnel. All must be exercised with a sophisticated regard for employee motivation, however, because the cumulative effect may result in a police state atmosphere that inhibits creativity and repels prospective employees.

Several farsighted R&D organizations are currently experimenting with plans which essentially delegate the responsibility for nondisclosure and nonuse of their trade secrets to the key employees themselves. These plans include pension and consulting programs operative for a specified post-employment period. In one company, for example, the pension plan provides that the corporate monies which are contributed to the employee pension fund in direct ratio to the employee's own contributions will remain in his pension package following his term of employment, providing he does not work for a competing firm for a specified number of years. In another company, the consulting plan provides that certain departing employees are eligible to receive an annual consulting fee for a given number of years following employment if they do not work for a competitor. The consulting fee is a preestablished percentage of the employee's annual salary at the time of his departure.

Obviously, such corporate plans are subject to employee abuse, but if limited to truly key employees, they may succeed without abuse in most cases. They not only have the merit of providing the employee with a choice, an equitable feature likely to incur employee loyalty, but they also have no apparent legal defects.

Another valid internal practice is the debriefing of departing employees. The debriefing session, carried out in a low-key atmosphere, affords management an excellent opportunity to retrieve company materials and information in physical form, to impart to the employee a sense of responsibility regarding trade secrets and sensitive areas, and to discuss mutual anxieties in full.

External Procedures

Several management responses relating to external company policies are worth noting, as they also serve to protect trade secrets in cases involving employee departures. Among several industries, such as in the chemical field, it is common to find gentlemen's agreements which provide mutuality in the nonhiring of competitor's key employees, following notice. Employees who have encountered this practice have not found the experience a pleasant one. This same practice is also found in other areas, such as the industrial machinery industry, that are in need of innovation; and it appears that the presence of such agreements helps to depict these industries in an unappealing fashion to the types of employees they need.

Another external response for management consideration is company reliance on trademarks. Given a good mark and subsequent public identification of the product with the mark, a company may be able to maintain markets despite the fact that its intellectual property is no longer a trade secret. Competitors may be hesitant about utilizing the former trade secrets of any company whose products are strongly identified with trademarks and with the company itself.

Some trade secrets are patentable, and management faced with the potential loss of such secrets should consider filing for patent protection. The application is treated confidentially by the U.S. Patent Office and some foreign patent offices up to the time of award. Moreover, if the application is rejected, the secrecy of the information is not legally diminished. In any case, the subject matter of the application remains secret throughout the two-to-three year period of time normally involved in U.S. Patent Office review.

CONCLUSION

A major concern of our society is progress through the promotion and utilization of new technology. To sustain and enhance this form of progress, it is necessary to optimize the flow of information and innovation all the way from conception to public use. This effort is now a tripartite affair involving federal agencies, industry, and universities. A unique feature of this tripartite relationship is the mobility of R&D managers, scientists, and engineers who follow contract funding and projects in accordance with their special competence. Neither the federal agencies not the universities rely on trade secret concepts for the protection of their intellectual property. However, industry still does, despite the fact that trade secret concepts bear the potential ancillary effect of interfering with employee mobility.

It is becoming increasingly clear that new societal values associated with the tripartite approach to new technology are now evolving, and that the common law dispensed by the courts has begun to reflect these values. A victim of sorts is trade secret law, which has not only never been clearly defined, but which has indeed been sustained by court concepts of unfair competition, equity, and confidence derived from other fields of law. The day when courts restrict employee mobility to preserve industrial trade secrets appears to have passed, except—as we noted earlier—in cases involving highly charged factors such as conspiracy, fraud, or theft.

In short, it is now unwise for management to rely on trade secret law and derivative employee contractual restraints to preserve trade secrets. Companies must now carefully weigh the nature and value of their intellectual property, present and potential employees, competition, and applicable laws in order to formulate sound management policies.

Programmed Approach

Regarding the challenge to the preservation of trade secrets posed by the mobile employee, sophisticated management will place its primary reliance on the inculcation of company loyalty in key employees, and on the continual satisfaction of such key employees. For example, management might consider adopting the following five-step basis for developing an overall approach to the challenge:

1. Devise a program for recognition of employee achievement in the trade secret area. At present, this form of recognition is even more neglected than is adequate recognition of employee inventions.

2. Make an appraisal of trade secret activities. This should result in a limitation of (a) personnel with access to trade secrets, (b) the extent of trade secrets available to such personnel, and (c) information which truly deserves the label of trade secret.

3. Review in-house procedures and the use of physical safeguards, such as restrictions on access to certain specified areas and on employee writings for outside publication. Restrictions may tend to stifle creativity by inhibiting communication and interaction conducive to innovation. Striking the balance between too few and too many safeguards is a delicate process and depends on the employee awareness of what is being sought and how it will benefit them.

4. Appraise the legal systems available for the protection of intellectual property. Utility and design patents may be advisable in some cases. The copyright system now offers some protection to certain types of industrial designs and computer software. Trademarks may be adroitly used to maintain markets.

5. Recognize that all efforts may fail to persuade a key employee from leaving. To cope with this contingency, the "gentle persuasion" of a pension or consulting plan in the postemployment period has proved effective and legally sound. A thorough debriefing is a further safeguard. Other cases wherein employee mobility is accompanied by fraud, unfair competition, or theft will be adequately dealt with by the courts.

The problem of the departing employee and the threatened loss of trade secrets is not solved by exhortations that scientists and engineers need courses in professional ethics. Management itself should display the standards of conduct expected of its employees and of other companies.

Finally, let me stress again that success probably lies in the inculcation of company loyalty in key employees, not in the enforcement of company desires or in misplaced reliance on the law to subsidize cursory management. Better employee relations—in fact, a total sensitivity to the needs and aspirations of highly educated employees—requires constant management concern. In the long run, total sensitivity will prove less costly and more effective than litigation and the use of questionable contractual restraints.

OF ACCEPTABLE RISK

William W. Lowrance

Few headlines are so alarming, perplexing, and personal in their implications as those concerning safety. Frightening stories jolt our early morning complacency so frequently that we wonder whether things can really be *that* bad. We are disturbed by what sometimes appear to be haphazard and irresponsible regulatory actions, and we can't help being suspicious of all the assaults on our freedoms and our pocketbooks made in the name of safety. We hardly know which cries of ''Wolf!'' to respond to; but we dare not forget that even in the fairy tale, the wolf really did come.

The issues: X-rays, cosmetics, DDT, lead, pharmaceuticals, toys, saccharin, intrauterine contraceptive devices, power lawn mowers, air pollutants, noise. . . .

The questions: How do we determine how hazardous these things are? Why is it that cyclamates one day dominate the market as the principal calorie-cutting sweetener in millions of cans of diet drinks, only to be banned the next day because there is a ''very slight chance'' they may cause cancer? Why is it that one group of eminent experts says that medical X-rays (or food preservatives, or contraceptive pills) are safe and ought to be used more widely, while another group of authorities, equally reputable, urges that exposure to the same things should be restricted because they are unsafe? At what point do debates such as that over DDT stop being scientific and objective and start being political and subjective? How can anyone gauge the public's willingness to accept risks? . . .

JUDGING SAFETY

. . . Safety is not measured. *Risks* are measured. Only when those risks are weighed on the balance of social values can safety be judged: *a thing is safe if its attendant risks are judged to be acceptable.*

Determining safety, then, involves two extremely different kinds of activities. . . .

Measuring risks—measuring the probability and severity of harm—is an empirical, scientific activity;

Judging safety—judging the acceptability of risks—is a normative, political activity.

Although the difference between the two would seem obvious, it is all too often forgotten, ignored, or obscured. This failing is often the cause of the disputes that hit the front pages.

We advocate use of this particular definition for many reasons. It encompasses the other, more specialized, definitions. By employing the word "acceptable," it emphasizes that safety decisions are relativistic and judgmental. It immediately elicits the crucial questions, "Acceptable in whose view?" and "Acceptable in what terms?" and "Acceptable for whom?" Further, it avoids all implication that safety is an intrinsic, absolute, measurable property of things.

In the following two examples, risk-measuring activity is described in Roman type, and safety-judging in italics. . . .

A scientific advisory committee is charged by the government with recommending radiation exposure standards. The committee reviews all the animal experiments, the occupational medical record, the epidemiological surveys of physicians and patients exposed to X-rays, and the studies of the survivors of the Nagasaki and Hiroshima explosions. It inventories the modes of exposure; it reviews present radiation standards, including those of other nations and international organizations; and it examines the practical possibility of reducing exposures. *It weighs all the risks, costs, and benefits, and then decides that the allowed exposure has been unacceptably high; it recommends that because the intensity of some major sources, such as medical X-rays, can be reduced at reasonable cost and with little loss of effectiveness, the standards should be made more restrictive.*

Over a three-year period, William Ruckelshaus, administrator of the Environmental Protection Agency, considered many different petitions from the various interested parties before acting on his agency's inquiry into the use of DDT. Finally, in 1972, he ruled that the scientific evidence led him to conclude that DDT is "an uncontrollable, durable chemical that persists in the aquatic and terrestrial environments" and "collects in the food chain," and that although the evidence regarding human tumorogenicity and other long-term effects was inconclusive, there was little doubt that DDT has serious ecological effects. Ruckelshaus reviewed the benefits of DDT in the protection of cotton and other crops and affirmed that other equally effective pesticides were available. *Summing the arguments, then, he ruled that "the long-range risks of continued use of DDT for use on cotton and most other crops is unacceptable and outweighs any benefits. . . ."*[1]

. . . In heading down the slopes a skier attests that he accepts the risks; at a later stage of his life he may reject those very same risks because of changes in his awareness, his physical fragility, or his responsibilities to family or firm. While one woman may accept the side effects of oral contraceptives because she doesn't want to risk pregnancy, another woman may so fear the pill that she judges a diaphragm to be a more acceptable compromise among the several risks. Even though he is fully aware of the mangled fingers, chronic coughs, or damaged eyes or ears of those around him, a worker may accept those risks rather than endure the daily nuisance and tedium of blade guards, respirators, goggles, or ear protectors; but his employer, for reasons of cost, paternalism, or government requirement, may find this risky behavior unacceptable. . . .

Acceptance may be just a passive, or even stoical, continuance of historical momentum, as when people accept their lot at a dangerous traditional trade or continue to live near a volcano. Acceptance may persist because no alternatives are seen, as in the case of automobiles and many other technological hazards. Acceptance may result from ignorance or misperception of risk: variations on ''I didn't know the gun was loaded'' and ''It won't happen to me'' show up in every area. Acceptance may be simply acquiescence in a majority decision, such as a referendum-based decision on fluoridation, or in a decision by some governing elite, as with the average person's tacit approval of most public standards. Acceptance may even be an expression of preference for modern but known risks over perhaps smaller but less well understood risks, as with preference for coal- and oil-fired power plants over nuclear plants. . . . It is important to appreciate that such decisions may or may not be—and are certainly not necessarily—fair, just, consistent, efficient, or rational.

There is a great deal of overlap between the two decisionmaking domains implied by our definition of safety. Scientists, engineers, and medical people are called upon by political officials to judge the desirability of certain courses for society. Panels of scientists recommend exposure limits. Physicians prescribe medicines and diets. Engineers design dams, television sets, toasters, and airplanes. All of these decisions are heavily, even if only implicitly, value-laden.

On the other hand, by adopting particular risk data in their deliberations, political and judiciary agents at least implicitly rule on the correctness of measurements. The business of determining risk must often be settled operationally in hearings or other political deliberations, because the day-to-day management of society can't always wait for scientists to complete their cautious, precise determinations, which may take years. Congressional committees and regulatory agencies conduct hearings and issue rulings on the risks of food additives and air pollutants. Courts rule on the dangers of DDT. Risk and its acceptability are weighed by both manufacturers and consumers in the push-and-pull of the marketplace.

Between the two activities—measuring risk and judging safety—lies a discomforting no-man's-land . . . or every-man's-land. Scientists on the fringe of the political arena, attempting to avoid charges of elitism, are looking for more objective ways to appraise society's willingness to accept various risks. At the same time, political officials confronted by scientifically controversial ''facts'' that never seem to gain the clarity promised by textbooks are exploring the possibilities of advisory assistance, fact-finding hearings, and formal technology assessments.

GUIDES TO ACCEPTABILITY

''Reasonableness.'' This is by far the most commonly cited and most unimpeachable principle in safety judgments. For instance, the legislative charter of the Consumer Product Safety Commission directs it to ''reduce

unreasonable risk of injury'' associated with consumer goods.[2] Panels of experts frequently invoke a ''rule of reason'' in rendering advice. The concept of reasonableness pervades economic analyses of hazard reduction and the structures of legal liability.

Unfortunately, reference to reasonableness is in a sense a phantom citation. It provides little specific guidance for public decisionmakers, for whom reasonableness is presumably a requirement for staying in office. Not surprisingly, the Consumer Product Safety Act does not venture to define reasonableness. As guidance, the Safety Commission quotes the description given by the final report of its progenitor, the National Commission on Product Safety:

> Risks of bodily harm to users are not unreasonable when consumers understand that risks exist, can appraise their probability and severity, know how to cope with them, and voluntarily accept them to get benefits that could not be obtained in less risky ways. When there is a risk of this character, consumers have reasonable opportunity to protect themselves; and public authorities should hesitate to substitute their value judgments about the desirability of the risk for those of the consumers who choose to incur it.
>
> But preventable risk is not reasonable
> (a) when consumers do not know that it exists; or
> (b) when, though aware of it, consumers are unable to estimate its frequency and severity; or
> (c) when consumers do not know how to cope with it, and hence are likely to incur harm unnecessarily; or
> (d) when risk is unnecessary in . . . that it could be reduced or eliminated at a cost in money or in the performance of the product that consumers would willingly incur if they knew the facts and were given the choice.[3]

The point of safety judgments is indeed to decide what is reasonable; it's just that any rational decision will have to be made on more substantive bases, such as the following, which are in a sense criteria for reasonableness.

Custom of usage. The Food and Drug Administration has designated hundreds of food additives as ''generally recognized as safe'' (GRAS). The GRAS list, established in 1958, includes such substances as table salt, vitamin A, glycerin, and baking powder, whose long use has earned them wide and generally unquestioned acceptance.[4] Being classified as GRAS exempts those substances from having to pass certain premarket clearances. From time to time this sanction is challenged, but most critics of the GRAS list have argued not so much that it should be abandoned as that individual items should be subjected to periodic review. In 1969, following its decision to ban the popular artificial sweetener cyclamate (until then GRAS), the Food and Drug Administration initiated a full review of the GRAS list. That review is still in progress, and ''so far nothing has been found to lead to any further bans similar to the one on cyclamate.''[5]

Prevailing professional practice. Long established as the criterion for physicians' clinical practice, this principle is increasingly being invoked in evaluating the protection that engineers, designers, and manufacturers provide their clients. Buildings are said to conform to the ''prevailing local standards." Toys are "of a common design." X-ray machines are operated "at normal intensities." In many instances the wisdom of such deference to convention can be questioned. The underlying assumption is that if a thing has been in common use it must be okay, since any adverse effects would have become evident, and that a thing sanctioned by custom is safer than one not tested at all.

Best available practice, highest practicable protection, and lowest practicable exposure. Air and water quality regulations have stipulated that polluters control their emissions by the "best available means." So have noise abatement laws. Obviously, although such a requirement does provide the public regulator with a vague rationale, he must still exercise judgment over what constitutes "best" practice for every individual case and what economic factors should be considered in defining "practicable." Hardware for pollution control or noise abatement may exist, but only at a cost that many allege to be prohibitive; is it to be considered "available"? . . .

"No detectable adverse effect." Although such a principle is applied frequently in our everyday lives, and although it has a certain operational value, it is a weak criterion which may amount to little more than an admission of uncertainty or ignorance. Many hazards now recognized, such as moderate levels of X-rays or asbestos or vinyl chloride, could at an earlier time have been said to have "no detectable adverse effect." . . .

The threshold principle. If it can be proven that there is indeed a level of exposure below which no adverse effect occurs, subthreshold exposures might be considered safe. But determining whether there really is a threshold, for the especially vulnerable as well as for the average populace, is usually a nearly impossible task. As we mentioned earlier, for loud noises there are clearly thresholds of annoyance, pain, and ear damage. But whether there are thresholds for effects of radiation, chemical carcinogens, and mutagens has never been firmly established. . . .

ON BEING, AND BEING HELD, RESPONSIBLE

In essence, the issue is posed by the following questions: Should technically trained people be expected to bear any social responsibilities different from those borne by others? Why? What are the unique obligations? And further, can all the obligations be met simply by individuals working alone, or are there in addition some responsibilities requiring technical people to act collectively? . . .

Scientists, engineers, designers, architects, physicians, public health experts, and other technically trained people *do* have special responsibilities to the rest of society with respect to personal safety. Some principal kinds of risks which ought to be taken upon the conscience of the technical community are:

1. Technically complex risks whose intricacies are comprehensible only to highly trained people;
2. Risks that can be significantly reduced by applying new technology or by improving the application of existing technology;
3. Risks constituting public problems whose technical components need to be

distinguished explicitly from their social and political components so that responsibilities are assigned properly;

4. Technological intrusions on personal freedom made in the pursuit of safety; and

5. Risks whose possible consequences appear so grave or irreversible that prudence dictates the urging of extreme caution, even before the risks are known precisely.

Notice that we have said that these problems *should be taken as matters of conscience* by the technical community. Whether the verb describing the action should be *protecting,* or *watching over,* or *looking out for,* or *issuing a warning,* depends on the situation. The specific response might be doing an experiment, raising an issue before a professional society, blowing the whistle on an employer, exerting political leverage, or aiding a legislator or administrator in untangling the parts of a public issue.

. . . These responsibilities have several deep origins. Basically they arise, in congruence with all major moral philosophies, from the conviction that every person has a general responsibility for the well-being of his fellow men. Reflecting this, the common law has held through the centuries that anyone who becomes aware of the possibility of danger has a responsibility to warn those at risk. But we are obliged to push further and ask whether, in this age of cultural specialization, there isn't more to the issue—for if we don't press, we may be left simply making vague exhortations to virtue.

When we examine what society expects, we find that it does look to the technical community for warning, guidance, and protection, in the kinds of situations we have described and in others as well. Highly trained people are definitely seen as having special status. Given this, a key to developing a compelling ethical argument, and to understanding why the lay public feels as it does, seems to reside in the notion of professionalism.

Over the years a tacit but nonetheless real compact has developed. Society *invests in* the training and professional development of scientists and other technical people. It invests heavily; substantial public subsidy of one form or another goes to virtually every college, university, medical school, field station, and research facility in the United States. By and large the professions are left free to govern themselves, control admission to membership, choose their direction of research, enforce the quality of work, and direct the allocation of public funds within their subject area.

Concomitantly, society *invests with* the professions and their institutions certain trusts, among them a trust that the professions will watch over the well-being of society, including its safety. As Berkeley sociologist William Kornhauser has expressed it, ''Professional responsibility is based on the belief that the power conferred by expertise entails a fiduciary relationship to society.''[6] This ''fiduciary relationship,'' or what we have called a tacit compact, is what gives rise to the ethical ''oughts.''

. . . As this century has careened along it has brought an increasing need for a collective shouldering of responsibility. The one-to-one personal relationships that once governed ethical conduct have been supplanted by more diffuse ones involving many intermediaries. Industrial scientists plan their research by committee. Engineers who design tunnels and dams interact with their ultimate public clients only indirectly, through managers, attorneys, and the officials who supervise public contracts. Physicians may still carry the wand of Aesculapius, but they do so in the context of one of the nation's largest businesses. Two sorts of diffuseness enlarge the collective dimension. First, the cliency is expanding, often in the interest of social justice: a national health care system that intends to reach every citizen has quite different ethical dimensions from a free-market private physician system. And second, as we confront hazards that are more diffuse, we often realize that *nobody* has considered that the problem was specifically his concern: there is no International Agency for the Supervision of the Ozone Layer.

We try to manage these problems by government action, building in mechanisms of accountability where possible; and we test the justice of specific actions in the courts, as when people feel that they are being unfairly denied medical care. Beyond that, and usually leading it, we have to depend on action by communities of scholars and coteries of professionals—hence the obligations we listed earlier.

Two current cases exemplify some of the difficulties. Three engineers in California, backed to a limited extent by several engineering societies, have pressed suit against the Bay Area Rapid Transit (BART) system for firing them after they publicly protested that the automatic train control systems their companies were developing for BART were inadequate and not up to the best professional standards with regards to passenger safety. The dispute raises complex questions about how great the risks really were, whether they should have been considered acceptable, how engineers should play their roles, how corporations should handle dissension, and what the professional societies should do.[7] In another case, an international group of biologists has voluntarily convened itself to discuss whether and how to control certain genetics experiments that would have bizarre, disastrous consequences if they ran amok.[8]

There is little precedent for either case, so it is not surprising that neither has been handled with assurance. In the BART case, the engineering societies were not well prepared to act and could muster only limited support. Perhaps for lack of experience and guidance, the three engineers party to the suit were not able to pursue the case through the courts to completion; the case has reportedly had to be settled out of court, thus setting only weak legal precedent. In the genetic experiments case, the scientists involved continue to suffer the anguish of not even being able to reach a firm consensus on the issue, and they are hard pressed to take any action other than to issue stern pronouncements, plead for prudence, and cross their collective fingers that researchers will be careful.

We have developed the above arguments because we believe they are important. They are by no means the sole guide to action. There can be no substitute for honesty, courage, sacrifice, and the other manifestations of high morality. Nor should legal and other sanctions fail to be applied: enforceable building codes can be adopted to supplement voluntary action; duties can be made a matter of contractual responsibility; and falsification of records is cause for lawsuit. There are many obligations in addition to ethical ones. The ethical ones are of a special sort, though, and urgently deserve to be developed.

The great questions of responsibility will remain with us. Is simply providing information or issuing warnings a sufficient response, or ought those with the knowledge do more? How is responsibility passed up through administrative and managerial hierarchies? In what sense is tacit acquiescence in a misleading scheme irresponsible (as when corporate scientists who know better say nothing when their company makes false claims for its products or evades pollution control laws)? To what extent should those who generate scientific and technological innovations be responsible for their subsequent application?

Notes

1. U.S. Environmental Protection Agency, "Consolidated DDT Hearings," *37 Federal Register,* 13369–13376 (July 7, 1972).
2. Consumer Product Safety Act, *Public Law 82–573* (1972).
3. National Commission on Product Safety, *Final Report,* 11 (1970).
4. *21 U.S. Code of Federal Regulations,* 121.101 (subpart B).
5. Alan T. Spiher, Jr., "Food ingredient review: where it stands now," *FDA Consumer,* 23–26 (June 1974).
6. William Kornhauser, *Scientists in Industry,* 1 (University of California Press, Berkeley, 1962).
7. Gordon D. Friedlander, *IEEE Spectrum,* 11, 69–76 (October 1974); Gordon D. Friedlander, "Fixing BART," *IEEE Spectrum,* 12, 43–45 (February 1975).
8. Nicholas Wade, "Genetics: Conference sets strict controls to replace moratorium," *Science 187,* 931–935 (1975); Stuart Auerbach, "And man created risks," *Washington Post* (March 9, 1975).

THE RIGHT TO RISK INFORMATION AND THE RIGHT TO REFUSE HEALTH HAZARDS IN THE WORKPLACE

Ruth R. Faden and Tom L. Beauchamp

In recent years, the right of employees to know about health hazards in the workplace has emerged as a major issue in occupational health policy.[1] A general consensus has gradually evolved that there is a right to know, and correlatively that there is a moral obligation to disclose relevant information to workers. For example, the National Institute for Occupational Safety and Health (NIOSH), and several other U.S. federal agencies, informed the U.S. Senate as early as July 1977 that ''workers have the right to know whether or not they are exposed to hazardous chemical and physical agents regulated by the Federal Government.''[2] In 1980, the Occupational Safety and Health Administration (OSHA) promulgated regulations guaranteeing workers access to medical and exposure records.[3] Legislation recently passed in the states of Connecticut and New York and the city of Philadelphia further supports the claim that workers have a right to know. The New York bill, for example, declares that employees and their representatives have a right to ''*all* information relating to toxic substances''—a right that cannot be ''waived as a condition of employment.''[4]

Although the general belief that workers have a right to information about health hazards is now well entrenched, there is no clear consensus—and scarcely any commentary—about the nature and extent of an employer obligation to disclose such information. There is also considerable ambiguity about the scope of the right, i.e., which protections and actions the right entails. For example, the 1980 OSHA regulation established a strong worker right of *access* to information. With few exceptions, employers under this regulation are obligated to provide information within fifteen days of having received a request for access to records by an employee or an employee's designated representative. On its own initiation, an employer is obligated to inform workers first entering employment (and at least yearly thereafter) about the *existence* of medical and exposure records, about the employee's rights of access to those records, and the person responsible for maintaining the records.[5] However, under the regulation, employers have no affirmative duty to provide the content of these records; only their existence must be disclosed. A direct employee request is necessary for disclosures of content. Also, the day after workers receive exposure records they have requested, an employer could introduce a new toxic substance into the manufacturing process and be under no obligation, pursuant to the regulation, to disclose new information to workers.

Although this workers' right of access to records and to employer analyses of these records is an important component of a general employee right in the United States, it is not solely sufficient to protect workers' interests. As Elihu Richter points out,[6] the difficulty with such access rights is that unless workers request the information, they may not possess even minimal risk information. If the right to know in the workplace is to be adequately protected, there must be an *affirmative duty to disclose* information about health hazards to workers *in addition to a duty to honor worker-initiated* requests for access to records.

This paper focuses on several philosophical and policy-oriented problems about the right to know and correlative duties to disclose. Also addressed are some related rights, such as the right to refuse hazardous work and the right to contribute to the development of safety standards in the workplace.

I

The belief that citizens in general—though not workers in particular—have a right to know about significant risks is reflected in a diverse set of recent laws and federal regulations in the United States. These include The Freedom of Information Act, The Federal Insecticide, Fungicide, and Rodenticide Amendments and Regulations, The Motor Vehicle and School Bus Safety Amendments, The Truth-in-Lending Act, The Pension Reform Act, The Real Estate Settlement Procedures Act, The Federal Food, Drug, and Cosmetic Act, The Consumer Product Safety Act, and The Toxic Substances Control Act. These acts commonly require guidebooks, explanations of products, and warranties; the implicit message is that manufacturing companies and other businesses have a moral (and obviously in some cases an explicit legal) obligation to disclose information without which individuals could not adequately decide about matters of participation, usage, employment, or enrollment.[7]

If the right to know in the workplace parallels these developments in upcoming years, and comes to include a corporate responsibility to provide adequate information to workers about hazards in the workplace, this development could potentially have a pervasive and revolutionary effect on major American corporations. Workers do not now routinely receive such information from their employers, as is evidenced by OSHA's conclusion that, at least prior to the 1980 regulation, *denial* of access to exposure records was a frequent, though not universal, employer practice.[8] More importantly, workers are exposed to many hazards on a wide scale. There are over 30,000 pesticides now in use in the United States. The annual Registry of Toxic Effects of Chemical Substances lists over 25,000 chemicals. An estimated 25 million largely uninformed workers in North America (1 in 4 workers) are exposed to toxic substances regulated by the federal government, and one per cent of the labor force is exposed to known carcinogens. Over 44,000 U.S. workers are exposed *full time* to OSHA-regulated carcinogens.[9] A representative sample of American corporations whose workplaces have encountered controversy in the past about how to control hazards includes Philco, Johns-Manville, General Electric, Kennecott Copper, Union Carbide, RCA Victor, Allied Chemical, Lockheed Aircraft, General Motors, The Raytheon Co., Bell Telephone, American Petroleum Institute (representing virtually all oil companies), Raybestos-Manhattan, and Dow Chemical. In every case unresolved questions remain about the acceptability of known hazards in the workplace.[10]

II

The most developed models of disclosure obligations and the right to know are presently found in the extensive literature on informed consent, which also deals with informed refusal.[11] This literature developed largely from contexts of fiduciary relationships between physicians and patients or investigators and subjects, where there are broadly recognized moral and legal obligations to disclose known risks (and benefits) associated with a proposed treatment or research maneuver. No parallel obligation traditionally has been legally recognized in nonfiduciary relationships, such as that between management and workers. Except for special and limited regulations that require warnings or signs about individual substances or conditions, there is currently no general legal requirement in the U.S. that employers actively warn workers about the above-mentioned hazards in the workplace. There may nonetheless be moral requirements, and the law may need substantial revision. We shall argue for both conclusions.

The recent history of informed consent requirements in fiduciary relationships clearly does provide important and relevant data for discussions of nonfiduciary contexts. It offers a model of disclosure that seems promising for the workplace. However, this model will prove to have only severely limited application in the workplace.

III

The nonfiduciary nature of the relationship between employers and employees certainly provides one sound reason for skepticism about applying an informed consent model to risk in the workplace. There are other reasons as well. There is currently no pervasive legal duty of disclosure in the workplace because risks in this environment have thus far been handled by workmen's compensation laws. These laws were originally designed for problems of accident in instances of immediately assessible damage. Duties to warn or to disclose are formally pointless under the no-fault conception operative in workmen's compensation, and there is no functional equivalent of the concept of an explicit voluntary assumption of a risk. To be compensated for an injury, a worker must show only that an injury occurred; there is no need to show that someone was responsible, and therefore no reason to show that there should have been a warning or a valid consent. The problem is one of legal causation: a physician may be sued by causing an injury through nondisclosure or underdisclosure; management may not, unless fraudulent misrepresentation is involved.

Reasons traditionally invoked for establishing such starkly different arrangements of responsibility, causation, and compensation for medicine and for industry are now crumbling. It has been relatively easy in the past to disassociate disclosure of information from causation of industrial "accidents" and from problems of compensation; but the fact that asbestos or cotton fibers, for example, present serious long-term risks of injury, disease, and death is different from the fact that radial saws and pathways along steel girders lead to similarly serious accidents. Every worker on the job already knows of the existence of the latter dangers—though not of the magnitude of those risks; e.g., plant injury rates are seldom known. (Moreover, as *Canterbury* and other cases make clear, there is no duty even in fiduciary contexts to disclose what a reasonable person in the situation would *already* know.) Recently discovered risks to health in the workplace thus carry with them a *greater need* for information on the basis of which a person may wish to take one or several actions, including choosing to forego employment completely, to refuse certain work environments within a place of employment, to wear protective devices, or to agitate for higher minimum exposure standards.

We are presently unprepared by our legal tradition to deal with these questions about the worker's need for information. Clearly the informed consent model cannot simply be transplanted to the workplace. We are therefore ripe for a discussion of the responsibility of employers—and perhaps other parties—to make disclosures about risks quite independently of current law.

IV

Unlike physician-patient relationships, employee-employer relationships invite disclosure requirements for risk information *because* no fiduciary relationship or common goal exists between the parties—the relationship often being confrontational, with few interests and goals shared in common, and therefore increased risks presented to workers.[12] The greater likelihood of harm to employees, and even their relative powerlessness in the employer-employee relationship, may not be sufficient to justify employer disclosure obligations in all cases, but placing relevant information in the hands of workers surely seems appropriate in at least some cases. By what criteria, then, shall such disclosure obligations be determined to begin and end, and how is negligence to be determined?

We must again resist all temptation to squeeze the analogy to medicine dry, for it is implausible to suppose that employers can be reconceived as fiduciaries. As customarily conceived, both government and unions have a relationship to employees more closely approximately a fiduciary relationship than do employers. This only indicates, however, that in some contexts the government or a union leader is a more likely candidate to be held culpable for not providing information than an employer.[13] The question still must be faced whether the moral point of view provides an adequate argument for the acceptance of a particular standard of disclosure in the workplace.

One plausible argument is the following: Because large employers, unions, and government agencies must deal with multiple employees and complicated causal conditions, no standard *more* demanding than the objective reasonable person standard is appropriate for general industry disclosures. That is, no party is to be held responsible for disclosing information beyond that needed to make an informed choice about the adequacy of safety precautions, industrial hygiene, long-term hazards, and the like, as determined by what the reasonable person would judge to be the worker's need for information material to a decision about employment or working conditions. It does not follow, however, that this general standard of disclosure—which would in practice be used for disclosures to unions who represent employees (or to groups of employees)—is adequate for all individual disclosures. At least in the case of extremely serious hazards—such as those involved in short-term, but concentrated doses of radiation—the subjective standard may be more appropriate.[14]

Accordingly, in cases where disclosures to *individual* workers may be expected to have significant subjective impact and variance, the reasonable person standard should perhaps be supplemented by a subjective standard that takes account of independent informational needs. An alternative that might be viable would be to include the following as a component of all general disclosures under the reasonable person standard: "If you are concerned about the possible effect of hazards on your individual health, and you seek clarification or personal information, a company physician may be consulted by making an appointment." An entirely subjective standard would be inappropriate, because workers will rarely know what information would be relevant for their deliberations and underdisclosures would therefore regularly occur. Perhaps the most satisfactory solution is a compromise standard: Whatever a reasonable person would judge material to the decision-making process should be disclosed, and in addition any remaining information material to an individual worker should be provided through a process of asking what he or she is concerned about as a special problem.[15]

V

Despite the direction of the arguments thus far, there are reasons why it will prove far more difficult in practice to honor the right to know for workers than corresponding rights for patients. There are, for example, more complicated questions about the kinds of information to be disclosed, as well as by whom, to whom, and under what conditions it ought to be released. There is also the problem of what to do if workers themselves are inhibited from reacting to information as they would otherwise act because of economic or other constraints—e.g., industries where ten persons stand in line for every available position. The intractability of these questions is magnified in the workplace by the massive numbers of persons directly affected and by the legitimate interests of third parties—in this case the federal government and the public whose cost concerns it represents. However, we must set these considerations aside here in order to consider what is perhaps the single greatest difficulty about the right to know about risks in the workplace: the right to refuse hazardous work assignments and to have effective mechanisms for workers to reduce the risks they face.

Several important issues turn on the options available to informed workers to reduce or remove personal risks. In a limited range of cases, it is possible for informed workers to reject employment because health and safety conditions are regarded as unacceptable. This decision is most likely to be reached in a job market where workers have alternative employment opportunities or where a worker is being offered a new assignment with the option of remaining in his or her current job. More commonly, however, workers are not in a position to respond to information about health hazards by seeking employment elsewhere. For the information to be useful, it must be possible for the worker to effect change while staying on the job.

The United States Occupational Safety and Health Act of 1970 (OSH

Act)[16] confers a series of rights on employees which appear to give increased significance to the duty to disclose hazards in the workplace. Specifically, the OSH Act grants workers the right to request an OSHA inspection if they believe an OSHA standard has been violated or an imminent hazard exists. Under the Act, employees also have the right to participate in OSHA inspections of the worksite and to consult freely with the inspection officer. Perhaps most importantly, employees requesting an inspection or otherwise exercising their rights under the OSH Act are explicitly protected in the Act from dischargement and from any form of discrimination by current or future employees.

While these worker rights under the OSH Act are important, it can be argued that they do not go far enough in insuring that workers have effective mechanisms for initiating inspections of suspected health hazards. It should be noted that federal, state, and municipal employees are not covered by the OSH Act and that unions are not afforded the same protections against discrimination as individual employees. There are also serious questions about the ability of the Occupational Safety and Health Administration to enforce provisions of the OSH Act. If workers are to make effective use of disclosed information about health hazards, they must have unimpeded access to an effective and efficient regulatory system.

It is also essential that workers have an adequately protected right to refuse unsafe work. It is difficult to determine the extent to which this right is legally protected at the present time. Although the OSH Act does not grant a general right to refuse unsafe work,[17] provisions to this effect exist in some state occupational safety laws. In addition, the Secretary of Labor has issued a regulation that interprets the OSH Act as including a limited right to refuse unsafe work, a right which was upheld by the U.S. Supreme Court in 1980.[18] A limited right of refusal is also protected explicitly in the Labor-Management Relations Act (LMRA) and implicitly in the National Labor Relations Act (NLRA).[19]

Unfortunately, these statutory protections vary significantly in the conditions under which they grant a right to refuse and the consequences which they permit to follow from such refusals. For example, the OSHA regulation allows workers to walk off the job where there is a "real danger of death or serious injury," while the LMRA permits refusals only under "abnormally dangerous conditions."[20] Thus, under the LMRA, the nature of the occupation determines the extent of danger justifying refusal, while under OSHA the character of the threat is determinative. By contrast, under the NLRA a walkout may be justified for even minimal safety problems, so long as the action can be construed as a concerted activity for mutual aid and protection and there does not exist a no-strike clause in any collective bargaining agreements.[21] While the NLRA would appear to provide the broadest protection to workers, employees refusing to work under the NLRA may lose the right to be reinstated in their positions if permanent replacements can be found.[22]

The relative merits of the different statutes are further confused by questions of overlapping authority. It is not always clear (1) when a worker is eligible to claim protection under each law, (2) which law affords a worker maximum protection in a particular circumstance, and (3) whether or under what conditions a worker can seek relief through more than one law or directly through the courts.

The overall legal situation concerning the right to refuse hazardous work in the United States is far too complicated to be adequately treated here. Any definitive treatment of the problem will need to consider not only narrow legal questions of jurisdiction and remedy but also important policy and moral questions raised by the conflicting interests of employees and employers. Unfortunately, these questions have not received much attention outside limited legal circles. Consider, for example, whether a meaningful right to refuse hazardous work entails an obligation to continue to pay nonworking employees, or to award the employees back-pay if the issue is resolved in their favor. It could be argued that workers without union strike benefits or other income protections are unable to exercise their right to refuse unsafe work because of undue economic pressures. On the other hand, it could be argued that to permit such workers to draw a paycheck is to legitimate strike with pay, a practice generally considered unacceptable by management and by Congress.

Also unresolved is whether the right to refuse unsafe work should be restricted to cases of obvious, imminent, and serious risks to health or life (the current OSHA and LMRA position) or expanded to include lesser risks and also uncertain risks—e.g., as discussed centrally in this paper, exposure to suspected toxic or carcinogenic substances. Certainly, if "the right to know" is to lead to meaningful worker action, workers must be able to remove themselves from exposure to *suspected* hazards, as well as *obvious* or *known* hazards.

Related to this issue is the question of the *proper standard* for determining whether a safety walkout is justified. At least three different standards have been proposed (and even imposed): a good-faith standard, which requires only a determination that the worker honestly (subjectively) believes that the health hazard exists; a reasonable person standard which requires that the belief be reasonable under the circumstances, as well as sincerely held; and an objective standard which requires evidence, generally established by expert witnesses, that the threat actually exists.[23] (The similarities between these three standards and the three standards for the duty to disclose discussed in Section IV are obvious and pertinent.) Although the possibility of worker abuse of the right to refuse has been a major factor in a current trend to reject the good faith standard, recent commentary has argued that this trend raises serious equity issues in the proper balancing of this concern with the needs of workers confronted with basic self-preservation issues.[24]

Still another related issue is whether the right to refuse hazardous work should be protected only until a review is initiated (at which time the worker must return to the job) or whether the walk-out should be permitted until the alleged hazard is at least temporarily removed. So long as the hazards covered under a right to refuse are restricted to those risks which are obvious in the environment and which are easily established as health hazards, this issue is relatively easy to resolve. However, if the nature of the risk is less apparent—as in the case of the risks treated in this paper—a major function of the right to refuse will be to call attention to an alleged hazard and to compel regulatory action. If this chain of events is set in motion, requiring workers to continue to be exposed while OSHA or the NLRB conduct investigations may be unacceptable to workers and certainly will be unacceptable if the magnitude of potential harm is perceived as great. On the other hand, compelling employers to remove suspected hazards during the evaluation period may result in intolerable economic burdens. We therefore need a delineation of the conditions under which workers may be compelled to return to work while an alleged hazard is being evaluated and the conditions under which employers must be compelled to remove alleged hazards. This problem is a special case of the aforementioned issue of setting standards for acceptable risks in the workplace.

VI

In conclusion, legal rights will be of no practical consequence if workers remain ignorant of their options. It is doubtful that many workers, particularly nonunion workers, are even aware that they have a legally protected right to refuse hazardous work, let alone that there are at least three statutory provisions protecting that right. Even if workers were aware of such a right, it is unlikely that they could weave their way through the maze of legal options unaided. If there is to be a meaningful right to know in the workplace, there will also have to be an adequate program to educate workers about their rights and how to exercise them, as well as adequate legal protection of this and related worker rights.[25]

Notes

1. See Elihu D. Richter, "The Worker's Right to Know: Obstacles, Ambiguities, and Loopholes," *Journal of Health Politics, Policy and Law* 6 (1981), p. 340; Gail Bronson, "The Right to Know," *The Wall Street Journal* (Eastern Edition), July 1, 1977, p. 4 and Editorial, January 1, 1979; George Miller, "The Asbestos Coverup," *Congressional Record* (May 17, 1979), pp. E2363–64, and "Asbestos Health Hazards and Company Morality," *Congressional Record* (May 24, 1979), pp. E2523–24.
2. NIOSH, *et al.*, "The Right to Know: Practical Problems and Policy Issues Arising from Exposures to Hazardous Chemical and Physical Agents in the Workplace," a report prepared at the request of the Subcommittee on Labor and Committee on Human Resources, U.S. Senate (Washington, D.C.: July 1977), pp. 1 and 5.
3. Occupational Safety and Health Administration, "Access to Employee Exposure and Medical Records—Final Rules," *Federal Register*, May 23, 1980, pp. 35212–77. (Hereafter referred to as OSHA regulations.)

4. State of New York, 1979–1980 Regular Sessions, 7103-D, Article 28, para. 880.
5. OSHA regulations, Section III, g., p. 35280.
6. Elihu D. Richter, *op. cit.,* p. 341.
7. On this point, cf. Harold J. Magnuson, "The Right to Know," *Archives of Environmental Health* 32 (1977), pp. 40–44.
8. OSHA regulations, p. 35214.
9. See NIOSH, *et al.,* "The Right to Know," pp. 3, 9.
10. For a useful public policy perspective, see P. Weiner, "Testimony to OSHA on Employee Access to Records" (December 5, 1978).
11. The issue of the right to know in the workplace could also be profitably explored through an examination of the literature on the analogous issue of the *patient's right to know,* and in particular, the literature on patient access to medical records. For a discussion of the relationship between this literature and the issue of workers' rights of access to employer records, see the OSHA regulations, particularly pp. 35228–35236.
12. However, we hasten to add that assertions of industry's reluctance to provide information and disclose risks may often be unduly exaggerated by critics. It is frequently in industry's long-term interest to report hazards and restructure environments.
13. There may of course be circumstances in which employers or other parties will *justifiably* withhold information from employees, just as the government or physicians will sometimes justifiably withhold information.
14. The special needs of *unrepresented* workers would also have to be considered in electing any general standard(s). For an account that in effect demands a subjective standard for carcinogens, see Andrea Hricko, "The Right to Know," in Thomas P. Vogl, ed., *Public Information in the Prevention of Occupational Cancer: Proceedings of a Symposium,* December 2–3, 1976, (Washington: National Academy of Sciences, 1977), esp. p. 72.
15. As more and more data are gathered regarding the effects of workplace hazards on particular predisposing conditions, the need for disclosure of such information can be identified through preemployment physical examinations without the worker's needing to ask questions.
16. 29 U.S.C. § 651–678 (1970).
17. Susan Preston, "A Right Under OSHA to Refuse Unsafe Work or a Hobson's Choice of Safety or Job?," *University of Baltimore Law Review* 8 (Spring 1979), pp. 519–550.
18. The Secretary's interpretation of the OSH Act was upheld by the Supreme Court on February 26, 1980, see *Law Week,* 48:33, pp. 4189–4195, for Feb. 26, 1980, and *The New York Times* (February 27, 1980), p. 15.
19. Susan Preston, "A Right Under OSHA to Refuse Unsafe Work or a Hobson's Choice of Safety or Job?," pp. 519–550.
20. 29 U.S.C. § 143 (1976), and 29 CFR § 1977.12 (1978).
21. Nicholas Ashford and Judith P. Katz, "Unsafe Working Conditions: Employee Rights Under the Labor Management Relations Act and the Occupational Safety and Health Act," *Notre Dame Lawyer* 52 (June 1977), pp. 802–837.
22. Susan Preston, "A Right Under OSHA to Refuse Unsafe Work or a Hobson's Choice of Safety or Job?," p. 543.
23. Nancy K. Frank, "A Question of Equity: Workers' 'Right to Refuse' Under OSHA Compared to the Criminal Necessity Defense," *Labor Law Journal* 31 (October 1980), pp. 617–626.

24. *Ibid.*
25. Work on this essay was supported by a grant from the National Library of
    Medicine. Earlier drafts were read at the Philosophy Department, University
    of Pittsburgh, at the School of Public Health, University of Minnesota, at the
    Hastings Center, and at the Philosophy Department, the University of Col-
    orado. We received valuable comments that altered the substance and form of
    the paper from Stephen Teret and Nancy King. We are also indebted to
    Alasdair MacIntyre, Terry Pinkard, Ron Giere, Arthur Caplan, Rachel
    Laudan, Kurt Baier, Nicholas Rescher, David Braybrooke, H. Tristram
    Engelhardt, Jr., Gilbert Omenn, and Deborah Kohrman for helpful com-
    ments and criticism.

BANYARD v.
NATIONAL LABOR RELATIONS BOARD

These consolidated petitions[1] for review of orders of the National Labor
Relations Board call into question the Board's application of its *Spielberg*
and *Collyer*[2] doctrines. Because we find the Board has erroneously applied
those doctrines in these cases, we remand for further proceedings.

I

Banyard's Case

. . . James Banyard worked as a truck driver for McLean Trucking Company and its predecessor for 22 years and also served as the Union's appointed shop steward since 1955. He was fired on 7 October 1969 for refusing to drive a truck admittedly overloaded in violation of Ohio state law.[3]
At the time of his discharge there was in effect between the Company and
the Union the National Master Freight Agreement and the Central States
Area Local Cartage Supplemental Agreement. Article 16 of the contract
provided that employees would not be required to violate any applicable
statute or a governmental regulation relating to safety.

On 6 October 1969 Banyard was dispatched to pick up 800 fifty-pound
sacks of breading at Specialty Products Company in Cleveland. He was
reluctant to haul what he considered an overweight load, but when he expressed his reluctance to a Specialty employee, he was told that he would
have to call his dispatcher if he wanted to reduce the size of the load.
Banyard telephoned the dispatcher and was told to "load the front end
light and the back end heavy, and . . . bring it in." He loaded the truck
and again telephoned the terminal. When he refused to "bring it in," he
was instructed to drop the trailer and return to the terminal. He was
discharged the following day.

Pursuant to Articles 8, 42, and 43 of the contract, the Union had pros-

---

505 Federal Reporter, 2d 342. Opinion by Judge Wilkey, United States Court of Appeals, District of Columbia Circuit.

ecuted Banyard's grievance through two stages of grievance procedure when on 2 January 1970 Banyard filed a charge with the National Labor Relations Board alleging violation by the Company of section 8(a) (1) and (3) of the National Labor Relations Act of 1947. On 23 July 1970 the trial examiner concluded that although the grievance proceedings were under way, there was no award for the Board to recognize. He went on to find that Banyard's discharge violated sections 8(a) (1) and (3) of the Act.

Although the Company filed timely exceptions, the Board reached no decision until after the Union's claim had been denied at the final stage of the contract grievance procedure. On 23 March 1973 the Board dismissed the unfair labor practice complaint, deferring to the decision of the National Grievance Procedure under *Spielberg.*

Ferguson's Case

Clay D. Ferguson worked as an over-the-road driver for Roadway Express, Inc., for nine years. He was fired on 24 March 1972 for refusing to drive a truck which he asserted was unsafe. At the time of Ferguson's discharge there was in effect between the Company and the Union the National Master Freight Agreement and the Carolina Freight Council Over the Road Supplemental Agreement. Article 16 of the contract provided that employees would not be required to operate vehicles not in safe operating condition.

On 20 March 1972 Ferguson was assigned a tractor to drive from Nashville, Tennessee, to Columbia, South Carolina. Finding it difficult to hold the road—and therefore believing the truck to be unsafe—he hailed a second Roadway driver who happened by and asked him to road test the tractor for possible defects. When the second driver confirmed the danger,[4] Ferguson proceeded with caution to Hageman's, a nearby truck stop, and telephoned his dispatcher who instructed him to allow the Hageman's mechanic to road test the vehicle. When the mechanic also expressed doubt over the vehicle's safety,[5] Ferguson again telephoned his dispatcher, refusing to proceed any farther, and was told to wait at Hageman's for Roadway personnel. Roadway sent a safety supervisor and a mechanic, both of whom indicated that the vehicle was safe, but Ferguson still refused to drive. Pursuant to Ferguson's request, a Department of Transportation Safety Investigator arrived, inspected (but did not drive) the tractor, and stated that he could find nothing wrong.[6] Roadway's replacement driver then drove the tractor ten or fifteen miles and reported it safe to drive. When Ferguson then refused to drive the tractor "unless somebody from Roadway Express signs a statement that they will be responsible for the unit," he was discharged.

Pursuant to Articles 43 and 44 of the contract, Ferguson's grievance was heard by the Carolina Joint Bi-State Grievance Committee and denied on 11 April 1972. Four days earlier, Ferguson had filed a charge with the National Labor Relations Board alleging violation by Roadway of section 8(a) (1) of the National Labor Relations Act. The opinion of the trial examiner deferring to the Joint Committee award and dismissing the complaint was affirmed by the Board on 25 April 1973.

II.

In *Spielberg* (post-arbitral) the Board established its policy of dismissing unfair labor practice complaints where the issues involved had been previously resolved by arbitral award. Under *Collyer* (pre-arbitral) the Board will withhold its processes until the parties first submit to those processes upon which they have privately agreed. If, after the Board has withheld under *Collyer,* the unfair labor practice issues are resolved by the arbitral tribunal, the Board will apply *Spielberg* and defer to the arbitral award.

[1] In three opinions this year by Judges Wright and Tamm of this court, the *Spielberg* and *Collyer* doctrines are analyzed. Recognizing that

> submission to grievance and arbitration proceedings of disputes which might involve unfair labor practices would be substantially discouraged if the disputants thought the Board would give *de novo* consideration to the issue which the arbitrator might resolve[,][7]

in Associated Press v. NLRB,[8] we approved the application of both *Spielberg* and *Collyer.* However, our acceptance of those doctrines was and is founded upon the premise that they are appropriately applied only where the resolution of the contractual issues is congruent with the resolution of the statutory unfair labor practice issues. In Local Union 2188 v. NLRB we held: "This congruence between the contractual dispute and the overlying unfair labor practice charge is significant. If it were not present, the Board's abstention might . . . constitute [ ] not deference, but abdication."[9] Moreover, shortly thereafter in Local Union 715 v. NLRB, we held that abstention is proper only where three prerequisites (established in the *Spielberg* opinion itself) are met: (1) fair and regular arbitral proceedings, (2) parties agreed to be bound by the arbitral award, and (3) a decision which is "not clearly repugnant to the purposes and policies of the National Labor Relations Act."[10]

Banyard

[2] As found by the trial examiner, the Company has engaged in the practice of requiring its employees to haul overloaded trucks in violation of state law. Banyard's attempts to protest the practice ultimately resulted in his discharge in 1969. We agree with the conclusion of the trial examiner:

> In the instant case, it is patent that the issue raised by the allegations of the complaint, namely, whether Banyard has been discharged by Respondent because of his concerted or union activity, is not one which falls within the special competence of an arbitrator, but is primarily one for resolution under the provisions of the Act which the Board has been mandated by Congress to enforce.

With respect to the issue whether the purpose of the Ohio law was for the protection of this driver, or other drivers on the highways, or for the protection of the highways, the Board majority refused to substitute its judgment for that of the Grievance Committee, but pointed out that no points were assessed against the license of any driver caught hauling an overload, and that during periods of suspension of a driver's license the Company agreed to provide employment at equivalent earnings. Whatever the primary purpose of the Ohio law (which we need not determine), aside from possible loss of license *vel non,* there are other valid reasons for refusing to haul overloads in violation of state law. The trial examiner found definite safety risks involved in the practice.[11] These risks pose a danger not only to the driver himself, but to the rest of the motoring public as well.

Our review of the transcript fails to reveal that the Committee considered such important issues as safety. Moreover, the actual Committee award does not indicate that the Committee's judgment was exercised at all on the crucial issues regarding violation of the Ohio statute. . . .

[3] Regardless of the purpose of the Ohio statute, it remains axiomatic that it was still the law; for this or any other company to require its employees to act in violation thereof can never be upheld by the Board or this court. We concur in the dissenting Board members' perception of the dispositive issue in this case, *viz.,* "No contract provision or arbitration award can permit an employer to require his employees to violate state laws or to create safety hazards for themselves or others." Left standing, the arbitral award below grants the Company a license to violate state law and as such is void as against public policy and repugnant to the purposes of the National Labor Relations Act.

[4] Congress recognized that neither employers, employees, nor labor organizations have "any right in [their] relations with each other to engage in acts or practices which jeopardize the public health, safety, or interest." Whether Banyard's discharge was violative of section 8(a) (1) of the Act was the proper issue for the Board's consideration, and this in turn necessarily embraced the admitted violations of Ohio law and their repugnance to public policy and the purposes of the Act. To the three prerequisites of *Spielberg* already listed in *Local Union 715, supra,* we would add that the *Spielberg* doctrine only applies if the arbitral tribunal (A) clearly decided the issue on which it is later urged that the Board should give deference, and (B) the arbitral tribunal decided an issue within its competence. Here the doctrine was misapplied as to these two prerequisites. Moreover, the arbitral tribunal's award appears repugnant to the statute.

Ferguson

[5] Section 7 of the Act extends to employees "the right . . . to engage in . . . concerted activities for the purpose of . . . mutual aid or protection. . . ." Ferguson contends that his refusal to drive was a protest against "abnormally dangerous" working conditions protected under section 502 of the Act and a protest on behalf of other employees against the unsafe condition of the vehicle and to secure its repair. He argues that such protest constitutes protected activity under section 7. The Board argues that its deferral under *Spielberg* was proper because the statutory question —whether in all the circumstances Ferguson was justified in refusing to operate the tractor because of unsafe operating conditions "was squarely faced by the Joint Committee since Article 16 of the contract prohibited

discharging Ferguson unless his refusal to drive based on safety factors 'is unjustified.''' Yet the Board's characterization of the contract and statutory issues as identical does not make them so, and our decisions make it clear that deferral on statutory issues is proper only where there is congruence with contractual issues.

We perceive the resolution of the statutory issue here as dependent upon whether, in the Board's own language, "the actual working conditions shown to exist by competent evidence might in the circumstances reasonably be considered 'abnormally dangerous.''' Rejecting the conclusion of the Third Circuit that "an employee's honest belief, no matter how unjustified, in the existence of 'abnormally dangerous conditions for work' necessarily invokes the protection of § 502," the Supreme Court in Gateway Coal Company v. United Mine Workers of America recently held that "a union seeking to justify a contractually prohibited work stoppage under § 502 must present 'ascertainable, objective evidence supporting its conclusion that an abnormally dangerous condition for work exists.'''

Our reluctance in the case *sub judice* to sanction the Board's deferral to the Joint Committee award stems from our uncertainty over whether the standard applied by the Joint Committee to the *contractual* issue before it is the correct standard to be applied to the *statutory* issue before the Board. Our concern is that the Joint Committee applied a "safe-in-fact" standard and thereby found that Ferguson was not contractually justified in refusing to drive the tractor. Under the more liberal *Gateway Coal* standard the Board might have concluded that Ferguson's belief that the tractor was unsafe was amply supported by "ascertainable, objective evidence."

Our approval of the Board's deferral under *Spielberg* of statutory issues to arbitral resolution along with contractual issues is conditioned upon the resolution by the arbitral tribunal of *congruent* statutory and contractual issues. In that situation "the arbitration award becomes the sole remedy for both contractual and statutory violations." If in the present case the Joint Committee applied to the issue before it a standard correct under the contract but not under judicial interpretation of section 502, then it cannot be said that the statutory issue was decided by the Joint Committee. In that event the Board's abstention goes beyond deferral and approaches abdication.

As in Banyard's case, the award of the Grievance Committee in this case was exceedingly brief. After merely summarizing the Company's and the Union's positions, the award states in its entirety:

Claim of Union denied.

The trial examiner, whose findings were adopted by the Board in this case, stated that the "Committee in reaching its conclusion to deny the grievance had to conclude that Ferguson's refusal to drive the vehicle was unjustified." Yet the failure of the Committee to amplify its decision forced the trial examiner to speculate by what standard the refusal was "unjustified." Neither the examiner, the Board, nor we are entitled to engage in such speculation.

Accordingly, these petitions are remanded with instructions that deferral not being appropriate, the Board should proceed to a consideration of the unfair labor practice issues in a manner not inconsistent with this opinion.

So ordered.

Notes

1. Spielberg Manufacturing Co., 112 N.L.R.B. 1080 (1955).
2. Collyer Insulated Wire, 192 N.L.R.B. 837 (1971).
3. The parties stipulated that Ohio law prohibited a weight exceeding 19,000 pounds plus three percent tolerance on the drive axle, and/or a weight exceeding 32,000 pounds plus three percent on the trailer axle. The trial examiner found that the 6 October shipment was in excess of the lawful weight under Ohio law and that Banyard did in fact refuse to pull an overload on that date. . . .
4. Testifying before the trial examiner, Roy Potts (the second driver) stated: "Well, it scared me. I thought maybe it was going to break in two. . . . I didn't see how that I could drive the truck because I thought it was unsafe." . . .
5. The mechanic testified that "I told him [Ferguson] that I wouldn't drive it, and that in my opinion the tractor was not safe to be on the road and get somebody else killed." . . .
6. Claude Gatlin, Jr., Safety Investigator of the Department of Transportation, would state neither that the tractor was safe nor that it was unsafe. Gatlin merely inspected the vehicle and could find nothing visibly wrong with it.
7. Associated Press v. NLRB, 160 U.S. App. D.C. 396, 401, 492 F.2d 662, 667 (1974).
8. *Ibid.*
9. Local Union 2188, AFL-CIO v. NLRB, 161 U.S.App.D.C. 168, 172, 494 F.2d 1087, 1091 (1974).
10. Local Union 715, AFL-CIO v. NLRB, 161 U.S.App.D.C. 217, 219, 494, F.2d 1136, 1138 (1974).
11. One employee testified that he had trouble maintaining traffic speed with an overload and that he could not brake an overload to a stop as he could a legal load. Both Banyard and another employee confirmed the difficult braking. Banyard also testified, and the trial examiner found, that overloading limits maneuverability. . . .

MAGRI v. *GIARRUSSO*

Plaintiff, Irvin L. Magri, Jr., was dismissed from his job as a sergeant with the New Orleans Police Department on July 18, 1974. As the letter of dismissal from the Superintendent of Police, Clarence B. Giarrusso,

379 F. Supp. 353. Opinion by Chief Judge Heebe, U.S. District Court E. D. Louisiana.

makes clear, this action was taken because of Magri's persistent public criticism of the superintendent, in violation of the regulations of the department. Suit was filed against the superintendent and the mayor, Moon Landrieu, pursuant to 28 U.S.C. § 1343 and 42 U.S.C. § 1983, seeking reinstatement due to the alleged infringements of rights protected by the First and Fourteenth Amendments.

After a lengthy hearing in which numerous problems relating to the administration of the police department and the city itself were aired, the following picture emerges. Giarrusso was appointed Police Superintendent in August of 1970, at which time Magri, then a patrolman on the force, was organizing the Patrolman's Association of New Orleans. In fact, he had been elected its president in November of 1969. From the time Giarrusso took office, relations between the two were, to say the least, strained. As president of the Patrolman's Association of New Orleans, Magri wrote literally hundreds of letters to the superintendent critical of the police department's practices and policies. Carbon copies of many of these letters were sent to local television and radio stations and the local newspapers. In the first several months of Giarrusso's tenure, Magri mailed to the superintendent over one hundred of such letters. In addition, Magri habitually held press conferences, issued press releases and appeared on television and radio to publicize a wide variety of the problems confronting the police department, such as low pay, deteriorating district stations and the lack of adequate equipment, problems, we note, which plague the police departments of many large cities across the nation. The radio appearances took the form of a weekly talk show. Although the superintendent also utilized the media to respond to Magri's public criticism of himself and his policies, there is evidence of only one occasion during this time when Magri was ordered to temper his remarks. . . . The Court thus finds that from 1969 through 1973 no attempt was made to curb Magri's comments on matters of public concern relating to the police department and its relationship with the union and the public. We, therefore, focus our attention on events which occurred in 1974, as Magri's firing was provoked by statements made during that time.

Before turning to these statements, it is necessary to detail to a certain extent the context in which they were made. Within approximately three months of the signing of the contract, the first crisis developed. The Collective Bargaining Contract provided, *inter alia:*

> Supervisory employees (including but not limited to the Superintendent of Police, Deputy Superintendent . . . *Sergeants, Desk Sergeants) . . . are specifically excluded from the provisions of this Agreement and from membership in the Patrolmen's Association of New Orleans.* (emphasis added)

On December 7, 1973, the city was informed that the Patrolman's Association of New Orleans and the Supervisor's Association of New Orleans had voted to merge into one union, effective December 31, 1973. The new union was to be known as the Policeman's Association of New Orleans. At approximately this time and at his own request, Magri was promoted to the rank of sergeant. He continued to serve as president of the new union.

The letter further stated that:

> More particularly, vindictive inflammatory remarks made by you without any proof, whatsoever and with a reckless disregard of the actual facts known to you, or personally discoverable by you, were apparently calculated and have tended to undermine the authority of my office in connection with the efficient administration of the Department as well as having an adverse effect on leadership and morale.

The letter went on to cite those particular statements quoted above upon which the superintendent relied in discharging Magri, statements which Magri has never denied having made. The superintendent concluded the letter by advising Magri that his intemperate remarks constituted a violation of several departmental regulations, including most importantly, Article 33 which reads in pertinent part as follows:

CRITICISM

> Members and employees shall not publicly criticize or ridicule the department, its policies or other employees by talking, writing or expressing in any other manner, where such talking, writing or other expression:

>   *   *   *   *   *   *

> d. tends to impair the operation of the department by interfering with its efficiency; interfering with the ability of supervisors to maintain discipline; or having been made with reckless disregard for truth or falsity.

Magri's major contention before this Court is that he was discharged from his position with the New Orleans Police Department in abrogation of his right to freedom of speech guaranteed by the First and Fourteenth Amendments to the Constitution. Additionally, he maintains that Article 33 is unconstitutionally vague and that the Police Department failed to accord him procedural due process in effectuating his dismissal. . . .

Plaintiff asserts that the language in the departmental regulation which prohibits public criticism of the department that *"tends* to impair the operation of the department by interfering with its efficiency; interfering with the ability of supervisors to maintain discipline; or having been made with reckless disregard for truth or falsity'' (emphasis added) is vague and overbroad on its face and therefore punishes constitutionally protected free speech. We note at the outset that this article has been added to the regulations since 1971 when this Court struck down several departmental regulations, in Flynn v. Giarrusso, 321 F.Supp. 1295 (E.D.La.1971), as being vague and overbroad. This new article was an attempt to rectify that which this Court found objectionable. In this regard we think it was successful. Article 33 does not distinguish between public and private speech, and it does limit the prohibition on speech to statements regarding the police department and its employees. Consequently, we do not find that the regulation is overbroad. Nor do we find that it is unconstitutionally vague in that there is now a standard against which a reviewing board or court can scrutinize the objectionable activity of a policeman. . . .

The instant Court would never intentionally put its stamp of approval on a regulation which includes language that would permit discharge of a public employee for exercising a constitutional right, as witnessed in Flynn

v. Giarrusso, *supra.* However, that does not mean that a court should strike down language as vague which sets out prohibitions on the speech of public employees " . . . in terms that the ordinary person exercising ordinary common sense can sufficiently understand and comply with, without sacrifice to the public interest."

Plaintiff next asserts that the manner of his discharge denied him his right to procedural due process. He complains that he was given no forewarning of the impending dismissal and was not granted a reasonable opportunity to respond to the superintendent prior to his discharge. . . . Under the current state of the law, we do not think it is required that a public employee, whether federal, state or municipal, be afforded a pre-termination hearing. . . . we do not agree that he was dismissed with no forewarning. The mayor of New Orleans, on several occasions, warned him that his abusive remarks concerning the superintendent could bring about his discharge. There undoubtedly are appropriate cases in which it would serve some useful purpose to reinstate a discharged employee and require that a notice of proposed removal provide for some type of hearing before the responsible authority. However, under the peculiar facts of this case, we think we would be performing a meaningless act. As previously pointed out, Magri has never denied publicly calling his superior a "liar" and a "coward" nor has there ever been any indication he would cease making such statements in the future.

Accordingly, we turn to the merits of this case to determine whether a police officer, who is both a sergeant on the force and president of the policemen's union, has a protected right to make public statements, which were previously quoted, such as Magri made. The controlling law dealing with public statements by public employees is found in Pickering v. Board of Education, 391 U.S. 563, 88 S.Ct. 1731, 20 L.Ed.2d 811 (1968), in which a teacher was dismissed by the Board of Education for publishing a letter in a newspaper which was critical of the Board. In *Pickering,* the Court held that ". . . absent proof of false statements knowingly or recklessly made by him, a teacher's exercise of his right to speak on issues of public importance may not furnish the basis for his dismissal from public employment." We could easily rest our decision on a finding that no constitutionally protected conduct on Magri's part was the basis of his discharge, i.e., that the false statements were knowingly or recklessly made. *See,* Whitsel v. Southeast Local School District, 484 F.2d 1222 (6th Cir. 1973). His statements that the superintendent was a "coward" and a "liar" were in response to statements of the superintendent in reference to matters about which Magri knew there was a difference of opinion. For example, he knew that the superintendent referred to him as "an alleged union president" because his official status as the union president had been challenged by the city under its contract with the patrolmen's association. Magri's statement that the superintendent impounded police overtime funds "to cause internal strife in the Police Department," which was obviously false, could only have been knowingly and recklessly made. Plaintiff introduced no evidence that Giarrusso did not have the welfare and best interests of his men at heart. On the contrary, this Court takes note, from the media over a period of years, of the superintendent's constant efforts to run a harmonious department.

However, even in *Pickering,* the Court made it clear that government employees may, in certain situations, be discharged for their speech without offending First Amendment guarantees. The Court stated in *Pickering, supra,* 391 U.S. at 568, 88 S.Ct. at 1734:

> At the same time it cannot be gain said that the State has interests as an employer in regulating the speech of its employees that differ significantly from those it possesses in connection with regulation of the speech of the citizenry in general. The problem in any case is to arrive at a balance between the interests of the teacher, as a citizen, in commenting upon matters of public concern and the interest of the State, as an employer, in promoting the efficiency of the public services it performs through its employees.

We are faced with the right of a policeman to speak out on matters of public concern against the superintendent's interest in promoting the efficiency of the police department. In balancing these conflicting interests, courts focus on those factors which the Court in *Pickering* indicated were absent from its case when it reinstated the plaintiff. These factors are succinctly set forth by the District Court for the District of Columbia in Tygrett v. Washington, 346 F. Supp. 1247, 1251 (1972):

1. Pickering's statements were not directed towards a person with whom he would normally be in contact in the course of his daily work as a teacher. 391 U.S. at 569–570, 88 S.Ct. at 1735;
2. Thus there was not present any question of maintaining discipline by immediate superiors and harmony among co-workers. *Id.* at 570, 88 S.Ct. at 1735;
3. Pickering's relationship with the Board of Education was not the kind of close working relationship for which it could be claimed that personal loyalty and confidence are essential. *Id.,* 88 S.Ct. at 1735;
4. Pickering's letter did not damage the professional reputation of the Board of Education and did not foment controversy and conflict among Pickering's co-workers. *Id.,* 88 S.Ct. at 1736.

All of these elements not found in the *Pickering* case are present in the instant one. It hardly needs pointing out that the superintendent needs the confidence and loyalty of his men in order to run an effective police department, in order to maintain an efficient and disciplined force. Magri's insubordinate remarks, bordering on the defamatory, worked to destroy this relationship between the superintendent and his men. That this is so was witnessed by the instant Judge who, in his courtroom, watched police supporters of Magri turn their backs on the superintendent of police as he entered and departed the courtroom on many occasions. The testimony of various ranking policemen of the force was to the same effect.

A public employee enjoys the rights of freedom of expression conferred by the First Amendment. This Court would have recognized and, indeed, encouraged responsible public criticism of the superintendent's policies, of the proposed police pay raise and of the proposed compulsory arbitration bill. But that does not include vitriolic remarks which this Court finds threatened significant working relationships vital to the administration of the police department.

Finally, Magri has argued that, as union president, he should be given wide latitude to criticize the superintendent and his policies. Although we agree that the extent of his criticism may be greater, his criticism in the capacity of union president has limits implicit in his status as a member of the police department. We have found those limits were overreached.

For the foregoing reasons,

It is ordered, adjudged and decreed that the relief of reinstatement sought by plaintiff in his Complaint and Application for Injunctive Relief, be, and the same is hereby, denied.

case 1: Jobs and Controversy

Philip Washburn, supervisor of urban affairs at a Pennsylvania plant of Mammoth Steel Corporation, was fired by his employer after local newspaper articles identified him as a member of the city's Civic League, a volunteer group that studied various social problems of the city where Mr. Washburn worked and lived. The newspaper described a report by the League that asserted that the relatively higher dropout rate among the city's black high school population was caused by limited local employment opportunities and that major employers in the area still had some way to go before they met reasonable affirmative action goals in both blue-collar and white-collar hiring and promotion. Mammoth Steel was the largest employer in the city and one of only two or three companies that could be called "major employers" there. A spokesman for Mammoth promptly issued a statement calling attention to Mammoth's "long-standing policy of nondiscrimination."

The president of Mammoth Steel later explained, in answer to a question raised at the annual stockholders meeting, that Mr. Washburn was not experienced in personnel matters and that the company believed there was a risk he might be regarded as speaking for Mammoth at the Civic League. Mr. Washburn, a white, 43-year-old father of three, whose job had involved the company's relations with various departments of the city government, replied to a reporter that he had made it clear "several times" he was acting on his own, as a private citizen, in the Civic League.

At about the time Mr. Washburn's case came to public notice, the *Wall Street Journal* news staff learned of two similar incidents. One concerned a 32-year-old lawyer who resigned from the most prestigious law firm in a large, older Alabama city after he wrote a letter to the Alabama superintendent of education protesting a state move to make Bible reading a regular part of the state-required curriculum. The young lawyer argued that this would defy the U.S. Supreme Court's ban on classroom prayers in public schools. The state superintendent mailed a copy of his reply to the partners of the young man's

This case was prepared by the Committee for Education in Business Ethics under a grant from the National Endowment for the Humanities.

law firm, "because," said the superintendent, "they're acquaintances of mine and I thought they should know about it."

The young man told the *Wall Street Journal* that "it was generally felt in the city that people shouldn't get involved in things like that. The feeling was enhanced if you were on the 'wrong' side of an issue. I wasn't asked to leave, but after that I decided I had a better future elsewhere." A partner in the law firm said it would be "professionally improper" for him to comment on the resignation.

Another such incident involved activity at the opposite end of the political spectrum. An executive of a Midwestern advertising agency resigned after his superiors ordered him to quit making speeches on Communist propaganda techniques. "They said the talks were right-wing, controversial, and bad for the agency," he recalled, "I disagreed with the right-wing part. I quit because I felt no one could tell me what to do with my own time."

The *Wall Street Journal* saw these as a crop of events worth investigating and went in search of executives who would comment on the occurrences. Most of the business officials interviewed claimed that their companies placed no limits on outside views or group membership of employees other than the obvious one of frowning upon illegal activities. There was general agreement, also, that an employee is liable for dismissal if outside interests interfere with his work.

Some executives candidly admitted, however, that their views were more restrictive. Said an official of a large New York metals processor:

We assume that people who hold higher jobs here won't do or say anything that might reflect negatively on the company, like speak for some radical political outfit or get tossed in jail for civil disobedience. If a customer doesn't like our product, okay. But we'd hate to lose out because someone doesn't like one of our men's ideas.

The chairman of the board of a large industrial conglomerate went further and told how his firm tried to avoid ever having to defend or dismiss an employee for community activity:

We don't try to tell employees what they can or can't do off the job, but we pick them carefully to begin with. Among other things, we don't go looking for people who'll go out looking for trouble.

Questions

1. Should an employee have the right in his/her role of private citizen to criticize his/her employer?
2. Should an employee be fired for belonging to a group which is critical of his/her employer?
3. Should an employer have the right to forbid an employee from belonging to any civic or social group, e.g., the American Civil Liberties Union, the Ku Klux Klan?
4. Should membership in civic or social groups be considered relevant in making hiring decisions?

case 2: Catching a Thief by Honesty Exams

Employee theft is a serious problem. The American Management Association estimates that as many as 20 percent of the firms that go out of business do so because of employee theft. Since the polygraph or lie detector has been restricted in at least twenty states, a number of firms have turned to honesty tests. As described in the Wall Street Journal, the tests are given in the employer's office, take about an hour, and are relatively cheap at $6 to $14 a test. Among the questions on the test are the following: What's your favorite alcoholic drink? Which drugs have you tried? Did you ever make a false insurance claim? Do you blush often? Have you ever gotten really angry at someone for being unfair to you?[1] Let us assume that the questions are statistically correlated with employee theft, that the tests are administered by the test manufacturer, and that persons failing the test are given an opportunity to establish their innocence on other grounds.

Many employees answer the questions openly and many provide damaging information. As one corporate spokesperson said, "You become amazed at how many people believe it is acceptable conduct to steal just a little bit, maybe 50 cents, maybe a dollar a day."

Nonetheless, the tests have come under severe criticism from some unions, some lawyers, and the American Civil Liberties Union. They criticize many of the questions as non-job-related and as violations of rights of privacy. Others find the use of the test intimidating.

Questions

1. Does the test violate an employee's right to privacy? Could a test be devised that didn't?
2. Is it a violation of an employee's right to privacy if the test is used to catch thieves, that is, if the questions asked the employee related solely to thefts that had actually occurred?
3. Suppose that data analysis indicates that 80 percent of the employees who steal from their employers blush often but that only 10 percent of those who do not steal blush often. If an employee who takes the tests blushes, should we conclude he has stolen from the employer?
4. Would one-way mirrors or management "plants" among employees in order to catch thieves violate employee rights?

Note

1. *Wall Street Journal,* August 3, 1981.

Case prepared by Norman Bowie. Reprinted by permission.

case 3: Old Secrets in a New Job

William Stapleton, a chemical engineer with considerable experience in offset printing processes, had been hired recently as an engineering supervisor in Western Chemical's Printing Products Division. Until then he had been employed as a research chemist by a competing firm and during the past two years had personally developed a new formula and manufacturing process for press blankets. The new blanket was now on the market and was gaining an increasing share of the market for Stapleton's former employer.

In the offset process, the rubber blanket cyclinder on the press receives the image from the inked printing plate and transfers this image to the paper. The blanket is thus an important determinant of printing quality. Stapleton's formula and manufacturing process resulted in a blanket which not only produced superior quality but also gave longer wear, reducing the cost of materials and the cost of press down-time for blanket changes.

Western executives who had interviewed Stapleton had made no mention to him of the new offset blanket. They had indicated it was his managerial potential which interested them since the company was expanding and would soon need many more managers with scientific experience than were presently available. Stapleton had been anxious to move out of the laboratory and into management work for some time, but his former employer had not afforded him the opportunity.

The responsibilities of supervision and administration had brought Stapleton to grips with new kinds of problems, as he had hoped would be the case. One problem, however, currently sitting on his desk in the form of a memo from George Curtis, the Division's director of Engineering, was giving him particular concern. It read as follows:

Please see me this afternoon for the purpose of discussing formulas and manufacturing processes for offset press blankets.

This was the first reference anyone had made to the use of specific past technical information in his new job. Stapleton realized he would have to decide immediately to what extent he would reveal data concerning the secret processes being used by his former employer.

Questions

1. Is the new formula and manufacturing process for press blankets the kind of trade secret that should be protected?
2. Suppose an employee knew quite a lot about the manufacturing process, but did not know the new formula. If the employee gave Western Chemical his knowledge of the manufacturing process, would that violate a legitimate trade secret?

Case prepared by William McInnes, S.J., Fairfield University. Reprinted by permission.

3. Would Stapleton violate a trade secret if his new employer were in a noncompetitive industry?
4. Is Stapleton morally obligated to refuse the information to Western, even if his refusal would cost him his job?

case 4:   OSHA Noncompliance and Seniority

TMW Corporation produces three-quarters of the world's micro-synchronizers, an integral part of apartment vacuum systems. This corporation has plants mostly in the Midwest, although a few are scattered on both the East and West Coasts. The plants in the Midwest employ members of the Electronic Worker's Union under a contract which became effective last August and is in force for three years. This union is very strong and the employees will do anything to preserve and maintain the strong union benefits that have been won.

Last year an OSHA official came on a visit to the St. Louis plant and found several discrepancies with the standards established by the act. These included the absence of safety goggles on employees whose job it is to weld tiny wires together, and an automatic shut-off switch on the wire-splicing machine. TMW was issued warnings of the noncompliances, and was told if they were not corrected, the next step would be drastic fines.

The company immediately set about correcting the problems. They had to shut parts of the plants down in the midwest on a rotating basis to take care of the wire-splicing machines. The union members were quite upset because the employer laid off older employees, not the new trainees on the machines. They threatened a walkout.

Another company problem with the OSHA compliances was with the safety goggles. When told of the need to wear their goggles the welders refused, saying they were not able to see as well. They did not have to wear them before. The welders said they would take the responsibility of not wearing them now. The union backed the welders in their refusal.

Questions

1. Was the TMW Company wrong in the lay-offs of the senior employees? Should the trainees be laid off instead?
2. If the union members walked off the job, would they have their jobs when the problem was settled?
3. Can the company force the welders to comply with the wearing of the safety goggles?

This case was prepared by Professor Kenneth A. Kovach of George Mason University. Distributed by HBS Case Services, Harvard Business School, Boston, Mass. 02163. All rights reserved to the contributors. Printed in the USA.

4. If an accident occurred to a welder because of the noncompliance with OSHA, would TMW be responsible, even though the welders and union said that they would assume the responsibility?
5. Could the OSHA official fine TMW for their employees not wearing the goggles? The union?

SUGGESTED SUPPLEMENTARY READINGS

Blades, Lawrence E. "Employment At Will vs. Individual Liberty: On Limiting the Abusive Exercise of Employment Power." *Columbia Law Review,* Vol. 67 (1967), pp. 1404–35.

Cherrington, David J. *The Work Ethic: Working Values and Values That Work.* New York: Amacom, 1980.

Comment, "The Scott Amendment to the Patent Revision Act: *Should Trade Secrets Receive Federal Protection?*" 1971, *Wisconsin Law Review,* pp. 900–921.

De George, Richard. *Business Ethics,* Chapter 9. New York: Macmillan Publishing Co. Inc., 1982.

Doerfer, Gordon L. "The Limits of Trade Secret Law Imposed by Federal Patent and Antitrust Supremacy." 80, *Harvard Law Review,* 1967, pp. 1432–1462.

Donaldson, Thomas. *Corporations and Morality,* Chapter 7. Englewood Cliffs, N.J.: Prentice Hall, Inc., 1982.

Ewing, David W. *Freedom Inside the Organization: Bringing Civil Liberties to the Workplace.* New York: E. P. Dutton, 1977.

———. "What Business Thinks About Employee Rights." *Harvard Business Review,* 55 (September–October 1977).

Garrett, Thomas M. *Business Ethics,* Chapters 3–5. New York: Appleton-Century Crofts, 1966.

Holloway, William J. "Fired Employees Challenging Terminable-At-Will Doctrine." *The National Law Journal,* 19 February 1979, p. 22.

Jackson, Dudley. *Unfair Dismissal: How and Why the Law Works.* Cambridge: Cambridge University Press, 1975.

Linowes, David F. "Is Business Giving Employees Privacy?" 32 *Business & Society Review* (Winter 1979–80), 47–49.

Mason, Ronald M. *Participatory and Workplace Democracy.* Carbondale, Ill.: The Southern Illinois University Press, 1982.

Milgrim, Roger M. *Trade Secrets.* New York: Matthew Bender, 1978, first publ. 1967.

———. *Protecting and Profiting from Trade Secrets.* Practicing Law Institute, 1979, New York.

Nickel, James. "Is There A Human Right to Employment?" *Philosophical Forum,* Vol. 10, Nos. 2–4 (Summer 1978–Winter 1979).

O'Connell, Brian J. "Secrecy in Business," *Society,* 16, May–June 1979, pp. 40–45.

Palmer, David C. "Free Speech and Arbitration: Implications for the Future." *Labor Law Journal,* May 1976, p. 287.

Powers, Charles W. "Individual Dignity and Institutional Identity: The Paradoxical Needs of the Corporate Employee." *The Work Ethic In Business,* W. Michael Hoffman and Thomas J. Wyly, eds., Cambridge, Mass.: Oelgeschlager, Gunn & Hain, Publishers, Inc. 1981.

PRESIDENT'S REPORT ON OCCUPATIONAL SAFETY AND HEALTH, 1979. Washington, D.C.: U.S. Government Printing Office, 1972.

SETTLE, RUSSELL F., AND BURTON A. WEISBROD. "Occupational Safety and Health and the Public Interest." *Public Interest Law,* Burton Weisbrod, Joel F. Handler, and Neil K. Komesar, eds., Berkeley: University of California Press, 1978.

STEVENS, GEORGE E. "The Legality of Discharging Employees For Insubordination." *American Business Law Journal,* V 18 # 3 (Fall, 1980), pp. 371–389.

WESTIN, ALAN F., and STEPHAN SALISBURY. *Individual Rights in the Corporation: A Reader on Employee Rights.* New York: Pantheon, 1980.

CHAPTER 4

CONFLICTS OF INTERESTS AND ROLES

INTRODUCTION

Perplexing issues arise in business ethics because of *conflicts of interest.* Among the conflict of interest cases to achieve national notoriety are the Bert Lance case and the Richard Allen case. Bert Lance was President Carter's Director of the Office of Management and Budget. After his confirmation by the Senate, several details of his past business practices in banking became public knowledge. An "enforcement agreement" between Lance's Georgia bank and the U.S. Comptroller of the Currency, which had been imposed after it was discovered Lance had regularly and heavily overdrawn his account, was lifted apparently through political influence. Lance had also received large personal loans from other banks in which he had deposited funds from his Georgia bank. Despite Lance's claims that these were acceptable practices in Southern banks, the public thought otherwise, and Lance resigned.

Richard Allen was Ronald Reagan's Director of the National Security Council. Soon after Reagan's election, he obtained an interview with Mrs. Reagan for a Japanese magazine. He received a payment of $1,000, which he put in his office safe. When the matter came to light several months later, Allen indicated that he had forgotten about the money. Although subsequent investigation discovered that he had received several watches as well, he was cleared of any serious wrongdoing. Nevertheless, he was forced to resign.

Other cases involve *conflicts of roles.* The "Death of a Salesman" graphically portrays the conflict which can result when one has obligations to employer and family. Other conflicts occur when the obligation to one's employer conflicts with one's role as a citizen and, hence, with one's obligation to protect the public interest. Several courageous persons have given priority to their obligation to the public interest and have blown the whistle on their former employer. Indeed, Ralph Nader has provoked the ire of many in the business community by advocating that employees *ought* "to blow the whistle" on corporate wrongdoing by revealing confidential information to the Securities and Exchange Commission, the Department of Justice, a board of directors, or some other official and appropriate body.

Finally, the rise of multinational corporations has created a number of conflict-of-interest situations. Most of these situations occur when a corporate action in pursuit of profit damages the interests of the home country (the country in which the corporation is chartered). For example, some critics have alleged that corporations have manipulated corporate funds and the foreign exchange rates in a way which undermines U.S. fiscal and monetary policy. Others have argued that corporate activities undercut U.S. foreign policy. In the 1970s, Congress responded to rumors that some companies doing business in Arab countries were honoring the Arab boycott of Israel. Congress made it illegal for American chartered companies to participate in the boycott. In this way American firms were legally prevented from undermining U.S. foreign policy toward Israel.

This chapter provides an analysis of these various types of conflict and some of the arguments which have been proposed to settle them.

CONFLICT OF INTEREST

A conflict of interest occurs in the world of business when a person has two or more interests, such that if both are pursued there might result an unjustified effect on another relevantly affected individual or individuals. Generally, such a conflict emerges where one's personal interest could be pursued to the detriment of the business one represents or with which one is engaged. The most celebrated cases have occurred in sales, banking, and purchasing transactions, but they can occur in any context where interests can conflict—monetary or nonmonetary, management or nonmanagement. For example, if a personnel director in charge of promotions is in a position to evaluate and promote his son, he has a conflict of interest. It does not follow that he is unqualified to evaluate his son or even that he will inevitably do something against the interests of the business. It only follows that he has been placed in a position such that his interest in the promotion is so substantial that it might affect his independent judgment in his business role.

The first two readings in this chapter analyze the concept of conflict of interest. Joseph M. McGuire provides what might be called an organizational definition. On his account "a conflict of interest exists when a subsystem attempts deliberately to enhance its own interests or those of an alien system to the detriment of the larger system of which it is a part." Suppose the members of a sales department engage in tactics which increase orders (and hence their commissions) beyond the capability of the company to produce the goods; as a result, long-term harm to the company is done. These members of the sales department are in a conflict of interest situation. The sales department, which is the subsystem, has advanced its own interest at the expense of the larger system of which it is a part. So far, so good. However, suppose we ask whether it is morally justifiable for the subsystem to advance its own interest at the expense of the larger system. Quite often, it is not justifiable. Unless there are special circumstances, it is probably not right for the sales department to put its own interests ahead of the interest of the company as a whole. But sometimes it is justifiable for the interests of the subsystem to prevail. For example, rigorous adherence to professional standards by the engineering department might slow the introduction of a new product and hence hurt the company's competitive position. Nonetheless, there are good arguments to show that in this case, the interests of the subsystem, the engineering department, should prevail.

To address this larger question, Ruth Macklin distinguishes various kinds of interest which create conflict of interest situations. There are the personal interests of the agent, the interests of the business or organization, and interests pertaining to society as a whole (the public interest). The conflict of interest situations discussed in this chapter are conflicts of two or more of these interests.

But how should conflict of interest situations be resolved? Perhaps in some cases they should not be resolved. After all, the three traditional means for avoiding or resolving conflicts of interest are (1) reduction in the opportunities for conflicts of interest, (2) codes or other formal guidelines, and (3) legislation. However, as McGuire argues, all of these devices have costs, and none can be totally successful. Hence, McGuire argues there is no ''quick fix'' for conflict of interest situations. When a conflict of interest presents a choice between a moral and an immoral (or less moral) alternative, then presumably one ought to choose the moral alternative. But, as other essays in this chapter point out, even that judgment must be conditional. Moreover, the conflict is often between two morally acceptable and recommended alternatives, only one of which can be chosen.

THE INDIVIDUAL IN CONFLICT WITH THE FIRM

In the 1950s, some corporate executives went to jail because they had been convicted of ''price fixing.'' Sending corporate executives to jail was a unique episode that has received considerable attention. A broad consensus exists that the executives did not fix prices in order to benefit themselves. Their companies' and not their *personal* interests were enhanced. That is, they acted contrary to what was legally declared the public good in order to benefit their companies. Given this objective, many believe their action was excusable, or certainly not so culpable as to merit a jail sentence.

This example shows that many employees allow their obligations to the company to override their obligations to obey the law. But can such an argument be justified? In his article, ''The Loyal Agent's Argument,'' Alex Michalos argues that the excuse ''I did it for the good of the company'' is not a legitimate excuse. Ultimately, the excuse ''I did it for the good of the company'' is seen to be a disguised version of the excuse ''I did it to protect my job.'' In other words, the grounds upon which the obligation to the company overrode the obligation to obey the law was based on personal interest.

In his essay, Walter Gulick denies that every "I did it for my boss" argument represents a conflict between personal interest and one's duty to law and morality. He contends psychological and sociological evidence indicate that employees can be motivated to act for the good of the company even when such action would not be in the interest of the employee. There are cases when the conflict is between moral obligations to one's company and one's other moral obligations, such as the obligation to obey the law. When the obligation to obey the law is at stake in a democracy, Gulick argues, the obligation to obey the law always has priority.

WHISTLEBLOWING

Perhaps the most publicized conflicts of obligation occur in so-called whistleblowing situations. An employee is often in a position to know about the illegal or immoral actions of a supervisor or employer, whether or not he or she is asked to participate in the act. Should an employee inform the public if he or she is asked to participate in an illegal, immoral, or questionable act, or if he or she witnesses such an action by a supervisor or employer? Despite the obviously good intentions of whistleblowers to protect the public interest (sometimes at great personal cost), many businesspersons hold that whistleblowers violate one of the chief duties of an employee—that of loyalty. This attitude is nicely captured in some remarks by James M. Roche, former president of General Motors.

> Some critics are now busy eroding another support of free enterprise—the loyalty of a management team, with its unifying values of cooperative work. Some of the enemies of business now encourage an employee to be disloyal to the enterprise. They want to create suspicion and disharmony, and pry into the proprietary interests of the business. However this is labelled—industrial espionage, whistleblowing, or professional responsibility—it is another tactic for spreading disunity and creating conflict.[1]

A plausible reading of Roche's comments is that loyalty is the *supreme* virtue for any employee. But that view is questionable (in light, for example, of the account of principles and duties presented in Chapter 1).

Loyalty is loyalty to something. Suppose one is loyal to an immoral cause or end. There is loyalty among thieves. One *should* be loyal; it is a prima facie duty. Yet the object of one's loyalty must be morally appropriate if loyalty is to be the overriding obligation. The virtue of loyalty does not require that one accept blindly the person or cause to which one is loyal. Nor does it require that when loyalty conflicts with other duties—such as respecting another's autonomy—that loyalty is always overriding. To be loyal to an employer thus clearly does not require that the employee should do what the employer says, come what may, or even that the employer must be obeyed under conditions that generally call for loyalty.

One cannot assume, on the other hand, that the claims of all whistleblowers are justified and that the denials of all employers are obviously false. Whistleblowers may be trying to seize more power within the company or trying to cover up genuine personal inadequacies—inadequacies that represent the real reason for their being disciplined or dismissed. What is needed is a careful definition of whistleblowing and a set of conditions indicating precise considerations that should be taken into account to justify acts of whistleblowing.

Sissela Bok explains why the stakes in a whistleblowing situation are so high, as well as why employers are often bitter when an employee has blown the whistle. She also attempts to characterize the nature of whistleblowing and, in so doing, raises a number of considerations which indicate when whistleblowing is justified. In his article, Alan F. Westin suggests new management policies and procedures which, if adopted, would render whistleblowing unnecessary. He thus proposes a preventive strategy that carries with it an implicit theory of good management.

CONFLICTS IN BUSINESS PRACTICE BY MULTINATIONALS

In the previous two sections, the conflicts under discussion are between the employee's obligation to the firm and the employee's duties to obey the dictates of law and morality. But some of the most publicized conflicts in the practice of multinationals involve the conflicting legal and moral dictates of two different cultures. An essential function of the multinational is to make a profit. Frequently a multinational can increase profit by manufacturing or selling products in foreign countries that it could not manufacturer or sell in the home country. Is it morally right for it to do so?

Some argue that all moral principles are culturally relative. What is right or wrong depends on the culture. Hence, "When in Rome, do as the Romans do." As noted in Chapter 1, serious questions have been raised about moral relativism as an ethical theory. One of the functions of normative ethical theory is to discover universal moral principles which are valid across all cultures. Using the specific issue of product safety, Norman Bowie argues that sometimes a company should follow the rules of the home country, while under other conditions it should follow the rules of the host country. What one ought to do depends on the nature of the conflict.

But what should a multinational do when the practices of the host country violate universal moral norms? Both bribery and racism are wrong. Yet both are practiced. Should American chartered multinationals be permitted to bribe? Should they be permitted to do business in racist countries? Mark Pastin and Michael Hooker examine the former question by considering the U.S. Foreign Corrupt Practices Act of 1977. This act applied U.S. laws on corporate bribery to activities of U.S. based multinationals outside the United States. Although the act does distinguish between a bribe and so-called "grease" payments (gratuities)—and distinguishes both from extortion—Pastin and Hooker argue that the law places an unfair burden on the practices of U.S. multinationals. Finally, Richard DeGeorge discusses the general question by considering the explosive issue of whether or not U.S. corporations should maintain facilities or otherwise invest in South Africa. DeGeorge provides the minimum conditions that must be met if corporations are to be justified in conducting business in South Africa.

These essays, as all others in this chapter, point to subtle difficulties for moral theory in determining what "ought" to be done. Often a proposed action has both good effects and bad effects, or involves fulfilling one obligation at the expense of another of equal importance. Even if no definitive answers are given, these essays provide important guides for reaching ethically acceptable decisions in an area where emotions run high and reasoned judgment has been sparse.

N.E.B

Note

1. James M. Roche, "The Competitive System, to Work, to Preserve, and to Protect," *Vital Speeches of the Day* (May 1971), p. 445.

CONFLICT OF INTEREST:
Whose Interest?
And What Conflict?

Joseph M. McGuire

THE CONCEPT OF CONFLICT OF INTEREST

. . . The term "conflict of interest" has become widely used in recent years, and is probably understood by most members of the adult population in the United States much in the way they understand such terms as "love," "faith," or "electricity." To define it precisely, however, so that it can be probed and analyzed is another matter.

A conflict of interest, in the public mind, may be synonymous with honest graft. However, to cover a wider range and variety of cases than those resulting only from the possession and use of inside information, we shall express our definition in the jargon of systems theory. Thus, *a conflict of interest exists when a subsystem attempts deliberately to enhance its own interests or*

Adapted from J. M. McGuire, "Conflict of Interest: Whose Interest and What Conflict?" in *Ethics, Free Enterprise, and Public Policy: Original Essays on Moral Issues in Business,* eds., R. T. DeGeorge and J. A. Pichler. Copyright © 1978 by Oxford University Press, Inc. Reprinted by permission.

those of an alien system to the detriment of the larger system of which it is a part. The use of the word "subsystem" broadens and depersonalizes the definition, but in no way is it intended that the individual be excluded. A subsystem, therefore, may be a person, but it also may be an agency of government, a division, department, or office in a corporation, or the member or group of any organization or society. An alien system is typically another organization, but it may be any person, nation, or other unit that is not an integral part of the larger system. Furthermore, this definition implies not only that the values and goals of the system and the subsystem are different, but that they must be diametrically opposed rather than merely complementary, so that attempts to increase subsystem gains will harm the interests of the larger system.

As the definition now stands, unfortunately, it does an injustice to what is commonly understood to be a conflict of interest, largely because it does not *a priori* judge that the interests of the system are "good" and "desirable," and the interests of the subsystem are "bad." In other words, the definition is flawed because it is value free. As such, it covers the generally accepted meaning of conflicts of interest. For example, the situation wherein the attempts of an alcoholic member to increase the duration or extent of his or her euphoric stupor harms the family system is included under this definition. So too is G.W. Plunkitt, seizing opportunities to purchase land at low prices and to resell it at high prices to the detriment of the community, covered. And those cases wherein directors profit financially from inside information at the expense of investor confidence and the corporate good. It is probable that, in these and similar cases, there would be general public agreement that conflicts of interest exist. However, it would not be correct to jump to the conclusion that, because these illustrations conform to the public impression of conflicts of interest, the definition above is satisfactory.

The problem with our definition is that it includes too many types of conflict which do not conform with the public image. For example, it covers those situations which might be considered ethically "neutral," such as the conflicts that the organizational models of Robert K. Merton and Philip Selznick consider normal.[1] Both of these organizational models take for granted the appearance of dysfunctional attitudes whereby subsystems establish barriers to the attainment of system goals. In the Selznick model, for example, the individuals in large and complex organizations will "naturally" resist efforts by top management to use them as means to organizational goals, and will attempt to substitute their own purposes for those of the larger system. In the Merton and Selznick theories, the attempt to advance the purposes of the organization results in unintended and undesired individual and subsystem behavior. Such conflicts, however, would probably not be included in the public notion of conflict of interest, although they are covered by our definition.

Most importantly, our definition of conflicts of interest includes those cases where right is on the side of the subsystem. This category of conflict situations would not ordinarily be included in the public definition. The individuals described in John F. Kennedy's book, *Profiles in Courage,* were elements of subsystems eventually applauded for their brave words and actions in the light of system goals. As the Nuremburg trials attest, individuals have been castigated for their failure to enter into conflicts with the larger system. The American public typically would approve the attempts of a small band of democratically inclined revolutionaries to overthrow a dictatorship.

The point of all this is, very simply, that: while there is nothing inherently wrong with our definition of conflict of interest, it does not conform with the commonly accepted notion of this term because it does not contain *a priori* ethical assumptions about the "rightness" of system and subsystem interests, goals, and values. In order to make our definition correspond to the public concept of conflict of interest, it would be essential to assume that the interests and values and goals of the system are ethically good and morally right, and that those of the subsystem are ethically wrong.

And, indeed, it is this underlying presumption of the ethical propriety of system goals, interests, and values that makes the concept of conflict of interest so complex and bothersome. It is this presumption, too, that may cause reforms to be undertaken ". . . for the wrong reasons and [to leave] behind the wrong remedies." Our definition of conflict of interest, if ethics must underlie it, is situational in nature. It does not prejudge whether the subsystem or system is right or wrong. In some situations, the subsystem conflict activities may be morally correct; in others, immoral. In the public concept, however, right always is attributed to the system. The latter rests upon an absolutist, or sometimes cultural, concept of ethics. Thus, espionage activities are basically conflicts of interest. However, when American spies are used in wartime situations, the public applauds them as heroes, while alien spies in the United States are obviously in the wrong.

Whose interests are harmed by conflicts of interest? The interests of the system. Is this good or bad? According to our definition of the concept, the results of a conflict of interest may be good, bad, or ethically neutral. To the public mind, however, it would appear that harm to the system is always wrong.

Given the public attitudes toward conflict of interest situations, therefore, it is not surprising that the remedies for rectifying those situations have consisted largely of removing temptation from, and imposing sanctions on, subsystems. We shall examine some of these reforms in the following section of this essay. At the same time, however, it is necessary to note that such reforms are not costless. There might be less freedom of speech and action in organizations and more demands for conformity to organizational values and goals. There will be a greater hesitancy on the part of some good people to take certain positions because of the "appearance" of conflicts of interest. There may be the imposition of righteous and rigid moral codes upon organizational members. And, finally, many of the efforts at reform are based on a rather dismal view of man, regarding people as basically weak, not to be trusted, and with a natural propensity to place their personal interests above the system's "good." We shall pursue these "costs" of conflict of interest reforms as we examine the reforms themselves in the following section.

Recent attempts to prevent conflicts of interest or to punish participants in them appear to fall into one or more of the following categories: (1) efforts to reduce the potential for conflicts of interest; (2) attempts to write or rewrite codes, guidelines, and policies to make clear and explicit what is not permitted by the organization so that members will know what the rules are and when their activities will be in conflict with these rules; and (3) legislation. We shall examine, through illustrations, each of these classes of reform.

1. Reduction in the Potential for Conflict of Interest

The furor over conflicts of interest has led some individuals and organizations to adopt an "arms-length" policy whereby they attempt to avoid all situations in which there exists the potential for conflict. This attitude has apparently produced a relatively widespread "don't question company goals" sentiment among corporate managers. For example, Archie Carroll recently conducted a survey of managers at various levels in approximately 240 randomly selected companies. One of his findings was that almost 65 percent of these executives believed they were currently under considerable pressure to compromise their personal standards to achieve company goals. About 60 percent of the respondents agreed that young executives in business would have loyally gone along with their bosses, just as the junior members of President Nixon's reelection committee did.[2] These remarkable results attest to the opinion, earlier expressed, that one way to avoid conflicts of interest is to sublimate one's own interests to those of the organization. If one is blindly unswerving in his or her loyalty to the organization, the only conflict that might occur is the inner one—but over time, probably even this trauma can be lessened if only one perseveres.

More sensitive individuals and organizations evidently are reducing the potential for conflicts of interest by simply refusing to serve or to ask others to serve. Thus, in a recent survey by Korn/Ferry International (an executive recruiting company) of 407 major corporations, it was found that the number of lawyers, commercial bankers, and investment bankers on the boards of directors of these enterprises had declined between 1973 and 1975. *Business Week* reports John L. Hanigan, chairman of Brunswick Corporation, as saying:

> I don't think we should have partners of investment banking firms or executives of commercial banks on the board. You have to ask, "Whose side are they on?" They sure have a conflict because they are trying to sell their services to you.[3]

A survey by Booz, Allen and Hamilton, Inc., of 30 top accounting, consulting, investment banking, and law firms found that only 6 of these companies encouraged their members to accept directorships, while 14 discouraged acceptance and 11 were neutral. Clifford E. Graese, a partner in Peat, Marwick, Mitchell and Company, says:

We want to avoid even the appearance of conflict of interest. The potential for conflict is too great. We could not have one partner on a bank's board, while the firm audits another bank.[4]

The sensitivity of these groups and individuals to serve on corporate boards has not been without its side effects. Thus, academicians, women, members of ethnic minorities, economists, and representatives of similar groups have increasingly become members of boards of directors in place of the lawyers, bankers, accountants and others who have refused, or been refused, membership.[5] Presumably, these latecomers are not concerned about the possibility of interest conflicts, or possibly none exist.

Some observers of these developments believe that the loss of legal, financial, and professional talent on corporate boards will make these boards (and, presumably, the companies themselves) less efficient. David C. David, former dean of the Graduate School of Business Administration at Harvard University, is reported to have said, for example, "that in his experience the men with the conflicts usually make excellent directors."[6] . . .

Efforts to solve potential conflict of interest situations typically consist of proposals to prohibit members or former members of alien systems from membership in "the system." The basis for such denials is that the possible allegiances to the alien system will be, or might be, troublesome. In dealing with conflicts of interest, then, as in other areas such as liquor, drugs, and pornography, mankind stands ready to protect the individual from his baser cravings. And, again, society stands alert; prepared to re-create the Garden of Eden by removing, in potential conflict cases, the possibility of temptation. This Victorian mentality regards mankind as weak and seeks to minimize the exposure of all individuals to the occasion of sin. As in similar situations, the blanket and heroic generalizations about the nature of mankind's frailties preclude the best and strongest, as well as the weak and unethical, from accepting positions of responsibility. Such assumptions, at their best, inhibit freedom of choice; differentiate between individuals on the basis of what may, indeed, be irrelevant but all-important criteria; impugn the image of man as an individual and ascribe to each person an all-important social identity; and find each person guilty of weaknesses in the face of temptation. It is difficult to understand why the efforts to protect persons from potential conflicts of interest should be condoned. Whether an individual will succumb to temptation in these situations, it would appear, depends more upon the character and integrity of the person than upon the nature of the conflict. To solve potential conflicts of interest through universal prohibition would appear, therefore, a somewhat childish way to prevent such situations.[7]

2. Codes, Guidelines, and Organizational Policies to Prohibit Conflict of Interests

In this part of this essay, however, we are not going to explore the task of writing an epistle to cover globally all possible areas where transgressions might occur in organizational life. But, in a somewhat limited way, we shall raise the question: "Is it possible to write (or rewrite) codes that will prevent conflicts of interest? And can these codes be effective?"

Raymond Baumhart, S.J., in conducting his well-known study of business ethics in 1961, included in his mail questionnaire to 5,000 executives several inquiries on ethical codes.[8] . . . Over 70 percent of Baumhart's respondents believed that codes of ethical practices in each industry would be a good idea. However, while such codes would raise the ethical level of industry, help executives by defining clearly the limits of acceptable conduct, and be useful aids when executives wanted to refuse unethical requests, most respondents also believed that such codes would be extremely difficult to enforce, and that people would violate them whenever they thought they could avoid detection. Surprisingly, perhaps, the majority of respondents also believed that these codes would operate more effectively if they were enforced by non-government regulatory groups external to the company rather than by company management. The cynicism and distrust evident in the responses about enforceability and the preference for regulation by external groups would appear to make even the least skeptical of Baumhart's readers doubtful of the utility of ethical codes, although it would indeed appear more satisfactory (for public relations reasons, if for no other) to have them than not.

Some conflict of interest situations, on the other hand, can be satisfactorily covered by organizational policies and guidelines. In two cases in particular—the extent of external affiliations and the acceptance of gifts by organizational members—organizational policies are frequently effective. Consequently, many businesses and government agencies have, at the very least, disclosure policies, wherein members are required to inform management or to make public their financial interests in other organizations. Some companies explicitly forbid their employees to have investments in suppliers, customers, or distributors. Others permit employees to own some percentage of stock in such organizations. Still others require disclosure of all outside business interests—financial, kinship, or whatever—by key executives and purchasing agents. Organizations often are fearful, too, that the acceptance by their members of gifts or entertainment might lead to a conflict of interest whereby the recipient might be disposed to give preferential treatment to the giver, and therefore frequently have policies covering these situations. In some organizations, employees cannot accept any gifts from external sources. In others, the value of the gift, its purpose, the circumstances surrounding it, the position of the recipient in the organization, and general practices in the organizational culture determine the policy that is established. Thus, in one company it might be acceptable to receive a calendar or a pencil with the donor's name on it, while in another there may be specific prohibitions against even such nominal gifts. Many organizations set an upper dollar value on gifts that might be accepted, assuming, implicitly, that items costing less than $10 or whatever will not result in preferential treatment for the donor. Entertainment of organizational members by alien systems also is frequently controlled by guidelines. . . .

Policies and guidelines designed to control situations which might create interest conflicts would appear to be desirable for all organizations, but it is clear that the totality of such conflicts is difficult to circumvent by organizational codes alone. Typically, if such codes are too strict, they inhibit member effectiveness, for they interfere with social conventions. On the other hand, if they permit reasonable latitude in member behavior, they are likely to be misinterpreted by the best of men and deliberately broken by the worst. In the last analysis, such codes, since they attempt to ward off temptation, have the same shortcomings as the efforts to remove the potential for interest conflicts discussed earlier. The one advantage that such codes have, however, is that they do provide limits beyond which organizational sanctions may be imposed, and thereby tend to act as a deterrent to some of the weaker organizational members. . . .

3. Legislation

. . . Much of the federal legislation that has been passed with regard to conflicts of interest has been directed toward the government system itself, or to its interface with external institutions, rather than toward external institutions such as businesses. The states, however, have been more active than the federal government, and in many ways some of their legislation has been more imaginative and interesting. We shall examine some of these laws, drawing our illustrations from the State of California.

The California Political Reform Act of 1974 requires that

> No public official . . . shall make, participate in making or in any way attempt to use his official position to influence a governmental decision in which he knows or has reason to know he has a financial interest.[9]

"Financial interests" are defined as direct or indirect investments of $1,000 or more, income totaling $250 or more received during the preceding year, or any company of which the public official is a member. The Act requires public officials to file statements of their financial interests annually with the Fair Political Practices Commission, an agency established by the law. The Commission is authorized to implement the Act, hold hearings, and, if it finds a violation has occurred, to issue cease and desist orders and/or impose fines up to $2,000.

Another part of the Political Reform Act of California requires campaign finance disclosure reports of the employer and the occupation of every contributor of $50 or more. Auditing and enforcement provisions can result in penalties against businesses that range up to $10,000 fines.

Perhaps the most discussed section of the Act is that which prohibits lobbyists from making gifts of more than $10 per month to state legislators or administrative officials. They are also required to register and to file complex monthly reports of their activities. Furthermore, under the provisions of the Act, any person who attempts to promote, support, influence, modify, oppose, or delay state legislation or administrative action is lobbying, and as soon as he or she spends $250 on such activities in a month (including the purchase of newspaper advertisements) a lobbying report must be filed.

Despite the fact that the Act contains over 20,000 words of definition, description, and discussion, there is considerable uncertainty still about the meaning of the law. For example, soon after the passage of the Act, the Fair Political Practices Commission spent a month just trying to define what a private-interest lobbyist is. These uncertainties have caused many companies and associations to take great precautions to conform with the law. Now, for example, the Pacific Gas and Electric Company has registered seventeen lobbyists, as compared with five in 1974![10] The California Taxpayers Association, unable to differentiate between research personnel and lobbyists, has registered all professionals in its Sacramento office. A number of companies initially failed to register at all as lobbyists, but have now done so, although they remain uncertain of their status. The Commission has been sued by such disparate groups as the California Bankers Association and the Socialist Workers Party. One of the more serious questions is whether lobbyists, such as those employed by the California Labor Federation, can advise their membership about legislators' voting records without breaking the law.

Some groups and individuals believe that the California Act, especially its lobbyists' provisions, interferes with that phrase in the First Amendment which guarantees "the right of the people . . . to petition the government for a redress of grievances," and the disclosure requirements imposed upon private persons and organizations violate the Fourth Amendment's privacy provisions.

Earlier comments about potential conflicts of interest and organizational policies to prevent conflicts or punish transgressions apply to much of the legislation that has been enacted at the state and federal levels in recent years. This legislation typically presumes not only that elected or appointed officials or bureaucrats must be "pure" but that they must prove their purity. It assumes they cannot withstand the blandishments and temptations and bribes of representatives of external systems, so the latter must not be permitted to offer the former apples—or anything more expensive. In order to keep these tempters away, legislation is devised that impinges on freedoms guaranteed by the Bill of Rights. It is doubtful that legislation will deter either legislators or other transgressors who are determined to corrupt or be corrupted. It may, however, prevent more ethical individuals from marginal, controversial, or even healthy activities. It is also doubtful that legislation will cleanse our political system of conflicts of interest. Persons who are capable of operating "off the record," and who are disposed toward unethical behavior, will undoubtedly continue to do so. Legislation will, however, make those who are crafty and unethical more careful.

CONCLUSIONS

If the remedies we have discussed, designed to resolve conflicts of interest, are not particularly attractive, why is this the case, and what might be more desirable solutions?

First, it should be recognized that not all conflicts of interest are undesirable. The definition presented in the first section of this essay, and the discussion surrounding it, tried to make clear and precise that attempts at subsystem gains are not necessarily unethical or evil. But, underlying the public concept of this term, is the presumption that such subsystem activities are per se "wrong." In their efforts to correct conflict of interest situations, therefore, private and public policy makers have attempted to prevent all conflicts of interest—the meritorious along with the harmful, the innocent or innocuous or "natural" along with the guilty. History has shown the folly of condemning large sectors of human activity because a part of this activity is deviant or abhorrent. Too many degrees of freedom are lost when general policies are written to prevent conflicts of interest.

Second, solutions to conflict of interest situations have focused on the occasion for offenses rather than on the offenders. One does not, in the United States, advocate the separation of the sexes to prevent rape, or (again in the United States) remove guns from the population in order to prevent murder. Yet, to prevent conflicts of interest, lobbyists are moved away from legislators, certain types of outsiders are prevented from organizational service, and it is suggested that relationships between regulators and regulated become more distant. A more satisfactory solution in all conflict cases might be one of cautious trust and careful screening, accompanied by the establishment of sanctions for those transgressors who, with evidence, can be found guilty of derelictions. Some conflicts of interest are improper and some are criminal. There should be laws and organizational policies directed at specific wrongdoers in conflict of interest situations. These laws and policies should identify the act as well as the guilt, and under them, wrongdoers should be punished—but with due process safeguards. Such guidelines and legislation will, however, require much more serious and detailed study of conflicts of interest than has been given to these situations in the past.

Notes

1. Robert K. Merton, *Social Theory and Social Structure,* revised and enlarged edition (New York: The Free Press of Glencoe, Inc., 1957), Chapter 1, especially pp. 50–54; and Philip Selznick, "Foundations of the Theory of Organization," *American Sociological Review,* Vol. XIII (February, 1948), pp. 25–35.
2. Archie B. Carroll, "A Summary of Managerial Ethics: Is Business Morality Watergate Morality?" *Business and Society Review,* No. 10 (Spring, 1975), pp. 58–60.
3. *Business Week,* March 29, 1976, p. 100.
4. *Ibid.*
5. It should be noted that there have been a number of court cases involving conflicts of interest by corporate board members. For example, in the Bar Chris Construction Corporation case, 1968, the court said that a lawyer on the board owed a higher duty to the shareholders than did other directors. And in *Feit* v. *Leasco,* an "outside" Leasco director was labeled an "insider" because he had helped, as a lawyer, to prepare a misleading tender offer. Theodore W. Kheel was singled out as principal in a conflict of interest case involving

Stirling Homex Corporation, where he was both a director and counsel negotiating a labor contract. *Forbes,* May 15, 1976, p. 118.

7. For an interesting discussion of a specific illustration of this point, see Eberhard Faber, "How I Lost Our Great Debate About Corporate Ethics," *Fortune,* Vol. XCIV, No. 5 (November, 1976), pp. 180–190.

8. Raymond C. Baumhart, S. J., "How Ethical Are Businessmen?" *Harvard Business Review,* Vol. 39, No. 4 (July–August, 1961), pp. 6–8.

9. Political Reform Act of 1974, California, Chapter 7, Section 87100.

10. "Will California's Lobbying Law Set a Trend?" *Business Week* (August 18, 1975), pp. 113–114, 116.

CONFLICTS OF INTEREST

Ruth Macklin

Cases of conflict of interest arise in all professions and professional activities, as well as in everyday life. Perhaps the most familiar concept of "interest" is one that denotes *financial* interest. Under this concept, a public official is prohibited from acting upon matters in which he has a personal pecuniary interest. For example, since many members of Congress are lawyers, statutes expressly limiting the type of law practice open to members of Congress have been enacted. There is even a statute called: "the Federal Conflict of Interest Act." Passed in 1962, it prohibits a member of Congress from receiving direct or indirect compensation for representation in "any proceeding . . . in which the United States is a party or has a direct and substantial interest, before any department, agency, court martial, officer, or any civil, military or naval commission. . . ."[1]

Conflict of interest in this narrow, financial meaning of the concept is not limited, of course, to members of Congress or to the law practices of public officials. In a well-known case that received public attention in recent years, Bert Lance—President Carter's first nominee for director of the Office of Management and Budget—was eventually forced to resign as a result of a series of incidents involving his financial interests. For one thing, he had regularly and heavily overdrawn, without the usual penalty, his own account with his Georgia bank. This resulted in an "enforcement agreement" between Lance's Georgia bank and the U.S. Comptroller of the Currency, who described the bank's practice as "unsafe and unsound." Another aspect of Lance's financial dealings concerned large personal loans he received from other banks. Ostensibly, those funds helped Lance's own bank receive additional banking services, but the loans also served as inducements for the other banks to make the personal loans to Lance. In the charges and defenses that ensued, Lance claimed that these practices were all "normal" in business. However, there is no guarantee that any practice—in business, government, or in the professions—is ethical simply because it is frequently done. The Lance case was construed as one involving morally unacceptable conflict of interests for a public official.

A wide range of situations, common to both the public and private sectors, are potentially open to conflicts of interest. If an executive recommends to his own organization a contract with another firm, in which he holds substantial stock, his actions are open to the charge of conflict of interests. Corporate officers or government officials who accept gifts from a firm whose contracts they must periodically renegotiate may be suspected of engaging in a conflict of interests. These are only two of the many examples of conflict of interest where "interests" are construed in the narrowly financial or pecuniary sense. But to think of moral problems of conflict of interest only in this narrow sense is both limiting and misleading. It is limiting because of the large variety of cases of nonmonetary conflicts of interest that share many of the same features with the financial instances. And it is misleading because the narrow conception fails to bring out fully the nature of moral concerns inherent in all such cases.

There is not very much in the way of systematic writing on moral problems of conflict of interests. What does exist in the literature is mostly either confined to a legal analysis of suits charging violation of laws or practices forbidding certain actions on the part of lawyers, businessmen, or public officials; or else it consists of analyses from the perspective of business ethics, which for the most part, take the concept of conflict of interest in the narrowly financial sense I've just described. If we try to approach the issue from a very general perspective, however, we find that the concept of "interest" is so broad and so vague that it can encompass virtually any moral consideration in which conflict occurs: conflict of obligations, of duty, of loyalty, and of principle. As a result of the breadth and vagueness of the concept of "interest" itself, as well as the diverse contexts in which various interests may come into conflict, it is hard to know what to infer from a judgment that a conflict of interest exists in a particular case, and even harder to come up with some general conclusions about the moral category of conflict of interests. In what follows, I will take a systematic look at this category, by making a few distinctions and by sorting out the different kinds of cases that fall into the category in an attempt to arrive at a picture of just where the moral wrong lies when one engages in actions involving a conflict of interest. Along the way, I'll draw on examples from practices and actions in various professions, by way of comparison and contrast. . . .

One philosopher, who has written recently on the notion of conflict of interest from a general perspective, poses the following questions in trying to become clear about the application of the concept in non-legal contexts:

> . . . the "old boy" system in the hiring of university faculty . . . , which obviously raises the issue, is very often ignored. It is often ignored in the moral domain as well. Is it a conflict of interest for a former student and beneficiary of

a senior professor, mentioned with thanks in the preface of that professor's newly published book, to review the book in a formal way in a professional journal? Is it a conflict of interest for a journal editor refereeing a submitted manuscript to suggest improving the paper by the addition of a brief discussion of two or three relevant authors including himself? Going a little farther afield, is it a conflict of interest for a theatre critic to party regularly with actors, playwrights, directors, the public reception of whose current work he will affect decisively? Is it a conflict of interest to referee a grant application when the applicant has already innocently suggested that he (the referee, not yet known as such) may be chosen to play an important part in the program proposed? Questions of these sorts demonstrate the ubiquity of our issue. There is no difference in principle between minor and major cases or between cases that can and cannot be monitored. The issue is one of fair play and, as such, is more a matter of conscience and intention than of consequences[2].

   What characterizes all of the cases in the questions just posed is that the interest in question may be described as a *personal* interest of some sort—some gain, financial or otherwise, that may accrue to the person faced with the conflict. In business and legal contexts, and at various levels of government, however, while personal gain of some sort may be at stake, it is just as common for cases of conflict of interest to involve gain for one's company or organization, at the expense of fair dealings. In these latter cases, the individual's own interest is presumably identical with that of his or her organization, but the motive or intention of the agent may have nothing to do with expected personal gains. A loyal or conscientious employee may be acting in what he or she believes to be the best interest of the organization, where such behavior may violate accepted practices or even rules of conduct.

   This distinction, between *personal* interests (financial or other gain) and the interests of one's organization or institution, suggests that not all cases of conflict of interest are ones in which self-interest is pitted against the interest of others, or against what fair play or ethical conduct requires. There is a range of other types of interests besides personal or self-interest, including interests that arise from roles that people occupy, from norms or standards governing professional conduct, and from the well-being of society as a whole. It is because of this wide range of things that can legitimately count as *interests,* where potential conflict of some sort exists, that it is so hard to draw general moral conclusions that offer practical guidance. Let me turn, then, to a minimal classification of *types* of interest, with some illustrations falling under each type. My aim is to see if this typology, along with the examples, sheds any light on the moral nature of the heterogeneous class of conflicts of interest.

TYPES OF INTEREST

1. *Personal Interest of the Agent*

This is the sort discussed above, and it can be thought of as synonymous with *self*-interest. It includes pecuniary interests, as mentioned in several of the earlier examples—the Bert Lance case, the example of members of

Congress receiving compensation for practicing law in cases where the United States is a party, receipt of gifts by corporate officers, governmental officials, etc. But the interest need not be financial. As in the examples cited in the quotation discussing academic practices, journal refereeing, and professional publications, personal interests can include those of status, prestige, power, reputation, or any other form of self-aggrandizement. It can also include various forms of nepotism, insofar as one's family can be thought of as an "extension" of oneself. Thus the potential conflict for the personnel director who is in a position to evaluate and promote his own son properly falls under the category of personal or self-interest, since the personnel director's own interests can be presumed identical with those of his family members.

Personal interests can conflict with those of one's employer or organization, but they may also be fully consonant with those interests and at odds with interests belonging to other persons, groups, or institutions, as will be evident in the remaining types in this classification scheme. There is one general observation I think is sound, which can be made about personal interests that come into conflict with other kinds. It will usually turn out that when self-interest is pitted against one of the other types, in cases of conflict of interests, to pursue one's self-interest is the immoral or less moral alternative. There are exceptions, of course. But this general observation accords with the widely accepted moral viewpoint that *ethical egoism* is not a valid or legitimate moral theory. This should not be taken to mean that there are never good reasons for acting that invoke personal gain or motives of some sort. It is, rather, to follow the many philosophical accounts that have argued for the view that egoism cannot properly be treated as providing *moral* reasons for acting. In his book, *The Moral Point of View*, Kurt Baier observes that

> . . . we employ principles of the superiority of one type of reason over another. We all believe that reasons of self-interest are superior to reasons of mere pleasure, that reasons of long-range interest outbalance reasons of short-range interest, and reasons of law, religion, and morality outweigh reasons of self-interest. On the other hand, there is considerable uncertainty about whether and when law is superior to morality, religion to law, and morality to religion[3].

2. Interests Belonging to One's Organization or Institution

This type of interest exists in all cases where an individual works for an organization or institution of some sort, be it a business, a law firm, a hospital, a military outfit, university, social work agency, or any level of government (municipal, state, or Federal). As in the case of personal interests, organizational interests are not limited to financial ones; they may also be those of power and authority, reputation and prestige. But beyond these similarities, a new complication enters into the attempt even to identify what the organization's interests are. In many instances, it will be obvious from common sense or experience: an organization's interests are those that increase rather than decrease its profits or financial stability; that enhance rather than diminish its power or prestige *vis á vis* competitors; and that contribute to its realizing its stated goals. But beyond those interests that can be identified through common-sense reflection or experience, there may be others embodied in an organization's rules or code of conduct for its own employees, some of which may not be obvious without directly consulting the code or rules. The following examples are taken from the Business Conduct Guidelines distributed by IBM to its employees:

a. Under "Financial Interests and Insider Information" the Guidelines state:

If you know someone in a business whose customers are mainly persons moving into newly purchased homes, you should not disclose information on new hires and transfers of IBM employees to anyone who might offer the service or product of that business to IBM employees.

b. Under "Fair Competition" the manual states:

From the very beginning, IBM has relied on one thing above all to sell its products: Excellence. It always has been IBM's policy to provide the best possible products and services to customers, and to sell on the merits of our own products and services—not by disparaging competitors, or their products and services . . . Disparaging remarks include not only false statements, but also information which is misleading or simply unfair. Even factually correct material can be disparaging if it's derogatory and irrelevant to the particular sales situation. This includes casting doubt on a competitor's capabilities or making unfair comparisons.

Subtle hints or innuendos are wrong, too. For instance, asking a customer or prospect what they've heard about the competitor's maintenance service. If your objective is to focus the prospect's attention on a known problem, don't do it.

c. And under "Reciprocity" the guidelines state:

You certainly can buy products and services from a supplier who buys products and services from IBM. But you cannot make an agreement to buy from suppliers on the condition that they agree to use IBM products and services. This means, quite clearly, that IBM's decision whether to use a supplier's services and products must be totally independent from his or her decision to use IBM as a supplier. You should not even *hint* to a supplier that, somehow, IBM's purchases from the supplier should be a reason why it ought to do business with us.

These published guidelines for IBM employees illustrate several points relevant to our topic. First, as mentioned in introducing these illustrations, they refer to conduct one might not think of as unethical without reference to the company's explicit regulations in such matters. To that extent, although they may be adopted by other businesses or organizations besides IBM, an IBM employee may be able to know these guidelines apply only after having consulting them. Secondly, a point that takes us back to the remarks of Joseph Margolis, cited earlier, these examples all revolve around *fairness* in some way. Recall that Margolis's general characterization of cases falling under the category of conflict of interest is "the issue is one of fair play, and, as such, is more a matter of conscience and intention than of consequences." Finally, the IBM guidelines just quoted express the company's policy about how its interests are to be served in a way that may bring about a conflict with the most obvious and straightforward interest a company has: increasing its profits. Thus the guidelines that expressly forbid disparaging a competitor's products may not serve the evident company interest of maximizing its profit (at least in the short term), since an employee might better succeed in making a sale by violating the precepts embodied in that policy. The same is true for the guideline that prohibits hinting to a supplier that if they do business with IBM, it will be reciprocated. In these guidelines, IBM is surely not mandating to its employees conduct that its chief executives believe will *lower* the company's long-range profits. But it is electing to put forth an image of a company dedicated to fair business practices—an image that requires a broader construal of what is in the company's interests. A company's overall reputation can rest, among other things, on its reputation for fairness. IBM's employees are instructed to view the company's interest not in the narrowly financial terms that might foster cutthroat business practices, but instead, in terms that require the organization to look good by virtue of its ethical stance, as well as its products.

3. Interests Pertaining to Society as a Whole: the Public Interest

This is the broadest notion of "interest" of all. Society's interest, or "the public interest," may come in conflict with an individual's personal interest (as in cases where an ordinary citizen, a professional, or a public servant seeks to prevent disclosure of confidential information of some sort); it can conflict with a company's interests, as in a wide range of cases concerning the environment, where industry seeks to prevent erosion of its profits at the expense of continued threats to the environment posed by air and water pollution; and the public interest at large may conflict with the interests of various special groups: the National Rifle Association, with its opposition to gun control; the automobile industry (including workers), who seek to curtail less expensive and more fuel-efficient Japanese imports; right-to-life groups whose interests are opposed to those of the larger society favoring not only the continued availability of abortions, but also the funding of abortions for poor women, to mention only a few examples.

To embark on a discussion of how conflicts between the public interest and those of special interest groups might be resolved would plunge us into the topic of pluralism and the political process in our own pluralistic society. But as a moral philosopher, rather than a political analyst, I prefer to confine my remarks to *ethical* instead of *political* considerations, bearing on problems of conflict of interest. The distinction between ethical and political concerns gives me the opportunity, in closing, to make some general observations about the difficulties of resolving conflicts of interest.

Some interests are short-term, others long-term. Some interests are public, some private. It seems evident that the public interest must be viewed as long-term; we would not call a policy or practice "in the public interest" if the benefits or gains occurred only in the short run, whether the policy concerned financial well-being, use of energy resources, military strength, the health of the population, or whatever. Officials or employees in the public as well as the private sector, however, are much more likely to act with regard to short-term interests. Whether the reasons for that are self-interest, the interest of the firm or institution one works for, or mere expediency, the pursuit of some person's or group's interests are limited by various contingencies and constraints. This is as true of the Federal government's practical policies as it is of those in managerial positions in industry or other institutions in the private sector. Political and economic factors often seem to override moral considerations in practice, even though adherence to ethical ideals is the more noble course of action. Ethics and politics are often at odds, which is why we cannot expect moral solutions always to come about as a result of the political process. When groups have different and conflicting interests, the political process in a democratic society presumably enables these interests to balance out. But even in that case, there is no guarantee that such balancing of competing interests will yield the morally best solution.

In conclusion, some conflicts of interest present a choice between one moral and one immoral (or less moral) alternative. Often, those can be avoided in advance if the individual takes steps to circumvent being placed in such a situation. Other cases are harder, though, because the contingencies of a situation give rise to conflicting interests, and a person may be caught in the middle. Here the choice need not be between one moral and one immoral alternative, but the situation may be covered in a professional code of conduct, or the preferred action may flow from the person's professional role. But codes often do not give clear practical guidance; so in many cases of conflict of interest, as elsewhere in moral behavior, the choice in the end is left to an individual's reflective, conscientious decision.

Notes

1. 76 Stat. 1121–122 (1962), 18 U.S.C. Paras. 203–205.
2. Joseph Margolis, "Conflict of Interest and Conflicting Interests," in Tom L. Beauchamp and Norman E. Bowie (eds.), *Ethical Theory and Business,* first edition (Englewood Cliffs: Prentice-Hall, Inc., 1979), p. 365.
3. Kurt Baier, *The Moral Point of View.* (New York: Random House, 1965), p. 35.

THE LOYAL AGENT'S ARGUMENT

Alex C. Michalos

INTRODUCTION

According to the Report of the Special Review Committee of the Board of Directors of Gulf Oil Corporation:

> It is not too much to say that the activity of those Gulf officials involved in making domestic political contributions with corporate funds during the period of approximately fourteen years under review [1960–1974] was shot through with illegality. The activity was generally clandestine and in disregard of federal, as well as a number of state, statutes.[1]

Nevertheless, and more importantly for our purposes, the Committee apparently endorsed the following judgment, which was submitted by their lawyers to the U.S. Securities and Exchange Commission.

> No evidence has been uncovered or disclosed which establishes that any officer, director or employee of Gulf personally profited or benefited by or through any use of corporate funds for contributions, gifts, entertainment or other expenses related to political activity. Further, Gulf has no reason to believe or suspect that *the motive of the employee or officer* involved in such use of corporate funds was anything other than *a desire to act solely in what he considered to be the best interests of Gulf and its shareholders*.[2] [Emphasis added.]

If we accept the views of the Committee and their lawyers, then we have before us an interesting case of individuals performing illegal actions with altruistic motives. What they did was admittedly illegal, but they meant well. They had good intentions, namely, to further "the best interests of Gulf and its shareholders." Furthermore, there is no suggestion in these passages or in the rest of the report that the officials were ordered to commit such acts. They were not ordered. On the contrary, the acts seem to have emerged as practically natural by-products of some employees' zeal in looking after their employer's interests. They are, we might say, the result of overzealous attempts of agents to fulfill their fiducial obligations.

In the following paragraphs I am going to pursue this apparently plausible account of overzealous behavior to its bitter end. That is, I'm going to assume for the sake of argument that there really are reasonable people who would and do perform immoral and illegal actions with altruistic motives, i.e., there are people who would and do perform such actions with reasons that they regard as good in some fairly general sense. It's not to be assumed that they are shrewd enough to see that their own interests lie in the advancement of their employer's or client's interests. They are not, I'm assuming, cleverly egoistic. If anything, they are stupidly altruistic by

This paper was written for the Conference on Ethics and Economics at the University of Delaware, Newark, Delaware, November 10–12, 1977. Copyright © 1978 by Alex C. Michalos. Reprinted by permission of the author.

247

hypothesis. But that's beside the point now. What I want to do is construct a generalized form of an argument that I imagine would be attractive to such agents, whether or not any of them has or will ever formulate it exactly so. Then I want to try to demolish it once and for all.

THE ARGUMENT

What I will call the Loyal Agent's Argument (LAA) runs as follows:

1. *As a loyal agent of some principal, I ought to serve his interests as he would serve them himself if he had my expertise.*
2. *He would serve his own interests in a thoroughly egoistic way.*
   Therefore, as a loyal agent of this principal, I ought to operate in a thoroughly egoistic way in his behalf.

Some clarification is in order. First, in order to make full use of the fairly substantial body of legal literature related to the *law of agency,* I have adopted some of the standard legal jargon. In particular, following Powell, I'm assuming that *"an agent is a person who is authorised to act for a principal and has agreed so to act, and who has power to affect the legal relations of his principal with a third party."*[3] The standard model is an insurance agent who acts in behalf of an insurance company, his principal, to negotiate insurance contracts with third parties. More generally, lawyers, real estate agents, engineers, doctors, dentists, stockbrokers, and the Gulf Oil zealots may all be regarded as agents of some principal. Although for some purposes one might want to distinguish agents from employees, such a distinction will not be necessary here. The definition given above is broad enough to allow us to think of coal miners, Avon Ladies, zoo attendants, and Ministers of Parliament as agents.

Second, as our definition suggests, there are typically three important relationships involved in agency transactions, namely, those between agent and principal, agent and third party, and principal and third party. The law of agency has plenty to say about each of these relationships, while LAA is primarily concerned with only the first, the fiducial relation between agent and principal. It would be a mistake to regard this as mere oversight. Few of us are immune to the buck-passing syndrome. Most of us are inclined to try to narrow the range of activities for which we are prepared to accept responsibility and, at the same time, widen the range of activities for which we are prepared to accept authority. Notwithstanding the psychological theory of cognitive dissonance, most human beings seem to have sufficient mental magnanimity to accommodate this particular pair of incompatible inclinations. Like the insects, we are very adaptable creatures.

Third, I imagine that someone using an argument like LAA would, in the first place, be interested in trying to establish the fact that agents have a moral obligation to operate in a thoroughly egoistic way in their principals' behalf. If most LAA users in fact are primarily concerned with establishing their legal obligations, then perhaps what I have to say will be less interesting than I imagine to most people. Nevertheless, I'm assuming that the force of "ought" in the first premise and conclusion is moral rather than legal. For our purposes it doesn't matter what sort of an ontological analysis one gives to such obligations or what sort of a moral theory one might want to use to justify one's moral principles. It only has to be appreciated that LAA is designed to provide a moral justification for the behavior prescribed in its conclusion.

Fourth, an agent may be regarded as operating in a thoroughly egoistic way if all his actions are designed to optimize his own interests and he has no inclination at all to identify the interests of anyone else with his own. (Throughout the essay I usually let the masculine "he" abbreviate "he or she.") He may very well be a self-confident, self-starting, self-sustaining, and self-controlled individual. These are all commendable personal characteristics. But he must be selfish, self-centered, and/or self-serving. In conflict situations when there are not enough benefits to satisfy everyone, he will try to see that his own needs are satisfied, whatever happens to the needs of others. He is more interested in being first than in being nice, and he assumes that everyone else is too. He may harbor the suspicion that if everyone behaved as he does, the world's resources would be used in a maximally efficient way and everyone would be materially better off. But these are secondary considerations at best. His first consideration, which he regards as only prudent or smart, is to look out for *Número Uno,* himself.

Fifth, to say that an agent is supposed to operate in a thoroughly egoistic way in behalf of his principal is just to say that the agent is supposed to act as he believes his principal would act if his principal were an egoist. The agent is supposed to conduct the affairs of his principal with the single-minded purpose of optimizing the latter's interests and not yielding them to anyone else's interests.

THE SECOND PREMISE

Now we should be talking the same language. The question is: Is the Loyal Agent's Argument sound? Can its conclusion be established or even well-supported by its premises? I think there are good reasons for giving a negative answer to these questions. Moreover, since the argument has been deliberately formulated in a logically valid form, we may proceed immediately to a closer investigation of the content of its premises.

Let's consider the second premise first. This premise can only be regarded as true of real people *a priori* if one of the assumptions we have made for the sake of argument about human motivation is false. Following the quotations from the Special Review Committee, it was pointed out that the case involved agents who apparently performed illegal actions with altruistic motives. What they did wrong, they did in behalf of Gulf Oil Corporation. Fair enough. However, if it's possible to perform illegal but altruistically motivated acts, it must be possible to perform legal but altruistically motivated acts as well. The very assumption required to give the argument initial plausibility also ensures that its second premise cannot be assumed to be generally true *a priori.* Since some people can perform nonegoistically motivated actions, the second premise of LAA requires some defense. Moreover, broadly speaking there are two directions such a defense might take, and I will consider each in turn.

Granted that users of LAA cannot consistently regard every individual as a thoroughly egoistic operator and hence guarantee the truth of the second premise *a priori*, it is still possible to try to defend this premise as a well-confirmed empirical hypothesis. That is, admitting that there are exceptions, one might still claim that if one acted as if the second premise were true, much more often than not one would be right. This is the sort of line economists have traditionally taken toward their idealized rational economic man. They realize that people are capable of altruistic action, but they figure that the capability is seldom exercised and they design their hypotheses, laws, and theories accordingly.

So far as business is concerned, the egoistic line seems to be translated into profit maximization. According to Goodman, for example:

> The Wall Street rule for persons legally charged with the management of other people's money runs as follows: Invest funds in a company with the aim of gaining the best financial return with the least financial risk for the trust beneficiaries. If you later come to disagree with the company's management, sell the stock.[4]

Similarly, in a cautious version of LAA, Friedman has claimed that:

> In a free-enterprise, private-property system, a corporate executive is an employee of the owners of the business. He has a direct responsibility to his employers. That responsibility is to conduct the business in accordance with their desires, which generally will be to make as much money as possible while conforming to the basic rules of the society, both those embodied in law and those embodied in ethical custom.[5]

Instead of challenging the accuracy of these assessments of the motives of people generally or of businessmen in the marketplace in particular now, I want to grant it straightaway for the sake of the argument. The question is: How does that affect LAA?

As you may have guessed, users of LAA are not much better off than they were. If it's a good bet that the second premise is true, then it's an equally good bet that anyone inclined to defend his actions with LAA is not an altruistic operator. No one can have it both ways. Evidence for the empirical hypothesis that people generally act as egoists is evidence for the truth of the second premise and the falsehood of the alleged altruistic motives of anyone using LAA. In short, the premise is still self-defeating.

CORPORATE PRINCIPALS

Instead of regarding the second premise as an empirical claim about real people and attempting to support it inductively, one might treat it as a logical claim justifiable by an appeal to the definitions of some of its key terms. This looks like a very promising strategy when one considers the fact that many contemporary principals, like Gulf Oil Corporation, for example, are abstract entities. Corporate persons are, after all, nothing but fictional persons invented by people with fairly specific aims. In particular, corporations have been invented to assist in the accumulation of material assets. While they typically accomplish many different tasks, the accumulation of assets is generally regarded as their basic aim. Thus, if one's principal happens to be a corporation, one might reasonably argue that it is by definition thoroughly egoistic. The business of such entities is certainly business, because that is their very reason for being, the very point of inventing them in the first place. So, the second premise of LAA could be substantiated by definitional fiat. . . .

Apparently, then, morally conscientious corporate agents may find themselves facing lawsuits if they assume their principals are not self-serving profit maximizers and act accordingly. Legal niceties aside, there is a thought-provoking moral argument in favor of agents acting as if their principals were just as the designers of corporate law imagine them. That is, if any particular stockholder wants to give his money away or to pursue any aims other than profit maximization, he is free to do so. Investors should be and almost certainly are aware that corporations are designed to make money. If they have other aims, they shouldn't be investing in corporations. If they don't have other aims and they go into corporations with their eyes wide open, then they should appreciate and respect the interests of others who have gone in with them.

In principle the defense of the second premise of LAA on the grounds of the defining characteristic of corporations may be challenged as before. Insofar as corporations are defined as egoistic corporate persons (a rough abbreviated definition, to be sure), a serious question arises concerning the morality of becoming an agent for them—not to mention inventing them in the first place. The evils of unbridled egoism are well known and they aren't mitigated by the fact that the egoist in question is a corporate person. If anything, they are magnified because of the difficulties involved in assigning responsibility and holding corporations liable for their activities. It is demonstrably certain that if everyone only attends to what he perceives as his own interests, a socially self-destructive result may occur. That is the clear message of prisoner's dilemma studies. It's also the message of two kids in a playpen who finally tear the toys apart rather than share them.

As before, it will not help to argue that in developed countries most people work for corporations or they don't work at all. Again, self-preservation is not altruism. To serve an evil master in the interests of survival is not to serve in the interests of altruism, and users of LAA are supposed to be motivated by altruism. On the other hand, insofar as corporations are not defined as egoistic corporate persons and are granted more or less benevolent if not downright altruistic aims, the truth of the second premise of LAA is again open to question. In either case, then, an agent trying to salvage LAA with this sort of definitional defense is bound to find the task self-defeating.

THE FIRST PREMISE

Let's turn now to the first premise of LAA. In a way it's as innocuous as motherhood and apple pie. Every discussion I've read of the duties of agents according to agency law in North America and the United

Kingdom has included some form of this premise. For example, Powell says, ''An agent has a general duty to act solely for the benefit of his principal in all matters connected with the execution of his authority.''[6] *The American Restatement of the Law of Agency* says that ''an agent is subject to a duty to his principal to act solely for the benefit of the principal in all matters connected with his agency.''[7] According to a standard Canadian textbook on business law, ''Good faith requires that the agent place the interest of his principal above all else except the law.''[8]

The only trouble with the premise is that its limitations are not clearly built into it. In this respect it is like most moral principles and rules of law. Short of turning every principle and rule into a self-contained treatise, it's impossible to indicate every possible exception. . . . However, the *American Restatement of the Law of Agency* makes it quite clear that ''In no event would it be implied that an agent has a duty to perform acts which . . . are illegal or unethical.''[9] Moreover, ''In determining whether or not the orders of the principal to the agent are reasonable . . . business or professional ethics . . . are considered.''[10] Powell also remarks that agents have no duty ''to carry out an illegal act.''[11] . . . Thus, there is no doubt at all that the first premise of LAA cannot be regarded as a licence to break the law. No respectable court would permit it. In fact, although the courts have no special jurisdiction over moral law, they have shown no reluctance to condemn immoral acts allegedly performed in the interests of fulfilling fiduciary obligations.

Illegality and immorality aside, the first premise still gives up much more than any sane person should be willing to give up. It virtually gives a principal a licence to use an agent in any way the principal pleases, so long as the agent's activity serves the principal's interest. For example, suppose a life insurance agent agrees to sell State Farm Insurance on commission. It would be ludicrous to assume that the agent has also committed himself to painting houses, washing dogs, or doing anything else that happened to give his principal pleasure. It would also be misleading to describe such an open-ended commitment as an agreement to sell insurance. It would more accurately be described as selling oneself into bondage. Clearly, then, one must assume that the first premise of LAA presupposes some important restrictions that may have nothing to do with any sort of law.

Since they are apparently drawn from and applicable to ordinary affairs and usage, perhaps it would be instructive to mention some of the principles developed in the law of agency to address this problem. You may recall that the definition of an agent that we borrowed from Powell explicitly referred to a person being ''authorised to act for a principal.'' An agent's duties are typically limited to a set of activities over which he is granted authority by his principal. . . . [This] . . . would be sufficient to prevent the exploitation of the hypothetical insurance agent in the preceding paragraph.

Besides a carefully developed set of principles related to the granting of authority, the law of agency recognizes some other general duties of agents like the previously considered duty of good faith. For example, an agent is expected to ''exercise due care and skill in executing his authority.''[12] This obviously serves the interests of all concerned, and there are plenty of principles and precedents available to explain "due care and skill." . . . He is expected to "keep proper accounts," i.e., accounts that clearly distinguish his principal's assets from his own.[13] . . .

Keeping the preceding guidelines in mind, perhaps some form of LAA can be salvaged by tightening up the first premise. Let's suppose I'm in the advertising business and I want to use LAA by suitably restricting the scope of the first premise thus:

> **1a.** *As a loyal advertising agent of some company, I ought to advertise its products as they would advertise them if they had my expertise.*

That would require a consistent modification of the second premise and conclusion, but we need not worry about that. The question is: Does this reformulated premise 1a escape the kinds of criticism leveled against premise 1?

Certainly not. If the company happens to be run by a bunch of thoroughly unscrupulous thugs, it could be immoral and illegal to advertise their products as they would if they had the agent's expertise. Even if the company is run by fools who really don't know what they make, it could be immoral and illegal to advertise their products as they would if they had the agent's expertise. For example, if the company's directors are smart enough to know that they can make more money selling drugs than they can make selling candy, but dumb enough to think that the candy they make is an effective drug, an agent could hardly be under any obligation to advertise their product as a marvelous new drug, i.e., assuming that the agent was smart enough to know that his employers were only capable of producing candy.

If you think the agent could have such an obligation, what would be its source? Clearly it is not enough to say that the agent is employed by the company. That would be tantamount to appealing to LAA in order to establish a version of its own first premise, i.e., it would be a circular salvaging effort. Something else is required to support premise 1a. . . .

CONCLUSION

The announced aim of this essay was to destroy LAA once and for all. I think that has been done. It is perhaps worthwhile to emphasize that if people use LAA when, as we saw earlier, the real reason for their actions is fear (or job preservation) then they will be circulating a distorted view of the world and decreasing the chances of reform. Thus, in the interests of a clear perception and resolution of social problems related to responsible human agency, LAA deserves the sort of treatment it has received here.

Notes

1. J. J. McCloy, N. W. Pearson, and B. Matthews, *The Great Oil Spill* (New York: Chelsea House, 1976), p. 31.
2. *Ibid*, p. 13.

3. R. Powell, *The Law of Agency* (London: Sir Isaac Pitman and Sons, Ltd., 1965), p. 7.
4. W. Goodman, "Stocks Without Sin," *Minneapolis Star and Tribune Co., Inc.* Reprinted in *Ethical Arguments for Analysis,* ed. R. Baum (New York: Holt, Rinehart & Winston, 1975), p. 206.
5. M. Friedman, "The Social Responsibility of Business Is to Increase Its Profits," *The New York Times Magazine,* September 13, 1970. Reprinted in *Ethical Arguments for Analysis,* ed. R. Baum (New York: Holt, Rinehart & Winston, 1975), p. 205.
6. Powell, *The Law of Agency,* p. 312.
7. Section 387 as quoted in P. I. Blumberg, "Corporate Responsibility and the Employee's Duty of Loyalty and Obedience: A Preliminary Inquiry," *The Corporate Dilemma,* ed. D. Votaw and S. P. Sethi (Englewood Cliffs, N.J.: Prentice-Hall, Inc., 1973), p. 87.
8. J. E. Smyth and D. A. Soberman, *The Law and Business Administration in Canada* (Toronto: Prentice-Hall of Canada, Ltd., 1968), p. 360.
9. Section 385 as quoted in Blumberg, "Corporate Responsibility," p. 86.
10. *Ibid.*
11. Powell, *The Law of Agency,* p. 302.
12. *Ibid,* p. 303.
13. *Ibid,* p. 321.

LOYALTY AND RESPONSIBILITY IN THE CORPORATION*

Walter B. Gulick

Alex Michalos seeks to demonstrate that no employee can legitimately pass off personal responsibility for breaking the law by claiming that it was a moral action done out of loyalty to one's employer or corporation.[1] I share Michalos' concern for asserting the importance of the principle of personal responsibility, but ultimately I am not persuaded that his line of reasoning illuminates any actual temptations to illegality. His success at demolishing the LAA is achieved largely because his hypothetical agent and imaginary principal are constructed of straw rather than flesh. The first section of this paper will attempt to show that Michalos' loyal agent is a straw man that would not be attractive to agents in the way he seems to expect. Moreover, his notion of a principal is too constricted; it does not take adequate account of the various types of principals actually to be found. In a second section I will set forth a revised version of the LAA that I think would appeal to many employees loyal to a corporation, a version that does justice to the ethical dilemmas involved in the notion of loyalty. Finally, I will argue that even this revised version of the LAA fails to provide moral grounds for breaking the law in a covert manner. The principle of individual responsibility will be upheld, but on different, and I think stronger, grounds than those suggested by Michalos.

I. THE LOYAL AGENT'S ARGUMENT (LAA)

Michalos begins his investigation of the limits of loyalty to a corporation or employer by examining the reported motives of Gulf Oil officials who made illegal political contributions with corporate funds. He is suspicious of claims that these employees broke the law, not for direct personal benefits, but for the good of the corporation and its shareholders (p. 247). Without presuming to render a judgment in the Gulf Oil case, he constructs the Loyal Agent's Argument as a synopsis of the type of argument that might be appealed to by Gulf Oil officials or any other employees wishing to defend illegal activities as necessary to serve the best interests of their employers.

The LAA runs as follows:

1. As a loyal agent of some principal, I ought to serve his interests as he would serve them himself if he had my expertise.
2. He would serve his own interests in a thoroughly egoistic way.
   Therefore, as a loyal agent of this principal, I ought to operate in a thoroughly egoistic way in his behalf. (p. 248)

Would the LAA in fact be attractive to the average employee? Would it express a justification actually believed in by a lawbreaking employee? I think not. Some of the reasons the LAA would not be actually accepted are detailed by Michalos when he demolishes the LAA. No reasonable employee would obey a self-interested principal's instructions to carry out illegal or immoral activities and still think that such involvement could be laundered into taint-free purity because the activities were done in the name of loyalty. Someone apprehended for a business-related crime might clutch at the LAA in a desperate attempt to provide the semblance of moral justification for the illegal acts, but that is hardly the same as believing in the LAA or finding it attractive.

If there is little to suggest the LAA would be attractive to an average employee, there seems to be nothing at all to suggest the Gulf Oil officials (or anybody primarily loyal to a corporation) would accept the LAA as adequately expressing their motivations. In developing his argument, Michalos does not distinguish clearly between the different types of agents and principals involved in the business world.[2] The human superior to a middle management employee is quite a different kind of principal than the "corporate principal" Michalos discusses (pp. 250–251). An agent has a different sort of allegiance to a human superior than to a corporation. There is no evidence to suggest that the Gulf Oil officials carried out their illegal political activities in unthinking obedience to some corporate directive or because of blind loyalty to some boss. Rather they appear to be motivated primarily by a shared vision of the worth of the corporate principal, a view not at all captured by the LAA.

Now it might be objected that I assume too much in regarding the effective principal of the Gulf Oil officials as the corporation itself. All corporate employees, including even the chief executive officer (CEO), are responsible to some superior or principal as listed on an organizational structure chart. The CEO would be responsible to the board of directors, which would in turn be at least responsive to the shareholders. Thus, it might be concluded, the person (or board) to whom one is responsible is one's actual principal, not the corporation itself.

Without being tied to the specifics of the Gulf Oil case, however, this objection can be answered along several lines. It should be recognized that currently most boards of directors formulate general policy but leave the specifics of corporate direction to the executives. Thus executives tend to be rather loosely responsible to the board, not tied to a demanding principal. In addition, those whose work is obviously motivated by self-interest alone generally do not work their way to the top of the corporate hierarchy. The team worker, subservient to corporate needs, advances. The importance of the team simile cannot be overemphasized. A junior executive may report to a senior executive in what may seem to be a traditional agent-principal relationship; however, that relationship is overshadowed in importance by the way each executive contributes to the welfare of the team itself, the corporation. The CEO or board of directors sponsors cooperation for the good of the corporation much as a basketball coach emphasizes teamwork as the key to team victory. Therefore, many corporate executives are in effect trained to consider corporate welfare as that which motivates and justifies their actions. Because boards of directors are usually primarily composed of members who have themselves had executive experience, corporate leaders as a whole (board and administration) tend to subordinate themselves to the welfare of the corporation itself, their effective principal.

How is this corporate principal conceptualized? It tends to be thought of as a structural entity transcending its employees, organizational structures, or even profit-making capacity. The corporation is likely conceived as an institution dispensing services or goods for society while simultaneously providing the amenities of life for its employees. Such a beneficial organization may well be thought to have a moral right to exist and to thrive. It is this moral aura of the corporation (which for some may even have quasi-religious overtones) that would justify illegal acts on the part of those guarding its welfare. Its leaders might claim that some illegal actions can be morally justified, especially those which protect the corporation against harmful incursions on the part of government or other antagonistic interests. The LAA would not be utilized as a rationale for such illegal actions because its premises do not reflect corporate reality as corporate leaders conceive it.

Let us return to the Gulf Oil officials. Michalos quotes the following analysis of the Gulf Oil situation:

> No evidence has been uncovered or disclosed which establishes that any officer, director or employee of Gulf personally profited or benefited by or through any

use of corporate funds for contributions, gifts, entertainment or other expenses related to political activity. Further, Gulf has no reason to believe or suspect that *the motive of the employee or officer* involved in such use of corporate funds was anything other than a desire to act *solely in what he considered to be the best interest of Gulf and its shareholders.* [3]

Michalos seems to regard these claims as attempts to provide a phoney altruistic cover for what were essentially self-interested (egoistic) acts. In contrast, I have tried to show that these claims may well be true (although the statement would be more accurate if "solely" were excised). If the Gulf Oil officials believed that their illegal contributions would further the good of their own beneficent corporation and advance society in general, their illegal actions could be regarded as also being altruistic. On the other hand, it is to be doubted that their actions were *purely* altruistic in nature (if such an abstraction as pure altruism can exist). When people have invested their careers in a corporation's advancement, it is not so easy to separate personal and corporate interests as Michalos seems to assume. For top executives, the company's success is personal success, and vice versa. When such a close identification exists between personal and corporate interests, the alternatives of either altruism or egoism are not neatly sifted out in an analysis. Both are involved.

Michalos is convincing in the way he destroys the LAA, but because few would be attracted to it in the first place, little is accomplished thereby. Few are attracted to it because in order to prove his point he resorts to populating his world with unrealistic black and white opposites. He makes his agent a purely altruistic (other-regarding) figure committed to becoming subordinate to a thoroughly egoistic (self-regarding) principal out of loyalty. Thus the LAA's logical force depends upon two straw men: a purely altruistic agent loyal to a purely egoistic principal. Can a psychologically more astute argument, one recognizing the messy gray of human reality, be constructed which people such as the Gulf Oil officials would believe is adequate to justify their actions?

II. The Loyal Agent's Argument Revised (LAAR)

I do believe it is possible to construct a Loyal Agent's Argument Revised (LAAR) which would deal with the *corporation* conceived as principal in a way which at first glance seems to justify some illegal activities. The revised argument runs as follows:

1. The formation of corporations and the enactment of legislation are alternative and complementary ways of seeking the public good.
2. As a loyal agent of my corporation, I ought to work for the furtherance of the corporate goals which society affirms as good in chartering the corporation.
3. Some laws are promulgated which serve special interests rather than the public good, undermine the socially affirmed goals to which my corporation is committed, or otherwise diminish the public good.

   Therefore, as a loyal agent of my corporation, I ought to work against such laws, breaking them if necessary to serve the greater public good.

The LAAR links the corporate good with the public good[4] and thus provides some firm footing for seeing loyalty to the corporation as having a moral basis. The LAAR might have been utilized by the Gulf Oil officials in conjunction with a justification such as this:

> Political Party Y stands for sensible economic policies that are in the best interests of our corporation and the country as a whole. Party Z has engineered restrictive laws limiting what we can contribute to Party Y. These laws are for their narrow self-interest and oppose all that we stand for. Our conception of the public good is broader than that embodied in the restrictive laws, and since we have no power to change these laws, we are morally justified in breaking them in order to contribute to the greater corporate and public good.

If this is a plausible reconstruction of the rationale of the Gulf Oil officials, their argument might seem to follow an honorable line of forebears in the tradition of civil disobedience. To be sure, because their actions were covert, they would not be equivalent to public acts in defiance of an unjust law, acts calculated to bring about changes in the law. The illegal contributions are not like the sit-ins at segregated lunch counters during the civil rights movement. But the Gulf Oil case has some similarity to the example set by Dietrich Bonhoeffer.

As is well known, Bonhoeffer was a German clergyman opposed to Nazism during the 1930s and 1940s. The Nazi government developed vast power to repress and stamp out any public resistance to their policies. Consequently, resistance was driven underground. Bonhoeffer came to see Hitler as so evil that he felt justified in joining a plot to murder him, even though the prohibition against murder has the strongest moral, legal, and religious support. Bonhoeffer's decision to break the law against murder, a decision that ultimately led to his own death, was motivated by considerations of the public good analogous to those articulated in the LAAR.

From our present perspective, Bonhoeffer is regarded as a hero and a martyr. If the Gulf Oil officials broke the law to further public welfare, are they not also deserving of our approbation? The answer hinges upon an analysis of 1) the moral worth of the end sought, and 2) the extent to which the moral actor(s) had less morally objectionable alternatives to accomplish their end. Bonhoeffer's decision to help murder Hitler is judged to be morally justified because 1) Hitler was responsible for incalculable evil which could not be stopped unless he were removed from power, and 2) his use of the Gestapo to obliterate opposition meant that he could be successfully removed from power only through secret and extreme means. Considering the consequences of inaction and the lack of feasible alternatives, the decision to murder Hitler was indeed moral and commendable. Can the same be said for the illegal political contributions?

Although the Gulf Oil officials' actions seem supported by the LAAR, I can find no plausible grounds for affirming their actions as moral. The officials' actions can be sustained neither through an analysis of the situation according to the two criteria of the previous paragraph nor through reliance on the LAAR, which I believe is flawed. Turning first to the two criteria, it is clear that the moral worth of the officials' objective, supporting Party Y because its program was perceived to be more in the public interest than was Party Z's, is certainly open to debate. Moreover, the political structure in place in America provides for ways in which the debate may be legally settled. In any case, it was perfectly possible for the officials to give contributions privately and legally in support of their beliefs. Thus the situation facing Bonhoeffer was quite different from the one facing the Gulf Oil officials, and the officials could not legitimately claim a comparable precedent had been established by Bonhoeffer.

Ultimately, I believe the LAAR does not merit support. It goes astray, I believe, in its very first premise. While both corporations and governments are concerned to contribute to the public good, their contributions are not appropriately regarded as complementary. The chartering process of corporations is not subject to wide public input. Essentially corporate viability is an economic phenomenon related to fulfilling the perceived needs and desires of the customer. Corporations have considerable room to seek out and develop markets and thereby contribute to public welfare. Yet most corporations are "voted for" (through sales) by a very narrow and select segment of the public, and the voting is done in terms of the relative price and quality of its products or services. The corporate goals are not of prime interest to the consuming public; they tend to be decided upon apart from public scrutiny. In essence, contributing goods or services to the public is primarily a way of enhancing the private welfare of shareholders and employees.

In contrast, governments in general and legislatures in particular are in theory immediately responsive to public needs and goals. Democratic elections of persons representing publicly known viewpoints contribute to legislatures which pass legislation in full public view. This is of course an ideal never fully realized. Certainly some laws are passed that serve special interests. Certainly there are many corruptions of the democratic ideal. But our democratic governmental process is so devised that the public can remedy the worst abuses of governmental power through recall, the judicial system, or the elective process. Even deliberately and publicly breaking the law can be used as moral means of bringing about change. This approach has greatest moral force when the lawbreaker is willing to suffer the legal consequences (following the examples set by Gandhi and Martin Luther King). Thus there are several ways to change legislation that does not represent dominant public interests. Since there are legitimate ways to work to change laws that counter corporate goals, in no instance can the corporation find moral grounds for claiming it is above the law. To reiterate, corporate actions and legislative acts are not even complementary. Societies as well as corporations have their hierarchical structures. The law, representing public interests, is superior to the corporation, representing private interests. The latter is an agent of the legislature, owing it loyalty, but not blind obedience.

To conclude, I will revise the LAAR so that it assumes a form I can support. (Precedent suggests that it be called the LAARR. Some respect for our language suggests it be called something else—almost anything else.)

III. THE LOYAL AGENT'S CREDO (LAC)

1. The function of corporations is to enhance private interests by serving the public within the limitations imposed by economic processes, legislative restrictions or regulations, and such fundamental moral considerations as respect for human rights and attention to questions of justice.
2. As a loyal agent of my corporation, I ought to work for the furtherance of those goals whereby the corporation contributes usefully, legally and morally to both public well-being and private interests.
3. Some laws are promulgated which serve special rather than public interests, undermine the socially affirmed goals to which my corporation is committed, or otherwise diminish public welfare.

   Therefore, as a loyal agent of my corporation, I ought to use legal and moral means, *for which I assume responsibility,* to work against those laws which counter the legitimate goals to which my corporation is committed.

If the LAC is accepted as the fundamental guide for agents, then the Gulf Oil officials, whether primarily agents of a human or a corporate principal, would have to be judged culpable for their offenses even though they may have been committed for altruistic reasons. Loyalty, as a recognition of claims upon one that may run counter to immediate self-interest, is an admirable quality. But loyalty to a human principal has its limits, and so does loyalty to a corporation. The Gulf Oil employees transgressed limits indicated in the LAC. Loyalty, important as it is to efficient corporate functioning, does not override personal responsibility. There may be times, such as during Nazi control of Germany, when the LAC is superceded because the democratic institutions, which it presupposes, are inoperative. But in contemporary America I believe the LAC provides a realistic and workable guideline for understanding the place of loyalty and responsibility in the corporation.

Notes

* The author acknowledges with appreciation support from the Center for the Study of Values, University of Delaware.
1. Alex Michalos, "The Loyal Agent's Argument," in Tom L. Beauchamp and Norman E. Bowie, eds., *Ethical Theory and Business* (Englewood Cliffs, N.J.: Prentice-Hall, 1979), First Edition, pp. 338–348, Second Edition pp. 247–254. Page references in the text are to the Second Edition.
2. Whether one takes the second premise as applying to a human or corporate principal, it is problematically stated, even considering the arguments Michalos finally marshalls against the whole LAA. Most human principals are themselves agents of higher principals, and are thus not free to act in the thoroughly egoistic way Michalos suggests to be plausible. All employees are subject to corporate objectives, which serve to limit unbounded egoism. The corporation as the ultimate principal is chartered by society to fulfill certain useful functions. As subject to legal and moral restrictions, it is not appropriately thought of as "thoroughly egoistic" in the sense suggested by Michalos in his fourth clarification on page 249.

3. Michalos cites on p. 247 the Report of the Special Review Committee of the Board of Directors of Gulf Oil Corporation, itself quoted in J.J. McCloy, N.W. Pearson, and B. Matthews, *The Great Oil Spill* (New York: Chelsea House, 1976), p. 13. Michalos has added the emphases.
4. I recognize that it is problematic to speak of the public good in an unqualified way. Such usage may suggest there is one such monolithic and homogeneous structure. I tend to be sympathetic with Robert Paul Wolff, James Ogilvy and others who insist on the pluralistic nature of public goods, but to make this point in the LAAR would blur the force of the argument. I do assume heterogeneous goods in the Loyal Agent's Credo at the conclusion of the article.

WHISTLEBLOWING AND PROFESSIONAL RESPONSIBILITY

Sissela Bok

"Whistleblowing" is a new label generated by our increased awareness of the ethical conflicts encountered at work. Whistleblowers sound an alarm from within the very organization in which they work, aiming to spotlight neglect or abuses that threaten the public interest.

The stakes in whistleblowing are high. Take the nurse who alleges that physicians enrich themselves in her hospital through unnecessary surgery; the engineer who discloses safety defects in the braking systems of a fleet of new rapid-transit vehicles; the Defense Department official who alerts Congress to military graft and overspending: all know that they pose a threat to those whom they denounce and that their own careers may be at risk.

MORAL CONFLICTS

Moral conflicts on several levels confront anyone who is wondering whether to speak out about abuses or risks or serious neglect. In the first place, he must try to decide whether, other things being equal, speaking out is in fact in the public interest. This choice is often made more complicated by factual uncertainties: Who is responsible for the abuse or neglect? How great is the threat? And how likely is it that speaking out will precipitate changes for the better?

In the second place, a would-be whistleblower must weigh his responsibility to serve the public interest against the responsibility he owes to his colleagues and the institution in which he works. While the professional ethic requires collegial loyalty, the codes of ethics often stress responsibility to the public over and above duties to colleagues and clients. Thus the

Adapted from Sissela Bok, "Whistleblowing and Professional Responsibility," *New York University Education Quarterly* Vol. II, *4* (1980), 2–7. Reprinted with permission.

United States Code of Ethics for Government Servants asks them to "expose corruption wherever uncovered" and to "put loyalty to the highest moral principles and to country above loyalty to persons, party, or government."[1] Similarly, the largest professional engineering association requires members to speak out against abuses threatening the safety, health, and welfare of the public.[2]

A third conflict for would-be whistleblowers is personal in nature and cuts across the first two: even in cases where they have concluded that the facts warrant speaking out, and that their duty to do so overrides loyalties to colleagues and institutions, they often have reason to fear the results of carrying out such a duty. However strong this duty may seem in theory, they know that, in practice, retaliation is likely. As a result, their careers and their ability to support themselves and their families may be unjustly impaired.[3] A government handbook issued during the Nixon era recommends reassigning "undesirables" to places so remote that they would prefer to resign. Whistleblowers may also be downgraded or given work without responsibility or work for which they are not qualified; or else they may be given many more tasks than they can possibly perform. Another risk is that an outspoken civil servant may be ordered to undergo a psychiatric fitness-for-duty examination,[4] declared unfit for service, and "separated" as well as discredited from the point of view of any allegations he may be making. Outright firing, finally, is the most direct institutional response to whistleblowers.

Add to the conflicts confronting individual whistleblowers the claim to self-policing that many professions make, and professional responsibility is at issue in still another way. For an appeal to the public goes against everything that "self-policing" stands for. The question for the different professions, then, is how to resolve, insofar as it is possible, the conflict between professional loyalty and professional responsibility toward the outside world. The same conflicts arise to some extent in all groups, but professional groups often have special cohesion and claim special dignity and privileges.

The plight of whistleblowers has come to be documented by the press and described in a number of books. Evidence of the hardships imposed on those who chose to act in the public interest has combined with a heightened awareness of professional malfeasance and corruption to produce a shift toward greater public support of whistleblowers. Public service law firms and consumer groups have taken up their cause; institutional reforms and legislation have been proposed to combat illegitimate reprisals.[5]

Given the indispensable services performed by so many whistleblowers, strong support is often merited. But the new climate of acceptance makes it easy to overlook the dangers of whistleblowing: of uses in error or in malice; of work and reputations unjustly lost for those falsely accused; of privacy invaded and trust undermined. There comes a level of internal prying and mutual suspicion at which no institution can function. And it is a fact that the disappointed, the incompetent, the malicious, and the paranoid all too often leap to accusations in public. Worst of all, ideological persecution throughout the world traditionally relies on insiders willing to inform on their colleagues or even on their family members, often through staged public denunciations or press campaigns.

No society can count itself immune from such dangers. But neither can it risk silencing those with a legitimate reason to blow the whistle. How then can we distinguish between different instances of whistleblowing? A society that fails to protect the right to speak out even on the part of those whose warnings turn out to be spurious obviously opens the door to political repression. But from the moral point of view there are important differences between the aims, messages, and methods of dissenters from within.

Nature of Whistleblowing

Three elements, each jarring, and triply jarring when conjoined, lend acts of whistleblowing special urgency and bitterness: dissent, breach of loyalty, and accusation.

Like all dissent, whistleblowing makes public a disagreement with an authority or a majority view. But whereas dissent can concern all forms of disagreement with, for instance, religious dogma or government policy or court decisions, whistleblowing has the narrower aim of shedding light on negligence or abuse, or alerting to a risk, and of assigning responsibility for this risk.

Would-be whistleblowers confront the conflict inherent in all dissent: between conforming and sticking their necks out. The more repressive the authority they challenge, the greater the personal risk they take in speaking out. At exceptional times, as in times of war, even ordinarily tolerant authorities may come to regard dissent as unacceptable and even disloyal.[6]

Furthermore, the whistleblower hopes to stop the game; but since he is neither referee nor coach, and since he blows the whistle on his own team, his act is seen as a violation of loyalty. In holding his position, he has assumed certain obligations to his colleagues and clients. He may even have subscribed to a loyalty oath or a promise of confidentiality. Loyalty to colleagues and to clients comes to be pitted against loyalty to the public interest, to those who may be injured unless the revelation is made.

Not only is loyalty violated in whistleblowing, hierarchy as well is often opposed, since the whistleblower is not only a colleague but a subordinate. Though aware of the risks inherent in such disobedience, he often hopes to keep his job.[7] At times, however, he plans his alarm to coincide with leaving the institution. If he is highly placed, or joined by others, resigning in protest may effectively direct public attention to the wrongdoing at issue.[8] Still another alternative, often chosen by those who wish to be safe from retaliation, is to leave the institution quietly, to secure another post, and then to blow the whistle. In this way, it is possible to speak with the authority and knowledge of an insider without having the vulnerability of that position.

It is the element of accusation, of calling a "foul," that arouses the strongest reactions on the part of the hierarchy. The accusation may be of neglect, of willfully concealed dangers, or of outright abuse on the part of colleagues or superiors. It singles out specific persons or groups as responsible for threats to the public interest. If no one could be held responsible—as in the case of an impending avalanche—the warning would not constitute whistleblowing.

The accusation of the whistleblower, moreover, concerns a present or an imminent threat. Past errors or misdeeds occasion such an alarm only if they still affect current practices. And risks far in the future lack the immediacy needed to make the alarm a compelling one, as well as the close connection to particular individuals that would justify actual accusations. Thus an alarm can be sounded about safety defects in a rapid-transit system that threaten or will shortly threaten passengers, but the revelation of safety defects in a system no longer in use, while of historical interest, would not constitute whistleblowing. Nor would the revelation of potential problems in a system not yet fully designed and far from implemented.[9]

Not only immediacy, but also specificity, is needed for there to be an alarm capable of pinpointing responsibility. A concrete risk must be at issue rather than a vague foreboding or a somber prediction. The act of whistleblowing differs in this respect from the lamentation or the dire prophecy. An immediate and specific threat would normally be acted upon by those at risk. The whistleblower assumes that his message will alert listeners to something they do not know, or whose significance they have not grasped because it has been kept secret.

The desire for openness inheres in the temptation to reveal any secret, sometimes joined to an urge for self-aggrandizement and publicity and the hope for revenge for past slights or injustices. There can be pleasure, too—righteous or malicious—in laying bare the secrets of co-workers and in setting the record straight at last. Colleagues of the whistleblower often suspect his motives: they may regard him as a crank, as publicity-hungry, wrong about the facts, eager for scandal and discord, and driven to indiscretion by his personal biases and shortcomings.

For whistleblowing to be effective, it must arouse its audience. Inarticulate whistleblowers are likely to fail from the outset. When they are greeted by apathy, their message dissipates. When they are greeted by disbelief, they elicit no response at all. And when the audience is not free to receive or to act on the information—when censorship or fear of retribution stifles response—then the message rebounds to injure the whistleblower. Whistleblowing also requires the possibility of concerted public response: the idea of whistleblowing in an anarchy is therefore merely quixotic.

Such characteristics of whistleblowing and strategic considerations for achieving an impact are common to the noblest warnings, the most vicious personal attacks, and the delusions of the paranoid. How can one distinguish the many acts of sounding an alarm that are genuinely in the public interest from all the petty, biased, or lurid revelations that pervade our querulous and gossip-ridden society? Can we draw distinctions between different whistleblowers, different messages, different methods?

We clearly can, in a number of cases. Whistleblowing may be starkly inappropriate when in malice or error, or when it lays bare legitimately private matters having to do, for instance, with political belief or sexual life. It can, just as clearly, be the only way to shed light on an ongoing unjust practice such as drugging political prisoners or subjecting them to electroshock treatment. It can be the last resort for alerting the public to an impending disaster. Taking such clearcut cases as benchmarks, and reflecting on what it is about them that weighs so heavily for or against speaking out, we can work our way toward the admittedly more complex cases in which whistleblowing is not so clearly the right or wrong choice, or where different points of view exist regarding its legitimacy—cases where there are moral reasons both for concealment and for disclosure and where judgments conflict. Consider the following cases:[10]

A. As a construction inspector for a federal agency, John Samuels (not his real name) had personal knowledge of shoddy and deficient construction practices by private contractors. He knew his superiors received free vacations and entertainment, had their homes remodeled and found jobs for their relatives—all courtesy of a private contractor. These superiors later approved a multimillion no-bid contract with the same "generous" firm.

Samuels also had evidence that other firms were hiring nonunion laborers at a low wage while receiving substantially higher payments from the government for labor costs. A former superior, unaware of an office dictaphone, had incautiously instructed Samuels on how to accept bribes for overlooking sub-par performance.

As he prepared to volunteer this information to various members of Congress, he became tense and uneasy. His family was scared and the fears were valid. It might cost Samuels thousands of dollars to protect his job. Those who had freely provided Samuels with information would probably recant or withdraw their friendship. A number of people might object to his using a dictaphone to gather information. His agency would start covering up and vent its collective wrath upon him. As for reporters and writers, they would gather for a few days, then move on to the next story. He would be left without a job, with fewer friends, with massive battles looming, and without the financial means of fighting them. Samuels decided to remain silent.

B. Engineers of Company "A" prepared plans and specifications for machinery to be used in a manufacturing process and Company "A" turned them over to Company "B" for production. The engineers of Company "B," in reviewing the plans and specifications, came to the conclusion that they included certain miscalculations and technical deficiencies of a nature that the final product might be unsuitable for the purposes of the ultimate users, and that the equipment, if built according to the original plans and specifications, might endanger the lives of persons in proximity to it. The engineers of Company "B" called the matter to the attention of appropriate officials of their employer who, in turn, advised Company "A." Company "A" replied that its engineers felt that the design and specifications for the equipment were adequate and safe and that Company "B" should proceed to build the equipment as designed and specified. The officials of Company "B" instructed its engineers to proceed with the work.

C. A recently hired assistant director of admissions in a state university begins to wonder whether transcripts of some applicants accurately reflect their accomplishments. He knows that it matters to many in the university community, including alumni, that the football team continue its winning tradition. He has heard rumors that surrogates may be available to take tests for a fee, signing the names of designated applicants for admission, and that some of the transcripts may have been altered. But he has no hard facts. When he brings the question up with the director of admissions, he is told that the rumors are unfounded and asked not to inquire further into the matter.

INDIVIDUAL MORAL CHOICE

What questions might those who consider sounding an alarm in public ask themselves? How might they articulate the problem they see and weigh its injustice before deciding whether or not to reveal it? How can they best try to make sure their choice is the right one? In thinking about these questions it helps to keep in mind the three elements mentioned earlier: dissent, breach of loyalty, and accusation. They impose certain requirements—of accuracy and judgment in dissent; of exploring alternative ways to cope with improprieties that minimize the breach of loyalty; and of fairness in accusation. For each, careful articulation and testing of arguments are needed to limit error and bias.

Dissent by whistleblowers, first of all, is expressly claimed to be intended to benefit the public. It carries with it, as a result, an obligation to consider the nature of this benefit and to consider also the possible harm that may come from speaking out: harm to persons or institutions and, ultimately, to the public interest itself. Whistleblowers must, therefore, begin by making every effort to consider the effects of speaking out versus those of remaining silent. They must assure themselves of the accuracy of their reports, checking and rechecking the facts before speaking out; specify the degree to which there is genuine impropriety; consider how imminent is the threat they see, how serious, and how closely linked to those accused of neglect and abuse.

If the facts warrant whistleblowing, how can the second element—breach of loyalty—be minimized? The most important question here is whether the existing avenues for change within the organization have been explored. It is a waste of time for the public as well as harmful to the institution to sound the loudest alarm first. Whistleblowing has to remain a last alternative because of its destructive side effects: it must be chosen only when other alternatives have been considered and rejected. They may be rejected if they simply do not apply to the problem at hand, or when there is not time to go through routine channels, or when the institution is so corrupt or coercive that steps will be taken to silence the whistleblower should he try the regular channels first.

What weight should an oath or a promise of silence have in the conflict of loyalties? One sworn to silence is doubtless under a stronger obligation because of the oath he has taken. He has bound himself, assumed specific obligations beyond those assumed in merely taking a new position. But even such promises can be overridden when the public interest at issue is strong enough. They can be overriden if they were obtained under duress or through deceit. They can be overridden, too, if they promise something that is in itself wrong or unlawful. The fact that one has promised silence is no excuse for complicity in covering up a crime or a violation of the public's trust.

The third element in whistleblowing—accusation—raises equally serious ethical concerns. They are concerns of fairness to the persons accused of impropriety. Is the message one to which the public is entitled in the first place? Or does it infringe on personal and private matters that one has no right to invade? Here, the very notion of what is in the public's best "interest" is at issue: "accusations" regarding an official's unusual sexual or religious experiences may well appeal to the public's interest without being information relevant to "the public interest."

Great conflicts arise here. We have witnessed excessive claims to executive privilege and to secrecy by government officials during the Watergate scandal in order to cover up for abuses the public had every right to discover. Conversely, those hoping to profit from prying into private matters have become adept at invoking "the public's right to know." Some even regard such private matters as threats to the public: they voice their own religious and political prejudices in the language of accusation. Such a danger is never stronger than when the accusation is delivered surreptitiously. The anonymous accusations made during the McCarthy period regarding political beliefs and associations often injured persons who did not even know their accusers or the exact nature of the accusations.

From the public's point of view, accusations that are openly made by identifiable individuals are more likely to be taken seriously. And in fairness to those criticized, openly accepted responsibility for blowing the whistle should be preferred to the denunciation or the leaked rumor. What is openly stated can more easily be checked, its source's motives challenged, and the underlying information examined. Those under attack may otherwise be hard put to defend themselves against nameless adversaries. Often they do not even know that they are threatened until it is too late to respond. The anonymous denunciation, moreover, common to so many regimes, places the burden of investigation on government agencies that may thereby gain the power of a secret police.

From the point of view of the whistleblower, on the other hand, the anonymous message is safer in situations where retaliation is likely. But it is also often less likely to be taken seriously. Unless the message is accompanied by indications of how the evidence can be checked, its anonymity, however safe for the source, speaks against it.

During this process of weighing the legitimacy of speaking out, the method used, and the degree of fairness needed, whistleblowers must try to compensate for the strong possibility of bias on their part. They should be scrupulously aware of any motive that might skew their message: a desire for self-defense in a difficult bureaucratic situation, perhaps, or the urge to seek revenge, or inflated expectations regarding the effect their message will have on the situation. (Needless to say, bias affects the silent as well as the outspoken. The motive for holding back important information about abuses and injustice ought to give similar cause for soul-searching.)

Likewise, the possibility of personal gain from sounding the alarm ought to give pause. Once again there is then greater risk of a biased message. Even if the whistleblower regards himself as incorruptible, his profiting from revelations of neglect or abuse will lead others to question his motives and to put less credence in his charges. If, for example, a government employee stands to make large profits from a book exposing the iniquities in his agency, there is danger that he will, perhaps even unconsciously, slant his report in order to cause more of a sensation.

A special problem arises when there is a high risk that the civil servant who speaks out will have to go through costly litigation. Might he not justifiably try to make enough money on his public revelations—say, through books or public speaking—to offset his losses? In so doing he will not strictly speaking have *profited* from his revelations: he merely avoids being financially crushed by their sequels. He will nevertheless still be suspected at the time of revelation, and his message will therefore seem more questionable.

Reducing bias and error in moral choice often requires consultation, even open debate:[11] methods that force articulation of the moral arguments at stake and challenge privately held assumptions. But acts of whistleblowing present special problems when it comes to open consultation. On the one hand, once the whistleblower sounds his alarm publicly, his arguments will be subjected to open scrutiny: he will have to articulate his reasons for speaking out and substantiate his charges. On the other hand, it will then be too late to retract the alarm or to combat its harmful effects, should his choice to speak out have been ill-advised.

For this reason, the whistleblower owes it to all involved to make sure of two things: that he has sought as much and as objective advice regarding his choice as he can *before* going public; and that he is aware of the arguments for and against the practice of whistleblowing in general, so that he can see his own choice against as richly detailed and coherently structured a background as possible. Satisfying these two requirements once again has special problems because of the very nature of whistleblowing: the more corrupt the circumstances, the more dangerous it may be to seek consultation before speaking out. And yet, since the whistleblower himself may have a biased view of the state of affairs, he may choose not to consult others when in fact it would be not only safe but advantageous to do so; he may see corruption and conspiracy where none exists.

Notes

1. Code of Ethics for Government Service passed by the U.S. House of Representatives in the 85th Congress (1958) and applying to all government employees and office holders.
2. Code of Ethics of the Institute of Electrical and Electronics Engineers, Article IV.
3. For case histories and descriptions of what befalls whistleblowers, see: Rosemary Chalk and Frank von Hippel, "Due Process for Dissenting Whistle-Blowers," *Technology Review* 81 (June–July 1979): 48–55; Alan S.

Westin and Stephen Salisbury, eds., *Individual Rights in the Corporation* (New York: Pantheon, 1980); Helen Dudar, "The Price of Blowing the Whistle," *New York Times Magazine,* 30 October 1979, pp. 41–54; John Edsall, *Scientific Freedom and Responsibility* (Washington, D.C.: American Association for the Advancement of Science, 1975), p. 5; David Ewing, *Freedom Inside the Organization* (New York: Dutton, 1977); Ralph Nader, Peter Petkas, and Kate Blackwell, *Whistle Blowing* (New York: Grossman, 1972); Charles Peter and Taylor Branch, *Blowing the Whistle* (New York: Praeger, 1972).

4. Congressional hearings uncovered a growing resort to mandatory psychiatric examinations. See U.S. Congress, House Committee on Post Office and Civil Service, Subcommittee on Compensation and Employee Benefits, *Forced Retirement/Psychiatric Fitness for Duty Exams,* 95th Cong., 2nd sess., 3 November 1978, pp. 2–4. See also the Subcommittee hearings of 28 February 1978. Psychiatric referral for whistleblowers has become institutionalized in government service, but it is not uncommon in private employment. Even persons who make accusations without being "employed" in the organization they accuse have been classified as unstable and thus as unreliable witnesses. See, e.g., Jonas Robitscher, "Stigmatization and Stone-Walling: The Ordeal of Martha Mitchell," *Journal of Psychohistory,* 6, 1979, pp. 393–407.

5. For an account of strategies and proposals to support government whistleblowers, see Government Accountability Project, *A Whistleblower's Guide to the Federal Bureaucracy* (Washington, D.C.: Institute for Policy Studies, 1977).

6. See, e.g., Samuel Eliot Morison, Frederick Merk, and Frank Friedel, *Dissent in Three American Wars* (Cambridge: Harvard University Press, 1970).

7. In the scheme worked out by Albert Hirschman in *Exit, Voice and Loyalty* (Cambridge: Harvard University Press, 1970), whistleblowing represents "voice" accompanied by a preference not to "exit," though forced "exit" is clearly a possibility and "voice" after or during "exit" may be chosen for strategic reasons.

8. Edward Weisband and Thomas N. Franck, *Resignation in Protest* (New York: Grossman, 1975).

9. Future developments can, however, be the cause for whistleblowing if they are seen as resulting from steps being taken or about to be taken that render them inevitable.

10. Case A is adapted from Louis Clark, "The Sound of Professional Suicide," *Barrister,* Summer 1978, p. 10; Case B is Case 5 in Robert J. Baum and Albert Flores, eds., *Ethical Problems of Engineering* (Troy, N.Y.: Rensselaer Polytechnic Institute, 1978), p. 186.

11. I discuss these questions of consultation and publicity with respect to moral choice in chapter 7 of Sissela Bok, *Lying* (New York: Pantheon, 1978); and in *Secrets* (New York: Pantheon Books, 1982) Ch. IX and XV.

WHAT CAN AND SHOULD BE DONE TO PROTECT WHISTLE BLOWERS IN INDUSTRY

Alan F. Westin

INTRODUCTION

. . . As we begin the 1980s, two basic judgments seem justified by the experiences of . . . whistle blowers of the past decade:

1. The harm that can be done to worker and public health, consumer safety, and the environment by corporate mistakes or disregard of law has grown so serious, and its future effects so awesome, that we need to improve the mechanisms of decision making within the corporation, to weigh risks and costs more effectively from the standpoint of the public interest. Greater internal-dissent and error-detection procedures are vital to such an improved process, along with a better early warning system to alert society at large to dangers *before* their consequences engulf us.
2. The internal and external protections of legitimate whistle blowing that began to be applied in the late 1970s are still very fragile and isolated blooms in a rocky organizational and legal soil. It is simply not enough that a few dozen companies out of 10,000 large enterprises have adequate employee-rights programs that affect whistle-blowing matters. As for the law, the opinions of the majority of courts in the 1970s make it clear that most judges are still uncomfortable with "public policy" exceptions to employer firing powers. Also most government agencies do not give enough help within a reasonable time to whistle blowers who have been the victims of reprisal actions.

My conclusion is that our society needs to rethink the current definitions of loyalty and dissent in corporate life. We must come up with a strategy that will apply a combination of new remedies to increase the protection of legitimate whistle blowing. And, we have to start discussing this issue with some urgency now, if we are to take the actions that the public interest requires for the 1980s and beyond.

THE COMPLEXITIES TO BE CONSIDERED IN FRAMING NEW POLICIES

Having stated this conclusion, it may seem that this presents a relatively straightforward problem for American law and social policy: just create some new procedures to protect whistle blowers. But the problem is not at all simple. Consider the following factors that have to be taken into account in framing new public policies.

1. *Not all whistle blowers are correct in what they allege to be the facts of management's conduct, and determining the accuracy of whistle-blowing charges is not always easy.* Even though we presented ten examples where corporate employees

Adapted from A. F. Westin, "What Can and Should Be Done to Protect Whistle Blowers in Industry," in *Whistle Blowing! Loyalty and Dissent in the Corporation,* ed. A. F. Westin (New York: McGraw-Hill, 1981), pp. 131–165. Reprinted by permission.

seem to have been in the right, this is often not the case. If it were possible to collect all the instances of corporate-employee whistle-blowing charges in the United States in a given year and then determine how often managements were justified in their actions and the employees mistaken, my guess is that employers would deserve to win many of these disputes. This has been the experience under independent labor arbitration, when unionized workers challenge dismissals as not being for "just cause." It is also the experience when government employees have appealed to the courts to vindicate free-expression rights in government whistle-blowing cases. Putting the whistle to one's lips does not guarantee that one's facts are correct.

2. *There is always the danger that incompetent or inadequately performing employees will take up the whistle to avoid facing justified personnel sanctions.* Forbidding an employer to dismiss or discipline an employee who protests against illegal or improper conduct by management invites employees to take out "antidismissal insurance" by lodging a whistle-blowing complaint. Any new system to protect whistle blowers must find ways to deal with this possibility.

3. *Employees can choose some ways of blowing the whistle that would be unacceptably disruptive, regardless of the merits of their protest.* Suppose an employee at a chemical plant takes out an ad in the local newspaper that says, "My company is violating the law by polluting the town reservoir." Or suppose a black employee of the XYZ Corporation comes to work on the assembly line one day wearing a large button that says "XYZ is a Honkie Firm that Practices Racism against its Black Workers." Finally, suppose an automobile design engineer, without raising the issue with his supervisor or upper management, reports to the National Transportation Safety Board that he believes the gas tank of a new model just entering production will pose grave safety problems. These illustrations demonstrate that any system to protect rights of employee expression must consider the time, place, and manner in which an employee voices that dissent.

4. *Some whistle blowers are not protesting unlawful or unsafe behavior but social policies by management that the employee considers unwise.* When this is the case, should such an employee be entitled to remain on the job? In considering this, it helps to recall that whistle blowing can come in a wide variety of ideological stripes. Most government and corporate whistle blowers have recently been people who are asserting liberal values when they call for changes in corporate policies. But in the late 1940s and early fifties, the most celebrated whistle blowers were persons leaking information to anti-Communist legislators or the press about allegedly "soft-on-communism" policies by members of the Truman administration or their private employers. It was Senator Richard M. Nixon who proposed legislation in 1951 to protect the jobs of such federal-employee whistle blowers if they revealed classified information about corruption or pro-Communists to congressional committees. At that moment, liberals and civil libertarians defended the need for autonomy and confidentiality in the Executive Branch, and deplored the totalitarian "informer" mentality being championed by the McCarthyites. This suggests that any policy protecting whistle blowers must reckon with the likelihood of shifting ideological directions

among protesting employees, and consider how often society wants social policies to be determined in the private sector through whistle-blowing disputes.

5. *The legal definitions of what constitutes a safe product, danger to health, or improper treatment of employees are often far from clear or certain.* It usually takes years and many test cases before the courts and regulatory agencies define just what is required in a given situation. This leaves open a wide range of judgments and choices as to what is proper compliance activity. Until the law becomes clear, shouldn't management have the authority to select compliance strategies, since management bears the legal responsibility for meeting standards? This is especially true since the harsh realities of foreign business competition and rising production expenses create legitimate concerns for management about containing costs, including the costs of complying with government regulations. In addition, the jobs of millions of corporate employees, the well-being of local communities in which companies operate, and the strength of the national economy are all involved in the determination of reasonable risk-to-cost calculations.

6. *The efficiency and flexibility of personnel administration could be threatened by the creation of legal rights to dissent and legalized review systems.* If it becomes legally protected to challenge management policies and procedures and to appeal directives to outside authorities, this could lead to a flood of unjustified and harassing employee complaints. It could require personnel managers to document every action as a defense to possible litigation, and embroil managements in constant employee litigation. It could also create an "informer ethos" at work that would threaten the spirit of cooperation and trust on which sound working relationships depend.

7. *There can be risks to the desirable autonomy of the private sector in expanding government authority too deeply into internal business policies.* Although democratic societies have a major interest in allowing private organizations to run their own affairs and to make their own personnel decisions, they insist that these private organizations are also subject to obeying the law. Having courts or government tribunals pass on the validity of a wide range of personnel decisions could give the government more authority to define loyalty and disloyalty for 80 million private-sector employees than would be desirable, and could also give government too much authority to control what products are produced and how they are manufactured.

This catalogue of institutional and social problems does *not* mean that we should abandon the effort to install new whistle-blower protections in the private sector. It does suggest that we need to be sensitive to the multifaceted aspects of the task, and to recognize that care now could save much regret later over the "unanticipated consequences" of a new policy. . . .

New Management Policies and Procedures: The Inside Mechanisms

The single most important element in creating a meaningful internal system to deal with whistle blowing is to have top leadership accept this as a management priority. This means that the chief operating officer and his senior colleagues have to believe that a policy which encourages discussion and dissent, and deals fairly with whistle-blowing claims, is a good and important thing for their company to adopt. Executives of American business have to be convinced that such protection of dissent is, in both the short and the long run, important for their company's progress. They have to see such an approach as essential if their firms are to operate effectively in the risk-heavy environment of the 1980s, and to secure the best efforts of an increasingly rights-conscious workforce. They have to see it, in their own terms, as a moral duty of good private enterprise. . . .

. . . The next step is the drafting of principles and policy statements that apply management's intention throughout the company, and the communication of this policy to all employees. It is especially important not only that middle and line managers be informed about the policy, and given concrete training in its meaning and application, but also that adherence to such policy be built into the reward and penalty structure of management. . . .

Even the best drafted policy statements and management training programs will not resolve all the questions of illegal, dangerous, or improper conduct that might arise. There has to be a clear process of receiving complaints, conducting impartial investigations, defining standards of judgment, providing a fair-hearing procedure, and reaching the most objective and responsible decision possible. Such a procedure has to be fair both to the complaining employee and to company officials if morale is to be preserved and general confidence in management's integrity is to be the general expectation of the work force.

When collective bargaining contracts for unionized employees and their grievance machinery are not involved, the great majority of American corporations use three elements to handle employee complaints: the immediate supervisor; the personnel department; and some kind of "Open Door" appeal to management.[1] Many whistle-blowing issues involving personnel decisions (race and sex discrimination, sexual harassment, age discrimination, etc.) can and probably should be handled through this traditional chain of appeal. But the personnel department does not have the substantive skills or the authority within the company to handle issues of product design, dangerous work processes, environmental pollution, or other alleged violation of regulatory standards.

As it has traditionally been administered, the Open Door program of appeal to a plant manager, division head, or company chief executive has been more of a promise than an operating reality. The weakness in practice has usually been the absence of a well-publicized and easily accessible means to lodge an appeal; a well-staffed investigative system; a powerful enough commitment of time and attention by the chief executive officer to create a "without-fear-or-favor" approach to reaching decisions; and a publicized record of decisions that indicate enough rulings adverse to management to satisfy employee concerns for impartial judgment. IBM is an example of a company in which the conditions for effective use of the Open Door exist and could be applied in whistle-blowing situations.[2] But very few companies that I know of have such carefully administered Open Door programs.

A few companies, such as General Electric's Aircraft Frame Division,

Control Data Corporation, Singer, and McDonald's, have created Ombudsmen programs that provide a single official to receive, investigate, and respond to employee complaints.[3] This can be an important forum for the employee who believes illegal or improper conduct is taking place, especially if the Ombudsman is an experienced executive who enjoys the open and determined support of the company's chief executive officer. For many situations, especially overzealousness by middle managers or violation of the company's own rules and ethical guides, the Ombudsman can be an effective resource. However, very few companies have adopted the Ombudsman technique so far. And, the problem with using the Ombudsman in some whistle-blowing situations is that the Ombudsman may not be able to deal effectively with a charge of illegal or improper conduct by a "line function" such as design, production, or sales. There is likely to be even greater difficulty when senior executives of the company are actively promoting this conduct as a company imperative.

In recognition of this problem, Citibank created a special procedure in 1980 that its employees can use when whistle-blowing issues arise.[4] While Citibank already had a Good Practices Committee of its Board of Directors, this was a general supervisory mechanism and not one specifically addressed to the whistle-blowing problem. Also, Citibank had experienced an employee complaint of alleged illegality that had drawn headlines in 1978–79.[5] Believing that a more explicit policy for receiving and reviewing complaints was needed, Citibank personnel set out to draft a new procedure to handle accusations by employees of questionable, unethical, or illegal practices, and one that would apply to Citibank's activities worldwide, not just in the United States. (Taking into account the diversity of laws and practices in the many countries in which Citibank operates proved the biggest difficulty, a Citibank executive noted. "If it had only been for the United States, we could have issued it a year ago.")[6] . . .

For companies that have scientific, technical, and professional employees working for them, and recognizing the growing problems of risk-assessment involved in product safety, employee safety, and environmental protection, managements might consider developing a special procedure along the lines installed in mid-1980 by the U.S. Nuclear Regulatory Commission.[7] The NRC policy grows out of the First Amendment free speech rights of government employees, their right to communicate with Congress, and the whistle-blower protections of the 1978 Civil Service Reform Act, so that it unfolds in a very different legal and organizational climate than private employment. However, its philosophy and procedures are worth consideration in the corporate world.

The NRC defines a "differing professional opinion" as "a conscientious expression of professional judgment on any matter relating to NRC's mission or organizational activities. . . ." To handle those differing opinions that cannot be resolved through normal discussions with co-workers and supervisors, or by the agency's Open Door system, the employee submits a written statement to NRC management outlining the existing policy or practice, the employee's disagreement and the basis for it, the consequences that could arise if the policy is not changed, and any previous reviews or reconsiderations of the policy that the employee is aware of. From that point on, a written record is created, a hearing process is provided, and an appropriate management executive either accepts the recommended change or decides it is not persuasive.

The NRC's Office of Management and Program Analysis provides the Commission with quarterly reports of all such differing professional opinions filed and their outcomes, and these are also filed in the public document room so that experts, the public, and the media can learn of them. The NRC expressly forbids retaliation against an employee for filing a differing professional opinion, spelling out all the informal means of harassment as well as direct retaliation that are not to be used. Each year, a Special Review Panel of NRC employees and outsiders will go over the handling of differing professional opinions not only to see that the system is working properly but also to suggest merit awards for employees whose differing professional opinions "made significant contributions to the agency or to public safety. . . ."

All of these internal complaint and appeal mechanisms offer important procedures to institutionalize the enforcement of the company's principles and policies. . . .

Notes

1. For overviews of these mechanisms in the corporate world, see *Policies for Unorganized Employees,* Personnel Policies Forum Survey No. 125, Bureau of National Affairs, April 1979, and *Nonunion Complaint Systems: A Corporate Appraisal,* Report No. 770, The Conference Board, 1980.
2. For a description of IBM's policy, see "IBM's Guidelines to Employee Privacy: An Interview with Frank T. Cary," *Harvard Business Review,* Volume 54, Number 5, September–October 1976, pp. 82–90.
3. These companies made presentations on their Ombudsman programs at the First and Second National Seminars on Individual Rights in the Corporation, in 1978 and 1979. They are to be published in a casebook on employee rights programs to be issued by McGraw-Hill in 1981.
4. Materials provided by Citibank, N.A., February 1980; official promulgation by Citibank was to take place later in 1980.
5. *Edwards* v. *Citibank,* 418 N.Y.S. 2d 269 (1979), dismissing the complaint under the employment-at-will doctrine.
6. Statement to Alan F. Westin by Citibank personnel executive, December, 1979.
7. "Proposed Policy and Procedures for Differing Professional Opinions," "NUREG-0567," 1979. This was about to be promulgated early in 1980 after completion of a period for public comments in the latter part of 1979.

WHEN IN ROME,
SHOULD YOU DO AS THE ROMANS DO?

Norman E. Bowie

In developing this paper, I wish to use certain features of Joseph Margolis' distinction between a conflict of interest and conflicting interests. A conflict of interest is a collision of interests where the resolution of the conflict requires that only one of the interests be met and that all other interests in the conflict must yield and not be fulfilled at all. Conflicting interests, on the other hand, represent legitimate interests which cannot be fulfilled and where resolution of the conflict permits a balancing of the interests so that all the interests could be partially fulfilled. "Where conflicting interests obtain, an unfortunate agent is somehow bound to act properly in accord with both; where a conflict of interest obtains, he must not undertake the relevant ventures conjointly; he must divert himself of at least one."[1] If all this seems unnecessarily abstract, perhaps some examples will clear things up. Let us begin with a domestic issue in product safety.

Case I

Company x discovers that one of its products has serious, harmful side effects while the competing product produced by another company apparently does not. Should Company x stop production on this profitable product?

Case II

Company x produces an artificial sweetener which has great health value to diabetics and overall health benefits to Americans suffering from overweight. However, there is some evidence that the artificial sweetener will cause a small number of persons to contract cancer. There is no available substitute. In the absence of laws governing the case, should Company x stop producing the artificial sweetener?

Using our distinction between conflicting interests and a conflict of interest, we can give a very different analysis of the two cases. Case I presents a genuine conflict of interest—the interest of Company x in marketing a profitable product and the interest of consumers in not having their health endangered. In this case, there is no balancing to be done; the health of the consumers is to take precedence over the interest of the company. The reason for this should be obvious. By using the competitive product, no consumers are harmed. Preventing health hazards has a higher moral priority than the profits of an individual company. With this particular product, the interest of Company x is not to count at all.

Adapted from Norman E. Bowie, "A Taxonomy for Discussing the Conflicting Responsibilities of a Multinational Corporation" in *Responsibilities of Multinational Corporations to Society* (Arlington, Va.: Council of Better Business Bureau, 1978), pp. 21–43. Reprinted by permission.

Case II is very different however. We are not simply balancing off the profits of Company x against the harms to consumers. Rather, we are balancing off the harms to some consumers if the artificial sweetener is produced against the harms to other consumers if the artificial sweetener is not produced. In this case we have conflicting interests where the notions of weighing and balancing are much more in order. In this case it is not obvious which interest should predominate.

For some situations, it will not be clear whether we have a case of conflict of interest or a case of conflicting interests. However, there are always borderline cases.

I. Illusory Cases of Conflicting Responsibilities

Far too many of the discussions of multinational corporations focus on situations which really present pseudo-moral issues. I believe the central cause of this mistake is the emphasis on the different practices, customs, mores, and laws which exist among nations. Even if there are great differences in social practices, nothing logically follows concerning conflict. It is an obvious logical fallacy to conclude from ''practice x is different from practice y'' that ''practice x is in conflict with practice y.'' I adopt one set of practices for dealing with my family, another for relations with my colleagues and still another for casual interactions with shopkeepers, repairmen, and bureaucrats. Although the practices are different, they do not conflict. It is not simply the *difference* in practices which creates conflicting responsibilities.

With this in mind, consider some of the alleged conflicts which occur as a result of the activities of multinationals. Sometimes the errors result when we are excessively concerned with different legal standards or moral customs. Should there be worldwide standards of health, safety, wages, and training benefits? When a company operates in many countries, does it have ethical obligations in relation to its home country's ethics, laws, standards? The answer to the first question is ''no.'' The answer to the second question is ''it all depends.'' If we mean does a multinational have an obligation to *our* ethics, laws, or standards when operating in another country the answer is ''sometimes yes, but usually no.'' A discussion of some cases will confirm these conclusions.

Case III

Multinational x produces a drug in a foreign country for a foreign market which it could not produce in the U.S. The drug had not been certified as safe by government authorities even though as yet no dangerous or harmful side effects have been discovered. Multinational x produces the drug abroad.

Case IV

Multinational x produced a drug in the U.S. which was later found to be a potential carcinogen. The company accepted the findings. Nonetheless, safety requirements in a foreign country are not so strict. Multinational x produces the drug abroad.

Case V

Multinational x produces baby formula. It is, of course, safe for use in the U.S. The company tries to expand its markets in underdeveloped countries and aggressively advertises the formula there, knowing full well that most families in underdeveloped countries do not have the storage and preparation facilities to make the product safe and effective. As a result of general ignorance on the part of poor families, countless infants will be undernourished and hence physically harmed; thousands will die. Multinational x produces the product abroad.

Now I have heard multinationals condemned for all the activities described in Cases III–V. That seems to me to be a mistake. All the cases present excellent illustrations of my main point that there should not be worldwide standards of health, safety, wages, and training benefits and that we do not always have an obligation to take the home country's ethics, laws, and standards into account. The cases also illustrate the point that different standards between home and host countries need not represent conflicting standards.

In Case V, concerning infant formula, behavior which is morally appropriate in the home country is clearly immoral in the host country. However, there is no conflict of responsibilities here. Different cultural factors in the host country require different standards of behavior.

In Case III there are no conflicts at all. There are a number of possible rules for product safety. One is that the company prove in advance that the product is safe. Another is that after certain minimum test procedures a product be presumed safe until it is proved harmful. If two countries adopt different rules for determining product safety, there is no reason why a multinational cannot legitimately, and without any sense of conflicting responsibilities, market product x in one country but not in another.

Case IV is more complicated and it points out how the philosophy of relativism (When in Rome, do as the Romans do) can be abused. Case IV could be reduced to either a Case I situation where there is a genuine conflict of interest or to a Case II situation where there are conflicting interests. If the product in Case IV was an artificial sweetener, there would be no conflicting responsibilities for the reasons given in our analysis of Case III. The fact that the U.S. has made one decision concerning the trade-offs among conflicting interests does not require foreign countries to follow our lead. It is not immoral for a multinational to market an artificial sweetener in a country which reached a decision on product safety different from our own.

But shouldn't there be worldwide standards? I think not. It is not clear which of the possible rules concerning product safety is best. Is it better that a product be proved safe or is it better that, after minimum testing, it be presumed safe until proven guilty? The former rule will prevent harmful products, but it will delay the introduction of many very useful products. The latter rule will have the converse effect. By having national states using different rules, we have an experimental situation for testing various rules. We also enhance individual liberty since a person in a country with a conservative rule on product safety might be able to get a desired product in another country with a more permissive rule. On balance, I think multiple standards are better than worldwide standards.

I do not wish to leave the impression that I endorse ethical relativism. If the product in Case IV is one like that discussed earlier in Case I, I think the multinational ought not to market it there. This is because I would contend that there are some moral rules that transcribe national boundaries, or, in other words, that some moral principles are absolute. The injunction that one ought to avoid deliberately harming another person when such harm is easily avoidable is one such moral absolute. Many corporate executives are no more ethical relativists than I. Richard Heckert, senior vice president of DuPont, has argued:

> . . . the general rule is that when you're in another country you should behave like a guest—but what do you do when the safety situation is unacceptable?
>
> Our answer is to move aggressively and demand higher standards even if it upsets local practices. We do this on the grounds that protecting human life is more important than maintaining good manners.[2]

If there are universal moral rules, we must be careful in how we talk about conflicting responsibilities. For example, we would not speak of conflicting responsibilities to home and host countries but rather of conflicting responsibilities to a local practice and a universal moral rule. In such cases, however, it seems clear that our ultimate responsibility is to the universal moral rule. The most typical case would be a country (like South Africa) whose own moral practices are in violation of universal moral principles. Since the universal moral rules take precedence over the social norms of the deviant country, it seems clear that the course for the multinational is set. It should conform to universal moral rules.

In summary, I have presented some arguments to show that a multinational operating in host countries usually has *no* obligations in relation to its home country's ethics, laws, and standards. It is only when the host country's ethics and standards depart from universal moral rules that obligations are incurred.

Notes

1. Joseph Margolis, "Conflict of Interest and Conflicting Interests," in Thomas Beauchamp and Norman Bowie, eds., *Ethical Theory in Business,* first edition, (Englewood Cliffs, N.J.: Prentice-Hall, Inc., 1979). Margolis provides many more defining conditions for a conflict of interest than the ones here.
2. Richard E. Heckert, "Business Ethics In An International Setting," address before American Institute of Chemical Engineers, Atlanta, 2/27/78.

ETHICS AND THE
FOREIGN CORRUPT PRACTICES ACT

Mark Pastin and Michael Hooker

One aspect of the recent attention paid to corporate morality is the controversy surrounding payments made by American corporations to foreign officials for the purpose of securing business abroad. Like any law or system of laws, the Foreign Corrupt Practices Act (FCPA), designed to control or eliminate such payments, should be grounded in morality, and should therefore be judged from an ethical perspective. Unfortunately, neither the law nor the question of its repeal has been adequately addressed from that perspective.

HISTORY OF THE FCPA

On December 20, 1977 President Carter signed into law S.305, the Foreign Corrupt Practices Act (FCPA), which makes it a crime for American corporations to offer or provide payments to officials of foreign governments for the purpose of obtaining or retaining business. The FCPA also establishes record keeping requirements for publicly held corporations to make it difficult to conceal political payments proscribed by the Act. Violators of the FCPA, both corporations and managers, face severe penalties. A company may be fined up to $1 million, while its officers who directly participated in violations of the Act or had reason to know of such violations, face up to five years in prison and/or $10,000 in fines. The Act also prohibits corporations from indemnifying fines imposed on their directors, officers, employees, or agents. The Act does not prohibit "grease" payments to foreign government employees whose duties are primarily ministerial or clerical, since such payments are sometimes required to persuade the recipients to perform their normal duties.

At the time of this writing, the precise consequences of the FCPA for American business are unclear, mainly because of confusion surrounding the government's enforcement intentions. Vigorous objections have been raised against the Act by corporate attorneys and recently by a few government officials. Among the latter is Frank A. Weil, former Assistant Secretary of Commerce, who has stated, "The questionable payments problem may turn out to be one of the most serious impediments to doing business in the rest of the world."[1]

The potentially severe economic impact of the FCPA was highlighted by the fall 1978 report of the Export Disincentives Task Force, which was created by the White House to recommend ways of improving our balance

Adapted from M. Pastin and M. Hooker, "Ethics and the Foreign Corrupt Practices Act," *Business Horizons* (1980), 43–47. Reprinted with permission.

of trade. The Task Force identified the FCPA as contributing significantly to economic and political losses in the United States. Economic losses come from constricting the ability of American corporations to do business abroad, and political losses come from the creation of a holier-than-thou image.

The Task Force made three recommendations in regard to the FCPA:

> The Justice Department should issue guidelines on its enforcement policies and establish procedures by which corporations could get advance government reaction to anticipated payments to foreign officials.
>
> The FCPA should be amended to remove enforcement from the SEC, which now shares enforcement responsibility with the Department of Justice.
>
> The administration should periodically report to Congress and the public on export losses caused by the FCPA.

In response to the Task Force's report, the Justice Department, over SEC objections, drew up guidelines to enable corporations to check any proposed action possibly in violation of the FCPA. In response to such an inquiry, the Justice Department would inform the corporation of its enforcement intentions. The purpose of such an arrangement is in part to circumvent the intent of the law. As of this writing, the SEC appears to have been successful in blocking publication of the guidelines, although Justice recently reaffirmed its intention to publish guidelines. Being more responsive to political winds, Justice may be less inclined than the SEC to rigidly enforce the Act.

Particular concern has been expressed about the way in which bookkeeping requirements of the Act will be enforced by the SEC. The Act requires that company records will "accurately and fairly reflect the transactions and dispositions of the assets of the issuer." What is at question is the interpretation the SEC will give to the requirement and the degree of accuracy and detail it will demand. The SEC's post-Watergate behavior suggests that it will be rigid in requiring the disclosure of all information that bears on financial relationships between the company and any foreign or domestic public official. This level of accountability in record keeping, to which auditors and corporate attorneys have strongly objected, goes far beyond previous SEC requirements that records display only facts material to the financial position of the company.

Since the potential consequences of the FCPA for American businesses and business managers are very serious, it is important that the Act have a rationale capable of bearing close scrutiny. In looking at the foundation of the FCPA, it should be noted that its passage followed in the wake of intense newspaper coverage of the financial dealings of corporations. Such media attention was engendered by the dramatic disclosure of corporate slush funds during the Watergate hearings and by a voluntary disclosure program established shortly thereafter by the SEC. As a result of the SEC program, more than 400 corporations, including 117 of the Fortune 500, admitted to making more than $300 million in foreign political payments in less than ten years.

Throughout the period of media coverage leading up to passage of the

FCPA, and especially during the hearings on the Act, there was in all public discussions of the issue a tone of righteous moral indignation at the idea of American companies making foreign political payments. Such payments were ubiquitously termed "bribes," although many of these could more accurately be called extortions, while others were more akin to brokers' fees or sales commissions.

American business can be faulted for its reluctance during this period to bring to public attention the fact that in a very large number of countries, payments to foreign officials are virtually required for doing business. Part of that reluctance, no doubt, comes from the awkwardly difficult position of attempting to excuse bribery or something closely resembling it. There is a popular abhorrence in this country of bribery directed at domestic government officials, and that abhorrence transfers itself to payments directed toward foreign officials as well.

Since its passage, the FCPA has been subjected to considerable critical analysis, and many practical arguments have been advanced in favor of its repeal.[2] However, there is always lurking in back of such analyses the uneasy feeling that no matter how strongly considerations of practicality and economics may count against this law, the fact remains that the law protects morality in forbidding bribery. For example, Gerald McLaughlin, professor of law at Fordham, has shown persuasively that where the legal system of a foreign country affords inadequate protection against the arbitrary exercise of power to the disadvantage of American corporations, payments to foreign officials may be required to provide a compensating mechanism against the use of such arbitrary power. McLaughlin observes, however, that "this does not mean that taking advantage of the compensating mechanism would necessarily make the payment moral."[3]

The FCPA, and questions regarding its enforcement or repeal, will not be addressed adequately until an effort has been made to come to terms with the Act's foundation in morality. While it may be very difficult, or even impossible, to legislate morality (that is, to change the moral character and sentiments of people by passing laws that regulate their behavior), the existing laws undoubtedly still reflect the moral beliefs we hold. Passage of the FCPA in Congress was eased by the simple connection most Congressmen made between bribery, seen as morally repugnant, and the Act, which is designed to prevent bribery.

Given the importance of the FCPA to American business and labor, it is imperative that attention be given to the question of whether there is adequate moral justification for the law.

ETHICAL ANALYSIS OF THE FCPA

The question we will address is not whether each payment prohibited by the FCPA is moral or immoral, but rather whether the FCPA, given all its consequences and ramifications, is itself moral. It is well known that morally sound laws and institutions may tolerate some immoral acts. The First Amendment's guarantee of freedom of speech allows individuals to utter racial slurs. And immoral laws and institutions may have some beneficial consequences, for example, segregationist legislation bringing deep-seated racism into the national limelight. But our concern is with the overall morality of the FCPA.

The ethical tradition has two distinct ways of assessing social institutions, including laws: *End-Point Assessment* and *Rule Assessment.* Since there is no consensus as to which approach is correct, we will apply both types of assessment to the FCPA.

The End-Point approach assesses a law in terms of its contribution to general social well-being. The ethical theory underlying End-Point Assessment is utilitarianism. According to utilitarianism, a law is morally sound if and only if the law promotes the well-being of those affected by the law to the greatest extent practically achievable. To satisfy the utilitarian principle, a law must promote the well-being of those affected by it at least as well as any alternative law that we might propose, and better than no law at all. A conclusive End-Point Assessment of a law requires specification of what constitutes the welfare of those affected by the law, which the liberal tradition generally sidesteps by identifying an individual's welfare with what he takes to be in his interests.

Considerations raised earlier in the paper suggest that the FCPA does not pass the End-Point test. The argument is not the too facile one that we could propose a better law. (Amendments to the FCPA are now being considered.[4]) The argument is that it may be better to have *no* such law than to have the FCPA. The main domestic consequences of the FCPA seem to include an adverse effect on the balance of payments, a loss of business and jobs, and another opportunity for the SEC and the Justice Department to compete. These negative effects must be weighed against possible gains in the conduct of American business within the United States. From the perspective of foreign countries in which American firms do business, the main consequence of the FCPA seems to be that certain officials now accept bribes and influence from non-American businesses. It is hard to see that who pays the bribes makes much difference to these nations.

Rule Assessment of the morality of laws is often favored by those who find that End-Point Assessment is too lax in supporting their moral codes. According to the Rule Assessment approach: A law is morally sound if and only if the law accords with a code embodying correct ethical rules. This approach has no content until the rules are stated, and different rules will lead to different ethical assessments. Fortunately, what we have to say about Rule Assessment of the FCPA does not depend on the details of a particular ethical code.

Those who regard the FCPA as a worthwhile expression of morality, despite the adverse effects on American business and labor, clearly subscribe to a rule stating that it is unethical to bribe. Even if it is conceded that the payments proscribed by the FCPA warrant classifications as bribes, citing a rule prohibiting bribery does not suffice to justify the FCPA.

Most of the rules in an ethical code are not *categorical* rules; they are *prima facie* rules. A categorical rule does not allow exceptions, whereas a prima facie rule does. The ethical rule that a person ought to keep promises is an example of a prima facie rule. If I promise to loan you a book on nuclear energy and later find out that you are a terrorist building a private atomic bomb, I am ethically obligated not to keep my promise. The rule that one ought to keep promises is "overridden" by the rule that one ought to prevent harm to others.

A rule prohibiting bribery is a prima facie rule. There are cases in which morality requires that a bribe be paid. If the only way to get essential medical care for a dying child is to bribe a doctor, morality requires one to bribe the doctor. So adopting an ethical code which includes a rule prohibiting the payment of bribes does not guarantee that a Rule Assessment of the FCPA will be favorable to it.

The fact that the FCPA imposes a cost on American business and labor weighs against the prima facie obligation not to bribe. If we suppose that American corporations have obligations, tantamount to promises, to promote the job security of their employees and the investments of shareholders, these obligations will also weigh against the obligation not to bribe. Again, if government legislative and enforcement bodies have an obligation to secure the welfare of American business and workers, the FCPA may force them to violate their public obligations.

The FCPA's moral status appears even more dubious if we note that many of the payments prohibited by the Act are neither bribes nor share features that make bribes morally reprehensible. Bribes are generally held to be malefic if they persuade one to act against his good judgment, and consequently purchase an inferior product. But the payments at issue in the FCPA are usually extorted *from the seller*. Further it is arguable that not paying the bribe is more likely to lead to purchase of an inferior product than paying the bribe. Finally, bribes paid to foreign officials may not involve deception when they accord with recognized local practices.

In conclusion, neither End-Point nor Rule Assessment uncovers a sound moral basis for the FCPA. It is shocking to find that a law prohibiting bribery has no clear moral basis, and may even be an immoral law. However, this is precisely what examination of the FCPA from a moral perspective reveals. This is symptomatic of the fact that moral conceptions which were appropriate to a simpler world are not adequate to the complex world in which contemporary business functions. Failure to appreciate this point often leads to righteous condemnation of business, when it should lead to careful reflection on one's own moral preconceptions.

Notes

1. *National Journal,* June 3, 1978: 880.
2. David C. Gustman, "The Foreign Corrupt Practices Act of 1977," *The Journal of International Law and Economics,* Vol. 13, 1979: 367–401, and Walter S. Surrey, "The Foreign Corrupt Practices Act: Let the Punishment Fit the Crime," *Harvard International Law Journal,* Spring 1979: 203–303.
3. Gerald T. McLaughlin, "The Criminalization of Questionable Foreign Payments by Corporations," *Fordham Law Review,* Vol. 46: 1095.

4. "Foreign Bribery Law Amendments Drafted," *American Bar Association Journal,* February 1980: 135.

U.S. FIRMS IN SOUTH AFRICA

Richard DeGeorge

The situation in South Africa illustrates one of the major difficulties in multinational operations. The Union of South Africa practices a policy of racial segregation, discrimination, and oppression known as apartheid. It is condemned as immoral by many in the United States and in other countries throughout the world. It is justified and defended by many whites in South Africa as the morally allowable lesser of two evils.

Under apartheid the blacks in South Africa suffer extreme repression. Although they constitute the overwhelming majority of the population, they are allowed to live on only 13 percent of the land. The other 87 percent is reserved for the whites, who constitute only 17 percent of the population. The whites control the gold and diamond mines, the harbors, and the industrial areas. Blacks who wish to work in these areas are required to live in townships outside of the major cities. Since only males are allowed in the townships, the workers are separated from their families for the major part of the year. The blacks cannot vote, own property, politically organize, or join unions. They are systematically paid less than whites for the same work. They are not allowed to hold managerial positions of even the lowest kind. They are forced to use segregated eating, dressing, and toilet facilities.

United States companies began moving into South Africa as early as the 1880s. At that time they employed only whites and sold their products almost exclusively to the white community. The white community was the economically advanced and productive sector of the country and supplied the market for goods. The blacks lived in their own sections of the country in their traditional tribal ways. The whites set up and controlled the government. The blacks did not take part in any governmental activities, were not educated, and were not considered able to run the government or to have any impact on it. A colonial type of paternalism was exercised by the whites over the blacks.

Whatever one considers the morality of such colonial paternalism, it is understandable how and why companies from the United States initially saw their market as the white community and their employees as coming from that same community. The intent of these companies was to expand their markets and make a profit, and South Africa was a ripe market to develop. With time and the changes of over half a century, colonialism fell

From R. T. DeGeorge, *Business Ethics* (New York: Macmillan Publishing Co., Inc., 1982), pp. 253–261. Reprinted with permission.

out of favor in Africa, the native inhabitants took over the reins of power in country after country and ran their own affairs. In South Africa, however, blacks did not succeed in gaining power and have been kept from doing so by the legal enforcement of apartheid. Some changes, however, did take place finally. Factories, as they expanded, found that there were not enough white people to fill the jobs available, and blacks were found able and willing to work in these factories. Fear of their achieving control in part motivated the government to draw up and enforce the apartheid laws. But as blacks entered the labor market, they also had money to buy goods and so represented a potential and as yet untapped market for goods.

American-controlled multinationals moved into South Africa in greater numbers to take advantage of the low wages they could pay blacks and the large market which South Africa represented. The profits earned by South African subsidiaries were often twice as much as the profits earned by the home-based mother company. Many black-dominated countries in Africa have placed embargoes on goods manufactured by U.S. companies operating in South Africa. But the local market is sufficient to make opera-tion of subsidiaries in South Africa profitable for IBM, Ford, General Motors, Goodyear, Firestone, Exxon, Mobil, Kellogg's, Eli Lilly, Kodak, Control Data, and over 300 other U.S. companies.

Despite the protestations of the whites in South Africa, most people acknowledge that apartheid is immoral. It is blatant racial segregation, discrimination, and oppression. Let us assume the majority view. The moral issues that have surfaced have been of two kinds, related though separable. One is the question of whether U.S. multinationals can morally operate in South Africa. The other is whether U.S. investors, especially university endowment associations and churches, should invest in com-panies that operate in South Africa.

1. U.S. MULTINATIONALS IN SOUTH AFRICA

U.S. multinationals would not open subsidiaries in South Africa unless it were profitable to do so. South Africa has four conditions that make it at-tractive to U.S. companies. First, it has a stable government. U.S. com-panies are reluctant to open plants in countries with unstable governments for fear of losing their investments through nationalization or constant domestic turmoil. U.S. companies therefore have an interest in helping preserve stable governments. They tend not to care whether the govern-ment is repressive or dictatorial. That, they claim, is a local, political mat-ter. But from a business point of view, a strong stable government is a guarantee of the safety of their investment. Second, South Africa has a large potential market. Its population is 28 million people. Even though only 17 percent of the population is white, that represents a market of close to 5 million people, the other 23 million people form a pool that can be in-creasingly tapped. The U.S. companies are the chief suppliers of consumer goods and of advanced technology. Third, South Africa has a large and cheap supply of labor. The standard of living of the blacks is extremely low and the scale paid them by South African firms is about one-fourth the wages paid to white workers. As more blacks are brought into the work force, the market for manufactured goods grows. Fourth, South Africa is rich in minerals. It can provide the materials necessary for manufacturing within its own borders, as well as shipping to the parent companies raw materials needed for production in the United States.

All four conditions supply both the reasons for multinationals to locate subsidiaries in South Africa and the reasons why critics of such firms charge them with immoral exploitation and with supporting repressive regimes.

United States firms have not been unaware of the charges of immorality. A few of them have responded to the charges by withdrawal. Polaroid is one such company. Citibank and the First Pennsylvania Bank no longer give loans to the South African government. But most of the other companies have not moved out. They have felt the moral pressure from stockholders and vocal groups in the United States, however, and have responded in a number of cases by adopting a set of principles drawn up in 1977 by Leon Sullivan, a black Philadelphia minister and a director of General Motors. The principles, known as the Sullivan Code, aim to end apartheid in the companies that adopt it. The code calls for desegregation of eating, toilet, and work facilities; equal pay for all people doing comparable jobs within the plant; equal opportunity for advancement regardless of race; apprenticeships and training of nonwhites; promotion of blacks and coloreds to supervisory positions; improvement of living conditions; and support of unionization by nonwhites.

The Sullivan Code, its supporters argue, works to break down apartheid from within and so is more effective than simply casting moral stones at the system from outside the country. It helps train nonwhites who would not get such training without the multinationals. It increases the pay of the nonwhites to that of the whites doing similar work. All of this is illegal. It violates South African law. But the South African government has not complained or sought to prevent the adoption of the Sullivan Code by American companies.

The critics of the Sullivan Code claim that it is not an effective way of breaking down apartheid. If it were, it would not be allowed by the South African government. The American firms pay taxes, and so provide revenue essential to the government to support and enforce its practice of repression throughout the country. The Sullivan Code, its critics claim, serves as a smoke screen behind which American companies can hide. They can sign the Code and claim to adhere to it, while in fact not doing so, or doing so only in token fashion. The Code, moreover, takes pressure off the companies to withdraw from the country, and gives them a moral excuse for continuing their profitable and exploitative operations.

The Sullivan Code was proposed in 1977 and has been adopted by a significant number of American-owned firms operating in South Africa. These facts alone throw into question the morality of the practices of these firms prior to 1977. Apartheid, we have acknowledged, is immoral. Consequently, firms that observe apartheid laws follow immoral practices. The arguments of the South Africans that they (South Africans) must enforce apartheid for the benefit of all cannot apply to the American-owned companies. The U.S. companies do not need their South African affiliates or subsidiaries in order to exist. The proportion of the assets of Ford or of IBM tied up in South Africa is relatively small in comparison with their total operation. They have a live option, which is withdrawal from South Africa. The fact that many U.S. firms adopted the Sullivan Code so readily, at least in principle, indicates both that such companies respond to some extent to moral pressure applied in the United States, and that they can still operate profitably (even if less profitably) while observing the Code.

If we admit that U.S. companies act immorally when following the apartheid laws, are they morally permitted to operate in South Africa if they follow the Sullivan principles? The question is not whether any American company follows the Sullivan principles completely, but rather, *if* a company diligently enforced the Sullivan Code in all its detail, would its continued operation in South Africa be morally justifiable? If we assume that the Sullivan Code negates all of the immoral aspects of apartheid, then a company that implements the Code would not be guilty of racial segregation, discrimination, or exploitation unless white employees were also exploited. To that extent its operation would not be immoral. But that is not the end of the matter. Through its taxes the company helps support the government, which in turn enforces apartheid in South African firms and in all other aspects of life within the country. Is such support of a repressive government morally justifiable?

The arguments here are not conclusive. Suppose we attempt to analyze the question from a utilitarian point of view. What are the consequences of the American firms operating within the country as opposed to withdrawing from the country? The critics of the American firms claim that if the firms left South Africa, much of the revenue needed to support the government would disappear. Furthermore, a wholesale withdrawal of American firms would leave the country in chaos. The government would not be able to keep the peace or run the economy. Because of the subsequent turmoil, blacks would have the opportunity to stage an effective revolution, seize control of the government, and put an end to apartheid. As a result, they claim, the repression of the blacks would be ended. The 23 million nonwhites would benefit incomparably more than the 5 million whites would suffer. The whites would suffer loss of their special position. But the blacks would gain respect as persons which they have been denied for a century. The American firms would not be substantially harmed by withdrawal, and after the revolution they might even return to the country to operate within a moral rather than an immoral context.

The scenario of the critics, however, is disputed by defenders of continuing American operations in South Africa. In the first place, they say, consider the benefits to the South African blacks and coloreds. The U.S. firms are the only places where they can get work at wages comparable to whites. They are the only firms at which they can learn skills and rise to supervisory positions. Hence those who work for American companies that follow the Sullivan Code gain much more by working in U.S.-owned plants than they would if these firms left South Africa. Second, a wholesale U.S. withdrawal would not bring the results claimed by the critics of the U.S. companies. As the U.S. left the country, its presence would be replaced by firms from other countries, most likely Japanese or German firms. It is less likely that these firms will follow the Sullivan Code than U.S. firms will. The South African government will continue to receive the revenue it needs from these firms. Hence the government will not be affected and the workers will be harmed. Less good will be achieved on the whole, therefore, by U.S. withdrawal than by continued U.S. presence. Third, the violation of the apartheid laws by U.S. companies is the first step, in the process of abolishing these laws. It is admittedly a small step, but it sets the stage for a gradual change in the laws. Breaking down the laws from within the country is more effective than simply condemning the laws from outside the country. Finally, the spokesmen for an American presence claim that if (counter to what they predict) a revolution does take place, there is little reason to believe such a revolution will produce more good on the whole than a continuation of the present system. The blacks have not been educated or trained in the skills required to run the economy or government of the country. There is little reason to believe that a stable black government will be formed or that whatever government is formed will be less repressive than the present government, even though the repression may express itself differently. Many black leaders fear what might happen if American companies were to leave. The conclusion on utilitarian grounds, defenders of a continued American presence argue, is that more good is achieved by the U.S. firms remaining in South Africa and following the Sullivan Code than would be achieved by their departure.

Which scenario is more likely? Which side's predictions of what would happen as a result of U.S. withdrawal should be believed? The evidence is not sufficiently clear to make a dogmatic judgment of the morality of American companies in South Africa. What is clear, however, is that any company operating in South Africa without adopting and fully enforcing the Sullivan Code directly practices apartheid and hence acts immorally.

2. Investing in Multinationals

Thus far we have focused on the morality of practices of multinationals that fall outside of the control of the United States government. But American-controlled multinationals do not fall outside of the control of the American parent company. And such companies are controlled by their respective boards of directors, which are in turn subject to the interests of the shareholders. American shareholders could, at least in theory, determine the practices of the U.S. multinationals.

Concerning those U.S. multinationals that operate in South Africa we can raise two moral issues. (a) Is it morally permissible for people or groups to hold stock in corporations that engage in immoral practices? (b) Should churches and universities in particular divest themselves of the stock of corporations that operate in South Africa?

(a) Every person has a moral obligation not to help others engage in immoral practices. Is it immoral for anyone to own stock in a company that engages in immoral practices? The simplest answer would be a flat yes. By owning part of a firm, a shareholder supplies the capital for its operation. If it operates immorally, the shareholder is helping it to do so. The answer to the above question would apply clearly in a company that had as its end some immoral purpose. For instance, no one could morally invest in Murders, Inc., if its purpose was to provide excellent hit men for those who wished to kill people they did not like. But few if any companies have as their purpose something that is outrightly immoral and the typical investor would not invest in such a firm if it did exist.

What makes a firm immoral? Is it enough that someone within the firm acts immorally? Is a firm immoral only if it habitually acts immorally? Is a firm immoral if it has one practice that is immoral? These questions cannot be answered with a simple yes or no. Clearly a firm is not immoral simply because someone within the firm acts immorally. If an employee of a firm, for instance, were to embezzle funds from the company, we would say that the employee and not the company was immoral. If a company made it a practice to exploit its workers, to discriminate against women and blacks, to overcharge its customers—and if it did all these things as a matter of ordinary practice—we could well say the company was immoral. It would therefore be immoral to invest in such a company, since such an investment would help promote the company's immoral practices.

But what are the moral responsibilities of an investor? Must he investigate from a moral point of view the activities of a company in which he is interested in investing? Is such a rule practical and reasonable, or does it ask too much of the typical, small investor? It is not always easy to obtain information about the immoral activities of companies. If the activities are questionable, it is unlikely the companies will publicize or publish them in their annual reports. Nor is there any guide to the moral index of companies for potential investors. There are many guides to the performance of companies from a financial and even from a management point of view. But there is no guide to the moral index of companies. Such a guide would be helpful to the morally conscientious investor. But in the absence of such information, an investor must make do with information that is available to him through the newspapers, any information on legal suits and charges brought against the company, and so on. Most scandals that reach the newspapers, however, bring about changes in corporate policy or personnel to reverse the scandalous practice. Yet despite all these difficulties we can assert that a moral investor should not support a firm that engages in immoral practices.

(b) Since individuals should not support firms that engage in immoral practices it follows that institutions also should not invest in such firms. Since corporate bodies usually make larger investments than individuals, they have a correspondingly greater responsibility concerning the investments they make. Critics have claimed that churches and universities should take the lead in ethical investment practices since they are appropriate models for moral behavior.

The critics of multinationals operating in South Africa have focused primarily on church and university investments. They have attempted to persuade these groups to divest themselves of their investments in American companies operating in South Africa. Their arguments are based on two premises. One is that companies operating in South Africa are engaged in immoral practices, even if they follow the Sullivan principles, since they help the government through their taxes. Secondly, they argue that the churches and universities can force the U.S. companies out of South Africa by selling their stock in protest.

We have already seen that those firms that do not follow the Sullivan principles act immorally. Since it is immoral to support such activity, those institutional as well as private investors who own stock in such companies should divest themselves of it. Many universities have followed this practice, for instance, with respect to banks that grant loans to the government of South Africa. Such banks do not help break down apartheid by hiring blacks, promoting them, or doing any of the things the Sullivan principles require. The banks help the government without attacking apartheid in any way. They thereby help support apartheid. Since this is immoral, many universities have protested this action by divestiture of their stock.

Two arguments that oppose such actions have been raised but neither is very convincing. One argument claims that no investor can be sure that some company in which he is investing is not engaged in immoral practices. Since no one can investigate all companies, it is unreasonable to expect corporate investors to be guided in their investments by moral considerations. The argument is not convincing because we can grant that no one is required to find out what he cannot in practice determine. But when it is clear that a company is engaging in an immoral practice, and when this is brought to one's attention, then he should act on that information. To refuse to act on that information concerning company *A* simply because he may not know whether company *B* is acting immorally is to choose knowingly to participate in an immoral practice. As stated before, the second argument is that South African operations for most American companies constitute a very small part of their total activities. Hence, if on the whole companies operate morally, a small immorality in a minor portion of their operations should not be blown out of proportion. The companies are on the whole moral. The corporate investors claim that they have obligations to their respective institutions to invest their funds to produce the greatest return. They must weigh this obligation against the obligation not to support a company that engages in an immoral practice in some small portion of its total operation. The equation, they claim, often comes out in favor of retaining their invested shares. The counterclaim, however, is that they would lose so little if they did divest themselves of the shares of those companies that not to do so is to condone the immoral practice.

The situation is far less clear, however, when we consider those firms that follow the Sullivan Code. Nor is it clear that the universities and churches could effect the withdrawal of these companies from South Africa by selling their stock in protest. If they were to sell their stock and drive the price of the stock down, it would simply be purchased by traders who would be delighted to get it at a lower price, confident that it will soon rise again in accordance with its actual worth. Some of the institutional shareholders claim that they are more effective voting from within the company than they would be voicing disapproval as outsiders. But they have not been effective insiders when they have sought to force a company to leave South Africa.

During the 1970s and the early part of 1980, groups on campuses around the country have sought to get their local endowment associations to divest themselves of companies operating in South Africa. These groups have in some cases been successful and in others unsuccessful. They show how pressure might be brought to bear on university endowment associations. But they have not accomplished much in the way of effecting withdrawal of companies from South Africa. One reason is that their protest has been in some ways too broad and in others too narrow. It has been too broad because they have tarred all U.S. corporations operating in South Africa with the same brush, instead of concentrating on those corporations that do not even adopt the Sullivan principles. Their protest has been too narrow because it has focused only on divestment by university endowment associations, groups which even together could not force a change in policy. But if Ford Motor Company and IBM are immoral, then the attack should not stop with refusal by a university to own stock in the company. Ford is helped more by millions of students and their families buying Ford cars than by some endowment associations owning Ford stock. IBM is helped more by universities buying or renting IBM computers, and by offices and individuals buying IBM typewriters than by endowment associations owning stock. If a practice is immoral, there are more effective ways to influence a company than by symbolic divestiture. But what are we to do if all the major carmakers operate in South Africa or if we prefer IBM computers or typewriters to those of other companies? This question gets to the crux of the issue. Those seriously interested in stopping immorality and who wish to protest the immoral practice of a company should not only want other people to make sacrifices and take action, but they should also be willing themselves to sacrifice and act accordingly.

Multinationals can be held accountable by their stockholders if the stockholders are truly interested in holding them accountable. Stockholders can demand to know what practices the companies follow in their subsidiaries abroad. If immoral practices are discovered in an operation abroad and enough people in the United States refuse to purchase the product of the manufacturer in question until the immoral practice is stopped, then it is safe to assume that the practice will be changed when the economics of the situation demand it.

The structures for controlling multinationals and for preventing practices that harm people have been slow in coming. They require international cooperation both on the part of governments and people organized either as workers or as consumers. Multinationals are helping bind the world closer together. As they do so, they help prepare the way for collective efforts by those affected by their actions.

EVERETT v. PHILLIPS I

The plaintiff is the owner of 100 shares of the "participating stock" of Empire Power Corporation. The issued and outstanding capital stock of the corporation consists of 77,000 shares of six percent cumulative preferred stock with a stated value of $7,133,000; 400,000 shares of "participating" stock with a stated value of $3,150,000, and 400,000 shares of common stock with a stated value of $1,000,000. The directors of the corporation and members of their families owned all the common stock and large amounts of the preferred stock and the "participating" stock. At the same time they also owned or controlled, directly or indirectly, 1,500,000 shares, constituting a majority of the common stock of Long Island Lighting Company. In 1931 and 1932 the Empire Power Corporation loaned to Long Island Lighting Company large sums of money. Payment of these loans was from time to time extended and the loans are still unpaid. Claiming that these loans and the extension of time of payment were *ultra vires* [beyond the power of] and were "not made to promote any business purpose of Empire Power Corporation, but were made for the sole purpose of promoting the interests of the individual defendants and that of Long Island Lighting Company," the plaintiff has brought an action in behalf of himself and other minority stockholders in which he has asked that directors of Empire Power Corporation named as individual defendants be compelled to demand payment of the indebtedness by Long Island Lighting Company and that "in the event that the said indebtedness cannot be collected from Long Island Lighting Company, then that the individual defendants shall be directed to pay the same." . . .

To establish his cause of action the plaintiff must show that the individual defendants in causing the Empire Power Corporation to loan the moneys to the Long Island Lighting Company and in failing to demand payment of such loans as they became due, have acted in disregard of the duties they owe Empire Power Corporation and that Empire Power Corporation has suffered, or at least may suffer, some detriment or loss. In a long line of decisions this court has held directors who control corporate action responsible for dereliction of duty where they have used the property of the corporation or managed its affairs to promote their own interests, disregarding the interests of the corporation. Power of control carries with it a trust or duty to exercise that power faithfully to promote the corporate interests, and the courts of the State will insist upon scrupulous performance of that duty. Yet, however high may be the standard of fidelity to duty which the court may exact, *errors of judgment by directors do not alone suffice to demonstrate lack of fidelity. That is true even though the errors may be so gross that they may demonstrate the unfitness of the directors to manage the corporate affairs.* [The "business judgment" rule—ED.]

The plaintiff here is asserting a cause of action for wrong done to the cor-

288 N.Y. 227, 43 N.E. 2d 18. Majority opinion by Judge Herbert Lehman, Court of Appeals of New York.

poration of which he is a minority stockholder. In such an action it is immaterial whether the minority stockholder who asserts it has a large or a small interest; but in determining whether those who have power to control the corporation have committed a wrong either to the corporation or to its stockholders, the corporate capital structure, the certificate of incorporation, and the corporate constitution or by-laws may be factors of great weight; for within limits prescribed by law these define to whom the power of control is entrusted, its scope and the manner in which it must be exercised. Directors are elected by the holders of stock which have voting rights. Here the certificate of incorporation of Empire Power Corporation provides that only the holders of common stock shall have voting rights. According to the testimony of the defendant Phillips, who has been president of the corporation from its formation in 1924 and who with George W. Olmsted, its vice-president until he died in 1940, owned or controlled, either directly or indirectly, all of its common stock, the corporation was "formed for the purpose of financing and taking care of the various companies in which we were then interested and later became interested further." They invited the public to subscribe to the capital of the corporation which would be managed by directors in whose election no other stockholders would have any part, and those who might furnish the capital which these directors would manage were not left under any illusion that the directors when acting for the corporation would be free from other interests which might prevent an unprejudiced exercise of judgment. The certificate of incorporation contained a provision that: "No contract or other transaction between the Corporation and any other corporation shall be affected or invalidated by the fact that any one or more of the directors of this Corporation is or are interested in, or is a director or officer, or are directors or officers of such other corporation, . . . and no contract, act or transaction of this Corporation with any person or persons, firm or corporation, shall be affected or invalidated by the fact that any director or directors of this Corporation is a party, or are parties to or interested in such contract, act or transaction, or in any way connected with such person or persons, firm or association, and each and every person who may become a director of this Corporation is hereby relieved from any liability that might otherwise exist from contracting with the Corporation for the benefit of himself or any firm, association or corporation in which he may be in anywise interested." It is against this background that the court must consider the claim of the appellant that he has established by the overwhelming weight of testimony that the directors were faithless to their trust.

The complaint of the plaintiff concerns, as we have said, loans made to Long Island Lighting Company. The defendants controlled that corporation. Their stock interest in it was large. According to the balance sheets of the corporation introduced in evidence by the plaintiff, the corporation in 1931 and also at the time of the trial had a very large surplus and was earning large profits, but needed money for the development of its business. Corporate balance sheets unfortunately do not always present a correct picture of the corporate finances. . . . The evidence establishes that unless it had succeeded in borrowing money it would have been obliged to discontinue payment of dividends, at least temporarily, and, to use all its earnings for needed improvements, and that perhaps the earnings might have provided insufficient moneys for its needs. The evidence establishes too that the defendants expected to derive benefit not only as stockholders but also in other ways from the moneys which, as directors, they caused Long Island Lighting Company to borrow. The question remains whether in seeking benefit for themselves and for the Long Island Lighting Company, which they controlled through stock ownership, they caused Empire Power Corporation, which the defendants also controlled through stock ownership, to make a loan, which might work harm to the Empire Power Corporation.

The Long Island Lighting Company at the end of 1930 owed banks approximately $10,500,000 on short term, unsecured notes. Though, according to the balance sheet of the Long Island Lighting Company, it had assets greatly in excess of its indebtedness, and had a net income of more than $3,000,000 a year, its financial position was not entirely safe or sound. The banks might press for payment of short term obligations at a time when Long Island Lighting Company might find it difficult to borrow elsewhere the money to pay such obligations. Moreover, the needs of the territory served by Long Island Lighting Company required constant extension of its plant. We may assume that prudent and conservative directors would, in such circumstances, have sought to obtain by an issue of bonds the money the corporation might require to refund its short term obligations and for new capital. . . .

. . . The Long Island Lighting Company did in 1932 apply to the Public Service Commission for permission to issue approximately $15,000,000 of refunding bonds. The directors of the Long Island Lighting Company preferred, however, to borrow the moneys under a plan which would not be subject to the restrictions which the Public Service Commission might impose as conditions to its approval. An inference that the directors were influenced by that consideration when they sought to borrow the moneys for Long Island Lighting Company upon notes payable within one year from that date might reasonably be drawn from the evidence in this case. The transaction would not be unlawful for that reason. The Legislature has in the public interest provided that bonds or notes evidencing loans for a longer period than one year may be issued only with the approval of the Commission. The Legislature has not decreed that the public interest requires similar safeguards for issues where the loans became due within the year. The Legislature has drawn the line, and "the very meaning of a line in the law is that you intentionally may go as close to it as you can if you do not pass it." . . .

The defendants can be charged with no wrong to the Empire Power Corporation on account of repeated renewals of the loans nor on account of the way in which they were handled, without proof that in these acts the defendants willfully failed to protect the interests of Empire Power Corporation in order to serve better their personal interests and the interests of the Long Island Lighting Company. There may be difference of opinion as to whether these defendants as directors of Empire Power Corporation acted wisely in the handling of the loans. There are many matters disclosed by the record which cast doubt upon the prudence, the wisdom, and the concern for the public interest shown by these directors. We are constrained, however, to agree with the Appellate Division that there is little, if any, evidence to sustain a finding that they have violated their trust or have failed to protect the interests of the Empire Power Corporation according to the dictates of their judgment, be that judgment good or bad. . . .

The provision of the certificate of incorporation of Empire Power Corporation expressly authorizing the directors to act even in matters where they have dual interest, has the effect of exonerating the directors, at least in part, "from adverse inferences which might otherwise be drawn against them." [*Spiegel* v. *Beacon Participations*, 297 Mass 398, 417, 8 N.E.2d 895, 907.] We may point out here also that if by reason of these loans Empire Power Corporation should sustain a loss, the loss would fall primarily upon these defendants as owners of the entire capital stock. The proportion of stock of all classes owned by these defendants in Empire Power Corporation whose moneys they are claimed to have diverted wrongfully, is, indeed, much greater than the proportion of the stock owned by them in Long Island Lighting Company which received these moneys. The loans were not excessive in relation to the capital assets and the income of the borrower as shown in the borrower's balance sheet. The evidence demonstrates that the defendants acting as the directors of the Long Island Lighting Company borrowed moneys from Empire Power Corporation because in their opinion the loans promoted the interests of the borrower and the stockholders of the borrower; the evidence does not demonstrate that the defendants acting as directors of the Empire Power Corporation in loaning its moneys to Long Island Lighting Company did not decide upon sufficient ground that the loans would also promote the interests of the lender and its stockholders.

The judgment should be affirmed, without costs.

EVERETT v. PHILLIPS II

At all the times of which we write, the individual defendants controlled both Long Island Lighting Company and Empire Power Corporation. In dealings between those corporations these individual defendants sat on both sides of the table. They caused Empire Power Corporation, from November, 1930, to February, 1933, to loan Long Island Lighting Company $5,330,000 on the latter's unsecured notes. These notes and various renewals thereof were all made for periods of less than a year. See Public Service Law, § 69. Interest has been paid regularly but, up to the beginning of this action, nothing was ever paid on principal. The lighting com-

---

288 N.Y. 227, 43 N.E. 2d 18. Dissenting opinion by Judge Charles S. Desmond, Court of Appeals of New York.

pany needed these moneys—and used them—to pay off from time to time, notes held by banks which were asking for payment. In 1930, when Empire made its first loan to the lighting company, the latter owed the banks more than $10,000,000 and found it increasingly difficult to persuade the banks to accept renewals of their unsecured notes. The banks had suggested to the individual defendants that the lighting company discontinue paying cash dividends, so that it might accumulate in its treasury funds with which to pay off the bank loans. This the individual defendants, who owned or controlled half of the lighting company's common stock, were unwilling to do. An application to the Public Service Commission for authority to issue mortgage bonds to raise money to pay off the banks was pending but undetermined. There was only one other convenient source of funds. A lender had to be found who would supply, without security and without question, the cash needed from time to time to satisfy the banks. Such a lender was ready at hand in Empire Power Corporation, completely controlled by these individual defendants themselves.

During 1930 and 1932 these defendants arranged loans aggregating $4,500,000 from the power corporation to the lighting company, most, if not all, of the proceeds going to pay off the bank loans. In March, 1932, when the lighting company owed the power corporation about $4,500,000 and the banks about $8,750,000, an agreement was made between the lighting company and the banks whereby the latter accepted renewals of their notes for six months, and agreed to accept renewals for another six months if necessary, on condition that the lighting company make certain payments which were intended to come from, and did come from, Empire Power Corporation. It was part of this arrangement that the whole of the lighting company's debt to Empire Power Corporation should be post-dated to that of the banks, post-dated rather than subordinated because it was felt that subordination "would be openly subject to attack on account of the unity of interest between Empire Power and Long Island Lighting."

A little later Empire's directors passed a resolution agreeing on behalf of Empire "to extend and keep extended the time of payment" of the lighting company's notes to Empire Power Corporation until the banks should be paid in full. An agreement to the same effect was made by defendant Phillips on behalf of Empire, in 1933, and approved by Empire's board of directors. Later that same year the Public Service Commission granted permission to the lighting company to sell the issue of bonds above referred to, but sale at the stipulated price was found to be impossible. Again the bank notes had to be renewed, and again Empire Power Corporation was caused to agree to subordinate its claims to those of the bank. Finally, in 1934, the authorized bond issue was sold by the lighting company under a contract which provided that the indebtedness to Empire Power Corporation would not be paid, discharged or secured by the issuance of any bonds of the lighting company secured by a lien prior to or on a parity with the lien of the bond issue. All of the proceeds of this bond issue went to the banks, none to Empire Power Corporation. In 1936 the lighting company paid off all its unsecured indebtedness, except that owing to Empire Power

Corporation. Among the creditors so paid off were the common directors of the two corporations and their relatives and corporations controlled by them. Thus Empire Power Corporation, starting out with short term loans to the lighting company, ended up with what amounted to a "permanent investment" of $5,000,000 in the lighting company, in the form of unsecured notes, payment of which, if this suit fails, must await the pleasure of the defendants. . . .

A court will not attempt to pass upon questions of expediency or to control the corporate managers in the faithful exercise of their discretion. [*City Bank Farmers' Trust Co.* v. *Hewitt Realty Co.*, 257 N.Y. 62, 177 N.E. 309, 76 A.L.R. 881; *United Copper Securities Co.* v. *Amalgamated Copper Co.*, supra; *Burden* v. *Burden*, supra.] To make a case for the invalidation of such a contract there must be shown circumstances tending to prove that the contract was made in bad faith, fraud or other breach of trust, including a biased exercise of judgment. [*Globe Woolen Co.* v. *Utica Gas & Electric Co.*, *Sage* v. *Culver*, *United Copper Securities Co.* v. *Amalgamated Copper Co.*, *Koral* v. *Savory, Inc.*, supra.] Given such a showing, the burden is then upon those who would maintain the contract to establish its fairness [*Sage* v. *Culver*, supra.] particularly when they themselves are shown to have exercised the dominating influence in effecting the contract. [*Geddes* v. *Anaconda Copper Mining Co.*, supra.] Whether the particular contract between these two corporations having the same directors was or was not made under circumstances amounting to a breach of the directors' fiduciary duty, is a question of fact.

Here the individual defendants who arranged the loans by Empire Power Corporation to Long Island Lighting Company, were completely aware of the latter's financial difficulties at the times the loans and renewals were made. They and their families owned the majority of the lighting company's stock; they directed its policies and managed its affairs; some of them were unsecured creditors of the lighting company in substantial amounts. It was to their interest individually, that the lighting company's urgent need of funds to pay its unsecured and demanding bank creditors be met. They met it by loaning Empire's money to Long Island on such terms that Empire's capital funds were used to pay off Long Island's bank loans in part, then these loans were made subordinate to the balances owing to the banks and finally remained wholly unpaid when all Long Island's other creditors of the same class were taken care of by the proceeds of a bond issue. The inference is unescapable that in the making of these loans, and renewals, the welfare of Empire Power Corporation was ignored and that the purpose of defendants was to benefit Long Island Lighting Company, and themselves. It is no answer to all this that Empire's financial structure may have resilience enough to absorb the risk or the damage of the loans, or that the individual defendant's stake in Empire is large and the plaintiff's small. Plain disclosure of the inequity of the situation and of the unfairness of the risk to the Empire Corporation, makes a strong appeal to the conscience of the court. It is not answered by defendants' protestations that Empire has a good investment in these loans, that they would surely be paid on a liquidation of the lighting company, that the lighting company's credit is good, etc., or by the provision in Empire Power Corporation's charter concerning contracts between that corporation and other corporations with the same officers or directors.

A court of equity in such a case as this does not stand aside and await the outcome of defendants' conduct. It acts promptly and effectively. It sets the whole transaction aside without waiting, or compelling minority stockholders to wait, to see whether those who unlawfully put a corporation's property at risk, may possibly at some undetermined time, have the skill, or luck, to get it back intact for the corporation.

The judgment of the Appellate Division should be reversed and that of the Special Term reinstated, with costs.

PIERCE v.
ORTHO PHARMACEUTICAL CORPORATION

Plaintiff, a physician employed in research by defendant pharmaceutical company, filed a complaint seeking damages resulting from the termination of her employment with defendant, even though such employment was pursuant to an ''at-will'' relationship. The trial judge granted defendant's motion for summary judgment on the ground that even if plaintiff were constructively discharged and did not actually resign from her employment, by reason of the fact that this was an employment at will, defendant nevertheless had the right to terminate it for any reason whatsoever. This appeal followed.

Since the matter involves a summary judgment motion, the facts set forth below are such as are gleaned from the proofs before the court on that motion, giving plaintiff the benefit of all of such evidence, and the reasonable inferences therefrom, in her favor.

Plaintiff commenced employment with defendant in May 1971 as Associate Director of Medical Research. The terms of her employment were not fixed by contract. In March 1973 she became Director of Medical Research/Therapeutics, a section that studied nonreproductive drugs.

One of the projects pursued by plaintiff was development of loperamide, a liquid treatment for acute and chronic diarrhea to be used by infants, children, older persons and those unable to take a solid form of medication. The formulation contained a high concentration of saccharin, apparently 44 times higher than that which is permitted by the Food and Drug Administration in 12 ounces of an artificially sweetened soft drink. It does not appear, however, that there are any promulgated standards for use of saccharin in drugs. At least one of the experts, a Ph.D., employed by defendant indicated that he did not know of any preparation whose saccharin level was as high as that contained in the loperamide formula and that it

399 A.2d. Opinion by Judge Kole, Superior Court of New Jersey, Appellate Division.

was "not desirable" to use such an excessively high level for a pediatric formulation.

Plaintiff worked in conjunction with a project team on the loperamide development. At a meeting of the team on March 6, 1975 it was unanimously agreed that the existing loperamide formula, which had apparently been marketed in Europe, was unsuitable for use in the United States due to the unusually high saccharin content. At the time it was felt that an alternate formulation would require at least three months of development.

The team apparently began to receive pressure to proceed with clinical or human testing of the existing formula, and in late March 1975 it finally acceded to the demands of management in this regard. Plaintiff, however, given her status as the only medical person on the team and her responsibility for recommending the drug for clinical use, maintained her opposition to the high saccharin formula, especially in light of indications that an alternative formula would soon be available. She refused to submit a drug containing such a high level of saccharin for clinical testing, as she could not in good conscience give the formula to old people and children in light of saccharin's potential carcinogenic attributes. She felt that such refusal was required by the Hippocratic Oath.

After indicating that she was unable to pursue clinical testing for the foregoing reasons, plaintiff was relieved of this project and informed by her supervisor, also a physician, that she was being demoted. He advised her that notice of this demotion would be posted. She was also told that she was considered nonpromotable, irresponsible and lacking in judgment, and that she had exhibited unacceptable productivity, inability to work with marketing people and failure to behave as a Director. She had not received such criticism from her supervisor before.

Plaintiff thereafter resigned, feeling that she was being punished for refusing to perform a task which she considered to be unethical. The resignation was accepted.

This action followed. Plaintiff sought to recover damages resulting from the termination of her employment. Essentially, the complaint alleged that because of defendant's actions she sustained damage to her professional reputation, interruption of her career, forfeiture of interesting and remunerative employment, monetary loss, deprivation of retirement benefits, loss of four years' seniority, physical and mental distress, and pain and suffering, and other damage was sustained by her and the public; that defendant breached its contract in refusing to permit her to use her expertise, skills and best medical judgment; that defendant, by its actions, violated plaintiff's property right in the form of her expertise and skill in medical and pharmaceutical research; that defendant interfered with plaintiff's employment contract and relationships, and that defendant violated and interfered with plaintiff's right to object to the appropriate regulatory bodies, presumably with regard to the safety of loperamide, the drug with which plaintiff had previously been working.

The trial judge denied defendant's summary judgment motion to the extent that it was based on plaintiff's written resignation, since there was a fact issue as to whether she was, in fact, induced to resign by defendant's actions. This determination is not assailed on this appeal and was proper. However, the judge did grant the summary judgment predicated on his conclusion that under New Jersey law there was no showing that the rule relating to at-will private employees did not apply—namely, that such an employment may be terminated at the will of either employer or employee, with or without justification, in the absence of a contractual or statutory provision to the contrary. See *English v. College of Medicine and Dentistry of N.J.*, 73 *N.J.* 20, 23-24, 372, *A.*2d 295 (1977). See also *Nicoletta v. North Jersey Dist. Water Supply Comm'n*, 77 *N.J.* 145, 150, 390, *A.*2d 90 (1978).

The trial judge held that even if the facts could be construed to indicate that plaintiff was constructively discharged—that is, she resigned by reason of wrongful acts of defendant employer—defendant, nonetheless, had the right to terminate her employment for any reason whatsoever. The judge acknowledged the existence in other jurisdictions of an exception to that rule as to termination of at-will employment when the motivation therefor contravened public policy. He stated that it may be that "public policy will develop to a degree that professionals, even though employees at will, will be permitted to resist what they consider to be a professionally unsound and unethical decision without fear of demotion or discharge." He was of the view that that question had to be decided by the Supreme Court, rather than a trial judge. In any event, he found plaintiff's case to be distinguishable from the out-of-state cases permitting relief on public policy grounds, and that "even if plaintiff's termination [is considered] in the light that it has been presented by the plaintiff, the most that can be said is that she was discharged because of a conflict in a medical viewpoint concerning the advisability of testing the drug loperamide."

We reverse and remand for a trial on all of the issues raised by the pleadings.

This case presents a novel question in this State relating to relief for wrongful discharge of an employee at will where the termination involves a claimed violation of public policy. See *O'Sullivan v. Mallon*, 160 *N.J.Super.* 416, 390 *A.*2d 149 (Law Div. 1978). We note in this regard that a growing minority of jurisdictions has created an exception to the traditional employment at-will rule, which generally bars an action for wrongful discharge, so as to permit recovery where the employment termination contravenes a clear mandate of public policy. [citations omitted]. . .

This new doctrine seems particularly pertinent to professional employees whose activities might involve violations of ethical or like standards having a substantial impact on matters of public interest, including health and safety.

Arguably, the time may have arrived to permit recovery, predicated either on a theory of contract or of tort, for the terminated at-will employee where the circumstances involving the discharge contravene a clear and important public policy. We do not now decide whether any such new doctrine should be adopted in this State or whether this case presents the appropriate vehicle in which to determine that question.

[1] We note that a public policy exception would represent a departure

from the well-settled common law employment-at-will rule. If such a departure is to be made, care is required in order to insure that the reasons underlying the rule will not be undermined. Most notably in this regard, the employer's legitimate interests in conducting his business and employing and retaining the best personnel available cannot be unjustifiably impaired. Thus, it cannot change the present rule which holds that just or good cause for the discharge of an employee at will or the giving of reasons therefor are not required. [citations omitted] In addition the exception must guard against a potential flood of unwarranted disputes and litigation that might result from such a doctrine, based on vague notions of public policy. Hence, if there is to be such an exception to the at-will employment rule, it must be tightly circumscribed so as to apply only in cases involving truly significant matters of clear and well-defined public policy and substantial violations thereof. If it is to be established at all, its development must be on a case-to-case basis.

For these reasons, the adoption of any such new doctrine must be grounded in a specific factual and legal context resulting from a plenary hearing, at which the proofs and public policy considerations involved will be fully developed and taken into account in the final determination. As indicated, we express no views on this issue. The matter should be decided in the first instance by the trial court after a hearing.

We merely hold that the grant of the summary judgment here was premature and a determination of the significant novel question projected by plaintiff, with respect to which such judgment was granted, should have been based upon a full record at a trial. Only in this fashion may the trial court, and if necessary, an appellate court render an appropriate decision on the issue thus presented. . . .

[2] The present record cannot serve as the predicate for determining whether the exception should be adopted and, if so, whether it should be applied in this case. For example, we are satisfied that, using the standard applicable to a summary judgment motion, the court below erred in finding that, even if there were public policy reasons which might be relevant to plaintiff's discharge, "the most that can be said is that she was discharged because of a conflict in a medical viewpoint concerning the advisability of testing the drug loperamide." There is a genuine fact issue as to that matter. Moreover, the question of whether plaintiff resigned or was constructively discharged, which remains unresolved, appears to be so intertwined with that relating to whether a public policy exception should be adopted and applied here, that it is desirable that both issues be tried and determined at a plenary hearing.

Additionally, we note that the instant case seems to implicate (1) an endeavor to compel a physician to violate what appears to be a reasonably supportable ethical standard and (2) the safety of the public in connection with the testing of drugs. If the court decides that plaintiff was discharged, unless the proofs at trial indicate otherwise, the determination of whether relief should be granted by reason of a substantial violation of a clear matter of public policy would be limited to that factual pattern. In ruling on whether a public policy exception should be adopted and applied here, the court may have to determine whether a bona fide dispute between a physician and her superior, also a physician, as to medical ethics relating to a matter of public health and safety is an appropriate consideration under the facts developed at trial. The court may also wish to consider, in addition to the Hippocratic Oath relied on by plaintiff as the ethical standard to which she claims to have adhered, the statutory provisions as to licensing of, and governing, physicians, such as *N.J.S.A.* 45:9–6 and 45:9–16.

Reversed and remanded for trial. We do not retain jurisdiction.

case 1:   Bendix Politics

On September 24, 1980, William Agee, chairman of Bendix Corporation was scheduled to address a special meeting of 600 company staff members at Bendix headquarters in Southfield, Michigan. There was plenty to talk about since under Agee's leadership the company was undergoing a major change in direction and a controversial major internal reorganization. Not only were employees concerned that theirs might be one of the dozens of jobs that would be cut from the new organization, there was also some residual uneasiness over Agee's firing of William Panny, the former president, and the simultaneous resignation of Jerome Jacobson, the former executive vice-president for strategic planning. At the meeting Agee planned to announce his choice for Jacobson's replacement: Mary Cunningham, a young (twenty-nine year old) Harvard Business School Graduate who had been with Bendix for fifteen months. There was a problem, however.

As he usually did when preparing a meeting, Agee solicited reports from his senior executives concerning what they felt were the most significant issues on the minds of Bendix employees. One of the items that appeared was a concern over the nature of the relationship between Agee and Cunningham and the rising rumors over what was termed "this whole female thing." Since Mary Cunningham's arrival at Bendix she had been working closely with Bill Agee, and he had quickly promoted her from his executive assistant to vice-president for corporate and public affairs. Both handsome people, the two necessarily worked and traveled together and gossip started when first Cunningham and then Agee separated from their spouses. As one Bendix staff member put it:

> There were rumors for a long time, and they just grew and grew. The two of them were seen together at the GOP convention [in July 1980]. The TV camera panned in on them, with Agee on one side of Gerald Ford and Mary on [Agee's] other [side], and people thought it was really stupid of them to be seen like that. But they acted like they didn't care. And with her being his top business aide, they traveled all over the country together. That got tongues to wagging. It was almost inevitable.[1]

Manuel G. Velasquez, *Business Ethics: Concepts and Cases,* © 1982, pp. 340–341. Reprinted by permission of Prentice-Hall, Inc., Englewood Cliffs, N.J.

Agee decided to deal with the rumors. At the September 24th meeting with 600 employees present, he announced Mary Cunningham's promotion to vice-president for strategic planning, and then made the following statement:

> I know it has been buzzing around that Mary Cunningham's rise in this company is very unusual and that it has something to do with a personal relationship we have. Sure it's unusual. Her rise in this company is unusual because she's a very unusual and very talented individual. It is true that we are very close friends and she's a very close friend of my family. But that has nothing to do with the way that I and others in this company evaluate performance. Her rapid promotions are totally justified.[2]

Questions

1. In cases of an appearance of a conflict of interest, should we trust the judgment of the individual or should such matters be settled by company policy?
2. Does open disclosure and a public confrontation of the appearance of a conflict of interest help (succeed?) in eliminating the conflict of interest?
3. Should there be a company policy prohibiting supervisors from dating those they supervise?
4. Some businesses forbid a spouse from working for a spouse. Although that policy wouldn't apply to this case, it does address a similar conflict of interest situation. Do you think such a policy is morally appropriate?

Notes

1. *The Detroit News,* 5 October 1980, p. 4C.
2. See *Newsweek,* 6 October 1980, p. 79; and *Wall Street Journal,* 26 September 1980, p. 33.

case 2:   The Antitrust Case

One of the most troubling criminal cases in recent U.S. history arose when the antitrust division of the U.S. Department of Justice formally charged virtually every firm in a segment of the heavy machinery industry with having joined in a conspiracy to fix prices of their products. The case ended with a federal judge imposing fines for criminal violation of the Sherman Act on twenty-nine

This case was prepared by the Committee for Education in Business Ethics under a grant from the National Endowment for the Humanities.

corporations. The judge also fined forty-four executives of the firms and sentenced thirty of these men to thirty days in jail. No testimony about the alleged offences had been heard by the judge, since all defendants pleaded guilty.

Lawyers for the convicted men had pleaded for leniency at the time of sentencing, using arguments about men acting on orders of superiors and caught in a system that had been operating for years. The men were pictured as community leaders, active in church, fund raising, and other civic activities.

After the federal judge had meted out fines and jail sentences, Worldwide saw to it that all sixteen of its sentenced employees resigned from the firm, though all of them were granted severance pay. Cunningham allowed its five sentenced executives to return to their jobs when they were released from jail. Indeed, Cunningham had continued to pay the salaries of these men while they served their jail terms. Cunningham's president issued a public statement of the considerations influencing management's attitude:

1. While their actions cannot in any way be condoned, these men did not act for personal gain, but in the belief—misguided though it may have been—that they were furthering the company's interest.
2. Punishment incurred by them already is harsh. They have suffered the anguish of the period of indictment and of the period while they awaited sentence. They now have suffered severe sentences by the court. No further penalties would serve any useful purpose.
3. Each of these individuals is in every sense a reputable citizen, a respected and valuable member of his community and of high moral character. They have made—and can continue to make—valuable technological contributions to the industry which have benefited consumers throughout the country.
4. And finally, these men above all others can be relied upon in the future to make absolutely certain that every aspect of their conduct and performance is in full compliance with the laws and with corporate policies governing legal and ethical conduct. They can be expected to enforce company policies in this respect relentlessly within their respective jurisdictions.

Questions

1. Should the fact that the employees acted for the good of the company rather than for personal gain count as a legitimate reason for a reduced sentence?
2. If the employees were in fact acting on orders from superiors, where does ultimate responsibility for the illegal activity rest?
3. Was the prison sentence unduly harsh?
4. And finally, were the guilty executives treated justly by their employers after the indictments were handed up and after the case had ended?

case 3: Whistleblowing—Alpha Corporation

You are purchasing manager for Alpha Corporation. You are responsible for buying two $1 million generators. Your company has a written policy prohibiting any company buyer from receiving a gratuity in excess of $50 and requiring that all gratuities be reported. The company has no company policy regarding *whistleblowing*. A sales person for a generator manufacturer offers to arrange it so that you can buy a $12,000 car for $4,000. The car would be bought from a third party. You decline the offer.

This case was prepared by the Committee for Education in Business Ethics under a grant from the National Endowment for the Humanities.

Questions

1. If you reported the offer to your superior, would your action count as whistleblowing?
2. If you reported the offer to your salesperson's superior, would your action count as whistleblowing or is it merely tattling?
3. Should Alpha Company have a rule requiring that you report such offers to your superior?
4. Should Alpha Company have a policy of informing a salesperson's company, when a salesperson makes offers like those described in the case?

case 4: Foreign Payments

In 1974, CYC Corporation decided to follow the lead of Crown Cork and Seal, Continental Can and American Can and develop its operations in international markets. The container and packaging industry, in searching for new fields in which to grow, had sought opportunities in the international markets for their canning and bottling operations. The CYC Corporation, recognized as one of the top ten firms in the industry with approximately a 9 percent market share in the canning and bottling of consumer products, felt that it must follow the lead of others in the industry in the hope that new markets would bring the sales growth it so desperately needed without having to rely on technological breakthroughs.

The CYC Corporation felt that its major competitors had overwhelming advantages in most of the major developed countries of Europe because of earlier entrance into those markets. Consequently, CYC felt that its best strategic

This case was prepared by the Committee for Education in Business Ethics under a grant from the National Endowment for the Humanities.

move would be the establishment of manufacturing and marketing operations for beer and soft drink cans and bottles in developing countries, especially in Africa. It reasoned that by not having to compete with the giants of the industry on a head-to-head basis in the international markets and by maintaining its own manufacturing operations in the underdeveloped countries, it could control its own segment of the market.

When CYC approached the Emperor of Utopia through diplomatic channels late in 1974, the idea of the establishment of manufacturing operations was warmly received. However, as negotiations proceeded with the Secretary of Commerce of Utopia it became clear that CYC would not be hiring as many citizens of that country as the officials desired. Because its operations were so highly mechanized, CYC required skilled American workers and managers for its operations and could employ Utopians in small numbers and only then as menial laborers. Still, the Utopian government was anxious to attract industry from the West and encouraged CYC to begin construction of its plants.

By late 1976, CYC Corporation had completed the land clearing and external construction of its three plant operations in Utopia. Shipments of machinery from its U.S. operations were due to arrive by early 1977. Then, in what CYC considered to be a surprise move, the Commerce officials of Utopia informed the CYC-African-management that their operations could not begin as planned in mid-1977. The Utopian officials mentioned a myriad of regulations not previously considered and the failure to hire natives as reasons for the hold-up. However, the officials explained that all of these matters could be resolved immediately and operations could begin as scheduled if certain payments were made both to the officials themselves and to the Emperor's staff. These payments were to be in U.S. dollars and were to be a one-time payment. Unfortunately, the Utopians would not allow these "payments for administrative costs" to be publicly recorded.

Questions

Assume that a payment would not violate U.S. law.
1. Would it be immoral for CYC Corporation to make the one-time payment?
2. If the payment could be recorded as "payment for administrative services," would it be morally permissible to make the payment?
3. If other corporations were making similar payments, would it be morally permissible for CYC to make the payment?
4. Should there be a law like the current one forbidding U.S. firms from making such payments?

SUGGESTED SUPPLEMENTARY READINGS

BARNET, RICHARD, and RONALD MUELLER. *Global Reach: The Power of Multinational Corporations.* New York: Simon & Schuster, Inc., 1974.

BAUM, ROBERT J., and ALBERT FLORES. *Ethical Problems in Engineering.* New York: Center for the Study of the Human Dimensions of Science and Technology, 1978.

BEARD, EDMUND. "Conflict of Interest and Public Service," *Ethics, Free Enterprise and Public Policy,* Richard De George, ed., New York: Oxford University Press, 1978.

ELBINGER, "Are Sullivan's Principles Folly In South Africa?" *Business and Society Review,* 30 (Summer 1979) 34–40.

ELLISTON, FREDERICK A. "Civil Disobedience and Whistleblowing: A Comparative Appraisal of Two Forms of Dissent," *Journal of Business Ethics,* Vol. 1 (February 1982).

―――― "Anonymous Whistleblowing: A Conceptual and Ethical Analysis," *Business and Professional Ethics Journal,* Vol. 1 (Winter 1982).

GARRETT, THOMAS M. *Business Ethics,* Chapter 4. New York: Appleton-Century Crofts, 1966.

Hearings before the Subcommittee on Labor-Management Relations, Committee on Education and Labor, House of Representatives, *Pressures in Today's Workplace.* Washington, D.C.: U.S. Government Printing Office, 1979, Vols. 1 and 2, 1979.

HIRSCHMAN, ALBERT L. *Exit, Voice, and Loyalty.* Cambridge: Harvard University Press, 1970.

JOHNSTON, DOUGLAS. "A Glimpse at Nesties' Anti-Boycott Strategy," *Business and Society Review,* 37 (Spring 1980–81) 65–67.

NADER, RALPH, PETER J. PETKAS, and KATE BLACKWELL (eds.). *Whistle Blowing: The Report of the Conference on Professional Responsibility.* New York: Grossman Publishers, 1972.

PETERS, CHARLES and TAYLOR BRANCH. *Blowing the Whistle: Dissent in the Public Interest.* New York: Pineger Publishers, 1972.

POWERS, CHARLES W., ed. *People/Profits: The Ethics of Investments.* New York: Council on Religion and International Affairs, 1972.

SCHWAMM, HENRI and DIMITRI GERMIDIS. *Codes of Conduct for Multinational Companies: Issues and Positions.* Brussels: European Centre for Study and Information on Multinational Corporations, 1977.

SIMON, JOHN G., CHARLES POWERS, and JON P. GUNNEMANN. *The Ethical Investor.* New Haven, Conn.: Yale University Press, 1972.

TURNER, LOUIS. *Multinational Companies and the Third World.* New York: Hill and Wang, 1973.

VAUGHN, ROBERT G. *Conflict of Interest Regulation in the Federal Executive Branch.* Lexington, Mass.: Lexington Books, 1979.

VON HIPPEL, FRANK. "Protecting the Whistle Blowers," *Physics Today* (October 1977).

WALTERS, KENNETH. "Your Employee's Right to Blow the Whistle." *Harvard Business Review,* July-August 1975.

WEISBAND, EDWARD AND THOMAS M. FRANK. *Resignation in Protest.* New York: Grossman, 1975.

CHAPTER 5

ADVERTISING AND INFORMATION DISCLOSURE

INTRODUCTION

LYING, BLUFFING, AND DECEPTION

Everyone agrees that lying is morally wrong under most circumstances and hence that any business practice which involves actual lying has the weight of morality stacked against it. However, there is less agreement on what constitutes a lie, especially in situations where bluffing is practiced or where information is withheld.

One does not need extensive experience in business to know that there are many deceptive practices, like bluffing, that are both widely practiced and widely accepted. It is common knowledge that auto dealers do not expect people to pay the sticker price for automobiles. A certain amount of haggling, quoting of competitors, and bargaining is part of the game. A similar situation prevails in real estate transactions, where the asking price for a house is seldom the selling price. Labor leaders overstate wage demands at bargaining sessions, and management also understates the wage increases it is willing to grant. In his article "Is Business Bluffing Ethical?" Albert Carr recognizes that such practices are characteristic of business, which he takes to be analogous to the game of poker. Just as conscious misstatement, concealment of pertinent facts, exaggeration, and bluffing are morally acceptable in poker, they are also morally acceptable in business. What makes such practices morally acceptable, Carr seems to suggest, is that all parties understand the rules of the game. In the instance of advertising, for example, exaggeration and bluffing are understood to be part of the selling game.

But surely there are moral limits? Suppose that I am willing to sell my home for $60,000 if that is the best price I can get. I ask $70,000. A potential buyer's initial offer is $60,000. I turn it down and tell him that $65,000 is my rock bottom price. He purchases the home for $65,000. Many people would characterize my behavior as shrewd bluffing rather than as an immoral lie. Most people would think more of me rather than less. However, suppose that I had manufactured the claim that someone else had promised me that they were in the process of writing up a contract for $65,000 for the house, but that I would sell it to him since we were both members of Rotary International. In this case most people would agree that I had told an immoral lie. It also would not improve the moral character of my action to have my brother pretend to make me an offer so that the prospective buyer would be pressured to buy. That would be a case of an immoral lie as well.

Perhaps the debate on the difference between harmless exaggeration and immoral deception is most intense in the discussion of advertising ethics. In his article, Burton Leiser provides some vivid examples of deceptive advertising. Language changes its meaning in many ads. "Noncancellable" and "guaranteed renewable" have technical meanings which one might not expect. Often age stipulations are thrown in. Testimonials, until recently, were also under attack. And so it goes. To many, these practices indicate that advertising is an inherently deceptive industry.

Yet others would argue that much of what critics call "deceptive advertising" is nothing more than harmless bluffing. They argue that the purpose of advertising is to sell a product. To sell a product, you must put a product in its best light, you must emphasize its good points, you must exaggerate a bit. So long as this commercial context is understood, exaggeration, puffery, and hyperbole are not deceptive. The claim that one's product is the best or the use of other such superlatives should not cause anyone problems. Indeed we all try to sell ourselves. Whether searching for a job or searching for a mate, we engage in exaggeration, puffery, and hyperbole about ourselves. We expect others to do the same. Perhaps the world would be a better place if human beings could avoid hyperbole or puffery, but that would require an unlikely change in human nature.

Moreover, as Phillip Nelson argues, the emphasis on the exaggeration and hyperbole in advertisements obscures the essential feature of advertising—providing information. Indeed it is this informational feature of advertising which receives the attention of economists. Efficiency is optimized when all parties in an economic transaction have maximum information. Consider the grocery ads in your local newspapers. This price information enables you to shop for the best buys week after week. Sometimes you buy turkey at the Acme, sometimes at the A & P. As a result of the information provided by the grocery ads, you maximize your food dollar. Since all other rational consumers behave as you do, efficiency in the market is improved and a general social good results. Nelson also argues that truthful advertising pays. Since it pays to advertise winners rather than losers, more heavily advertised brands are likely to be winners and, on the whole, larger selling brands which are advertised more provide the better value per dollar.

A consensus exists that good and sufficient information promotes rational decision making. My résumé provides information to a prospective employer. The grocery ads provide information to shoppers. Moreover the rational decision making is aided even when we know that the claims in the information we receive have been exaggerated or that negative information has not been disclosed. Our knowledge of distortion in the information system serves as a corrective. Where acceptable bluffing or nondisclosure ends and deception begins constitutes the ethical issue. Criteria to distinguish the relatively harmless cases of puffery from the immoral lies and deceptions are needed.

To decide if information is deceptive, the intention of the informer, the sophistication of the audience, and standard practice all need to be considered. In his article, Arnold Isenberg focuses on the intention of the person or agency providing the information. A lie might be defined as a false statement uttered with the intention to mislead. The addition of the intentionality condition is extremely important. It allows many false statements not to be lies. Fortunately, mistaken utterances, although false, are not lies; otherwise, most of us would be frequent, if not habitual, liars. Neither are poetic utterances considered lies. "He has the heart of a lion" is not a lie, although it is literally false. Sometimes advertisements are akin to exaggeration in poetry. "Esso puts a tiger in your tank" is false, but surely it is not a lie, because it is never intended to mislead.

The federal regulatory agencies that grapple with these questions focus on the audience, the recipients of the information. Most agencies like the Federal Trade Commission appeal to two competing standards—the reasonable consumer standard and the ignorant consumer standard. Ivan Preston describes the history behind the use of these two standards by the FTC and provides some analysis of the strengths and weaknesses of them. A decision as to which standard is appropriate has important implications for whether ads should be viewed as inherently deceptive or simply given to harmless exaggeration.

Another way to handle this debate over where to draw the line between harmless exaggeration and immoral deception is to appeal to a criterion of public openness. A business practice may not be deceptive if that business acknowledges the rules it is playing under. The ads for the auto dealers and for real estate make it perfectly clear that the "asking price" is not the "real price." An ad for a home that says "asking $120,000" virtually announces that the homeowner is in a mood to deal. Auto ads for individual dealers stress the fact that they will match any other deal in town. They explicitly acknowledge the bargaining aspect of auto sales. Grocery store ads by and large contain none of this bargaining language. The price of oranges is not a function of an individual bargain worked out between the individual purchaser and the supermarket. Deception enters when a businessperson announces that he or she is playing by one set of rules when in fact he or she is playing by another. Of course immorality also enters when one partner to a contract breaks his or her end of the deal. But as long as the rules of the game are known and people are in an equal bargaining position, then most people will accept consequences of business practice that they might not accept in other circumstances.

In their article, Thomas Carson, et al. deny that lying, even when it is accepted as standard practice in daily life, can be justified. However, if in certain business contexts everyone else is bluffing, you are justified in bluffing as well. But doesn't this show that business practice is ethically flawed? Carson et al. think not. They argue that business practice can be defended on grounds of procedural justice. In Chapter 1 we indicated that the practices of social institutions which yielded some unjust results might nonetheless be justified if that social institution represented the best we could do. For example, in our criminal justice system, procedural safeguards enable some guilty persons to go free. However, this is the price we pay for protecting the innocent (although innocent persons can be convicted). The practices of our criminal justice system, despite some unjust results, are defended on the grounds that this is the best we can do. Perhaps business practices are similar to these practices in that respect.

ADVERTISING, FREE WILL, AND RATIONAL DECISION MAKING

As Nelson noted, one classic defense of American business practice is that it gives the public what it wants: in the American free enterprise system, the consumer is king, and the market responds to consumer demands. This response to consumer demand allegedly represents one of the chief strengths of a market economy over a collectivist economy. In the latter economy, consumption patterns are severely constrained by government bureaucrats. In a competitive free enterprise economy, freedom of consumer choice is presumably protected.

However, critics of advertising, such as John Kenneth Galbraith in this chapter, point out that the effectiveness of advertising destroys the benefits of consumer sovereignty. Contrary to a popular myth, they say, the market does not respond to consumer demand; rather it creates demand through advertising. If consumer preferences were taken as given, the only advertising that society would need would be strictly informational. But as every good market researcher knows, one must create and/or encourage a demand for one's product. The market does not simply respond to consumers; rather, consumers respond to the market under the pressure of advertising and other forms of sales techniques.

Given human nature, Galbraith argues that the fact that business firms must often create a market for their products should come as no surprise. The necessity for demand creation can be anticipated from one of the "laws" of economic theory—specifically the law of diminishing marginal utility. Under the law of diminishing utility, a consumer's satisfaction from each additional unit of a product increases but at a decreasing rate. Stripped of its academic jargon, this simply means that a child does not enjoy the third ice cream as much as the first one. Let us apply the law of diminishing marginal utility to material goods in general. As our standard of living increases, we do not get the same satisfaction from fulfilling desires for luxuries as we do from the products that meet more basic needs. Given the desirability of increased economic growth, the so-called law of diminishing marginal utility will need to be repealed. In an affluent society, industry needs to create a demand for more goods and services. Advertising represents one means for effecting this repeal. If business really lived by the creed of consumer sovereignty, this heavily persuasive type of advertising would be unnecessary.

In a stinging critique of Galbraith's views, Friedrich von Hayek, although quite willing to accept Galbraith's distinction between different levels of need, is unwilling to accept the conclusions Galbraith draws from this distinction. For example, von Hayek argues that it is not true that culturally induced needs are of comparatively little value. If that were true, the products of music, painting, and literature would be of little value. Moreover, even though nonbasic needs may not *originate* with the consumer, that fact does not show that such needs were not *freely* adopted. When a student develops the need to hear Beethoven rather than popular music, has his or her music teacher forced this need upon him or her? Surely not, von Hayek argues: Consumers are of necessity influenced, but to be influenced is not to be *unduly* influenced and therefore unfree.

The underlying dispute turns at least in part on an old philosophical issue—the conditions of human freedom. Galbraith thinks that some advertising is unduly manipulative and even coercive, and hence undermines human freedom and consumer sovereignty. Von Hayek, on the other hand, agrees that advertising influences consumers but denies that it coerces or unduly influences.

Some philosophers have distinguished two kinds of freedom—negative freedom and positive freedom. Negative freedom is the absence of external constraints such as coercion or pressure by other human beings. Most of the freedoms enumerated in the Bill of Rights protect negative freedoms. These rights protect certain individual activities from the coercive power of other citizens or agents of the state. Positive freedom, on the other hand, is a broader concept; it moves beyond the absence of external constraint to freedom from internal restraints such as ignorance and lack of ability and thus to the freedom to govern oneself. Positive freedom thus includes the important notion of personal autonomy. On this view, one cannot be genuinely free or autonomous if one is under the sway of one's own compulsive desires or overwhelmed by depression. In summary, a person has negative freedom if he or she is not coerced, pressured, manipulated, etc. by others, and a person has positive freedom to do something if he or she has the resources and psychological ability to do that thing.

If advertising endangers freedom, it does not pose dangers to negative freedom unless it constrains by manipulation or coercion. While there can be circumstances of this description—for example, subliminal advertising—the main threat from advertising has generally been thought to be to positive freedom. As the critics of advertising point out, advertising can diminish genuine consumer choice, can play on ignorance, and can mold desires in such a way that one's self-governance is undermined. If the critics are right, some advertising represents an assault on positive freedom.

However, such contentions by the critics of advertising have not gone unchallenged. The difficulty centers on the notion of autonomy. Under what conditions is a person autonomous or truly self-governing? Either the individual decides, or the decision is made by some external authority. Suppose that, as a result of advertising, a person purchases consumer goods at the expense of an adequate savings account or investment program for the future? If the consumer indicates that the decision represents what he or she genuinely wants to do, on what basis can an outsider deny that the decision was freely made? Is the person deceived about his or her own preferences? Suppose one buys toothpaste on the basis that it gives your mouth sex appeal. One might disagree with the *reason* the person had for buying the toothpaste, but it scarcely follows that the decision was not freely made, for the person after all does choose *based on a reason.*

Stanley Benn's concluding article focuses on the legitimate and illegitimate uses of influence and persuasion. Even if most advertising does not violate either negative or positive freedom, the standard persuasive techniques of advertising might nonetheless be morally inappropriate. Benn argues that what is needed is a distinction between legitimate and illegitimate influence; the key is whether the persuasion is directed toward human beings as both rational and autonomous agents. Benn concludes with the provocative, but undeveloped, suggestion that nonrational persuasion is illegitimate when it influences people to choose on grounds that reflect a corrupt understanding of human nature. If Benn is right, a fair amount of advertising is morally suspect.

CONCLUSION

The discussions of deceptive advertising and the impact of advertising on human freedom have an important element in common. Whether an ad is deceptive or interferes with positive freedom depends in large part on the knowledge and resistance of the consumer. The consumer who knows the rules of the game and is equipped to play the game neither loses freedom nor is deceived. Perhaps a minimum condition for business practice is that the rules of the business game be made common knowledge and the players be on roughly equal bargaining ground. This openness condition, as we shall call it, serves as one basis of information disclosure. People should be free to speculate in stocks, but if an accountant, lawyer, or other person obtains inside information, that person is not free to buy or sell the stock of that company or the stock of any other company that would be significantly affected if the inside information were publicly known. In a context in which bluffing and exaggeration are permitted, open access to relevant information and knowledge of the rules of the activity one is engaged in are a moral necessity. Otherwise, the bluffing game of standard business practice is unfair, just as poker is unfair when some of the players do not know the rules or standard practice.

N.E.B.

CONDITIONS FOR LYING

Arnold Isenberg

In the following analysis of the lie, I shall keep to those points that have some connection with issues in ethics.

A lie is a statement made by one who does not believe it with the intention that someone else shall be led to believe it.

This definition leaves open the possibility that a person should be lying, even though he says what is true: for example, a man who does not know that his watch is one hour slow says, "It is ten o'clock," thinking that it is nine. He gives what he thinks is the wrong time; but it happens to be the right time. The dictionary definition—"a falsehood uttered or acted for the purpose of deception"—rules out this awkward possibility but has, I believe, other things the matter with it. Any short definition will leave some queer possibilities open. The differences among customary definitions are not very material for the ethics of lying.

The essential parts of the lie, according to our definition, are three. (1) A statement—and we may or may not wish to divide this again into two parts, a proposition and an utterance. (2) A disbelief or a lack of belief on the part of the speaker. (3) An intention on the part of the speaker. Since (1) and (2) are obvious, I shall elaborate only on (3).

The intention is essential. If the speaker does not intend to make someone believe what he himself does not believe, he is not lying. Examples: (a) A *mistaken* utterance is not as such a lie. (b) The deliberate utterance of a statement that the speaker *knows* to be false need not be a lie. "There is a camel in my closet." This is not a lie if the person addressed is one whom the speaker believes intelligent and informed. (c) *Poets* do not often lie, even when they say what they know is false; for they do not often wish or expect to be believed. Plato, who tries to show that poetry is false, if not mendacious, touches only on what is relatively credible in Homer and the other poets; not on any of the real whoppers which Lucian was to list later on—one-eyed giants, caves of the winds, men turned into swine. These were not "dangerous" untruths; for they would not be believed.

Since the author of the lie wants to be believed, he will have some opinions beforehand about the people he is speaking to and will shape his lie accordingly. This means that the element of intention interlocks, causally, if not logically, with the other two elements in the lie, as they do with each other. For example, the liar will not only have reason for not believing his own words, but will have some opinion as to their "inherent credibility," that is, their plausibility relative to the general information that he thinks is available to the members of his audience. If the listener is believed to be very foolish or very ignorant, the inherent credibility of the lie need not be

From "Deontology and the Ethics of Lying" by Arnold Isenberg, in *Philosophy and Phenomenological Research,* vol. 24, no. 3. March 1964. Reprinted by permission.

great. And since, among the supposed grounds of the listener's credence, there is a certain opinion about the speaker and the likelihood of his telling the truth, there will enter into the speaker's intention an opinion about *that* opinion: he will reckon upon what he believes to be the other man's opinion of him.

Thus there appears another, decidedly complex element which, though it may not belong to the definition of the lie, is always present: a set of estimates by the speaker, apart from his main opinion of the statement he makes, of the existing evidence for that statement, the probability of the statement upon various portions of that evidence, the listener's mentality and cognitive situation. Liars, dupes, and cognitive situations are of many different kinds; and so the combination of elements within the lie can be very numerous.

Now, what *is* the liar's intention? I believe we have to say that what is common to every lie is the wish to make someone believe something—the same motive that so often prompts us to tell the truth. We should beware of ascribing a stronger intention to the liar, e.g., the "wish to deceive." One can lie without wishing to deceive. A man who tells a creditor that he has no money on his person wants the other to believe what he says, not to be mistaken in what he is led to believe: it might suit this man very well, in fact, if he *had* no money just then and could say so truthfully. On the other hand, it can be the liar's intention to produce an *erroneous* belief—for example, about a future point of attack in time of war. But the "wish to deceive" is stronger still. That phrase implies that deception is the end and suggests, therefore, that a man would look about at random for a false story to perpetrate upon others. Such a motive, or something like it, is to be found in the April Fool's Day joke, where the joker indeed does not care what it is that he gets the other to believe, so long as it is false—for he wishes "to deceive." If there were a devil who enjoyed the thought of our being in perpetual error, he would be regularly governed by a will to deceive. But it is obvious that we should be letting too many people off if we said that no one is a liar who does not wish to deceive. . . .

Since there is bound to be a considerable vagueness in our conception of the lie, there will be many doubtful cases, (i) If the *statement* is very vague, it can hardly be the subject of a definite lie. A celebrated case, formerly pending in the courts, turned upon the question whether a man can lie in saying that he did not "follow the Communist line." But there are vaguer statements still; and though we could accuse their authors of some kind of imposture, we could not accuse them of lying. Besides, the usage of the word "lie" restricts the subject of the lie to questions of information in a fairly narrow sense; it does not permit us to speak of lying about matters of theory. Suppose that a scientist, who is to be the referee in a bet on the laws of motion, has been bribed to distort the truth. I do not think we would say he was lying; but if he were supposed to be reporting scientific *opinion* about the laws of motion, we should call it a lie. Yet usage is capricious; and if an adult were to tell a child that the world was full of demons, without believing it himself, we should probably call that a lie. Other types of statement could be mentioned which can only questionably figure in lies. (ii) *Belief* and *disbelief* are strong or weak and also vary in a good many other ways. If a speaker thinks it very probable that a proposition, *p,* is true but intentionally communicates to another a degree of confidence slightly greater than his own, the question of mendacity may well be doubtful. (iii) And the *intention* may be strong or weak, definite or indefinite. The large and irregular fringe which surrounds the concept of intention is, as a matter of fact, the source of most of our uncertainties, in judging the veracity of others. An advertiser who ''boosts'' his product beyond its merits, knowing that everyone expects him to exaggerate and that no one will believe what he says, is probably not to be called a liar. But an advertiser who makes a false claim for his product in the hope that, though *most* will not believe him, *some* people may, is a liar. And an advertiser who makes exorbitant claims in the hope of creating, through suggestion, a partial or subconscious belief in the consumer is a borderline liar.

IS BUSINESS BLUFFING ETHICAL?

Albert Z. Carr

A respected businessman with whom I discussed the theme of this article remarked with some heat, ''You mean to say you're going to encourage men to bluff? Why, bluffing is nothing more than a form of lying! You're advising them to lie!''

I agreed that the basis of private morality is a respect for truth and that the closer a businessman comes to the truth, the more he deserves respect. At the same time, I suggested that most bluffing in business might be regarded simply as game strategy—much like bluffing in poker, which does not reflect on the morality of the bluffer.

I quoted Henry Taylor, the British statesman who pointed out that ''falsehood ceases to be falsehood when it is understood on all sides that the truth is not expected to be spoken''—an exact description of bluffing in poker, diplomacy, and business. I cited the analogy of the criminal court, where the criminal is not expected to tell the truth when he pleads ''not guilty.'' Everyone from the judge down takes it for granted that the job of the defendant's attorney is to get his client off, not to reveal the truth; and this is considered ethical practice. I mentioned Representative Omar Burleson, the Democrat from Texas, who was quoted as saying, in regard to the ethics of Congress, ''Ethics is a barrel of worms''[1]—a pungent summing up of the problem of deciding who is ethical in politics.

I reminded my friend that millions of businessmen feel constrained every day to say *yes* to their bosses when they secretly believe *no* and that this is generally accepted as permissible strategy when the alternative might be the loss of a job. The essential point, I said, is that the ethics of business are game ethics, different from the ethics of religion.

He remained unconvinced. Referring to the company of which he is president, he declared: "Maybe that's good enough for some businessmen, but I can tell you that we pride ourselves on our ethics. In 30 years not one customer has ever questioned my word or asked to check our figures. We're loyal to our customers and fair to our suppliers. I regard my handshake on a deal as a contract. I've never entered into price-fixing schemes with my competitors. I've never allowed my salesmen to spread injurious rumors about other companies. Our union contract is the best in our industry. And, if I do say so myself, our ethical standards are of the highest!"

He really was saying, without realizing it, that he was living up to the ethical standards of the business game—which are a far cry from those of private life. Like a gentlemanly poker player, he did not play in cahoots with others at the table, try to smear their reputations, or hold back chips he owed them.

But this same fine man, at that very time, was allowing one of his products to be advertised in a way that made it sound a great deal better than it actually was. Another item in his product line was notorious among dealers for its "built-in obsolescence." He was holding back from the market a much-improved product because he did not want it to interfere with sales of the inferior item it would have replaced. He had joined with certain of his competitors in hiring a lobbyist to push a state legislature, by methods that he preferred not to know too much about, into amending a bill then being enacted.

In his view these things had nothing to do with ethics; they were merely normal business practice. He himself undoubtedly avoided outright falsehoods—never lied in so many words. But the entire organization that he ruled was deeply involved in numerous strategies of deception.

PRESSURE TO DECEIVE

Most executives from time to time are almost compelled, in the interests of their companies or themselves, to practice some form of deception when negotiating with customers, dealers, labor unions, government officials, or even other departments of their companies. By conscious misstatements, concealment of pertinent facts, or exaggeration—in short, by bluffing—they seek to persuade others to agree with them. I think it is fair to say that if the individual executive refuses to bluff from time to time—if he feels obligated to tell the truth, the whole truth, and nothing but the truth—he is ignoring opportunities permitted under the rules and is at a heavy disadvantage in his business dealings.

But here and there a businessman is unable to reconcile himself to the bluff in which he plays a part. His conscience, perhaps spurred by religious idealism, troubles him. He feels guilty; he may develop an ulcer or a nervous tic. Before any executive can make profitable use of the strategy of the bluff, he needs to make sure that in bluffing he will not lose self-respect or become emotionally disturbed. If he is to reconcile personal integrity and high standards of honesty with the practical requirements of business, he must feel that his bluffs are ethically justified. The justification rests on the fact that business, as practiced by individuals as well as by corporations, has the impersonal character of a game—a game that demands both special strategy and an understanding of its special ethics.

The game is played at all levels of corporate life, from the highest to the lowest. At the very instant that a man decides to enter business, he may be forced into a game situation, as is shown by the recent experience of a Cornell honor graduate who applied for a job with a large company.

> This applicant was given a psychological test which included the statement, "Of the following magazines, check any that you have read either regularly or from time to time, and double-check those which interest you most. *Reader's Digest, Time, Fortune, Saturday Evening Post, The New Republic, Life, Look, Ramparts, Newsweek, Business Week, U.S. News & World Report, The Nation, Playboy, Esquire, Harper's, Sports Illustrated.*"

His tastes in reading were broad, and at one time or another he had read almost all of these magazines. He was a subscriber to *The New Republic,* an enthusiast for *Ramparts,* and an avid student of the pictures in *Playboy.* He was not sure whether his interest in *Playboy* would be held against him, but he had a shrewd suspicion that if he confessed to an interest in *Ramparts* and *The New Republic,* he would be thought a liberal, a radical, or at least an intellectual, and his chances of getting the job, which he needed, would greatly diminish. He therefore checked five of the more conservative magazines. Apparently it was a sound decision, for he got the job.

He had made a game player's decision, consistent with business ethics.

A similar case is that of a magazine space salesman who, owing to a merger, suddenly found himself out of a job:

> This man was 58, and, in spite of a good record, his chance of getting a job elsewhere in a business where youth is favored in hiring practice was not good. He was a vigorous, healthy man, and only a considerable amount of gray in his hair suggested his age. Before beginning his job search he touched up his hair with a black dye to confine the gray to his temples. He knew that the truth about his age might well come out in time, but he calculated that he could deal with that situation when it arose. He and his wife decided that he could easily pass for 45, and he so stated his age on his résumé.

This was a lie: yet within the accepted rules of the business game, no moral culpability attaches to it.

THE POKER ANALOGY

We can learn a good deal about the nature of business by comparing it with poker. While both have a large element of chance, in the long run the winner is the man who plays with steady skill. In both games ultimate victory requires intimate knowledge of the rules, insight into the psychology of the other players, a bold front, a considerable amount of self-discipline, and the ability to respond swiftly and effectively to opportunities provided by chance.

No one expects poker to be played on the ethical principles preached in churches. In poker it is right and proper to bluff a friend out of the rewards of being dealt a good hand. A player feels no more than a slight twinge of sympathy, if that, when—with nothing better than a single ace in his hand— he strips a heavy loser, who holds a pair, of the rest of his chips. It was up to the other fellow to protect himself. In the words of an excellent poker player, former President Harry Truman, ''If you can't stand the heat, stay out of the kitchen.'' If one shows mercy to a loser in poker, it is a personal gesture, divorced from the rules of the game.

Poker has its special ethics, and here I am not referring to rules against cheating. The man who keeps an ace up his sleeve or who marks the cards is more than unethical; he is a crook, and can be punished as such—kicked out of the game or, in the Old West, shot.

In contrast to the cheat, the unethical poker player is one who, while abiding by the letter of the rules, finds ways to put the other players at an unfair disadvantage. Perhaps he unnerves them with loud talk. Or he tries to get them drunk. Or he plays in cahoots with someone else at the table. Ethical poker players frown on such tactics.

Poker's own brand of ethics is different from the ethical ideals of civilized human relationships. The game calls for distrust of the other fellow. It ignores the claim of friendship. Cunning deception and concealment of one's strength and intentions, not kindness and openheartedness, are vital in poker. No one thinks any the worse of poker on that account. And no one should think any the worse of the game of business because its standards of right and wrong differ from the prevailing traditions of morality in our society. . . .

'WE DON'T MAKE THE LAWS'

Wherever we turn in business, we can perceive the sharp distinction between its ethical standards and those of the churches. Newspapers abound with sensational stories growing out of this distinction:

> We read one day that Senator Philip A. Hart of Michigan has attacked food processors for deceptive packaging of numerous products.[2]
>
> The next day there is a Congressional to-do over Ralph Nader's book, *Unsafe At Any Speed,* which demonstrates that automobile companies for years have neglected the safety of car-owning families.[3]
>
> Then another Senator, Lee Metcalf of Montana, and journalist Vic Reinemer show in their book, *Overcharge,* the methods by which utility companies elude regulating government bodies to extract unduly large payments from users of electricity.[4]

These are merely dramatic instances of a prevailing condition; there is hardly a major industry at which a similar attack could not be aimed. Critics of business regard such behavior as unethical, but the companies concerned know that they are merely playing the business game.

Among the most respected of our business institutions are the insurance companies. A group of insurance executives meeting recently in New England was startled when their guest speaker, social critic Daniel Patrick Moynihan, roundly berated them for "unethical" practices. They had been guilty, Moynihan alleged, of using outdated actuarial tables to obtain unfairly high premiums. They habitually delayed the hearings of lawsuits against them in order to tire out the plaintiffs and win cheap settlements. In their employment policies they used ingenious devices to discriminate against certain minority groups.[5]

It was difficult for the audience to deny the validity of these charges. But these men were business game players. Their reaction to Moynihan's attack was much the same as that of the automobile manufacturers to Nader, of the utilities to Senator Metcalf, and of the food processors to Senator Hart. If the laws governing their businesses change, or if public opinion becomes clamorous, they will make the necessary adjustments. But morally they have in their view done nothing wrong. As long as they comply with the letter of the law, they are within their rights to operate their businesses as they see fit.

The small business is in the same position as the great corporation in this respect. For example:

> In 1967 a key manufacturer was accused of providing master keys for automobiles to mail-order customers, although it was obvious that some of the purchasers might be automobile thieves. His defense was plain and straightforward. If there was nothing in the law to prevent him from selling his keys to anyone who ordered them, it was not up to him to inquire as to his customers' motives. Why was it any worse, he insisted, for him to sell car keys by mail, than for mail-order houses to sell guns that might be used for murder? Until the law was changed, the key manufacturer could regard himself as being just as ethical as any other businessman by the rules of the business game.[6]

Violations of the ethical ideals of society are common in business, but they are not necessarily violations of business principles. Each year the Federal Trade Commission orders hundreds of companies, many of them of the first magnitude, to "cease and desist" from practices which, judged by ordinary standards, are of questionable morality but which are stoutly defended by the companies concerned.

In one case, a firm manufacturing a well-known mouthwash was accused of using a cheap form of alcohol possibly deleterious to health. The company's chief executive, after testifying in Washington, made this comment privately:

> "We broke no law. We're in a highly competitive industry. If we're going to stay in business, we have to look for profit wherever the law permits. We don't make the laws. We obey them. Then why do we have to put up with this 'holier than thou' talk about ethics? It's sheer hypocrisy. We're not in business to promote ethics. Look at the cigarette companies, for God's sake! If the ethics aren't embodied in the laws by the men who made them, you can't expect businessmen to fill the lack. Why, a sudden submission to Christian ethics by businessmen would bring about the greatest economic upheaval in history!"

It may be noted that the government failed to prove its case against him.

Talk about ethics by businessmen is often a thin decorative coating over the hard realities of the game. . . .

The illusion that business can afford to be guided by ethics as conceived in private life is often fostered by speeches and articles containing such phrases as, "It pays to be ethical," or, "Sound ethics is good business." Actually this is not an ethical position at all; it is a self-serving calculation in disguise. The speaker is really saying that in the long run a company can make more money if it does not antagonize competitors, suppliers, employees, and customers by squeezing them too hard. He is saying that oversharp policies reduce ultimate gains. That is true, but it has nothing to do with ethics. The underlying attitude is much like that in the familiar story of the shopkeeper who finds an extra $20 bill in the cash register, debates with himself the ethical problem—should he tell his partner?—and finally decides to share the money because the gesture will give him an edge over the s.o.b. the next time they quarrel.

I think it is fair to sum up the prevailing attitude of businessmen on ethics as follows:

We live in what is probably the most competitive of the world's civilized societies. Our customs encourage a high degree of aggression in the individual's striving for success. Business is our main area of competition, and it has been ritualized into a game of strategy. The basic rules of the game have been set by the government, which attempts to detect and punish business frauds. But as long as a company does not transgress the rules of the game set by law, it has the legal right to shape its strategy without reference to anything but its profits. If it takes a long-term view of its profits, it will preserve amicable relations, so far as possible, with those with whom it deals. A wise businessman will not seek advantage to the point where he generates dangerous hostility among employees, competitors, customers, government, or the public at large. But decisions in this area are, in the final test, decisions of strategy, not of ethics.

. . . If a man plans to make a seat in the business game, he owes it to himself to master the principles by which the game is played, including its special ethical outlook. He can then hardly fail to recognize that an occasional bluff may well be justified in terms of the game's ethics and warranted in terms of economic necessity. Once he clears his mind on this point, he is in a good position to match his strategy against that of the other players. He can then determine objectively whether a bluff in a given situation has a good chance of succeeding and can decide when and how to bluff, without a feeling of ethical transgression.

To be a winner, a man must play to win. This does not mean that he must be ruthless, cruel, harsh, or treacherous. On the contrary, the better his reputation for integrity, honesty, and decency, the better his chances of victory will be in the long run. But from time to time every businessman, like every poker player, is offered a choice between certain loss or bluffing within the legal rules of the game. If he is not resigned to losing, if he wants to rise in his company and industry, then in such a crisis he will bluff—and bluff hard. . . .

In the last third of the twentieth century even children are aware that if a man has become prosperous in business, he has sometimes departed from the strict truth in order to overcome obstacles or has practiced the more subtle deceptions of the half-truth or the misleading omission. Whatever the form of the bluff, it is an integral part of the game, and the executive who does not master its techniques is not likely to accumulate much money or power.

Notes

1. *The New York Times,* March 9, 1967.
2. *The New York Times,* November 21, 1966.
3. New York, Grossman Publishers, Inc., 1965.
4. New York, David McKay Company, Inc., 1967.
5. *The New York Times,* January 17, 1967.
6. Cited by Ralph Nader in "Business Crime," *The New Republic,* July 1, 1967, p. 7.

BLUFFING IN LABOR NEGOTIATIONS: LEGAL AND ETHICAL ISSUES

Thomas L. Carson, Richard E. Wokutch, Kent F. Murrmann

More than a decade ago a *Harvard Business Review* article entitled 'Is Business Bluffing Ethical?' (Carr, 1968) created a storm of controversy when the author defended bluffing and other questionable business practices on the grounds that they are just part of the game of business. The controversy over the ethics of bluffing and alleged deception in business negotiations erupted again recently with the publication of the *Wall Street Journal* article, 'To Some at Harvard, Telling Lies Becomes a Matter of Course' (Bulkeley, 1979). This detailed a negotiations course taught at Harvard Business School in which students were allowed to bluff and deceive each other in various simulated negotiation situations. Student's grades were partially determined by the settlements they negotiated with each other, and hence some alleged that this course encouraged and taught students to bluff, lie to, and deceive negotiating partners. These controversies raised issues concerning the morality, necessity, and even the legality of bluffing in business negotiations which were never adequately resolved. It is the aim of this paper to shed some light on these issues.

In the first section of the paper we will describe briefly the nature of the collective bargaining process and then examine the role of bluffing in that process. The second section of the paper is a discussion of labor law as it

Journal of Business Ethics 1 (1982) 13–22. *Copyright* © 1982 *by D. Reidel Publishing Company,* Dordrecht, Holland.

relates to bluffing. Then, in the third and fourth sections of the paper we will argue that bluffing and other deceptive practices in labor negotiations typically do constitute lying. Nevertheless, we will argue that bluffing is typically morally permissible but for different reasons than those put forth by Carr. In our conclusion we consider whether it is an indictment of our present negotiating practices and our economic system as a whole that, given the harsh realities of the market-place, bluffing *is* usually morally acceptable.

1. THE NATURE OF COLLECTIVE BARGAINING

Collective bargaining is fundamentally a competitive process in which labor and management dispute and eventually decide the terms of employment. Through bargaining each party attempts to reach an agreement which each perceives to be at least minimally acceptable if not highly favorable in light of its vital interests.

Typically there is a range of possible settlement points on wages (and other bargained issues) that each party would accept rather than fail to reach an agreement. This range exists with respect to wages, for instance, because the minimum wage that an employer could pay and still attract the needed employees is typically lower at any point in time than the maximum wage the employer could pay and still manage to operate a competitive business. Neither party knows the exact location of these extreme points. And, ordinarily there is no one economically optimal wage level within the range that can be established through reference to objective criteria that are acceptable to both parties.[1] Each party attempts to move the wage agreement toward its preferred end of the range. Also, each attempts to define a point on the range beyond which it would rather endure a work stoppage than accept a settlement. Thus, in practice, the top end of the range becomes the highest wage that management would pay rather than endure a work stoppage. The bottom end of the range becomes the minimum wage that labor would accept rather than endure a work stoppage. These extreme positions are the parties' respective 'sticking points.'

1.1. Factors Affecting Bargaining Success

Two factors are instrumental to the ability of either party to negotiate a favorable agreement, i.e., an agreement that both perceive to be more than minimally acceptable. The first factor is the ability to impose significant costs on the other party, or to credibly threaten the imposition of such costs, in order to pressure the other party to make concessions. Thus, in order to bargain successfully, labor must be able to instill in management the belief that labor would initiate a work stoppage, or other form of costly noncooperation, in order to secure what it considers to be reasonable terms of employment. Likewise, in order for management to bargain successfully, it must convey to labor the perception that it would endure a work stoppage rather than accept what it believes to be unreasonable conditions.

The other key factor that affects one's bargaining success is the ability to accurately discern the other party's minimum acceptable conditions while vigilantly concealing one's own minimum terms. Such knowledge enables one to confidently drive the bargain to more favorable terms without risking an unwanted and costly work stoppage.

1.2. *Bluffing and Bargaining Success*

Bluffing typically plays a very important part concerning both of these factors. Bluffing is an act in which one attempts to misrepresent one's intentions or overstate the strength of one's position in the bargaining process. This is possible because neither party knows for sure the other party's true intentions or 'sticking point.' Bluffing often involves making deceptive statements. For instance, the union bargaining representative may boldly state, "There is no way that our people will accept such a small wage increase," when he/she knows full well that they would gladly accept management's offer rather than go out on strike. However, bluffing can be entirely nonverbal. Nodding confidently as one raises the bet while holding a poor hand in a game of poker is a paradigm case of bluffing. Getting up from the bargaining table in a huff and going out the door is another example of nonverbal bluffing. Through these and similar types of statements and behavior either party can convey to the other an exaggerated portrayal of its ability to impose or endure costs, and thereby can increase its actual ability to gain concessions in the bargaining process.

In addition, aggressive bluffing can be used to test the other party's resolve or otherwise prod the other party to concede certain points. This use of bluffing on different bargaining issues over a period of time, say, spanning several bargaining sessions, can significantly increase one's understanding of the other party's true strength, and thus can enhance one's ability to accurately estimate the other party's sticking points on various issues.

There can be no doubt that bluffing is an important bargaining tool. It can be employed to create impressions of enhanced strength as well as to probe the other party to find out the level of its critical sticking points. Through these methods either party can attempt to gain a more favorable settlement than the other party would otherwise be willing to allow. And, labor and management alike are more apt to fully abide by those terms of employment that they know were established through a free and vigorous use of their best bargaining skills.

1.3. *The Alleged Necessity of Bluffing*

While bluffing can obviously be advantageous in labor negotiations, one might ask whether it is 'economically necessary.' This does not appear to be the case. Where one of the parties has an extremely strong negotiating position (e.g. an employer in a one company town with a high unemployment rate, a slavemaster, or a surgeon who is the only one capable of performing a new surgical procedure necessary to save one's life), wages and working conditions can simply be dictated by the stronger party.

What about the claim that bluffing is a necessary part of the negotiation of any *voluntary* labor agreement between parties of relatively equal power? This also seems false. Suppose that two very scrupulous parties are attempting to reach a wage settlement and neither wants to engage in bluffing. Assuming that they trust each other and honestly reveal their 'sticking points,' they could agree to some formula such as splitting the difference between the sticking points. This is of course unlikely to occur in real life, but only because few individuals are honest or trusting enough for our assumptions to hold.

2. THE LEGAL STATUS OF BLUFFING

The National Labor Relations Act, as amended (1970), provides the legal framework within which the collective bargaining process in the private sector of our economy is carried out. Sections 8(a)(5) and 8(b)(3) of the National Labor Relations Act provide that it shall be an unfair labor practice for a union or an employer in a properly constituted bargaining relationship to fail to bargain in good faith. The statute left it to the National Labor Relations Board and the courts to establish criteria for determining whether a party is bargaining in good faith. Over the years numerous such criteria have been established by the Board and the courts.

2.1. The Honest Claims Doctrine

Of particular interest with respect to the legal status of bluffing is the 'honest claims' doctrine, established by the U.S. Supreme Court in its Truitt Mfg. Co. decision (*NLRB* v. *Truitt Mfg. Co.*, 1956). This states that "good faith necessarily requires that claims made by either party should be honest claims." The central issue in the Truitt Case was whether the employer would be required to substantiate its claim that it could not afford to pay a certain wage increase. In addition to enunciating its 'honest claims' doctrine, the court declared that if an "inability to pay argument is important enough to present in the give and take of bargaining it is important enough to require some sort of proof of its accuracy" (*NLRB* v. *Truitt Mfg. Co.*, 1956, p. 152). This 'honest claims' policy has been consistently upheld and applied in numerous court decisions to this day. Thus, it is clear that the law requires honesty in collective bargaining. However, the 'honest claims' requirement applies only to those types of claims that pertain directly to issues subject to bargaining and the employer's ability to provide certain conditions of employment. Thus, the 'honest claims' policy requires a union to refrain from presenting false information to management concerning the level of wages and fringe benefits provided by employers under other union contracts. Likewise, the employer must refrain from falsely claiming an inability to provide a certain benefit.

2.2. Bluffing and the Honest Claims Doctrine

How does the 'honest claims' doctrine apply to the practice of bluffing? It is clear that bluffing that involves the presentation of false information about issues subject to bargaining (i.e., wages, hours, and condition of employment) is a violation. However bluffing about objective issues not subject to negotiation such as one's ability to withstand a strike (e.g., the size of the union strike fund, or the union membership's vote on the question of whether or not to go out on strike) is allowable. Also, bluffing that is limited to representations of one's bargaining intentions or one's willingness to impose or endure costs in order to win a more favorable contract does not constitute a violation. Of course, this type of bluffing is more effective and more prevalent because it cannot be as easily discredited through reference to objective information as can false statements about working conditions. In sum, though the Truitt decision requires honesty with regard to the making of claims concerning bargaining topics, it does not proscribe the more effective and important forms of bluffing commonly used in bargaining today.

3. Bluffing and the Concept of Lying

Suppose (example 1) that I am a management negotiator trying to reach a strike settlement with union negotiators. I need to settle the strike soon and have been instructed to settle for as much as a 12% increase in wages and benefits if that is the best agreement I can obtain. I say that the company's final offer is a 10% increase. Am I lying? Consider also whether any of the following examples constitute lying:

(2) Management negotiators misstating the profitability of a subsidiary to convince the union negotiating with it that the subsidiary would go out of business if management acceded to union wage demands.
(3) Union officials misreporting the size of the union strike fund to portray a greater ability to strike than is actually the case.
(4) Management negotiators saying, "We can't afford this agreement," when it would not put the firm out of business but only reduce profits from somewhat above to somewhat below the industry average.
(5) Union negotiators saying, "The union membership is adamant on this issue," when they know that while one half of the membership is adamant, the other half couldn't care less.
(6) Union negotiators saying, "If you include this provision, we'll get membership approval of the contract," when they know they'll have an uphill battle for approval even with the provision.

3.1. Defining Lying

What is lying? A lie must be a false statement,[2] but not all false statements are lies. If I am a salesman and say that my product is the best on the market and *sincerely believe this to be the case,* my statement is not a lie, even if it is untrue. A false statement is not a lie unless it is somehow deliberate or intentional. Suppose that we define a lie as an intentional false statement. According to this definition, I am telling a lie when I say, "This aftershave will make you feel like a million bucks." This definition implies that we lie when we exaggerate, e.g., a negotiator representing union workers making $10/hour but seeking a substantial raise says, "These are slave wages you're paying us." When I greatly exaggerate or say something in jest, I know that it is very improbable that the other person(s) will believe what I say. The reason that these examples do not appear to be lies is that they do not involve the intent to deceive. This suggests the following definition of lying:

(1) A lie is a deliberate[3] false statement intended to deceive another person.

This definition is inadequate in cases in which a person is compelled to make false statements. For example, I may lie as a witness to a jury for fear of being killed by the accused. But is doesn't follow that I hope or intend to deceive them.[4] I may hope that my statements don't deceive anyone. We might say that what makes my statements lies is that I realize or foresee that they are likely to deceive others. This then suggests the following definition of lying:

> (2) A lie is a deliberate false statement which is thought to be likely to deceive others by the person who makes it.

This definition is also lacking because a person can lie even if he or she has almost no hope of being believed. A criminal protesting his or her innocence in court is lying no matter how unlikely it is that he/she thinks the argument will be convincing to the judge or jury. The following definition is more plausible than either (1) or (2):

> (3) A lie is a deliberate false statement which is either intended to deceive others or foreseen to be likely to deceive others.

3.11. Implications for bluffing. It appears that this definition implies that the statements in our first three examples constitute lies. In examples (1) and (2) one is making deliberate false statements with the intent of deceiving others about matters relevant to the negotiations. In the first case I am making a deliberate false statement with the intent to deceive the other party into thinking that I am unwilling to offer more than 10%. One might object that this needn't be my intent in example (1). No one familiar with standard negotiating practices is likely to take at face value statements which a person makes about a 'final offer.' One might argue that in the two cases in question I intend and expect my statement that 10% is my best offer to be taken to mean my highest possible offer is something around 12%. If this is my intention and expectation, then my bluffing does not constitute a lie. To this we might add the observation that such intentions are quite uncommon in business negotiations. Even if I don't *expect* you to believe that 10% is my final position, I probably still *hope* or intend to deceive you into thinking that I am unwilling to offer as much as 12%. Examples (2) and (3) are clear instances of lying—they involve deliberate false statements intended to deceive others. It's not so clear, however, that examples (4), (5) and (6) constitute instances of lying. These cases do seem to involve the intent to deceive, but the statements involved are sufficiently ambiguous that it is not clear that they are untrue. We can still say that these are cases in which one affirms (or represents as true) statements which one knows to be dubious with the intent to deceive others. Morally speaking this may be just as bad or wrong as straightforward instances of lying.

3.12. An alternative definition of lying. Our proposed definition of lying implies that bluffing in standard negotiation settings constitutes lying. There is at least one other approach to defining the concept of lying which does not have this consequence and it would be well for us to consider it here. In his *Lectures on Ethics* (1775–1780), Immanuel Kant holds that a deliberate false statement does not constitute a lie unless the speaker has "expressly given" the other(s) to believe that he/she intends to speak the truth.[5] According to Kant's original view, when I make a false statement to a thief about the location of my valuables, I am not lying because "the thief knows full well that I will not, if I can help it, tell him the truth and that he has no right to demand it of me" (1775–1780, p. 227). According to this view, false statements uttered in the course of business negotiations do not constitute lies except in the very unusual circumstances that one promises to tell the truth during the negotiations. Kant's definition is open to serious objections. It seems to rule out many common cases of lying. For example, suppose that a child standing in line to see an X-rated movie claims to be 18 when he or she is only 15. This is a lie in spite of the fact that no explicit promise to tell the truth was made to the ticket seller. There does seem to be one relevant difference between the two cases in question. The ticket taker has a right to be told the truth and a right to the information in question, the thief has no right to the information on one's valuables. This suggests the following revision of Kant's definition:

> (4) A lie is a deliberate false statement which is (i) either intended to deceive others or foreseen to be likely to deceive others, and (ii) either the person who makes the statement has promised to be truthful or those to whom it is directed have a right to know the truth.

Many would take it to be a virtue of (4) that it implies that deliberate false statements made during the course of certain kinds of competitive activities do not constitute lies. Carr quoted the British statesman Henry Taylor who argued that "falsehood ceases to be falsehood when it is understood on all sides that the truth is not expected to be spoken" (1968, p. 143). Carr argued that in poker, diplomacy, and business, individuals (through mutually implied consent) forfeit their rights to be told the truth. It seems at least plausible to say this with respect to standard cases of negotiation. However, it is surely not the case in situations in which one of the parties is unfamiliar with standard negotiating procedures (e.g. children, immigrant laborers, naive individuals or the mentally impaired), and who enters into the discussion assuming that all of the parties will be perfectly candid.

If (4) is a correct definition of lying, then it does seem plausible to say that bluffing typically does not amount to lying. So, in order to defend our earlier claim, that bluffing usually involves lying, we need to give reasons for thinking that (3) is preferable to (4). We are inclined to think that deliberate falsehoods uttered in the course of games and diplomacy as well as business do constitute lies, and are thus inclined to prefer (3) to (4). This is a case about which people have conflicting intuitions; it cannot be a decisive reason for preferring (3) or (4) or vice versa. A more decisive consideration in favor of (3) is the following case. Suppose that a management negotiator asks a union negotiator the size of the union strike fund. The union negotiator responds by saying it is three times its actual amount. Definition (4) implies that this statement is not a lie since the management negotiator didn't have a right to know the information in question and the union didn't explicitly promise to tell the truth about this. But surely this is a lie. The fact that management has no right to know the truth is just cause for withholding the information, but responding falsely is a lie nonetheless.

There is, to the best of our knowledge, no plausible definition of lying which allows us to say that typical instances of bluffing in labor and other sorts of business negotiations do not involve lying. We should stress that it is only bluffing, which involves making false statements which constitutes lying. One is not lying if one bluffs another by making the true statement "We want a 30% pay increase." Similarly, it is not a lie if one bluffs without making any statements as in a game of poker or overpricing (on a price tag) a product where bargaining is expected (e.g., a used car lot or antique store).

3.2. The Concept of Deception

At this point it would be useful to consider the relationship between lying and the broader concept of deception. Deception may be defined as intentionally causing another person to have false beliefs. . . . As we have seen, lying always involves the intent to deceive others, or the expectation that they will be deceived as a result of what one says, or both. But one can lie without actually deceiving anyone. If you don't believe me when I lie and tell you that 10% is our final offer, then I haven't succeeded in deceiving you about anything. It is also possible to deceive another person without telling a lie. . . . Only deception which involves making false statements can be considered lying.

It seems that one can often avoid lying in the course of a business negotiation simply by phrasing one's statements very carefully. In negotiations, instead of lying and saying that 10% is the highest wage increase we will give, I could avoid lying by making the following true, but equally deceptive statement: "Our position is that 10% is our final offer" (without saying that this position is subject to change). It is questionable whether this is any less morally objectionable than lying. Most people prefer to deceive others by means of cleverly contrived true statements, rather than lies. Some who have strong scruples against lying see nothing wrong with such ruses. It is doubtful, however, whether lying is any worse than mere deception. . . .

4. Moral Issues in Lying

Common sense holds that lying is a matter of moral significance and that lying is *prima facie* wrong, or wrong everything else being equal. This can also be put by saying that there is a presumption against lying, and that lying requires some special justification in order to be considered permissible. Common sense also holds that lying is not always wrong, it can sometimes be justified (Ross, 1930). . . .

Assuming the correctness of this view about the morality of lying and deception, and assuming that we are correct in saying that bluffing involves lying, it follows that bluffing and other deceptive business practices require some sort of special justification in order to be considered permissible.

We will now attempt to determine whether there is any special justification for the kind of lying and deception which typically occurs in labor and other sorts of business negotiations. Bluffing and other sorts of deceptive strategies are standard practice in these negotiations and they are generally thought to be acceptable. Does the fact that these things are standard practice or 'part of the game' show that they are justified? We think not. The mere fact that something is standard practice, legal, or generally accepted is not enough to justify it. Standard practice and popular opinion can be in error. Such things as slavery were once standard practice, legal, and generally accepted. But they are and *were* morally wrong. Bluffing constitutes an attempt to deceive others about the nature of one's intentions in a bargaining situation. The *prima facie* wrongness of bluffing is considerably *diminished* on account of the fact that the lying and deception involved typically concern matters about which the other parties have no particular right to know. The others have no particular right to know one's bargaining position—one's intentions. However, there is still some presumption against lying or deceiving other people, even when they have no right to the information in question. A stranger has no right to know how old I am. I have no obligation to provide him/her with this information. Other things being equal, however, it would still be wrong for me to lie to this stranger about my age.

In our view the main justification for bluffing consists in the fact that the moral presumption against lying to or deceiving someone holds only when the person or persons with whom you are dealing is/are not attempting to lie to or deceive you. Given this, there is no presumption against bluffing or deceiving someone who is attempting to bluff or deceive you on that occasion. The prevalence of bluffing in negotiations means that one is safe in presuming that one is justified in bluffing in the absence of any special reasons for thinking that one's negotiating partners are not bluffing (e.g., when one is dealing with an unusually naive or scrupulous person).

5. CONCLUSIONS

Granted that bluffing and deception can be permissible given the exigencies and harsh realities of economic bargaining in our society, isn't it an indictment of our entire economic system that such activities are necessary in so many typical circumstances? Even those who defend the practice of bluffing (Carr, 1968) concede that a great deal of lying and deception occurs in connection with the economic activities of our society. Much of this (particularly in the area of bargaining or negotiating) is openly condoned or encouraged by both business and labor. While lying and deception are not generally condoned in other contexts, they often occur as the result of pressures generated by the highly competitive nature of our society. For example, few would condone the behavior of a salesperson who deliberately misrepresents the cost and effectiveness of a product. However, a salesperson under pressure to sell an inferior product may feel that he/she must either deceive prospective customers or else find a new job.

Many people would argue that our economic system is flawed in that it allegedly encourages dishonesty and thus corrupts our moral character and makes us worse persons than we would have been otherwise. Such criticisms are frequently found in Marxist literature. . . . The so-called competitive business 'rat race' has also been cited as a cause of personal treachery, backbiting, and sycophantic behavior. This, it seems to us, is a very serious criticism which warrants careful consideration. We suggest the following three lines of response.

(1) One could concede that the economic arrangements of our society are such as to elicit a great deal of unethical conduct, but argue that this is the case in any viable economic system—including various forms of socialism and communism. If this is so then the existence of immoral conduct which is associated with economic activities in our own society cannot be a reason to prefer some other sort of economic system. The record of the major socialist and communist countries would tend to support this view. There is deception in the bargaining involved in such things as the allocation of labor and raw materials for industry and setting production quotas for industry. There is also the same kind of gamesmanship involved in competing for desirable positions in society and (by all accounts) much greater opportunity and need for bribery. However, there have been viable feudalistic and caste societies which are much less competitive than our own which function with much less deception or occasion for deception. If one's place in society is determined by birth, then one will simply not have occasion to get ahead by deception.

(2) While it must be conceded that there are other types of economic systems which involve less dishonesty than our own, these systems have other undesirable features which outweigh this virtue. In a feudal society or a centrally planned 'command' economy there might well be less occasion for bargaining about wages and prices and thus also less occasion for deceiving other people about such things. But such a society is surely less free than our own and also very likely to be less prosperous. There are strong reasons to desire that wages be determined by voluntary agreements, even if that allows for the possibility of dishonesty in negotiations.

(3) It can be argued that the present objections to competitive economic systems such as our own rest on a mistaken view about the nature of moral goodness and the moral virtues. One's moral goodness and honesty are not a direct function of how frequently one tells lies. . . . The fact that a businessperson who has a monopoly on a vital good or service does not misrepresent the price or quality of his/her goods or services does not necessarily mean that he/she is honest. There is simply no occasion or temptation to be dishonest. . . . Competitive economic arrangements do not usually *cause* people to become dishonest or treacherous, etc. However these arrangements often actualize dispositions to act dishonestly or treacherously which people had all along. . . .

Notes

1. It could however be argued on utilitarian grounds that, given a decreasingly marginal utility for money, there is a presumption to settle as favorably as possible for the employees since they are *generally* poorer than the stockholders.
2. Arnold Isenberg however disputes this in 'Conditions for Lying' in *Ethical Theory and Business,* Tom Beauchamp and Norman Bowie (eds.) (Englewood Cliffs, N.J., Prentice-Hall, Inc., 1979), pp. 466–468. He holds that a true statement can be a lie provided that one does not believe it. He defines a lie as

follows: "A lie is a statement made by one who does not believe it with the intention that someone else be led to believe it. This definition leaves open the possibility that a person should be lying even though he says what is true. . ." (p. 466). We feel that this is most implausible. For if what one says is true, this is always sufficient to defeat the claim that it is a lie.

3. There is however some question here as to what it means to make a *deliberate* false statement. Must one believe that what one says is false or is it enough that one not believe it? Roderick Chisholm and Thomas Feehan hold that the latter is all that is necessary in "The Intent to Deceive," *Journal of Philosophy,* 74 (1977), 143–159. This makes the concept of lying broader than it would otherwise be.

4. Frederick Siegler considers this kind of example in "Lying," *American Philosophical Quarterly,* 3 (1966), 128–136. But he argues that it does not count against the view that a necessary condition of a statement's being a lie is that it is intended to deceive someone. The example only shows that it is not necessary that the liar, him/herself, intend to deceive the others. But it does not count against the view that the lie must be intended *by someone* to deceive others. For, in our present example, *the criminal intends* that the witness' statements deceive others. However, a slight modification of the present example generates a counter-example to his claim that a lie must be intended by someone or other to deceive. Suppose that a witness makes a deliberate false statement, *x* for fear of being killed by the friends of the accused. He/she is lying even if the accused's friends believe that *x* is true, in which case neither they nor anyone else intend that the witness' statements deceive the jury.

5. Kant's analysis of lying offered here differs from the one presented in Kant's later and more well known work, "On the Supposed Right to Tell Lies from Benevolent Motives" (1797) in Barauch Brody (ed.), *Moral Rules and Particular Circumstances* (Englewood Cliffs, N.J., Prentice-Hall, Inc., 1970), pp. 31–36. There he says that any intentional false statement is a lie (p. 32). Kant also gives a different account of the morality of lying in these two works. His well-known absolute prohibition against lying is set forth only in the latter work.

DECEPTIVE PRACTICES IN ADVERTISING

Burton Leiser

This paper is deliberately designed to point out some of the problems that arise as a result of advertising industry's failure to develop meaningful ethical guidelines for its members' use. While considerable attention is devoted to such well-known and frequently discussed practices as deception, fraud, and the like, some issues that are not so frequently discussed are raised as well. . . .

MISLEADING STATEMENTS OR CONTEXTS

Campbell's Soups concocted a television commercial that showed a thick, creamy mixture that the announcer suggested was Campbell's vegetable soup. Federal investigators, intrigued by the fact that the soup shown in the commercial was much thicker than any Campbell's vegetable soup they had ever seen, discovered that the bowl shown in the commercial had been filled with marbles to make it appear to be thicker than it really was and to make it seem to contain more vegetables than it did. Max Factor promoted a wave-setting lotion, Natural Wave, by showing how a drinking straw soaked in the lotion curled up. The FTC pointed out, however, that it did not logically follow that human hair would react as drinking straws did. The implication left in the viewer's mind, therefore, was false, because, in fact, straight hair did not curl after being soaked in Natural Wave. . . .

Misleading words and phrases, particularly when those words and phrases have special technical meanings, are often employed to create false impressions in the minds of persons who are not familiar with the jargon of particular businesses. And ordinary language may be used in such a way as to suggest to the uninitiated that certain conditions exist which do not in fact exist at all. For example, in describing insurance coverage, the terms *all, full, complete, comprehensive, unlimited, up to, as high as,* and the like can be extremely deceptive. "This policy will pay your hospital and surgical bills" suggests (though it does not *literally* say) that *all* of the hospital and surgical bills of the insured will be paid; and "This policy will replace your income" suggests that *all* of a person's income will be replaced if he becomes disabled—when in fact, only a very small portion of his bills or his income will be paid or replaced. The use of several synonymous terms (e.g., to describe the same condition or disease) may suggest to the uninitiated that he is buying much broader coverage than is in fact the case. Offering a "family" contract suggests to the unwary that each member of his family will receive equal coverage—the coverage that is announced in bold type—when in fact, his spouse and/or his children will receive substantially less coverage than the policyholder will.

When an ad says that a given policy "pays full coverage," it does not mean what it seems to mean. It *seems* to say that it will pay the full costs of (e.g.) the policyholder's hospitalization and doctors bills. But it *really* says that it will pay as much as the policy stipulates that it will pay—that is, it pays as much as you contract for, not as much as you may have to pay. (In other words, it utters a meaningless, uninformative tautology which the consumer misinterprets.)

An ad that proclaims that "This policy pays $10,000 for hospital room and board expenses" may not make it clear that there is a daily limit, a maximum time limit, and complete exclusion of all hospital expenses.

Most potential insurance buyers are unaware of the fact that "noncancellable" and "guaranteed renewable" are technical terms which have very definite meanings within the insurance industry that may not mean anything like what the layman thinks they mean. A noncancellable policy is one which the insured has the right to keep in force by timely payment of premiums until at least age 50, or, if the policy is issued after age 44, for at least five years after the date of issue. The insurer may not unilaterally change any provision of the policy while it is in force. But it does *not* guarantee the insured that he will be able to keep the policy in force *after* he reaches age 50 (or after five years)—though he might very well suppose that that is what it means.[1]

Similarly, "guaranteed renewable" means that the insured has the right to keep his policy in force by timely premium payments until at least age 50 or, if he purchases the policy after age 44, for five years from the date of issue, and that insurer may not unilaterally change any provision of the policy, but that the insurer may change the premium rates by classes.[2]

The use of such terms is misleading unless the ad makes it clear that the insured does *not* have the option of renewing his policy indefinitely.

Similarly, advertising "Eligible—ages 18 to 65" suggests that if a person buys the policy, he will be covered until he reaches age 65—when in fact, what is meant is that anyone who is under 65 may *purchase* the policy—but the policy itself may not be renewed by the insurer.

Life insurance ads often read, "This policy is flexible and can be changed as your needs change—you may convert it to permanent life insurance," or "This policy (ANNUAL PREMIUM, ONLY $_____) is flexible and can be changed to fit your needs—you may convert it to permanent life insurance." Such ads don't even *suggest* that conversion will entail payment of much higher rates based upon the insured's age at the time of conversion.

The same is true of policies that are advertised as offering "generous loan privileges at low interest rates." Nowhere is it made clear that the policy has no loan or cash value for several years, or that the "low" interest rates may not be low at all relative to bank rates that might prevail at the time the loan might be made.

One of the most misleading mail order insurance ads was described in FTC Consumer Bulletin No. 1. The ad said:

> Maximum Policy Benefits. For Hospital Care $5,000. For Death Natural Cause $10,000. For Accidental Death $20,000. . . . this big Family Plan for only $6.25 monthly.

In fact, the policy was written in such a way that the insurer was not obliged to pay more than $500 in any one year for any one person. Only $2,000 was payable for each death by natural causes and $4,000 for accidental death. Any full benefits did not accrue until after the policy had been in effect for a considerable period of time. . . .

The land promoter who sends a glossy pamphlet advertising his "retirement city" in Arizona may not make a single false statement in the entire pamphlet. But by filling it with beautiful color photographs of swimming pools, golf links, and lush vegetation, none of which exist within 100 miles of the land he is selling, he leads his prospects to believe that certain features exist within the area which do *not* exist. Thus, without uttering or printing a single false statement, he is able to lead his prospects to believe what he knows is not true. . . .

In none of these cases could one say that false statements were made. Strictly speaking, these advertisers are not guilty of lying to the public, if *lying* is defined as the deliberate utterance of an untrue statement. For, taken literally, none of the statements made in these advertisements is untrue. But the messages of the ads are misleading. Because of the pictorial matter in them, the reader or viewer makes inferences that are false; and the advertiser juxtaposes those pictures with the narrative in such a way that false inferences *will* be made. It is through those false inferences that he expects to earn enough money to pay for the ad and to have something left over for himself. . . .

THE EXPLOITATION OF ILLUSIONS

Closely related to misleading pictures and statements is the use made by manufacturers and advertisers of illusions in selling their goods. This is best illustrated by the use merchandisers make of certain optical illusions in their choice of packaging. Cereal boxes would be much more stable, less apt to spill over, if they were short and squat. But the packaging experts at Kellogg's, General Foods, and General Mills know that if housewives are given the choice between two boxes of cereal, one short and squat and the other tall and narrow, they will almost invariably choose the tall and narrow box, *even if it contains less cereal and costs more.* Most housewives judge by the outward appearance of the box and do not look for the net weight and attempt to calculate the price per ounce (a project that is virtually impossible anyway, unless one is equipped with a slide rule). Two lines of equal length, one horizontal and the other vertical, do not *appear* to be of equal length. The vertical line always appears to be longer. Tall boxes appear to be larger than short ones, and the housewife doing her shopping thinks she is getting more in the tall box than she would be getting if she were to purchase the short box.

Bottles follow the same principle. Shampoos, for example, are packaged in tall, narrow bottles—often with the waist pinched to make them even taller—to give the illusion of quantity. Some jars and bottles are manufactured with inner compartments, or double glass walls, so that the actual quantity of goods in the container is much less than it appears to be. Fruit and other goods are canned in large quantities of syrup, and cookies, nuts, and other dry foods are packed in tins or cartons that are stuffed with cardboard—allegedly to prevent breakage, but more realistically to reduce the quantity of goods in the package while giving the customer the illusion that he is purchasing more than is actually to be found in the package.

Manufacturers argue that these stuffings are necessary to prevent breakage, that there is a certain amount of "settling" in some products that results in their packages being a third empty when they reach the consumer, and that their machines have been designed in any case to fill the packages by weight so that the customer always receives an honest measure, regardless of the size or shape of the package. But these explanations do not explain the hiss of air that escapes from my toothpaste tube when I open it (the tube seemed full and firm until then, but turns out to have been full of air); and it does not explain the manufacturers' aversion to standardized weights and their vigorous battle against requirements that the net weight be printed boldly and prominently on the front of the package. Until recent legislation was passed, the net weight of many products was printed in obscure corners of the packages, in microscopic type, and in a color that was just two shades lighter than the background color of the package (e.g., red against a dark red background) so that it was almost impossible for the normal shopper to find out how much merchandise was contained in the package.

However, the producer and the manufacturer may have legitimate excuses for some of these practices. A relatively small macaroni company, for example, may produce a number of different products, in different shapes and with a variety of densities. By standardizing all of its packages by *dimensions* rather than by *weight*, it is able to purchase packages and cases in great quantities and to save considerable money both for itself and, one would hope, for its customers. If it were required to standardize its packages by *weight*, it would have to invest a considerable amount of money in new plant and equipment, and the time during which its plant and equipment were standing idle would be increased significantly, thus raising its costs and, eventually, the cost to the consumer.[3] If standardized packaging were suddenly legislated into existence, it is conceivable that a number of smaller firms would be forced out of business because of their inability to absorb the added costs, and that the giant corporations would be bequeathed an even larger share of the total market than they now have. Still, none of these considerations should apply to a requirement that all packages bear, in clear and unmistakable type, a true and unambiguous statement of the nature of their contents and their weight.

Merchants and producers have many ways of concealing truth from the customers—not by lying to them, but simply by not telling them facts that are relevant to the question of whether they ought to purchase a particular product or whether they are receiving full value for their money. A particularly good example of this is the great ham scandal that broke into the open a few years ago. Major packers, including Swift, Armour, and others, were selling ham that was advertised as being particularly juicy. The consumer was not told, however, that the hams were specially salted and that hypodermic syringes were used to inject large quantities of water into them. The "juice" was nothing but water that evaporated away during cooking, leaving a ham some 40 percent smaller than the one that had been put into the oven. The housewife purchasing such a ham had no advance warning that she was purchasing water for the price of ham, unless she knew that the words *artificial ham* that were printed in small letters on the seal of the package meant that that was the case. Even that small warning, if it can be called such, was added only because of pressure brought to bear against the packers by the FTC. And there was no publicity to arouse the consumer to the special meaning of that odd term, *artificial ham.*[4]

Probably the most common deception of this sort is price deception, the technique some high-pressure salesmen use to sell their goods by grossly inflating their prices to two, three, and even four times their real worth. Again, there may be no "untruth" in what they say; but they conceal the important fact that the same product, or one nearly identical to it, can be purchased for far less at a department or appliance store. It is not the business of salesmen and businessmen to send their clients to their competitors, but it is certainly unethical for them to fail to tell their customers that they are not getting full value for their money.

A common form of deception involves a company advertising a product as if the product were on sale at a reduced price, when in fact, the product is never sold at the so-called original or regular price. This sometimes hurts the little man, as it did in the case of *FTC* v. *Mary Carter Paint Company,* in which a small paint manufacturer advertised: "Buy 1 gallon for $6.98 and get a second gallon free." The company claimed that it used this method to compete with national companies who normally sold similar paint at $6.98 per gallon. It feared that if it sold paint at half price, the public would think that its product was inferior. It therefore used the "one gallon free" device to achieve the same result. The FTC found that the practice was deceptive, since the paint in question was *never* sold at $6.98 per gallon, and the Supreme Court upheld the FTC's decision.

Encyclopedia and book salesmen are notorious for their deceptive practices. Almost everyone has had an encyclopedia salesman come to the door misrepresenting himself as an agent for the school board, or as a person taking a public opinion survey, or as a representative of some "educational" organization. And we are all familiar with the gimmick used by them, in which they claim that they are "placing"—they never "sell" anything, of course—encyclopedias or "earning programs" in homes at no cost whatever to the lucky recipient. It is all part of their advertising or public relations program, they say. "All we ask is that you give us five or ten references, and that you allow us to use your name. In addition, there will be a small monthly service charge for the ten-year extension service, or the ten-year research service," which will allegedly make a scholar out of your son or daughter and guarantee him or her a place in law school (*FTC* v. *Standard Education Society*). . . .

Perhaps it may be put as follows: A burglar or a thief may be heavily fined or sent to jail for many months for stealing a relatively small amount of money or valuables from a single person. But a salesman who cheats hundreds of people out of equal sums of money that total, in the aggregate, hundreds of thousands of dollars, is immune to prosecution, and may, in fact, be one of the community's most respected citizens. If Armour and Swift and other large corporations can bilk their customers out of enormous sums of money and do it with impunity, why, one might ask, should the petty thief be subjected to such severe penalties for his activities? He may plead that he desperately needs the money he derives from his dishonest activities, but that excuse would hardly be credible if it was uttered by corporate executives.

TESTIMONIALS

Too many "testimonials" are phony. By now, most people probably know that the people who offer testimonials on TV and in printed ads are paid for their services, and they must suspect that there isn't an ounce of sincerity in them. They must rightly believe that the so-called testimonials are written by admen, and not by the people who read them. But it is reasonable to assume that there are still some unsuspecting, gullible, and naive people who believe that the people who speak to them from their TV screens are honest and are persuaded by what they hear. At least the admen must think so, for otherwise it would be difficult to understand why they would continue to use this ancient device.

When football and basketball stars promote foods, their expertise in home economics ought at least to be brought into question by those who watch their ads. Pearl Bailey is a fine singer, but her singing ability is irrelevant to her ability to judge kitchen ranges. ("There's just two cooks allowed in Pearl's kitchen, me and this handsome devil by White-Westinghouse. Me, I've been filling hungry mouths with my scrumptious cooking . . . since most of you were making mud pies. So any assistant that Pearl lets in has got to be real able." [Two-page ad in *Better Homes and Gardens,* November 1976. Notice the deliberately poor grammar.]) Even worse are the actors and models who are posed in white coats and stethoscopes, or are dressed in dark business suits and filmed in hospital corridors or seated behind huge desks in book-lined studies, suggesting that they are physicians, lawyers, or high-paid executives; or in laboratories, suggesting that they are distinguished scientists or engineers. Far from reporting information derived from their own expert appraisal of the facts, they merely mouth the words prepared for them by advertising men—in deep voices and with profound conviction—sometimes seeming to read from beautifully bound "reports" prepared by the same advertising men. . . .

A Final Word on Advertising

Advertising has an important and constructive role to play in the life of the nation. It is not true that all advertising men are unscrupulous or that all businessmen are concerned only with selling, no matter what the cost to the customers. Nor is it true that advertisements are necessarily misleading or fraudulent.

David Ogilvy, one of the most successful advertising executives in the United States, is the creator of such successful advertising images as Schweppes's Commander Whitehead and Hathaway Shirt's man with the eye patch.[5] In his discussion of techniques for building a successful advertising campaign, he says:

> Give the Facts. Very few advertisements contain enough factual information to sell the product. There is a ludicrous tradition among copywriters that consumers aren't interested in facts. Nothing could be farther from the truth. Study the copy in the Sears, Roebuck catalogue; it sells a billion dollars' worth of merchandise every year by giving *facts*. In my Rolls-Royce advertisements I gave nothing but facts. No adjectives, no "gracious living."
>
> The consumer isn't a moron; she is your wife. You insult her intelligence if you assume that a mere slogan and a few vapid adjectives will persuade her to buy anything. She wants all the information you can give her.[6]

And he adds the following bit of advice that bears directly on our subject:

> You wouldn't tell lies to your own wife. Don't tell them to mine. Do as you would be done by.
>
> If you tell lies about a product, you will be found out—either by the Govern-

ment, which will prosecute you, or by the consumer, who will punish you by not buying your product a second time.

Good products can be sold by *honest* advertising. If you don't think the product is good, you have no business to be advertising it. If you tell lies, or weasel, you do your client a disservice, you increase your load of guilt, and you fan the flames of public resentment against the whole business of advertising. . . .[7]

Some 2,000 years ago there was a debate between the scholars of two great academies as to whether it was proper to praise the beauty of an ugly bride. According to one faction, the principle that one should refrain from uttering any falsehood required that the honest man refrain from praising the ugly bride. The other group, however, insisted that principles of kindness should prevail and that even if one had to lie, one was obliged to add to the newlyweds' happiness rather than to detract from it. They went on to say that in a matter of far less moment to a man than his marriage, the principle of kindness should take precedence, so that if a person had made a bad bargain at the market, one should not rub it in by telling him so.[8] If they were here to participate in a discussion on the issue presently under consideration, it is not hard to imagine what they might say:

Thousands of men and women are too poor to afford foreign travel, or large and flashy automobiles, or Hathaway shirts, or expensive liquors or costly cosmetics. What useful purpose is served by dangling these luxuries before their eyes? To some, perhaps, the enticing display of such luxuries may serve as an incentive, spurring them on to greater achievement so that they too may enjoy what their more affluent neighbors take for granted. But to many, and perhaps to most, the display may arouse feelings of frustration, anger, and hurt. "Why," they may ask, "are we unable to have all of these things, when so many others do? Why can we not give our children what those ads show other people giving their children? Why can we not share the happiness that is depicted here?" Before a man is married, it might be appropriate to point out some of his fiancée's faults; but at the wedding, when it's obviously too late, it's unkind to dwell on them. For those who cannot afford the luxuries—and they are luxuries, whatever Ogilvy may say—offered in advertisements that are often directed *specifically at them,* it is cruel to hurt them by offering them what they cannot buy, or to seduce them with false promises of happiness or prestige or success into neglecting their primary obligations in order to seek the fantasy world portrayed in advertisements.

Everyone wants a beautiful bride, I suppose, and it may be good that the working classes no longer desire to live Spartan lives, if they ever did. But some men learn to live very happily with women whose proportions are not even close to those that are currently considered to be the standard of beauty, and it is wrong to jeopardize their happiness by constantly reminding them of that fact; and it would be infinitely worse to parade well-proportioned beauties before them and to urge them to switch. No one is married to a life of poverty. But some people, unable to escape from such a life themselves, have made the adjustment and have found that it is possible to be happy and respectable even on a severely limited income. Is it right to parade the latest fashions in "good living" before their eyes at every opportunity, urging them to buy them *"Now, while our limited supply lasts!''*? Men who have been seduced into discontentment over their wives have been known to commit murder. So have some who have been seduced into dissatisfaction with their style of life. Some of the latter may be partially attributable to advertising.

This is not to say that all advertising is bad; but even when the message is not distorted, those who use the mass media to disseminate it should do so with some sense of social and public responsibility. It is far worse, though, when the message is distorted. And even David Ogilvy, for all his insistence on honesty in advertising, admits that he is "continuously guilty of *suppressio veri* (the suppression of the truth). Surely it is asking too much to expect the advertiser to describe the shortcomings of his product. One must be forgiven for putting one's best foot forward."[9] So the consumer is *not* to be told all the relevant information; he is *not* to be given all the facts that would be of assistance in making a reasonable decision about a given purchase. In particular, he will *not* be told about the weaknesses of a product, about its shock hazards, for example, if it is an electrical appliance; about the danger it poses to the consumer's health if it is a cleaning fluid; about the danger it poses to his life if it is an automobile tire that is not built to sustain the heavy loads of today's automobile at turnpike speeds; or, if one carries the doctrine to its final conclusion, about the possibly harmful side effects of a new drug that is advertised to the medical profession. Telling the truth combined with *"suppressio veri"* is *not* telling the truth. It is *not* asking too much of the advertiser to reveal such facts when they are known to him, and he should *not* be forgiven for "putting his best foot forward" at his customer's expense.

Notes

1. Cf. Richard L. Ismond, *Insurance Advertising: Ethics and Law* (New York: Roberts Publishing Company, 1968), pp. 101ff.
2. *Ibid,* pp. 103ff.
3. See "The Consumer," an address by Lloyd E. Skinner, president of the Skinner Macaroni Company, in *Vital Speeches of the Day,* vol. 33 (January 1, 1967), pp. 189ff., reprinted in Grant S. McClellan, "The Reference Shelf," vol. 40, no. 3, *The Consuming Public* (New York: H. W. Wilson Company, 1968), pp. 143ff. He explains that his company produces some nineteen or twenty different kinds of macaroni products, all packaged in the same containers. If his firm were required to standardize by weight, rather than by volume, he would have to invest $86,000 in new machinery over the $300,000 investment in packaging machinery that he already has, as well as $100,000 in new plant facilities to accommodate the new machines. As opposed to the 90 percent operating time of the packaging machinery that he had at the time, the new machinery would have been operating only 40 to 50 percent of the time, according to his estimates. This would have resulted in an increase of 1 to 2 cents per package in the cost of producing macaroni.
4. Cf. *Consumer Reports,* March and August 1961, follow-up reports April and August 1962.

5. The firm is Ogilvy, Benson, and Mather.
6. David Ogilvy, *Confessions of an Advertising Man* (New York: Atheneum, 1963), pp. 95f.
7. *Ibid,* p. 99.
8. Babylonian Talmud, *Ketuvot,* p. 17a. The academies were those that went under the names of Shammai and Hillel, respectively. The "debate" was not comparable to the kind of oratory contest that might be staged by college debating teams. It was a serious discussion on matters of legal and moral principle.
9. Ogilvy, *Confessions,* pp. 158f.

ADVERTISING AND ETHICS

Phillip Nelson

THE MARKET SYSTEM AND ADVERTISING

There are two possible routes one can take to ethics. One can exhort others to take account of social well-being in their behavior—"to love one another" and act accordingly. Or one can try to design institutions such that people will, indeed, benefit society, given the motivations that presently impel their behavior. Most economists, whatever their political position, adopt the latter view; ethical behavior is behavior that, in fact, benefits society, not necessarily behavior that is motivated to benefit society.

Those of us who advocate the market as an appropriate institution are following the lead of Adam Smith: that the market, more or less, acts as if there were an invisible hand, converting individual actions motivated by the pursuit of private gain into social benefit. The selfish employer, for example, callously firing employees when he no longer needs them, helps in the reallocation of labor to activities where it is more useful.

This is not the stuff of poetry. In novels—and quite possibly in the interpersonal relations upon which novels generally focus—selfish people act in ways disastrous to those around them. But novels are hardly the basis for determining social policy, though novelists and their compatriots, literary critics, are often in the forefront in the espousal of "social causes." They have been the consciences of society. Because of their focus on motivation, they have generated a guilt complex when guilt is totally unjustified.

It must be admitted that the market is not a perfect instrument, that the invisible hand wavers a bit. Some individual actions will not lead to social well-being. However, popular perceptions tend to exaggerate market imperfections. For example, the available evidence indicates that the monopoly problem is not terribly serious in the United States. More importantly, the popular view fails to evaluate the problems of alternative institutions. The record of government regulation to make the market behave has been distinguished by case after case where the cure has been worse than the disease, where often there has been no disease at all.

I want to look at the ethics of advertising, given this perspective. Advertising is ethical not because of the motivations of its practitioners but because of the consequences of its operation. The invisible hand strikes again! The market power of consumers will force advertisers to act in ways that benefit society. Advertising will by no means be an "ideal" institution. But it will do an effective job of getting information to consumers.

Advertising bothers its critics not only because its practitioners are selfishly motivated. The advertising itself is often distasteful. Celebrities endorse that brand that pays them the highest price. Advertisers lie if it pays. Advertisers often make empty statements. Nobel prizes for literature have not yet been awarded to the classics of the advertising art. But the crucial question is not whether advertising is aesthetically satisfying, or whether its practitioners are noble, or even whether they occasionally lie. The question is whether advertising generates social well-being. Some of the former questions are not irrelevant in determining the answer to the latter question. In particular, as I discuss later, the role that truth plays in generating socially useful advertising is an important question.

ADVERTISING AND INFORMATION

Before resolving the fundamental ethical issue about advertising, it is important to understand how advertising behaves. I support a simple proposition about the behavior of advertising: that all advertising is information. This is not a statement with which the critics of advertising would agree. What bothers them is that advertising is paid for by the manufacturers of the brands whose products are being extolled. How can information be generated by such a process? Clearly, some kind of mechanism is required to make the self-interested statements of manufacturers generate information. But such a mechanism exists—consumer power in the product markets.

The nature of consumer control over advertising varies with the character of consumer information. Consumers can get some information about certain qualities of products prior to purchase. For example, they can try on a dress, find out about the price of the product, or see how new furniture looks. I call these "search qualities." In the case of search qualities, a manufacturer is almost required by the nature of his business to tell the truth. The consumer can determine before he buys the product whether indeed this is the dress or the piece of furniture that has been advertised; and in consequence, it will pay the advertiser to be truthful. This is a situation where the famous ditty of Gilbert and Sullivan would be appropriate:

This haughty youth, he tells the truth
Whenever he finds it pays;
And in this case, it all took place
Exactly like he says.

Now, there are other qualities that the consumer cannot determine prior to purchase. It is very difficult for the consumer to determine the taste of a brand of tuna fish before he buys the tuna fish, or to determine how durable a car will be until he's experienced it; but even in these cases, the consumer can get information about a product. The character of his experiences when using the brand will generate information to the consumer. This information will not be useful for initial purchases, but it will govern whether the consumer repeatedly purchases the brand or not. The repeat purchase of consumers provides the basis of consumer control of the market in the case of "experience qualities."

In this case, there will be certain characteristics of the advertising which are truthful. It will pay the advertiser to relate correctly the function of the brand. It pays the manufacturer of Pepto-Bismol to advertise his brand as a stomach remedy rather than as a cure for athlete's foot because, obviously, he is going to be able to get repeat purchases if Pepto-Bismol does something for stomachs and people are taking it for stomachs. If they're taking the stomach remedy for athlete's foot, they're in trouble. So the effort to get repeat purchasers will generate a lot of truthfulness in advertising. Another example: it pays the manufacturer of unsweetened grapefruit juice to advertise the product as unsweetened. This is the effective way to get repeat purchases; hence people can believe it.

There are other qualities about the brand for which the incentive of truthfulness does not exist. It pays the manufacturer of Pepto-Bismol to advertise his brand as the most soothing stomach remedy even if it were the least soothing stomach remedy around. It pays somebody to say that a piece of candy tastes best even if the candy has an unpleasant taste. Even here, however, there is information for the consumer to obtain through advertising. The advertising message is not credible, but the fact that the brand is advertised is a valuable piece of information to the consumer. The consumer rightly believes that there is a positive association between advertising and the better buy. The more advertising he sees of the product, the more confidence he has prior to purchasing the product. Simply put, it pays to advertise winners. It does not pay to advertise losers. In consequence, the brands that are advertised the most heavily are more likely to be the winners.

The mechanism that is operating is the repeat purchasing power of the consumer. Brands that are good after purchase will be brands that consumers buy more. In consequence, there is a negatively sloped demand curve. People buy more as the price per unit of utility of a good goes down, even when it takes experience on the part of consumers to determine this utility. As quantity goes up, the amount of advertising will also go up. This is a well-established relationship.[1] The positive association between quantity and advertising and the negative association between quantity and price per unit of utility generates a negative association between advertis-

ing and price per unit of utility. In other words, the "better buys" advertise more; and, in consequence, the *amount* of advertising provides information to consumers.

Considering that we have no direct measure of "better buys," there is a
good deal of evidence to support this proposition. First, it pays a firm to expand its sales if it can produce what consumers want more cheaply than
other firms. It can increase its sales either by increasing advertising or
lowering prices. I maintain that it does both at the same time, just as plants
usually increase both their capital and their labor when they expand output
on a permanent basis. But the critics say that the larger selling brand
advertises more; therefore, it charges more to cover the costs of advertising.

The only way the critics could be right is if diminishing returns in advertising did not exist. By diminishing returns in advertising, I mean that the
more a manufacturer spends on advertising, the less he gets in additional
sales per dollar of advertising. When there are diminishing returns, the
advertising of the larger selling brand is less efficient; it gets fewer sales per
dollar. When advertising is less efficient in that sense, the larger advertiser
will have a greater incentive to get additional sales by lowering the price.
With diminishing returns in advertising, then, the larger selling brand
both advertises more and gives greater value per dollar. There is considerable evidence that there are, indeed, diminishing returns in advertising.[2]

There is a second strand of evidence in support of my position. One can
successfully predict which products get advertised most intensively by
assuming that advertising provides information in the way I have described. It can be shown that it requires more advertising to provide the indirect advertising for experience goods than the direct advertising of search
goods. Indeed, the advertising/sales ratios are greater for experience goods
than search goods.

There is another important piece of evidence that winners are advertised
more. If it is true that the larger-selling brand provides better value per
dollar on the average than smaller-selling brands, wouldn't it pay a brand
to advertise its rank in its product class more, the higher the rank? Consumers would prefer to buy top sellers rather than bottom sellers. The
evidence is overwhelming that more brands say that they are Number One
than declare any other rank.

One could argue, I suppose, that consumers are brainwashed into
believing that larger-selling brands are better, when the contrary is true.
But how could this be? A lot more advertisers have an interest in brain-
washing the consumers into believing the contrary. Yet, the "big is
beautiful" message wins. The only reasonable explanation is that this is
the message which is confirmed by the consumers' own experiences. The
brainwashing explanation is particularly hard to accept, given the industries in which brands most frequently advertise their Number One
status. It pays consumers to make much more thoughtful decisions about
durables than non-durables because the cost to them of making a mistake is
so much greater in that case. Yet, the "I am Number One" advertising
occurs more frequently for durables than for non-durables.[3] Even more

convincing is the evidence that the advertising of Number One rank is not confined to possibly gullible consumers. That same message is used in advertising directed to businessmen. They too must have been brainwashed if the critics are right. But such soft-headed businessmen could hardly survive in the market.

The evidence seems inescapable: larger-selling brands do, on the whole, provide the better value per dollar. The evidence also shows—and all would admit—that larger-selling brands advertise more. In consequence, the more advertised brands are likely to be the better buys.

It is frequently alleged that advertised brands are really no better than non-advertised brands. A case that is often cited in this connection is Bayer Aspirin. But aspirins do, indeed, vary in their physical characteristics. Soft aspirins dissolve in the stomach both more rapidly and more certainly than hard aspirins. In consequence, the soft aspirin are better. They are also more expensive to produce. It is no accident that the most heavily advertised brand of aspirin is a soft aspirin. Of course, there are also non-advertised soft aspirins that sell for less than Bayer Aspirin. But the issue is not whether the best unadvertised aspirin is as good as the most heavily advertised aspirin. The issue is whether purchasing one of the more heavily advertised aspirins at random gives one a better product, on the average, then getting an unadvertised aspirin at random. The existence of unadvertised soft aspirin, when the consumer does not know which aspirin fits into that category, is of little help to the consumer.

Advertising can provide this information without consumers being aware of its doing so. Advertising as information does not require intelligent consumer response to advertising, though it provides a basis for such intelligent response. Consumers who actually believe paid endorsements are the victims of the most benign form of deception. They are deceived into doing what they should do anyhow.

It does not pay consumers to make very thoughtful decisions about advertising. They can respond to advertising for the most ridiculous, explicit reasons and still do what they would have done if they made the most careful judgments about their behavior. ''Irrationality'' is rational if it is cost-free.

Whatever their explicit reasons, consumers' ultimate reason for responding to advertising is their self-interest in so doing. That is, it is no mere coincidence that thoughtful and unthoughtful judgments lead to the same behavior. If it were not in consumers' self-interest to respond to advertising, they would no longer pay attention to advertising. . . .

Notes

1. This is borne out by data from the Internal Revenue Service *Source Book of Income,* 1957. For every industry, firms with larger sales advertise more.
2. See Phillip Nelson, ''Advertising as Information Once More'', *Journal of Political Economy* 4 (1982), 729–774.
3. In the May, 1955, issue of *Life* magazine, there were twelve durable and three non-durable, ''I am Number One'' advertisements.

REASONABLE CONSUMER OR IGNORANT CONSUMER?
How the FTC Decides

Ivan L. Preston

Introduction

Is the Federal Trade Commission obligated to protect only reasonable, sensible, intelligent consumers who conduct themselves carefully in the marketplace? Or must it also protect ignorant consumers who conduct themselves carelessly?

Since its origin in 1914, the Commission has varied its answer to these questions. It has committed itself at all times to prohibit sellers' claims which would deceive reasonable people, but has undergone changes of direction on whether to ban claims which would deceive only ignorant people. At times it has acted on behalf of the latter by invoking the "ignorant man standard."[1] At other times it has been ordered by courts to ignore these people and invoke the "reasonable man standard." In still other cases it has chosen voluntarily to protect certain ignorant persons but not others.

The significance of the issue is that the FTC will rule against the fewest types of sellers' claims under the reasonable man standard, and against the most under the ignorant man standard. The latter guideline therefore means, in the eyes of many, the greatest protection for the consuming public. Some consumerists may feel, in fact, that such a standard should be mandatory on the grounds that a flat prohibition is needed against all sellers' deceptions which would deceive anyone at all.

The FTC, however, works under a constraint which makes it necessary to temper its allegiance to the ignorant man standard. The constraint is that the Commission may proceed legally only in response to substantial public interest.[2] Over the years the Commissioners have been sensitive to the argument that there is no public interest in prohibiting messages which would deceive only a small number of terribly careless, stupid or naive people. To explain the compelling nature of this argument, I would like to describe a deception of that sort.

An Example

In my hometown of Pittsburgh, Pennsylvania, there appears each Christmas-time a brand of beer called Olde Frothingslosh. This quaint item is nothing but Pittsburgh Brewing Company's regular Iron City Beer in its holiday costume, decked out with a specially designed label to provide a few laughs. The label identifies the product as "the pale stale ale for the pale stale male," and there is similar wit appended, all strictly nonsense.

From *Journal of Consumer Affairs,* vol. 8, no. 2, Winter 1974. Reprinted by permission.

One of the best is a line saying that Olde Frothingslosh is the only beer in which the foam is on the bottom.

A customer bought some Olde Frothingslosh to amuse friends at a party and was disturbed to find the claim was nothing but a *big lie:* the foam was right up there on top where it always is! She wanted her money back from the beer distributor, couldn't get it, and went to a lawyer with the intention of bringing suit. The true story ended right there because the lawyer advised her there was no chance of success. The reasonable man (woman! person!) standard would be applied to her suit, and her reliance on the belief about the foam would be judged unreasonable.

Had the ignorant man standard applied she would possibly have succeeded, which illustrates the difference the choice of standards makes. It also illustrates the essential weakness, in conjunction with definite strengths, possessed by a legal standard which sets out to protect everybody from everything. Many of the resulting prohibitions would eliminate only infinitesimal amounts of deception.

Problems of the Ignorant Man Standard

There are other reasons, too, for the FTC's cautious attitude toward the ignorant man standard. A pragmatic point is that the Commission does not have the resources to prosecute all cases, therefore those which are investigated might better be ones which endanger greater numbers of people. Another problem is that an extreme concern for the ignorant could lead to repression of much communication content useful to consumers, and could lead as well to possible violation of the First Amendment's freedom of speech guarantee.

Probably the most important objection to the ignorant man standard is that the reasonable man standard was traditional in the common law which preceded the development of the FTC in 1914. The common law held that to avoid being negligent a person must act as a reasonable person would act under like circumstances.[3] Mention of the reasonable or prudent person first appeared in an English case of 1837,[4] and has been in widespread use since.

In many of its applications the reasonable man concept has been applied to the defendant; did he, for example, act negligently in causing an accident which injured the plaintiff? In the law of misrepresentation, however, the concept is applied to the plaintiff, the deceived consumer. He brings a suit against the deceptive seller, and the question is whether he is guilty of contributory negligence which the deceiver may use as a defense. The rules require the plaintiff to assert and show that he relied upon the false representation, and that the damages he suffered were a result of such reliance. In addition, he must show that his reliance was justified—that is, his reliance must pass the test of the conduct of a reasonable man. He may not claim to have relied on a statement which sensible and prudent people would recognize as preposterous. If he does, he is guilty of contributory negligence which the deceiver may use as a reason for having the suit dismissed.[5]

This rule usually does not apply in the case of a fraudulent misrepresentation, where the deceiver consciously knows the representation was false and deliberately seeks to deceive with it. If that is shown, the person deceived is entitled to rely without having to justify the action as reasonable conduct.[6] But where the deceit is not intentional (or not so proved!) the reasonable man standard applies and the seller's falsity will not amount legally to deception where it is felt that the buyer should have known better than to rely on it. Various types of sellers' statements thereby escape legal liability under the reasonable man standard, beginning with those such as the Olde Frothingslosh claim which are physically impossible and therefore presumed obviously false. Also included are the exaggerations and superlatives called puffery—"The Greatest Show on Earth" and the claims that psycho-social values are present in products—"Ultra-Brite gives your mouth sex appeal."

The Transition to the Ignorant Man Standard

At the time the FTC was created, the only specific law on these matters was the common law just described. The FTC Act stated nothing explicitly about what persons the Commission was authorized to protect; it said only that proceedings must be in the interest of the public. The most obvious procedure therefore would have been to follow the common law precedents and embrace the reasonable man standard. Instead, the FTC did the unexpected and flaunted the reasonable man standard in many of its early cases. Neither that concept nor a replacement standard were discussed explicitly, but numerous early cases show that the Commission was applying an ignorant man standard or a close approximation of it. In 1919 it ordered a manufacturer to stop advertising that its automobile batteries would "last forever."[7] One might assume that no reasonable person even in that year would have relied upon this claim literally, especially when the same ads offered a service by which "the purchaser pays 50 cents per month and is entitled to a new battery as soon as the old one is worn out." The FTC saw the latter phrase, however, as confirming the falsity and deceptiveness rather than the sheer frivolousness of "last forever." The case indicates that the Commission was developing a policy of stopping deceptions which would deceive only a minority.[8]

The switch to the ignorant man standard appeared questionable legally; precedent did not support it. But before we describe the eventual court considerations of this matter, we should acknowledge that there was much argument against the reasonable man standard in common sense if not in law. The legal conception of the buyer who failed to be reasonable in the marketplace was that of a person who made a stupid purchase through his own fault—he should have known better. It was this conception with which common sense could disagree. Some so-called stupid choices may be made not through carelessness but through the impossibility of obtaining and assessing information even when great caution and intelligence are applied. The world of goods and services was once simple, but has become terribly technical. Many poor choices were being made by persons who *couldn't* have known better.

These problems might have been incorporated into the reasonable man standard by adjusting that standard to the realities of the market. Consider a store scene in which a product was available at six cans for a dollar while one can was 16 cents. In considering whether a reasonable person would be deceived, the law might have taken into account that many people are slow at arithmetic, and that the bustle of a market and the need to make many other choices in the same few minutes rendered it unlikely they would fully use the mathematical capacity they possessed. The competence assumed of a "reasonable person" might have been reduced accordingly, and the traditional standard, altered in this way, might still have been applied.

Something bordering the opposite actually occurred in legal actions. The reasonable man came to be regarded as a *better* than average person, as someone who was never negligent and who therefore was entirely fictitious outside the courtroom.[9] He was "an ideal creature. . . . The factor controlling the judgment of [his] conduct is not what *is*, but *what ought to be*." The law, apparently, had created an unreasonable conception of the reasonable man.

It was this problem the FTC sought to correct. We do not know, because the point was not discussed as such, whether the Commission regarded its new conception as a move to the ignorant man standard or as a redefinition of the reasonable man standard by the method described above. But the practical effect was the same in either case—the Commission moved toward protecting the public from deceptions which regulators previously had ignored because they did not harm the fictitiously reasonable man.

COURT INTERPRETATIONS

Considerations of the reasonable and ignorant man standards eventually were made explicit through the intervention of appeals court decisions into FTC affairs. In 1924 the Commission outlawed a sales method which offered an encyclopedia "free" provided a purchaser paid $49 for two supplementary updating services.[10] The seller appealed and won a reversal on the grounds that no deception was involved.[11] "It is conceivable," the opinion stated, "that a very stupid person might be misled by this method of selling books, yet measured by ordinary standards of trade and by ordinary standards of the intelligence of traders, we cannot discover that it amounts to an unfair method of competition. . . ."

The FTC did not adopt the reasonable man standard as a result of this ruling; its subsequent activities reflected instead a posture of resistance.[12] When it stubbornly invoked a similar restraint against a different encyclopedia company[13] it was again reversed by an appeals court.[14] Circuit Judge Learned Hand was most adamant in declaring that

. . . a community which sells for profit must not be ridden on so short a rein that it can only move at a walk. We cannot take seriously the suggestion that a man who is buying a set of books and a ten years' extension service, will be fatuous enough to be misled by the mere statement that the first are given away, and that he is paying only for the second. Nor can we conceive how he could be damaged were he to suppose that that was true. Such trivial niceties are too impalpable for practical affairs, they are will-o-the-wisps which divert attention from substantial evils.[15]

This time, however, the FTC took the case to the U.S. Supreme Court, where a new justice delivering his first opinion told Learned Hand that the encyclopedia decision *was* a substantial evil. Hugo Black's opinion in *FTC v. Standard Education* of 1937[16] restored the Commission's use of the ignorant man standard:

> The fact that a false statement may be obviously false to those who are trained and experienced does not change its character, nor take away its power to deceive others less experienced. There is no duty resting upon a citizen to suspect the honesty of those with whom he transacts business. Laws are made to protect the trusting as well as the suspicious. The best element of business has long since decided that honesty should govern competitive enterprises, and that the rule of *caveat emptor* should not be relied upon to reward fraud and deception.

Though Black mentioned the name of neither standard, his words suggest he was rejecting the reasonable man standard rather than proposing merely to adjust it. It was his words, above all, which led to the concept of an "ignorant man standard" for the FTC in place of what went before.

Just how *Standard Education* was supported by precedent is a curious question. Justice Black's opinion cited none. It affirmed that the sales method not merely had deceptive capacity but clearly deceived many persons,[17] and it also stated that the deception was committed knowingly and deliberately.[18] This suggests the Supreme Court was invoking the common law notion that the reasonable man standard should not apply in case of deliberate deception. Something left unclarified, however, is what significance such a ruling should have for an agency such as FTC which routinely did not make findings of deliberate deception. Deliberate intent to deceive undoubtedly occurs in many cases where no one can prove it. The whole advantage of FTC procedure, in comparison with what went before, was that it could rule sellers' messages out of the marketplace *without* bothering with the traditional requirement of having to prove intent. What was the advantage, then, of obtaining the right to use the ignorant man standard only in conjunction with proven intent to deceive?

The result, strangely, was that the FTC, on the basis of *Standard Education,* began applying the ignorant man standard liberally without regard for determining intent, and in some cases without regard for the fact that intent to deceive was almost surely absent. The appeals courts, also via *Standard Education,* approved this procedure. The trend was thoroughly questionable but was pursued decisively, particularly by the Second Circuit Court of Appeals, the one which *Standard Education* had reversed. In *General Motors* v. *FTC,*[19] involving a "6% time payment plan" which actually charged 11½% interest, the Second Circuit's Judge Augustus Hand concluded:

> It may be there was no intention to mislead and that only the careless or the incompetent could be misled. But if the Commission, having discretion to deal with these matters, thinks it best to insist upon a form of advertising clear

enough so that, in the words of the prophet Isaiah, "wayfaring men, though fools, shall not err therein," it is not for the courts to revise their judgment.

The influence of the *Standard Education* reversal was unmistakable on the one Hand—and on the other Hand as well. When Judge Learned Hand considered an appeal to the Second Circuit of the Commission's finding of deception in an admittedly untrue claim that "one Moretrench wellpoint is as good as any five others," he said:

> It is extremely hard to believe that any buyers of such machinery could be misled by anything which was patently no more than the exuberant enthusiasm of a satisfied customer, but in such matters we understand that we are to insist upon the most literal truthfulness. *Federal Trade Commission* v. *Standard Education Society*. . . .[20]

It was clear that the Second Circuit's Hands were tied. Substitution of the ignorant man standard for the reasonable man standard proceeded in additional Second Circuit cases,[21] and in others as well.[22] Under these liberal interpretations the FTC appeared during most of the 1940's to be knocking down right and left every advertising claim it thought had the slightest chance of deceiving even the most ignorant person. There was a good bit of unchecked exuberance in this spree,[23] reaching an extreme when Clairol was forbidden to say that its dye will "color hair permanently."[24] The FTC thought the public would take this as a claim that all the hair a person grows for the rest of her life will emerge in the Clairol color. That expectation was based on the testimony of a single witness who said she thought somebody might think that—although she added that *she* wouldn't.

On Clairol's appeal the Second Circuit said it couldn't imagine *anybody* believing the claim, but in accordance with *Standard Education* it said it had to support the FTC.[25] No hint was offered that the Clairol claim was used with intent to deceive, and no acknowledgment was made by the Second Circuit that *Standard Education* might have been intended by the Supreme Court to apply only where such intent was evident. We may speculate that if the Olde Frothingslosh matter had been appealed to the Second Circuit in the same year as the Clairol case, 1944, the purchaser might have recovered damages because the beer's foam wasn't on the bottom!

RETURN TO THE REASONABLE MAN STANDARD

We have now seen the development of a strong emphasis on the ignorant man standard. The next task is to describe how this emphasis came to be diluted, a matter which involved additional curious events. One of the arbitrary facts of life in U.S. law is that the various Circuit Courts of Appeal are sometimes inconsistent in their rulings. They need not take each other's decisions into account, so a case may be decided differently in one than in another. The Second Circuit was the one reversed by *Standard Education,* and we have seen that this court in subsequent cases applied the ignorant man standard assiduously. This included the prohibition of puffery in *Moretrench,* even though puffery had traditionally been called nondeceptive. With its long-standing immunity, puffery might have been expected to resist the courts even if nothing else did, but under the ignorant man standard the Second Circuit moved to eliminate this kind of falsity along with everything else.

But the time came, in 1946, when a puffery case was appealed to the Seventh Circuit rather than the Second, and the difference was significant. *Carlay*[26] involved a claim that Ayds candy mints make weight-reducing easy, which FTC said was false. On appeal the Seventh Circuit,[27] which had tended earlier to object to the ignorant man standard,[28] said the claim of "easy" was "mere puffing or dealer's talk upon which no charge of misrepresentation can be based." The court cited previous non-FTC cases which had allowed puffery, and completely ignored the cases stemming from Justice Black and the Second Circuit, which would have supported the FTC's outlawing of "easy."

As a result the FTC had a contradiction on its hands. The Second Circuit told it to protect the ignorant man; the Seventh Circuit told it to permit puffery which could deceive the ignorant man. The contradiction might have been resolved by the Supreme Court, but was never considered there. The FTC's resolution was to allow puffery thereafter, which tended to dilute the ignorant man standard.

An example of the dilution occurred in *Bristol-Myers,*[29] in which the Commission issued a complaint against the "Smile of Beauty" phrase used by Ipana tooth paste. Apparently it felt the line amounted to a claim that Ipana would straighten out people's crooked teeth.[30] The complaint was issued in 1942, about the same time as the Clairol *(Gelb)* case and prior to *Carlay* which legitimized puffery. But the final decision was made in 1949, post-*Carlay,* and produced a change of mind in which the Commission decided that "the reference to beautification of the smile was mere puffery, unlikely, because of its generality and widely variant meanings, to deceive anyone factually."

The trend away from the extreme ignorant man standard had begun, but only slightly. Cases followed in which the FTC retained a strong protective stance on behalf of ignorant consumers.[31] But in 1963 the FTC finally commented that the standard could be carried too far. *Heinz W. Kirchner*[32] was a case about an inflatable device to help a person stay afloat and learn to swim. Called Swim-Ezy, it was worn under the swimming suit and was advertised as being invisible. It was not invisible, but the FTC found it to be "inconspicuous," and ruled that that was all the claim of invisibility would mean to the public:

> The possibility that some persons might believe Swim-Ezy is, not merely inconspicuous, but wholly invisible or bodiless, seems to us too far-fetched to warrant intervention.

But what about the few persons who would accept this far-fetched belief? The Commission made clear it no longer intended to protect such ignorant persons:

> True . . . the Commission's responsibility is to prevent deception of the gullible and credulous, as well as the cautious and knowledgeable. . . . This princi-

ple loses its validity, however, if it is applied uncritically or pushed to an absurd extreme. An advertiser cannot be charged with liability in respect of every conceivable misconception, however outlandish, to which his representations might be subject among the foolish or feeble-minded. . . . A representation does not become "false and deceptive" merely because it will be unreasonably misunderstood by an insignificant and unrepresentative segment of the class of persons to whom the representation is addressed.

That is the position the FTC has followed since. It holds no longer to the strict ignorant man standard by which it would protect everyone from everything which may deceive them.[33] It would rule out consideration, for example, of the Olde Frothingslosh claim which apparently fooled only one stray individual. Perhaps we may call the new stance a modified ignorant man standard which protects only those cases of foolishness which are committed by significant numbers of people.

Some observers may protest that any behaviors which are customary for a substantial portion of the population shouldn't be called "ignorant." They might rather call the new stance a modified reasonable man standard in which what is reasonable has been equated more closely than before with what is average or typical. Whatever the name, however, the FTC's present position appears to remain closer to the spirit and practice of the strict ignorant man standard of the 1940's than to the reasonable man standard of tradition.[34]

Notes

1. "Ignorant man standard" is my own term, which I feel is correctly blunt. The terms "credulous man standard" and "lowest standard of intelligence," which lack semantic punch, have been used elsewhere.
2. FTC Act, #5(b), 15 *U. S. C.* #45(b).
3. *Restatement of Torts (Second),* Section 283 (1965). Section 283A states that a child must act as would a reasonable person of like age, intelligence, and experience under like circumstances.
4. Vaughan v. Menlove, 3 Bing N.C. 468, 132 Eng. Rep. 490 (1837). For other cases and references see Reporter's Notes to Section 283 in *Restatement of Torts (Second) Appendix.*
5. The terminology "contributory negligence" is not always used, but the idea of denying recovery for unreasonable reliance on misrepresentations is based on that concept; William L. Prosser, *Torts,* 4th ed., p. 717 (1971).
6. Prosser, *ibid.,* p. 716.
7. FTC v. Universal Battery, 2 FTC 95 (1919).
8. See also FTC v. A. A. Berry, 2 FTC 427 (1920); FTC v. Alben-Harley, 4 FTC 31 (1921); FTC v. Williams Soap, 6 FTC 107 (1923); Alfred Peats, 8 FTC 366 (1925).
9. #283, *Restatement of Torts (Second),* comment c.
10. *John C. Winston,* 8 FTC 177 (1924).
11. John C. Winston v. FTC, 3 F.2d 961 (3rd Cir., 1925).
12. *Nugrape,* 9 FTC 20 (1925); *Ostermoor,* 10 FTC 45 (1926), but set aside, Ostermoor v. FTC, 16 F.2d 962 (2d Cir., 1927); *William F. Schied,* 10 FTC 85 (1926), *Good Grape,* 10 FTC 99 (1926); *Hobart Bradstreet,* 11 FTC 174 (1927);

Frank P. Snyder, 11 FTC 390 (1927); *Dr. Eagan,* 11 FTC 436 (1927); *Berkey &
Gay Furniture,* 12 FTC 227 (1928), but set aside, Berkey & Gay Furniture v.
FTC, 42 F.2d 427 (6th Cir., 1930); *Northam-Warren,* 15 FTC 389 (1931), but
set aside, *Northam-Warren* v. *FTC,* 59 F.2d 196 (2d Cir., 1932); *Fairyfoot,* 20
FTC 40 (1934), affirmed in Fairyfoot v. FTC, 80 F.2d 684 (7th Cir., 1935).

13. *Standard Education Society,* 16 FTC 1 (1931).
14. FTC v. Standard Education Society, 86 F.2d. 692 (2d Cir., 1936).
15. *Ibid.*
16. 302 U.S. 112, 58 S.C. 113 (1937).
17. *Ibid,* p. 117.
18. "It was clearly the practice of respondents through their agents, in accor-
    dance with a well matured plan, to mislead customers . . ." *Ibid.,* p. 116.
19. 114 F.2d 33 (2d Cir., 1940).
20. Moretrench v. FTC, 127 F.2d 792 (2d Cir., 1942). Turning to another
    literally untrue Moretrench claim, that its product had an advantage to which
    "contractors all over the world testify," Hand stated, "It is again hard to im-
    agine how anyone reading it could have understood it as more than puffing;
    yet for the reasons we have just given, if the Commission saw fit to take notice
    of it, we may not interfere." This was the same judge who once had rejected
    similar claims on the grounds that "There are some kinds of talk which no
    man takes seriously, and if he does he suffers from his credulity. . . . Neither
    party usually believes what the seller says about his opinions, and each knows
    it. Such statements, like the claims of campaign managers before election, are
    rather designed to allay the suspicion which would attend their absence than
    to be understood as having any relationship to objective truth." Vulcan
    Metals v. Simmons, 248 F. 853 (2d Cir., 1918).
21. Charles of the Ritz v. FTC, 143 F.2d 676 (2d Cir., 1944); Gelb v. FTC, 144
    F.2d 580 (2d Cir., 1944).
22. D.D.D. v. FTC, 125 F.2d 679 (7th Cir., 1942); Aronberg v. FTC, 132 F.2d
    165, (7th Cir., 1942); Gulf Oil v. FTC, 150 F.2d 106 (5th Cir., 1945); Parker
    Pen v. FTC, 159 F.2d 509 (7th Cir., 1946). In the latter case the FTC's role
    was said to be to "protect the casual, one might say the negligent, reader, as
    well as the vigilant and more intelligent. . . ." A much-used quote, cited in
    Aronberg and *Gulf Oil,* above, and in *Gelb, op. cit.,* was from Florence v. Dowd,
    178 F. 73 (2d Cir., 1910): "The law is not made for the protection of experts,
    but for the public—that vast multitude which includes the ignorant, the un-
    thinking, and the credulous, who, in making purchases, do not stop to
    analyze, but are governed by appearances and general impressions." This
    was a pre-FTC case with evidence of deliberate deception.
23. *Charles of the Ritz, op. cit.*
24. *Gelb,* 33 FTC 1450 (1941).
25. Gelb v. FTC, op. cit. "There is no dispute that it imparts a permanent col-
    oration to the hair to which it is applied, but the commission found that it has
    'no effect upon new hair,' and hence concluded that the representation as to
    permanence was misleading. It seems scarcely possible that any user of the
    preparation could be so credulous as to suppose that hair not yet grown out
    would be colored by an application of the preparation to the head. But the
    commission has construed the advertisement as so representing it. . . . Since
    the Act is for the protection of the trusting as well as the suspicious, as stated in
    Federal Trade Commission v. Standard Education Society . . . we think the
    order must be sustained on this point."
26. 39 FTC 357 (1944).
27. Carlay v. FTC 153 F.2d 493 (1946).

28. Allen B. Wrisley v. FTC, 113 F.2d 437 (7th Cir., 1940); also later in Buchsbaum v. FTC, 160 F.2d 121 (7th Cir., 1947).
29. 46 FTC 162 (1949).
30. "The beauty of human teeth depends primarily upon their conformation, color, arrangement in the mouth and other natural physical features, and teeth which do not possess these natural qualities will not be rendered beautiful by the use of Ipana tooth paste." *Ibid.*
31. Lorillard v. FTC, 186 F.2d 52 (4th Cir., 1950); Goodman v. FTC, 244 F.2d 584 (9th Cir., 1957); FTC v. Sewell, 353 U.S. 969 (1957); Exposition Press v. FTC, 295 F.2d 869 (2d Cir., 1961); Colgate v. FTC, 310 F.2d 89 (1st Cir., 1962): Giant Food v. FTC, 322 F.2d 977 (D.C. Cir., 1963).
32. 63 FTC 1282 (1963).
33. In *Papercraft*, 63 FTC 1965, 1997 (1963), Commissioner MacIntyre protested that the retreat from the extreme ignorant man position was unfortunate. The majority opinion had withdrawn from protecting the "foolish or feeble-minded," and MacIntyre dissented: "Should this observation be construed as a retreat from our long-held position that the public as a whole is entitled to protection, including even 'the ignorant, the unthinking, and the credulous,' then the result may well be confusion."
34. "It might be said that the test of consumer competence generally employed by the Commission appears to approximate the least sophisticated level of understanding possessed by any substantial portion of the class of persons to whom the advertisement is addressed." Personal correspondence to Peter B. Turk from Gale T. Miller, law clerk, Bureau of Consumer Protection, Federal Trade Commission, December 6 (1971). The "class of persons" assumed in the present article is that of adults. Special consideration for representations made to children (see footnote 3) was recognized in FTC v. Keppel, 291 U.S. 304, 54 S.C. 423 (1934). As for other groups, Miller wrote, "It is the position of the staff that advertising geared towards other special audiences, such as the ghetto dweller, the elderly, and the handicapped, might also be subjected to a more rigorous test than is applied to advertisements addressed to the public at large."

THE DEPENDENCE EFFECT

John Kenneth Galbraith

The theory of consumer demand, as it is now widely accepted, is based on two broad propositions, neither of them quite explicit but both extremely important for the present value system of economists. The first is that the urgency of wants does not diminish appreciably as more of them are satisfied or, to put the matter more precisely, to the extent that this happens it is not demonstrable and not a matter of any interest to economists or for economic policy. When man has satisfied his physical needs, then psychologically grounded desires take over. These can never be satisfied or, in any case, no progress can be proved. The concept of satiation has very little standing in economics. It is neither useful nor scientific to speculate on the comparative cravings of the stomach and the mind.

The second proposition is that wants originate in the personality of the consumer or in any case, that they are given data for the economist. The latter's task is merely to seek their satisfaction. He has no need to inquire how these wants are formed. His function is sufficiently fulfilled by maximizing the goods that supply the wants. . . .

The notion that wants do not become less urgent the more amply the individual is supplied is broadly repugnant to common sense. It is something to be believed only by those who wish to believe. Yet the conventional wisdom must be tackled on its own terrain. Intertemporal comparisons of an individual's state of mind do rest on doubtful grounds. Who can say for sure that the deprivation which afflicts him with hunger is more painful than the deprivation which afflicts him with envy of his neighbor's new car? In the time that has passed since he was poor his soul may have become subject to a new and deeper searing. And where a society is concerned, comparisons between marginal satisfactions when it is poor and those when it is affluent will involve not only the same individual at different times but different individuals at different times. The scholar who wishes to believe that with increasing affluence there is no reduction in the urgency of desires and goods is not without points for debate. However plausible the case against him, it cannot be proved. In the defence of the conventional wisdom this amounts almost to invulnerability.

However, there is a flaw in the case. If the individual's wants are to be urgent they must be original with himself. They cannot be urgent if they must be contrived for him. And above all they must not be contrived by the process of production by which they are satisfied. For this means that the whole case for the urgency of production, based on the urgency of wants, falls to the ground. One cannot defend production as satisfying wants if that production creates the wants.

Were it so that a man on arising each morning was assailed by demons which instilled in him a passion sometimes for silk shirts, sometimes for kitchenware, sometimes for chamber-pots, and sometimes for orange squash, there would be every reason to applaud the effort to find the goods, however odd, that quenched this flame. But should it be that his passion was the result of his first having cultivated the demons, and should it also be that his effort to allay it stirred the demons to ever greater and greater effort, there would be question as to how rational was his solution. Unless restrained by conventional attitudes, he might wonder if the solution lay with more goods or fewer demons.

So it is that if production creates the wants it seeks to satisfy, or if the wants emerge *pari passu* with the production, then the urgency of the wants can no longer be used to defend the urgency of the production. Production only fills a void that it has itself created. . . .

The even more direct link between production and wants is provided by the institutions of modern advertising and salesmanship. These cannot be reconciled with the notion of independently determined desires, for their central function is to create desires—to bring into being wants that previously did not exist.[1] This is accomplished by the producer of the goods or at his behest. A broad empirical relationship exists between what is spent on production of consumers' goods and what is spent in synthesizing the desires for that production. A new consumer product must be introduced with a suitable advertising campaign to arouse an interest in it. The path for an expansion of output must be paved by a suitable expansion in the advertising budget. Outlays for the manufacturing of a product are not more important in the strategy of modern business enterprise than outlays for the manufacturing of demand for the product. None of this is novel. All would be regarded as elementary by the most retarded student in the nation's most primitive school of business administration. The cost of this want formation is formidable. In 1956 total advertising expenditure— though, as noted, not all of it may be assigned to the synthesis of wants—amounted to about ten thousand million dollars. For some years it had been increasing at a rate in excess of a thousand million dollars a year. Obviously, such outlays must be integrated with the theory of consumer demand. They are too big to be ignored.

But such integration means recognizing that wants are dependent on production. It accords to the producer the function both of making the goods and of making the desires for them. It recognizes that production, not only passively through emulation, but actively through advertising and related activities, creates the wants it seeks to satisfy.

The businessman and the lay reader will be puzzled over the emphasis which I give to a seemingly obvious point. The point is indeed obvious. But it is one which, to a singular degree, economists have resisted. They have sensed, as the layman does not, the damage to established ideas which lurks in these relationships. As a result, incredibly, they have closed their eyes (and ears) to the most obtrusive of all economic phenomena, namely modern want creation.

This is not to say that the evidence affirming the dependence of wants on advertising has been entirely ignored. It is one reason why advertising has so long been regarded with such uneasiness by economists. Here is something which cannot be accommodated easily to existing theory. More pervious scholars have speculated on the urgency of desires which are so obviously the fruit of such expensively contrived campaigns for popular attention. Is a new breakfast cereal or detergent so much wanted if so much must be spent to compel in the consumer the sense of want? But there has been little tendency to go on to examine the implications of this for the theory of consumer demand and even less for the importance of production and productive efficiency. These have remained sacrosanct. More often the uneasiness has been manifested in a general disapproval of advertising and advertising men, leading to the occasional suggestion that they shouldn't exist. Such suggestions have usually been ill received.

And so the notion of independently determined wants still survives. In the face of all the forces of modern salesmanship it still rules, almost undefiled, in the textbooks. And it still remains the economist's mission—and on few matters is the pedagogy so firm—to seek unquestioningly the means for filling these wants. This being so, production remains of prime urgency. We have here, perhaps, the ultimate triumph of the conventional wisdom in its resistance to the evidence of the eyes. To equal it one must imagine a humanitarian who was long ago persuaded of the grievous shortage of hospital facilities in the town. He continues to importune the passers-by for money for more beds and refuses to notice that the town doctor is deftly knocking over pedestrians with his car to keep up the occupancy.

And in unravelling the complex we should always be careful not to overlook the obvious. The fact that wants can be synthesized by advertising, catalysed by salesmanship, and shaped by the discreet manipulations of the persuaders shows that they are not very urgent. A man who is hungry need never be told of his need for food. If he is inspired by his appetite, he is immune to the influence of Messrs. Batten, Barton, Durstine and Osborn. The latter are effective only with those who are so far removed from physical want that they do not already know what they want. In this state alone men are open to persuasion.

The general conclusion of these pages is of such importance for this essay that it had perhaps best be put with some formality. As a society becomes increasingly affluent, wants are increasingly created by the process by which they are satisfied. This may operate passively. Increases in consumption, the counterpart of increases in production, act by suggestion or emulation to create wants. Or producers may proceed actively to create wants through advertising and salesmanship. Wants thus come to depend on output. In technical terms it can no longer be assumed that welfare is greater at an all-round higher level of production than at a lower one. It may be the same. The higher level of production has, merely, a higher level of want creation necessitating a higher level of want satisfaction. There will be frequent occasion to refer to the way wants depend on the process by which they are satisfied. It will be convenient to call it the Dependence Effect. . . .

The final problem of the productive society is what it produces. This manifests itself in an implacable tendency to provide an opulent supply of some things and a niggardly yield of others. This disparity carries to the point where it is a cause of social discomfort and social unhealth. The line which divides our area of wealth from our area of poverty is roughly that which divides privately produced and marketed goods and services from publicly rendered services. Our wealth in the first is not only in startling contrast with the meagreness of the latter, but our wealth in privately produced goods is, to a marked degree, the cause of crisis in the supply of public services. For we have failed to see the importance, indeed the urgent need, of maintaining a balance between the two.

This disparity between our flow of private and public goods and services is no matter of subjective judgment. On the contrary, it is the source of the most extensive comment which only stops short of the direct contrast being made here. In the years following World War II, the papers of any major city—those of New York were an excellent example—told daily of the shortages and shortcomings in the elementary municipal amd metropolitan services. The schools were old and overcrowded. The police force was under strength and underpaid. The parks and playgrounds were insufficient. Streets and empty lots were filthy, and the sanitation staff was underequipped and in need of men. Access to the city by those who work there was uncertain and painful and becoming more so. Internal transportation was overcrowded, unhealthful, and dirty. So was the air. Parking on the streets had to be prohibited, and there was no space elsewhere. These deficiencies were not in new and novel services but in old and established ones. Cities have long swept their streets, helped their people move around, educated them, kept order, and provided horse rails for vehicles which sought to pause. That their residents should have a non-toxic supply of air suggests no revolutionary dalliance with socialism.

The contrast was and remains evident not alone to those who read. The family which takes its mauve and cerise, air-conditioned, power-steered, and power-braked car out for a tour passes through cities that are badly paved, made hideous by litter, blighted buildings, billboards, and posts for wires that should long since have been put underground. They pass on into a countryside that has been rendered largely invisible by commercial art. (The goods which the latter advertise have an absolute priority in our value system. Such aesthetic considerations as a view of the countryside accordingly come second. On such matters we are consistent.) They picnic on exquisitely packaged food from a portable icebox by a polluted stream and go on to spend the night at a park which is a menace to public health and morals. Just before dozing off on an air-mattress, beneath a nylon tent, amid the stench of decaying refuse, they may reflect vaguely on the curious unevenness of their blessings. Is this, indeed, the American genius? . . .

The case for social balance has, so far, been put negatively. Failure to keep public services in minimal relation to private production and use of goods is a cause of social disorder or impairs economic performance. The matter may now be put affirmatively. By failing to exploit the opportunity to expand public production we are missing opportunities for enjoyment which otherwise we might have had. Presumably a community can be as well rewarded by buying better schools or better parks as by buying bigger cars. By concentrating on the latter rather than the former it is failing to maximize its satisfactions. As with schools in the community, so with public services over the country at large. It is scarcely sensible that we should satisfy our wants in private goods with reckless abundance, while in the case of public goods, on the evidence of the eye, we practice extreme self-denial. So, far from systematically exploiting the opportunities to derive use and pleasure from these services, we do not supply what would keep us out of trouble.

The conventional wisdom holds that the community, large or small, makes a decision as to how much it will devote to its public services. This decision is arrived at by democratic process. Subject to the imperfections and uncertainties of democracy, people decide how much of their private income and goods they will surrender in order to have public services of which they are in greater need. Thus there is a balance, however rough, in the enjoyments to be had from private goods and services and those rendered by public authority.

It will be obvious, however, that this view depends on the notion of independently determined consumer wants. In such a world one could with some reason defend the doctrine that the consumer, as a voter, makes an independent choice between public and private goods. But given the dependence effect—given that consumer wants are created by the process by which they are satisfied—the consumer makes no such choice. He is subject to the forces of advertising and emulation by which production creates its own demand. Advertising operates exclusively, and emulation mainly, on behalf of privately produced goods and services.[2] Since management and emulative effects operate on behalf of private production, public services will have an inherent tendency to lag behind. Car demand which is expensively synthesized will inevitably have a much larger claim on income than parks or public health or even roads where no such influence operates. The engines of mass communication, in their highest state of development, assail the eyes and ears of the community on behalf of more beer but not of more schools. Even in the conventional wisdom it will scarcely be contended that this leads to an equal choice between the two.

The competition is especially unequal for new products and services. Every corner of the public psyche is canvassed by some of the nation's most talented citizens to see if the desire for some merchantable product can be cultivated. No similar process operates on behalf of the nonmerchantable services of the state. Indeed, while we take the cultivation of new private wants for granted we would be measurably shocked to see it applied to public services. The scientist or engineer or advertising man who devotes himself to developing a new carburetor, cleanser, or depilatory for which the public recognizes no need and will feel none until an advertising campaign arouses it, is one of the valued members of our society. A politician or a public servant who dreams up a new public service is a wastrel. Few public offences are more reprehensible.

So much for the influences which operate on the decision between public and private production. The calm decision between public and private consumption pictured by the conventional wisdom is, in fact, a remarkable example of the error which arises from viewing social behaviour out of context. The inherent tendency will always be for public services to fall behind private production. We have here the first of the causes of social imbalance.

Notes

1. Advertising is not a simple phenomenon. It is also important in competitive strategy, and want creation is, ordinarily, a complementary result of efforts to shift the demand curve of the individual firm at the expense of others or (less importantly, I think) to change its shape by increasing the degree of product

differentiation. Some of the failure of economists to identify advertising with want creation may be attributed to the undue attention that its use in purely competitive strategy has attracted. It should be noted, however, that the competitive manipulation of consumer desire is only possible, at least on any appreciable scale, when such need is not strongly felt.

2. Emulation does operate between communities. A new school or a new highway in one community does exert pressure on others to remain abreast. However, as compared with the pervasive effects of emulation in extending the demand for privately produced consumer's goods there will be agreement, I think, that this intercommunity effect is probably small.

THE *NON SEQUITUR* OF
THE "DEPENDENCE EFFECT"

F. A. von Hayek

For well over a hundred years the critics of the free enterprise system have resorted to the argument that if production were only organized rationally, there would be no economic problem. Rather than face the problem which scarcity creates, socialist reformers have tended to deny that scarcity existed. Ever since the Saint-Simonians their contention has been that the problem of production has been solved and only the problem of distribution remains. However absurd this contention must appear to us with respect to the time when it was first advanced, it still has some persuasive power when repeated with reference to the present.

The latest form of this old contention is expounded in *The Affluent Society* by Professor J. K. Galbraith. He attempts to demonstrate that in our affluent society the important private needs are already satisfied and the urgent need is therefore no longer a further expansion of the output of commodities but an increase of those services which are supplied (and presumably can be supplied only) by government. Though this book has been extensively discussed since its publication in 1958, its central thesis still requires some further examination.

I believe the author would agree that his argument turns upon the "Dependence Effect" explained in Chapter XI of the book. The argument of this chapter starts from the assertion that a great part of the wants which are still unsatisfied in modern society are not wants which would be experienced spontaneously by the individual if left to himself, but are wants which are created by the process by which they are satisfied. It is then represented as self-evident that for this reason such wants cannot be urgent or important. This crucial conclusion appears to be a complete *non sequitur* and it would seem that with it the whole argument of the book collapses.

From *Southern Economic Journal*, April 1961. Reprinted by permission.

The first part of the argument is of course perfectly true: we would not desire any of the amenities of civilization—or even of the most primitive culture—if we did not live in a society in which others provide them. The innate wants are probably confined to food, shelter, and sex. All the rest we learn to desire because we see others enjoying various things. To say that a desire is not important because it is not innate is to say that the whole cultural achievement of man is not important.

This cultural origin of practically all the needs of civilized life must of course not be confused with the fact that there are some desires which aim, not as a satisfaction derived directly from the use of an object, but only from the status which its consumption is expected to confer. In a passage which Professor Galbraith quotes, Lord Keynes seems to treat the latter sort of Veblenesque conspicuous consumption as the only alternative ''to those needs which are absolute in the sense that we feel them whatever the situation of our fellow human beings may be.'' If the latter phrase is interpreted to exclude all the needs for goods which are felt only because these goods are known to be produced, these two Keynesian classes describe of course only extreme types of wants, but disregard the overwhelming majority of goods on which civilized life rests. Very few needs indeed are ''absolute'' in the sense that they are independent of social environment or of the example of others, and that their satisfaction is an indispensable condition for the preservation of the individual or of the species. Most needs which make us act are needs for things which only civilization teaches us to exist at all, and these things are wanted by us because they produce feelings or emotions which we would not know if it were not for our cultural inheritance. Are not in this sense probably all our esthetic feelings ''acquired tastes''?

How complete a *non sequitur* Professor Galbraith's conclusion represents is seen most clearly if we apply the argument to any product of the arts, be it music, painting, or literature. If the fact that people would not feel the need for something if it were not produced did prove that such products are of small value, all those highest products of human endeavor would be of small value. Professor Galbraith's argument could be easily employed, without any change of the essential terms, to demonstrate the worthlessness of literature or any other form of art. Surely an individual's want for literature is not original with himself in the sense that he would experience it if literature were not produced. Does this then mean that the production of literature cannot be defended as satisfying a want because it is only the production which provokes the demand? In this, as in the case of all cultural needs, it is unquestionably, in Professor Galbraith's words, ''the process of satisfying the wants that creates the wants.'' There have never been ''independently determined desires for'' literature before literature has been produced and books certainly do not serve the ''simple mode of enjoyment which requires no previous conditioning of the consumer.'' Clearly my taste for the novels of Jane Austen or Anthony Trollope or C. P. Snow is not ''original with myself.'' But is it not rather absurd to conclude from this that it is less important than, say, the need for education? Public education indeed seems to regard it as one of its tasks to instill a taste for literature in the young and even employs producers of literature for that purpose. Is this want creation by the producer reprehensible? Or does the fact that some of the pupils may possess a taste for poetry only because of the efforts of their teachers prove that since "it does not arise in spontaneous consumer need and the demand would not exist were it not contrived, its utility or urgency, ex contrivance, is zero?"

The appearance that the conclusions follow from the admitted facts is made possible by an obscurity of the wording of the argument with respect to which it is difficult to know whether the author is himself the victim of a confusion or whether he skillfully uses ambiguous terms to make the conclusion appear plausible. The obscurity concerns the implied assertion that the wants of the consumers are determined by the producers. Professor Galbraith avoids in this connection any terms as crude and definite as "determine." The expressions he employs, such as that wants are "dependent on" or the "fruits of" production, or that "production creates the wants" do, of course, suggest determination but avoid saying so in plain terms. After what has already been said it is of course obvious that the knowledge of what is being produced is one of the many factors on which it depends what people will want. It would scarcely be an exaggeration to say that contemporary man, in all fields where he has not yet formed firm habits, tends to find out what he wants by looking at what his neighbours do and at various displays of goods (physical or in catalogues or advertisements) and then choosing what he likes best.

In this sense the tastes of man, as is also true of his opinions and beliefs and indeed much of his personality, are shaped in a great measure by his cultural environment. But though in some contexts it would perhaps be legitimate to express this by a phrase like "production creates the wants," the circumstances mentioned would clearly not justify the contention that particular producers can deliberately determine the wants of particular consumers. The efforts of all producers will certainly be directed towards that end; but how far any individual producer will succeed will depend not only on what he does but also on what the others do and on a great many other influences operating upon the consumer. The joint but uncoordinated efforts of the producers merely create one element of the environment by which the wants of the consumers are shaped. It is because each individual producer thinks that the consumers can be persuaded to like his products that he endeavours to influence them. But though this effort is part of the influences which shape consumers' tastes, no producer can in any real sense "determine" them. This, however, is clearly implied in such statements as that wants are "both passively and deliberately the fruits of the process by which they are satisfied." If the producer could in fact deliberately determine what the consumers will want, Professor Galbraith's conclusions would have some validity. But though this is skillfully suggested, it is nowhere made credible, and could hardly be made credible because it is not true. Though the range of choice open to the consumers is the joint result of, among other things, the efforts of all producers who vie with each other in making their respective products appear more attractive than those of their competitors, every particular consumer still has the choice between all those different offers.

A fuller examination of this process would, of course, have to consider how, after the efforts of some producers have actually swayed some consumers, it becomes the example of the various consumers thus persuaded which will influence the remaining consumers. This can be mentioned here only to emphasize that even if each consumer were exposed to pressure of only one producer, the harmful effects which are apprehended from this would soon be offset by the much more powerful example of his fellows. It is of course fashionable to treat this influence of the example of others (or, what comes to the same things, the learning from the experience made by others) as if it amounted all to an attempt of keeping up with the Joneses and for that reason was to be regarded as detrimental. It seems to me that not only the importance of this factor is usually greatly exaggerated but also that it is not really relevant to Professor Galbraith's main thesis. But it might be worthwhile briefly to ask what, assuming that some expenditure were actually determined solely by a desire of keeping up with the Joneses, that would really prove? At least in Europe we used to be familiar with a type of persons who often denied themselves even enough food in order to maintain an appearance of respectability or gentility in dress and style of life. We may regard this as a misguided effort, but surely it would not prove that the income of such persons was larger than they knew how to use wisely. That the appearance of success, or wealth, may to some people seem more important than many other needs, does in no way prove that the needs they sacrifice to the former are unimportant. In the same way, even though people are often persuaded to spend unwisely, this surely is no evidence that they do not still have important unsatisfied needs.

Professor Galbraith's attempt to give an apparent scientific proof for the contention that the need for the production of more commodities has greatly decreased seems to me to have broken down completely. With it goes the claim to have produced a valid argument which justifies the use of coercion to make people employ their income for those purposes of which he approves. It is not to be denied that there is some originality in this latest version of the old socialist argument. For over a hundred years we have been exhorted to embrace socialism because it would give us more goods. Since it has so lamentably failed to achieve this where it has been tried, we are now urged to adopt it because more goods after all are not important. The aim is still progressively to increase the share of the resources whose use is determined by political authority and the coercion of any dissenting minority. It is not surprising, therefore, that Professor Galbraith's thesis has been most enthusiastically received by the intellectuals of the British Labour Party where his influence bids fair to displace that of the late Lord Keynes. It is more curious that in this country it is not recognized as an outright socialist argument and often seems to appeal to people on the opposite end of the political spectrum. But this is probably only another instance of the familiar fact that on these matters the extremes frequently meet.

FREEDOM AND PERSUASION

Stanley I. Benn

I

Some time in the fifties, everyone became conscious of the menace of the hidden persuaders. Whether as commercial advertisers or as political propagandists, they formed, it was said, an invisible power elite, corrupting taste and manipulating opinion for private gain or sectional power. We learnt with alarm that having the sense of choosing freely was no guarantee that one really had a free choice; choices could be rigged by skillful operators who could make us want what they or their clients wanted us to want.

This scandal of our age seems to have been exaggerated. It is now the fashion to take a more sober view of the claims of the persuasion industry and its supporting "motivational research." Propaganda and advertising, we are assured, can shape beliefs and attitudes only within limits; people resist suggestions that run counter to their basic personality characteristics. So a film intended to counter a prejudice may actually reinforce it. Though authoritarian personalities can be readily switched from fascism to communism, they make poor liberals. "Brain-washing" is effective only with alienated and anomic individuals—and its effects even on them are relatively short-lived once they leave the reinforcing environment.

All the same, although mass persuasive techniques are less successful in changing attitudes than the alarmists would have us suppose, they seem to be very effective in reinforcing already existing tendencies to change. Furthermore, all the research done so far has been on "campaign effects" i.e., on the kind of short-term effects which are typically the goals of publicity and advertising; little is known as yet of the long-term effects of mass persuasive influences. Besides, the reassurances that have been given amount only to saying that not much progress has been made so far. As yet, our minds cannot readily be made up for us unless we are initially indifferent (as, for instance, between one kind of soap and another, or, maybe, between one brand of authoritarianism and another); altering basic attitudes is very much more difficult. Propaganda may "boomerang"; human personality is not infinitely plastic; psychologists have much to learn about the formation of human attitudes, and propagandists about how to manipulate them. In much the same way one might have been assured at the end of the last century that fear of aerial warfare was fantastic—pioneers had barely succeeded in getting a heavier-than-air machine off the ground. For the fact remains that there are interested people who are spending a great deal to find out what makes a man believe and behave as he does, and who clearly live in hope that out of it will come more efficient ways of influenc-

From *The Australasian Journal of Philosophy*, vol. 45, December 1967. Reprinted by permission.

ing both. Discovering why primitive techniques have only limited effectiveness is the first step to more effective ones.

My intention here, however, is not to assess the claims of the persuasion industry, but rather to examine what the expressions of alarm that these claims evoke presuppose about freedom and the social interactions of aims and influences, and to gain from this an insight into certain liberal ways of thinking about politics and society. . . .

. . . The classic discussions of political obligation have all been concerned with what constitutes a good reason for requiring a man to put aside his own wishes or opinions and to act instead in accordance with someone else's. The problem presented by propagandists, advertisers and public relations experts is quite different. They aim not at overruling contrary intentions by threats of coercion but, by persuasion, to create a willing—if possible an enthusiastic—accord. They seek to avoid or dissolve conflict, not to overrule it. . . .

. . . But liberalism has never taken much notice of how men come to want what they do want—or rather, the traditional target for liberal critics like Milton, Jefferson, and Mill, has been censorship, the monopolistic control of the supply of ideas, not the techniques used to persuade people to adopt some ideas rather than others. Pinning their faith to human rationality, they believed that to drive out error truth needed no special privilege beyond the opportunity to be heard; the shoddy tricks of those who exploited credulity could not survive exposure to rational criticism. This faith never faced the challenge that there might be non-rational techniques for persuading a person to believe certain things or to adopt certain desired attitudes—that is, techniques for inducing him to want to do or be something that someone else had decided upon, even though arguments and evidence to the contrary remained fully accessible. Would the classical liberals have said that a person who was able to do what he wanted without interference, but whose preferences had been shaped by such techniques, was free because he was "left to do or be what he wanted to do or be, without interference by other persons"?

The classical liberals might have objected that the techniques of persuasion that modern liberals fear do in fact "interfere"—not, certainly, with a man's doing what he wants to do, but with his freely *deciding* what he wants to do. But making this move commits the liberal to some way of distinguishing forms of persuasion that interfere from those that do not. For in defining social and political freedom, the liberal relies on a conception of a free market in ideas, a conception which actually presupposes that men will attempt to influence one another's beliefs. Accordingly, he must allow that there are some ways at least of getting people to change their minds that are not in his sense interferences. . . .

II

The liberal emphasis on rationality may suggest that the distinction sought for, between persuasion that is consistent with autonomy and persuasion that is not, would be the distinction between rational and non-rational persuasion. This distinction can indeed be made, and, as I hope to show, can be useful, but it will not take us the whole way we have to go. Persuasion is rational in so far as the persuasiveness lies in the substance of the arguments rather than in the manner of presentation, the authority of the persuader, or some other special relationship by virtue of which one party is particularly susceptible to suggestions from the other. Rational persuasion, in short, is impersonal, in the sense that it is the argument not the person that persuades—the same argument advanced by anyone else would be as effective. Of course, not any kind of reason will do. To give as a reason the injury you will do to me if I reject your suggestions is to threaten me, not to use rational persuasion. However, some neutral or disinterested person with no control over your behaviour would be using rational persuasion if *he* warned me of what you would do to me if I disobeyed you. The distinctive feature of rational persuasion is that it invites and responds to criticism. The would-be persuader is committed to changing his opinion too if the persuadee gives sufficient reasons for rejecting it. Rational persuasion is therefore essentially a dialogue between equals. Although the man who warns me of the probable consequences of what I am doing may be trying to stop me doing it, and perhaps succeeds, he is not acting inconsistently with my autonomy; for though I might have preferred to remain ignorant of the inconvenient facts—or even to have gone on disregarding what I already really knew—still, he has not made my mind up for me, but, on the contrary, has made it more possible for me to make a rational decision for myself. Indeed, by offering reasons why I should make one decision rather than another, so far from abusing my rational autonomy he recognizes and respects it. It was because the liberal classics took this as the paradigm of persuasion that they never felt the necessity for defining the relation between persuasion and power.

I said above that persuasion is rational *in so far as* it seeks to convince by giving reasons, and consequently in so far as it is impersonal. This is not to say that we can distinguish sharply between the case of pure rational persuasion and others. Most cases combine rational and nonrational elements; any argument, however good, can be spoilt by bad presentation, and its effect heightened by fitting eloquence. Still, we can envisage a case of successful persuasion in which the persuader is so distasteful to the persuadee, his presentation so graceless and his whole demeanour so repellent, that almost anyone else could have done it better. Unless the persuadee is over-compensating for his personal dislike, we shall have to attribute the persuader's success entirely to the rational merits of his argument.

The possibility of distinguishing rational and non-rational persuasion does not imply, however, that an instance of persuasion is an invasion of personal freedom or autonomy precisely to the extent that it involves non-rational elements, like appeals to emotion or prejudice. The pretty girl in the tooth paste advertisement may be captivating, but do her charms really make slaves of us? While, therefore, we can confidently say that rational persuasion is consistent with freedom, we still have to distinguish among different forms of non-rational persuasion those that are not.

A is not unfree merely because his conduct is influenced (i.e., affected) by someone else's actions or communications of some kind other than rational arguments. Suppose, for instance, that he confides in B a plan from which he has great hopes; B, while offering no criticism, treats it scornfully; A, discouraged, gives up. Should we say that A's freedom had been infringed? Has B interfered with A, because B's non-rational influence upon A has put him off? Or should we not rather say that A must have been unusually weak-minded to be put off so easily?

This example suggests that whether a man is really master of himself or whether he is being interfered with, does not depend solely on the kind of influence another man exerts, nor on its actual effects; it depends *also* on whether it would be reasonable to expect him, in the given conditions, to withstand influence of that kind.

I suggested earlier that to say that a man was not free to do what he would certainly be punished for doing is not to say that no one, faced with the same consequence, has ever chosen to do such a thing, but rather that the choice is not one we could reasonably expect a man to make. Similarly a temptation or a provocation is not irresistable merely because someone has in fact failed to resist it; but neither is the fact that someone has resisted it proof that it is not irresistible. A temptation is said to be irresistible only if a man *could not reasonably be expected* to resist it, even though others might actually have resisted it in the past.

These are instances of a class of judgements which cannot be satisfactorily elucidated without using some standard of "the normal man." Judgements about freedom, influence, power, and interference are, I believe, of the same class. What does it mean to say that a man does not withstand an influence? It is not simply that he falls in with what is proposed. For the idea of withstanding it suggests some inner source of strength, some kind of disposition, interest, or motive for not falling in with it. It is not merely that the influence fails in its intent, but that it fails on account of something about the patient, not simply on account of the ineptitude of the agent. Consider the following dialogue:

CUSTOMER: I want a cake of soap, please.
SHOPKEEPER: Which brand?
CUSTOMER: Which do you recommend?
SHOPKEEPER: *Pongo.* (Aside) It's no different from any of the others, and I make a quarter cent more profit per bar.
CUSTOMER: Very well, I'll take *Pongo.*

Clearly, he could have said no. But why should he have done so? To say that he failed to withstand the suggestion seems to presuppose, what is not the case in this example, that he had some contrary interest or disposition, that he knew, for instance, that he was allergic to *Pongo.* Even then, one would not say that the grocer's influence was irresistible. For any other customer in his place would have said: "No, not that one—I'm allergic to it."

Bribery raises similar issues. If A asks B for a service in return for a sum of money, there is no reason *prima facie* why B should be expected to refuse the offer; and if B accepts it, we should not say that he failed to withstand or resist it. If, however, he accepts, having an interest that could provide a counter-motive, or a duty, e.g., as a public official, not to do what A asks, one could properly say that he did not resist. Furthermore, if we wanted to plead irresistible temptation in his defence, we should have to argue that no one under the exceptional conditions in which B was placed (whatever they may have been) could *reasonably be expected* to resist. That a man has been provided with a counter-motive is not enough to make it impossible for him to do his duty, though it may sufficiently explain why he did not do it. In the absence of exceptional conditions, attempting to corrupt him does not deprive him of free choice. On the contrary, his freedom is an indispensable condition for his being held responsible should he give in to the temptation. Similarly one cannot plead by way of excuse that a man has been subject to non-rational persuasive influence, unless one can also maintain that no one, despite an interest counter to the suggestion, could reasonably have been expected not to fall in with it.

The problem for the liberal, then, is to establish tests by which to identify non-rational influences that a person could not reasonably be expected to resist, supposing that he has some interest in doing so. One such test is whether the patient can be aware of what is happening to him. For if one cannot know that an attempt is being made to manipulate one's preferences, and if one has no way of distinguishing a manipulated preference, one cannot be on one's guard against it. Subliminal suggestion would probably prove objectionable by this test (though there appear to be subconscious censors operating even here to inhibit out-of-character responses). An extension of the same principle would cover propaganda, supported and protected by censorship. For supposing the subject to have some initial disposition, presumed interest, or duty not to accept it, an apparently well-supported suggestion in the complete absence of any counter-evidence might fairly be called irresistible. Beyond these rather obvious criteria we should have to rely on the results of psychological research. If we want to discuss whether protection from mass persuasive techniques is necessary or even desirable, we must first have some idea of the kinds of influence that a person of normal firmness of purpose and with normal interests could reasonably be expected to withstand in a given situation. Moreover, there may be classes of persons, like children, who are peculiarly vulnerable to particular techniques, or to suggestions of particular kinds; principles of protection may very possibly have to use different norms for different purposes. Information like this is as important to the defenders of freedom as it is to the manipulators, and may well be among the fruits of psychologists' investigations into the effectiveness of advertising and propaganda techniques.

III

To what extent can such criteria for distinguishing forms of persuasion inconsistent with freedom suggest moral criteria for the use and control of persuasion and manipulative techniques? The liberal presupposition that every man has a right not to be interfered with unless he is doing something that itself interferes with the freedom or well-being of someone else, applies as much to the persuader as to the persuadee. Unless a form of persuasion itself interferes with the freedom or interests either of the persuadee or someone else, to interfere with it would be an invasion of the rights of the persuader. On the other hand, the persuadee can properly claim as a condition for *his* freedom, that he be protected from hidden manipulation aimed at political or economic exploitation. From these considerations we can elicit, in the first place, criteria for any advertising or propaganda that is designed to promote the interests of the persuaders. We can say, provisionally, that there is no ground for objecting to such influences if they do not infringe the freedom of the persuadee, and constitute no threat to the interests of anyone else. It is up to the persuadee to determine whether his own interests would be served or impaired by letting himself fall in with what is suggested to him. It is not consistent, in other words, with liberal presuppositions about human nature and its characteristic excellence that he should be protected from every kind of influence that might lead him to do things against his own interests. If men allow themselves to be exploited, through lack of reasonable caution or of the exercise of normal critical judgement, they have only themselves to blame. As rational and autonomous beings, they are responsible within reason for safeguarding their own interests—*caveat emptor* applies to ideas and tastes as well as to goods. There is a case, of course, for protection against misrepresentation of both ideas and goods. But this is not to protect the consumer against freely choosing what is damaging to his own interests; it is rather that in determining where his interest lies he shall not be deliberately and unfairly deceived by a lack of information he cannot remedy or by false information that he cannot reasonably be expected to check. Lying newspapers are at least as objectionable as false statements of the weight of soap powder in a King Size packet. Though there may be no objection to manufacturers attracting customers by putting small amounts of soap in large packets, the consumer who wants to make a reasoned choice between brands is entitled to know the weight of soap he is buying without the inconvenience of carrying his own scales or insisting on having the alternative packages weighed before he decides. Of far greater importance is his right to be told the truth in news reports, on which he has to base rational judgements on public affairs, and which he simply cannot confirm for himself. Of course, insisting that newspapers tell the truth is far more problematic and politically hazardous than insisting on the truth about soap powders. Since governments are interested parties there are no doubt good reasons for leaving it to the reader to check one against the other.

Applying the criteria to techniques which, designed to get under the consumer's guard, may be incompatible with his autonomy, is rather more complicated. A practice which simply exploits the consumer (or the voter) presents no theoretical difficulty; if it is both an infringement of the consumer's freedom and an attack on his interest, it is indefensible. But how firmly can the liberal turn down a plea that a manipulative technique is being used in the general interest, or in the interests of the individual himself?

Pace Mill, it is difficult to sustain unqualified the doctrine that "the sole end for which mankind are warranted, individually or collectively, in interfering with the liberty of action of any of their number is self-protection" and that "his own good . . . is not a sufficient warrant."[1] Mill's equivocation in the matter of the unsafe bridge[2] is evidence of his own uneasiness; and one can have legitimate doubts about his plea that poisons and dangerous drugs be freely available without medical prescription. What kind of an interest, however, would justify interference for a man's own good?

Consider a possible advertiser's argument that, by persuading a consumer to want G (which the consumer can afford and the manufacturer can supply), he makes it possible for the former to satisfy his wants; moreover, creating a want he can also satisfy, he is acting in the consumer's own interests by maximizing his satisfactions. (If this be a man of straw, this particular kind of straw can still be illuminating.)

The argument would be mistaken, in my view, firstly in identifying the consumer's wants with his interests. Tobacco manufacturers who by advertising create tobacco customers, may cultivate their customers' wants but are questionably serving their interests. And this is not because the experience might not be "really satisfying." For once the habit is formed, smoking undoubtedly satisfies a craving, and deprivation is so unpleasant that many smokers accept the risk of lung cancer rather than give it up. One has to recognize that people often want what is conspicuously bad for them, and that what satisfies their desires may not be in their interests. Suppose, however, the desire were for something reasonably harmless; what value would we attach to satisfying it, once it were seen as the deliberate creation of someone else? If the advertiser succeeds in producing a mass demand for a product that no one wanted before, is his product valuable and his activity worthwhile, simply because it now meets a demand? Or are we entitled to look critically at the sorts of things that men are encouraged to demand, and to decide that some demands may be unworthy of satisfaction?

Writers in the empirical, liberal tradition, and most notably, of course, writers in the utilitarian tradition, have been inclined to treat as a reason in favour of any performance or provision whatsoever that someone wanted it. Though this reason might be overridden in a given instance by other people's wishes, or by the expectation of harmful consequences, these would weigh as reasons against doing something that would still have been intrinsically worth doing simply as satisfying a desire. Moreover, if the thing were not done, there would be a presumption in favour of saying that the person desiring it had been deprived of a satisfaction, that the result had been to his disadvantage, and that he would have been better off had he got what he wanted. So *ceteris paribus* a world in which many desires were satisfied would seem to be a better world than one in which fewer were satisfied, whether because some remained unsatisfied or because people had fewer desires.

Though this view is persuasive when stated generally, I have difficulty in extending this presumption in favour of satisfying desires to desires demonstrably contrived by someone else, especially if contrived for his own purposes. That is not to say that no contrived desire would ever be worth satisfying; one might properly claim that some kind of experience for which one had induced a desire in someone else, for whatever purpose, was worth having, and that he would consequently be better off if his desire for it were satisfied. But this would be to recognize a distinction between experiences which were worth having, for which the corresponding desires would be worth satisfying, and those which were not. This is quite different from allowing a residual kind of worth in the satisfaction of any desire, simply as such and irrespective of its object.

It might be objected, as a general negative reason for satisfying desires, that a desire unsatisfied is a source of suffering. Certainly, if a drug addict had no hope of cure, what he suffered from his unsatisfied desire would be a strong reason, perhaps sufficient reason, for satisfying it. It is surely a mistake, however, to assimilate all desires to cravings; to be disappointed is not necessarily to suffer, or, at any rate, to suffer in the same sense in which deprived addicts suffer. Furthermore, there is something repugnant about saying that, in a case of deliberate torturing a saving factor in an otherwise totally deplorable situation is that the sadistic desires of the torturer have been satisfied. Malicious satisfaction makes a situation worse, not better.

The view I am challenging depends for its persuasiveness in part on a meaning shift in the word "satisfaction." I may get satisfaction from contemplating a picture or reading a novel, but this is not necessarily because a desire to look at a picture has been satisfied. On the other hand, if I desire X and get X my desire is satisfied but it may give me no satisfaction. I may discover that what I wanted was not worth having. And this may not be because I was misinformed about the nature of the thing; I may have got precisely what I desired and expected, yet still be no better off for having it. The quality of the life into which it enters may be no better for it—it may have no function in my life, and add nothing to me as a person. My wanting it may have been factitious, in the sense that the desire arose from no integral tendency in my nature, no search for a mode of expression, no recognizable need. I could have set my heart on almost anything else, or on nothing at all, and have been no worse off. Now, if my desires were simply the contrivance of persuaders, they might very well be like this. In that case one would be led to ask whether the mere fact of a desire could really be a reason for satisfying it or whether what gives value to the satisfaction of a desire is the quality of the life of which it forms a part and in which it has a function. Satisfying a desire would be valuable then if it sustained or made possible a valuable kind of life. To say this is to reject the argument that in creating the wants he can satisfy, the advertiser (or the manipulator of mass emotion in politics or religion) is necessarily acting in the interests of his public. What their interests are depends now on some objective assessment of what constitutes excellence in human beings, not on what they happen, for whatever reason, to want. If this is true, advertising that presents consumption as a self-justifying activity, that attributes value to things, rather than to what they do to and for a person, is essentially corrupting in that it promotes a misconception of the nature of man. Misunderstanding what we are, we are misled about the nature of the enterprize in which as men we are engaged.

This does not mean that we ought to repudiate the cautious liberal approach to protection "in one's own interests." For everything depends on what one takes to be the characteristic human excellences. The liberal concept of man, as sustained by Kant and Mill, places at the top of the list a man's capacity for making responsible choices among alternative ways of life, for striving no matter how mistakenly or unsuccessfully to make of himself something worthy of his own respect. This is a creative enterprise calling for experiment, intelligent self-appraisal, and criticism. Consequently, it cannot be fostered by denying men the opportunity to make false starts and to learn from experience. Men have an overriding interest in liberty itself.

This account of human interests suggests an important qualification to my earlier provisional statement, that there was no ground for objecting to persuasion that did not infringe the freedom of the persuadee, and constituted no threat to the interests of anyone else, since it was for him to determine whether his own interests would be served or impaired by falling in with it. For we can now suggest a case for protecting a man from any influence, irresistible or not, which if successful would lead to a condition like drug addiction in which his ability to make further rational choices would be permanently and irremediably impaired. For though the mode of persuasion might not itself be an interference, nevertheless, if successful, it would impair freedom, understood as rational self-mastery.

I do not expect everyone to agree on the application of this criterion, on whether, for instance, it would rule out advertising by cigarette manufacturers, or advertising of the type mentioned earlier, which corrupts by promoting the worship of consumption for its own sake. It is arguable, on the one hand, that advertisements of this latter kind are not, taken severally, irresistible, nor would responding to them irremediably impair the individual's capacity for discovering for himself what kinds of things are valuable and why. Indeed, the very opposite might be the case. On the other hand, the cumulative influence of an environment filled with a variety of advertisements all with the same underlying message hidden by its very ubiquity may be more closely analogous to influences like subliminal suggestions that one cannot directly perceive than to a straightforward appeal to emotions.

The same basic principles on which I have relied for criteria justifying protection from persuasion also provide criteria for the use of irresistible manipulative techniques. Just as the sole ground for protecting a man from an influence which is not irresistible is that he should not risk impairing his capacity for choosing rationally and for making critical appraisals of his own experience and achievements, so the justification for manipulation must be that he is suffering from some impediment or handicap, which inhibits such activities, and which he could not remedy by his own efforts. This would justify, for instance, the use in psychotherapy of hypnosis and "truth-drugs"; for the aim of the treatment is not to dominate nor to mould the patient, but to restore his capacity for making his own rational appraisals of his environment, and for deciding for himself what would be his appropriate adjustment to it. Here again one has to rely heavily on conceptions of normality; for to be handicapped is to lack capacities that a man normally enjoys.

I have said that these criteria are not easy to apply, and there would be plenty of argument about any particular application. Nevertheless since we are bound to make decisions of this kind, it is well that we should be conscious of what we are about in making them.

Notes

1. John Stuart Mill, *On Liberty,* Everyman Edition (New York: E. B. Dutton Company, 1910), pp. 72–73.
2. *Ibid.,* pp. 151–152.

FEDERAL TRADE COMMISSION v. COLGATE-PALMOLIVE CO. ET AL.

The basic question before us is whether it is a deceptive trade practice, prohibited by § 5 of the Federal Trade Commission Act, to represent falsely that a televised test, experiment, or demonstration provides a viewer with visual proof of a product claim, regardless of whether the product claim is itself true.

The case arises out of an attempt by respondent Colgate-Palmolive Company to prove to the television public that its shaving cream, "Rapid Shave," outshaves them all. Respondent Ted Bates & Company, Inc., an advertising agency, prepared for Colgate three one-minute commercials designed to show that Rapid Shave could soften even the toughness of sandpaper. Each of the commercials contained the same "sandpaper test." The announcer informed the audience that, "To prove RAPID SHAVE'S super-moisturizing power, we put it right from the can onto this tough, dry sandpaper. It was apply . . . soak . . . and off in a stroke." While the announcer was speaking, Rapid Shave was applied to a substance that appeared to be sandpaper, and immediately thereafter a razor was shown shaving the substance clean.

The Federal Trade Commission issued a complaint against respondents Colgate and Bates charging that the commercials were false and deceptive. The evidence before the hearing examiner disclosed that sandpaper of the type depicted in the commercials could not be shaved immediately following the application of Rapid Shave, but required a substantial soaking period of approximately 80 minutes. The evidence also showed that the substance resembling sandpaper was in fact a simulated prop, or "mock-

U.S. Reports 380 U.S. 374, 85 S. Ct. 1035, 13 L Ed. 2nd 904. Majority opinion by Chief Justice Earl Warren, U.S. Supreme Court.

up,'' made of plexiglass to which sand had been applied. However, the examiner found that Rapid Shave could shave sandpaper, even though not in the short time represented by the commercials, and that if real sandpaper had been used in the commercials the inadequacies of television transmission would have made it appear to viewers to be nothing more than plain, colored paper. The examiner dismissed the complaint because neither misrepresentation—concerning the actual moistening time or the identity of the shaved substance—was in his opinion a material one that would mislead the public.

The Commission, in an opinion dated December 29, 1961, reversed the hearing examiner. It found that since Rapid Shave could not shave sandpaper within the time depicted in the commercials, respondents had misrepresented the product's moisturizing power. Moreover, the Commission found that the undisclosed use of a plexiglass substitute for sandpaper was an additional material misrepresentation that was a deceptive act separate and distinct from the misrepresentation concerning Rapid Shave's underlying qualities. Even if the sandpaper could be shaved just as depicted in the commercials, the Commission found that viewers had been misled into believing they had seen it done with their own eyes. As a result of these findings the Commission entered a cease-and-desist order against the respondents.

An appeal was taken to the Court of Appeals for the First Circuit which rendered an opinion on November 20, 1962. That court sustained the Commission's conclusion that respondents had misrepresented the qualities of Rapid Shave, but it would not accept the Commission's order forbidding the future use of undisclosed simulations in television commercials. It set aside the Commission's order and directed that a new order be entered. On May 7, 1963, the Commission, over the protest of respondents, issued a new order narrowing and clarifying its original order to comply with the court's mandate. The Court of Appeals again found unsatisfactory that portion of the order dealing with simulated props and refused to enforce it. We granted certiorari, 377 U.S. 942, to consider this aspect of the case and do not have before us any question concerning the misrepresentation that Rapid Shave could shave sandpaper immediately after application, that being conceded. . . .

We are not concerned in this case with the clear misrepresentation in the commercials concerning the speed with which Rapid Shave could shave sandpaper, since the Court of Appeals upheld the Commission's finding on that matter and the respondents have not challenged the finding here. We granted certiorari to consider the Commission's conclusion that even if an advertiser has himself conducted a test, experiment or demonstration which he honestly believes will prove a certain product claim, he may not convey to television viewers the false impression that they are seeing the test, experiment or demonstration for themselves, when they are not because of the undisclosed use of mock-ups.

We accept the Commission's determination that the commercials involved in this case contained three representations to the public: (1) that sandpaper could be shaved by Rapid Shave; (2) that an experiment had been conducted which verified this claim; and (3) that the viewer was seeing this experiment for himself. Respondents admit that the first two representations were made, but deny that the third was. The Commission, however, found to the contrary, and, since this is a matter of fact resting on an inference that could reasonably be drawn from the commercials themselves, the Commission's finding should be sustained. For the purposes of our review, we can assume that the first two representations were true; the focus of our consideration is on the third, which was clearly false. The parties agree that § 5 prohibits the intentional misrepresentation of any fact which would constitute a material factor in a purchaser's decision whether to buy. They differ, however, in their conception of what "facts" constitute a "material factor" in a purchaser's decision to buy. Respondents submit, in effect, that the only material facts are those which deal with the substantive qualities of a product.[1] The Commission, on the other hand, submits that the misrepresentation of *any* fact so long as it materially induces a purchaser's decision to buy is a deception prohibited by § 5.

The Commission's interpretation of what is a deceptive practice seems more in line with the decided cases than that of respondents. This Court said in *Federal Trade Comm'n* v. *Algoma Lumber Co.,* 291 U.S. 67, 78: "[T]he public is entitled to get what it chooses, though the choice may be dictated by caprice or by fashion or perhaps by ignorance." It has long been considered a deceptive practice to state falsely that a product ordinarily sells for an inflated price but that it is being offered at a special reduced price, even if the offered price represents the actual value of the product and the purchaser is receiving his money's worth.[2] Applying respondents' arguments to these cases, it would appear that so long as buyers paid no more than the product was actually worth and the product contained the qualities advertised, the misstatement of an inflated original price was immaterial.

It has also been held a violation of § 5 for a seller to misrepresent to the public that he is in a certain line of business, even though the misstatement in no way affects the qualities of the product. As was said in *Federal Trade Comm'n* v. *Royal Milling Co.,* 288 U.S. 212, 216:

> If consumers or dealers prefer to purchase a given article because it was made by a particular manufacturer or class of manufacturers, they have a right to do so, and this right cannot be satisfied by imposing upon them an exactly similar article, or one equally as good, but having a different origin.

The courts of appeals have applied this reasoning to the merchandising of reprocessed products that are as good as new, without a disclosure that they are in fact reprocessed. And it has also been held that it is a deceptive practice to misappropriate the trade name of another.

Respondents claim that all these cases are irrelevant to our decision because they involve misrepresentations related to the product itself and not merely to the manner in which an advertising message is communicated. This distinction misses the mark for two reasons. In the first place, the present case is not concerned with a mode of communication, but with a misrepresentation that viewers have objective proof of a seller's product claim over and above the seller's word. Secondly, all of the above cases, like the present case, deal with methods designed to get a consumer to purchase a product, not with whether the product, when purchased, will perform up to expectations. We find an especially strong similarity between the present case and those cases in which a seller induces the public to purchase an arguably good product by misrepresenting his line of business, by concealing the fact that the product is reprocessed, or by misappropriating another's trademark. In each the seller has used a misrepresentation to break down what he regards to be an annoying or irrational habit of the buying public—the preference for particular manufacturers or known brands regardless of a product's actual qualities, the prejudice against reprocessed goods, and the desire for verification of a product claim. In each case the seller reasons that when the habit is broken the buyer will be satisfied with the performance of the product he receives. Yet, a misrepresentation has been used to break the habit and, as was stated in *Algoma Lumber,* a misrepresentation for such an end is not permitted.

We need not limit ourselves to the cases already mentioned because there are other situations which also illustrate the correctness of the Commission's finding in the present case. It is generally accepted that it is a deceptive practice to state falsely that a product has received a testimonial from a respected source. In addition, the Commission has consistently acted to prevent sellers from falsely stating that their product claims have been "certified." We find these situations to be indistinguishable from the present case. We can assume that in each the underlying product claim is true and in each the seller actually conducted an experiment sufficient to prove to himself the truth of the claim. But in each the seller has told the public that it could rely on something other than his word concerning both the truth of the claim and the validity of his experiment. We find it an immaterial difference that in one case the viewer is told to rely on the word of a celebrity or authority he respects, in another on the word of a testing agency, and in the present case on his own perception of an undisclosed simulation.

Respondents again insist that the present case is not like any of the above, but is more like a case in which a celebrity or independent testing agency has in fact submitted a written verification of an experiment actually observed, but, because of the inability of the camera to transmit accurately an impression of the paper on which the testimonial is written, the seller reproduces it on another substance so that it can be seen by the viewing audience. This analogy ignores the finding of the Commission that in the present case the seller misrepresented to the public that it was being given objective proof of a product claim. In respondents' hypothetical the objective proof of the product claim that is offered, the word of the celebrity or agency that the experiment was actually conducted, does exist; while in the case before us the objective proof offered, the viewer's own perception of an actual experiment, does not exist. Thus, in respondents' hypothetical, unlike the present case, the use of the undisclosed mock-up does not conflict with the seller's claim that there is objective proof.

We agree with the Commission, therefore, that the undisclosed use of plexiglass in the present commercials was a material deceptive practice, independent and separate from the other misrepresentation found. We find unpersuasive respondents' other objections to this conclusion. Respondents claim that it will be impractical to inform the viewing public that it is not seeing an actual test, experiment or demonstration, but we think it inconceivable that the ingenious advertising world will be unable, if it so desires, to conform to the Commission's insistence that the public be not misinformed. If, however, it becomes impossible or impractical to show simulated demonstrations on television in a truthful manner, this indicates that television is not a medium that lends itself to this type of commercial, not that the commercial must survive at all costs. Similarly unpersuasive is respondents' objection that the Commission's decision discriminates against sellers whose product claims cannot be "verified" on television without the use of simulations. All methods of advertising do not equally favor every seller. If the inherent limitations of a method do not permit its use in the way a seller desires, the seller cannot by material misrepresentation compensate for those limitations.

Respondents also claim that the Commission reached out to decide a question not properly before it and has presented this Court with an abstract question. They argue that since the commercials in the present case misrepresented the time element involved in shaving sandpaper, this Court should not consider the additional misrepresentation that the public had objective proof of the seller's claim. As we have already said, these misrepresentations are separate and distinct, and we fail to see why respondents should be sheltered from a cease-and-desist order with respect to one deceptive practice merely because they also engaged in another.

Respondents finally object to what they consider to be the absence of an adequate record to sustain the Commission's finding. It is true that in its initial stages the case was concerned more with the misrepresentation about the product's underlying qualities than with the misrepresentation that objective proof was being given. Nevertheless, both misrepresentations were in the case from the beginning, and respondents were never prejudicially misled into believing that the second question was not being considered. Nor was it necessary for the Commission to conduct a survey of the viewing public before it could determine that the commercials had a tendency to mislead, for when the Commission finds deception it is also authorized, within the bounds of reason, to infer that the deception will constitute a material factor in purchaser's decision to buy. See *Federal Trade Comm'n* v. *Raladam Co.,* 316 U.S. 149, 152. We find the record in this case sufficient to support the Commission's findings.

We turn our attention now to the order issued by the Commission. . . . The Court of Appeals has criticized the reference in the Commission's order to "test, experiment or demonstration" as not capable of practical interpretation. It could find no difference between the Rapid Shave commercial and a commercial which extolled the goodness of ice cream while giving viewers a picture of a scoop of mashed potatoes appearing to be ice cream. We do not understand this difficulty. In the ice cream case the mashed potato prop is not being used for additional proof of the product claim, while the purpose of the Rapid Shave commercial is to give the viewer objective proof of the claims made. If in the ice cream hypothetical the focus of the commercial becomes the undisclosed potato prop and the viewer is invited, explicitly or by implication, to see for himself the truth of the claims about the ice cream's rich texture and full color, and perhaps compare it to a "rival product," then the commercial has become similar to the one now before us. Clearly, however, a commercial which depicts happy actors delightedly eating ice cream that is in fact mashed potatoes or drinking a product appearing to be coffee but which is in fact some other substance is not covered by the present order.

The crucial terms of the present order—"test, experiment or demonstration . . . represented . . . as actual proof of a claim"—are as specific as the circumstances will permit. If respondents in their subsequent commercials attempt to come as close to the line of misrepresentation as the Commission's order permits, they may without specifically intending to do so cross into the area proscribed by this order. However, it does not seem "unfair to require that one who deliberately goes perilously close to an area of proscribed conduct shall take the risk that he may cross the line," *Boyce Motor Lines, Inc.* v. *United States,* 342 U.S. 337, 340. In commercials where the emphasis is on the seller's word, and not on the viewer's own perception, the respondents need not fear that an undisclosed use of props is prohibited by the present order. On the other hand, when the commercial not only makes a claim, but also invites the viewer to rely on his own perception for demonstrative proof of the claim, the respondents will be aware that the use of undisclosed props in strategic places might be a material deception. We believe that respondents will have no difficulty applying the Commission's order to the vast majority of their contemplated future commercials. If, however, a situation arises in which respondents are sincerely unable to determine whether a proposed course of action would violate the present order, they can, by complying with the Commission's rules, oblige the Commission to give them definitive advice as to whether their proposed action, if pursued, would constitute compliance with the order.

Notes

1. Brief for Respondent Colgate, p. 16: "What [the buyer] is interested in is whether the actual product he buys will look and perform the way it appeared on his television set." *Id.,* at 17: "[A] buyer's real concern is with the truth of the substantive claims or promises made to him, not with the means used to make them." *Id.,* at 20: "[T]he Commission's error was to confuse the substantive claim made for a product with the means by which such claim was conveyed."

   Brief for Respondent Bates, pp. 2–3: "If the viewer or reader of the advertisement buys the product, and it will do exactly what the portrayal in the advertisement asserts it will do, can there be any unlawful misrepresentation?" *Id.*, at 13–14: "What induces the buyer to purchase is the claim that the product will perform as represented in the portrayed test. That is the material claim." *Id.*, at 25: "It is not a representation in any way relating to the product or to its purchase, so that even if the strained suggestion that there is such an implied representation were realistic, the representation plainly would be immaterial."

2. Federal Trade Comm'n v. Standard Education Society, 302 U.S. 112, 115–117, Kalwajtys v. Federal Trade Comm'n, 237 F.2d 654, 656 (C. A. 7th Cir. 1956), cert. denied, 352 U.S. 1025.

FEDERAL TRADE COMMISSION v. STERLING DRUG, INC.

The Federal Trade Commission, appellant here, instituted an action in the District Court for the Southern District of New York praying for a temporary injunction designed to prevent the dissemination of what the Commission alleged it had reason to believe was false and misleading advertising. Judge Dawson denied the injunction. . . .

I

The controversy has its roots in the December 29, 1962 issue of the *Journal of the American Medical Association,* which carried an article written by two physicians and a medical statistician,[1] titled "A Comparative Study of Five Proprietary Analgesic Compounds." The article analyzed the results of a study made of the efficacy as well as the unhappy after-effects of certain pain-relieving drugs, sold in pharmacies and supermarkets throughout the nation. These five were Bayer Aspirin, St. Joseph's Aspirin, Bufferin (aspirin with buffering agent), and two of the so-called "combination of ingredients" tablets, Anacin and Excedrin. Also used in the experiment, as a form of control, was a placebo, the name given a harmless non-medicinal substance administered in the form of a pill for those pill-poppers whose ailment is without organic origin and whose pain seems to be relieved by following the ritual of downing a tablet irrespective of size, shape, or content which the user believes has qualities of medicinal value; the placebo utilized by the three researchers was composed of lactose, or milk sugar, and a conventional cornstarch binder. After investigating the efficacy of the five analgesic agents as pain relievers, the study noted, "The data failed to show any statistically significant difference among any of the drugs (that is, excluding the placebo) at any of the check points [fifteen minutes through four hours] . . . [T]here are no important differences among the compounds studied in rapidity of onset, degree, or duration of analgesia." Fifteen minutes after the drugs were administered, so-called

The Federal Reporter 317 Fed 669. Opinion by Judge Irving R. Kaufman U.S. Court of Appeals Second Circuit.

"pain-relief scores" were computed, and Bayer earned a score of 0.94, while the next most effective drug at that point in time, Excedrin, earned a score of 0.90; the others were rated at 0.76 and lower. The chart on which these figures appeared indicated that the "standard error of mean," or the margin of statistical accuracy of the study, was 0.124. Upon investigating the incidence of stomach upset after the administration of the five drugs as well as the placebo, the researchers came to this conclusion: "Excedrin and Anacin form a group for which the incidence of upset stomach is significantly greater than is the incidence after Bayer Aspirin, St. Joseph's Aspirin, Bufferin, or the placebo. The rates of upset stomach associated with these last 4 treatments are not significantly different, one from the other." The accompanying table revealed that of the 829 doses taken of Bayer Aspirin, there were nine episodes of upset stomach, a rate of 1.1%; the placebo was administered in 833 cases, and caused stomach upset but seven times, a rate of 0.8%. The article concluded by stating, "This study was supported by a grant from the Federal Trade Commission, Washington, D.C."[2]

It is not difficult to understand the heartwarming reception this article received in the upper echelons of Sterling and its Madison Avenue colleagues; no sooner were the results of the study published in the *Journal of the American Medical Association* when Sterling Drug and its advertising agencies decided to make the most of them. This decision, we may fairly assume, did not surprise Sterling's competitors. The public had long been saturated with various claims proved by the study to be of doubtful validity. One of the products had boasted in its advertisements that it "works twice as fast as aspirin," and "protects you against the stomach distress you can get from aspirin alone"; another, that it "does not upset the stomach" and "is better than aspirin"; and yet another, that it is "50% stronger than aspirin." Believing that the Judgment Day has finally arrived and seeking to counteract the many years of hard-sell by what it now believed to be the hard facts, Sterling and its co-defendants prepared and disseminated advertising of which the following, appearing in *Life* Magazine and numerous newspapers throughout the country, is representative:

GOVERNMENT-SUPPORTED MEDICAL TEAM COMPARES BAYER ASPIRIN AND FOUR OTHER POPULAR PAIN RELIEVERS.

FINDINGS REPORTED IN THE HIGHLY AUTHORITATIVE JOURNAL OF THE AMERICAN MEDICAL ASSOCIATION REVEAL THAT THE HIGHER PRICED COMBINATION-OF-INGREDIENTS PAIN RELIEVERS UPSET THE STOMACH WITH SIGNIFICANTLY GREATER FREQUENCY THAN ANY OF THE OTHER PRODUCTS TESTED. WHILE BAYER ASPIRIN BRINGS RELIEF THAT IS AS FAST, AS STRONG, AND AS GENTLE TO THE STOMACH AS YOU CAN GET.

This important new medical study, supported by a grant from the federal government, was undertaken to compare the stomach-upsetting effects, the speed of relief and the amount of relief offered by five leading pain relievers, including Bayer Aspirin, aspirin with buffering, and combination-of-ingredients products. Here is a summary of the findings.

Upset Stomach

According to this report, the higher priced combination-of-ingredients products upset the stomach with significantly greater frequency than any of the other products tested, while Bayer Aspirin, taken as directed, is as gentle to the stomach as a plain sugar pill.

Speed and Strength

The study shows that there is no significant difference among the products tested in rapidity of onset, strength, or duration of relief. Nonetheless, it is interesting to note that within just fifteen minutes, Bayer Aspirin had a somewhat higher pain relief score than any of the other products.

Price

As unreasonable as it may seem, the products which are most likely to upset the stomach—that is, the combination-of-ingredients products—actually cost substantially more than Bayer Aspirin. The fact is that these products as well as the buffered product, cost up to 75% more than Bayer Aspirin.

II

In a proceeding such as this, the burden was upon the Commission, in seeking its temporary injunction against the advertising, to show that it had "reason to believe" that the advertisements were false and misleading, and that the injunction during the pendency of administrative proceedings which the Commission initiated against Sterling Drug in January 1963 "would be to the interest of the public."

The Commission alleged and sought to prove that the appellees' advertisements falsely represented, directly and by implication: (a) that the findings of the medical research team were endorsed and approved by the United States Government; (b) that the publication of the article in the *Journal of the American Medical Association* is evidence of endorsement and approval thereof by the association and the medical profession; (c) that the research team found that Bayer Aspirin is not upsetting to the stomach and is as gentle thereto as a sugar pill; (d) that the research team found that Bayer Aspirin, after fifteen minutes following administration, affords a higher degree of pain relief than any other product tested. An injunction was alleged to be in the public interest, since the consuming public would otherwise unwarrantedly rely upon the advertising to their "irreparable injury," and since competitors of Sterling Drug might be encouraged to engage in similar advertising tactics in order to maintain competitive standing.

The legal principles to be applied here are quite clear. The central purpose of the provisions of the Federal Trade Commission Act under discussion is in effect to abolish the rule of *caveat emptor* which traditionally defined rights and responsibilities in the world of commerce. That rule can no longer be relied upon as a means of rewarding fraud and deception, *Federal Trade Commission* v. *Standard Education Society*, 302 U.S. 112, 116, 58 S.Ct.

113, 82 L.Ed. 141 (1937), and has been replaced by a rule which gives to the consumer the right to rely upon representations of facts as the truth, *Goodman* v. *Federal Trade Commission,* 244 F.2d 584, 603 (9th Cir., 1957). In order best to implement the prophylactic purpose of the statute, it has been consistently held that advertising falls within its proscription not only when there is proof of actual deception but also when the representations made have a capacity or tendency to deceive, i.e., when there is a likelihood or fair probability that the reader will be misled. . . . For the same reason, proof of intention to deceive is not requisite to a finding of violation of the statute, *Gimbel Bros., Inc.* v. *Federal Trade Commission,* 116 F.2d 578 (2d Cir., 1941); since the purpose of the statute is not to punish the wrongdoer but to protect the public, the cardinal factor is the probable effect which the advertiser's handiwork will have upon the eye and mind of the reader. It is therefore necessary in these cases to consider the advertisement in its entirety and not to engage in disputatious dissection. The entire mosaic should be viewed rather than each tile separately. "[T]he buying public does not ordinarily carefully study or weigh each word in an advertisement. The ultimate impression upon the mind of the reader arises from the sum total of not only what is said but also of all that is reasonably implied." [*Aronberg* v. *Federal Trade Commission,* 132 F.2d 165, 167 (7th Cir., 1942).]

Unlike that abiding faith which the law has in the "reasonable man," it has very little faith indeed in the intellectual acuity of the "ordinary purchaser" who is the object of the advertising campaign.

> The general public has been defined as "that vast multitude which includes the ignorant, and unthinking and the credulous, who, in making purchases, do not stop to analyze but too often are governed by appearances and general impressions." The average purchaser has been variously characterized as not "straight thinking," subject to "impressions," uneducated, and grossly misinformed; he is influenced by prejudice and superstition; and he wishfully believes in miracles, allegedly the result of progress in science. . . . The language of the ordinary purchaser is casual and unaffected. He is not an "expert in grammatical construction" or an "educated analytical reader" and, therefore, he does not normally subject every word in the advertisement to careful study.

[Callman, Unfair Competition and Trademarks § 19.2(a) (1), at 341–44 (1950), and the cases there cited.][3]

It is well established that advertising need not be literally false in order to fall within the proscription of the act. Gone for the most part, fortunately, are the days when the advertiser was so lacking in subtlety as to represent his nostrum as superlative for "arthritis, rheumatism, neuralgia, sciatica, lumbago, gout, coronary thrombosis, brittle bones, bad teeth, malfunctioning glands, infected tonsils, infected appendix, gall stones, neuritis, underweight, constipation, indigestion, lack of energy, lack of vitality, lack of ambition and inability to sleep. . . ." See *Federal Trade Commission* v. *National Health Aids, Inc.,* 108 F.Supp. 340, 342 (D.Md. 1952). The courts are no longer content to insist simply upon the "most literal truthfulness," *Moretrench Corp.* v. *Federal Trade Commission,*

127 F.2d 792 at 795, for we have increasingly come to recognize that "Advertisements as a whole may be completely misleading although every sentence separately considered is literally true. This may be because things are omitted that should be said, or because advertisements are composed or purposefully printed in such way as to mislead." . . . There are two obvious methods of employing a true statement so as to convey a false impression: one is the half truth, where the statement is removed from its context and the nondisclosure of its context renders the statement misleading, see *P. Lorillard Co.* v. *Federal Trade Commission,* 186 F.2d 52, 58 (4th Cir., 1950); a second is the ambiguity, where the statement in context has two or more commonly understood meanings, one of which is deceptive.

III

The Federal Trade Commission asserts here that the vice of the Bayer advertisement is of these types. It concedes that none of the statements made therein is literally false, but it contends that the half-truths and ambiguities of the advertisement give it "reason to believe" that our hypothetical, sub-intelligent, less-than-careful reader will be misled thereby. Thus, we are told that the reference in large type to a "Government-Supported Medical Team" gives the misleading impression that the United States Government endorsed or approved the findings of the research team. Surely the fact that the word "supported" might have alternative dictionary definitions of "endorsed" or "approved" is not alone sufficient to show reason to believe that the ordinary reader will probably construe the word in this manner. Most words *do* have alternative dictionary definitions; if that in itself were a sufficient legal criterion, few advertisements would survive. Here, no impression is conveyed that the *product itself* has its source in or is being endorsed by the Government; for this reason, the cases cited by the Commission are inapt. If the reader of the advertisement believes that the Government in some way vouched for the soundness of the study's conclusions, then this impression would have also been conveyed had the advertisement "told the whole story," relating in full detail the extent of the Commission's participation: it selected the research team, supported the study with a grant, and authorized the publication of the report. The capsulized expression "Government-Supported" can not, therefore, be characterized as misleading. The commission indicated to us upon argument that it would have been equally unhappy had the advertisement stated that the medical team was "Government-Financed" or "Government-Subsidized." But surely the concise statement of an established fact, immediately thereafter expanded—"This important new medical study, supported by a grant from the federal government . . ."—cannot fairly be proscribed by the Commission; the alternatives are complete omission of the admittedly true statement or long-winded qualification and picayune circumlocution, neither of which we believe was in the contemplation of Congress.

The Commission's attack upon the use of the phrase "Findings reported in the highly authoritative *Journal of the American Medical Association*," as misleadingly connoting endorsement and approval, is similarly unfounded, for much the same reasons already discussed. To assert that the ordinary reader would conclude from the use of the word "authoritative" that the study was endorsed by the *Journal* and the Association is to attribute to him not only a careless and imperceptive mind but also a propensity for unbounded flights of fancy. This we are not yet prepared to do. If the reader's natural reaction is to think that the study, because of publication in the *Journal*, is likely to be accurate, intelligent, and well-documented, then the reaction is wholly justified, and one which the advertiser has every reason to expect and to seek to inculcate. We, as judges, know that an article on the law which has survived the rigorous selection and editing process of one of the major law publications is most probably more reliable and more thoroughly researched than the report of a recent trial or judicial decision carried in the *Podunk Daily Journal*. But we hardly think that there is "reason to believe" that either we or the lay observer would tend to construe the views expressed in the article as having secured the wholehearted endorsement and approval of the "authoritative" periodical in which it appears.[4]

The Commission's third objection deals with the probable vulnerability of the ordinary reader to Bayer's representations concerning stomach upset. We pass without comment the Commission's claim that the Bayer advertisement represented that no other available analgesic product was more gentle to the stomach; clearly, any comparative statements made in the advertisement could only be understood to refer to the four other products tested. More seriously pressed upon us is the claim that the reader will be deceived by the statement that "Bayer Aspirin, taken as directed, is as gentle to the stomach as a plain sugar pill." "Sugar pill," we are told, is misleading terminology; the advertisement should have used the word "placebo." Again, we are confronted by a simple problem of communication. For how can we expect our hypothetically slow-witted reader to react when he reads that "Bayer Aspirin is as gentle to the stomach as a placebo"! Most likely, he will either read on, completely unaware of the significance of the statement, or impatiently turn the page. Perhaps he will turn to his neighbor, and in response to a request for a definition of the troublesome word be greeted with the plausible query, "A *what?*" (This assumes that the reader will have been able to muster the correct pronunciation of the word.) But, all this aside, the pill used as a control in this case was indeed constituted of milk sugar, and the use of the term "sugar pill" was neither inaccurate nor misleading.

The Commission next shifts its focus to the words "as gentle as," alleging that it has reason to believe that the reader will conclude that Bayer is not in the slightest bit harmful to the stomach; this can be rectified, we are told, by stating that Bayer is "no more upsetting" than the placebo, which did in fact cause a very minor degree of stomach upset. Unlike the standard

of the average reader which the Commission avidly endorses throughout
these proceedings, it here would have us believe that he is linguistically and
syntactically sensitive to the difference between the phrases "as gentle as"
and "no more upsetting than." We do not find that the Commission has
reason to believe that this will be the case, and we therefore reject its contentions.

Finally, the Commission attacks the manner in which the Bayer advertisement treated results of the study on speed and effectiveness of pain
relief. As we understand the Commission's argument, no objection is
taken to the statement that "The study shows that there is no significant
difference among the products tested in rapidity of onset, strength, or
duration of relief." Indeed, no objection can properly be taken, for the
statement reproduces almost verbatim one of the conclusions enumerated
in the article. It is thought, however, that the advertisement improperly
represents greater short-run pain relief with Bayer Aspirin by stating that
"Nonetheless, it is interesting to note that within just fifteen minutes,
Bayer Aspirin had a somewhat higher pain relief score than any of the
other products." As we have seen, the statement is literally true, for
Bayer's "score" after fifteen minutes was 0.94 while its closest competitor
at that time interval was rated 0.90. The fact that the margin of accuracy of
that scoring system was 0.124—meaning that the second-place drug might
fare as well as or better than Bayer over the long run of statistical
tests—does not detract from the fact that on this particular test, Bayer apparently fared better than any other product in relieving pain within fifteen
minutes after its administration. It is true that a close examination of the
statistical chart drawn up by the three investigators reveals that they
thought the difference between all of the drugs at that time interval not to
be "significantly different." But that is precisely what the Bayer advertisement stated in the sentence preceding its excursion into the specifics of the
pain-relief scores. We cannot, therefore, conclude that Judge Dawson
clearly erred in finding that the Commission failed properly to carry its
statutory burden of proof, however slim that burden might be. Not even
the Commission contends that in a proceeding under section 13(a) the
judge is merely a rubber stamp, stripped of the power to exercise independent judgment on the issue of the Commission's "reason to believe."

The Commission relies heavily, especially as to the pain-relief aspects of
its case, upon *P. Lorillard Co.* v. *Federal Trade Commission*, 186 F.2d 52 (4th
Cir., 1950). There, *Reader's Digest* sponsored a scientific study of the major
cigarettes, investigating the relative quantities of nicotine, tars, and resins.
It accompanied its conclusions with a chart which revealed that, although
Old Gold cigarettes ranked lowest in these deleterious substances, the
quantitative differences between the brands were insignificant and would
have no effect in reducing physiological harm to the smoker. The tenor of
the study is revealed by its cheery words to the smoker "who need no
longer worry as to which cigarette can most effectively nail down his coffin.
For one nail is just about as good as another." Old Gold trumpeted its

dubious success, claiming that it was found lowest in nicotine, tars, and resins, and predicting that the reader upon examining the results of the study would say "From now on, my cigarette is Old Gold." The Court quite properly upheld a cease-and-desist order issued by the Commission. An examination of that case shows that it is completely distinguishable in at least two obvious and significant respects. Although the statements made by Old Gold were at best literally true, they were used in the advertisement to convey an impression diametrically opposed to that intended by the writer of the article. As the Court noted, "The company proceeded to advertise this difference as though it had received a citation for public service instead of a castigation from the *Reader's Digest.*" 186 F.2d at 57. Moreover, as to the specifics of brand-comparison, it was found that anyone reading the advertisement would gain "the very definite impression that Old Gold cigarettes were less irritating to the throat and less harmful than other leading brands of cigarettes. . . . The truth was exactly the opposite." 186 F.2d at 58. In the instant case, Sterling Drug can in no sense be said to have conveyed a misleading impression as to either the spirit[5] or the specifics of the article published in the *Journal of the American Medical Association.*

Notes

1. Dr. DeKornfeld was then chief of the department of anesthesiology, Baltimore City Hospitals. Dr. Lasagna was affiliated with Johns Hopkins School of Medicine. Mr. Frazier was director of the Bureau of Biostatistics, Baltimore City Health Department.
2. We find support in the record for the article's statement regarding the Commission's involvement in the study. For in January 1963, the Chairman of the Federal Trade Commission appeared before a special committee of the Senate, and testified, in response to the question "I understand that the Aspirin study was financed at least in part by a Federal Trade Commission grant. Is that so?" that "[W]e had these tests made, sir . . . we paid for the study. We obtained and entered into a contract to get that study made."
3. See Federal Trade Commission v. Standard Education Society, 302 U.S. 112, 116, 58 S.Ct. 113, 82 L.Ed. 141 (1937); Exposition Press, Inc. v. Federal Trade Commission, 295 F.2d 869, 872 (2d Cir., 1961), cert. denied, 370 U.S. 917, 82 S.Ct. 1554, 8 L.Ed.2d 497 (1962); Niresk Industries, Inc. v. Federal Trade Commission, 278 F.2d 337, 342 (7th Cir.), cert. denied, 364 U.S. 883, 81 S.Ct. 173, 5 L. Ed.2d 104 (1960); Book-of-the-Month Club, Inc. v. Federal Trade Commission, 202 F.2d 486 (2d Cir., 1953); Moretrench Corp. v. Federal Trade Commission, 127 F.2d 792, 795 (2d Cir., 1942); Charles of the Ritz Distributors Copr. v. Federal Trade Commission, supra; Florence Mfg. Co. v. J. C. Dowd & Co., 178 F. 73, 75 (2d Cir., 1910); Handler, "The Control of False Advertising under the Wheeler-Lea Act," 6 *Law & Contemp. Prob. 91, 98* (1939).
4. It is interesting to note that the American Medical Association, contemporaneously with the publication of the issue of the *Journal* in which the findings appeared, transmitted a press release throughout the country which called attention to the study, the fact of its publication in the *Journal,* and a detailed

summary of its findings. Subsequently, the AMA issued another press release, claiming that certain current advertising had been misinterpreted as statements of AMA endorsement of Bayer Aspirin. We note, however, that the press release, although disclaiming endorsement of the product itself, did not question either the findings of the article or the responsibility of the AMA in publishing them.

5. The Commission makes no contention here that the allegedly misleading advertising will cause or induce physical harm.

case 1:   The Firestone Tire and Rubber Case

The "Stop 25 Per Cent Quicker" ad read as follows:

Year after year, more races are won on Firestone tires than on any other kind.

But we're not racing just to win. We're in it to learn, too. And what we learn on the track goes into building safer tires for your car.

Like the original Super Sports Wide Oval tire.

It came straight out of Firestone racing research.

It's built nearly two inches wider than regular tires. To corner better, run cooler, stop 25 per cent quicker.

Before we sell a single tire, each new Firestone design is thoroughly tested on indoor test equipment, on our test track and in rigorous day-to-day driving conditions.

Firestone tires are custom-built and personally inspected for an extra margin of safety. So that when you buy a Firestone tire—no matter how much or how little you pay—you get a safe tire.[1]

Between 1967 and 1968, Firestone Tire and Rubber ran a series of ads which were challenged by the Federal Trade Commission on the grounds that the ads were deceptive in a way that endangered human life and safety. Although the Commission had specific criticisms for each ad, the "Stop 25 Per Cent Quicker" ad can serve as an accurate illustration of most of the Commission's criticisms. The Commission argued first that contrary to the implications of Firestone advertising, Firestone could not truthfully claim that every tire is "custom-built and personally inspected" in any way that could guarantee each and every tire to be free of defects. Second, Firestone testing procedures, particularly the tests for stopping, were not made over a wide variety of conditions. There were two different widths of tires tested on a wet, smooth, concrete surface. All tests were run on the same day under the same load and with the same level of tire inflation pressure. Third, the Commission argued that the general tone of the ad lulled the consumer into a sense of false security. To counteract this tendency, the Commission argued that Firestone's ads should indicate to the consumer, "that the safety of any tire is affected by conditions of use, such as inflation pressure, vehicle weight, or other operating conditions."[2]

This case was prepared by Norman E. Bowie. Reprinted by permission.

The Firestone Company challenged the FTC on all points, although Firestone ultimately lost in court. Firestone argued that they did in fact use the best quality control techniques known and that the vast majority of people never interpreted the ad as a guarantee of *absolute* safety. In defense of their testing procedures, Firestone contended that the conditions used were genuinely hazardous. There was no point in testing on a dry surface. Besides, it could be argued that performance would be even better on dry surfaces than on wet ones. Firestone had nothing but scorn for the requirement that ads contain explicit mention of the common-sense conditions that affect tire safety. The company said, "The Commission has reached the absurd conclusion that a tire cannot be advertised as safe . . . unless the advertisements also include a warning that air must be put in the tire. . . ."[3]

Notes

1. FTC v. Firestone, 481 F.2d 246 (1973), p. 249.
2. *Ibid.* p. 248.
3. "Firestone to Fight FTC on Ad Charges." *Wall Street Journal,* October 9, 1972, p. 9.

Questions

1. For a mass produced product is use of the phrase "custom-built and personally inspected" inherently deceptive?
2. Was Firestone right when they claimed that there was no point in testing on a dry surface?
3. Is the ad deceptive in lulling the buyer into a false sense of security? Does it give the impression that Firestone tires are absolutely safe?
4. Should tire ads in general make explicit mention of the common-sense conditions that affect tire safety?

case 2:   What Does "List Price" Mean?

Giant Food, Inc. is a supermarket chain, which sells housewares and appliances in some of its stores. Its advertising in the Washington, D.C. area sometimes appeared in the form:

Sunbeam Mixmaster	$24.00—Manufacturer List Price $37.95
Regina Twin Brush Waxer	$25.47—Manufacturer List $66

The advertisements also contained the following note at the bottom of each page:

The manufacturer's list prices referred to in this advertisement are inserted to assist you in identification of the products and to allow you to compare accurately the selling prices offered here and elsewhere. The use of the term manufacturer's list, or similar terminology in our advertising, is not to imply that Giant has ever sold the advertised product at such list prices, or that the products are being offered for sale generally in the area at such list prices. Many reputable national brand manufacturers issue to retailers, from time to time, suggested retail list prices that are intended to afford reasonable profits to all retailers based upon their traditional costs of marketing. Giant's employment of self-service supermarket techniques enables it usually to sell below suggested list prices. Consumers, however, have come to recognize most brand merchandise by the list prices, rather than model numbers, consequently Giant includes these manufacturer's list prices so that you may make simple, intelligent comparisons between our selling prices and those of others.

According to buyers from three companies in the Washington area, their stores never sold at the list prices advertised by Giant. Thus where Giant had advertised a Sunbeam appliance as selling for $13.97 with a list of $21, the three stores charged the following prices for the same item: $16.49, $14.97 and $13.49.

Giant contended that at least some stores in the Washington area had advertised the product for sale at the manufacturer's list price. Furthermore, Giant's comparison shoppers had discovered stores which actually sold the advertised products at the list price. In addition the manufacturers themselves had used these list prices in *Life, Look,* and *McCall's.*

The Federal Trade Commission claimed that despite the note inserted by Giant, the term *manufacturer's list price* meant that this was the price at which the item was usually and customarily sold in that area.

The matter was taken to the U.S. Court of Appeals of the District of Columbia, which had to decide whether the FTC has the right—when an advertisement has two meanings, one of which is deceptive—to demand the termination of such advertising. The court was also expected to rule on whether the insertion itself tended to reinforce the deception.

Questions

1. Does the addition of the note make any difference in determining whether or not Giant Food Inc.'s ad is deceptive?
2. Would the placement of the note or the size of the type make any difference?
3. If advertisers use words which have two distinct meanings, does that make the ad deceptive?
4. In terms of determining deception, does it matter if only one store had sold the items at the manufacturer's list price? if one store had never sold at the manufacturer's list price? if Giant Food Inc., had never sold at the manufacturer's list price?

From Thomas Garrett, Raymond C. Baumhart, Theodore Purcell, and Perry Roets, eds. *Cases in Business Ethics.* Copyright © 1968 by Appleton-Century Crofts, New York. Reprinted by permission of Prentice-Hall, Inc.

case 3:   The Case of the Giant Quart

Your company sells only in the state of New Wyoming. State law does not prohibit marketing your cola in "giant quarts." A quart is a standard measure, so a giant quart is the same size as an ordinary quart. A survey conducted by your firm indicates that 40 percent of cola buyers think that a giant quart is larger than a regular quart.

Questions

1. Would it be deceptive advertising to call your bottle a giant quart?
2. In deciding whether this ad is deceptive, does it make any difference what percentage of cola buyers think that a giant quart is larger than a regular quart?
3. Suppose a firm sold a half gallon of soda for 89¢. In ads, the half gallon size was called the giant size. The firm finds it necessary to increase the price of the soda to 99¢. With the new price comes a new name—the "giant economy" size. Is the use of the new name deceptive?
4. Should there be a standard according to product for large, extra large, giant, and family sizes?

This case was prepared by the Committee for Education in Business Ethics under a grant from the National Endowment for the Humanities.

case 4:   Zeroing in on the Joneses

The technology now exists to tailor ads for individual families. Experiments are now under way in several cities to study the effectiveness of these ads and the initial results have been enthusiastically received by the advertising industry. Consumers in the test areas are asked if they would permit their purchases to be monitored at supermarket checkout counters. They are promised anonymity. They are often rewarded with food discounts and other inducements. They are also told that the ads they see on their cable TV may differ from those seen by their neighbors. Advertisers are then able to beam ads promoting competing products into the consumer's home. If the Joneses use brand X, the competitor can beam ads for brand Y into the Joneses home. The Civil Liberties Union takes a dim view of these developments. An ACLU spokesperson has characterized the experiments as "shocking," and an invasion of privacy.

This case was prepared by Norman E. Bowie. Reprinted by permission.

Questions

1. Do you think such ads directed toward specific families undermine human freedom?
2. Even if you think they don't invade human freedom, do you find them objectionable on grounds of the invasion of privacy?
3. Does this individualized method of advertising undermine rational decision-making?
4. Is the description of the experiment given to potential participants at the supermarket checkout counters deceptive?

SUGGESTED SUPPLEMENTARY READINGS

ARRINGTON, ROBERT L. "Advertising and Behavior Control." *Journal of Business Ethics,* Vol. 1, No. 1 (February 1982).

BOK, SISSELA. *Lying: Moral Choice in Public and Private Life.* New York: Pantheon Books, 1978.

CLASEN, EARL A. "Marketing Ethics and the Consumer," *Harvard Business Review,* (January–February 1967).

FINN, DAVID. " Struggle for Ethics in Public Relations," *Harvard Business Review,* (January–February 1959).

FRIED, CHARLES. *Right and Wrong,* Chapter 3. Cambridge, Mass.: Harvard University Press, 1978.

GARDNER, DAVID M. "Deception in Advertising: A Conceptual Approach," *Journal of Marketing,* 39 (January 1975).

GREYSER, STEPHEN A. "Advertising: Attacks and Counters," *Harvard Business Review,* 50 (March 10, 1972).

HENTOFF, NAT. "Would You Run This Ad?" *Business and Society Review,* 14 (Summer 1975).

KEANE, JOHN G. "On Professionalism in Advertising," *Journal of Advertising,* Fall 1974.

LUCAS, JOHN T., and RICHARD GURMAN. *Truth in Advertising.* New York: American Management Association, 1972.

MILLUM, TREVOR. *Images of Woman: Advertising in Women's Magazines.* Totowa, N.J.: Rowman and Littlefield, 1975.

MOSKIN, J. ROBERT, ed. *The Case for Advertising.* New York: American Association of Advertising Agencies, 1973.

MURPHY, PAT, and BEN M. ENIS. "Let's Hear the Case Against Brand X." *Business and Society Review,* 12 (Winter 1974–75).

PACKARD, VANCE. *The Hidden Persuaders.* New York: Pocket Books, 1957.

PRESTON, IVAN L. *The Great American Blow-up: Puffery in Advertising and Selling.* Madison: University of Wisconsin Press, 1975.

REILLY, JOHN H., JR. "A Welfare Critique of Advertising," *American Journal of Economics and Sociology,* 31 (July 1972).

SANDAGE, C. H., and VERNON FRYBURGER. *Advertising Theory and Practice* (9th ed.). Homewood, Ill.: Richard D. Irwin, Inc., 1975.

STUART, FREDERICK, ed. *Consumer Protection from Deceptive Advertising.* Hempstead, N.Y.: Hofstra University, 1974.

CHAPTER 6

THE ENVIRONMENT

INTRODUCTION

Most of the controversy about the environment has emerged in the last two decades, a period which has caught business, government, and the general public equally unprepared for discussion about environmental problems. The reason we have been caught off guard is that environmental issues were formerly handled by relatively simple procedures which balanced conflicting interests. Those who polluted, for example, could be prosecuted and fined. It was thought that the community's interests were protected by such standard legal maneuvers, and it was largely unsuspected that the environment, once properly tended to, was not sufficiently resilient to return to its former state. More recently it has been argued that this optimistic outlook is naive. The contention is that technology, production, and their consequent environmental impact have advanced to the point where unrectifiable and uncontrollable global imbalances may emerge. Thus, whole sections of leading periodicals such as *National Geographic* now devote sections almost monthly to such topics as the dangers of "acid rain."

Well-know writers such as Garrett Hardin depict the environment as analogous to a pasture where competing herdsmen graze so many cattle in the quest for profits (as is economically rational for each cattleman to do) that eventually the common land is overgrazed and can no longer support even a single animal. Hardin argues that as each businessperson pursues his or her own best economic interest, they work toward the ruin of all—"the tragedy of the commons," as he puts it.[1] This analogy has been widely disputed in various sectors of business, which tend to see present environmental problems as sometimes involving unfortunate tradeoffs, but not irreversible damage to "the commons."

This battle has not emerged simply because we now *know* a great deal more than we used to know about ecosystems and the environmental sciences. The struggle has emerged because human life, animal life, and plant life seem threatened in new ways by our use of the environment. On the other hand, certain business interests are equally threatened by public policies protecting the environment against further encroachment. Classic conflicts between public and private interests have resulted. For example, there have been attempts to show that fluorocarbons in aerosol spray cans sufficiently damage the earth's ozone shield that serious repercussions may follow from continued use: e.g., melting of polar ice caps, flooding of cities along the world's coasts, and radioactive contamination. The food industry has been charged with raping the land by its failure to balance high-level methods of food production with the land's actual lower-level capacity to produce. The timber industry has been accused of deforestation without replenishment. And responsibility for various forms of pollution has been laid at the door of the bottle and can industries, plastics industries, smelters, the chemical industry, and the oil industry.

In this chapter these problems of environmental protection, as balanced against the interests of business, will concern us. In particular, the following problems will be discussed: What sort of framework of ethical principles is needed to attack these environmental issues? Does this framework grant *rights* either to citizens, corporations, animals, or natural objects? What balancing considerations between business and public interests can be validly institutionalized as public policies? What are the facts about the extent of the environmental crisis, and how do these facts bear on moral problems and questions of industry responsibility?

RELEVANT ETHICAL PRINCIPLES

Those who promote a radically new environmental ethic argue that there is a special problem produced by overpowering habits and background beliefs prevalent in Western culture. For example, there are religious beliefs about nature which inform the attitudes of many persons. According to some religious teachings human beings alone have intrinsic value; the rest of nature is inferior and is to be used for human enjoyment and betterment. From this view, humans are not conceived so much as a part of the ecosystem as external to it. Those who believe differently point out that such beliefs run deep in Western culture and will be difficult to eliminate short of overturning the entire religious tradition. Hence they call for a new environmental ethic.

Others disagree with this protective approach. They argue that we need to view the environment in a different way only to the extent that doing so would improve our quality of life and continued existence, now and in the future. That is, they argue that environmental concerns are valid only to the extent that they improve the human situation, and not because animals and plants have some sort of rights. This approach emphasizes the freedom of businesses to continue a heavy use of the environment, subject to limitations only insofar as they harm other individuals in society by this use of the environment.

The articles in this chapter by Neil Chamberlain, Alasdair MacIntyre, Richard DeGeorge, and R. G. Frey all exhibit limited sympathy for some aspect of this thesis, but none would accept the above contentions without heavy qualification. MacIntyre emphasizes the vital role that industry can play in a situation of public choice about the environment. Chamberlain argues that stronger environmental controls than those now operative "would require a larger sacrifice of immediate pleasures and preferences than the public is willing to make." DeGeorge looks to the welfare of future generations and ponders our present obligations to those generations. He too contends that many uncertainties attend such speculation, and that we are obliged to be extremely cautious with natural resources only if our own sacrifice is not too great.

In a separate article, William T. Blackstone takes a substantially different view. He asks whether a livable environment is merely a *desirable* outcome or one to which all persons have a *right*. After developing a theory of human rights, he argues that we do have a right to a livable environment because it is a necessary condition of human flourishing. He also contends that this moral right should be made a legal right (compatible with some qualifications in presently operative property rights). Blackstone urges his program because he thinks "we cannot expect private business to provide solutions to the multiple pollution problems for which they themselves are responsible." He explicitly argues against the self-regulation proposals advanced in some quarters: "We are deluding ourselves if we think that private business can function as its own pollution police." Blackstone then offers a series of arguments that focus on the incompatibility of the notions of economic profit and altruistic interest in a clean environment.

OBLIGATIONS TO ANIMALS AND NATURAL OBJECTS

Others take a starkly different view from those thus far mentioned. They disagree with the premise that nature should be protected if and only if it is in our best interest. This general problem about ethics and business appears repeatedly throughout this book: To justify something as being in one's own interest is quite different from justifying a position on grounds that moral duties and rights demand a certain action. (This problem was explored in Chapter 1 under the two topics of rights and egoism.) In the present case, those who support a strong environmental ethic—Christopher D. Stone and Peter Singer in the present chapter—do so because they believe we have an obligation to nature, or at least to the animals in it, not to destroy the ecosystem. From this perspective there are valuable aspects of nature quite independent of nature's usefulness to us, and it is important to protect those values. Because business interests can conflict with these "primary values," business's values must sometimes take second place. It does not follow from such a view that the value of the environment outweighs all human values, but only that it can outweigh the interests of the *business* community.

Many philosophers have maintained that human life alone deserves the special protections afforded by law and morality, but others have urged that special protections not be restricted to human life. At the root of much of this discussion is the philosophical claim that we cannot justify our "exploitation" of animals and other parts of the human environment on any rational philosophical basis, although human prejudice may lead us to believe we are justified. Recently a host of philosophers, including Feinberg and Singer in this chapter, have argued that there is no morally relevant difference between human life and animal life sufficient to justify the claim that *only* human life deserves these protections. What is it, Singer asks, that distinguishes the life of a human infant from the life of an adult chimpanzee so that infants are protected and chimpanzees are not? Do businesses and indeed all of us not have moral obligations to take the interests of animals into account when chopping down forests, preparing meals, and poisoning pests?

Singer's belief is that there is no consistent way to draw a line between human and animal life that will exclude one and include the other on as many occasions as we have traditionally thought. It cannot be merely the human capacity to feel pleasure and pain that makes the difference, for many animals share that capacity almost equally with humans. Nor can it be, for example, that humans have reason, the use of language, or the capacity to interact with the human community in ways animals to do not, for in these respects the retarded and irreversibly comatose infants fall into the same category as animals. From Singer's perspective, no matter where one draws the line between animals and humans, one is going to let in too much or exclude too little. If the *only* reason we offer for excluding animals is *merely* that they are not human, Singer believes we are guilty of "speciesism," a blind prejudice in favor of one's own species, and one dangerously akin to racism and sexism. Singer concludes that animals should have at least some rights to freedom from cruel treatment.

This line of argument has been attacked on the grounds that we have only limited obligations to animals, who possess no intrinsic rights. We have, for example, a society for the prevention of cruelty to animals, but support of this society does not entail acknowledgment of animal rights of any sort. This perspective is defended by R. G. Frey, who argues that both Feinberg and Singer are guilty of many undefended assumptions in their arguments favoring animal protections.

THE LAW AND THE COURTS

Some writers, including both Stone and Supreme Court Justice William O. Douglas, have argued that in various ways plants and animals—and perhaps even other natural objects such as oceans and trees—should be given legal standing. Only this maneuver, they argue, will provide natural objects with sufficient environmental status to protect them. While these natural entities cannot initiate court action, others could institute such actions on their behalf—just as guardians now do for children, the comatose, and the retarded. These natural objects could then be defended against the actions of corporations. Corporations will sometimes *win,* because they have some clear rights to use the environment; but if these entities themselves have rights, corporations cannot use environmental entitites in any way they please, and this conclusion is Stone's larger objective. Moreover, in his view these objects would have stricter legal standing than would corporations, which are mere legal "fictions." Natural objects, he argues, would themselves have rights that are based on their needs and interests: those who support this point of view argue that these needs and interests generate moral obligations to these entities, and this moral basis supplies the grounds for the grant of legal rights.

Stone admits that this proposal is "bound to sound odd or frightening or laughable" to some, but he thinks this psychological reaction occurs only because we already categorize natural entities as "things" rather than as "bearers of rights." He is calling, then, for an environmental liberation that parallels the "black liberation" and "women's liberation" movements that have resulted in expanded rights for blacks and women. The radically revisionary conclusions to which Stone is led are challenged, in the final selections in this section, by Feinberg and DeGeorge. Feinberg's article serves to synthesize many of the arguments found throughout the chapter. He begins with a careful analysis of the nature of rights. He argues that only entities capable of having *interests* possess rights—and therefore vegetables, trees, etc. cannot have rights. However, Feinberg argues that both animals and future generations of persons can be meaningfully said to have rights. These rights morally require that we of the present generation protect the environment in order to protect their interests. DeGeorge's article presents a sharp and direct reply to these claims.

These issues also bear on the problem of social and political control over industry. Many believe that severe curbs on industry and severe judicial penalties provide the only viable ways to protect the environment, while others believe that the filing of environmental impact statements and other currently employed practices will be sufficient. Still others believe that there is now a severe overregulation or underregulation in the face of the actual problem. Almost everyone believes that there will in the future be some loss of the liberty to use property as businesses see fit. Like all important values, some liberties must be balanced against other liberties. The heart of the environmental problem is the way in which the balancing is to be done, and especially how role considerations of justice, rights, and liberty (in the form of the free market so important to business) are themselves to be protected.

A second court opinion besides Douglas's is a composite of two opinions in a single case, *Reserve Mining Company* v. *United States*. Both opinions were delivered by Judge Myron Bright, but on separate dates. This case is among the best demonstrations of the complexity and uncertainty of evaluating environmental hazards. It occurred during a critical transistional phase of American environmental law. Prior to this case, the courts had held that the burden of proof in showing hazardous environmental conditions rested with the government, rather than there being a burden on industry to prove that the effects of its discharges are nonhazardous. Several cases in the mid-1970s, including this one, indicate a shift of perspective in the judiciary (a changing "environmental ethic"): the courts began to hold that the burden of proof was on industry rather than on the government. The *Reserve Mining* case began as a controversy over the effects of water pollution on aquatic life. However, on June 8, 1973, the focus shifted from fish to people—specifically, to the public health implications of Reserve Mining's discharge of asbestiform particles into the air and water.

There appears to be some sympathy in Judge Bright's first opinion (on June 4, 1974) for the position that the government must prove that a hazardous condition prevails. However, in his second opinion he seems to conclude that the identical evidence does prove that a public health hazard exists, and hence that the burden is on industry to take positive steps to end the pollution. Still, the matter of proof is not quite this simple. The larger thesis spanning these two opinions is that the burden of proof is always heavier on the government if it seeks an injunction to stop an industry from producing its products on grounds of pollution. The burden is lighter on the government when it seeks only to force industry to reduce the amount of its discharge, thereby cleaning up the environment but without stopping production. This approach by courts is now a familiar one, and its general framework is utilitarian: industry's pollution must be justified on a cost/benefit basis. If it costs the community more than it profits the community, then the company must either cease production or improve the quality of its environmental discharges. However, if it benefits the community more than it places the community at risk, then the balance of justification tips in the direction of industry.

PROBLEMS OF FACTUAL EVIDENCE AND INDUSTRY RESPONSIBILITY

Problems of judicial and agency rulings are touched on at several points in this chapter. In the aforementioned article by Chamberlain, for example, it is argued that governmental and judicial regulations are inevitable. However, he argues strongly for self-regulation and responsible cooperation in order that external interventions be kept at a minimum. In other quarters, governmental regulation of business through environmental control is even more strongly resisted. Opponents of regulation argue: (1) that there are inadequate statistics and predictions about energy resources and their destruction or depletion; (2) that there are presently no acceptable cost/benefit studies to show that governmental regulation serves the public interest more than it hurts; (3) that we have yet to understand how government can aid in balancing the public interest against private interests better than private interests themselves; and (4) that the problem of the environment is a problem created not only by business but also by public facilities (such as inadequate sewage treatment) and by poor government planning.

Judge Bright's second opinion in *Reserve Mining* is again illustrative. In this opinion he made reference to epidemiological studies of occupational exposure to asbestos and to the difficulty of applying this data to an assessment of the environmental hazard. In addition, this second opinion attempted to weigh the danger of possible "future harm" to the environment and to the public against the immediate economic hardship and loss which would be caused by closing the Silver Bay Mining facility. Judge Bright finds these problems of factual evidence to be almost impenetrable to reason.

Opponents of strict government regulation point as well to the need for greater education about the environment and for larger incentives (in contrast to regulation) to clean it up. They attempt to provide facts supporting unfettered or only mildly fettered business control. For example, they adduce facts to show that far from there being a food shortage created by poor agricultural land use, there is excellent land use and we possess the capacity to feed twice the number of persons now on the earth. These arguments, if correct in their premises, lead inescapably to the conclusion that voluntary controls and incentives should dominantly control business. But are the factual and ethical claims used in these arguments correct?

T.L.B.

Note

1. See the discussion of these problems in F. R. Anderson, *et al., Environmental Improvement Through Economic Incentives* (Baltimore: The Johns Hopkins University Press, 1977).

CORPORATIONS AND THE PHYSICAL ENVIRONMENT

Neil W. Chamberlain

The centrality of consumption as a social value is splendidly displayed in the matter of environmental quality. Public alarms over pollution and resource exhaustion lead to legislative controls and regulatory actions. These can be modulated, "within reason," with incremental effects on the environment. But if they begin to bite, in the sense of threatening consumption through higher prices and taxes, industry can count on a reduction in the alarm level. Not only industry's ox but society's own horsepower is being gored. Industry's responsibility to the environment is thus limited by society's conception of the good life—a conception that . . . can be traced back ultimately to values inculcated by the corporate system itself.

No single corporation—whatever its size or however socially sensitive its management—can break out of this institutionalized constraint.

THE DARK UNDERSIDE OF ECONOMIC GROWTH

Concern for the conservation of natural resources has a long history. Originating in aesthetic revulsion at the commercial despoliation of natural resources such as timberlands, scenic areas, and animal life, it eventually extended also to outcries against the unrestricted and wasteful exploitation of land and fossil fuels. Concern with pollution also has a long history. It early expressed itself in abhorrence of the concentration of smoke in Europe's growing cities and the fetid atmosphere of the "Satanic mills" of the industrial revolution. This latter, however, was viewed as a matter of entrepreneurial greed, a kind of class conflict rather than a general social disaster.

Present fears concerning depletion and pollution are more widespread, embracing imminent dangers both to life as we know it and to life itself. They are expressed in picturesque concepts such as "spaceship earth," which views the planet as a vessel in space, whose stock of provisions are all there is to sustain whatever the number of passengers, and so both provisions and number of passengers must be managed carefully. Others have described ours as a "throughput economy," which mines the earth for the materials out of which it fashions articles of consumption for temporary enjoyment; these, once used, are thrown back on the earth as though it were a dumpheap. The "mines" become exhausted and the dumpheap grows.

Let us agree at the outset that the problems of depletion and pollution are basically the same in that both involve the using up of natural resources. Pollution uses up air and water, just as extraction uses up minerals. Pollution reduces people to using air and water of inferior quality, just as mineral extraction drives producers to lower-grade ores. Presumably the producer bears the cost in the latter case but not in the former, but in both cases it is the consumer who ultimately pays, either a money cost or a real cost, and in any event this distinction is one that could conceivably be erased by appropriate forms of taxation on the producer, a subject with which we shall deal later. Production that takes place without pollution may nevertheless involve depletion, by dispersing scarce natural resources, but that distinction too, if important, could presumably be met by some form of "recovery" tax or regulation. The antipollution movement is founded on the "discovery" that air and water are natural resources that should not be squandered as though they were unlimited in quantity. They are now appreciated as scarce resources requiring economic use like any other resource. Thus, whether our discussion deals with one or the other, it relates to both . . . .

GOVERNMENT RESPONSE TO ENVIRONMENTAL CONCERNS

As concern for the environment spread from a handful of conservationists to a more general public, the federal government reacted with legislation to curb pollution. But how does a government go about such a task, when "the problem" has scarcely been defined and means of combating it are in a trial-and-error stage? The consumer-protection movement offers something of a model. Modest legislation takes a few hesitant steps forward. Thus in 1955 the Public Health Service was authorized to conduct limited research on air pollution and to offer technical assistance to state and local governments. The Clean Air Act of 1963 moved a little further by providing grants to the states to establish and maintain air-pollution control agencies and by authorizing federal authorities to initiate proceedings against interstate polluters. A 1965 amendment to this act for the first time recognized automobile exhaust as a contributor to unclean air and empowered the Secretary of Health, Education, and Welfare to set emission standards. This was followed by the Air Quality Act of 1967, which retained the provisions of the preceding legislation, but also called for collaboration of federal and state governments and major industrial corporations in setting standards for the most seriously polluted regions. . . .

In 1970 the Environmental Protection Agency (EPA) was established under administrative reorganization procedure, bringing together the water-quality office lodged in the Department of the Interior, the air-pollution control group in the Department of Health, Education, and Welfare, the pesticide control function then in the Department of Agriculture, and nuclear-radiation control previously under the jurisdiction of the Atomic Energy Commission. The new agency was mandated to conduct research, and to set and enforce standards with respect to air, water, and solid-waste pollution. . . .

If public awareness of environmental decay is recent, government response has been relatively quick and extensive. Indeed, the Nixon Administration by 1972 had moved to the position that Congress was overreacting and that such measures as the Water Pollution Control bill (enacted later that same year), which required total elimination of all effluent discharges into the nation's waterways by 1985, are wasteful, if not capricious. The Chairman of the Council on Environmental Quality has pointed out that the cost of pollution control, too, has an exponential aspect, so that removal of the last 1 percent of contaminant may cost as much as the removal of the first 99 percent. "Zero discharge" may thus be a goal that diverts substantial resources away from other more badly needed public works to an unnecessarily finicky scrubbing of air and water. In any event, we are safe in concluding that once the public had recognized pollution as a problem, the political authorities vied with one another in doing "something," piling laws on administrative agencies and legislative amendments on regulatory orders.

BUSINESS REACTION

Could anything be more predictable than the response of business to this flurry of political activity? . . . The first reaction is defensive and bitter: business is being made a scapegoat for society's own failings; politicians are pandering to a panicky public; the cleanup demanded will bankrupt many companies and increase the public's cost of living more than it realizes. After this initial irritation, business professionalism reasserts itself: the public-relations offices take over with the soothing message that industry is busily coping with an admittedly serious problem. Millions of dollars are being spent on the research needed to take effective action, even as billions are being spent to improve old equipment and develop new equipment in line with what is already known. This is the period when resistance to remedial action shades over into acceptance of the inevitability of some action, but this is accompanied by pressures for making standards "practical" and the time period for their enforcement "reasonable."

This reaction pattern is wholly understandable. It suggests that at least in some respects the Supreme Court was not too far afield in picturing the corporation as human. When, within the space of a decade, a cause takes on the dimensions of a crusade, with industry assuming the role of the infidels, what else but a defensive reaction can be expected? With pollution controls entailing costs running into literally unknown but clearly massive sums loosely spoken of as the "ransom" that would be legislatively demanded of business to permit it freedom to operate, how else could business feel but victimized, at least in the first fresh shock of recognition that the contest was "for real"?

The instinct to fight back, with whatever arguments come to hand, is surely understandable. Thus one leading businessman informed—mistakenly—a college audience that "U.S. Department of Commerce figures show that 219 plants last year were forced to shut down because of environmental pressures."[1] As a House-Senate conference committee pondered legislation to set strict limits on automobile pollution emissions in 1975, the executive vice president of Ford Motor Company, urging a specially called meeting of principal Ford suppliers and dealers to initiate a telegram campaign to their Washington representatives, "went so far as to claim that the bill 'could prevent continued production of automobiles after January 1, 1975.'"[2] The president of a steel company, speaking before a group of university economists, emphasized the adverse effects of ill-advised pollution control legislation: "The thrust for an improved environment has caused many of us in the steel industry to close and/or drastically alter plant operations; . . . shifted vital funds away from essential revenue producing activities, including research and development; increased the competitive advantage of foreign competitors; placed an additional annual operating cost burden on our industry of about $412 million."[3]

A sanitation engineering consultant, speaking of Detroit's costly and largely "wasted" efforts to control discharges into Lake Erie, drew more lurid conclusions: "This excessive expenditure diverts funds from other environmental blights in Detroit such as crime on the streets, ghettos, malnutrition, and the needs of education. Can Detroit afford to have such a warped concept of environmental priorities? Why can't a child be as important as a fish?"[4] Such costly public ventures into pollution control obviously increase business taxes and provide undesirable examples of what might be expected of business itself. A suspicious business partisan might conclude and feel justified in suggesting to others that there are "efforts afoot, avowedly to control the quality of the environment but more accurately to control industrial operations and the American way of life."[5]

Business's counterattack has included undercover efforts to "defuse" the public. A "news" item describing the movement against leaded gasoline as "misleading and irrelevant" asserted that no evidence existed that lead in the atmosphere poses a health hazard. *Natural History,* a magazine published by New York's American Museum of Natural History, traced the story to *Editor's Digest,* a division of Planned Communications Services, Inc., "a company that writes and distributes stories to small-circulation newspapers on behalf of corporate and industrial clients. This story, it turns out, originated with the Lead Industries Association. . . ."[6]

Corporate leadership is, on the whole, too sophisticated to rely solely on opposition when a problem has been shown to be real and demand for its solution has generated a popular following, however misguided. One time-tested device is to join the opposition in calling for a "common" effort. "We" have erred, but "we" can make up for our folly. Again Atlantic Richfield Company, employing reproductions of contemporary art to illustrate its "cultural" concern, offers what might paradoxically be referred to as a "good" example:

> The ideal: Seas that are permanently protected from man's abuse.
> The real: Thoughtlessly, man spews waste into the world's oceans. From the air, from the stream, from ships, all of it from ourselves.
> We must find new and better ways to guard our waters from ourselves. Our solutions must be swift. They must be creative and mature. For tomorrow the waters of the world will inherit what we do today.
> Throughout the world, man must learn to function without fouling the oceans—and the air and earth that adjoin them. Until then, we cannot protect the environment in which life began—and on which our lives still depend.[7]

In place of such soothing syrup, the steel industry prefers the language of hard cash: "Our industry has put its money where its mouth is. Companies producing about 98% of the nation's iron and steel spent slightly over $735 million between '66 and '71. In '71, they spent $161.5 million, equal to 10.3% of our total capital expenditures . . . the largest of any industry and twice the average for all manufacturing. Last year, environmental control spending accounted for about 20% of net profits. An additional 12% of initial construction costs, or $142,000,000 a year, must be spent annually to keep equipment working."[8]

But communicating with the public is not enough in a situation where the stakes are so high. The real objective is to help mold the legislation which cannot be avoided. Industry finds itself, willy-nilly, engaged in a bargaining process with politicians over the shape of pollution-control laws that will satisfy the public. The politicians can ignore neither the interests of large-scale industry, which after all exercises enormous, if not dominant, influence over the very structure and functioning of the American society,[9] nor the wishes and interests of their popular constituencies, whose votes must return them to office. Bargaining is something at which both politicians and industrialists have long been adept.

The passage of the Air Quality Act of 1967 nicely illustrates this process. Although the whole story of such an event can never be reassembled, it appears that the White House was more interested in the political than the pollution effect of endorsing *national* emission standards and actually offered little support for its own bill when introduced into the Senate. Industry lobbyists, at first alarmed over the bill's stringent provisions, became reassured during the course of informal meetings with staff members of the Air and Water Pollution Subcommittee of the Public Works Committee. In these discussions details were hashed out over such issues as how *regional* criteria would work, timetables for coordinating state standards, whether the federal government should be given powers to subpoena company records and monitor industry emissions. . . .

Controls over industry there are, and there will be more, but any which pose a threat to continuity of the corporate system as we know it are likely to be curbed not by the government's "knuckling under" to blatant industry demands, but simply by tempering the regulatory process. This can be done through jurisdictional ambiguities, budgetary curtailment, concessions to other competing political objectives, uncertainties in standard setting, and weakness in enforcement.

ACCEPTABILITY OF LIMITED PROGRESS

These limitations on the legislative and administrative protection of the environment do not mean that public interest will be slighted and the public's will thwarted. On the contrary, such incremental measures as are forthcoming to alleviate, in whatever degree, the discomforts of pollution will probably be sufficient to satisfy public pressures. This is because any more effective environmental controls would require a larger sacrifice of immediate pleasures and preferences than the public is willing to make.

When the costs of achieving more stringent standards of air and water purity drastically affect the prices of consumer goods, we can expect public resistance to the higher standards. We have already noted the contribution made by divided political objectives to less effective pollution control. In the kind of consumption-oriented society that we encountered in the preceding chapter, consumer goods and clean environment become seriously competing objectives. If, as has been estimated, the standards for automobile emissions now set for 1976 will add between $390 and $425 to the price of a car, we may confidently anticipate an outcry by the automobile-buying public. I concur with René Dubos when he says: "We would like to improve our polluted and cluttered environments, but we like gadgets and economic prosperity even more. In fact, values such as political power and gross national income so dominate our collective lives that we shall undertake the social and technological reforms essential for environmental control only if we are forced into action by some disaster."[10]

This consumption-mindedness of the American public goes beyond a desire for more goods. It is linked to a way or style of life that those goods make possible. It is thus not only the price increase that irritates car buyers, but the fact that even present emission controls increase fuel consumption and reduce engine performance. One consequence has been that some car owners have had emission controls disconnected. The manager of the auto-diagnostic clinic of the Missouri Automobile Club reported that one-fourth of the late-model cars going through his clinic had their emission controls tampered with. A Detroit automobile mechanic says that thirty of the forty automobile tune-ups he does every month involve modifications of the control system.[11]

The former head of EPA had no illusions about the unpopularity of actions necessary for effective pollution control if these begin to affect people's private lives. It has been popular to talk about "changing life styles," he observed, "but when someone finds out that means bicycling or carpooling to work, or going home at a different time, he may not be for it."[12] Nor do the politicians have any illusions on this score. When the iconoclast Admiral Hyman G. Rickover testified at House hearings on the prospects of a national energy shortage, he suggested the desirability of banning "nonessential" air conditioners and putting a high tax on such "luxuries" as clothes driers. A congressman thereupon "observed with undisguised disdain that the admiral had never run for office. 'What do you think we can do and still stay in office?' " he asked. John B. Connally, then Secretary of the Treasury and a former governor of Texas, advised the House committee that he too "was too much of a pragmatist" to embrace the Rickover program. He could live without air conditioning but would "hate to give it up." People can "save a tremendous amount of energy just by going around and turning off a few lights," Mr. Connally counseled reassuringly.[13]

Ambivalence over priorities in establishing political objectives ripens into profound disagreement between the disadvantaged minorities and the more advantaged majority within the general public. Blacks and Latins, large numbers of whom have suffered from lack of social amenities in matters of housing, health, education, and employment, often believe that the billions of dollars of expenditures that they hear advocated for clean air and water should be redirected into improving their general way of life. Appeals of the conservationists to save the marshlands near urban areas or the Everglades of Florida sound like an almost callous disregard for more fundamental reforms needed in the ghettos. It is not that the ghetto residents do not suffer from bad air and bad water; if anything, they are more the victims than the suburban whites. The polluted beaches characteristic of most large cities deprive black children of desirable recreation far more than they adversely affect white children who have access to less polluted waters of remoter areas, not to mention backyard swimming pools. Nevertheless, to blacks fighting against what often appears as a hopeless existence, pollution control emerges as a political objective rather far down the list. Consumption is more important than environment.

As one black leader put the matter: "We suffer from pollution as much as anyone, but we're not the beneficiaries of the affluence that produced the pollution."[14] For the government to institute stricter controls over industry, an action that causes the latter to pass along higher costs in the form of higher prices, thus appears to shut the blacks off from any opportunity of achieving the material advancement that they seek. It would be as though the government had capriciously increased the cost of the goods they buy by 10 or 20 percent at the very time it professed to be seeking to improve their standard of living.

Blacks and Latins are not the only groups who see their economic interests jeopardized by the campaign to clean up the environment. Workers whose jobs appear threatened by new pollution standards have often joined in opposition. The previously cited example of community persecution of a citizen group that secured a court order against the Blackwell, Oklahoma, zinc smelter of American Metal Climax has numerous counterparts. The 1972 National Conference on Strip Mining, meeting in Kentucky to pass a resolution urging abolition of this form of coal extraction, was harassed by some hundred strip miners from neighboring counties, wearing their work clothes and hard hats decorated with stickers proclaiming "I Dig Coal" and "Coal Puts Bread on My Table." "'I think you can understand the feelings of the men,' and Paul Patton, the young president of the Kentucky Elkhorn Company, who is a leading spokesman for the smaller operations. 'These people [the conferees] have the emotions of idealism, but my men have the emotions of their livelihood, which is a lot stronger.'"[15]

Although a number of national unions have adopted positions favorable to environmental protection, local union leaders often find themselves placed in an ambiguous position when the employment of their members seems to be the price of a cleaner environment.

A United Steelworkers local in El Paso lobbied hard and successfully in the city council recently to help an American Smelting & Refining Co. plant to obtain more time in which to bring its air-cleanup equipment up to par; many of the plant's 1,000 employees faced possible layoffs.

Representatives of the Teamsters Union, Glass Bottle Blowers Association and Steelworkers helped in September to stymie efforts by New Jersey legislators to impose restrictions on nonreturnable containers; there were warnings that up to 30,000 jobs were threatened.

Local 1 of the United Papermakers and Paperworkers in Holyoke, Mass., has replaced its customary fall job-safety campaign with a drive "to save jobs by halting the ecology steamroller." Union officials contend a local paper company had to abolish more than 150 jobs this year because of the "excessive cost of a pollution-control system. . . ."

A Maine labor representative arguing for a new oil refinery along the state's picturesque coast maintains, "We can't trade off the welfare of human beings for the sake of scenery. . . ."

United Auto Workers President Leonard Woodcock recently told a congressional subcommittee that "their economic circumstances require them to think first of jobs, paychecks and bread on the table. . . ."

Even A. F. Grospiron, president of the Oil, Chemical and Atomic Workers, which has taken a tougher antipollution stand than most unions, warns: "We will oppose those theoretical environmentalists who would make air and water pure without regard to whether or not people have food on their tables."[16]

Nor has management failed to perceive the advantage of encouraging closer collaboration with organized labor in opposition to more stringent environmental legislation or adminstrative regulation. "One of the things industry and labor have to do is get together to protect ourselves from these ecology groups that have one-track minds," one manager comments.[17] Corporate officials have also played on labor's fears and self-interest by pointing out that costly pollution standards required by the U.S. government, but not matched by foreign governments, would put American industry at a competitive disadvantage and thus would cause further loss of employment. The same argument has been used in support of federal assistance to industrial research and development and to such industry projects as the supersonic transport plane, which has been condemned by numerous scientists for both known and potential adverse environmental effects. The president's special consultant on technology asserted that the United States "needed" the program to stay competitive in technology with foreign countries.[18]

The consumer culture is too closely allied with corporate interests to subordinate the latter to ecological considerations. The dominant role of the corporation in American society derives from its ability to satisfy a mass-consumption appetite, not from its contribution to an unpolluted environment.

Notes

1. *The New York Times,* June 4, 1972. Subsequently a Department of Commerce employee denied that any such figure had been released and suggested that the speaker had taken his statistic from a business-news syndicate that had misinterpreted a federal study.
2. *Business Week,* December 5, 1970.
3. Reynold C. MacDonald, "Steel and the Environment: Today," an address before the Steel Industry Seminar, University of Chicago, June 14, 1972.
4. John E. Kinney, "Economic Effects of Ecological Efforts," Earhart Foundation Lecture, University of Detroit, March 30, 1971.
5. *Ibid.*
6. *Natural History,* December 1971, p. 6.
7. From a series of advertisements, this one appearing in *Intellectual Digest,* June 1972, p. 48.
8. MacDonald, "Steel and the Environment: Today."
9. As I have delineated in *The Place of Business in America's Future: A Study in Social Values* (New York: Basic Books, 1973).
10. René Dubos, *Reason Awake* (New York: Columbia University Press, 1970), pp. 193–194.
11. *Wall Street Journal,* June 22, 1972. In most states there is nothing illegal about this operation; only automobile manufacturers and dealers are covered by federal law.
12. William D. Ruckelshaus, quoted in *Business Week,* August 21, 1971, p. 58.
13. *The New York Times,* April 23, 1972.
14. James Spain, urban affairs director of Allied Chemical Corp. and president of the Association for the Integration of Management, quoted in "To Blacks, Ecology is Irrelevant," *Business Week,* November 14, 1970, p. 49.

15. *The New York Times,* June 19, 1972.
16. *Wall Street Journal,* November 19, 1971. Not all local union leaders have allowed fear of unemployment to blunt their demands for pollution control.
17. Walter Sherman, vice president of the Flambeau Paper Co., quoted in the *Wall Street Journal,* November 19, 1971.
18. William G. Magruder, quoted in *The New York Times,* May 23, 1972.

ETHICS AND ECOLOGY

William T. Blackstone

Much has been said about the right to a decent or livable environment. In his 22 January 1970 state of the union address, President Nixon stated: "The great question of the seventies is, shall we surrender to our surroundings, or shall we make our peace with Nature and begin to make the reparations for the damage we have done to our air, our land, and our water? . . . Clean air, clean water, open spaces—these would once again be the birthright of every American; if we act now, they can be." It seems, though, that the use of the term *right* by President Nixon, under the rubric of a "birthright" to a decent environment, is not a strict sense of the term. That is, he does not use this term to indicate that one has or should have either a legal right or a moral right to a decent environment. Rather he is pointing to the fact that in the past our environmental resources have been so abundant that all Americans did in fact inherit a livable environment, and it would be *desirable* that this state of affairs again be the case. Pollution and the exploitation of our environment is precluding this kind of inheritance.

Few would challenge the desirability of such a state of affairs or of such a "birthright." What we want to ask is whether the right to a decent environment can or ought to be considered a right in a stricter sense, either in a legal or moral sense. In contrast to a merely desirable state of affairs, a right entails a correlative duty or obligation on the part of someone or some group to accord one a certain mode of treatment or to act in a certain way.[1] Desirable states of affairs do not entail such correlative duties or obligations.

THE RIGHT TO A LIVABLE ENVIRONMENT
AS A HUMAN RIGHT

Let us first ask whether the right to a livable environment can properly be considered to be a human right. For the purposes of this paper, however, I want to avoid raising the more general question of whether there are any human rights at all. Some philosophers do deny that any human rights exist.[2] In two recent papers I have argued that human rights do exist (even though such rights may properly be overridden on occasion by other morally relevant reasons) and that they are universal and inalienable (although the actual exercise of such rights on a given occasion is alienable).[3] My argument for the existence of universal human rights rests, in the final analysis, on a theory of what it means to be human, which specifies the capacities for rationality and freedom as essential, and on the fact that there are no relevant grounds for excluding any human from the opportunity to develop and fulfill his capacities (rationality and freedom) as a human. This is not to deny that there are criteria which justify according human rights in quite different ways or with quite different modes of treatment for different persons, depending upon the nature and degree of such capacities and the existing historical and environmental circumstances.

If the right to a livable environment were seen as a basic and inalienable human right, this could be a valuable tool (both inside and outside of legalistic frameworks) for solving some of our environmental problems, both on a national and on an international basis. Are there any philosophical and conceptual difficulties in treating this right as an inalienable human right? Traditionally we have not looked upon the right to a decent environment as a human right or as an inalienable right. Rather, inalienable human or natural rights have been conceived in somewhat different terms; equality, liberty, happiness, life, and property. However, might it not be possible to view the right to a livable environment as being entailed by, or as constitutive of, these basic human or natural rights recognized in our political tradition? If human rights, in other words, are those rights which each human possesses in virtue of the fact that he is human and in virtue of the fact that those rights are essential in permitting him to live a human life (that is, in permitting him to fulfill his capacities as a rational and free being), then might not the right to a decent environment be properly categorized as such a human right? Might it not be conceived as a right which has emerged as a result of changing environmental conditions and the impact of those conditions on the very possibility of human life and on the possibility of the realization of other rights such as liberty and equality? Let us explore how this might be the case.

Given man's great and increasing ability to manipulate the environment, and the devastating effect this is having, it is plain that new social institutions and new regulative agencies and procedures must be initiated on both national and international levels to make sure that the manipulation is in the public interest. It will be necessary, in other words, to restrict or stop some practices and the freedom to engage in those practices. Some look upon such additional state planning, whether national or international, as unnecessary further intrusion on man's freedom. Freedom is, of course, one of our basic values, and few would deny that excessive state control of human action is to be avoided. But such restrictions on individual freedom now appear to be necessary in the interest of overall human welfare and the rights and freedoms of *all* men. Even John Locke with his stress on freedom as an inalienable right recognized that this right must be construed so that it is consistent with the equal right to freedom of others. The whole point of the state is to restrict unlicensed freedom and to provide the conditions for equality of rights for all. Thus it seems to be perfectly consistent with Locke's view and, in general, with the views of the founding fathers of this country to restrict certain rights or freedoms when it can be shown that such restriction is necessary to insure the equal rights of others. If this is so, it has very important implications for the rights to freedom and to property. These rights, perhaps properly seen as inalienable (though this is a controversial philosophical question), are not properly seen as unlimited or unrestricted. When values which we hold dear conflict (for example, individual or group freedom and the freedom of all, individual or group rights and the rights of all, and individual or group welfare and the welfare of the general public) something has to give; some priority must be established. In the case of the abuse and waste of environmental resources, less individual freedom and fewer individual rights for the sake of greater public welfare and equality of rights seem justified. What in the past had been properly regarded as freedoms and rights (given what seemed to be unlimited natural resources and no serious pollution problems) can no longer be so construed, at least not without additional restrictions. We must recognize both the need for such restrictions and the fact that none of our rights can be realized without a livable environment. Both public welfare and equality of rights now require that natural resources not be used simply according to the whim and caprice of individuals or simply for personal profit. This is not to say that all property rights must be denied and that the state must own all productive property, as the Marxist argues. It is to insist that those rights be qualified or restricted in the light of new ecological data and in the interest of the freedom, rights, and welfare of all.

The answer then to the question, Is the right to a livable environment a human right? is yes. Each person has this right *qua* being human and because a livable environment is essential for one to fulfill his human capacities. And given the danger to our environment today and hence the danger to the very possibility of human existence, access to a livable environment must be conceived as a right which imposes upon everyone a correlative moral obligation to respect.

The Right to a Livable Environment as a Legal Right

If the right to a decent environment is to be treated as a legal right, then obviously what is required is some sort of legal framework which gives this right a legal status. Such legal frameworks have been proposed. Sen. Gaylord Nelson, originator of Earth Day, recently proposed a Constitutional Amendment guaranteeing every American an inalienable right to a decent environment.[4] Others want to formulate an entire "environmental bill of rights" to assist in solving our pollution problems. Such a bill of rights or a constitutional revision would provide a legal framework for the enforcement of certain policies bearing on environmental issues. It would also involve the concept of "legal responsibility" for acts which violate those rights. Such legal responsibility is beginning to be enforced in the United States. President Nixon on 23 December 1970 signed an executive order requiring industries to obtain federal permits before dumping pollutants. He issued the order not under the authority of new legislation but under the Refuse Act of 1899, which was originally designed to control discharges in connection with dredging and water construction operations but now has been broadened by Supreme Court decisions to cover pollution resulting from industrial operations. (The extension of this act is similar to my suggestion above, namely, the extension of the constitutional rights to equality, liberty, and property to include the right to a livable environment.)

Others propose that the right to a decent environment also be a cardinal tenet of international law. Pollution is not merely a national problem but an international one. The population of the entire world is affected by it, and a body of international law, which includes the right to a decent environment and the accompanying policies to save and preserve our environmental resources, would be an even more effective tool than such a framework at the national level. Of course, one does not have to be reminded of the problems involved in establishing international law and in eliciting obedience to it. Conflicts between nations are still settled more by force than by law or persuasion. The record of the United Nations attests to this fact. In the case of international conflict over environmental interests and the use of the environment, the possibility of international legal resolution, at least at this stage of history, is somewhat remote; for the body of enforceable international law on this topic is meager indeed. This is not to deny that this is the direction in which we should (and must) move.

A good case can be made for the view that not all moral or human rights should be legal rights and that not all moral rules should be legal rules. It may be argued that any society which covers the whole spectrum of man's activities with legally enforceable rules minimizes his freedom and approaches totalitarianism. There is this danger. But just as we argued that certain traditional rights and freedoms are properly restricted in order to insure the equal rights and welfare of all, so also it can plausibly be argued that the human right to a livable environment should become a legal one in order to assure that it is properly respected. Given the magnitude of the present dangers to the environment and to the welfare of all humans, and the ingrained habits and rules, or lack of rules, which permit continued waste, pollution, and destruction of our environmental resources, the legalized status of the right to a livable environment seems both desirable and necessary.

Such a legal right would provide a tool for pressing environmental transgressions in the courts. At the present the right to a livable environment, even if recognized as a human right, is not generally recognized as a legal one. One cannot sue individuals or corporations for polluting the environment, if the pollution harms equally every member of a community. One can sue such individuals or corporations if they damage one's private property but not if they damage the public environment. It is true that public officials have a legal standing in cases of generalized pollution, but unfortunately they have done little to exercise that standing.

Since public officials are failing to take steps to protect the environment, Joseph Sax, professor of law at the University of Michigan, argues that the right to take environmental disputes to court must be obtained as a right of private citizens: "The No. 1 legal priority of those concerned with environmental protection now is that the old restraints of the public nuisance doctrine and other archaic rules be rooted out of the law and be replaced with the recognition of every citizen's opportunity to enforce at law the right to a decent environment."[5] Sax himself drafted a model environmental law which was presented to the Michigan legislature, which "empowered any person or organization to sue any private or public body and to obtain a court order restraining conduct that is likely to pollute, impair, or destroy the air, water, or other material resources or the public trust therein."[6] This bill has now become law, and a similar bill is pending in the U.S. Congress, having been introduced by Senators McGovern and Hart and Representative Udall. I concur with Sax that this law, which provides an enforceable right to a decent environment and which places the burden of proof on a polluter or would-be polluter to show that his action affecting the environment is consistent with public health and welfare, "offers the promise of a dramatic legal break-through in the effort to protect environmental quality."[7] Although it may add to the clogged conditions of the courts, it should also have the effect of encouraging careful planning of activities which affect the environment.

The history of government, in this country and elsewhere, has been that of the gradual demise of a laissez-faire philosophy of government. Few deny that there are areas of our lives where government should not and must not intrude. In fact, what we mean by a totalitarian government is one which exceeds its proper bounds and attempts to control nearly all human activities. But in some areas of human life, it has been seen that the "keep-government-out-of-it" attitude just will not work. The entire quality of life in a society is determined by the availability and distribution of goods and services in such vital areas as education, housing, medical treatment, legal treatment, and so on. In the field of education, for example, we have seen the need for compulsory education and, more recently, for unitary school systems in order to provide equality of educational opportunity. . . .

In the same way, it is essential that government step in to prevent the potentially dire consequences of industrial pollution and the waste of environmental resources. Such government regulations need not mean the death of the free enterprise system. The right to private property can be made compatible with the right to a livable environment, for if uniform antipollution laws were applied to all industries, then both competition and private ownership could surely continue. But they would continue within a quite different set of rules and attitudes toward the environment. This extension of government would not be equivalent to totalitarianism. In fact it is necessary to insure equality of rights and freedom, which is essential to a democracy.

We suggested above that it is necessary to qualify or restrict economic or property rights in the light of new ecological data and in the interest of the freedom, rights, and welfare of all. In part, this suggested restriction is predicated on the assumption that we cannot expect private business to provide solutions to the multiple pollution problems for which they themselves are responsible. Some companies have taken measures to limit the polluting effect of their operations, and this is an important move. But we are deluding ourselves if we think that private business can function as its own pollution police. This is so for several reasons: the primary objective of private business is economic profit. Stockholders do not ask of a company, ''Have you polluted the environment and lowered the quality of the environment for the general public and for future generations?'' Rather they ask, ''How high is the annual dividend and how much higher is it than the year before?'' One can hardly expect organizations whose basic norm is economic profit to be concerned in any great depth with the long-range effects of their operations upon society and future generations or concerned with the hidden cost of their operations in terms of environmental quality to society as a whole. Second, within a free enterprise system companies compete to produce what the public wants at the lowest possible cost. Such competition would preclude the spending of adequate funds to prevent environmental pollution, since this would add tremendously to the cost of the product—unless all other companies would also conform to such antipollution policies. But in a free enterprise economy such policies are not likely to be self-imposed by businessmen. Third, the basic response of the free enterprise system to our economic problems is that we must have greater economic growth or an increase in gross national product. But such growth many ecologists look upon with great alarm, for it can have devastating long-range effects upon our environment. Many of the products of uncontrolled growth are based on artificial needs and actually detract from, rather than contribute to, the quality of our lives. A stationary economy, some economists and ecologists suggests, may well be best for the quality of man's environment and of his life in the long run. Higher GNP does not automatically result in an increase in social well-being, and it should not be used as a measuring rod for assessing economic welfare. This becomes clear when one realizes that the GNP

> aggregates the dollar value of all goods and services produced—the cigarettes as well as the medical treatment of lung cancer, the petroleum from offshore wells as well as the detergents required to clean up after oil spills, the electrical energy produced and the medical and cleaning bills resulting from the air-pollution fuel used for generating the electricity. The GNP allows no deduction for negative production, such as lives lost from unsafe cars or environmental destruction perpetrated by telephone, electric and gas utilities, lumber companies, and speculative builders.[8]

To many persons, of course, this kind of talk is not only blasphemy but subversive. This is especially true when it is extended in the direction of additional controls over corporate capitalism. (Some ecologists and economists go further and challenge whether corporate capitalism can accommodate a stationary state and still retain its major features.)[9] The fact of the matter is that the ecological attitude forces one to reconsider a host of values which have been held dear in the past, and it forces one to reconsider the appropriateness of the social and economic systems which embodied and implemented those values. Given the crisis of our environment, there must be certain fundamental changes in attitudes toward nature, man's use of nature, and man himself. Such changes in attitudes undoubtedly will have far-reaching implications for the institutions of private property and private enterprise and the values embodied in these institutions. Given that crisis we can no longer look upon water and air as free commodities to be exploited at will. Nor can the private ownership of land be seen as a lease to use that land in any way which conforms merely to the personal desires of the owner. In other words, the environmental crisis is forcing us to challenge what had in the past been taken to be certain basic rights of man or at least to restrict those rights. And it is forcing us to challenge institutions which embodied those rights. . . .

ETHICS AND TECHNOLOGY

I have been discussing the relationship of ecology to ethics and to a theory of rights. Up to this point I have not specifically discussed the relation of technology to ethics, although it is plain that technology and its development is responsible for most of our pollution problems. This topic deserves separate treatment, but I do want to briefly relate it to the thesis of this work.

It is well known that new technology sometimes complicates our ethical lives and our ethical decisions. Whether the invention is the wheel or a contraceptive pill, new technology always opens up new possibilities for human relationships and for society, for good and ill. The pill, for example, is revolutionizing sexual morality, for its use can preclude many of the bad consequences normally attendant upon premarital intercourse. *Some* of the strongest arguments against premarital sex have been shot down by this bit of technology (though certainly not all of them). The fact that the use of the pill can prevent unwanted pregnancy does not make premarital sexual intercourse morally right, nor does it make it wrong. The pill is morally neutral, but its existence does change in part the moral base of the decision to engage in premarital sex. In the same way, technology at least in principle can be neutral—neither necessarily good nor bad in its impact on other aspects of the environment. Unfortunately, much of it is bad—very bad. But technology can be meshed with an ecological attitude to the benefit of man and his environment.

I am not suggesting that the answer to technology which has bad environmental effects is necessarily more technology. We tend too readily to assume that new technological developments will always solve man's problems. But this is simply not the case. One technological innovation often seems to breed a half-dozen additional ones which themselves create more environmental problems. We certainly do not solve pollution problems, for example, by changing from power plants fueled by coal to power plants fueled by nuclear energy, if radioactive waste from the latter is worse than pollution from the former. Perhaps part of the answer to pollution problems is less technology. There is surely no real hope of returning to nature (whatever that means) or of stopping *all* technological and scientific development, as some advocate. Even if it could be done, this would be too extreme a move. The answer is not to stop technology, but to guide it toward proper ends, and to set up standards of antipollution to which all technological devices must conform. Technology has been and can be used to destroy and pollute an environment, but it can also be used to save and beautify it.

Notes

1. This is a dogmatic assertion in this context. I am aware that some philosophers deny that rights and duties are correlative. Strictly interpreted this correlativity thesis is false, I believe. There are duties for which there are no correlative rights. But space does not permit discussion of this question here.
2. See Kai Nielsen's "Scepticism and Human Rights," *Monist,* 52, no. 4 (1968): 571–594.
3. See my "Equality and Human Rights," *Monist,* 52, no. 4 (1968): 616–639; and my "Human Rights and Human Dignity," in Laszlo and Gotesky, eds., *Human Dignity.*
4. *Newsweek,* 4 May 1970, p. 26.
5. Joseph Sax, "Environment in The Courtroom," *Saturday Review,* 3 October 1970, p. 56.
6. *Ibid.*
7. *Ibid.*
8. See Melville J. Ulmer, "More Than Marxist," *New Republic,* 26 December 1970, p. 14.
9. See Murdock and Connell, "All about Ecology," *Center Magazine,* 3, no. 1 (January–February 1970): 63.

POWER INDUSTRY MORALITY

Alasdair MacIntyre

We are in one of those phases, recurrent in American history, in which morality has been rediscovered yet once again. It is characteristic of such phases that a hunt for scapegoats ensues, focusing our concerns in precisely the wrong way on precisely the wrong issues. Blaming and punishing individuals becomes a substitute for asking what it was in the structures of our common life that at the very least made possible and perhaps even positively engendered moral fault and failure.

From Alasdair MacIntyre, "Power Industry Morality," in *Symposium,* a Report from The Edison Electric Institute, Advertising Supplement to the *New York Review of Books,* pp. 7–9. Reprinted by permission.

The present fashionable concern with morality in general and the practice of scapegoating in particular concentrate their concern almost exclusively upon breaches of the kind of moral rule that tells us only what we ought not to do. Our very concern with an emphasis upon negative, prohibiting rules leads us to lose sight of what is, in fact, centrally important to morality and thus, in turn, to fail to give due importance to these self-same negative, prohibiting rules.

The record of the electric power industry, in abstaining from breaking such negative, prohibiting rules, is by and large an exemplary one. Paradoxically enough, insofar as I am inclined to question the moral resources of the electric power industry, it is because in one way its moral record is as good as it is. The morality of the industry has been essentially a negative one of proved abstinence from wrongdoing.

Since the end of the Great Depression, the electric power industry has inflexibly interpreted its legally mandated task, at the heart of which is the requirement to supply electric power on demand. The American electric power industry not only supplied power with a success unparalleled in human history, but actually participated in creating the demand that made that success necessary to the rest of American industry. All this was achieved in such a way that neither the more general question: "Growth for what?" nor the more specific question: "Electric power for what?" needed to be raised, let alone answered. Those questions implicitly were held to be questions only for consumers, just as questions of the legal constraints to be imposed on the provision and use of electric power were held to be questions for the Congress and for citizens.

The morality required and practiced by the industry was generally a strict morality of non-intervention in every area but that which it and others regarded as its own legitimate realm. There was one positive aspect to the morality: its basic assumption, so firmly held as scarcely needing to be stated, was that the providing of electric power within the limits set by these negative constraints was an unqualified good.

Environmental concerns did not emerge until the very end of the period about which I am speaking; and the obvious connections between the provision of electric power and the possibilities both of providing employment for an increasing work force and of increasing the comfort of domestic life reinforced this assumption. The consequence was that a whole range of decisions came to be treated as purely or almost purely technical decisions to be handed over to the economists and the engineers: what types of plants should be built, where should they be sited, at what points should investment be made, what skills did the industry need. Congress provided the mandate, the consumer provided the data for prediction, the executives of the industry provided the commercial integrity and the skills for answering such questions, but the questions themselves were technical, not moral.

The electric power industry—and in this it has been no different from the rest of us in modern society—has allowed its moral perspectives to be defined too much in terms of the negative prohibiting and constraining rules and not enough in terms of positive goods that ought to inform its tasks. It is those goods that provide the distinctive moral dimension in any definition of the future tasks of the electric power industry. We can very happily take for granted the need to observe the requirements of the negative rules; what we do need is a more explicit assertion of the industry's positive moral tasks.

One positive moral task of the industry is to assume a large public responsibility in areas that it has hitherto treated with a scrupulous but, if I am right, partly misplaced respect as the responsibility either of the Congress or the executive branch of government or of the industrial, commercial and private consumer. That responsibility is to urge, cajole and compel our society to make certain choices and to make those choices in as open, as explicit and as rational a way as possible. There are two different kinds of reason why this responsibility falls to the electric power industry. The first is concerned with its unrivaled strategic position in the supply of power and with the scale and scope of its resources, especially the industry's accumulation of relevant knowledge and relevant skills. Both government and the general public have to learn what are the applications and consequences of alternative energy sources under specific local conditions of particular communities and environments. Engineering, economic, environmental and social considerations are going to have to be presented within a framework of political choice.

It is perhaps obvious that the members of the electric power industry are, as a group, uniquely well-fitted to present such choices. It would be required of them that they transcend their position as one special interest group among others. Would we then be asking them to become moral supermen? There is no simple, glib answer. But part of the complex answer is that we have asked no less from a variety of special interest groups in times of national crisis, especially during the Second World War.

The second type of reason for suggesting that the industry has this special and relatively new responsibility is that so far those who have been conveniently assigned this task by the democratic process have signally failed to discharge it in any but the most inadequate ways.

We have in our society only two institutionalized methods for coordinating individual preferences and transforming them into public choices: those of the market and its allied institutions, and those of government legislation, taxation and regulation. It is scarcely surprising that public debate has focused, explicitly and implicitly, on energy questions as elsewhere on the choice between those two, and that the form of public debate has been largely that of an indictment of each of these methods by the proponents of the other. The sad fact of course is that both parties are right; both methods are grossly defective, and specifically so with respect to the kind of choices that our society now needs to formulate.

Consider first some defects of the mechanisms of the market. Markets only provide mechanisms for coordinating individual preferences once those preferences have been formulated and expressed in acts of consumption. The market, therefore, is of no help to us in those areas of life where we have to decide what our patterns of consumption are to be, how our preferences are to be ranked, how our desires are to be ordered. The debate on energy is centrally about investment; and it is a debate that has to be conducted within what Daniel Bell has felicitously called the "public household." We need to reason together in order to discover with what choices we want to enter the market. We are, that is to say, at a point in the argument where to tell us to rely on the mechanisms of the market is not so much mistaken as irrelevant.

There are weaknesses and defects in our system of political decision-making that correspond precisely to the weaknesses and defects of the market. It, like the market, is responsive to the pressures of the present much more rationally than to those of the future, partly because our ability to predict the future accurately is in general extraordinarily limited. And it, like the market, is far more effective at expressing already formulated choices on familiar issues than at formulating new possibilities of choice in unfamiliar areas. Neither the market nor the political system will provide the ordinary citizen with an adequate arena for formulating and expressing radically new choices of the kind that the energy debate thrusts upon us. And if public discussion that will enable ordinary citizens to formulate and express radically new choices does not take place, then the political and economic outcomes will inevitably be sadly defective.

But who is to begin the debate necessary to supplement our conventional economic and political institutions? Who is to educate the educators? I see very few individuals or institutions who are both capable of taking up this task and who possess the resources and the strategic position to carry it through, apart from those individuals and institutions comprised by the electric power industry. Their work compels them to interact with both producers and consumers at essential points. They have a peculiar responsibility, which arises from the fact that if they do not discharge it, it is unlikely that anyone else will. If the industry does embark on this task, it will perhaps be accused of trying to preempt the democratic process; but if it does not take action that will render it liable to such accusations, the democratic process itself may fail us.

What then is the task, and why does it have moral dimensions? In order to answer this question, I shall have to state briefly and unoriginally what I take the energy crisis to be. There is no more of a shortage of available energy now than at any other time; what has suddenly become unavailable is energy at the kind of low price to us to which we had become accustomed. What we now have to debate is what we are prepared to pay for what and to whom and how are we going to pay for it. The major possibility that we confront is of a gigantic shift in patterns of investment. And if we invest massively in new energy sources or in new ways and to new extents in existing sources, then we shall necessarily by shifting our investment away from something else important to our lives. Hence the energy crisis is a crisis about our whole way of life and not just about energy.

It is not difficult to see that when we rethink the wide range of questions facing America as questions about energy, four different kinds of moral concern must arise. The first is a concern for complexity. Oversimplification, the sacrifice of complexity, is in fact a crucial form of the vice of untruthfulness. Yet this is not the only morally damaging harm that is likely to arise from oversimplification of the issues. Just because so many different kinds of issues of policy and practice interlock at the point of energy use, there is no simple way to assess the costs and benefits that will arise from any particular proposal. How, for example, are we to weigh as considerations relevant to the same proposal the harm of damage to the environment against the harm of making fewer jobs available to those who badly need work, and both against the harm of injury and death to a certain number of presently unidentifiable individuals? It is always much easier for us to consider these issues in a piecemeal, local way, in which some particular compromise—determined through bargaining by local circumstances and balance of power—will, in the short run, at least, satisfy the particular, local contending parties. Our whole political and legislative process is biased towards oversimplified statements of problems and, consequently, not only oversimplified but unjust solutions.

Because our culture possesses no general set of standards that will enable us to evaluate costs and benefits of very different types in a single rational argument, it is all the more important that our evaluations satisfy two minimal requirements of justice. The first is that everyone relevantly involved—and where energy is concerned that means everyone—should have a chance to say what is to count as a cost and what as a benefit. The second is that, so far as possible, those who receive the benefits should also be those who pay the costs and vice versa. Neither the former nor the latter principle has received anything like adequate attention in recent debates. When environmentalists urge policies that will significantly reduce the number of jobs that might otherwise be available, it is rarely, perhaps never, the case that they are able to show *either* that those who would lose their opportunities of work are the same people who would benefit from the environment *or* that those who would lose their opportunities to work have had a part in shaping the conception and criteria of costs and benefits involved. Environmentalists in the present have sometimes been as untrammeled in endangering other people's jobs as industrialists in the past were in endangering other people's investments. Equally, when opponents of nuclear power stations urge policies that will significantly increase our future dependence on coal, the lives that will be lost as a result of their policies are not their own. Justice demands not only that everyone have a voice and a vote, but that some people—the populations that will bear the relevant risks and dangers, or most of them—have more of a voice and more of a vote than others.

There is at least one further requirement that must be met if justice is to be served. Because the energy crisis is primarily a crisis about the investment of resources, ordinary citizens are going to have no opportunity to understand how the costs and benefits of different investment policies do and will impinge upon them, if the costs are systematically concealed by subsidy. For the inhabitants of most advanced countries, the cheapness of energy to the consumer in the past 50 years has disguised its true costs. Ordinary citizens respond to their everyday experience and, if their everyday experience conceals what they are really paying for energy in all sorts of disguised ways, then no amount of theoretical education is likely to succeed. Only if there is a widespread perception of what the costs and benefits of different energy policies are can we decide both democratically and rationally how it is just to distribute costs and benefits.

Justice and truthfulness are not the only virtues central to determining energy production and use. Another is the ability to live with unpredictability.

We need to plan on a large scale, but we also have to recognize that our plans are for a future that is always apt to surprise us with its unexpectedness. In part, our social future is unpredictable because of the ways in which the future development of mathematics, science and technology are unpredictable. An obvious and obviously crucial example is the mathematics of Turing or of von Neumann, work essential to the development of modern computing science and engineering, and work whose outcome could not have been rationally predicted in advance.

In changing the social world and its national environment, we also change ourselves. No matter how sophisticated our social planning with respect to energy or to anything else, we can never rule out the possibility that in the course of implementing our plans we shall acquire views, interests and desires markedly different from those that led us to draw up and implement our original plans. Hence it is crucial that our planning is not so inflexible that it leaves our future selves—let alone successor generations—with no or few options acceptable to them because we were, at an early stage, too rigidly insistent on what is now acceptable to us.

It follows that there are great moral as well as practical dangers in making too many large-scale irreversible investment decisions that foreclose on future choices. This is especially a danger because the urgency of our immediate needs always tempts us towards short-term solutions.

Some of my statements about justice might seem supportive to the advocates of massive investment in nuclear power, while what I am now saying about the need for an ability to live with unpredictability may seem to endorse what some of their critics have said. But what matters at this juncture is not so much the particular policy implications of particular points; rather, it is the need to underline the fact that we ought not to expect moral considerations all to point in one single policy direction. There is a genuinely tragic dimension to the energy debate in that any particular policy direction is going to involve the sacrifice of some authentic goods for the sake of others. Our culture lacks any clear sense of how to handle tragic situations, situations that reveal our moral and human limitations in relation to the tasks imposed upon us.

Because we have never learned to face up to our moral limitations, we have lost to a large degree our vision of positive possibility. We have trudged for so long into a future of apparently limitless consumption that we do not now find it easy to remember who we are and what links us to others. The notion of possibility is always the notion of some future form of community that provides us now with standards and goals by which to diagnose our various forms of inadequacy and to set about remedying them. Just such a common vision—partial, not always coherent, but providing the essential sustenance for our constitution—was implicit in the founding of this republic.

What I am suggesting is this: that to press forward in the public arena the debate about energy, in such a way as to make its moral dimensions clear so far as possible to the whole society, will reveal to that society that it is, to a degree that a good deal of political rhetoric conceals from us, involved in a moral crisis as well as in an energy crisis. The prospect is a dismaying one and requires courage: we do not know how to reason together morally in an effective way. And this lack—just because it is something wanting in the social order as a whole—will never be remedied unless we face it as a society.

SHOULD TREES HAVE STANDING?— TOWARD LEGAL RIGHTS FOR NATURAL OBJECTS

Christopher D. Stone

Throughout legal history, each successive extension of rights to some new entity has been, theretofore, a bit unthinkable. We are inclined to suppose the rightlessness of rightless "things" to be a decree of Nature, not a legal convention acting in support of some status quo. It is thus that we defer considering the choices involved in all their moral, social, and economic dimensions. And so the United States Supreme Court could straight-facedly tell us in *Dred Scott* that Blacks had been denied the rights of citizenship "as a subordinate and inferior class of beings, who had been subjugated by the dominant race. . . ."[1] In the nineteenth century, the highest court in California explained that Chinese had not the right to testify against white men in criminal matters because they were "a race of people whom nature has marked as inferior, and who are incapable of progress or intellectual development beyond a certain point . . . between whom and ourselves nature has placed an impassable difference."[2] The popular conception of the Jew in the 13th Century contributed to a law which treated them as "men *ferae naturae,* protected by a quasi-forest law. Like the roe and the deer, they form an order apart."[3] Recall, too, that it was not so long ago that the foetus was "like the roe and the deer." In an early suit attempting to establish a wrongful death action on behalf of a negligently killed foetus (now widely accepted practice), Holmes, then on the Massachusetts Supreme Court, seems to have thought it simply inconceivable "that man might owe a civil duty and incur a conditional prospective liability in tort to one not yet in being."[4] The first woman in Wisconsin who thought she might have a right to practice law was told that she did not, in the following terms:

From *Southern California Law Review,* vol. 45 (1972) pp. 453–460, 463–464, 480–481, 486–487. Reprinted by permission.

The law of nature destines and qualifies the female sex for the bearing and nurture of the children of our race and for the custody of the homes of the world. . . .[A]ll life-long callings of women, inconsistent with these radical and sacred duties of their sex, as is the profession of the law, are departures from the order of nature; and when voluntary, treason against it. . . . The peculiar qualities of womanhood, its gentle graces, its quick sensibility, its tender susceptibility, its purity, its delicacy, its emotional impulses, its subordination of hard reason to sympathetic feeling, are surely not qualifications for forensic strife. Nature has tempered woman as little for the juridical conflicts of the court room, as for the physical conflicts of the battle field. . . .[5]

The fact is, that each time there is a movement to confer rights onto some new "entity," the proposal is bound to sound odd or frightening or laughable. This is partly because until the rightless thing receives its rights, we cannot see it as anything but a *thing* for the use of "us"—those who are holding rights at the time. In this vein, what is striking about the Wisconsin case above is that the court, for all its talk about women, so clearly was never able to see women as they are (and might become). All it could see was the popular "idealized" version of *an object it needed.* Such is the way the slave South looked upon the Black. There is something of a seamless web involved: there will be resistance to giving the thing "rights" until it can be seen and valued for itself; yet, it is hard to see it and value it for itself until we can bring ourselves to give it "rights"—which is almost inevitably going to sound inconceivable to a large group of people.

The reason for this little discourse on the unthinkable, the reader must know by now, if only from the title of the paper. I am quite seriously proposing that we give legal rights to forests, oceans, rivers and other so-called "natural objects" in the environment—indeed, to the natural environment as a whole.

As strange as such a notion may sound, it is neither fanciful nor devoid of operational content. In fact, I do not think it would be a misdescription of recent developments in the law to say that we are already on the verge of assigning some such rights, although we have not faced up to what we are doing in those particular terms. We should do so now, and begin to explore the implications such a notion would hold.

Toward Rights for the Environment

Now, to say that the natural environment should have rights is not to say anything as silly as that no one should be allowed to cut down a tree. We say human beings have rights, but—at least as of the time of this writing—they can be executed. Corporations have rights, but they cannot plead the fifth amendment; *In re Gault* gave 15-year-olds certain rights in juvenile proceedings, but it did not give them the right to vote. Thus, to say that the environment should have rights is not to say that it should have every right we can imagine, or even the same body of rights as human beings have. Nor is it to say that everything in the environment should have the same rights as every other thing in the environment.

But for a thing to be *a holder of legal rights,* something more is needed than that some authoritative body will review the actions and processes of those who threaten it. As I shall use the term, "holder of legal rights," each of three additional criteria must be satisfied. All three, one will observe, go towards making a thing *count* jurally—to have a legally recognized worth and dignity in its own right, and not merely to serve as a means to benefit "us" (whoever the contemporary group of rights-holders may be). They are, first, that the thing can institute legal actions *at its behest;* second, that in determining the granting of legal relief, the court must take *injury to it* into account; and, third, that relief must run to the *benefit of it.*

THE RIGHTLESSNESS OF NATURAL OBJECTS AT COMMON LAW

Consider, for example, the common law's posture toward the pollution of a stream. True, courts have always been able, in some circumstances, to issue orders that will stop the pollution. . . . But the stream itself is fundamentally rightless, with implications that deserve careful reconsideration.

The first sense in which the stream is not a rights-holder has to do with standing. The stream itself has none. So far as the common law is concerned, there is in general no way to challenge the polluter's actions save at the behest of a lower riparian—another human being—able to show an invasion of *his* rights. This conception of the riparian as the holder of the right to bring suit has more than theoretical interest. The lower riparians may simply not care about the pollution. They themselves may be polluting, and not wish to stir up legal waters. They may be economically dependent on their polluting neighbor. And, of course, when they discount the value of winning by the costs of bringing suit and the chances of success, the action may not seem worth undertaking. . . .

The second sense in which the common law denies "rights" to natural objects has to do with the way in which the merits are decided in those cases in which someone is competent and willing to establish standing. At its more primitive levels, the system protected the "rights" of the property owning human with minimal weighing of any values: *"Cujus est solum, ejus est usque ad coelum et ad infernos."* Today we have come more and more to make balances—but only such as will adjust the economic best interests of identifiable humans.

. . . None of the natural objects, whether held in common or situated on private land, has any of the three criteria of a rights-holder. They have no standing in their own right; their unique damages do not count in determining outcome; and they are not the beneficiaries of awards. In such fashion, these objects have traditionally been regarded by the common law, and even by all but the most recent legislation, as objects for man to conquer and master and use—in such a way as the law once looked upon "man's" relationships to African Negroes. Even where special measures have been taken to conserve them, as by seasons on game and limits on timber cutting, the dominant motive has been to conserve them *for us*—for the greatest good of the greatest number of human beings. Conservationists, so far as I am aware, are generally reluctant to maintain otherwise. As the name implies, they want to conserve and guarantee *our* consumption and *our* enjoyment of these other living things. In their own right, natural objects have counted for little, in law as in popular movements. . . .

As I mentioned at the outset, however, the rightlessness of the natural environment can and should change; it already shows some signs of doing so.

Toward Having Standing in Its Own Right

It is not inevitable, nor is it wise, that natural objects should have no rights to seek redress in their own behalf. It is no answer to say that streams and forests cannot have standing because streams and forests cannot speak. Corporations cannot speak either; nor can states, estates, infants, incompetents, municipalities or universities. Lawyers speak for them, as they customarily do for the ordinary citizen with legal problems. One ought, I think, to handle the legal problems of natural objects as one does the problems of legal incompetents—human beings who have become vegetable. If a human being shows signs of becoming senile and has affairs that he is de jure incompetent to manage, those concerned with his well-being make such a showing to the court, and someone is designated by the court with the authority to manage the incompetent's affairs. The guardian (or "conservator" or "committee"—the terminology varies) then represents the incompetent in his legal affairs. Courts make similar appointments when a corporation has become "incompetent"—they appoint a trustee in bankruptcy or reorganization to oversee its affairs and speak for it in court when that becomes necessary.

On a parity of reasoning, we should have a system in which, when a friend of a natural object perceives it to be endangered, he can apply to a court for the creation of a guardianship. . . .

. . . One reason for making the environment itself the beneficiary of a judgment is to prevent it from being "sold out" in a negotiation among private litigants who agree not to enforce rights that have been established among themselves. Protection from this will be advanced by making the natural object a party to an injunctive settlement. Even more importantly, we should make it a beneficiary of money awards. . . .

The idea of assessing damages as best we can and placing them in a trust fund is far more realistic than a hope that a total "freeze" can be put on the environmental status quo. Nature is a continuous theatre in which things and species (eventually man) are destined to enter and exit. In the meantime, co-existence of man and his environment means that *each* is going to have to compromise for the better of both. Some pollution of streams, for example, will probably be inevitable for some time. Instead of setting an unrealizable goal of enjoining absolutely the discharge of all such pollutants, the trust fund concept would (a) help assure that pollution would occur only in those instances where the social need for the pollutant's product (via his present method of production) was so high as to enable the polluter to cover *all* homocentric costs, plus some estimated costs to the environment *per se,* and (b) would be a corpus for preserving monies, if necessary, while the technology developed to a point where repairing the damaged portion of the environment was feasible. Such a fund might even finance the requisite research and development.

I do not doubt that other senses in which the environment might have rights will come to mind, and, as I explain more fully below, would be more apt to come to mind if only we should speak in terms of their having rights, albeit vaguely at first. "Rights" might well lie in unanticipated areas. It would seem, for example, that Chief Justice Warren was only stating the obvious when he observed in *Reynolds* v. *Sims* that "legislators represent people, not trees or acres." Yet, could not a case be made for a system of apportionment which *did* take into account the wildlife of an area? It stikes me as a poor idea that Alaska should have no more congressmen than Rhode Island primarily *because there are in Alaska all those trees and acres, those waterfalls and forests.* I am not saying anything as silly as that we ought to overrule *Baker* v. *Carr* and retreat from one man-one vote to a system of one man-or-tree one vote. Nor am I even taking the position that we ought to count each acre, as we once counted each slave, as three-fifths of a man. But I am suggesting that there is nothing unthinkable about, and there might on balance even be a prevailing case to be made for, an electoral apportionment that made some systematic effort to allow for the representative "rights" of non-human life. And if a case can be made for that, which I offer here mainly for purpose of illustration, I suspect that a society that grew concerned enough about the environment to make it a holder of rights would be able to find quite a number of "rights" to have waiting for it when it got to court.

Notes

1. Dred Scott v. Sandford, 60 U.S. (19 How.) 396, 404–5 (1856).
2. People v. Hall, 4 Cal. 399, 405 (1854).
3. Schechter, "The Rightlessness of Medieval English Jewry," 45 *Jewish Q. Rev.,* 121, 135 (1954) quoting from M. Bateson, *Medieval England,* 139 (1904).
4. Dietrich v. Inhabitants of Northampton, 138 Mass. 14, 16 (1884).
5. *In re* Goddell, 39 Wisc. 232, 245 (1875).

THE RIGHTS OF ANIMALS AND UNBORN GENERATIONS

Joel Feinberg

Every philosophical paper must begin with an unproved assumption. Mine is the assumption that there will still be a world five hundred years from now, and that it will contain human beings who are very much like

From *Philosophy and Environmental Crisis,* ed. William T. Blackstone. Copyright © 1974 by University of Georgia Press, Athens. Reprinted by permission of the publisher.

us. We have it within our power now, clearly, to affect the lives of these creatures for better or worse by contributing to the conservation or corruption of the environment in which they must live. I shall assume furthermore that it is psychologically possible for us to care about our remote descendants, that many of us in fact do care, and indeed that we ought to care. My main concern then will be to show that it makes sense to speak of the rights of unborn generations against us, and that given the moral judgment that we ought to conserve our environmental inheritance for them, and its grounds, we might well say that future generations *do* have rights correlative to our present duties toward them. Protecting our environment now is also a matter of elementary prudence, and insofar as we do it for the next generation already here in the persons of our children, it is a matter of love. But from the perspective of our remote descendants it is basically a matter of justice, of respect for their rights. My main concern here will be to examine the concept of a right to better understand how that can be.

THE PROBLEM

To have a right is to have a claim[1] *to* something and *against* someone, the recognition of which is called for by legal rules or, in the case of moral rights, by the principles of an enlightened conscience. In the familiar cases of rights, the claimant is a competent adult human being, and the claimee is an officeholder in an institution or else a private individual, in either case, another competent adult human being. Normal adult human beings, then, are obviously the sorts of beings of whom rights can meaningfully be predicated. Everyone would agree to that, even extreme misanthropes who deny that anyone in fact has rights. On the other hand, it is absurd to say that rocks can have rights, not because rocks are morally inferior things unworthy of rights (that statement makes no sense either), but because rocks belong to a category of entities of whom rights cannot be meaningfully predicated. That is not to say that there are no circumstances in which we ought to treat rocks carefully, but only that the rocks themselves cannot validly claim good treatment from us. In between the clear cases of rocks and normal human beings, however, is a spectrum of less obvious cases, including some bewildering borderline ones. Is it meaningful or conceptually possible to ascribe rights to our dead ancestors? to individual animals? to whole species of animals? to plants? to idiots and madmen? to fetuses? to generations yet unborn? Until we know how to settle these puzzling cases, we cannot claim fully to grasp the concept of a right, or to know the shape of its logical boundaries.

One way to approach these riddles is to turn one's attention first to the most familiar and unproblematic instances of rights, note their most salient characteristics, and then compare the borderline cases with them, measuring as closely as possible the points of similarity and difference. In the end, the way we classify the borderline cases may depend on whether we are more impressed with the similarities or the differences between them and the cases in which we have the most confidence.

It will be useful to consider the problem of individual animals first because their case is the one that has already been debated with the most thoroughness by philosophers so that the dialectic of claim and rejoinder has now unfolded to the point where disputants can get to the end game quickly and isolate the crucial point at issue. When we understand precisely what *is* at issue in the debate over animal rights, I think we will have the key to the solution of all the other riddles about rights.

Individual Animals

Almost all modern writers agree that we ought to be kind to animals, but that is quite another thing from holding that animals can claim kind treatment from us as their due. Statutes making cruelty to animals a crime are now very common, and these, of course, impose legal duties on people not to mistreat animals; but that still leaves open the question whether the animals, as beneficiaries of those duties, possess rights correlative to them. We may very well have duties *regarding* animals that are not at the same time duties *to* animals, just as we may have duties regarding rocks, or buildings, or lawns, that are not duties *to* the rocks, buildings, or lawns. Some legal writers have taken the still more extreme position that animals themselves are not even the directly intended beneficiaries of statutes prohibiting cruelty to animals. During the nineteenth century, for example, it was commonly said that such statutes were designed to protect human beings by preventing the growth of cruel habits that could later threaten human beings with harm too. Prof. Louis B. Schwartz finds the rationale of the cruelty-to-animals prohibition in its protection of animal lovers from affronts to their sensibilities. "It is not the mistreated dog who is the ultimate object of concern," he writes. "Our concern is for the feelings of other human beings, a large proportion of whom, although accustomed to the slaughter of animals for food, readily identify themselves with a tortured dog or horse and respond with great sensitivity to its sufferings."[2] This seems to me to be factitious. How much more natural it is to say with John Chipman Gray that the true purpose of cruelty-to-animals statutes is "to preserve the dumb brutes from suffering."[3] The very people whose sensibilities are invoked in the alternative explanation, a group that no doubt now includes most of us, are precisely those who would insist that the protection belongs primarily to the animals themselves, not merely to their own tender feelings. Indeed, it would be difficult even to account for the existence of such feelings in the absence of a belief that the animals deserve the protection in their own right and for their own sakes.

Even if we allow, as I think we must, that animals are the intended direct beneficiaries of legislation forbidding cruelty to animals, it does not follow directly that animals have legal rights, and Gray himself, for one,[4] refused to draw this further inference. Animals cannot have rights, he thought, for the same reason they cannot have duties, namely, that they are not genuine "moral agents." Now, it is relatively easy to see why animals cannot have duties, and this matter is largely beyond controversy. Animals cannot be "reasoned with" or instructed in their responsibilities; they are inflexible and unadaptable to future contingencies; they are subject to fits of instinctive passion which they are incapable of repressing or controlling, postponing or sublimating. Hence, they cannot enter into contractual agreements, or make promises; they cannot be trusted; and they cannot (except within very narrow limits and for purposes of conditioning) be blamed for what would be called ''moral failures'' in a human being. They are therefore incapable of being moral subjects, of acting rightly or wrongly in the moral sense, of having, discharging, or breeching duties and obligations.

But what is there about the intellectual incompetence of animals (which admittedly disqualifies them for duties) that makes them logically unsuitable for rights? The most common reply to this question is that animals are incapable of *claiming* rights on their own. They cannot make motion, on their own, to courts to have their claims recognized or enforced; they cannot initiate, on their own, any kind of legal proceedings; nor are they capable of even understanding when their rights are being violated, of distinguishing harm from wrongful injury, and responding with indignation and an outraged sense of justice instead of mere anger or fear.

No one can deny any of these allegations, but to the claim that they are the grounds for disqualification of rights of animals, philosophers on the other side of this controversy have made convincing rejoinders. It is simply not true, says W. D. Lamont,[5] that the ability to understand what a right is and the ability to set legal machinery in motion by one's own initiative are necessary for the possession of rights. If that were the case, then neither human idiots nor wee babies would have any legal rights at all. Yet it is manifest that both of these classes of intellectual incompetents have legal rights recognized and easily enforced by the courts. Children and idiots start legal proceedings, not on their own direct initiative, but rather through the actions of proxies or attorneys who are empowered to speak in their names. If there is no conceptual absurdity in this situation, why should there be in the case where a proxy makes a claim on behalf of an animal? People commonly enough make wills leaving money to trustees for the care of animals. Is it not natural to speak of the animal's right to his inheritance in cases of this kind? If a trustee embezzles money from the animal's account,[6] and a proxy speaking in the dumb brute's behalf presses the animal's claim, can he not be described as asserting the animal's *rights?* More exactly, the animal itself claims its rights through the vicarious actions of a human proxy speaking in its name and in its behalf. There appears to be no reason why we should require the animal to understand what is going on (so the argument concludes) as a condition for regarding it as a possessor of rights.

Some writers protest at this point that the legal relation between a principal and an agent cannot hold between animals and human beings. Between humans, the relation of agency can take two very different forms, depending upon the degree of discretion granted to the agent, and there is a continuum of combinations between the extremes. On the one hand, there is the agent who is the mere ''mouthpiece'' of his principal. He is a ''tool'' in much the same sense as is a typewriter or telephone; he simply transmits the instructions of his principal. Human beings could hardly be the agents or representatives of animals in this sense, since the dumb brutes could no more use human ''tools'' than mechanical ones. On the other hand, an agent may be some sort of expert hired to exercise his professional judgment on behalf of, and in the name of, the principal. He may be given, within some limited area of expertise, complete independence to act as he deems best, binding his principal to all the beneficial or detrimental consequences. This is the role played by trustees, lawyers, and ghostwriters. This type of representation requires that the agent have great skill, but makes little or no demand upon the principal, who may leave everything to the judgment of his agent. Hence, there appears, at first, to be no reason why an animal cannot be a totally passive principal in this second kind of agency relationship.

There are still some important dissimilarities, however. In the typical instance of representation by an agent, even of the second, highly discretionary kind, the agent is hired by a principal who enters into an agreement or contract with him; the principal tells his agent that within certain carefully specified boundaries ''You may speak for me,'' subject always to the principal's approval, his right to give new directions, or to cancel the whole arrangement. No dog or cat could possibly do any of those things. Moreover, if it is the assigned task of the agent to defend the principal's rights, the principal may often decide to release his claimee, or to waive his own rights, and instruct his agent accordingly. Again, no mute cow or horse can do that. But although the possibility of hiring, agreeing, contracting, approving, directing, canceling, releasing, waiving, and instructing is present in the typical (all-human) case of agency representation, there appears to be no reason of a logical or conceptual kind why that *must* be so, and indeed there are some special examples involving human principals where it is not in fact so. I have in mind legal rules, for example, that require that a defendant be represented at his trial by an attorney, and impose a state-appointed attorney upon reluctant defendants, or upon those tried *in absentia,* whether they like it or not. Moreover, small children and mentally deficient and deranged adults are commonly represented by trustees and attorneys, even though they are incapable of granting their own consent to the representation, or of entering into contracts, of giving directions, or waiving their rights. It may be that it is unwise to permit agents to represent principals without the latters' knowledge or consent. If so, then no one should ever be permitted to speak for an animal, at least in a legally binding way. But that is quite another thing than saying that such representation is logically incoherent or conceptually incongruous—the contention that is at issue. . . .

Now, if a person agrees with the conclusion of the argument thus far, that animals are the sorts of beings that *can* have rights, and further, if he accepts the moral judgment that we ought to be kind to animals, only one further premise is needed to yield the conclusion that some animals do in fact have rights. We must now ask ourselves for whose sake ought we to treat (some) animals with consideration and humaneness? If we conceive our duty to be one of obedience to authority, or to one's own conscience merely, or one of consideration for tender human sensibilities only, then we might still deny that animals have rights, even though we admit that they are the kinds of beings that *can* have rights. But if we hold not only that we ought to treat animals humanely but also that we should do so for the animals' own sake, that such treatment is something we owe animals as their due, something that can be claimed for them, something the withholding of which would be an injustice and a wrong, and not merely a harm, then it follows that we do ascribe rights to animals. I suspect that the moral judgments most of us make about animals do pass these phenomenological tests, so that most of us do believe that animals have rights, but are reluctant to say so because of the conceptual confusions about the notion of a right that I have attempted to dispel above.

Now we can extract from our discussion of animal rights a crucial principle for tentative use in the resolution of the other riddles about the applicability of the concept of a right, namely, that the sorts of beings who *can* have rights are precisely those who have (or can have) interests. I have come to this tentative conclusion for two reasons: (1) because a right holder must be capable of being represented and it is impossible to represent a being that has no interests, and (2) because a right holder must be capable of being a beneficiary in his own person, and a being without interests is a being that is incapable of being harmed or benefited, having no good or "sake" of its own. Thus, a being without interests has no "behalf" to act in, and no "sake" to act for. My strategy now will be to apply the "interest principle," as we can call it, to the other puzzles about rights, while being prepared to modify it where necessary (but as little as possible), in the hope of separating in a consistent and intuitively satisfactory fashion the beings who can have rights from those which cannot.

VEGETABLES

It is clear that we ought not to mistreat certain plants, and indeed there are rules and regulations imposing duties on persons not to misbehave in respect to certain members of the vegetable kingdom. It is forbidden, for example, to pick wildflowers in the mountainous tundra areas of national parks, or to endanger trees by starting fires in dry forest areas. Members of Congress introduce bills designed, as they say, to "protect" rare redwood trees from commercial pillage. Given this background, it is surprising that no one[7] speaks of plants as having rights. Plants, after all, are not "mere things"; they are vital objects with inherited biological propensities determining their natural growth. Moreover, we do say that certain conditions are "good" or "bad" for plants, thereby suggesting that plants, unlike rocks, are capable of having a "good." (This is a case, however, where "what we say" should not be taken seriously: we also say that certain kinds of paint are good or bad for the internal walls of a house, and this does not commit us to a conception of walls as beings possessed of a good or welfare of their own.) Finally, we are capable of feeling a kind of affection for particular plants, though we rarely personalize them, as we do in the case of animals, by giving them proper names.

Still, all are agreed that plants are not the kinds of beings that can have rights. Plants are never plausibly understood to be the direct intended

beneficiaries of rules designed to "protect" them. We wish to keep redwood groves in existence for the sake of human beings who can enjoy their
serene beauty, and for the sake of generations of human beings yet unborn.
Trees are not the sorts of beings who have their "own sakes," despite the
fact that they have biological propensities. Having no conscious wants or
goals of their own, trees cannot know satisfaction or frustration, pleasure
or pain. Hence, there is no possibility of kind or cruel treatment of trees. In
these morally crucial respects, trees differ from the higher species of
animals.

Yet trees are not mere things like rocks. They grow and develop according to the laws of their own nature. Aristotle and Aquinas both took trees to
have their own "natural ends." Why then do I deny them the status of beings with interests of their own? The reason is that an interest, however the
concept is finally to be analyzed, presupposes at least rudimentary
cognitive equipment. Interests are compounded out of *desires* and *aims,*
both of which presuppose something like *belief,* or cognitive awareness. . . .

FUTURE GENERATIONS

We have it in our power now to make the world a much less pleasant
place for our descendants than the world we inherited from our ancestors.
We can continue to proliferate in ever greater numbers, using up fertile soil
at an even greater rate, dumping our wastes into rivers, lakes, and oceans,
cutting down our forests, and polluting the atmosphere with noxious gases.
All thoughtful people agree that we ought not to do these things. Most
would say that we have a duty not to do these things, meaning not merely
that conservation is morally required (as opposed to merely desirable) but
also that it is something due our descendants, something to be done for
their sakes. Surely we owe it to future generations to pass on a world that is
not a used up garbage heap. Our remote descendants are not yet present to
claim a livable world as their right, but there are plenty of proxies to speak
now in their behalf. These spokesmen, far from being mere custodians, are
genuine representatives of future interests.

Why then deny that the human beings of the future have rights which
can be claimed against us now in their behalf? Some are inclined to deny
them present rights out of a fear of falling into obscure metaphysics, by
granting rights to remote and unidentifiable beings who are not yet even in
existence. Our unborn great-great-grandchildren are in some sense
"potential" persons, but they are far more remotely potential, it may
seem, than fetuses. This, however, is not the real difficulty. Unborn
generations are more remotely potential than fetuses in one sense, but not
in another. A much greater period of time with a far greater number of
causally necessary and important events must pass before their potentiality
can be actualized, it is true; but our collective posterity is just as certain to
come into existence "in the normal course of events" as is any given fetus
now in its mother's womb. In that sense the existence of the distant human

future is no more remotely potential than that of a particular child already on its way.

The real difficulty is not that we doubt whether our descendants will ever be actual, but rather that we don't know who they will be. It is not their temporal remoteness that troubles us so much as their indeterminancy—their present facelessness and namelessness. Five centuries from now men and women will be living where we live now. Any given one of them will have an interest in living space, fertile soil, fresh air, and the like, but that arbitrarily selected one has no other qualities we can presently envision very clearly. We don't even know who his parents, grandparents, or great-grandparents are, or even whether he is related to us. Still, whoever these human beings may turn out to be, and whatever they might reasonably be expected to be like, they will have interests that we can affect, for better or worse, right now. That much we can and do know about them. The identity of the owners of these interests is now necessarily obscure, but the fact of their interest-ownership is crystal clear, and that is all that is necessary to certify the coherence of present talk about their rights. We can tell, sometimes, that shadowy forms in the spatial distance belong to human beings, though we know not who or how many they are; and this imposes a duty on us not to throw bombs, for example, in their direction. In like manner, the vagueness of the human future does not weaken its claim on us in light of the nearly certain knowledge that it will, after all, be human.

Doubts about the existence of a right to be born transfer neatly to the question of a similar right to come into existence ascribed to future generations. The rights that future generations certainly have against us are contingent rights: the interests they are sure to have when they come into being (assuming of course that they will come into being) cry out for protection from invasions that can take place now. Yet there are no actual interests, presently existent, that future generations, presently nonexistent, have now. Hence, there is no actual interest that they have in simply coming into being, and I am at a loss to think of any other reason for claiming that they have a right to come into existence (though there may well be such a reason). Suppose then that all human beings at a given time voluntarily form a compact never again to produce children, thus leading within a few decades to the end of our species. This of course is a wildly improbable hypothetical example but a rather crucial one for the position I have been tentatively considering. And we can imagine, say, that the whole world is converted to a strange ascetic religion which absolutely requires sexual abstinence for everyone. Would this arrangement violate the rights of anyone? No one can complain on behalf of presently nonexistent future generations that their future interests which give them a contingent right to protection have been violated since they will never come into existence to be wronged. My inclination then is to conclude that the suicide of our species would be deplorable, lamentable, and a deeply moving tragedy, but that it would violate no one's rights. Indeed if, contrary to fact, all human beings could ever agree to such a thing, that very agreement would be a symptom of our species' biological unsuitability for survival anyway.

For several centuries now human beings have run roughshod over the lands of our planet, just as if the animals who do live there and the generations of humans who will live there had no claims on them whatever. Philosophers have not helped matters by arguing that animals and future generations are not the kinds of beings who can have rights now, that they don't presently qualify for membership, even "auxiliary membership," in our moral community. I have tried in this essay to dispel the conceptual confusions that make such conclusions possible. To acknowledge their rights is the very least we can do for members of endangered species (including our own). But that is something.

Notes

1. I shall leave the concept of a claim unanalyzed here, but for a detailed discussion, see my "The Nature and Value of Rights," *Journal of Value Inquiry,* 4 (Winter 1971): 263–277.
2. Louis B. Schwartz, "Morals, Offenses and the Model Penal Code," *Columbia Law Review,* 63 (1963): 673.
3. John Chipman Gray, *The Nature and Sources of the Law,* 2d ed. (Boston: Beacon Press, 1963), p. 43.
4. And W. D. Ross for another. See *The Right and the Good* (Oxford: Clarendon Press, 1930), app. 1, pp. 48–56.
5. W. D. Lamont, *Principles of Moral Judgment* (Oxford: Clarendon Press, 1946), pp. 83–85.
6. Cf. H. J. McCloskey, "Rights," *Philosophical Quarterly,* 15 (1965): 121, 124.
7. Outside of Samuel Butler's *Erewhon.*

THE ENVIRONMENT, RIGHTS, AND FUTURE GENERATIONS

Richard T. DeGeorge

The rapid growth of technology has outstripped our moral intuitions, which are consequently unclear and contradictory on many environmental issues. As we try to handle new moral problems we stretch and strain traditional moral concepts and theories. We do not always do so successfully.

From R. T. DeGeorge "The Environment, Rights, and Future Generations" in *Ethics and Problems of the 21st Century,* eds. K. E. Goodpaster and K. M. Sayre (Notre Dame, Ind.: University of Notre Dame Press, 1979), pp. 93–103. Reprinted by permission.

The difficulties, I believe, become apparent as we attempt to deal with the moral dimension of the depletion of nonrenewable resources.

Consider the use of oil, presently our chief source of energy. The supply of oil is limited. Prudence demands that we not waste it. But who has a right to the oil or to its use? From one point of view the owners of the oil have a right to it. And we each have a right to the amount we are able to buy and use. From another point of view everyone has a right to oil, since it is a natural resource which should be used for the good of all. Americans, as we know, use a great deal more oil than most other people in the world. Is it moral of us to do so? Will our use preclude people in other parts of the world from having it available to them when they will need it for uses we presently take for granted? Will some unborn generations not have the oil they will probably need to live as we presently do?

These questions trouble many people. They have a vague sense of moral uneasiness, but their intuitions concerning the proper answers are not clear. They feel that they should not waste oil or fuel or energy. They feel that they should not keep their houses as cool in summer and as warm in winter as they used to. They feel that they should impose these conditions on their children. Yet they are not, simply on moral grounds, ready to give up too much in the way of comfort. Once forced to do so by economics, they will. But they are somewhat uneasy about their own attitude. Is it morally proper that affluent individuals or nations are able to live in greater comfort and will have to make fewer sacrifices than the less well-to-do, simply because they have more money?

My intuitions on the issue of energy and oil are in no way privileged. I do not know how much oil or energy I have a right to; nor can I say with any certainty how much those in underdeveloped countries presently have a right to, or how much should be saved for them, or how much should be saved for generations yet to come. Nor do I know clearly how to weigh the claims to oil of the people in underdeveloped countries vis-á-vis the future claims to oil of generations yet unborn. If all presently existing members of the human race used energy at the rate that the average American does, there would obviously be much less left for future generations. Does this mean that others in the world should not use as much oil as Americans; or that Americans should use less, so that those in other countries will be able to use more; or that people in less developed countries should not use more in order that future generations of Americans will be able to use as much as present-day Americans?

Though our intuitions are not very clear on these issues, there is some consensus that present people have moral obligations vis-á-vis future generations. Yet stating the grounds for even these obligations is not an easy task and it is one that I do not think has been adequately accomplished. The attempt to state them in terms of rights has not been fruitful. And the utilitarian or consequentialist approach has fared no better. Lack of clarity about collective responsibility further magnifies the complexity of the problem.

In this paper I shall not be able to solve the question either of the proper use of oil or of the basis of our obligations to future generations. I shall attempt only to test the ability of some moral theories and language to express them adequately. I shall negatively show why some approaches are not fruitful lines to pursue. And positively I shall argue for some considerations which I think are applicable, though by themselves they are not adequate to solve the moral problems at issue.

Talk about rights has proliferated in recent years.[1] Moral feelings and concerns have been put in terms of rights in a great many areas. It does not fit in some of them. Thus for instance some people concerned with the environment have come to speak of the rights of nature, or the rights of trees, or the rights of a landscape.[2] The intent of people who use such language is easy enough to grasp. They are concerned about man's abuse of the environment, his wanton cutting of trees, or his despoiling the countryside. But those who wish to attribute rights to nature or trees or landscapes must come up with some way of interpreting the meaning of rights which makes their assertions plausible. The usual ways of unpacking rights in terms of justifiable moral claims, or in terms of interests, or in terms of freedom do not apply to nature or trees.[3] Yet failure to provide an interpretation which both grounds the purported rights of trees and relates them to the rights of humans, while accounting for the obvious differences between them, leads to confusion and precludes arriving at a satisfactory solution to the moral problems posed.

These attempts are nonetheless instructive. For rights can be ascribed and rights-talk can be used with respect to almost anything,[4] even if the claims involved cannot always be adequately defended. When we restrict our use of rights-talk to human beings, therefore, it should be clear that the question of whether people have rights is not a factual one comparable to the question of whether they have brains, or whether they usually have two arms or two legs. The question of whether future generations have rights is similarly not one simply of fact; and the answer is compounded because there is no consensus and little precedent. Thus simply looking at ordinary language, or simply unpacking the concepts of person or rights, will not yield a definitive answer. Since the question is not a factual one, it is to be solved in part by making a decision. It is possible to say that future generations have rights. But I shall argue that we avoid more problems if we maintain that, properly speaking, future generations do not presently have rights, than if we say they do.

Future generations by definition do not now exist. They cannot now, therefore, be the present bearer or subject of anything, including rights. Hence they cannot be said to have rights in the same sense that presently existing entities can be said to have them. This follows from the briefest analysis of the present tense form of the verb 'to have.' To claim that what does not now exist cannot now have rights in any strong sense does not deny that persons who previously existed had rights when they existed, or that persons who will exist can properly be said to have rights when they do exist, or that classes with at least one presently existing member can correctly be said to have rights now. Nor does it deny that presently existing persons can and sometimes do make rights claims for past or future persons. It emphasizes, however, that in ascribing rights to persons who do not exist it is the existing person who is expressing his interests or concerns.

Those who claim that present existence is not necessary for the proper ascription of present rights sometimes cite the legal treatment of wills as a counterexample. In this instance, they argue, the courts act as if the deceased continued to have rights, despite the fact that he no longer exists. But this is not the only way of construing wills or the actions of courts. If we consider those countries in which inheritance laws were suddenly changed so that all the property of a deceased went to the state rather than to the heirs named in a will, it would be more plausible to argue that the rights of a particular heir were violated rather than the rights of the deceased. Equally plausible construals can, I believe, be made for each of the other standard supposed counterexamples.[5]

Consider next the supposed present rights of some future individual. Before conception potential parents can and should take into account the obligations they will have in connection with caring for the children they might produce. They can and should consider the rights their children will have if they come into being. But since the children do not yet exist, we should properly say they do not now have rights. Among the rights they do not have (since they have none) is the right to come into existence. By not bringing them into existence we do not violate *that* right, and we can obviously prevent their having any other rights. Now if we attempt to speak otherwise, I suggest, we invite confusion. What sense would it make to say that some entity which was not conceived had a right to be conceived? We cannot sensibly or intelligibly answer the question of whose right was infringed when there is no bearer of the right.

A similar difficulty, and therefore a similar reason for not using rights-talk, arises in speaking of the rights of future generations, providing we mean by that term some generation no members of which have presently been conceived and so in no sense presently exist. Such future generations could at least in theory be prevented from coming into existence. If they were never produced it would be odd to say that their rights had been violated. For since they do not now exist they can have no right to exist or to be produced. Now, they have no present rights at all.

Nonetheless possible future entities can be said to have possible future rights. And future generations when they exist will have rights at that time. But the temptation to consider all rights as temporally on a par should be resisted. Moreover, the weight which should now be given to the rights claims which future individuals or future generations will have should be proportional to the likelihood that such individuals will exist, and by analogy with the case of parents the obligations should be borne by those individuals (and collectively by those groups) most responsible for bringing the individuals into existence.

Future persons do not, individually or as a class, presently have the right to existing resources. They differ from presently existing persons who in general have the right to the judicious use of the goods necessary for them to continue in existence. And if some of these goods, because of present rational demands, are used up, then it is a mistake to say that future persons or future generations have or will have a right to *those* goods and that we violate their rights by using them up. Future generations or future individuals or groups should correctly be said to have a right only to what is available when they come into existence, and hence when their possible future rights become actual and present.

Many people feel that this is incorrect and that future persons and generations have as much right as presently existing persons to what presently exists, for example, in the way of resources. A few considerations, however, should suffice to show that such a view is mistaken. The first consideration is conceptual. Only once a being exists does *it* have needs or wants or interests. It has a right only to the kind of treatment or to the goods available to it at the time of its conception. It cannot have a reasonable claim to what is not available. Consider this on an individual level. Suppose a couple are so constituted that if they have a child, the child will have some disease, for example, sickle-cell anemia. Suppose the woman conceives. Does the fetus or baby have a right not to have sickle-cell anemia? Before it was conceived there was no entity to have any rights. Once it is conceived, its genetic make-up is such as it is. It makes no sense to speak of *its* having the right not to have the genetic make-up it has, since the alternative is its not being. . . .

Second, suppose we attempt to speak otherwise. Suppose we assume that all future generations have the same right to oil as we do; and suppose that since it is a nonrenewable resource, it is used up—as it is likely to be —by some future generation. What of the next generation that follows it? Should we say that since that generation cannot be produced without violating its right to oil it has a right not to be produced? Surely not. Or should we say that if it is produced one of its rights is necessarily infringed, and that the right of all succeeding generations will similarly necessarily be infringed? It is possible to speak that way; but to do so is at least confusing and at worst undermines the whole concept of rights by making rights claims vacuous.

The third reason for not speaking of the rights of future generations as if their rights were present rights is that it leads to impossible demands on us. Suppose we consider oil once again. It is a nonrenewable resource and is limited in quantity. How many generations in the future are we to allow to have present claim to it? Obviously if we push the generations into the unlimited future and divide the oil deposits by the number of people, we each end up with the right to a gallon or a quart or a teaspoon or a thimble full. So we must reconstrue the claim to refer to the practical use of oil. But this means that we inevitably preclude some future generation from having oil. And if all future generations have equal claim, then we necessarily violate the rights of some future generations. It is clear, then, that we do not wish to let unending future claims have equal weight with present claims. The alternative, if we do not consistently treat future rights differently from the rights of presently existing persons, is arbitrarily to treat some rights, those of sufficiently distant generations, as less deserving of consideration than the same claims of generations closer to us. What I have been arguing is that our approach turns out to be less arbitrary and more consistent if we refuse to take even the first step in considering future rights as anything other than future, and if we do not confuse them or equate them with the rights of presently existing people.

To ascribe present rights to future generations is to fall into the trap of being improperly motivated to sacrifice the present to the future, on the grounds that there will possibly (or probably) be so innumerably many future generations, each of which has a presently equal right to what is now available, as to dwarf the rights of present people to existing goods. The trap can be avoided by maintaining that present existence is a necessary condition for the possession of a present right. To the extent that rights-talk tends to be nontemporal and future generations are considered to have present rights, such talk tends to confuse rather than clarify our obligations for the future, and the ground for such obligations. For this and similar reasons future generations should not be said to have present rights.

If the argument so far is correct, however, we have not solved a problem, but merely seen how not to approach it if we want a solution. That future generations do not have present rights does not mean that present people, individually and collectively, have no obligations to try to provide certain kinds of environment and to leave open as many possibilities as feasible for those who will probably come after them, consistent with satisfying their own rational needs and wants. How are we to describe this felt moral imperative? . . .

There is another dimension to the problem, however, which I have ignored thus far and which it would be well to consider at least briefly. With respect to the use of oil and future generations I have spoken of "we" and "they" and have traded on our common understanding of the terms. Moral obligation and responsibility, however, have for the most part been discussed in individual terms. The notion of collective responsibility and collective obligation and other collectively applied moral terms are in need of clarification. The concept of collective responsibility, for instance, despite some of the work that has been done on it,[6] remains in many cases obscure.

One difficulty arises in attempting to allocate individual responsibility under conditions in which individual effort has no real effect by itself. Who is responsible for preserving the environment for our children and grandchildren? The answer may be all of us. But what is required of each of us individually is far from clear. How responsible for strip mining is a carpenter in New York City? How responsible for oil depletion is someone who drives to work in a car? Is he morally obliged to drive less or not at all or to buy and use a smaller car? What if smaller cars are not available or if he cannot afford to buy one or if none of his neighbors drive less or buy smaller cars? Is the collective responsibility to fall primarily on collective agencies—on corporations and government? But this collective responsibility must also be allocated to individuals. Does each person have a responsibility to preserve resources no matter what others do? Or is it a prima facie obligation which becomes a real obligation only when our action and the action of others will effect the results desired? Are we therefore individually freed of our responsibility when others do not do their share? Does collective failure to fulfill a collective moral obligation absolve an individual of his individual obligation to do what he should under the collective obligation on the grounds that his sacrifice without that of the others is inefficacious? My claim is not that these questions do not have answers but that they have not been sufficiently discussed and that until we get clear about the answers we are unlikely to feel the pressure of the moral obligations we may have or to be able to weigh them against the individual moral pressures we feel with respect, for instance, to supplying our children or our fellow citizens with as high a quality of life as we can.

Consider further the questions of resources in the light of populations. If the population of one country grows unchecked to the detriment of the people of that country and to the exhaustion of that country's resources, do the people of other countries have the obligation to keep alive the individuals produced by parents who had no regard for whether the children could be supported? Who is the "we" who should preserve resources, and for whom should they be preserved? If the people of one nation sacrifice, should it be the heirs of that nation's people who reap the rewards of such sacrifice, or should it be all people wherever they might be and whoever they are? On the one hand our intuitions tell us that no country can do everything for the whole world, that people have to help themselves, and that each country's primary responsibility is to its own people and their descendents. On the other hand we have the unrelieved plight of human misery and death, some of which could be alleviated if some peoples would share more of what they have. By what right do some use many times more in the way of natural resources than others, especially when it is not by merit but partially by luck that they have natural riches available to them that are not available in their own countries to other people?

I mentioned earlier that our moral intuitions were still inadequate to some of the moral problems which seem to be looming before us. Part of the reason is that we have no precedent on which to build. Another is that we have no adequate institutions and practices on a global scale with which to relate global moral problems. Morality is a social institution and moral obligations are often closely tied to particular social practices. The moral obligations of parents with respect to their children, for instance, are different in a society with a nuclear family in which parents have almost exclusive responsiblity for the support and care of their children, and in a society in which all children are raised by the state, cared for in communal nurseries, state schools, and so on. Moral problems about the use of resources and the preservation of the environment transcend national boundaries. Yet we have no world institutions or practices adequate to help ground pertinent moral judgments. . . .

I have been arguing that environmental problems have developed faster than our intuitions, theories, practices, and institutions, and that some attempts to stretch our theories to fit our vague intuitions have not been successful. Yet I do not wish to imply that we are at a total loss from a moral point of view with respect to environmental problems or that they are ultimately unsolvable. I shall briefly argue three points, the first of which, I believe, is relatively uncontroversial and requires little defense. . . . [First] if the population of one country goes unchecked to the detriment of the people of that country, it is not clear that other countries have the obligation to keep alive the individuals so produced. It may be that richer countries have some obligations in this regard. But it is clear that the obligation of the members of a society to care for their own people is greater than the obligation to care for people of other societies.

My two other claims are more controversial and may seem to some mistaken; hence they deserve more comment. The first is that we do not owe to others, either outside our society or to those who will come after us, what we need to maintain a reasonable quality of life and dignity for the present members of our society; the second is that we do not owe others, either in other societies or those who will come after us, a better life than we ourselves are able to attain and enjoy. Present sacrifice for a better future for others may be a noble, altruistic goal. But it is not morally demanded and cannot be legitimately forced on those who do not wish to be noble, altruistic, or heroic.

Moral theorists have long argued that each human being, if the resources are available, deserves enough of the goods of life so that he can enjoy at least a minimal standard of living required for human dignity. My claim is consistent with that view. It allows room for the moral obligation of those who are well off to help bring those below the minimal standard of dignity up to that standard. How that is to be done within our own society is easier to determine than how that is to be effectively achieved on a global scale. But my claim denies that any generation or people have to fall below that level in order to help others rise above it. The argument for that is fairly straightforward.

Starting from the equality of all persons qua persons my good for me is as valuable as your good for you. Other things being equal your good is not better or more important than mine. Hence, again other things being equal, there is no reason why, given a choice, I should be morally obliged to choose your good over mine. Otherwise, by like reasoning you would have to choose my good over yours. Secondly, my claim is that other things being equal those who, where it is possible to avoid it, bring misery on themselves or on those close to them, are the ones who should bear the brunt of consequences of their actions. This is part of what it means to accept the moral responsibility for one's actions. Hence there are limits to the sacrifice which can be morally required of one people to help those less well off than they. One limit is that equality is not required; what is required is simply helping those below the minimal standard to rise up to it. Another limit is that those who are aided can legitimately be expected, as a condition of such aid, to take the means available to them to help themselves.

My second more controversial claim was that there is no moral imperative that requires each generation to sacrifice so that the next generation may be better off than it is. Parents do not owe their children better lives than they had. They may wish their children to have better lives; but they do not owe it to them. If there is to be a peak followed by a decline in the standard of living, and if such a peak is tied to the use of natural resources, then providing there is no profligate waste, there is no reason why the present rather than a future generation should enjoy that peak. For no greater good is served by any future group enjoying the peak, since when its turn comes, if enjoying the peak is improper for us, it will be improper for them also.

We do not owe future generations a better life than we enjoy nor do we owe them resources we need for ourselves. When dealing with renewable resources, other things being equal, they should not be used up faster than they can be replaced. When they are needed at a greater rate than they can be replaced, they raise the same problem raised by nonrenewable resources. We should use what we *need*, but we should keep our needs rational, avoid waste, and preserve the environment as best we can. How this is to be translated into the specific allocation of goods and resources is not to be determined a priori or by the fiat of government but by as many members of the society at large who are interested and aware and informed enough to help in the decision-making process. Part of that process must involve clarifying the moral dimensions of the use of resources and developing the moral theory to help us state consistently and evaluate our moral intuitions.

Up until relatively recent times it may have seemed that each generation was better off than the previous one, and that just as each successive generation had received a better lot than its predecessor, it had an obligation to continue the process. But we are now at the stage where our own efforts are frequently counterproductive. Our progress in transportation has led to pollution; our progress in pest control has led to new strains of insects resistant to our chemicals or has resulted in pollution of our food; our expansion of industry has taken its toll in our rivers and in the ocean; and so on. We are now faced with shortages of the type we used to experience only during war times. So we can argue that in some ways we are already over the peak and will all be forced to cut down on certain kinds of consumption. That our children have to bear our fate is no reason for reproach. What would be reprehensible on the individual level is if we lived in luxury and allowed our children to exist at a subsistence level. It is appropriate that we help them to live as well as we, where that is possible. But we have no responsiblity for helping them live better at great expense to ourselves.

Notes

1. See Rex Martin and James W. Nickel, "A Bibliography on the Nature and Foundations of Rights 1947–1977," *Political Theory* (forthcoming).
2. See, for example, Aldo Leopold, *A Sand Country Almanac and Sketches Here and There* (New York: Oxford University Press, 1949); Christopher Stone, *Should Trees Have Standing?: Toward Legal Rights for Natural Objects* (Los Altos, Ca.: Kaufmann, 1974).
3. H. L. A. Hart, "Are There Any Natural Rights?," *Philosophical Review*, 64 (1955): 175–191 argues that the natural right of men to be free is basic; Joel Feinberg, "Duties, Rights and Claims," *American Philosophical Quarterly*, 3 (1966): 137–144; David Lyons "The Correlativity of Rights and Duties," *Nous*, 4 (1970): 45–57.
4. H. J. McCloskey, "Rights," *Philosophical Quarterly*, 15 (1965): 115–127, raises the question of whether art objects can have rights. A number of philosophers have recently argued for the rights of animals: Andrew Linzey, *Animal Rights* (London: S. C. M. Press, 1976); Peter Singer, *Animal Liberation* (London: Jonathan Cape, 1976); on the other hand, see Joseph Margolis, "Animals Have No Rights and Are Not Equal to Humans," *Philosophic Exchange*, 1 (1974): 119–123.

5. Joel Feinberg, "The Rights of Animals and Unborn Generations," *Philosophy and Environmental Crisis,* ed. William T. Blackstone (Athens: University of Georgia Press, 1974), pp. 43–68, defends the opposite view.
6. See Peter A. French, ed., *Individual and Collective Responsibility: Massacre at My Lai* (Cambridge, Mass.: Schenkman 1972); Joel Feinberg, "Collective Responsibility," *Journal of Philosophy,* 45 (1968): 674–687; W. H. Walsh, "Pride, Shame and Responsibility," *The Philosophical Quarterly,* 20 (1970): 1–13; D. E. Cooper, "Collective Responsibility" *Philosophy,* 43 (1968): 258–268.

THE PLACE OF NONHUMANS IN ENVIRONMENTAL ISSUES

Peter Singer

NOT FOR HUMANS ONLY

When we humans change the environment in which we live, we often harm ouselves. If we discharge cadmium into a bay and eat shellfish from that bay, we become ill and may die. When our industries and automobiles pour noxious fumes into the atmosphere, we find a displeasing smell in the air, the long-term results of which may be every bit as deadly as cadmium poisoning. The harm that humans do the environment, however, does not rebound solely, or even chiefly, on humans. It is nonhumans who bear the most direct burden of human interference with nature.

By "nonhumans" I mean to refer to all living things other than human beings, though for reasons to be given later, it is with nonhuman animals, rather than plants, that I am chiefly concerned. It is also important, in the context of environmental issues, to note that living things may be regarded either collectively or as individuals. In debates about the environment the most important way of regarding living things collectively has been to regard them as species. Thus, when environmentalists worry about the future of the blue whale, they usually are thinking of the blue whale as a species, rather than of individual blue whales. But this is not, of course, the only way in which one can think of blue whales, or other animals, and one of the topics I shall discuss is whether we should be concerned about what we are doing to the environment primarily insofar as it threatens entire species of nonhumans, or primarily insofar as it affects individual nonhuman animals.

The general question, then, is how the effects of our actions on the environment of nonhuman beings should figure in our deliberations about what we ought to do. There is an unlimited variety of contexts in which this

From P. Singer, "The Place of Nonhumans in Environmental Issues," in *Ethics and Problems of the 21st Century,* eds. K. E. Goodpaster and K. M. Sayre (Notre Dame, Ind.: University of Notre Dame Press, 1979), pp. 191–198. Reprinted by permission.

issue could arise. To take just one: Suppose that it is considered necessary to build a new power station, and there are two sites, A and B, under consideration. In most respects the sites are equally suitable, but building the power station on site A would be more expensive because the greater depth of shifting soil at that site will require deeper foundations; on the other hand to build on site B will destroy a favored breeding ground for thousands of wildfowl. Should the presence of the wildfowl enter into the decision as to where to build? And if so, in what manner should it enter, and how heavily should it weigh?

In a case like this the effects of our actions on nonhuman animals could be taken into account in two quite different ways: directly, giving the lives and welfare of nonhuman animals an intrinsic significance which must count in any moral calculation; or indirectly, so that the effects of our actions on nonhumans are morally significant only if they have consequences for humans. . . .

The view that the effects of our actions on other animals has no direct moral significance is not as likely to be openly advocated today as it was in the past; yet it is likely to be accepted implicitly and acted upon. When planners perform cost-benefit studies on new projects, the costs and benefits are costs and benefits for human beings only. This does not mean that the impact of the power station or highway on wildlife is ignored altogether, but it is included only indirectly. That a new reservoir would drown a valley teeming with wildlife is taken into account only under some such heading as the value of the facilities for recreation that the valley affords. In calculating this value, the cost-benefit study will be neutral between forms of recreation like hunting and shooting and those like bird watching and bush walking—in fact hunting and shooting are likely to contribute more to the benefit side of the calculations because larger sums of money are spent on them, and they therefore benefit manufacturers and retailers of firearms as well as the hunters and shooters themselves. The suffering experienced by the animals whose habitat is flooded is not reckoned into the costs of the operation; nor is the recreational value obtained by the hunters and shooters offset by the cost to the animals that their recreation involves.

Despite its venerable origins, the view that the effects of our actions on nonhuman animals have no intrinsic moral significance can be shown to be arbitrary and morally indefensible. If a being suffers, the fact that it is not a member of our own species cannot be a moral reason for failing to take its suffering into account. This becomes obvious if we consider the analogous attempt by white slaveowners to deny consideration to the interests of blacks. These white racists limited their moral concern to their own race, so the suffering of a black did not have the same moral significance as the suffering of a white. We now recognize that in doing so they were making an arbitrary distinction, and that the existence of suffering, rather than the race of the sufferer, is what is really morally significant. The point remains true if "species" is substituted for "race." The logic of racism and the logic of the position we have been discussing, which I have elsewhere referred to as "speciesism," are indistinguishable; and if we reject the former then consistency demands that we reject the latter too.[1]

It should be clearly understood that the rejection of speciesism does not imply that the different species are in fact equal in respect of such characteristics as intelligence, physical strength, ability to communicate, capacity to suffer, ability to damage the environment, or anything else. After all, the moral principle of human equality cannot be taken as implying that all humans are equal in these respects either—if it did, we would have to give up the idea of human equality. That one being is more intelligent than another does not entitle him to enslave, exploit, or disregard the interests of the less intelligent being. The moral basis of equality among humans is not equality in fact, but the principle of equal consideration of interests, and it is this principle that, in consistency, must be extended to any nonhumans who have interests.

There may be some doubt about whether any nonhuman beings have interests. This doubt may arise because of uncertainty about what it is to have an interest, or because of uncertainty about the nature of some nonhuman beings. So far as the concept of "interest" is the cause of doubt, I take the view that only a being with subjective experiences, such as the experience of pleasure or the experience of pain, can have interests in the full sense of the term; and that any being with such experiences does have at least one interest, namely, the interest in experiencing pleasure and avoiding pain. Thus consciousness, or the capacity for subjective experience, is both a necessary and a sufficient condition for having an interest. While there may be a loose sense of the term in which we can say that it is in the interests of a tree to be watered, this attenuated sense of the term is not the sense covered by the principle of equal consideration of interests. All we mean when we say that it is in the interests of a tree to be watered is that the tree needs water if it is to continue to live and grow normally; if we regard this as evidence that the tree has interests, we might almost as well say that it is in the interests of a car to be lubricated regularly because the car needs lubrication if it is to run properly. In neither case can we really mean (unless we impute consciousness to trees or cars) that the tree or car has any preference about the matter.

The remaining doubt about whether nonhuman beings have interests is, then, a doubt about whether nonhuman beings have subjective experiences like the experience of pain. I have argued elsewhere that the commonsense view that birds and mammals feel pain is well founded;[2] but more serious doubts arise as we move down the evolutionary scale. Vertebrate animals have nervous systems broadly similar to our own and behave in ways that resemble our own pain behavior when subjected to stimuli that we would find painful; so the inference that vertebrates are capable of feeling pain is a reasonable one, though not as strong as it is if limited to mammals and birds. When we go beyond vertebrates to insects, crustaceans, mollusks and so on, the existence of subjective states becomes more dubious, and with very simple organisms it is difficult to believe that they could be conscious. As for plants, though there have been sensational claims that plants are not only conscious, but even psychic, there is no hard evidence that supports even the more modest claim.[3]

The boundary of beings who may be taken as having interests is therefore not an abrupt boundary, but a broad range in which the assumption that the being has interests shifts from being so strong as to be virtually certain to being so weak as to be highly improbable. The principle of equal consideration of interests must be applied with this in mind, so that where there is a clash between a virtually certain interest and a highly doubtful one, it is the virtually certain interest that ought to prevail.

In this manner our moral concern ought to extend to all beings who have interests. Unlike race or species, this boundary does not arbitrarily exclude any being; indeed it can truly be said that it excludes nothing at all, not even "the most contemptible clod of earth" from equal consideration of interests—for full consideration of no interests still results in no weight being given to whatever was considered, just as multiplying zero by a million still results in zero.[4]

Giving equal consideration to the interests of two different beings does not mean treating them alike or holding their lives to be of equal value. We may recognize that the interests of one being are greater than those of another, and equal consideration will then lead us to sacrifice the being with lesser interests, if one or the other must be sacrificed. For instance, if for some reason a choice has to be made between saving the life of a normal human being and that of a dog, we might well decide to save the human because he, with his greater awareness of what is going to happen, will suffer more before he dies; we may also take into account the likelihood that it is the family and friends of the human who will suffer more; and finally, it would be the human who had the greater potential for future happiness. This decision would be in accordance with the principle of equal consideration of interests, for the interests of the dog get the same consideration as those of the human, and the loss to the dog is not discounted because the dog is not a member of our species. The outcome is as it is because the balance of interests favors the human. In a different situation—say, if the human were grossly mentally defective and without family or anyone else who would grieve for it—the balance of interests might favor the nonhuman.[5]

The more positive side of the principle of equal consideration is this: where interests are equal, they must be given equal weight. So where human and nonhuman animals share an interest—as in the case of the interest in avoiding physical pain—we must give as much weight to violations of the interest of the nonhumans as we do to similar violations of the human's interest. This does not mean, of course, that it is as bad to hit a horse with a stick as it is to hit a human being, for the same blow would cause less pain to the animal with the tougher skin. The principle holds between similar amounts of felt pain, and what this is will vary from case to case.

It may be objected that we cannot tell exactly how much pain another animal is suffering, and that therefore the principle is impossible to apply. While I do not deny the difficulty and even, so far as precise measurement is concerned, the impossibility of comparing the subjective experiences of members of different species, I do not think that the problem is different in kind from the problem of comparing the subjective experiences of two members of our own species. Yet this is something we do all the time, for instance when we judge that a wealthy person will suffer less by being taxed at a higher rate than a poor person will gain from the welfare benefits paid for by the tax; or when we decide to take our two children to the beach instead of to a fair, because although the older one would prefer the fair, the younger one has a stronger preference the other way. These comparisons may be very rough, but since there is nothing better, we must use them; it would be irrational to refuse to do so simply because they are rough. Moreover, rough as they are, there are many situations in which we can be reasonably sure which way the balance of interests lies. While a difference of species may make comparisons rougher still, the basic problem is the same, and the comparisons are still often good enough to use, in the absence of anything more precise. . . .

The difficulty of making the required comparison will mean that the application of this conclusion is controversial in many cases, but there will be some situations in which it is clear enough. Take, for instance, the wholesale poisoning of animals that is euphemistically known as "pest control." The authorities who conduct these campaigns give no consideration to the suffering they inflict on the "pests," and invariably use the method of slaughter they believe to be cheapest and most effective. The result is that hundreds of millions of rabbits have died agonizing deaths from the artificially introduced disease, myxomatosis, or from poisons like "ten-eighty"; coyotes and other wild dogs have died painfully from cyanide poisoning; and all manner of wild animals have endured days of thirst, hunger, and fear with a mangled limb caught in a leg-hold trap.[6] Granting, for the sake of argument, the necessity for pest control—though this has rightly been questioned—the fact remains that no serious attempts have been made to introduce alternative means of control and thereby reduce the incalculable amount of suffering caused by present methods. It would not, presumably, be beyond modern science to produce a substance which, when eaten by rabbits or coyotes, produced sterility instead of a drawn-out death. Such methods might be more expensive, but can anyone doubt that if a similar amount of human suffering were at stake, the expense would be borne?

Another clear instance in which the principle of equal consideration of interests would indicate methods different from those presently used is in the timber industry. There are two basic methods of obtaining timber from forests. One is to cut only selected mature or dead trees, leaving the forest substantially intact. The other, known as clear-cutting, involves chopping down everything that grows in a given area, and then reseeding. Obviously when a large area is clear-cut, wild animals find their whole living area destroyed in a few days, whereas selected felling makes a relatively minor disturbance. But clear-cutting is cheaper, and timber companies therefore use this method and will continue to do so unless forced to do otherwise.[7] . . .

It is not merely the act of killing that indicates what we are ready to do to other species in order to gratify our tastes. The suffering we inflict on the animals while they are alive is perhaps an even clearer indication of our speciesism than the fact that we are prepared to kill them.[8] In order to have meat on the table at a price that people can afford, our society tolerates methods of meat production that confine sentient animals in cramped, unsuitable conditions for the entire durations of their lives. Animals are treated like machines that convert fodder into flesh, and any innovation that results in a higher "conversion ratio" is liable to be adopted. As one authority on the subject has said, "cruelty is acknowledged only when profitability ceases."[9] So hens are crowded four or five to a cage with a floor area of twenty inches by eighteen inches, or around the size of a single page of the *New York Times*. The cages have wire floors, since this reduces cleaning costs, though wire is unsuitable for the hens' feet; the floors slope, since this makes the eggs roll down for easy collection, although this makes it difficult for the hens to rest comfortably. In these conditions all the birds' natural instincts are thwarted: They cannot stretch their wings fully, walk freely, dust-bathe, scratch the ground, or build a nest. Although they have never known other conditions, observers have noticed that the birds vainly try to perform these actions. Frustrated at their inability to do so, they often develop what farmers call "vices," and peck each other to death. To prevent this, the beaks of young birds are often cut off.

This kind of treatment is not limited to poultry. Pigs are now also being reared in cages inside sheds. These animals are comparable to dogs in intelligence, and need a varied, stimulating environment if they are not to suffer from stress and boredom. Anyone who kept a dog in the way in which pigs are frequently kept would be liable to prosecution, in England at least, but because our interest in exploiting pigs is greater than our interest in exploiting dogs, we object to cruelty to dogs while consuming the produce of cruelty to pigs. Of the other animals, the condition of veal calves is perhaps worst of all, since these animals are so closely confined that they cannot even turn around or get up and lie down freely. In this way they do not develop unpalatable muscle. They are also made anaemic and kept short of roughage, to keep their flesh pale, since white veal fetches a higher price; as a result they develop a craving for iron and roughage, and have been observed to gnaw wood off the sides of their stalls, and lick greedily at any rusty hinge that is within reach.

Since, as I have said, none of these practices cater to anything more than our pleasures of taste, our practice of rearing and killing other animals in order to eat them is a clear instance of the sacrifice of the most important interests of other beings in order to satisfy trivial interests of our own. To avoid speciesism we must stop this practice, and each of us has a moral obligation to cease supporting the practice. Our custom is all the support that the meat industry needs. The decision to cease giving it that support may be difficult, but it is no more difficult than it would have been for a white Southerner to go against the traditions of his society and free his slaves; if we do not change our dietary habits, how can we censure those slaveholders who would not change their own way of living?

Notes

1. For a fuller statement of this argument, see my *Animal Liberation* (New York: A New York Review Book, 1975), especially ch. 1.
2. *Ibid.*

3. See, for instance, the comments by Arthur Galston in *Natural History,* 83, no. 3 (March 1974): 18, on the "evidence" cited in such books as *The Secret Life of Plants.*

4. The idea that we would logically have to consider "the most contemptible clod of earth" as having rights was suggested by Thomas Taylor, the Cambridge Neo-Platonist, in a pamphlet he published anonymously, entitled *A Vindication of the Rights of Brutes* (London, 1792) which appears to be a satirical refutation of the attribution of rights to women by Mary Wollstonecroft in her *Vindication of the Rights of Women* (London, 1792). Logically, Taylor was no doubt correct, but he neglected to specify just what interests such contemptible clods of earth have.

5. Singer, *Animal Liberation,* pp. 20–23.

6. See J. Olsen, *Slaughter the Animals, Poison the Earth* (New York: Simon and Schuster, 1971), especially pp. 153–164.

7. See R. and V. Routley, *The Fight for the Forests* (Canberra: Australian National University Press, 1974), for a thoroughly documented indictment of clear-cutting in Australia; and for a recent report of the controversy about clear-cutting in America, see *Time,* May 17, 1976.

8. Although one might think that killing a being is obviously the ultimate wrong one can do to it, I think that the infliction of suffering is a clearer indication of speciesism because it might be argued that at least part of what is wrong with killing a human is that most humans are conscious of their existence over time, and have desires and purposes that extend into the future—see, for instance, M. Tooley, "Abortion and Infanticide," *Philosophy and Public Affairs,* vol. 2, no. 1 (1972). Of course, if one took this view one would have to hold—as Tooley does—that killing a human infant or mental defective is not in itself wrong, and is less serious than killing certain higher mammals that probably do have a sense of their own existence over time.

9. Ruth Harrison, *Animal Machines* (Stuart, London, 1964). This book provides an eye-opening account of intensive farming methods for those unfamiliar with the subject.

THE CASE AGAINST ANIMALS

R. G. Frey

Moral Rights: Some Doubts

The question of whether non-human animals possess moral rights is once again being widely argued. Doubtless the rise of ethology is partly responsible for this: as we learn more about the behaviour of animals, it seems inevitable that we shall be led to focus upon the similarities between them and us, with the result that the extension of moral rights from human

From R. G. Frey, "The Case Against Animals," in *Interests and Rights: The Case Against Animals* by R. G. Frey. © R. G. Frey 1980. Reprinted by permission of Oxford University Press.

beings to non-human animals can appear, as the result of these similarities, to have a firm basis in nature. But the major impetus to renewed interest in the subject of animal rights almost certainly stems from a heightened and more critical awareness, among philosophers and non-philosophers alike, of the arguments for and against eating animals and using them in scientific research. For if animals *do* have moral rights, such as a right to live and to live free from unnecessary suffering, and if our present practices systematically tread upon these rights, then the case for eating and experimenting upon animals, especially when other alternatives are for the most part readily available, is going to have to be a powerful one indeed.

It is important, however, not to misconstrue the question: the question is not about *which* rights animals may or may not be thought to possess or about whether their alleged rights in a particular regard are on a par with the alleged rights of humans in this same regard but rather about the more fundamental issue of whether animals—or, in any event, the 'higher' animals—can be the logical subject of rights.

One enormously influential position on this issue is that which links the possession of rights to the possession of interests. In *A System of Ethics,* Leonard Nelson is among the first, if not the first, to propound the view that all and only beings which have interests can have rights,[1] a view which has attracted an increasingly wide following ever since. For example, in recent years, H. J. McCloskey has embraced this view but gone on to deny that animals have interests,[2] whereas Joel Feinberg has embraced the view but gone on to affirm that animals have interests.[3] Nelson himself is emphatic that animals as well as human beings are, as he puts it, 'carriers of interests,'[4] and he concludes, accordingly, that animals possess moral rights, rights which both deserve and warrant our respect. For Nelson, then, it is because animals have interests that they can be the logical subject of rights, and his claim that animals *do possess* interests forms the minor premiss, therefore, in an argument for the moral rights of animals:

> All and only beings which (can) have interests (can) have moral rights;
> Animals as well as humans (can) have interests;
> Therefore, animals (can) have moral rights.

McCloskey, Feinberg, and a host of others have accepted the major premiss of this argument, which I shall dub the interest requirement, but have disagreed over the truth of the minor premiss; and it is apparent that the minor premiss is indeed the key to the whole matter. For given the truth of the interest requirement, it is still the case that only the truth of the minor premiss would result in the inclusion of creatures other than human beings within the class of right-holders. Accordingly, since I desire to meet and confound my opponents on their own ground, it is the minor premiss of this argument which will concern me. But, first, there are two aspects of the major premiss that warrant attention, the second of which raises very large and important issues.

The major premiss as given by Nelson and endorsed by McCloskey and

Feinberg does not show that the possession of interests is a necessary and sufficient condition for the possession of moral rights but simply states that it is, and it is as well to bear in mind that other suggestions in this regard are thick on the ground. The possession of rationality, language, free will, choice, and culture; the capacity to experience pain, to recognize and discharge moral obligations; the acceptance of and participation within societal and communal relationships; these have all at one time or another had their advocates. (I shall return to several of these later.) It is not that the presence of so many suggested necessary (and perhaps also sufficient) conditions for the possession of moral rights *shows* that none of these is in fact such a condition; it is rather that the extent and variety of suggestions serves as a useful antidote to any unthinking presumption that the major premiss of Nelson's argument really does encapsulate a necessary and sufficient condition for the possession of moral rights. Perhaps it does; but it is at least not obvious that it does.

More importantly, however, the major premiss implicitly assumes that there are moral rights, and it is not at all clear to me that there are. The same assumption is made when it is asked, as it constantly is today, whether there are some moral rights, such as a right to live and to live free from unnecessary suffering, which can be extended from human beings to animals. The history of ethics reveals, however, that it is by no means an easy task to show that human beings do possess moral rights. And if they do not, then the question of the extension of such rights from humans to animals does not arise; there is, so to speak, nothing to extend. Arguments for animals rights which either explicitly or implicitly turn upon such an extension will accordingly be vitiated. . . .

My reason for doubting that there are any moral rights is perfectly straightforward and can be briefly put.

What is it to have a right? Doubtless the most prominent answer to this question today is Joel Feinberg's, as set out in his papers 'Duties, Rights and Claims'[5] and 'The Nature and Value of Rights'.[6] To have a right, according to Feinberg, whose answer is drawn up around the notion of a legal right, is to have a claim to something or against others. To have a legal right to the collection of rent is to have a claim to prompt payment from one's tenants; to have a legal right to privacy in one's home is to have a claim against others not to invade one's privacy through trespass, and so on. Thus, to have a legal right is to be able to make claims, claims which can be enforced, which one can properly insist upon having enforced, and which the courts, properly petitioned, will see are enforced. In this way, being able to make claims, enforced and backed by sanctions, forms an important part of what it is for a person to function in society, which is why the deprivation of one's legal rights, as in the case, for instance, of some Soviet dissidents, is such a severe loss, even though one remains at liberty in society.

But what if one lacks the ability to make claims at all? This problem, obviously of concern, for example, to animal and environmental rightists, since neither dogs nor trees can make or insist upon or petition the courts on behalf of their claims, is held to be solved by appealing to the cases of small children, the very seriously infirm, and the mentally subnormal, all of whom are conceded legal rights but in respect of whom the courts, if necessary, appoint persons to make and exercise claims and to petition for legal proceedings on their behalf. It is arguable that nothing prevents a similar treatment of dogs[7] and trees.[8]. . .

To my mind, then, either moral rights are superfluous or we are not yet in a position to affirm that there are any; whichever it is, I cannot see that anything is lost by giving up claims to moral rights altogether. If such rights are superfluous, we do not require them in order to discuss our treatment of women or animals or the environment; and if there are not any, or it cannot be affirmed that there are, surely we would do better to concentrate directly on our treatment of women, animals, and the environment and upon the task of working out among us both principles of rightness and justification of treatment and criteria of adequacy for the assessment of the theories of which these principles will form a part?

MENTAL STATES AND MORAL STANDING

Lacking experiences or mental states, the things which make up non-sentient creation lack not only moral rights but also what I shall call moral standing. By this, I mean that, in the absence of experiences or mental states, they are not themselves the bearers or repositories of value in their own right; they have, in a word, no value in themselves. Feinberg, who is an animal rightist, is emphatic about this:

> A mere thing, however valuable to others, has no good of its own. The explanation of that fact, I suspect, consists in the fact that mere things have no conative life. . . . Interests must be compounded somehow out of conations; hence mere things have no interests. *A fortiori,* they have no interests to be protected by legal or moral rules. Without interests a creature can have no "good" of its own, the achievement of which can be its due. Mere things are not loci of value in their own right, but rather their value consists entirely in their being objects of other beings' interests.[9]

Feinberg's position here is this: mere things are not loci of value in their own right because they lack interests, and they lack interests because they lack a conative life, which . . . he includes under 'sentience'; ultimately, therefore, it is because they lack sentiency that they have no good of their own and are not loci of value in their own right. In this way, because the things which comprise it lack a good of their own and are not loci of value in their own right, non-sentient creation comes to lack even moral standing. . . .

If the beings which comprise sentient creation are loci of value in their own right, it is on the sentiency criterion because of their having experiences or mental states. Accordingly, what appears to be at the very basis of a sentiency criterion is the view that having experiences or mental states is valuable in its own right. It is just because the beings which comprise sentient creation do and/or can have experiences or mental states that they have moral standing and so are in a position to possess moral rights.

What, then, is the support animal rightists bring for the view that having experiences or mental states is valuable in its own right? I have been unable to find any in their writings; and the truth of the matter, in fact, is that they *implicitly assume* that having experiences or mental states is valuable in its own right. Indeed, I think they have to assume this; for unless one either argues for or assumes that having experiences or mental states is valuable in its own right and suffices to confer moral standing upon creatures who have or are capable of having them, what reason has one for thinking that sentiency is a criterion for the possession of *moral* rights at all, that sentiency has anything whatever to do with morality?

Put differently, why are shrubs (i) not loci of value in their own right and (ii) completely lacking in moral rights? It would make no sense for Feinberg to say that it is because they lack this or that *kind* of experiences or mental states, such as hopes or experiences of pain; for the whole point is that plants, trees, shrubs, forests, valleys, etc. lack any and all kinds of experiences and mental states whatever. They are not non-sentient because they lack this or that kind of mental state but because they lack mental states altogether; and it is this fact which, on a sentiency criterion, denies them moral standing and places them beyond the realm of those things, as Feinberg would have it, which have a good the achievement of which can be their due. . . .

In this way, then, the implicit assumption that having experiences or mental states is valuable in its own right lies at the very basis of a sentiency criterion and is used to confer moral standing and moral rights upon one part of creation and to refuse them to another. Quite simply, an assumption of this magnitude and importance to the cause of animal rights requires argument in its support: it is by no means obviously true, nor can I see any immediate reason to give way in the fact of it. For if asked to name those things one regarded as intrinsically valuable, I think many people would reply that, *if anything* is intrinsically valuable, in order by this formulation to leave open the very real possiblity, which philosophers and others have argued for, that nothing is, then such things as deep and lasting friendships in the fullest of senses and the development of one's talents are. What I strongly suspect is that virtually no one would cite having experiences or mental states *per se* as among the class of the intrinsically valuable.

Pain, Interests, and Vegetarianism

An enormous volume of material has already appeared on the conditions under which animals live and die on factory farms,[10] and more is almost certainly on the way. Much of this material is upsetting in the extreme, and it is difficult to imagine any normal person reading or hearing of it without being revolted. Indeed, our feelings of revulsion may be so intense that we simply can no longer bring ourselves to eat meat. In other words, we become vegetarians, not through any decision of principle, but through being unable to bring ourselves to continue to dine upon the flesh of animals. . . .

[In his book *Animal Liberation,* Peter Singer] links the principle of the equal consideration of interests to animals. For without such a link, Singer cannot use this principle as the moral basis of his vegetarianism, and this, after all, is the point of his book (pp. 24, 257). This link is provided by the claim that animals have interests, since, obviously, only if animals *have* interests can the moral principle of the equal consideration of interests apply to them and require us to take their interests into account and accord them equal weight with the like interests of human beings. Thus, only if the claim that animals have interests is established can vegetarianism have the moral basis Singer alleges it has. In other words, I can deprive Singer of his moral basis to vegetarianism by severing the link between the principle of the equal consideration of interests and animals, and I can sever this link by showing, quite apart from my own, earlier arguments, that he has not established that animals do have interests.

Animals have interests, according to Singer, in virtue of the fact that they can suffer; and he emphasizes a number of times that the capacity for suffering is a 'prerequisite' for having interests at all (pp. 8, 9, 17, 185, 254). By 'prerequisite', I understand 'something required', in this case that the condition of being able to suffer be satisfied, if a creature is to have interests. That is, a prerequisite is *at least a necessary* condition, whereby I mean to allow that satisfaction of the condition may also suffice to establish the point at issue. In the United States, Philosophy 101 is a prerequisite for admission into Philosophy 201, in the sense that the successful completion of course 101 is at least a necessary condition for admission into course 201, while, in Britain, successful completion of Part I of the BA degree is a prerequisite or at least a necessary condition for admission into Part II of the degree. Singer is claiming, then, I take it, that the capacity for suffering is a necessary condition for the possession of interests, which condition, if satisfied, may also suffice for the possession of interests. . . .

Curiously enough, in view of its central importance, this prerequisite of Singer's for having interests is initially simply stated (pp. 8–9) and thereafter merely assumed (e.g., p. 185); and the fact that Singer *presumes* its truth and does not argue in its support shows, no doubt, that he has not *established* it. Nevertheless, it could still be true; so I myself am in need of an argument if I am going to cast doubt upon its truth. My argument is simply this: Singer's prerequisite for having interests is dubious, if not false, since we can and do speak of interests in cases where the capacity for feeling pain is muted in non-trivial ways and where this capacity is entirely absent. . . .

[A] type of case which is relevant to the evaluation of Singer's prerequisite is that exemplified by Karen Quinlan,[11] in which an individual does not and cannot feel pain as the result of being in a comatose state, which state can last from a few hours to decades. Does Karen Quinlan have interests? Once again, since she cannot feel pain, on Singer's prerequisite it appears that she does not. . . .

Many people agree with Singer that we can harm the interests of future generations by wholesale pollution of the environment and by indiscriminately using up natural resources, whereas, by curbing our destructive tendencies in the name of progress and by conserving and even in some cases increasing our natural resources, they think we can protect, if not benefit, the interests of future generations.[12] But none of these future beings whose interests they think we can presently harm and benefit now feel pain or have the capacity to feel pain; if, then, these beings have interests, as more and more people, including the courts, appear to believe, it cannot be in virtue of the structure of their nervous system. Here, also, we find that we can distinguish between hurting individuals and harming their interests; for though by destroying the quality of the environment we cannot hurt individuals who do not now exist, it is increasingly thought that we can harm their interests, which more and more people are convinced must be protected by legislation.

But such cases as these are not necessary to make the point; there are, after all, the more mundane cases, which by no means spring from our only recently revived concern with the environment. For instance, to give the best-known example, it has long been the policy in many Scandinavian communities to plant a tree for every tree cut. The interests of future generations are held to be straightforwardly affected by (and responsible for) this policy, which is vigorously policed, since nearly all of the trees planted will not reach their maturity and so be cut for decades, long after those who planted them have gone and new generations have appeared to cut and thereby to earn a living by means of them.

. . . I conclude that Singer is mistaken in thinking that being able to feel pain is a prerequisite or at least a necessary condition for having interests. He has not, therefore, even begun to establish that animals actually have any interests, so that his link between the moral principle of the equal consideration of interests and animals is severed. . . .

POSTSCRIPT

I am out of sympathy with the present trend of suddenly discovering this or that, which it so happens one has wanted or wanted to be the case all along, to be a moral right, a trend which increasingly knows no bounds, what with the recent formation of pressure groups to lobby and demonstrate on behalf of our moral right to sunshine, a car-free environment, a degree from university (failure produces avoidable mental anguish and often physical distress and so avoidable unhappiness, freedom from which is a right), and a society completely rid of aerosol sprays. So far as I can see, our alleged moral rights proliferate daily; and though some claims to moral rights, such as a moral right to abortion on demand, are obviously much more momentous than others, all such claims, including the momentous ones, presently are foundering in a sea of charges and countercharges over the existence of moral rights and thereby over the acceptability of the particular normative theses, standards, or principles in which these claims are allegedly grounded and upon which they rely and especially over the adequacy of the normative ethical theories of which these theses etc. form a part.

As I say, I strongly suspect that such claims have become nothing more than means to the end of securing what one or one's group wants; they have become attempts, and not very subtle attempts, to extract by force concessions from those who do not agree with one's view of the rightness or wrongness of this or that. . . .

The implications of this over-all view, however, do not run merely to the denial of moral rights to animals: they extend also, and doubtless more unpalatably, to a denial of moral rights to human beings. And one important thing this means is that we have no moral right to an animal's confinement in zoos, to its ceaseless drudgery and labour on our behalf, to its persistent exploitation in the name of cosmetics, clothing, entertainment, and sport, to its blindness, dismemberment, and ultimate death in the name of science, and, to be sure, to its appearance on our dining-tables. . . .

But can animals be wronged, even if they have no interests? Yes, they can. For I have allowed that the 'higher' animals can suffer unpleasant sensations and so, in respect of the distinction between harm and hurt, can be hurt; and wantonly hurting them, just as wantonly hurting human beings, demands justification, if it is not to be condemned. I do not mean to deny that, even here, fundamental questions of value will not have to be thrashed out; after all, one is only going to agree that wantonly hurting animals amounts to wronging them if one can be brought to agree that wantonly inflicting unpleasant sensations upon them is wrong, and, here as elsewhere, simply presenting some *unargued* value judgement in this regard is unlikely to bring this about. So, even here, problems may remain; but, importantly, they are not problems about moral rights. The point is that once the question is raised of whether our treatment of animals or our treatment of women is right and/or justified, we begin to set about the task not only of working out acceptable theses of rightness and justification of treatment but also of developing and working out answers to those absolutely critical questions about the adequacy of the normative ethics of which these theses are a part.

Notes

1. Leonard Nelson, *A System of Ethics,* trans. Norbert Guterman (Yale University Press, New Haven, 1956), Part I, Section 2, Ch. 7, pp. 136–144. See T. Regan, 'Introduction', in *Animal Rights and Human Obligations,* ed. T. Regan, P. Singer (Prentice-Hall, Englewood Cliffs, N.J., 1976), pp. 16 f. See also J. Passmore, *Man's Responsiblity for Nature* (Duckworth, London, 1974), pp. 113–116.
2. H.J. McCloskey, "Rights," *Philosophical Quarterly,* 15, (1965), 115–127.
3. J. Feinberg, "The Rights of Animals and Unborn Generations," in *Philosophy and Environmental Crisis,* ed. W.T. Blackstone (University of Georgia Press, Athens, Georgia, 1974), pp. 43–68.
4. *Op cit.* 138.
5. J. Feinberg, "Duties, Rights and Claims," *American Philosophical Quarterly,* iv (1966), 137–144.
6. J. Feinberg, "The Nature and Value of Rights," *Journal of Value Inquiry,* iv (1970), 243–260.
7. Cf. J. Feinberg, "The Rights of Animals and Unborn Generations," pp. 46 ff.; Regan, in *Animal Rights and Human Obligations,* p. 15.

8. Cf. C. Stone, *Should Trees Have Standing? Toward Legal Rights for Natural Objects* (Avon Books, New York, 1975), especially Ch. 2. In the United States, the remarks of Justice William O. Douglas, in the important US Supreme Court decision in *Sierra Club* v. *Morton* [405 U.S. 727, 1972], in which reference was made to Stone's work, aided enormously in popularizing the movement for extending legal and moral rights to natural objects.
9. J. Feinberg, "The Rights of Animals and Unborn Generations," p. 50.
10. For the uninitiated, a good introduction to this material is to be found in Singer's *Animal Liberation,* pp. 96–166. The notes to these pages, pp. 167–170, give the many sources of his material.
11. The case of Karen Ann Quinlan has become familiar, as the result of the publicity surrounding her parents' petition to allow her to die and her doctors' refusal to go along with this. (Both parties, of course, clearly believed that she was not already dead; see Ch. III, n. 11). Among the books on the case, see M.D. Heifetz *et al., The Right to Die* (Berkley Publishing Corporation, New York, 1975); and B.D. Colen, *Karen Ann Quinlan: Dying in the Age of Eternal Life* (Nash Publishing Co., New York, 1976). Of related interest is *Ethical Issues in Death and Dying,* eds. T.L. Beauchamp, S. Perlin (Prentice-Hall, Englewood Cliffs, N.J., 1978), Part IV.
12. Singer, then, distinguishes the case of future people from the case of foetuses. Strange as it may seem to many, this is not at all uncommon today; see, for example, Feinberg, "The Rights of Animals and Unborn Generations," pp. 64 ff.

SIERRA CLUB v. *MORTON*

The critical question of "standing" would be simplified and also put neatly in focus if we fashioned a federal rule that allowed environmental issues to be litigated before federal agencies or federal courts in the name of the inanimate object about to be despoiled, defaced, or invaded by roads and bulldozers and where injury is the subject of public outrage. Contemporary public concern for protecting nature's ecological equilibrium should lead to the conferral of standing upon environmental objects to sue for their own preservation.[1] This suit would therefore be more properly labeled as *Mineral King* v. *Morton.*

Inanimate objects are sometimes parties in litigation. A ship has a legal personality, a fiction found useful for maritime purposes. The corporation sole—a creature of ecclesiastical law—is an acceptable adversary and large fortunes ride on its cases.[2] The ordinary corporation is a "person" for purposes of the adjudicatory processes, whether it represents proprietary, spiritual, aesthetic, or charitable causes.

So it should be as respects valleys, alpine meadows, rivers, lakes, estuaries, beaches, ridges, groves of trees, swampland, or even air that feels the destructive pressures of modern technology and modern life. The river, for example, is the living symbol of all the life it sustains or nourishes—fish, aquatic insects, water ouzels, otter, fisher, deer, elk,

401 U.S. 907 (1972). Dissenting opinion by Justice William O. Douglas, United States Supreme Court.

bear, and all other animals, including man, who are dependent on it or who enjoy it for its sight, its sound, or its life. The river as plaintiff speaks for the ecological unit of life that is part of it. Those people who have a meaningful relation to that body of water—whether it be a fisherman, a canoeist, a zoologist, or a logger—must be able to speak for the values which the river represents and which are threatened with destruction.

I do not know Mineral King. I have never seen it nor travelled it, though I have seen articles describing its proposed "development.". . . The Sierra Club in its complaint alleges that "One of the principal purposes of the Sierra Club is to protect and conserve the national resources of the Sierra Nevada Mountains." The District Court held that this uncontested allegation made the Sierra Club "sufficiently aggrieved" to have "standing" to sue on behalf of Mineral King.

Mineral King is doubtless like other wonders of the Sierra Nevada such as Tuolumne Meadows and the John Muir Trail. Those who hike it, fish it, hunt it, camp in it, or frequent it, or visit it merely to sit in solitude and wonderment are legitimate spokesmen for it, whether they may be a few or many. Those who have intimate relation with the inanimate object about to be injured, polluted, or otherwise despoiled are its legitimate spokesmen.

The Solicitor General . . . takes a wholly different approach. He considers the problem in terms of "government by the Judiciary." With all respect, the problem is to make certain that the inanimate objects, which are the very core of America's beauty, have spokesmen before they are destroyed. It is, of course, true that most of them are under the control of a federal or state agency. The standards given those agencies are usually expressed in terms of the "public interest." Yet "public interest" has so many differing shades of meaning as to be quite meaningless on the environmental front. Congress accordingly has adopted ecological standards . . . and guidelines for agency action have been provided by the Council on Environmental Quality of which Russell E. Train is Chairman.

Yet the pressures on agencies for favorable action one way or the other are enormous. The suggestion that Congress can stop action which is undesirable is true in theory; yet even Congress is too remote to give meaningful direction and its machinery is too ponderous to use very often. The federal agencies of which I speak are not venal or corrupt. But they are notoriously under the conrol of powerful interests who manipulate them through advisory committees, or friendly working relations, or who have that natural affinity with the agency which in time develops between the regulator and the regulated. As early as 1894, Attorney General Olney predicted that regulatory agencies might become "industry-minded," as illustrated by his forecast concerning the Interstate Commerce Commission:

> "The Commission is or can be made of great use to the railroads. It satisfies the public clamor for supervision of the railroads, at the same time that supervision is almost entirely nominal. Moreover, the older the Commission gets to be, the more likely it is to take a business and railroad view of things." M. Josephson, The Politicos 526 (1938).

Years later a court of appeals observed, "the recurring question which has plagued public regulation of industry [is] whether the regulatory agency is unduly oriented toward the interest of the industry it is designed to regulate, rather than the public interest it is supposed to protect."

The Forest Service—one of the federal agencies behind the scheme to despoil Mineral King—has been notorious for its alignment with lumber companies, although its mandate from Congress directs it to consider the various aspects of multiple use in its supervision of the national forests.

The voice of the inanimate object, therefore, should not be stilled. That does not mean that the judiciary takes over the managerial functions from the federal agency. It merely means that before these priceless bits of Americana (such as a valley, an alpine meadow, a river, or a lake) are forever lost or are so transformed as to be reduced to the eventual rubble of our urban environment, the voice of the existing beneficiaries of these environmental wonders should be heard.

Perhaps they will not win. Perhaps the bulldozers of "progress" will plow under all the aesthetic wonders of this beautiful land. That is not the present question. The sole question is, who has standing to be heard?

Those who hike the Appalachian Trail into Sunfish Pond, New Jersey, and camp or sleep there, or run the Allagash in Maine, or climb the Guadalupes in West Texas, or who canoe and portage the Quetico Superior in Minnesota, certainly should have standing to defend those natural wonders before courts or agencies, though they live 3,000 miles away. Those who merely are caught up in environmental news or propaganda and flock to defend these waters or areas may be treated differently. That is why these environmental issues should be tendered by the inanimate object itself. Then there will be assurances that all of the forms of life which it represents will stand before the court—the pileated woodpecker as well as the coyote and bear, the lemmings as well as the trout in the streams. Those inarticulate members of the ecological group cannot speak. But those people who have so frequented the place as to know its values and wonders will be able to speak for the entire ecological community.

Ecology reflects the land ethic; and Aldo Leopold wrote in A Sand County Almanac 204 (1949), "The land ethic simply enlarges the boundaries of the community to include soils, waters, plants, and animals, or collectively, the land."

That, as I see it, is the issue of "standing" in the present case and controversy.

Notes

1. See Stone, Should Trees have Standing? Toward Legal Rights for Natural Objects, 45 S. Cal. L. Rev. 450 (1972). [Reprinted above.]
2. At common law, an office holder, such as a priest or the King, and his successors constituted a corporation sole, a legal entity distinct from the personality which managed it. Rights and duties were deemed to adhere to this device rather than to the office holder in order to provide continuity after the latter retired. The notion is occasionally revived by American courts.

RESERVE MINING CO. v. UNITED STATES

Opinion I (June 4, 1974)

Reserve Mining Company is a jointly owned subsidiary of Armco Steel Corporation and Republic Steel Corporation which mines low-grade iron ore, called "taconite," near Babbitt, Minnesota. The taconite is shipped by rail to Reserve's "beneficiating" plant at Silver Bay, Minnesota, on the north shore of Lake Superior, where it is concentrated into "pellets" containing some 65 percent iron ore. The process involves crushing the taconite into fine granules, separating out the metallic iron with huge magnets, and flushing the residue into Lake Superior. Approximately 67,000 tons of this waste product, known as "tailings," are daily discharged into the lake.

The use of Lake Superior for this purpose was originally authorized by the State of Minnesota in 1947, and Reserve commenced operations in 1955. In granting this permit to Reserve, the State of Minnesota accepted Reserve's theory that the weight and velocity of the discharge would insure that the tailings would be deposited at a depth of approximately 900 feet in the "great trough" area of the lake, located offshore from Reserve's facility. The permit provides that:

> [T]ailings shall not be discharged . . . so as to result in any material adverse effects on fish life or public water supplies or in any other material unlawful pollution of the waters of the lake. . . .

Until June 8, 1973, the case was essentially a water pollution abatement case, but on that date the focus of the controversy shifted to the public health impact of Reserve's discharge of asbestiform particles into the air and water. Hearings on a motion for preliminary injunction were consolidated with the trial on the merits, and on April 20, 1974, after 139 days of trial extending over a nine month period and after hearing more than 100 witnesses and examining over 1,600 exhibits, Judge Miles Lord of the United States District Court for the District of Minnesota entered an order closing Reserve's Silver Bay facility. In an abbreviated memorandum opinion, Judge Lord held that Reserve's water discharge violated federal water pollution laws and that its air emissions violated state air pollution regulations, and that both were common law nuisances. Most importantly to the question now before this court, Judge Lord concluded in Findings 9 and 10 of his opinion that:

9. The discharge into the air substantially endangers the health of the people of Silver Bay and surrounding communities as far away as the eastern shore of Wisconsin.

10. The discharge into the water substantially endangers the health of the people who procured their drinking water from the western arm of Lake Superior, including the communities of Silver Bay, Beaver Bay, Two Harbors, Cloquet, Duluth [Minnesota], and Superior, Wisconsin.

498 F.2d 1073 and 514 Federal Reporter, 2nd Series, 492 (1975). Majority Opinion by Judge Myron H. Bright, Eighth Circuit Court of Appeals.

Defendants Reserve, Armco, and Republic noticed their appeal to this court and moved for a stay of the district court's injunction pending the appeal. Judge Lord denied this request and Reserve applied to us for a stay. . . .

. . . The question now before us is whether, considering all facts and circumstances, the injunction order should be stayed pending Reserve's appeal. We grant the stay subject to certain conditions and limitations as stated herein.

Although there is no dispute that significant amounts of waste tailings are discharged into the water and dust is discharged into the air by Reserve, the parties vigorously contest the precise nature of the discharge, its biological effects, and, particularly with respect to the waters of Lake Superior, its ultimate destination. Plaintiffs contend that the mineral commingtonite-grunerite, which Reserve admits to be a major component of its taconite wastes and a member of the mineral family known as amphiboles, is substantially identical in morphology (or shape and form) and similar in chemistry to amosite asbestos, a fibrous mineral which has been found, in certain occupational settings, to be carcinogenic. The plaintiffs further argue that the mineral fibers discharged represent a serious health threat, since they are present in the air of Silver Bay and surrounding communities and, by way of dispersion throughout Lake Superior, in the drinking water of Duluth and other communities drawing water from the lake. . . .

The suggestion that particles of the cummingtonite-grunerite in Reserve's discharges are the equivalent of amosite asbestos raised an immediate health issue, since inhalation of amosite asbestos at occupational levels of exposure is a demonstrated health hazard resulting in asbestosis and various forms of cancer. However, the proof of a health hazard requires more than the mere fact of discharge; the discharge of an agent hazardous in one circumstance must be linked to some present or future likelihood of disease under the prevailing circumstances. An extraordinary amount of testimony was received on these issues. . . .

The theory by which plaintiffs argue that the discharges present a substantial danger is founded largely upon epidemiological studies of asbestos workers occupationally exposed to and inhaling high levels of asbestos dust. A study by Dr. Selikoff of workers at a New Jersey asbestos manufacturing plant demonstrated that occupational exposure to amosite asbestos poses a hazard of increased incidence of asbestosis and various forms of cancer. Similar studies in other occupational contexts leave no doubt that asbestos, at sufficiently high dosages, is injurious to health. However, in order to draw the conclusion that environmental exposure to Reserve's discharges presents a health threat in the instant case, it must be shown either that the circumstances of exposure are at least comparable to those in occupational settings, or, alternatively, that the occupational studies establish certain principles of asbestos-disease pathology which may be applied to predicting the occurrence of such disease in altered circumstances.

Initially, it must be observed that environmental exposure from Reserve's discharges into air and water is simply not comparable to that typical of occupational settings. The occupational studies involve direct exposure to and inhalation of asbestos dust in high concentrations and in confined spaces. This pattern of exposure cannot be equated with the discharge into the outside air of relatively low levels of asbestos fibers. . . .

. . . In order to make a prediction, based on the occupational studies, as to the likelihood of disease at lower levels of exposure, at least two key findings must be made. First, an attempt must be made to determine, with some precision, what that lower level of exposure is. Second, that lower level of exposure must be applied to the known pathology of asbestos-induced disease, i.e., it must be determined whether the level of exposure is safe or unsafe.

Unfortunately, the testimony of Dr. Arnold Brown[1] indicates that neither of these key determinations can be made. Dr. Brown testified that, with respect to both air and water, the level of fibers is not readily susceptible of measurement. This results from the relatively imprecise state of counting techniques and the wide margins of error which necessarily result, and is reflected in the widely divergent sample counts received by the court. . . .

Even assuming that one could avoid imprecision and uncertainty in measuring the number of fibers at low levels, there remains vast uncertainty as to the medical consequences of low levels of exposure to asbestos fibers. . . .

. . . In commenting on the statement, "This suggests that there are levels of asbestos exposure that will not be associated with any detectable risk," Dr. Brown stated:

> As a generalization, yes, I agree to that. But I must reiterate my view that I do not know what that level is. . . .

A fair review of this impartial testimony by the court's own witnesses—to which we necessarily must give great weight at this interim stage of review—clearly suggests that the discharges by Reserve can be characterized only as presenting an unquantifiable risk, i.e., a health risk which either may be negligible or may be significant, but with any significance as yet based on unknowns. This conclusion is simply a logical deduction from the following facts: (1) that fiber levels are not at occupational levels; (2) that the low levels present cannot be expressed or measured as a health risk; and (3) that, in any event, threshold values and dose-response relationships are undetermined. In other words, it is not known what the level of fiber exposure is, other than that it is relatively low, and it is not known what level of exposure is safe or unsafe. Finally, no basis exists, save a theoretical one, for assuming that drinking water, otherwise pure but containing asbestos-like particles, is dangerous to health. . . .

Considering all of the above, we think one conclusion is evident: although Reserve's discharges represent a possible medical danger, they have not in this case been proven to amount to a health hazard. The discharges may or may not result in detrimental health effects, but, for the present, that is simply unknown. . . .

Our stay of the injunction rests upon the good faith preparation and implementation of an acceptable plan. Therefore, we grant a 70-day stay upon these conditions:

1. Reserve's plans shall be promptly submitted to plaintiff-states and to the United States for review and recommendations by appropriate agencies concerned with environmental and health protection. Such plan shall be filed with the district court and submitted to all plaintiffs in no event later than 25 days from the filing of this order.
2. Plaintiffs shall then have an additional 20 days within which to file their comments on such plan.
3. The district court shall consider Reserve's plan and any recommendations made by the United States and plaintiff-states and make a recommendation, within 15 days following submission of plaintiffs' comments, whether or not a stay of the injunction should be continued pending the appeal.
4. Based on these plans, comments, and recommendations, this court will then review the status of its stay order within the time remaining.

OPINION II (APRIL 8, 1975)

On June 4, 1974, [this] court issued an opinion granting Reserve a 70-day stay of the injunction. *Reserve Mining Co.* v. *United States,* 498 F.2d 1073 (8th Cir. 1974). The court conditioned the stay upon Reserve taking prompt steps to abate its air and water discharges, and provided for further proceedings to review whether Reserve had proceeded with the good faith preparation and implementation of an acceptable plan. . . .

The initial, crucial question for our evaluation and resolution focuses upon the alleged hazard to public health attributable to Reserve's discharges into the air and water. . . .

In this preliminary review, we did not view the evidence as supporting a finding of substantial danger. We noted numerous uncertainties in plaintiff's theory of harm which controlled our assessment, particularly the uncertainty as to present levels of exposure and the difficulty in attempting to quantify those uncertain levels in terms of a demonstrable health hazard. . . .

We reached no preliminary decision on whether the facts justified a less stringent abatement order.

As will be evident from the discussion that follows, we adhere to our preliminary assessment that the evidence is insufficient to support the kind of demonstrable danger to the public health that would justify the immediate closing of Reserve's operations. We now address the basic question of whether the discharges pose any risk to public health and, if so, whether the risk is one which is legally cognizable. . . .

As we noted in our stay opinion, much of the scientific knowledge regarding asbestos disease pathology derives from epidemiological studies of asbestos workers occupationally exposed to and inhaling high levels of asbestos dust. Studies of workers naturally exposed to asbestos dust have shown "excess" cancer deaths and a significant incidence of asbestosis. The principal excess cancers are cancer of the lung, the pleura (mesothelioma) and gastrointestinal tract ("gi" cancer).

Studies conducted by Dr. Irving Selikoff, plaintiffs' principal medical witness, illustrated these disease effects. Dr. Selikoff investigated the disease experience of asbestos insulation workers in the New York-New Jersey area, asbestos insulation workers nationwide, and workers in a New Jersey plant manufacturing amosite asbestos. Generally, all three groups showed excess cancer deaths among the exposed populations. . . .

Several principles of asbestos-related disease pathology emerge from these occupational studies. One principle relates to the so-called 20-year rule, meaning that there is a latent period of cancer development of at least 20 years. [A.10:284–285.] Another basic principle is the importance of initial exposure, demonstrated by significant increases in the incidence of cancer even among asbestos manufacturing workers employed for less than three months (although the incidence of disease does increase upon longer exposure). [A.10:279–280.] Finally, these studies indicate that threshold values and dose-response relationships, although probably operative with respect to asbestos-induced cancer, are not quantifiable on the basis of existing data. [A.10:280, 317–319.]

Additionally, some studies implicate asbestos as a possible pathogenic agent in circumstances of exposure less severe than occupational levels. For example, several studies indicate that mesothelioma, a rare but particularly lethal cancer frequently associated with asbestos exposure, has been found in persons experiencing a low level of asbestos exposure.

Plaintiffs' hypothesis that Reserve's air emissions represent a significant threat to the public health touches numerous scientific disciplines, and an overall evaluation demands broad scientific understanding. We think it significant that Dr. Brown, an impartial witness whose court-appointed task was to address the health issue in its entirety, joined with plantiffs' witnesses in viewing as reasonable the hypothesis that Reserve's discharges present a threat to public health. Although, as we noted in our stay opinion, Dr. Brown found the evidence insufficient to make a scientific probability statement as to whether adverse health consequences would in fact ensue, he expressed a public health concern over the continued long-term emission of fibers into the air. . . .

The . . . discussion of the evidence demonstrates that the medical and scientific conclusions here in dispute clearly lie "on the frontiers of scientific knowledge." . . .

As we have demonstrated, Reserve's air and water discharges pose a danger to the public health and justify judicial action of a preventive nature.

In fashioning relief in a case such as this involving a possibility of future harm, a court should strike a proper balance between the benefits conferred and the hazards created by Reserve's facility.

Reserve must be given a reasonable opportunity and a reasonable time to construct facilities to accomplish an abatement of its pollution of air and water and the health risk created thereby. In this way, hardship to employees and great economic loss incident to an immediate plant closing may be avoided. . . .

We cannot ignore, however, the potential for harm in Reserve's discharges. This potential imparts a degree of urgency to this case that would otherwise be absent from an environmental suit in which ecological pollution alone were proved. Thus, any authorization of Reserve to continue operations during conversion of its facilities to abate the pollution must be circumscribed by realistic time limitations. Accordingly, we direct that the injunction order be modified as follows.

A. The Discharge into Water

Reserve shall be given a reasonable time to stop discharging its wastes into Lake Superior. A reasonable time includes the time necessary for Minnesota to act on Reserve's present application to dispose of its tailings at Milepost 7. . . .

Upon receiving a permit from the State of Minnesota, Reserve must utilize every reasonable effort to expedite the construction of new facilities. . . .

B. Air Emissions

Pending final action by Minnesota on the present permit application, Reserve must promptly take all steps necessary to comply with Minnesota law applicable to its air emissions. . . .

We wish to make it clear that we view the air emission as presenting a hazard of greater significance than the water discharge. Accordingly, pending a determination of whether Reserve will be allowed to construct an on-land disposal site or will close its operations, Reserve must immediately proceed with the planning and implementation of such emission controls as may be reasonably and practically effectuated under the circumstances. . . .

Finally, this court deems it appropriate to suggest that the national interest now calls upon Minnesota and Reserve to exercise a zeal equivalent to that displayed in this litigation to arrive at an appropriate location for an on-land disposal site for Reserve's tailings and thus permit an important segment of the national steel industry, employing several thousand people, to continue in production. As we have already noted, we believe this controversy can be resolved in a manner that will purify the air and water without destroying jobs.

The existing injunction is modified in the respects stated herein.

EDITOR'S POSTSCRIPT—1982

For several years after this decision by the Eighth Circuit Court of Appeals, various courts witnessed arguments to show whether, as the Court of Appeals had put it, "the probability of harm is more likely than not." Neither side ever succeeded in providing definitive scientific evidence, and the focus of the controversy over Reserve Mining shifted to the problem of finding a satisfactory on-land disposal site. Reserve complained bitterly about the costs that would be involved in constructing on the site the state of Minnesota preferred. (Their separate cost estimates varied by $50–60 million.)

Every health question mentioned above by the Eighth Circuit remained in dispute. Reserve repeatedly threatened to close down its Silver Bay facility permanently in the face of costs imposed by courts and the state.

Finally, a bargain was struck: on July 7, 1978, Reserve agreed both to build a new facility to satisfy stringent conditions the state insisted upon for approval of the permits. The total investment in the new facility was set at $370 million. The company agreed to stop all discharges into Lake Superior by April 15, 1980. It faithfully carried out this promise and the new facility began operations in August, 1980.

Several scientific studies of health hazards had been completed by July, 1978, and subsequent studies were also eventually completed. These studies, several of which were sponsored by Reserve, have not shown any significant increase in disease related to asbestos in the region or in workers at the plant. By mid-1982 studies had not shown a build-up of asbestiform bodies in lung tissue (of sufficient size to be detected), or in the bloodstream, among persons drinking the water from Lake Superior. Reserve's work force has not shown a significant problem of asbestosis or any similarly caused disease. On the other hand, just as government officials have never been able to show any increased incidence of disease as a result of the Silver Bay facility, so Reserve has no way of showing that there will not be latent and serious long-term effects in 15–20 years—as is commonly the case with asbestos-cased diseases.

T.L.B.

Note

1. Dr. Brown, a research pathologist associated with the Mayo Clinic of Rochester, Minnesota, served the court both in the capacity of a technical advisor and that of an impartial witness.

case 1: Velsicol Chemical Corporation

On December 24, 1975, the administrator of the Environmental Protection Agency of the United States Government, Russell E. Train, issued an order suspending some uses of the pesticides heptachlor and chlordane. A Federal act seemed to give him authority to do so, but both the Secretary of the Department of Agriculture and the manufacturer of the pesticides, Velsicol Chemical Corporation, joined hands in asking for a public hearing on the decision. Train and the EPA adduced considerable evidence to indicate that these pesticides, which were widely used in the environment to control pests, produced cancer in laboratory animals. Testing on laboratory animals was the sole basis for the inference that the pesticides posed a cancer threat to humans, although it also was conclusively demonstrated that residues of the chemical were widely present in the human diet and in the human tissues of those exposed.

Velsicol Chemical stood to lose a substantial amount of money unless ex-

This case was prepared by Tom L. Beauchamp. Reprinted by permission.

isting stocks could be sold, and the EPA administrator did allow them to sell limited stock for use on corn pests (for a short period of time). The Environmental Defense Fund felt strongly that no sale should be permitted, and sought an injunction against continued sale. During the course of the public hearing, Velsicol argued both that its product should not be suspended unless the governmental agency could demonstrate that it is unsafe, and that any other finding would be a drastic departure from past federal policy. However, both the agency and the judge argued that *the burden of proof is on the company;* i.e., the company must be able to prove that its product is safe. Since most issues about environmental and human safety turn on a demonstration of either safety or hazardousness, this burden-of-proof argument was strongly contested in the hearing. The judge found in favor of the agency largely because he believed the animal tests demonstrated a "substantial likelihood" of serious harm to humans. EPA officials subsequently considered backing down on this suspension ruling.

Questions

1. Should Velsicol have been allowed to sell its existing stock?
2. Why should the "burden of proof" be placed on the company rather than the government (if it should)? Are there parallels between the burden-of-proof arguments in this case and in the *Reserve Mining* case?
3. Are there any respects in which Velsicol was treated unfairly by the government?

case 2: The Peking Duck

In 1982 China had almost 6 million visitors from other nations. Most of these visitors were at some point served "Peking Duck"—a dish regarded by Chinese and vistors alike as one of the great delicacies in Peking. In order to meet the demand from restaurants, several million ducks per year are force-fed four times a day. In brief, this process involves forcing grain mash down the duck's gullet through a rubber tube. So fed, the ducks double their weight in approximately 2 1/2 weeks. While being fed, the ducks flap their wings wildly, make unusually loud noises, and attempt to flee from the scene of the feeding. Some ducks die from intestinal malfunctions produced by the force feeding, but most do not and are ready for shipping to restaurants approximately fifty days after hatching.

The railrods in China are particularly important to this business. They are slow and unreliable, but are the only available system of transport. The trains often either do not come on time, in which case the ducks are force-fed up to a month longer than usual, or they are so slow that some ducks die en route from the summer heat.

Almost every part of the duck is eventually served in the restaurant. This effi-

This case was prepared by Tom L. Beauchamp. Reprinted by permission.

cient use of duck parts yields the restaurants large annual profits. Because of transportation problems, however, the duck farms often lose money.

Questions

1. Do factory-farm ducks have rights? interests? desires?
2. Are there moral limits to the way ducks may be raised? If so, have the limits been exceeded in this case? If not, is it because no obligations whatever are owed to animals?
3. Is there a morally relevant difference in the way these ducks are raised in Peking and the way chickens are raised in Western nations?
4. Do low profit margins and losses justify feeding techniques that otherwise would be objectionable?

case 3: Tocks Island Dam

Between 1962 and 1975 a protracted controversy erupted over whether or not to build a dam in the remote regions of Tocks Island, New Jersey. The dam was designed to provide flood control, an additional water supply, a new electrical source, and a recreation center. On the other hand, it would have destroyed some local communities, ecological systems, and natural beauty. Opposition emerged between business and allied state interests in promoting economic growth (and recreational facilities) and the interests of environmentalists in preserving nature against further destruction. Terrible floods and severe drought had preceded plans for the dam and were responsible for the initial commission to build the dam. In 1962 the project was expected to cost $98 million, but by 1975 the projected figure moved to $400 million. Originally environmental groups favored the project, because it would limit growth in the area and would provide a recreation area run by the conservation-minded National Park Service. However, after cost/benefit studies were completed, environmentalists, governors, senators, and congressmen turned against the project for environmental reasons. It appeared that the dam would encourage heavy industrial and residential development, as well as tourism (9.4 million visitors annually was the projected figure). While this outcome would be extremely good for business in the area, for water and power companies, and for the growth of tourist facilities, there also would be ineliminable traffic congestion, waste disposal problems, lake eutrophication, damage to fisheries, the destruction of the last free-flowing river in the Eastern United States, the destruction of several forms of aquatic life in the area, and the flooding of a picturesque and historical valley. Although it was clearly demonstrated that business in the region would be spurred, that the community's tax base would be increased, and that the economic benefits outdistanced the economic costs, the project was eventually voted down by the states immediately af-

This case was prepared by Tom L. Beauchamp. Reprinted by permission.

fected by its construction. New York, New Jersey, and Delaware voted against the project, while Pennsylvania voted in favor of it.

Questions

1. Is there any way to decide this case rationally, or is it a classic tradeoff case that is impenetrable by a rational method?
2. Do almost all controversial problems of environmental usage involve difficult tradeoffs of the sort found in this case?
3. Is there any injustice involved in the decision which was finally reached?

case 4: The OSHA Plant Inspection

Tom Rosco is sipping his morning coffee in his office in the legal department at the headquarters of a major steel producer when he receives a call from an Occupational Safety and Health Administration (OSHA) inspector. The OSHA inspector wants Tom to accompany him on an inspection of the firm's local coking facility which had previously received a citation for excessive workplace air pollution. Stalling for time, Tom tells the inspector he has to take a long distance call, but will call back in a few minutes.

Tom proceeds to call the cokeworks plant manager to discuss the request. The plant manager tells Tom that because of current high production rates and stagnation due to a temperature inversion, the plant almost certainly contained more than the allowed levels of sulfur dioxide and other particulates. He fears that the OSHA inspector might very well shut the plant down. He tells Tom that he should do whatever he can to prevent the inspection.

Tom knows that excessive pollution can lead to lung cancer, emphysema, heart disease, and related maladies but he along with the plant manager feels that the mandated pollution levels are too low. The firm had invested millions of dollars to clean up the outdated coke ovens but it had been decided by the company that it was not economically feasible to meet the standards. If forced on the matter they would shut the plant down, throwing one thousand men out of work. Moreover, the union and individual employees had made it clear that should the choice come down to clean air or jobs, they wanted the jobs.

Questions

1. What options are available to Tom? Which are ethical, which are unethical? What would you do?
2. What are the ethical considerations for the OSHA inspector?
3. Do employees have a "right" to work in an unsafe environment if they so choose?

This case was prepared by Richard E. Wokutch. Copyright 1981 by Richard E. Wokutch and reprinted with permission.

SUGGESTED SUPPLEMENTARY READINGS

Environmental Issues

ACKERMAN, ROBERT W. *The Social Challenge to Business.* Cambridge, Mass.: Harvard University Press, 1975.

ANDERSON, FREDERICK R., et al. *Environmental Improvement Through Economic Incentives.* Baltimore: The Johns Hopkins University Press, 1977.

BARBOUR, IAN G., ed. *Western Man and Environmental Ethics.* Reading, Mass.: Addison-Wesley Publishing Co., 1973.

——. *Technology, Environment, and Human Values.* New York: Praeger Publishers, 1980.

BLACKSTONE, WILLIAM T., ed. *Philosophy and Environmental Crisis.* Athens: University of Georgia Press, 1974.

BRUNNER, DAVID L., *et al.*, eds. *Corporations and the Environment: How Should Decisions be Made?* Stanford, Calif.: Committee on Corporate Responsibility, 1981.

COMMONER, BARRY. *The Closing Circle.* New York: Alfred A. Knopf, 1971.

Environmental Ethics. "An Interdisciplinary Journal Dedicated to the Philosophical Aspects of Environmental Problems," 1979.

GOODPASTER, K. E., and K. M. SAYRE, eds. *Ethics and Problems of the 21st Century.* Notre Dame, Ind.: University of Notre Dame Press, 1979.

HARDIN, GARRETT, and JOHN BADEN. *Managing the Commons.* San Francisco: W. H. Freeman and Co., 1977.

JACOBY, NEIL H. *Corporate Power and Social Responsibility.* New York: Macmillan Publishing Co., 1973, Chapter 10.

KAPP, K. WILLIAM. *The Social Costs of Private Enterprise.* New York: Shocken Books, 1971.

KHARE, R. S., J. W. KOLKA, and C. A. POLLIS. *Environmental Quality and Social Responsibility.* Green Bay, Wisc.: University of Wisconsin-Green Bay, 1972.

LEOPOLD, ALDO. "The Land Ethic." In *A Sand County Almanac.* New York: Oxford Unversity Press, 1966.

METZGER, MICHAEL B. "Perspective: Private Property and Environmental Sanity." *Ecology Law Quarterly,* 5 (1975).

PARTRIDGE, ERNEST, ed. *Responsibilities to Future Generations: Environmental Ethics.* Buffalo: Prometheus Books, 1981.

PASSMORE, JOHN. *Man's Responsibility for Nature.* New York: Charles Scribner's Sons, 1974.

ROLSTON, HOLMES. "Is There an Ecologic Ethic?" *Ethics,* 85 (January 1975).

ROUTLEY, VAL. "Critical Notice: Passmore's *Man's Responsibility for Nature.*" *Australasian Journal of Philosophy,* 53 (August 1975).

SAGOFF, MARK. "On Preserving the Natural Environment." *The Yale Law Journal,* 84 (December 1974).

SAYRE, KENNETH, ed. *Values in the Electric Power Industry.* Notre Dame, Ind.: University of Notre Dame Press, 1977.

SCHUMAKER, E. F. *Small Is Beautiful.* New York: Harper and Row, 1973.

TRIBE, LAURENCE. "Ways Not to Think About Plastic Trees." *The Yale Law Journal,* 83 (1974).

——, CORRINE S. SCHELLING, and JOHN VOSS, eds. *When Values Conflict: Essays on Environmental Analysis, Discourse, and Decision.* Published for the American Academy of Arts and Sciences. Cambridge, Mass.: Ballinger Publishing Co., 1976.

VELASQUEZ, MANUEL G. *Business Ethics: Concepts and Cases.* Englewood Cliffs, N.J.: Prentice-Hall, 1982, Chapter 5.

WHITE, LYNN. "The Historical Roots of Our Ecologic Crisis." *Science,* 155 (March 10, 1967).

WOODCOCK, LEONARD. "Labor and the Economic Impact of Enviromental Control Requirements." In Robert M. Solow, et al., eds. *Jobs and the Environment.* San Francisco: Institute of Industrial Relations, University of California, Berkeley, 1972.

The Treatment of Animals

FEINBERG, JOEL. "Human Duties and Animal Rights." In Morris and Fox, eds. *On the Fifth Day.* Washington, D.C.: Acropolis Press, 1978.

FOX, MICHAEL. "'Animal Liberation': A Critique." *Ethics,* 88 (January 1978).

FREY, R. G. "Animal Rights." *Analysis,* 37 (June 1977).

——. *Interests and Rights: The Case Against Animals.* Oxford: Clarendon Press, 1980.

Inquiry (Summer 1979). Special Issue on Animals.

JAMIESON, DALE and TOM REGAN. "Animal Rights: A Reply to Frey." *Analysis,* 38 (January 1978).

LOCKWOOD, MICHAEL. "Singer on Killing and the Preference for Life." *Inquiry,* 22, (1979).

McCLOSKEY, H. J. "Moral Rights and Animals." *Inquiry,* 22 (1978).

MORRIS, RICHARD KNOWLES and MICHAEL W. FOX, eds. *On the Fifth Day: Animal Rights and Human Ethics.* Washington D.C.: Acropolis Press, 1978.

PATERSON, D. A., and RICHARD RYDER, eds. *Animal Rights: A Symposium.* London: Centaur Press, 1979.

REGAN TOM. "Feinberg on What Sorts of Beings Can Have Rights." *Southern Journal of Philosophy* (Winter 1976).

——. "Frey on Interests and Animal Rights." *Philosophical Quarterly,* 27 (October 1977).

——. *Humans, Animals, Nature: Essays on Animal Rights and Environmental Ethics.* Berkeley: University of California Press, 1982.

——, and PETER SINGER, eds. *Animal Rights and Human Obligations.* Englewood Cliffs, N.J.: Prentice-Hall, 1976.

ROLLIN, BERNARD. *Animal Rights and Human Morality.* Buffalo: Prometheus Books, 1981.

SINGER, PETER. "Animal Liberation." *New York Review of Books,* 20 (April

5, 1973). [A review of *Animals, Men and Morals,* Godlovitch and Harris, eds. New York: Grove Press, 1973.]

———. *Animal Liberation.* A New York Review Book. New York: Random House, 1975.

———. "Animals and the Value of Life." In Tom Regan, ed. *Matters of Life and Death.* New York: Random House, 1979.

———. "Killing Humans and Killing Animals." *Inquiry,* 22 (1979).

STEINBOCK, BONNIE. "Speciesism and the Idea of Equality." *Philosophy,* 53 (April 1978).

WATSON, RICHARD A. "Self-Consciousness and the Rights of Non-Human Animals and Nature." *Environmental Ethics,* 1 (Summer 1979).

CHAPTER 7

PREFERENTIAL HIRING AND REVERSE DISCRIMINATION

INTRODUCTION

In recent years government policies intended to ensure fairer opportunities for women and minority groups have provoked sustained controversy. Target goals, timetables, and quotas seem to many citizens not merely to be preferential treatment but actually to discriminate against more talented applicants who are excluded yet would be hired or accepted on their merits were it not for the preferential advancement of others. Such government policies are said to create a situation of "reverse discrimination." By balancing or compensating for past discrimination against persons on the basis of (morally irrelevant) characteristics such as race, sex, nationality, and religion, these policies now require discrimination in favor of such persons and therefore against the members of other previously favored classes. These policies seem unfairly discriminatory to some, because they violate basic principles of justice and equal protection. Others believe this conclusion incorrect for a variety of reasons. In this chapter we will study whether some compulsory government policies and even some policies voluntarily adopted by private industry would result in preferential treatment of persons and, if so, whether such policies are justifiable.

The articles in this chapter by Sidney Hook and Thomas Nagel address ethical issues which have emerged from recent congressional, executive, and judicial determinations. These issues include moral and legal responsibilities of businesses to eradicate discrimination, and the problem of whether there should be hiring quotas. Hook and Nagel specifically address issues of the role and responsibilities of the federal government. It gradually becomes apparent in these articles that most of the contemporary controversy about hiring is centered on (1) affirmative action programs and (2) preferential programs which might result in reverse discrimination. It is sometimes said in popular literature that "affirmative action" is synonymous with "reverse discrimination," but this equation can be misleading, as we shall now see.

AFFIRMATIVE ACTION AND REVERSE DISCRIMINATION

"Affirmative action" basically means the taking of positive steps to hire persons from groups previously discriminated against in educational and employment situations. Passive nondiscrimination is thus not sufficient to qualify as affirmative action. Federal requirements at a minimum impose on business the responsibility to advertise jobs fairly and to seek as employees members of those groups discriminated against in the past. The projected means for the fulfillment of these responsibilities are generally called employment *goals*. A "goal" in this context is a targeted employment outcome (intended to eliminate discrimination) planned by an institution, probably after consultation with government officials. A goal is commonly distinguished from a *quota,* which is construed in this context as a hard and fast figure or proportion—usually expressed in percentages. Goals and quotas sound to many ears like the same thing, and it is often difficult to know which an author has in mind. However, there is a crucial *symbolic* difference between the two. Goals have come largely to symbolize federally mandated or negotiated targets and timetables, whereas quotas have come to symbolize policies resulting in reverse discrimination. But what is "reverse discrimination" and how does it differ from both "affirmative action" and "preferential hiring"?

Writers on the subject of discrimination often use the term "reverse discrimination" in different ways. At a minimum this term means discrimination on behalf of a less qualified person or persons on the grounds that the group to which the person belongs was previously discriminated against. Some also assert or assume that, by definition, reverse discrimination occurs only as a result of policies involving *blanket* preferential treatment on the basis of sex or race for whole groups of persons who are members of those classes. Yet this understanding of reverse discrimination is questionable on at least two counts. First, properties other than race or sex may be used—religion or nationality, for example. Second, and more importantly, there is no reason why (by definition) a policy of compensation resulting in a reversal of discrimination must apply in blanket fashion to whole groups rather than more restrictedly to a limited number of individuals who are members of those groups. Suppose an industry-wide preferential policy were adopted that competitively advantaged the job applications of all blacks earning less than $10,000 per year (and which discriminated against competitive whites earning equivalent amounts) but did not advantage blacks who earned more than that figure. This policy would qualify as reverse discrimination (based on race), but the *entire* racial group would not have been given blanket preferential treatment.

This issue is important because it is often said that affluent women and minority group members would be advantaged, and disadvantaged poor whites or males would be discriminated against, by preferential hiring policies. Some authors have seemed to favor this outcome: "The mere fact of a person's being black in the United States is a sufficient reason for providing compensatory techniques even though that person may in some ways appear fortunate in his personal background."[1] But this is a particular *moral* thesis about the justifiability of reverse discrimination. It does not explicate the term's *meaning*. Hence, one can advocate even radical policies of compensation resulting in reverse discrimination and at the same time advocate nonblanket, perhaps highly restrictive policies of preferential treatment. This issue, though without this conclusion, is discussed in Robert Simon's critique of Judith Thomson in this chapter.

We can now summarize the basic outlines of the concept of reverse discrimination: reverse discrimination is a discriminatory action or practice based on a (normally) morally irrelevant property; policies resulting in reverse discrimination may also apply to individual persons or groups and need not involve unqualified blanket preferential treatment; and, finally, any morally irrelevant property could be used—not simply race and sex.

It should also be noted that *both* minimal affirmative action programs *and* policies possibly productive of reverse discrimination involve what is referred to as "preferential hiring." This notion refers to hiring that gives preference in recruitment and ranking to women, minority groups, and others previously discriminated against. This preference can be practiced either by the use of goals or quotas, or merely by choosing blacks, women, etc. whenever their credentials are *equal* to those of other candidates. However, "preferential hiring" carries connotations for some persons of reverse discrimination or at least of quotas. Accordingly, one should be careful to understand the term's exact use in any document or article in which it appears. This warning should be observed in the case of the articles by Thomson and Simon in this chapter, which explicitly discuss preferential hiring.

MORAL ISSUES IN PREFERENTIAL POLICIES

We sometimes think that a severe injustice has been done to a *group* of persons. Naturally we wish to restore the balance of justice by compensating them for their loss. The *principle of compensatory justice* says that whenever an injustice has been committed, just compensation or reparation is owed the injured parties. It is now a widespread view that minority groups discriminated against in the past, including women, blacks, North American Indians, and French Canadians, should be recompensed for these injustices by compensatory policies such as affirmative action or equal opportunity programs. Whatever one may think of this proposal, it is not difficult to understand why this view is espoused. For years deliberate barriers or quotas were placed on opportunities for blacks, women, and other groups to participate in some of society's most desirable institutions (universities, business, law, etc.). Even when barriers were formally dropped, matters often did not improve. Inequalities, many came to think, are rooted in early training in public schools or in unfair testing. They further charged that our systems of screening and promotion discriminate not intentionally *against* certain groups so much as unintentionally *in favor of* other groups. All of these factors have conspired to produce a range of government programs, which are in effect compensatory measures.

Because of this history of discrimination and its persistence, it is widely believed that we could restore the balance of justice by making it easier for previously discriminated-against groups to obtain admission to educational institutions and job interviews. Presumably, special programs also avoid the problem of mere *token* approval of more equal distribution. This system seems clearly, however, to involve an extensive network of preferential treatments, and many have asked the following question: If quotas or social policies require that, for example, a woman or a black be given preference over a white man otherwise better qualified (i.e., if the circumstances had been anonymous the white man would have been selected), is this an acceptable instance of compensatory justice or is it a simple case of treating the white man unjustly? In answer to this question it has been argued variously that such practices of preferential treatment are (a) just, (b) unjust, or (c) not just but *permitted* nonetheless by principles other than those of justice and equality.

a. Those who claim that such compensatory measures are just, or perhaps required by justice, argue that the past lives in the present: the victims of past discrimination against blacks are still handicapped or discriminated against, while the families of past slave owners are still being unduly enriched by inheritance laws. Those who have inherited wealth which was accumulated by iniquitous practices do not have as much right to the wealth, it is argued, as do the sons of slaves, who at least have a right of compensation. In the case of women it is argued that culture equips them with a lack of self-confidence, prejudicially excludes them from much of the work force, and treats them as a low-paid auxiliary labor unit. Hence only extraordinarily independent women can be expected to compete even psychologically with males. Sometimes a slightly stronger argument is advanced: compensation is fair even if some inequalities cannot be removed by offering the best available training measures. The compensation is said to be fair simply because it is *owed* to those who in the past suffered unjust treatment. As Judith Thomson argues in this chapter, we may think veterans are owed preferential treatment because of their service and sacrifice to country, and thus we may similarly think blacks and women are owed preferential treatment because of their economic sacrifices, systematic incapacitation, and consequent personal and group losses.

b. Those who claim that compensatory measures are unjust argue variously that no criteria exist for measuring compensations, that the extent of discrimination is now minor (insufficiently broad to justify preferential treatment), and that none of those actually harmed in previous eras is available now to be compensated. Instead of providing compensation, they argue, we should continue to guide justice by strict equality and merit, while attacking the roots of discrimination. Also, some now successful but once underprivileged minority groups argue that their long struggle for equality is jeopardized by programs of "favoritism" to blacks and women. Their view is that they either will suffer unfairly, having already suffered enough, or else will not suffer only because they too will be compensated for past oppressions. Is it not absurd, they say, to suggest that *all* past oppressed groups—blacks and women being only two among a great many—should receive compensatory reparations? Are we not compounding initial injustices with a vastly complicated system of further injustices? Some of these arguments are carefully developed in the articles below by Robert Simon and William Blackstone.

   c. The third possible view is that some strong compensatory measures are *not just,* because they violate principles of justice, and yet *are justifiable* by appeal to principles other than justice. This view is argued in this chapter by Tom Beauchamp. Because his argument is a straightforward attempt to justify reverse discriminatory policies in general, we may now shift to this topic.

THE MORAL PROBLEM OF REVERSE DISCRIMINATION

Among those writers who would permit policies of reverse discrimination, a fairly standard approach is taken: They attempt to justify reverse discrimination by showing that under certain conditions compensation owed for *past* wrongs justifies (for varying reasons) *present* policies productive of reverse discrimination. Thomson takes one form of this approach in this chapter. By contrast, Beauchamp argues that because of past wrongs to classes of persons, we have special and strong obligations to see that these wrongs do not continue. His argument differs from Thomson's and the more usual ones based on compensatory justice because he holds that reverse discrimination is permitted and even required in order that we might eliminate *present* discriminatory practices against classes of persons. He therefore introduces factual evidence for his claim of present, continuing discrimination, and this evidence in turn is supposed to support his claim that reverse discrimination is sometimes justified. Beauchamp's contention is that because these larger social conditions prevail, policies producing reverse discrimination are justified. These policies are morally *permitted* because they are social measures necessary for the protection of those harmed by intractable social attitudes and selection procedures. This argument—in the language of the first chapter of this book—is a utilitarian argument.

   In the final selection in this chapter William T. Blackstone argues against utilitarian justifications of reverse discrimination, on grounds that principles of justice override the principle of utility. Blackstone and Beauchamp thus come into direct controversy over a fundamental issue in ethical theory: utilitarian versus nonutilitarian justifications.

   Blackstone and many other opponents of policies which might result in reverse discrimination argue that reverse discrimination violates fundamental and overriding principles of justice. It is argued in this literature that since reverse discriminatory policies create injustices, they cannot be justified. The most widely defended thesis is that policies productive of reverse discrimination violate the equality of persons by discriminating for or against a group, thus favoring them with special privileges and damaging the rule of law by replacing it with power struggles. Other reasons proposed as supplementary to this primary argument include the following: (1) Some who are innocent of and not responsible for the past invidious discrimination pay the price (e.g., qualified young white males); but this treatment is discriminatory because such persons are penalized solely on the basis of their race. (2) Male members of minority groups such as Poles, Irish, and Italians—themselves discriminated against in the past—will bear a heavy and unfair burden of the cost of compensating women and minority groups such as blacks. (3) Many members of the *class* selected for preferential treatment will have never themselves been unjustly treated and will not deserve preferential policies. (4) There are some relevant differences between the sexes which justify differential expectations and treatment. (Men are naturally better at some things, women at others.) (5) Compensation can be provided to *individuals* treated unfairly in the past without resort to reverse discrimination, which is the result of blanket treatment for groups. The last reason (5) is presumably not only a reason against reverse discrimination, but an alternative *policy,* as well.

As indicated by the controversial court cases in this chapter—*Griggs* v. *Duke Power* and *United Steelworkers* v. *Weber*—problems of preferential and discriminatory hiring remain troublesome and surprisingly complicated.

T.L.B.

Note

1. Graham Hughes, "Reparations for Blacks?" *New York University Law Review,* 43 (December 1968), p. 1073.

DISCRIMINATION, COLOR BLINDNESS, AND THE QUOTA SYSTEM

Sidney Hook

Every humane and fair-minded person must approve of the presidential executive order of 1965, which forbade discrimination with respect to race, religion, national origin or sex by any organization or group that receives financial support from the government in the course of fulfilling its contractual obligations with it. The difficulties in enforcing this order flow not

From *Measure,* no. 30, (Summer 1974). Reprinted by permission of the author and University Centers for Rational Alternatives.

from its ethical motivation and intent, but in establishing the criteria of evidence that discrimination has been practiced. Very rarely are the inequities explicitly expressed in the provisions guiding or regulating employment. They must be inferred. But they cannot be correctly inferred from the actual figures of employment independently of the *availability* of different minority groups, their *willingness* to accept employment, and the objective *qualifications* of those able and willing to apply. To be sure, the bigoted and prejudiced can distort these considerations in order to cover up flagrant discriminatory practices. But only the foolish and unperceptive will dismiss these considerations as irrelevant and assume that reference to them is an obvious sign of prejudice.

There is, unfortunately, evidence that some foolish and unperceptive persons in the Office of Civil Rights of the Department of Health, Education, and Welfare are disregarding these considerations and mechanically inferring from the actual figures of academic employment in institutions of higher learning the existence of discriminatory practices. What is worse, they are threatening to cancel federal financial support, without which many universities cannot survive, unless, within a certain period of time, the proportion of members of minorities on the teaching and research staff of universities approximate their proportion in the general population. Further, with respect to women, since it is manifestly absurd to expect that universities be staffed in an equal sexual ratio in all departments, the presence of discrimination against them is to be inferred if the composition of the teaching and research staffs does not correspond to the proportion of *applicants*—independently of the qualifications of the applicants.

In the light of this evidence, a persuasive case can be made that those who have issued these guidelines and ultimata to universities, whether they are male or female, black or white, Catholic, Jewish, or Protestant are unqualified for the offices they hold and therefore unable to properly enforce the presidential executive order. For they are guilty of fostering the very racialism and discrimination an executive order was issued to correct and forestall.

It is not hard to demonstrate the utter absurdity of the directives issued by the Office of Civil Rights of the Department of Health, Education, and Welfare. I shall use two simple instances. A few years ago, it was established that more than 80 percent of the captains of tugboats in the New York Harbor were Swedish. None were black. None were Jewish. And this in a community in which blacks and Jews outnumbered Swedes by more than a hundred to one. If one were to construe these figures along the lines laid down by the office of Civil Rights of HEW, this would be presumptive proof of crass discrimination against Negroes and Jews. But it is nothing of the sort. Negroes and Jews, for complex reasons we need not here explore, have never been interested in navigating tugboats. They have not applied for the positions. They have therefore never been rejected.

The faculties of many Negro colleges are overwhelmingly black out of all proportion to their numbers in the country, state, or even local community. It would be a grim jest therefore to tax them with discriminatory practices. Until recently, they have been pathetically eager to employ qualified white teachers, but they have been unable to attract them.

The fact that HEW makes a distinction between women and minorities, judging sexual discrimination not by simple proportion of women teachers and researchers in universities to their proportion in the general population, but only to their proportion among *applicants,* shows that it has a dim understanding of the relevant issue. There are obviously various occupational fields—military, mining, aeronautical, and so forth, for which women have, until now, shown little inclination. Neither the school nor the department can be faulted for the scarcity of female applications. But the main point is this: no matter how many applicants there are for a post, whether they are male or female, the only relevant criterion is whether or not they are qualified. Only when there is antecedent determination that the applicants, with respect to the job or post specifications are equally or even roughly equally qualified, and there is a marked and continued disparity in the relative numbers employed, is there legitimate ground for suspicion and inquiry.

The effect of the ultimata to universities to hire blacks and women under threat of losing crucial financial support is to compel them to hire *unqualifed* Negroes and women, and to discriminate *against* qualified nonblacks and men. This is just as much a manifestation of racism, even if originally unintended, as the racism the original presidential directive was designed to correct. Intelligent, self-respecting Negroes and women would scorn such preferential treatment. The consequences of imposing any criterion other than that of qualified talent on our educational establishments are sure to be disastrous on the quest for new knowledge and truth as well as subversive of the democratic ethos. Its logic points to the introduction of a quota system, of the notorious *numerus clausus* of repressive regimes of the past. If blacks are to be hired merely on the basis of their color and women merely on the basis of their sex, because they are *under*represented in the faculties of our universities, before long the demand will be made that Jews or men should be fired or dismissed or not hired as Jews or men, no matter how well qualified, because they are *over*represented in our faculties.

The universities should not yield to the illiberal ultimata of the Office of Civil Rights of HEW. There is sufficient work for it to do in enforcing the presidential directive in areas where minorities are obviously qualified and are obviously suffering from unfair discrimination. It undoubtedly is true, as some members of UCRA who have long been active in the field of civil rights have long pointed out, that some educational institutions or their departments have been guilty of obvious religious and racial discrimination. The evidence of this was flagrant and open and required no elaborate questionnaires to establish. The Office of Civil Rights could cooperate with the Department of Justice here. Currently, its activities in the field of higher education are not only wasting time, effort, and the taxpayer's money but debasing educational standards as well. It is bringing confusion and conflict into an area where, prior to its intervention, the issues were well understood and where voluntary efforts to hire qualified women and members of minorities were being made with increasing success.

A DEFENSE OF AFFIRMATIVE ACTION

Thomas Nagel

The term "affirmative action" has changed in meaning since it was first introduced. Originally it referred only to special efforts to ensure equal opportunity for members of groups that had been subject to discrimination. These efforts included public advertisement of positions to be filled, active recruitment of qualified applicants from the formerly excluded groups, and special training programs to help them meet the standards for admission or appointment. There was also close attention to procedures of appointment, and sometimes to the results, with a view to detecting continued discrimination, conscious or unconscious.

More recently the term has come to refer also to some degree of definite preference for members of these groups in determining access to positions from which they were formerly excluded. Such preference might be allowed to influence decisions only between candidates who are otherwise equally qualified, but usually it involves the selection of women or minority members over other candidates who are better qualified for the position.

Let me call the first sort of policy "weak affirmative action" and the second "strong affirmative action." It is important to distinguish them, because the distinction is sometimes blurred in practice. It is strong affirmative action—the policy of preference—that arouses controversy. Most people would agree that weak or precautionary affirmative action is a good thing, and worth its cost in time and energy. But this does not imply that strong affirmative action is also justified.

I shall claim that in the present state of things it is justified, most clearly with respect to blacks. But I also believe that a defender of the practice must acknowledge that there are serious arguments against it, and that it is defensible only because the arguments for it have great weight. Moral opinion in this country is sharply divided over the issue because significant values are involved on both sides. My own view is that while strong affirmative action is intrinsically undesirable, it is a legitimate and perhaps indispensable method of pursuing a goal so important to the national welfare that it can be justified as a temporary, though not short-term, policy for both public and private institutions. In this respect it is like other policies that impose burdens on some for the public good.

THREE OBJECTIONS

I shall begin with the argument against. There are three objections to strong affirmative action: that it is inefficient; that it is unfair; and that it damages self-esteem.

Testimony before the Subcommittee on the Constitution of the Senate Judiciary Committee, June 18, 1981. Reprinted by permission of Professor Nagel.

The degree of inefficiency depends on how strong a role racial or sexual preference plays in the process of selection. Among candidates meeting the basic qualifications for a position, those better qualified will on the average perform better, whether they are doctors, policemen, teachers, or electricians. There may be some cases, as in preferential college admissions, where the immediate usefulness of making educational resources available to an individual is thought to be greater because of the use to which the education will be put or because of the internal effects on the institution itself. But by and large, policies of strong affirmative action must reckon with the costs of some lowering in performance level: the stronger the preference, the larger the cost to be justified. Since both the costs and the value of the results will vary from case to case, this suggests that no one policy of affirmative action is likely to be correct in all cases, and that the cost in performance level should be taken into account in the design of a legitimate policy.

The charge of unfairness arouses the deepest disagreements. To be passed over because of membership in a group one was born into, where this has nothing to do with one's individual qualifications for a position, can arouse strong feelings of resentment. It is a departure from the ideal—one of the values finally recognized in our society—that people should be judged so far as possible on the basis of individual characteristics rather than involuntary group membership.

This does not mean that strong affirmative action is morally repugnant in the manner of racial or sexual discrimination. It is nothing like those practices, for though like them it employs race and sex as criteria of selection, it does so for entirely different reasons. Racial and sexual discrimination are based on contempt or even loathing for the excluded group, a feeling that certain contacts with them are degrading to members of the dominant group, that they are fit only for subordinate positions or menial work. Strong affirmative action involves none of this: it is simply a means of increasing the social and economic strength of formerly victimized groups, and does not stigmatize others.

There is an element of individual unfairness here, but it is more like the unfairness of conscription in wartime, or of property condemnation under the right of eminent domain. Those who benefit or lose out because of their race or sex cannot be said to deserve their good or bad fortune.

It might be said on the other side that the beneficiaries of affirmative action deserve it as compensation for past discrimination, and that compensation is rightly exacted from the group that has benefited from discrimination in the past. But this is a bad argument, because as the practice usually works, no effort is made to give preference to those who have suffered most from discrimination, or to prefer them especially to those who have benefited most from it, or been guilty of it. Only candidates who in other qualifications fall on one or other side of the margin of decision will directly benefit or lose from the policy, and these are not necessarily, or even probably, the ones who especially deserve it. Women or blacks who don't have the qualifications even to be considered are likely to have been handicapped more by the effects of discrimination than those who receive preference. And the marginal white male candidate who is turned down can evoke our sympathy if he asks, ''Why me?'' (A policy of explicitly *compensatory* preference, which took into account each individual's background of poverty and discrimination, would escape some of these objections, and it has its defenders, but it is not the policy I want to defend. Whatever its merits, it will not serve the same purpose as direct affirmative action.)

The third objection concerns self-esteem, and is particularly serious. While strong affirmative action is in effect, and generally known to be so, no one in an affirmative action category who gets a desirable job or is admitted to a selective university can be sure that he or she has not benefited from the policy. Even those who would have made it anyway fall under suspicion, from themselves and from others: it comes to be widely felt that success does not mean the same thing for women and minorities. This painful damage to esteem cannot be avoided. It should make any defender of strong affirmative action want the practice to end as soon as it has achieved its basic purpose.

Justifying Affirmative Action

I have examined these three objections and tried to assess their weight, in order to decide how strong a countervailing reason is needed to justify such a policy. In my view, taken together they imply that strong affirmative action involving significant preference should be undertaken only if it will substantially further a social goal of the first importance. While this condition is not met by all programs of affirmative action now in effect, it is met by those which address the most deep-seated, stubborn, and radically unhealthy divisions in the society, divisions whose removal is a condition of basic justice and social cohesion.

The situation of black people in our country is unique in this respect. For almost a century after the abolition of slavery we had a rigid racial caste system of the ugliest kind, and it only began to break up twenty-five years ago. In the South it was enforced by law, and in the North, in a somewhat less severe form, by social convention. Whites were thought to be defiled by social or residential proximity to blacks, intermarriage was taboo, blacks were denied the same level of public goods—education and legal protection—as whites, were restricted to the most menial occupations, and were barred from any positions of authority over whites. The visceral feelings of black inferiority and untouchability that this system expressed were deeply ingrained in the members of both races, and they continue, not surprisingly, to have their effect. Blacks still form, to a considerable extent, a hereditary social and economic community characterized by widespread poverty, unemployment, and social alienation.

When this society finally got around to moving against the caste system, it might have done no more than to enforce straight equality of opportunity, perhaps with the help of weak affirmative action, and then wait a few hundred years while things gradually got better. Fortunately it decided instead to accelerate the process by both public and private institutional action, because there was wide recognition of the intractable character of the problem posed by this insular minority and its place in the nation's history and collective consciousness. This has not been going on very long, but the results are already impressive, especially in speeding the advancement of blacks into the middle class. Affirmative action has not done much to improve the position of poor and unskilled blacks. That is the most serious part of the problem, and it requires a more direct economic attack. But increased access to higher education and upper-level jobs is an essential part of what must be achieved to break the structure of drastic separation that was left largely undisturbed by the legal abolition of the caste system.

Changes of this kind require a generation or two. My guess is that strong affirmative action for blacks will continue to be justified into the early decades of the next century, but that by then it will have accomplished what it can and will no longer be worth the costs. One point deserves special emphasis. The goal to be pursued is the reduction of a great social injustice, not proportional representation of the races in all institutions and professions. Proportional racial representation is of no value in itself. It is not a legitimate social goal, and it should certainly not be the aim of strong affirmative action, whose drawbacks make it worth adopting only against a serious and intractable social evil.

This implies that the justification for strong affirmative action is much weaker in the case of other racial and ethnic groups, and in the case of women. At least, the practice will be justified in a narrower range of circumstances and for a shorter span of time than it is for blacks. No other group has been treated quite like this, and no other group is in a comparable status. Hispanic-Americans occupy an intermediate position, but it seems to me frankly absurd to include persons of oriental descent as beneficiaries of affirmative action, strong or weak. They are not a severely deprived and excluded minority, and their eligibility serves only to swell the numbers that can be included on affirmative action reports. It also suggests that there is a drift in the policy toward adopting the goal of racial proportional representation for its own sake. This is a foolish mistake, and should be resisted. The only legitimate goal of the policy is to reduce egregious racial stratification.

With respect to women, I believe that except over the short term, and in professions or institutions from which their absence is particularly marked, strong affirmative action is not warranted and weak affirmative action is enough. This is based simply on the expectation that the social and economic situation of women will improve quite rapidly under conditions of full equality of opportunity. Recent progress provides some evidence for this. Women do not form a separate hereditary community, characteristically poor and uneducated, and their position is not likely to be self-perpetuating in the same way as that of an outcast race. The process requires less artificial acceleration, and any need for strong affirmative action for women can be expected to end sooner than it ends for blacks.

I said at the outset that there was a tendency to blur the distinction between weak and strong affirmative action. This occurs especially in the use of numerical quotas, a topic on which I want to comment briefly.

A quota may be a method of either weak or strong affirmative action, depending on the circumstances. It amounts to weak affirmative action—a safeguard against discrimination—if, and only if, there is independent evidence that average qualifications for the positions being filled are no lower in the group to which a minimum quota is being assigned than in the applicant group as a whole. This can be presumed true of unskilled jobs that most people can do, but it becomes less likely, and harder to establish, the greater the skill and education required for the position. At these levels, a quota proportional to population, or even to representation of the group in the applicant pool, is almost certain to amount to strong affirmative action. Moreover it is strong affirmative action of a particularly crude and indiscriminate kind, because it permits no variation in the degree of preference on the basis of costs in efficiency, depending on the qualification gap. For this reason I should defend quotas only where they serve the purpose of weak affirmative action. On the whole, strong affirmative action is better implemented by including group preference as one factor in appointment or admission decisions, and letting the results depend on its interaction with other factors.

I have tried to show that the arguments against strong affirmative action are clearly outweighed at present by the need for exceptional measures to remove the stubborn residues of racial caste. But advocates of the policy should acknowledge the reasons against it, which will ensure its termination when it is no longer necessary. Affirmative action is not an end in itself, but a means of dealing with a social situation that should be intolerable to us all.

PREFERENTIAL HIRING

Judith Jarvis Thomson

Many people are inclined to think preferential hiring an obvious injustice.[1] I should have said "feel" rather than "think": it seems to me the matter has not been carefully thought out, and that what is in question, really, is a gut reaction.

I am going to deal with only a very limited range of preferential hirings: that is, I am concerned with cases in which several candidates present themselves for a job, in which the hiring officer finds, on examination, that all are equally qualified to hold that job, and he then straightway declares for the black, or for the woman, because he or she *is* a black or a woman. And I shall talk only of hiring decisions in the universities, partly because I am most familiar with them, partly because it is in the universities that the most vocal and articulate opposition to preferential hiring is now

Judith Jarvis Thomson, "Preferential Hiring," *Philosophy & Public Affairs* 2, no. 4 (Summer 1973). Copyright © 1973 by Princeton University Press. Excerpts reprinted by permission.

heard—not surprisingly, perhaps, since no one is more vocal and articulate than a university professor who feels deprived of his rights.

I suspect that some people may say, Oh well, in *that* kind of case it's all right, what we object to is preferring the less qualified to the better qualified. Or again, What we object to is refusing even to consider the qualifications of white males. I shall say nothing at all about these things. I think that the argument I shall give for saying that preferential hiring is not unjust in the cases I do concentrate on can also be appealed to to justify it outside that range of cases. But I won't draw any conclusions about cases outside it. Many people do have that gut reaction I mentioned against preferential hiring in *any* degree or form; and it seems to me worthwhile bringing out that there is good reason to think they are wrong to have it. Nothing I say will be in the slightest degree novel or original. It will, I hope, be enough to set the relevant issues out clearly.

I

But first, something should be said about qualifications.

I said I would consider only cases in which the several candidates who present themselves for the job are equally qualified to hold it; and there plainly are difficulties in the way of saying precisely how this is to be established, and even what is to be established. Strictly academic qualifications seem at a first glance to be relatively straightforward: the hiring officer must see if the candidates have done equally well in courses (both courses they took, and any they taught), and if they are recommended equally strongly by their teachers, and if the work they submit for consideration is equally good. There is no denying that even these things are less easy to establish than first appears: for example, you may have a suspicion that Professor Smith is given to exaggeration, and that this "great student" is in fact less strong than Professor Jones's "good student"—but do you *know* that this is so? But there is a more serious difficulty still: as blacks and women have been saying, strictly academic indicators may themselves be skewed by prejudice. My impression is that women, white and black, may possibly suffer more from this than black males. A black male who is discouraged or down-graded for being black is discouraged or down-graded out of dislike, repulsion, a desire to avoid contact; and I suspect that there are very few teachers nowadays who allow themselves to feel such things, or, if they do feel them, to act on them. A woman who is discouraged or down-graded for being a woman is not discouraged or down-graded out of dislike, but out of a conviction she is not serious. . . .

II

. . . Suppose two candidates for a civil service job have equally good test scores, but that there is only one job available. We could decide between them by coin-tossing. But in fact we do allow for declaring for A straightway, where A is a veteran, and B is not.[2] It may be that B is a nonveteran through no fault of his own: perhaps he was refused induction for flat feet, or a heart murmur. That is, those things in virtue of which B is a nonveteran may be things which it was no more in his power to control or change than it is in anyone's power to control or change the color of his skin. Yet the fact is that B is not a veteran and A is. On the assumption that the veteran has served his country, the country owes him something. And it seems plain that giving him preference is a not unjust way in which part of that debt of gratitude can be paid.

And now, . . . we should turn to those debts which are incurred by one who wrongs another. It is here we find what seems to me the most powerful argument for the conclusion that the preferential hiring of blacks and women is not unjust.

I obviously cannot claim any novelty for this argument: it's a very familiar one. Indeed, not merely is it familiar, but so are a battery of objections to it. It may be granted that if we have wronged A, we owe him something: we should make amends, we should compensate him for the wrong done him. It may even be granted that if we have wronged A, we must make amends, that justice requires it, and that a failure to make amends is not merely callousness, but injustice. But (a) are the young blacks and women who are amongst the current applicants for university jobs amongst the blacks and women who were wronged? To turn to particular cases, it might happen that the black applicant is middle class, the son of professionals, and has had the very best in private schooling; or that the woman applicant is plainly the product of feminist upbringing and encouragement. Is it proper, much less required, that the black or woman be given preference over a white male who grew up in poverty, and has to make his own way and earn his encouragements? Again, (b), did we, the current members of the community, wrong any blacks or women? Lots of people once did; but then isn't it for them to do the compensating? That is, if they're still alive. For presumably nobody now alive owned any slaves, and perhaps nobody now alive voted against women's suffrage. And (c) what if the white male applicant for the job has never in any degree wronged any blacks or women? If so, *he* doesn't owe any debts to them, so why should *he* make amends to them?

These objections seem to me quite wrong-headed.

Obviously the situation for blacks and women is better than it was a hundred and fifty, fifty, twenty-five years ago. But it is absurd to suppose that the young blacks and women now of an age to apply for jobs have not been wronged. Large-scale, blatant, overt wrongs have presumably disappeared; but it is only within the last twenty-five years (perhaps the last ten years in the case of women) that it has become at all widely agreed in this country that blacks and women must be recognized as having, not merely this or that particular right normally recognized as belonging to white males, but all of the rights and respect which go with full membership in the community. Even young blacks and women have lived through downgrading for being black or female: they have not merely not been given that very equal chance at the benefits generated by what the community owns which is so firmly insisted on for white males, they have not until lately even been felt to have a right to it.

And even those who were not themselves down-graded for being black or female have suffered the consequences of the down-grading of other blacks and women: lack of self-confidence, and lack of self-respect. For where a community accepts that a person's being black, or being a woman, are right and proper grounds for denying that person full membership in the community, it can hardly be supposed that any but the most extraordinarily independent black or woman will escape self-doubt. All but the most extraordinarily independent of them have had to work harder—if only against self-doubt—than all but the most deprived white males, in the competition for a place amongst the best qualified.

If any black or woman has been unjustly deprived of what he or she has a right to, then of course justice does call for making amends. But what of the blacks and women who haven't actually been deprived of what they have a right to, but only made to suffer the consequences of injustice to other blacks and women? *Perhaps* justice doesn't require making amends to them as well; but common decency certainly does. To fail, at the very least, to make what counts as public apology to all, and to take positive steps to show that it is sincerely meant, is, if not injustice, then anyway a fault at least as serious as ingratitude.

Opting for a policy of preferential hiring may of course mean that some black or woman is preferred to some white male who as a matter of fact has had a harder life than the black or woman. But so may opting for a policy of veterans' preference mean that a healthy, unscarred, middle class veteran is preferred to a poor, struggling, scarred, nonveteran. Indeed, opting for a policy of settling who gets the job by having all equally qualified candidates draw straws may also mean that in a given case the candidate with the hardest life loses out. Opting for any policy other than hard-life preference may have this result.

I have no objection to anyone's arguing that it is precisely hard-life preference that we ought to opt for. If all, or anyway all of the equally qualified, have a right to an equal chance, then the argument would have to draw attention to something sufficiently powerful to override that right. But perhaps this could be done along the lines I followed in the case of blacks and women: perhaps it could be successfully argued that we have wronged those who have had hard lives, and therefore owe it to them to make amends. And then we should have in more extreme form a difficulty already present: how are these preferences to be ranked? shall we place the hard-lifers ahead of blacks? both ahead of women? and what about veterans? I leave these questions aside. My concern has been only to show that the white male applicant's right to an equal chance does not make it unjust to opt for a policy under which blacks and women are given preference. That a white male with a specially hard history may lose out under this policy cannot possibly be any objection to it, in the absence of a showing that hard-life preference is not unjust, and, more important, takes priority over preference for blacks and women.

Lastly, it should be stressed that to opt for such a policy is not to make the young white male applicants themselves make amends for any wrongs done to blacks and women. Under such a policy, no one is asked to give up a job which is already his; the job for which the white male competes isn't his, but is the community's, and it is the hiring officer who gives it to the black or woman in the community's name. Of course the white male is asked to give up his equal chance at the job. But that is not something he pays to the black or woman by way of making amends; it is something the community takes away from him in order that *it* may make amends.

Still, the community does impose a burden on him: it is able to make amends for its wrongs only by taking something away from him, something which, after all, we are supposing he has a right to. And why should *he* pay the cost of the community's amends-making?

If there were some appropriate way in which the community could make amends to its blacks and women, some way which did not require depriving anyone of anything he has a right to, then that would be the best course of action for it to take. Or if there were anyway some way in which the costs could be shared by everyone, and not imposed entirely on the young white male job applicants, then that would be, if not best, then anyway better than opting for a policy of preferential hiring. But in fact the nature of the wrongs done is such as to make jobs the best and most suitable form of compensation. What blacks and women were denied was full membership in the community; and nothing can more appropriately make amends for that wrong than precisely what will make them feel they now finally have it. And that means jobs. Financial compensation (the cost of which could be shared equally) slips through the fingers; having a job, and discovering you do it well, yield—perhaps better than anything else—that very self-respect which blacks and women have had to do without.

But of course choosing this way of making amends means that the costs are imposed on the young white male applicants who are turned away. And so it should be noticed that it is not entirely inappropriate that those applicants should pay the costs. No doubt few, if any, have themselves, individually, done any wrongs to blacks and women. But they have profited from the wrongs the community did. Many may actually have been direct beneficiaries of policies which excluded or down-graded blacks and women—perhaps in school admissions, perhaps in access to financial aid, perhaps elsewhere; and even those who did not directly benefit in this way had, at any rate, the advantage in the competition which comes of confidence in one's full membership, and of one's rights being recognized as a matter of course.

Of course it isn't only the young white male applicant for a university job who has benefited from the exclusion of blacks and women: the older white male, now comfortably tenured, also benefited, and many defenders of preferential hiring feel that he should be asked to share the costs. Well, presumably we can't demand that he give up his job, or share it. But it seems to me in place to expect the occupants of comfortable professorial chairs to contribute in some way, to make some form of return to the young white male who bears the cost, and is turned away. It will have been plain that I find the outcry now heard against preferential hiring in the universities objectionable; it would also be objectionable that those of us who are now securely situated should placidly defend it, with no more than a sigh of regret for the young white male who pays for it.

III

One final word: "discrimination." I am inclined to think we so use it that if anyone is convicted of discriminating against blacks, women, white males, or what have you, then he is thereby convicted of acting unjustly. If so, and if I am right in thinking that preferential hiring in the restricted range of cases we have been looking at is *not* unjust, then we have two options: (a) we can simply reply that to opt for a policy of preferential hiring in those cases is not to opt for a policy of discriminating against white males, or (b) we can hope to get usage changed—e.g., by trying to get people to allow that there is discriminating against and discriminating against, and that some is unjust, but some is not.

Best of all, however would be for that phrase to be avoided altogether. It's at best a blunt tool: there are all sorts of nice moral discriminations [*sic*] which one is unable to make while occupied with it. And that bluntness itself fits it to do harm: blacks and women are hardly likely to see through to what precisely is owed them while they are being accused of welcoming what is unjust.

Notes

1. This essay is an expanded version of a talk given at the Conference on the Liberation of Female Persons, held at North Carolina State University at Raleigh, on March 26-28, 1973, under a grant from the S & H Foundation. I am indebted to James Thomson and the members of the Society for Ethical and Legal Philosophy for criticism of an earlier draft.
2. To the best of my knowledge, the analogy between veterans' preference and the preferential hiring of blacks has been mentioned in print only by Edward T. Chase, in a Letter to the Editor, *Commentary,* February 1973.

PREFERENTIAL HIRING:
A REPLY TO JUDITH JARVIS THOMSON

Robert Simon

Judith Jarvis Thomson has recently defended preferential hiring of women and black persons in universities.[1] She restricts her defense of the assignment of preference to only those cases where candidates from pre-

Robert Simon, "Preferential Hiring: A Reply to Judith Jarvis Thomson," *Philosophy & Public Affairs* 3, no. 3 (Spring 1974). Copyright © 1974 by Princeton University Press. Excerpts reprinted by permission.

ferred groups and their white male competitors are equally qualified, although she suggests that her argument can be extended to cover cases where the qualifications are unequal as well. The argument in question is compensatory; it is because of pervasive patterns of unjust discrimination against black persons and women that justice, or at least common decency, requires that amends be made.

While Thomson's analysis surely clarifies many of the issues at stake, I find it seriously incomplete. I will argue that even if her claim that compensation is due victims of social injustice is correct (as I think it is), it is questionable nevertheless whether preferential hiring is an acceptable method of distributing such compensation. This is so, even if, as Thomson argues, compensatory claims override the right of the white male applicant to equal consideration from the appointing officer. For implementation of preferential hiring policies may involve claims, perhaps even claims of right, other than the above right of the white male applicant. In the case of the claims I have in mind, the best that can be said is that where preferential hiring is concerned, they are arbitrarily ignored. If so, and if such claims are themselves warranted, then preferential hiring, while *perhaps* not unjust, is open to far more serious question than Thomson acknowledges.

A familiar objection to special treatment for blacks and women is that, if such a practice is justified, other victims of injustice or misfortune ought to receive special treatment too. While arguing that virtually all women and black persons have been harmed, either directly or indirectly, by discrimination, Thomson acknowledges that in any particular case, a white male may have been victimized to a greater extent than have the blacks or women with which he is competing. However, she denies that other victims of injustice or misfortune ought automatically to have priority over blacks and women where distribution of compensation is concerned. Just as veterans receive preference with respect to employment in the civil service, as payment for the service they have performed for society, so can blacks and women legitmately be given preference in university hiring, in payment of the debt owed them. And just as the former policy can justify hiring a veteran who in fact had an easy time of it over a nonveteran who made great sacrifices for the public good, so too can the latter policy justify hiring a relatively undeprived member of a preferred group over a more disadvantaged member of a nonpreferred group.

But surely if the reason for giving a particular veteran preference is that he performed a service for his country, that same preference must be given to anyone who performed a similar service. Likewise, if the reason for giving preference to a black person or to a woman is that the recipient has been injured due to an unjust practice, then preference must be given to anyone who has been similarly injured. So, it appears, there can be no relevant *group* to which compensation ought to be made, other than that made up of and only of those who have been injured or victimized.[2] Although, as Thomson claims, all blacks and women may be members of that latter group, they deserve compensation *qua* victim and not *qua* black person or woman.

There are at least two possible replies that can be made to this sort of objection. First, it might be agreed that anyone injured in the same way as blacks or women ought to receive compensation. But then, ''same way'' is characterized so narrowly that it applies to no one except blacks and women. While there is nothing logically objectionable about such a reply, it may nevertheless be morally objectionable. For it implies that a nonblack male who has been terribly injured by a social injustice has less of a claim to compensation than a black or woman who has only been minimally injured. And this implication may be morally unacceptable.

A more plausible line of response may involve shifting our attention from compensation of individuals to collective compensation of groups.[3] Once this shift is made, it can be acknowledged that as individuals, some white males may have stronger compensatory claims than blacks or women. But as compensation is owed the group, it is group claims that must be weighed, not individual ones. And surely, at the group level, the claims of black persons and women to compensation are among the strongest there are.

Suppose we grant that certain groups, including those specified by Thomson, are owed collective compensation. What should be noted is that the conclusion of concern here—that preferential hiring policies are acceptable instruments for compensating groups—does not directly follow. To derive such a conclusion validly, one would have to provide additional premises specifying the relation between collective compensation to groups and distribution of that compensation to individual members. For it does not follow from the fact that some group members are compensated that the group is compensated. Thus, if through a computer error, every member of the American Philosophical Association was asked to pay additional taxes, then if the government provided compensation for this error, it would not follow that it had compensated the Association. Rather it would have compensated each member *qua* individual. So what is required, where preferential hiring is concerned, are plausible premises showing how the preferential award of jobs to group members counts as collective compensation for the group.

Thomson provides no such additional premises. Moreover, there is good reason to think that if any such premises were provided, they would count against preferential hiring as an instrument of collective compensation. This is because although compensation is owed to the group, preferential hiring policies award compensation to an arbitrarily selected segment of the group; namely, those who have the ability and qualifications to be seriously considered for the jobs available. Surely, it is far more plausible to think that collective compensation ought to be equally available to all group members, or at least to all kinds of group members.[4] The claim that although compensation is owed collectively to a group, only a special sort of group member is eligible to receive it, while perhaps not incoherent, certainly ought to be rejected as arbitrary, at least in the absence of an argument to the contrary.

Accordingly, the proponent of preferential hiring faces the following dilemma. Either compensation is to be made on an individual basis, in which case the fact that one is black or a woman is irrelevant to whether one ought to receive special treatment, or it is made on a group basis, in which case it is far from clear that preferential hiring policies are acceptable compensatory instruments. Until this dilemma is resolved, assuming it can be resolved at all, the compensatory argument for preferential hiring is seriously incomplete at a crucial point.

Notes

1. Judith Jarvis Thomson, "Preferential Hiring," *Philosophy & Public Affairs,* 2, no. 4 (Summer 1973), 364–384. All further page references to this article will be made within the text.
2. This point also has been argued for recently by J. L. Cowen, "Inverse Discrimination," *Analysis,* 33, no. I (1972), 10–12.
3. Such a position has been defended by Paul Taylor, in his "Reverse Discrimination and Compensatory Justice," *Analysis,* 33, no. 4 (1973), 177–182.
4. Taylor would apparently agree, *ibid,* 180.

THE JUSTIFICATION OF
REVERSE DISCRIMINATION IN HIRING

Tom L. Beauchamp

In recent years government policies intended to ensure fairer employment and educational opportunities for women and minority groups have engendered alarm. Although I shall in this paper argue in support of enlightened versions of these policies, I nonetheless think there is much to be said for the opposition arguments. In general I would argue that the world of business is now overregulated by the federal government, and I therefore hesitate to support an extension of the regulative arm of government into the arena of hiring and firing. Moreover, policies that would eventuate in reverse discrimination in present North American society have a heavy presumption against them, for both justice-regarding and utilitarian reasons: The introduction of such preferential treatment on a large scale could well produce a series of injustices, economic advantages to some who do not deserve them, protracted court battles, jockeying for favored position by other minorities, congressional lobbying by power groups, a lowering of admission and work standards in vital institutions, reduced social and economic efficiency, increased racial hostility, and continued suspicion that well-placed women and minority group members

Adapted from "The Justification of Reverse Discrimination" by Tom L. Beauchamp, in *Social Justice and Preferential Treatment,* ed. Blackstone and Heslep. Copyright © 1977 by University of Georgia Press, Athens. Reprinted by permission of the publisher.

received their positions purely on the basis of quotas. Conjointly these reasons constitute a powerful case against the enactment of policies productive of reverse discrimination in hiring.

I find these reasons against allowing reverse discrimination to occur both thoughtful and tempting, and I want to concede from the outset that policies of reverse discrimination can create serious and perhaps even tragic injustices. One must be careful, however, not to draw an overzealous conclusion from this admission. Those who argue that reverse discrimination creates injustices often say that, because of the injustice, such policies are *unjust*. I think by this use of "unjust" they generally mean "not justified" (rather than "not sanctioned by justice"). But a policy can create and even perpetuate injustices, as violations of the principle of formal equality, and yet be justified by other reasons. It would be an injustice in this sense to fire either one of two assistant professors with exactly similar professional credentials, while retaining the other of the two; yet the financial condition of the university or compensation owed the person retained might provide compelling reasons which justify the action. The first reason supporting the dismissal is utilitarian in character, and the other derives from the principle of compensatory justice. This shows both that there can be conflicts between different justice-regarding reasons and also that violations of the principle of formal equality are not in themselves sufficient to render an action unjustifiable.

A proper conclusion, then—and one which I accept—is that all discrimination, including reverse discrimination, is prima facie immoral, because a basic principle of justice creates a prima facie duty to abstain from such treatment of persons. But no absolute duty is created come what may, for we might have conflicting duties of sufficient weight to justify such injustices. The latter is the larger thesis I wish to defend: Considerations of compensatory justice and utility are conjointly of sufficient weight in contemporary society to neutralize and overcome the quite proper presumption of immorality in the case of some policies productive of reverse discrimination.

I

It is difficult to avoid accepting two important claims: (a) that the law ought never to sanction any discriminatory practices (whether plain old unadorned discrimination or reverse discrimination), and (b) that such practices can be eradicated by bringing the full weight of the law down on those who engage in discriminatory practices. The first claim is a moral one, the second a factual one. I contend in this section that it is unrealistic to believe, as *b* suggests, that in contemporary society discriminatory practices *can* be eradicated by legal measures which do not permit reverse discrimination. And because they cannot be eradicated, I think we ought to relax our otherwise unimpeachably sound reservations (as recorded in *a* and discussed in the first section) against allowing any discriminatory practices whatever.

My argument is motivated by the belief that racial, sexual, and no doubt other forms of discrimination are not antique relics but are living patterns which continue to warp selection and ranking procedures. In my view the difference between the present and the past is that discriminatory treatment is today less widespread and considerably less blatant. But its reduction has produced apathy; its subtleness has made it less visible and considerably more difficult to detect. Largely because of the reduced visibility of racisim and sexism, I suggest, reverse discrimination now strikes us as all too harsh and unfair. After all, quotas and preferential treatment have no appeal if one assumes a just, primarily non-discriminatory society. Since the presence or absence of seriously discriminatory conditions in our society is a factual matter, empirical evidence must be adduced to show that the set of discriminatory attitudes and selection procedures I have alleged to exist do in fact exist. The data I shall mention derive primarily from historical, linguistic, sociological, and legal sources.

Statistical Evidence

Statistical imbalances in employment and admission are often discounted because so many variables can be hypothesized to explain why, for non-discriminatory reasons, an imbalance exists. We can all think of plausible non-discriminatory reasons why 22% of Harvard's graduate students in 1969 were women but its tenured Arts and Sciences Faculty in the Graduate School consisted of 411 males and 0 females.[1] But sometimes we are able to discover evidence which supports the claim that skewed statistics are the result of discrimination. Quantities of such discriminatory findings, in turn, raise serious questions about the real reasons for suspicious statistics in those cases where we have *not* been able to determine these reasons—perhaps because they are so subtle and unnoticed. I shall discuss each factor in turn: (a) statistics which constitute prima facie but indecisive evidence of discrimination; (b) findings concerning discriminatory reasons for some of these statistics; and (c) cases where the discrimination is probably undetectable because of its subtleness, and yet the statistical evidence is overwhelming.

a. A massive body of statistics constituting prima facie evidence of discrimination has been assembled in recent years. Here is a tiny but diverse fragment of some of these statisical findings.[2] (1) Women college teachers with identical credentials in terms of publications and experience are promoted at almost exactly one-half the rate of their male counterparts. (2) In the United States women graduates of medical schools in 1965 stood at 7%, as compared with 36% in Germany. The gap in the number of women physicians was similar. (3) Of 3,000 leading law firms surveyed in 1957 only 32 reported a woman partner, and even these women were paid much less (increasingly so for every year of employment) than their male counterparts. (4) 40% of the white-collar positions in the United States are presently held by women, but only 10% of the management positions are held by women, and their pay again is significantly less (70% of clerical workers are women). (5) 8,000 workers were employed in May 1967 in the construction of BART (Bay Area Rapid Transit), but not a single electrician, ironworker, or plumber was black. (6) In the population as a whole in the United States, 3 out of 7 employees hold white-collar positions, but only 1 of 7 blacks holds such a position, and these latter jobs are clustered in professions which have the fewest jobs to offer in top-paying positions. (7) In the well-known A. T. & T. case, this massive conglomerate signed a settlement giving tens of millions of dollars to women and minority employees. A. T. & T. capitulated to this settlement based on impressive statistics indicating discriminatory treatment.

b. I concede that such statistics are far from decisive indicators of discrimination. But when further evidence concerning the reasons for the statistics is uncovered, they are put in a perspective affording them greater power—clinching power in my view. Consider (3)—the statistics on the lack of women lawyers. A survey of Harvard Law School alumnae in 1970 provided evidence about male lawyers' attitudes.[3] It showed that business and legal firms do not generally expect the women they hire to become lawyers, that they believe women cannot become good litigators, and that they believe only limited numbers of women should be hired since clients generally prefer male lawyers. Surveys of women applicants for legal positions indicate they are frequently either told that a woman will not be hired, or are warned that "senior partners" will likely object, or are told that women will be hired to do only probate, trust, and estate work. (Other statistics confirm that these are the sorts of tasks dominantly given to women.) Consider also (5)—a particular but typical case of hiring in non-white-collar positions. Innumerable studies have shown that most of these positions are filled by word-of-mouth recruitment policies conducted by all-white interviewers (usually all-male as well). In a number of decisions of the Equal Employment Opportunity Commission, it has been shown that the interviewers have racially biased attitudes and that the applications of blacks and women are systematically handled in unusual ways, such as never even being filed. So serious and consistent have such violations been that the EEOC has publicly stated its belief that word-of-mouth recruitment policies without demonstrable supplementary and simultaneous recruitment in minority group communities is in itself a "prima facie violation of Title VII."[4] Gertrude Ezorsky has argued, convincingly I believe, that this pattern of "special ties" is no less present in professional white collar hiring, which is neither less discriminatory nor more sensitive to hiring strictly on the basis of merit.[5]

c. Consider, finally, (1)—statistics pertaining to the treatment of women college teachers. The Carnegie Commission and others have assembled statistical evidence to show that in even the most favorable construal of relevant variables, women teachers have been discriminated against in hiring, tenuring, and ranking. But instead of summarizing this mountain of material, I wish here to take a particular case in order to illustrate the difficulty in determining, on the basis of statistics and similar empirical data, whether discrimination is occurring even where courts have been forced to find satisfactory evidence of discrimination. In December 1974 a decision was reached by the Commission against Discrimination of the Executive Department of the State of Massachusetts regarding a case at Smith College where the two complainants were women who were denied tenure and dismissed by the English Department.[6] The women claimed sex discrimination and based their case on the following: (1) Women at the full professor level in the college declined from 54% in 1958 to 21% in 1972, and in the English department from 57% in 1960 to 11% in 1972. These statistics compare unfavorably at all levels with Mt. Holyoke's, a comparable institution (since both have an all female student body and are located in Western Massachusetts). (2) Thirteen of the department's fifteen associate and full professorships at Smith belonged to men. (3) The two tenured women had obtained tenure under "distinctly peculiar experiences," including a stipulation that one be only part-time and that the other not be promoted when given tenure. (4) The department's faculty members conceded that tenure standards were applied subjectively, were vague, and lacked the kind of precision which would avoid discriminatory application. (5) The women denied tenure were at no time given advance warning that their work was deficient. Rather, they were given favorable evaluations of their teaching and were encouraged to believe they would receive tenure. (6) Some stated reasons for the dismissals were later demonstrated to be rationalizations, and one letter from a senior member to the tenure and promotion committee contradicted his own appraisal of teaching ability filed with the department. (7) The court accepted expert testimony that any deficiencies in the women candidates were also found in male candidates promoted and given tenure during this same period, and that the women's positive credentials were at least as good as the men's.

The commissioner's opinion found that "the Complainants properly used statistics to demonstrate that the Respondents' practices operate with a discriminatory effect." Citing *Parham* v. *Southwestern Bell Telephone Co.,*[7] the commissioner argued that "in such cases extreme statistics may establish discrimination as a matter of law, without additional supportive evidence." But in this case the commissioner found abundant additional evidence in the form of "the historical absence of women," "word-of-mouth recruitment policies" which operate discriminatorily, and a number of "subtle and not so subtle, societal patterns" existing at Smith.[8] On December 30, 1974 the commissioner ordered the two women reinstated with tenure and ordered the department to submit an affirmative action program within 60 days.

This case is interesting because there is little in the way of clinching proof that the members of the English Department actually held discriminatory attitudes. Yet so consistent a pattern of *apparently* discriminatory treatment must be regarded, according to this decision, as *de facto* discrimination. The commissioner's ruling and other laws are quite explicit that "intent or lack thereof is of no consequence." If a procedure constitutes discriminatory treatment, then the parties discriminated against must be recompensed. Here we have a case where irresistible statistics and other sociological evidence of "social exclusion" and "subtle societal patterns" provide convincing evidence that strong, court backed measures must be taken because nothing short of such measures is suffi-ciently strong to overcome the discriminatory pattern, as the Respondents' testimony in the case verifies.[9]

Some understanding of the attitudes underlying the statistical evidence thus far surveyed can be gained by consideration of some linguistic evidence now to be mentioned. It further supports the charge of widespread discrimination in the case of women and of the difficulty in changing discriminatory attitudes.

Linguistic Evidence

Robert Baker has assembled some impressive linguistic evidence which in-dicates that our language is male-slanted, perhaps male chauvinistic, and that language about women relates something of fundamental importance concerning the males' most fundamental conceptions of women.[10] Baker argues that as the term "boy" once expressed a paternalistic and dominating attitude toward blacks (and was replaced in our conceptual structure because of this denigrating association), so are there other English terms which serve similar functions in regard to women (but are not replaced because not considered by men as in need of replacement). Baker assembles evidence both from the language itself and from surveys of users of the language to show the following.

The term "woman" is broadly substitutable for and frequently inter-changed in English sentences such as "Who is that ____ over there?" by terms such as those in the following divisions:

A. Neutral Categories	B. Animal Categories	C. Plaything Categories	D. Gender Categories	E. Sexual Categories
lady	chick	babe	skirt	snatch
gal	bird	doll	hem	cunt
girl	fox	cuddly		ass
broad	vixen	thing		twat
(sister)	filly			piece
	bitch			lay
				pussy

Baker notes that (1) while there are differences in frequency of usage, all of these terms are standard enough to be recognizable at least by most male users of the language; (2) women do not typically identify themselves in sexual categories; and (3) typically only males use the nonneutral categories (B–E). He takes this to be evidence—and I agree—that the male conception of women differs significantly from the female conception and that the categories used by the male in classifying women are "prima facie denigrating." He then argues that it is clearly and not merely prima facie denigrating when categories such as C and E are used, as they are either derived from playboy male images or are outright vulgarities. Baker argues that it is most likely that B and D are similarly used in denigrating ways. His arguments center on the metaphorical associations of these terms, but the evidence cannot be further pursued here.

Although Baker does not remark that women do not have a similar language for men, it seems to me important to notice this fact. Generally, any negative categories used by women to refer to men are as frequently or more frequently used by men to apply to women. This asymmetrical relation does not hold, of course, for the language used by whites and blacks for denigrating reference. This fact perhaps says something about how blacks have caught onto the impact of the language as a tool of denigrating identification in a way women have yet to do, at least in equal numbers. It may also say something about the image of submissiveness which many women still bear about themselves—an image blacks are no longer willing to accept.

Baker concludes from his linguistic studies that "sexual discrimination permeates our conceptual structure. Such discrimination is clearly inimical to any movement toward sexual egalitarianism and virtually defeats its purpose at the outset."[11] His conclusion may somewhat overreach his premises, but when combined with the corroborating statistical evidence previously adduced, it seems apt. Linguistic dispositions lead us to categorize persons and events in discriminatory ways which are sometimes glaringly obvious to the categorized but accepted as "objective" by the categorizer. My contention, derived from Baker's and to be supported as we proceed, is that cautious, good faith movements toward egalitarianism such as affirmative action guidelines *cannot* succeed short of fundamental conceptual and ethical revisions. And since the probability of such revisions approximates zero (because discriminatory attitudes are covertly embedded in language and cultural habit), radical expedients are required to bring about the desired egalitarian results, expedients which may result in reverse discrimination.

Conclusions

Irving Thalberg has argued, correctly I believe, that the gravest contemporary problems with racism stem from its "protectively camouflaged" status, which he calls "visceral." Thalberg skillfully points to a number of attitudes held by those whites normally classified as unprejudiced which indicate that racism still colors their conception of social facts.[12] My alliance with such a position ought to be obvious by now. But my overall intentions and conclusions are somewhat different. I hold that because of the peculiarly concealed nature of the protective camouflage under which sexism and racism have so long thrived, it is not a reasonable expectation that the lightweight programs now administered under the heading of affirmative action will succeed in overcoming discriminatory treatment. I turn now directly to this topic.

II

The rawest nerve of the social and political controversy concerning reverse discrimination is exposed by the following question: What government policies are permissible and required in order to bring about a society where equal treatment of persons is the rule rather than the exception?

Fair-minded opponents of any government policy which might produce reverse discrimination—Carl Cohen and William Blackstone, for example—seem to me to oppose them largely because and perhaps only because of their *factual belief* that present government policies not causing reverse discrimination will, if seriously and sincerely pursued, prove sufficient to achieve the goal of equal consideration of persons.

Once again a significant factual disagreement has emerged: what means are not only fair but also sufficient? I must again support my contentions by adducing factual data to show that my pessimism is sustained by the weight of the evidence. The evidence cited here comes from government data concerning affirmative action programs. I shall discuss the affirmative action program in order to show that on the basis of present government guidelines (which, to my knowledge, are the best either in law or proposed as law by those who oppose reverse discrimination), discriminatory business as usual will surely prevail.

Affirmative Action

I begin with a sample of the affirmative action guidelines, as understood by those who administer them. I use the example of HHS guidelines for educational institutions receiving federal financial aid. These guidelines are not radically different from those directed at hiring practices throughout the world of business. Specifically, these guidelines cover three areas: admission, treatment of students, and employment. A sample of the sorts of requirements universities are under includes: (1) They may not advertise vacant positions as open only to or preferentially to a particular race or sex, except where sex is a legitimate occupational requirement. (2) The university sets standards and criteria for employment, but if these effectively work to exclude women or minorities as a class, the university must justify the job requirements. (3) An institution may not set different standards of admission for one sex, race, etc. (4) There must be active recruitment where there is an underrepresentation of women and minorities, as gauged by the availability of qualified members of these classes. However, the relevant government officials have from time to time made it clear that (1) quotas are unacceptable, either for admission or employment, though target goals and timetables intended to correct deficiencies are acceptable and to be encouraged. (2) A university is never under any obligation to dilute legitimate standards, and hence there is no conflict with merit hiring. (3) Reserving positions for members of a minority group (and presumably for the female sex) is "an outrageous and illegal form of reverse bias" (as one former director of the program wrote).[13] By affirmative action requirements I mean this latter interpretation and nothing stronger (though I have given only a sample set of qualifications, of course).

The question I am currently asking is whether these guidelines, assuming they will be vigorously pursued, can reasonably be expected to bring about their goal, which is the social circumstance of non-discriminatory treatment of persons. If they *are* strong enough, then Cohen, Blackstone, and others are right: Reverse discrimination is not under such cirsumstances justified. Unfortunately the statistical and linguistic evidence previously adduced indicates otherwise. The *Smith College* case is paradigmatic of the concealed yet serious discrimination which occurs through the network of subtle distortions, old-boy procedures, and prejudices we have accumulated. Only when the statistics become egregiously out of proportion is action taken or a finding of mistreatment possible. And that is one reason why it seems unlikely that substantial progress can be made, in any realistic sense of "can," by current government measures not productive of reverse discrimination. According to Peter Holmes, once the Director of the Office for Civil Rights and in charge of interpreting affirmative action guidelines: "It has been our policiy that it is the institutions' responsiblity to determine non-discriminatory qualifications in the first instance, and that such qualifications, in conjunction with other affirmative action steps, should yield results."[14] This is the received HHS view, but the last sentence contains an ambiguous use of the word "should." If the "should" in this statement is a moral "should," none will disagree. But if it is an empirical, predictive "should," as I take Mr. Holmes to intend, we are back to the core of the difficulty. I now turn to a consideration of how deficient such affirmative action steps have proven to be.

Government Data

The January 1975 Report of the United States Commission on Civil Rights contains a section on "compliance reviews" of various universities. These are government assessments of university compliance with Executive Orders pertaining to affirmative action plans. The report contains a stern indictment of the Higher Education Division (HED)—the division then in charge of overseeing all HHS civil rights enforcement activities in the area of higher education. It concludes that "HED has, in large part, failed to follow the procedures required of compliance agencies under the Executive order regulations."[15] But more interesting than this mere failure to enforce the law is the report's discussion of how very difficult it is to obtain compliance even when there is a routine attempt to enforce the law. The Commission reviewed four major campuses in the United States (Harvard, University of Michigan, University of Washington, Berkeley). They concluded that there is a pattern of inadequate compliance reviews, inordinate delays, and inexcusable failures to take enforcement action where there were clear violations of the Executive order regulations.[16]

Consider the example of the "case history of compliance contacts" at the University of California at Berkeley. According to HED's own staff a "conciliation agreement" with this university "is now being used as a model for compliance activities with other campuses." When the office for Civil Rights of HHS determined to investigate Berkeley (April 1971), after several complaints, including a class action sex discrimination complaint, the university refused to permit access to its personnel files and refused to permit the interviewing of faculty members without an administrator present. Both refusals are, as the report points out, "direct violations of the Executive order's equal opportunity clause," under which Berkeley held contracts. Despite this clear violation of the law, no enforcement action was taken. A year and one-half later, after negotiations and more complaints, the university was instructed to develop a written affirmative action plan to correct "documented deficiencies" of "pervasive discrimination." The plan was to include target goals and timetables wherever job underutilization had been identified.[17]

In January 1973 the university, in a letter from Chancellor Albert H. Bowker, submitted a draft affirmative action plan which was judged "totally unacceptable." Throughout 1973 Berkeley received "extensive technical assistance" from the government to aid it in developing a better plan. No such plan emerged, and OCR at the end of the year began to question "the university's commitment to comply with the executive order." The university submitted other unacceptable plans, and finally in March 1974 "a conciliation agreement was reached." However, "the document suffered from such extreme vagueness that, as of August 1974, the university and OCR were in substantial disagreement on the meaning of a number of its provisions," and "the agreement specifically violated OFCC regulations in a number of ways." These violations are extensive and serious, and the report characterizes one part as "outrageous." Four years after this "model" compliance case began, it was unresolved and no enforcement proceedings had been taken against the university. The report concludes: "In its Title VI reviews of colleges and universities, HEW routinely finds noncompliance, but it almost never imposes sanctions; instead HEW responds by making vague recommendations. Moreover, HEW does not routinely require the submission of progress reports or conduct sufficient followup to determine if its recommendations have been followed." [HHS was then HEW.]

III

No one could be happy about the conclusions I have reached or about the depressing and disturbing facts on which they are based. But I do take it to be a *factual* and not an *evaluative* conclusion both (1) that the camouflaged attitudes I have discussed exist and affect the social position of minority groups and women and (2) that they will in all likelihood continue to have this influence. It is, of course, an evaluative conclusion that we are morally permitted and even required to remedy this situation by the imposition of quotas, target goals, and timetables. But anyone who accepts my *interpretation* of the facts bears a heavy burden of moral argument to show that we ought not to use such means to that end upon which I take it we all agree, viz., the equal consideration of persons irrespective of race, sex, religion, or nationality.

By way of conclusion, it is important to set my arguments in the framework of a distinction between real reverse discrimination and merely apparent reverse discrimination. My evidence demonstrates present, ongoing barriers to the removal of discriminatory practices. My contentions set the stage for showing that *because* of the existence of what Thalberg calls "visceral racism," and because of visceral sexism as well, there will be many occasions on which we can only avoid inevitable discrimination by policies productive of reverse discrimination. Sometimes, however, persons will be hired or admitted—on a quota basis, for example—who appear to be displacing better applicants, but the appearance is the result of visceral discriminatory perceptions of the person's qualifications. In this case there will certainly appear to the visceral racist or sexist to be reverse discrimination, and this impression will be reinforced by knowledge that quotas were used; yet the allegation of reverse discrimination will be a mistaken one. On other occasions there will be genuine reverse discrimination, and on many occasions it will be impossible to determine whether or not this consequence is occurring. The evidence I have adduced is, of course, intended to support the contention that real and not merely apparent reverse discrimination is justified. But it is justified only as a means to the end of ensuring genuinely nondiscriminatory treatment of all persons.

Notes

1. From "Statement of Dr. Bernice Sandler," *Discrimination Against Women: Congressional Hearings on Equal Rights in Education and Employment,* ed. Catharine R. Stimpson (New York: R. R. Bowker Company, 1973), pp. 61, 415. Hereafter *Discrimination Against Women.*
2. All of the statistics and quotations cited are taken from the compilations of data in the following sources: (1) Kenneth M. Davidson, Ruth B. Ginsburg, and Herma H. Kay, eds., *Sex-Based Discrimination: Text, Cases, and Materials* (Minneapolis: West Publishing Company, 1974), esp. Ch. 3. Hereafter *Sex-Based Discrimination.* (2) *Discrimination Against Women,* esp. pp. 397–441 and 449–502. (3) Alfred W. Blumrosen, *Black Employment and the Law* (New Brunswick, N.J.: Rutgers University Press, 1971), esp. pp. 107, 122f. (4) *The Federal Civil Rights Enforcement Effort—1971,* A Report of the United States Commission on Civil Rights.
3. *Discrimination Against Women,* pp. 505f.
4. *Sex-Based Discrimination,* p. 516.
5. "The Fight Over University Women," *The New York Review of Books,* May 16, 1974, pp. 32–39.
6. *Maurianne Adams and Mary Schroeder* v. *Smith College,* Massachusetts Commission Against Discrimination, Nos. 72-S-53, 72-S-54 (December 30, 1974). Hereafter *The Smith College Case.*
7. 433 F.2d 421, 426 (8 Cir. 1970).
8. *The Smith College Case,* pp. 23, 26.
9. *Ibid.,* pp. 26f.
10. Robert Baker, "'Pricks' and 'Chicks': A Plea for Persons," in Richard Wasserstrom, ed., *Today's Moral Problems* (New York: Macmillan Publishing Company, 1975), pp. 152–170.
11. *Ibid.,* p. 170.
12. "Visceral Racism," *The Monist,* 56 (1972), 43–63, and reprinted in Wasserstrom.
13. J. Stanley Pottinger, "Race, Sex, and Jobs: The Drive Towards Equality," *Change Magazine,* 4 (Oct. 1972), 24–29.
14. Peter E. Holmes, "HEW Guidelines and 'Affirmative Action,'" *The Washington Post,* Feb. 15, 1975.

15. *The Federal Civil Rights Enforcement Effort*—1974, 3: 276.
16. *Ibid.,* p. 281.
17. *Ibid.,* all subsequent references are from pp. 281–286.

REVERSE DISCRIMINATION AND COMPENSATORY JUSTICE

William T. Blackstone

Is reverse discrimination justified as a policy of compensation or of preferential treatment for women and racial minorities? That is, given the fact that women and racial minorities have been invidiously discriminated against in the past on the basis of the irrelevant characteristics of race and sex—are we now justified in discriminating in their favor on the basis of the same characteristics? This is a central ethical and legal question today, and it is one which is quite unresolved. Philosophers, jurists, legal scholars, and the man-in-the-street line up on both sides of this issue. These differences are plainly reflected (in the Supreme Court's majority opinion and Justice Douglas's dissent) in *DeFunis* v. *Odegaard.* [1] . . .

I will argue that reverse discrimination is improper on both moral and constitutional grounds, though I focus more on moral grounds. However, I do this with considerable ambivalence, even "existential guilt." Several reasons lie behind that ambivalence. First, there are moral and constitutional arguments on both sides. The ethical waters are very muddy and I simply argue that the balance of the arguments are against a policy of reverse discrimination. [2] My ambivalence is further due not only to the fact that traditional racism is still a much larger problem than that of reverse discrimination but also because I am sympathetic to the *goals* of those who strongly believe that reverse discrimination as a policy is the means to overcome the debilitating effects of past injustice. Compensation and remedy are most definitely required both by the facts and by our value commitments. But I do not think that reverse discrimination is the proper means of remedy or compensation. . . .

I

Let us turn to the possibility of a utilitarian justification of reverse discrimination and to the possible conflict of justice-regarding reasons and those of social utility on this issue. The category of morally relevant reasons is broader, in my opinion, than reasons related to the norm of justice. It is broader than those related to the norm of utility. Also it seems to me that the norms of justice and utility are not reducible one to the other. We cannot argue these points of ethical theory here. But, if these assumptions are correct, then it is at least possible to morally justify injustice or invidious discrimination in some contexts. A case would have to be made that such injustice, though regrettable, will produce the best consequences for society and that this fact is an overriding or weightier moral reason than the temporary injustice. Some arguments for reverse discrimination have taken this line. Professor Thomas Nagel argues that such discrimination is justifiable as long as it is "clearly contributing to the eradication of great social evils."[3] . . .

Another example of what I would call a utilitarian argument for reverse discrimination was recently set forth by Congressman Andrew Young of Georgia. Speaking specifically of reverse discrimination in the context of education, he stated: "While that may give minorities a little edge in some instances, and you may run into the danger of what we now commonly call reverse discrimination, I think the educational system needs this. Society needs this as much as the people we are trying to help . . . a society working toward affirmative action and inclusiveness is going to be a stronger and more relevant society than one that accepts the limited concepts of objectivity. . . . I would admit that it is perhaps an individual injustice. But it might be necessary in order to overcome an historic group injustice or series of group injustices."[4] Congressman Young's basic justifying grounds for reverse discrimination, which he recognizes as individual injustice, are the results which he thinks it will produce: a stronger and more relevant education system and society, and one which is more just overall. His argument may involve pitting some justice-regarding reasons (the right of women and racial minorities to be compensated for past injustices) against others (the right of the majority to the uniform application of the same standards of merit to all). But a major thrust of his argument also seems to be utilitarian.

Just as there are justice-regarding arguments on both sides of the issue of reverse discrimination, so also there are utilitarian arguments on both sides. In a nutshell, the utilitarian argument in favor runs like this: Our society contains large groups of persons who suffer from past institutionalized injustice. As a result, the possibilities of social discord and disorder are high indeed. If short-term reverse discrimination were to be effective in overcoming the effects of past institutionalized injustice and if this policy could alleviate the causes of disorder and bring a higher quality of life to millions of persons, then society as a whole would benefit.

There are moments in which I am nearly convinced by this argument, but the conclusion that such a policy would have negative utility on the whole wins out. For although reverse discrimination might appear to have the effect of getting more persons who have been disadvantaged by past inequities into the mainstream quicker, that is, into jobs, schools, and practices from which they have been excluded, the cost would be invidious discrimination against majority group members of society. I do not think that majority members of society would find this acceptable, i.e., the disadvantaging of themselves for past inequities which they did not control and for which they are not responsible. If such policies were put into effect by government, I would predict wholesale rejection or noncooperation, the result of which would be negative not only for those who have suffered past inequities but also for the justice-regarding institutions of society. Claims and counter-claims would obviously be raised by other ethnic or racial minorities—by Chinese, Chicanos, American Indians, Puerto Ricans—and by orphans, illegitimate children, ghetto residents, and so on. Literally thousands of types or groups could, on similar grounds as blacks or women, claim that reverse discrimination is justified on their behalf. What would happen if government attempted policies of reverse discrimination for all such groups? It would mean the arbitrary exclusion or discrimination against all others relative to a given purpose and given group. Such a policy would itself create an injustice for which those newly excluded persons could then, themselves, properly claim the need for reverse discrimination to offset the injustice to them. The circle is plainly a vicious one. Such policies are simply self-destructive. In place of the ideal of equality and distributive justice based on relevant criteria, we would be left with the special pleading of self-interested power groups, groups who gear criteria for the distribution of goods, services, and opportunities to their special needs and situations, primarily. Such policies would be those of special privilege, not the appeal to objective criteria which apply to all.[5] They would lead to social chaos, not social justice.

Furthermore, in cases in which reverse discrimination results in a lowering of quality, the consequences for society, indeed for minority victims of injustice for which reverse discrimination is designed to help, may be quite bad. It is no easy matter to calculate this, but the recent report sponsored by the Carnegie Commission on Higher Education points to such deleterious consequences.[6] If the quality of instruction in higher education, for example, is lowered through a policy of primary attention to race or sex as opposed to ability and training, everyone—including victims of past injustice—suffers. Even if such policies are clearly seen as temporary with quite definite deadlines for termination, I am sceptical about their utilitarian value. . . .

II

The inappropriateness of reverse discrimination, both on utilitarian and justice-regarding grounds, in no way means that compensation for past injustices is inappropriate. It does not mean that those who have suffered past injustices and who have been disadvantaged by them are not entitled to compensation or that they have no moral right to remedy. It may be difficult in different contexts to translate that moral right to remedy into practice or into legislation. When has a disadvantaged person or group been compensated enough? What sort of allocation of resources will compensate without creating additional inequities or deleterious consequences? There is no easy answer to these questions. Decisions must be made in particular contexts. Furthermore, it may be the case that the effects of past injustices are so severe (poverty, malnutrition, and the denial of educational opportunities) that genuine compensation—the balancing of the scales—is impossible. The effects of malnutrition or the lack of education are often non-reversible (and would be so even under a policy of reverse discrimination). This is one of the tragedies of injustice. But if reverse discrimination is inappropriate as a means of compensation and if (as I have argued) it is unjust to make persons who are not responsible for the suffering and disadvantaging of others to suffer for those past injuries, then other means must be employed unless overriding moral considerations of another type (utilitarian) can be clearly demonstrated. That compensation must take a form which is consistent with our constitutional principles and with reasonable principles of justice. Now it seems to me that the Federal Government's Equal Opportunity and Affirmative Action Programs are consistent with these principles, that they are not only not committed to reverse discrimination but rather absolutely forbid it.[7] However, it also seems to me that some officials authorized or required to implement these compensatory efforts have resorted to reverse discrimination and hence have violated the basic principles of justice embodied in these programs. I now want to argue both of these points: first, that these federal programs reject reverse discrimination in their basic principles; secondly, that some implementers of these programs have violated their own principles.

Obviously our country has not always been committed constitutionally to equality. We need no review of our social and political heritage to document this. But with the Fourteenth Amendment, equality as a principle was given constitutional status. Subsequently, social, political, and legal practices changed radically and they will continue to do so. The Fourteenth Amendment declares that states are forbidden to deny any person life, liberty, or property without due process of law or to deny to any person the equal protection of the laws. In my opinion the principles of the Equal Opportunity and Affirmative Action Programs reflect faithfully this constitutional commitment. I am more familiar with those programs as reflected in universities. In this context they require that employers "recruit, hire, train, and promote persons in all job classifications without regard to race, color, religion, sex or national origin, except where sex is a bona fide occupational qualification."[8] They state explictly that "goals may not be rigid and inflexible quotas which must be met, but must be targets reasonably attainable by means of good faith effort."[9] They require the active recruitment of women and racial minorities where they are "underutilized," this being defined as a context in which there are "fewer minorities or women in a particular job classification than would reasonably be expected by their availability."[10] This is sometimes difficult to determine; but some relevant facts do exist and hence the meaning of a "good faith" effort is not entirely fluid. In any event the Affirmative Action Program in universities requires that "goals, timetables and affirmative action commitment, must be designed to correct any identifiable deficiencies," with separate goals and timetables for minorities and women.[11] It recognizes that there has been blatant discrimination against women and racial minorities in universities and elsewhere, and it assumes that there are "identifiable deficiencies." But it does not require that blacks be employed because they are black or women employed because they are women; that is, it does not require reverse discrimination with rigid quotas to correct the past. It requires a good faith effort in the present based on data on the availability of qualified women and racial minorities in various disciplines and other relevant facts. (Similar requirements hold, of course, for non-academic employment at colleges and universities.) It does not mandate the hiring of the unqalified or a lowering of standards; it mandates only equality of opportunity for all which, given the history of discrimination against women and racial minorities, requires affirmative action in recruitment.

Now if this affirmative action in recruitment, which is not only consistent with but required by our commitment to equality and social justice, is translated into rigid quotas and reverse discrimination by those who implement equal opportunity and affirmative action programs in the effort to get results immediately—and there is no doubt in my mind that this has occurred—then such action violates the principles of those programs.

This violation—this inconsistency of principle and practice—occurs, it seems to me, when employers hire with *priority emphasis* on race, sex, or minority-group status. This move effectively eliminates others from the competition. It is like pretending that everyone is in the game from the beginning while all the while certain persons are systematically excluded. This is exactly what happened recently when a judge declared that a certain quota or number of women were to be employed by a given agency regardless of their qualifications for the job,[12] when some public school officials fired a white coach in order to hire a black one,[13] when a DeFunis is excluded from law school on racial grounds, and when colleges or universities announce that normal academic openings will give preference to female candidates or those from racial minorities.

If reverse discrimination is prohibited by our constitutional and ethical commitments, what means of remedy and compensation are available? Obviously, those means which are consistent with those commitments. Our commitments assure the right to remedy to those who have been treated unjustly, but our government has not done enough to bring this right to meaningful fruition in practice. Sound progress has been made in recent years, especially since the Equal Employment Opportunity Act of 1972 and the establishment of the Equal Employment Opportunities Commission. This Act and other laws have extended anti-discrimination protection to over 60% of the population.[14] The Commission is now authorized to enforce anti-discrimination orders in court and, according to one report, it has negotiated out-of-court settlements which brought 44,000 minority workers over 46 million dollars in back-pay.[15] Undoubtedly this merely scratches the surface. But now the framework exists for translating the right to remedy into practice, not just for sloughing off race and sex as irrelevant criteria of differential treatment but other irrelevant criteria as well—age, religion, the size of hips (I am thinking of airline stewardesses), the length of nose, and so on.

Adequate remedy to overcome the sins of the past, not to speak of the present, would require the expenditure of vast sums for compensatory programs for those disadvantaged by past injustice in order to assure equal access. Such programs should be racially and sexually neutral, benefiting the disadvantaged of *whatever sex or race.* Such neutral compensatory programs would have a high proportion of blacks and other minorities as recipients, for they as members of these groups suffer more from the injustices of the past. But the basis of the compensation would be that fact, not sex or race. Neutral compensatory policies have definite theoretical and practical advantages in contrast to policies of reverse discrimination: Theoretical advantages, in that they are consistent with our basic constitutional and ethical commitments whereas reverse discrimination is not; practical advantages, in that their consistency, indeed their requirement by our constitutional and ethical commitments, means that they can marshall united support in overcoming inequalities whereas reverse discrimination, in my opinion, can not.

Notes

1. 94 S.Ct. 1704 (1974).
2. I hasten to add a qualification—more ambivalence!—resulting from discussion with Tom Beauchamp of Georgetown University. In cases of extreme recalcitrance to equal employment by certain institutions or businesses some quota requirement (reverse discrimination) may be justified. I regard this as distinct from a general policy of reverse discrimination.
3. "Equal Treatment and Compensatory Discrimination," *Philosophy and Public Affairs,* 2 (Summer 1974).
4. *The Atlanta Journal and Constitution,* Sept. 22, 1974, p. 20-A.
5. For similar arguments see Lisa Newton, "Reverse Discrimination as Unjustified," *Ethics,* 83 (1973).
6. Richard A. Lester, *Antibias Regulation of Universities* (New York, 1974); discussed in *Newsweek,* July 15, 1974, p. 78.
7. See The Civil Rights Act of 1964, especially Title VII (which created the Equal Employment Opportunity Commission), amended by The Equal Employment Opportunity Act of 1972, found in *ABC's of The Equal Employment Opportunity Act,* prepared by the Editorial Staff of The Bureau of National Affairs, Inc., 1972. Affirmative Action Programs came into existence with Executive Order 11246. Requirements for affirmative action are found in the rules and regulations 41-CFR Part 60-2, Order #4 (Affirmative Action Programs) generally known as Executive Order #4 and Revised Order #4 41-CFR 60-2 B. For discussion see Paul Brownstein, "Affirmative Action Programs," in *Equal Employment Opportunities Compliance,* Practising Law Institute, New York City (1972), pp. 73–111.
8. See Brownstein, "Affirmative Action Programs" and, for example, *The University of Georgia Affirmative Action Plan,* Athens, Ga., 1973–74, viii, pp. 133, 67.
9. Brownstein and *The University of Georgia Affirmative Action Plan,* Athens, Ga., 1973–74, p. 71.
10. *Ibid.,* p. 69.
11. *Ibid.,* p. 71.
12. See the *Atlanta Journal and Constitution,* June 9, 1974, p. 26-D.
13. See *Atlanta Constitution,* June 7, 1974, p. 13-B.
14. *Newsweek,* June 17, 1974, p. 75.
15. *Ibid.,* p. 75.

GRIGGS, ET AL. v. *DUKE POWER COMPANY*

In 1965 the Duke Power Company's Dan River Steam Station of Draper, North Carolina, employed 95 people, 14 of whom were black. As a result of Title VII of the Civil Rights Act of 1964, the company had just revised its employment and promotion requirements for this generating plant. These revisions were challenged by thirteen of the power company's black employees, who questioned in particular the requirements of a high school diploma and passing intelligence tests as a condition of employment and transfer to other positions in the plant.

The Dan River facility then consisted of five operating departments: Labor, Coal Handling, Operations, Maintenance, and Laboratory and Tests. Prior to July 2, 1965, when the Civil Rights Act went into effect, black workers were by design employed exclusively in the Labor Department. The highest paying job in this department paid less than the lowest paying job in the other four operating departments, which were staffed entirely by white employees. In 1955, the company had instituted requirements of a high school education for initial assignment to any department except Labor, regardless of the employee's race. The diploma was also required for a transfer from Coal Handling to one of the remaining three departments (Operations, Maintenance, or Laboratory and Tests). From 1955 until the suit brought by the thirteen black employees, white employees hired before the high school requirement was put into effect functioned well in the top four operating departments, and these employees continued to be granted promotions. Those white employees hired after the 1955 high school standard was instituted were, in principle, not offered the privileged opportunities that obtained for the previous white employees. However, the black employees in or entering the Labor Department were not affected.

Title VII of the Civil Rights Act became effective on July 2, 1965. It deals specifically with the equality of employment opportunities, and the removal of arbitrary barriers to minorities. With a clear intent to be in compliance, the Duke Power Company altered its employment and promotion requirements. While black employees were no longer restricted to the Labor Department, completion of high school was still required for transfer from Labor to any other department. This restriction also applied to Coal Handling, previously open only to the white, nongraduate employee.

Another employment requirement that applied to initial assignment in any department (except Labor) had also been initiated in July, 1965. In addition to a high school diploma, the prospective employee had to register satisfactory scores on two professionally prepared aptitude tests. Those currently employed with a high school education were, however, still eligible for transfer from Labor to the other departments without such testing. Two months later, in September 1965, the company further expanded its

The first, introductory half of this case was prepared by Nancy Blanpied and Tom L. Beauchamp. The second half is from *Griggs* et al. v. *Duke Power Co.*, 401 U.S. 424 (1970), United States Supreme Court. Majority opinion by Chief Justice Warren Burger.

promotion opportunities to incumbent employees who lacked the high school background. These longstanding employees could now qualify for advancement from the Labor or Coal Handling departments by scoring satisfactorily on two intelligence and comprehension tests (the Wonderlic Personnel Test and the Bennett Mechanical Comprehension Test).

This use of tests by employers was specifically in conformity to the requirements of Title VII, Section 703(h) of the Civil Rights Act. This section was specifically included to allow testing for qualified personnel and to protect employers from being forced to hire solely because of an applicant's minority status. However, the effect of the requirement constituted an implicit barrier to black advancement in the judgment of those who challenged Duke Power's arrangement.

The Wonderlic and Bennett scores required by the company for initial hiring and transfer were equivalent to the national median of high school graduates, which in effect statistically eliminated half of all high school graduates. The power company's statistical data on test scores had shown that 58% of all white applicants passed, as compared to 6% of all black applicants. These test results were generally consistent with the 1960 North Carolina census statistics, which included data on the state's segregated education system. That census had shown that 34% of white males had completed their high school education, while only 12% of the black males had graduated.

The power company's intent to upgrade its requirement for employment and transfer included a program to finance ⅔ of the cost of high school tuition to interested employees. However, the company's own statistics indicated that (at least between July 2, 1965 and November 14, 1966) white employees who did not have to meet the high school and test requirements continued to do very well in promotions within the company. In August 1966, the first black employee to be promoted out of the Labor Department was a high school graduate who had been with the power company since 1953. He was assigned to the Coal Handling Department.

The Duke Power Company's *intent* to improve and advance the level of its employment was never the point of challenge or argument in this case. When the Supreme Court of the United States heard this case it focused on the *effects* of these new standards and whether they were ultimately discriminatory. The Supreme Court ruled in favor of the thirteen employees of the company—thereby reversing a District Court and partially reversing a Court of Appeals. The crucial parts of the Supreme Court Opinion, written by Chief Justice Warren Burger, are as follows:

> We granted the writ in this case to resolve the question whether an employer is prohibited by the Civil Rights Act of 1964, Title VII, from requiring a high school education or passing of a standardized general intelligence test as a condition of employment in or transfer to jobs when (a) neither standard is shown to be significantly related to successful job performance, (b) both requirements operate to disqualify Negroes at a substantially higher rate than white applicants, and (c) the jobs in question formerly had been filled only by white employees as part of a longstanding practice of giving preference to whites. . . .
> The objective of Congress in the enactment of Title VII is plain from the

language of the statute. It was to achieve equality of employment opportunities and remove barriers that have operated in the past to favor an identifiable group of white employees over other employees. Under the Act, practices, procedures, or tests neutral on their face, and even neutral in terms of intent, cannot be maintained if they operate to "freeze" the status quo of prior discriminatory employment practices.

The Court of Appeals' opinion, and the partial dissent, agreed that, on the record in the present case, "whites register far better on the Company's alternative requirements" than Negroes. This consequence would appear to be directly traceable to race. Basic intelligence must have the means of articulation to manifest itself fairly in a testing process. Because they are Negroes, petitioners have long received inferior education in segregated schools and this Court expressly recognized these differences in *Gaston County* v. *United States,* 395 U.S. 285 (1969). . . . Congress did not intend by Title VII, however, to guarantee a job to every person regardless of qualifications. In short, the Act does not command that any person be hired simply because he was formerly the subject of discrimination, or because he is a member of a minority group. Discriminatory preference for any group, minority or majority, is precisely and only what Congress has proscribed. What is required by Congress is the removal of artificial, arbitrary, and unnecessary barriers to employment when the barriers operate invidiously to discriminate on the basis of racial or other impermissible classification.

. . . The Act proscribes not only overt discrimination but also practices that are fair in form, but discriminatory in operation. The touchstone is business necessity. If an employment practice which operates to exclude Negroes cannot be shown to be related to job performance, the practice is prohibited.

On the record before us, neither the high school completion requirement nor the general intelligence test is shown to bear a demonstrable relationship to successful performance of the jobs for which it was used. Both were adopted, as the Court of Appeals noted, without meaningful study of their relationship to job-performance ability. Rather, a vice president of the Company testified, the requirements were instituted on the Company's judgment that they generally would impove the overall quality of the work force.

The evidence, however, shows that employees who have not completed high school or taken the tests have continued to perform satisfactorily and make progress in departments for which the high school and test criteria are now used. The promotion record of present employees who would not be able to meet the new criteria thus suggests the possibility that the requirements may not be needed even for the limited purpose of preserving the avowed policy of advancement within the Company. . . .

The Court of Appeals held that the Company had adopted the diploma and test requirements without any "intention to discriminate against Negro employees." We do not suggest that either the District Court or the Court of Appeals erred in examining the employer's intent; but good intent or absence of discriminatory intent does not redeem employment procedures or testing mechanisms that operate as "built-in headwinds" for minority groups and are unrelated to measuring job capability.

The Company's lack of discriminatory intent is suggested by special efforts to help the undereducated employees through Company financing of two-thirds the cost of tuition for high school training. But Congress directed the thrust of the Act to the *consequences* of employment practices, not simply the motivation. More than that, Congress has placed on the employer the burden of showing that any given requirement must have a manifest relationship to the employment in question.

The facts of this case demonstrate the inadequacy of broad and general testing devices as well as the infirmity of using diplomas or degrees as fixed measures of capability. History is filled with examples of men and women who rendered highly effective performance without the conventional badges of accomplishment in terms of certificates, diplomas, or degrees. Diplomas and tests are useful servants, but Congress has mandated the commonsense proposition that they are not to become masters of reality.

The company contends that its general intelligence tests are specifically permited by § 703 (h) of the Act. That section authorizes the use of "any professionally developed ability test" that is not "designed, intended *or used* to discriminate because of race. . . ." [Emphasis added.]

The Equal Employment Opportunity Commission, having enforcement responsibility, has issued guidelines interpreting § 703 (h) to permit only the use of job-related tests. . . .

Nothing in the Act precludes the use of testing or measuring procedures; obviously they are useful. What Congress has forbidden is giving these devices and mechanisms controlling force unless they are demonstrably a reasonable measure of job performance. Congress has not commanded that the less qualified be preferred over the better qualified simply because of minority origins. Far from disparaging job qualifications as such, Congress has made such qualifications the controlling factor, so that race, religion, nationality, and sex become irrelevant. What Congress has commanded is that any tests used must measure the person for the job and not the person in the abstract.

The judgment of the Court of Appeals is, as to that portion of the judgment appealed from, reversed.

As a result of this opinion, testing was stopped at Duke Power Company.

UNITED STEELWORKERS AND KAISER ALUMINUM v. *WEBER*

Challenged here is the legality of an affirmative action plan—collectively bargained by an employer and a union—that reserves for black employees 50% of the openings in an in-plant craft-training program until the percentage of black craftworkers in the plant is commensurate with the percentage of blacks in the local labor force. The question for decision is whether Congress, in Title VII of the Civil Rights Act of 1964, 78 Stat 253, as amended, 42 USC §§ 2000e et seq. [42 USCS §§ 2000e et seq.], left employers and unions in the private sector free to take such race-conscious steps to eliminate manifest racial imbalances in traditionally segregated job categories. We hold that Title VII does not prohibit such race-conscious affirmative action plans.

443 U.S. 193, 61 L Ed 2d 480, 99 S. Ct. 2721 (1979). Majority opinion by Justice William Brennan, United States Supreme Court.

I

In 1974, petitioner United Steelworkers of America (USWA) and petitioner Kaiser Aluminum & Chemical Corp. (Kaiser) entered into a master collective-bargaining agreement covering terms and conditions of employment at 15 Kaiser plants. The agreement contained, inter alia, an affirmative action plan designed to eliminate conspicuous racial imbalances in Kaiser's then almost exclusively white craftwork forces. Black craft-hiring goals were set for each Kaiser plant equal to the percentage of blacks in the respective local labor forces. To enable plants to meet these goals, on-the-job training programs were established to teach unskilled production workers—black and white—the skills necessary to become craftworkers. The plan reserved for black employees 50% of the openings in these newly created in-plant training programs.

This case arose from the operation of the plan at Kaiser's plant in Gramercy, La. Until 1974, Kaiser hired as craft-workers for that plant only persons who had had prior craft experience. Because blacks had long been excluded from craft unions, few were able to present such credentials. As a consequence, prior to 1974 only 1.83% (5 out of 273) of the skilled craftworkers at the Gramercy plant were black, even though the work force in the Gramercy area was approximately 39% black.

Pursuant to the national agreement Kaiser altered its craft-hiring practice in the Gramercy plant. Rather than hiring already trained outsiders, Kaiser established a training program to train its production workers to fill craft openings. Selection of craft trainees was made on the basis of seniority, with the proviso that at least 50% of the new trainees were to be black until the percentage of black skilled craft-workers in the Gramercy plant approximated the percentage of blacks in the local labor force. See 415 F Supp 761, 764.

During 1974, the first year of the operation of the Kaiser-USWA affirmative action plan, 13 craft trainees were selected from Gramercy's production work force. Of these, seven were black and six white. The most senior black selected into the program had less seniority than several white production workers whose bids for admission were rejected. Thereafter one of those white production workers, respondent Brian Weber (hereafter respondent), instituted this class action in the United States District Court for the Eastern District of Louisiana.

The complaint alleged that the filling of craft trainee positions at the Gramercy plant pursuant to the affirmative action program had resulted in junior black employees, receiving training in preference to senior white employees, thus discriminating against respondent and other similarly situated white employees in violation of §§ 703(a)[1] and (d)[2] of Title VII. The District Court held that the plan violated Title VII, entered a judgment in favor of the plaintiff class, and granted a permanent injunction prohibiting Kaiser and the USWA "from denying plaintiffs, Brian F. Weber and all other members of the class, access to on-the-job training programs on the basis of race." App 171. A divided panel of the Court of Appeals for the Fifth Circuit affirmed, holding that all employment preferences based upon race, including those preferences incidental to bona fide affirmative action plans, violated Title VII's prohibition against racial discrimination in employment. 563 F2d 216 (1977). We granted certiorari. 439 US 1045, 58 L Ed 2d 704, 99 S Ct 720 (1978). We reverse.

II

We emphasize at the outset the narrowness of our inquiry. Since the Kaiser-USWA plan does not involve state action, this case does not present an alleged violation of the Equal Protection Clause of the Fourteenth Amendment. Further, since the Kaiser-USWA plan was adopted voluntarily, we are not concerned with what Title VII requires or with what a court might order to remedy a past proved violation of the Act. The only question before us is the narrow statutory issue of whether Title VII forbids private employers and unions from voluntarily agreeing upon bona fide affirmative action plans that accord racial preferences in the manner and for the purpose provided in the Kaiser-USWA plan. . . .

Congress' primary concern in enacting the prohibition against racial discrimination in Title VII of the Civil Rights Act of 1964 was with "the plight of the Negro in our economy." 110 Cong Rec 6548 (1964) (remarks of Sen. Humphrey). Before 1964, blacks were largely relegated to "unskilled and semi-skilled jobs." Ibid. (remarks of Sen. Humhrey); id., at 7204 (remarks of Sen. Clark); id., at 7379–7380 (remarks of Sen. Kennedy). Because of automation the number of such jobs was rapidly decreasing.

Given this legislative history, we cannot agree with respondent that Congress intended to prohibit the private sector from taking effective steps to accomplish the goal that Congress designed Title VII to achieve. The very statutory words [were] intended as a spur or catalyst to cause "employers and unions to self-examine and to self-evaluate their employment practices and to endeavor to eliminate, so far as possible, the last vestiges of an unfortunate and ignominious page in this country's history."

It would be ironic indeed if a law triggered by a Nation's concern over centuries of racial injustice and intended to improve the lot of those who had "been excluded from the American dream for so long," 110 Cong Rec 6552 (1964) (remarks of Sen. Humphrey), constituted the first legislative prohibition of all voluntary, private, race-conscious efforts to abolish traditional patterns of racial segregation and hierarchy.

Our conclusion is further reinforced by examination of the language and legislative history of § 703(j) of Title VII. Opponents of Title VII raised two related arguments against the bill. First, they argued that the Act would be interpreted to *require* employers with racially imbalanced work forces to grant preferential treatment to racial minorities in order to integrate. Second, they argued that employers with racially imbalanced work forces would grant preferential treatment to racial minorities, even if not required to do so by the Act. See 110 Cong Rec 8618–8619 (1964) (remarks of Sen. Sparkman). Had Congress meant to prohibit all race-conscious affirmative action, as respondent urges, it easily could have answered both objections by providing that Title VII would not require or *permit* racially preferential integration efforts. But Congress did not choose such a course. Rather Congress added § 703(j) which addresses only the first objection. The section provides that nothing contained in Title VII "shall be interpreted to *require* any employer . . . to grant preferential treatment . . . to any group because of the race . . . of such . . . group on account of" a de facto racial imbalance in the employer's work force. The section does *not* state that "nothing in Title VII shall be interpreted to *permit*" voluntary affirmative efforts to correct racial imbalances. The natural inference is that Congress chose not to forbid all voluntary race-conscious affirmative action.

The reasons for this choice are evident from the legislative record. Title VII could not have been enacted into law without substantial support from legislators in both Houses who traditionally resisted federal regulation of private business. Those legislators demanded as a price for their support that "management prerogatives, and union freedoms . . . be left undisturbed to the greatest extent possible." . . .

III

We need not today define in detail the line of demarcation between permissible and impermissible affirmative action plans. It suffices to hold that the challenged Kaiser-USWA affirmative action plan falls on the permissible side of the line. The purposes of the plan mirror those of the statute. Both were designed to break down old patterns of racial segregation and hierarchy. Both were structured to "open employment opportunities for Negroes in occupations which have been traditionally closed to them." 110 Cong Rec 6548 (1964) (remarks of Sen. Humphrey).

At the same time, the plan does not unnecessarily trammel the interests of the white employees. The plan does not require the discharge of white workers and their replacement with new black hirees. Cf. McDonald v Santa Fe Trail Transp. Co., 427 US 273, 49 L Ed 2d 493, 96 S Ct 2574 (1976). Nor does the plan create an absolute bar to the advancement of white employees; half of those trained in the program will be white. Moreover, the plan is a temporary measure; it is not intended to maintain racial balance, but simply to eliminate a manifest racial imbalance. Preferential selection of craft trainees at the Gramercy plant will end as soon as the percentage of black skilled craftworkers in the Gramercy plant approximates the percentage of blacks in the local labor force. See 415 F Supp, at 763.

We conclude, therefore, that the adoption of the Kaiser-USWA plan for the Gramercy plant falls within the area of discretion left by Title VII to the private sector voluntarily to adopt affirmative action plans designed to eliminate conspicuous racial imbalance in traditionally segregated job categories. Accordingly, the judgment of the Court of Appeals for the Fifth Circuit is reversed.

Notes

1. Section 703(a), 78 Stat 255, as amended, 86 Stat 109, 42 USC § 2000e-2(a) [42 USCS § 2000e-2(a)], provides:

    "(a) . . . It shall be an unlawful employment practice for an employer—

    "(1) to fail or refuse to hire or to discharge any individual, or otherwise to discriminate against any individual with respect to his compensation, terms, conditions, or privileges of employment, because of such individual's race, color, religion, sex, or national origin; or

    "(2) to limit, segregate, or classify his employees or applicants for employment in any way which would deprive or tend to deprive any individual of employment opportunities or otherwise adversely affect his status as an employee, because of such individual's race, color, religion, sex, or national origin."

2. Section 703(d), 78 Stat 256, 42 USC § 2000e-2(d) [42 USCS § 2000e-2(d)], provides:

    "It shall be an unlawful employment practice for any employer, labor organization, or joint labor-management committee controlling apprenticeship or other training or retraining, including on-the-job training programs to discriminate against any individual because of his race, color, religion, sex, or national origin in admission to, or employment in, any program established to provide apprenticeship or other training."

case 1: Secretarial Advancement

Patricia Maxwell was John Bennet's private secretary. She was a bright woman and an extremely competent secretary. Before getting her present spot, Patricia worked six months under Richard Green. The two functioned unusually well together and Richard gave her more responsibility than any of the other people on his staff. He was sure his early success at the headquarters was due to her abilities and it was a blow to his operations to lose her. He consoled himself with the fact that she deserved every opportunity to advance.

Patricia's last advancement had taken her to the highest level that a secretary could attain. She strongly believed she could function well above that plane. When an opening appeared in the personnel department a pay step higher than hers, she applied.

Green was quick to emphasize to J. P. Bennet, his boss, that she could handle the promotion. However, his superiors only paid lip service to Patricia's request. Assuring her that she would be given every consideration, they privately expressed to Green that they had no intention of giving her the job. When he questioned their reasoning, he was told the following:

1. Patricia was an excellent secretary and a satisfactory replacement would be very hard to locate. She could best serve the needs of the firm where she was.
2. She was married and had expressed a desire to have children. S.I.C. could never be sure when she might quit to raise a family. It was therefore clearly unwise to expend resources to train her for a new job.
3. Also, her income was supplemental to her husband's. There was no real need for her to work. It was Richard's superiors' belief that women in this category rarely developed a strong commitment and obligation to the company. They were less likely to rise and meet any unexpected pressures of their jobs. If things got rough, they might say "the money isn't worth my sanity" and leave.
4. Finally, the head of the personnel department was sure he would have a revolt if a woman was put in the open position. The girls on his staff had repeatedly expressed that they did not want to work under a woman. The department head surmised that they thought a woman supervisor would be harder on them than a man.

At the end of the discussion Bennet looked at Green reemphasizing that the firm didn't need a discrimination case, and that none of the staff must realize what was happening. Green had to play the game for the company's sake. Whenever Patricia asked how her chances were, Richard always smiled and assured her he was doing everything he could and that as far as he knew, she was still in the running.

S.I.C. eventually found a qualified man on the outside market, and as far as Richard could discern, Patricia never seemed to question his hiring. Still, he wondered if Patricia would stay with S.I.C. if she realized she had no chance for advancement.

Questions

1. Should Patricia Maxwell be informed of her position in S.I.C.?
2. Richard Green had to decide:
   a. Is he going to say anything? Will it be to his advantage?
   b. If he does say something, to whom should he speak? (Bennet? Maxwell?)

case 2:   Sing's Chinese Restaurant

The Bali Hai Corporation started as a small Chinese restaurant in Boston, Massachusetts in 1959. The restaurant was an exact replica of a Chinese pagoda. Over the years, the restaurant, owned and managed by Arnold Sing, became known for its food and atmosphere. Customers were made to feel as if they were actually in China. In the last few years Sing decided to incorporate and open other similar restaurants throughout the country. Sing, who had come to the United States from China in the early 1940s, was very strict in keeping up his reputation of good food and atmosphere, and had a policy of hiring only waiters of Oriental descent. He felt this added to his customers' dining pleasure and made for a more authentic environment. For kitchen positions, though, Sing hired any applicants who were qualified.

About a year ago in Sing's Bali Hai of Washington, D.C. there was a shortage of waiters. An advertisement was placed in the paper for waiters, and the manager of the store was instructed by Sing to hire only Orientals. The manager was also reminded of Bali Hai's commitment to a reputation of good food and atmosphere. Two young men, one black and one white, both with considerable restaurant experience, applied for the waiters' jobs. The manager explained the policy of hiring only Orientals to the young men, and he also told them he could get them work in his kitchen. The two men declined the positions and instead went directly to the area Equal Employment Office and filed a complaint. Sing's defense was that the policy was only to preserve the atmosphere of the restaurant. He said the Oriental waiters were needed to make it more authentic. Sing also added that he hired Blacks, Whites, and other races for his kitchen help.

Questions

1. Is Sing's defense a good one under the law? Why or why not?
2. Is Sing's defense a good one under the standards of morality? Why or why not?
3. Is this a case of "preferential hiring"? "reverse discrimination"?

case 3: T. H. Sandy Sportswear

The Millers, Brad and Mary, moved to Tallahassee, Florida in order for Mary to attend Law School at Florida State University. Brad graduated from Georgetown University with a degree in Business Administration and worked in retail management for five years. Brad graduated with top honors from Georgetown and had excellent recommendations from his former employers.

Tallahassee, Florida is basically a college town, centering around two universities and the Florida State Legislature. The two universities are Florida State University and Florida A & M University. There is only one large shopping mall and a few department stores in Tallahassee, and jobs in retail management are quite scarce.

Upon arriving in Tallahassee, Mary started classes at the Law School and Brad began looking for a job. There were absolutely no openings anywhere in town for retail managers, and Brad eventually had to settle for a teller position at a local bank. Brad kept abreast of the retail job market in Tallahassee, and finally an opportunity came open.

T. H. Sandy, a women's discount sportswear retailer advertised in the local newspaper for a store manager. Brad immediately made an appointment for an interview and sent in a resume, as requested in the ad. Brad arrived early for his interview and was given an application form to complete. The application form was a long one and included a question concerning sex of applicant. While completing the application form, Brad noticed that all the employees of T. H. Sandy were female and all of the other applicants waiting to be interviewed were also female. Brad was finally called in for his interview, which he thought went very well. The interviewer told Brad that they had two more days of interviewing before a decision would be made and that he would be hearing from them in about a week. The next week Brad received a letter from T. H. Sandy informing him that he had not been chosen for the position and thanking him for his interest in the company. The letter gave no reason for their decision. Since this job was so important to Brad, he decided to visit the store and talk with the lady who had interviewed him.

In his meeting with the interviewer, Brad found out that the company had been very impressed with his experience and credentials, but had decided against hiring him because he was a male. The interviewer showed Brad a job description for the manager's position and pointed out that one of the duties of the manager was to supervise all areas of the store, including the dressing room. Because of this particular duty, the company felt that the position should be filled with a female. Brad left the store upset and discouraged.

After discussing the situation with his wife, who was now studying Fair Employment Legislation, Brad considered filing suit against T. H. Sandy for discrimination based on sex under Title VII of the Civil Rights Act of 1964.

Questions

1. Was T. H. Sandy's decision concerning Brad Miller in conflict with Title VII of the Civil Rights Act of 1964?
2. Is sex a bona fide occupational qualification in this situation?
3. Is Brad a "victim" of reverse discrimination?

SUGGESTED SUPPLEMENTARY READINGS

ADELSON, JOSEPH. "Living With Quotas." *Commentary,* 65 (May 1978).

AMDUR, ROBERT. "Compensatory Justice: The Question of Costs." *Political Theory,* 7 (May 1979).

AXELSEN, DIANA. "With All Deliberate Delay: On Justifying Preferential Policies in Education and Employment." *Philosophical Forum,* 9 (Winter-Spring 1977–78).

BABCOCK, BARBARA, *et al. Sex Discrimination and the Law: Causes and Remedies.* Boston: Little, Brown and Company, 1975.

BEAUCHAMP, TOM L. and TERRY PINKARD, eds. *Ethics and Public Policy.* 2nd ed. Englewood Cliffs, N.J.: Prentice-Hall, 1983, Chapter 6.

BELL, DERRICK A., JR. "Racial Remediation: An Historical Perspective on Current Conditions." *Notre Dame Lawyer,* 52 (October 1976).

BLACKSTONE, WILLIAM T. "An Assessment of the Ethical Pros and Cons of Reverse Discrimination." *Philosophy and Public Policy.* Donnie E. Self, ed. Norfolk, Va.: Teagle & Little, Inc., 1977.

———, and ROBERT HESLEP, eds. *Social Justice and Preferential Treatment.* Athens: University of Georgia Press, 1977.

BLUMROSEN, ALFRED. "Quotas, Common Sense, and Law in Labor Relations: Three Dimensions of Equal Opportunity." *Rutgers Law Review,* 27 (Spring 1974).

———. "Strangers in Paradise: *Griggs* v. *Duke Power Co.* and the Concept of Employment Discrimination." *Michigan Law Review,* 71 (1975).

BOWIE, NORMAN E., and ROBERT L. SIMON. *The Individual and the Political Order,* Chapter 9. Englewood Cliffs, N.J.: Prentice-Hall, 1977.

BOXILL, BERNARD. "The Morality of Preferential Hiring." *Philosophy & Public Affairs,* 7 (Spring 1978).

BOYLE, M. BARBARA. "Equal Opportunities for Women is Smart Business." *Harvard Business Review* (May–June 1973).

CADEI, RAYMOND M. "Hiring Goals, California State Government, and Title VII: Is This Numbers Game Legal?" *Pacific Law Journal,* 8 (January 1977).

COHEN, CARL. "Why Racial Preference is Illegal and Immoral." *Commentary,* 67 (June 1979).

COHEN, MARSHALL, THOMAS NAGEL, and THOMAS SCANLON, eds. *Equality and Preferential Treatment.* Princeton, N.J.: Princeton University Press, 1977.

"Constitutionality of Remedial Minority Preferences in Employment." *Minnesota Law Review,* 56 (1972).

DORIOT, GEORGE, ed. *The Management of Racial Integration in Business.* New York: McGraw-Hill, 1965.

DWORKIN, RONALD. "How to Read the Civil Rights Act." *New York Review of Books,* 26 (December 20, 1979).

EDWARDS, HARRY T. "Race Discrimination in Employment: What Price Equality?" *University of Illinois Law Forum,* 1976 (1976).

EPSTEIN, E. M., and D. R. HAMPTON. *Black America and White Business.* Belmont, Calif.: Wadsworth Publishing Co., 1971.

EZORSKY, GERTRUDE. "Hiring Women Faculty." *Philosophy & Public Affairs,* 7 (Fall 1977).

FISS, OWEN. "A Theory of Fair Employment Laws." *University of Chicago Law Review,* 38 (Winter 1971).

FREEMAN, RICHARD B. "The New Job Market for Black Academicians." *Industrial and Labor Relations Review,* 30 (January 1977).

FRETZ, C. F., and JOANNE HAYMEN. "Progress for Women—Men are Still More Equal." *Harvard Business Review* (September–October 1973).

FULLINWIDER, ROBERT. *The Reverse Discrimination Controversy.* Totowa, N.J.: Rowman and Littlefield, 1980.

GLAZER, NATHAN. *Affirmative Discrimination: Ethnic Inequality and Public Policy.* New York: Basic Books, 1975.

GOLDMAN, ALAN. "Justice and Hiring by Competence." *American Philosophical Quarterly* (January 1977).

——. *Justice and Reverse Discrimination.* Princeton, N.J.: Princeton University Press, 1979.

GROSS, BARRY R. *Reverse Discrimination.* Buffalo, N.Y.: Prometheus Books, 1977.

HENKIN, LOUIS, "What of the Right to Practice a Profession?" *California Law Review,* 67 (January 1979).

HUGHES, GRAHAM. "The Right to Special Treatment." In *The Rights of Americans,* ed. Norman Dorsen. New York: Pantheon Books, 1971.

KATZNER, LOUIS. "Is the Favoring of Women and Blacks in Employment and Educational Opportunities Justified?" In *Philosophy of Law,* eds. Joel Feinberg and Hyman Gross. Belmont, Calif.: Wadsworth-Dickenson, 1975. Second Edition, 1980.

NAGEL, THOMAS. "Equal Treatment and Compensatory Discrimination." *Philosophy & Public Affairs,* 2 (Summer 1973).

NEWTON, LISA. "Reverse Discrimination as Unjustified." *Ethics,* 83 (1973).

——. *"Bakke* and *Davis:* Justice, American Style." *National Forum: The Phi Kappa Phi Journal,* LVIII (Winter 1978).

NOTE. "Weber v. Kaiser Aluminum & Chemical Corp.: The Challenge to Voluntary Compliance Under the Title VII." *Columbia Journal of Law and Social Problems,* 14 (1978).

PEMBERTON, JOHN DeJ., JR., ed. *Equal Employment Opportunity—Responsibiities, Rights, Remedies.* New York: Practicing Law Institute, 1975.

POPLIN, CAROLINE. "Fair Employment in a Depressed Economy: The Layoff Problem." *UCLA Law Review,* 23 (December 1975).

POSNER, RICHARD. "The *DeFunis* Case and the Constitutionality of Preferential Treatment of Racial Minorities." *The Supreme Court Review.* Ed. Philip Kurland. Chicago: University of Chicago Press, 1975.

——. "The *Bakke* Case and the Future of 'Affirmative Action'." *California Law Review,* 67 (January 1979).

PURCELL, THEODORE V., and GERALD F. CAVANAUGH. *Blacks in the Industrial World.* New York: The Free Press, 1972.

SETHI, S. PRAKASH. *Business Corporations and the Black Man.* Scranton, Pa.: Chandler Publishing Co., 1970.

SHER, GEORGE. "Justifying Reverse Discrimination in Employment." *Philosophy & Public Affairs,* 4, no. 2 (Winter 1975).

———. "Reverse Discrimination, the Future, and the Past." *Ethics,* 90 (October 1979).

SIMON, ROBERT L. "Statistical Justification of Discrimination." *Analysis* 38 (January 1978).

SINGER, PETER. "Is Racial Discrimination Arbitrary?" *Philosophia,* 8 (November 1978).

UNITED STATES SUPREME COURT. DeFunis v. Odegaard. 416 U.S. 312 (1974).

———. Frontiero v. Richardson. 411 U.S. 677 (1973).

———. McDonald v. Sante Fe Transportation Co. 427 U.S. 273 (1976).

———. Regents of the University of California v. Allan Bakke. 438 U.S. 265, 46 LW 4896 (1978).

VELASQUEZ, MANUEL G. *Business Ethics: Concepts and Cases.* Englewood Cliffs, N.J.: Prentice-Hall, 1982, Chapter 7.

VITTERITTI, JOSEPH P. *Bureaucracy and Social Justice: Allocation of Jobs and Services to Minority Groups.* Port Washington, N.Y.: Kennikat Press, 1979.

WASSERSTROM, RICHARD. "A Defense of Programs of Preferential Treatment," *National Forum: The Phi Kappa Phi Journal,* LVIII (Winter 1978) and a more inclusive article "Racism, Sexism, and Preferential Treatment: An Approach to the Topics," *UCLA Law Review,* 24 (1977).

CHAPTER 8

SELF-REGULATION AND GOVERNMENT REGULATION

INTRODUCTION

A corporation or group of corporations can be viewed as analogous to an individual who has committed himself or herself to a moral point of view and who now wishes to put that perspective into practice. Individuals face a distinctive problem in practicing their morality that is commonly referred to as "weakness of will." Simply put, individuals sometimes yield to the temptation to do what they know is morally wrong. They therefore face the question, "How should weakness of the will be compensated for or overcome?" There are two fundamental strategies for overcoming weakness of the will. One relies on internal mechanisms of self-control and the other on external constraints on behavior. These same two strategies have been adopted in the corporate setting to overcome weakness of will in business. Internal mechanisms for self-control include business codes of ethics and the corporate social audit. The chief external constraint is government regulation. In this chapter, the strengths and weaknesses of these mechanisms for self-regulation and of government regulation are discussed.

SELF-REGULATION

Most business persons agree that society can expect a high level of ethical conduct on the part of persons engaged in business only if the practices and reward-and-punishment structures of business reinforce that behavior. As James Weber points out in this chapter, ethics must be institutionalized into the corporation. There are many strategies for institutionalizing ethics. On some occasions, persons must be made responsible for making certain that ethical issues are raised. This is precisely the strategy adopted by the Federal Communications Commission in one case selected for this chapter. Instead of drafting a substantive regulation indicating specifically which drug lyrics are inappropriate for broadcast, a procedure is required: they order each radio station to make at least one person responsible for that decision.

One of the most common means of self-regulation is the code of ethics. Among the professional groups governed by codes are physicians, nurses, bankers, advertising agents, chemical engineers, and lawyers. There are several advantages to such codes: (1) they provide more stable, permanent guides to right and wrong conduct than do human personalities; (2) they provide guidance in ethically ambiguous situations and resolve conflict-of-interest situations (see Chapter 4, pp. 235–237); and (3) they act as a partial check on autocratic powers of employers. Nonetheless, codes of ethics must be enforced and they must be supported by top management and the corporate structure. A code of ethics is not sufficient as a tool for self-regulation.

In his article on codes of ethics, Kenneth Arrow shows how an industry-wide code potentially can serve as a viable alternative to government regulation. Sometimes the competitive nature of business makes it impossible for an individual corporation to do the morally appropriate act. Suppose, for example, that textile company A is polluting a river and that expensive technology is now available to enable company A to reduce pollution. On the basis of the harm analysis provided by Simon, Powers, and Gunnemann (see Chapter 2), it seems that company A ought to install the pollution control device. However, suppose that company A can show that all other textile companies are similarly polluting rivers. If company A installs the pollution control devices and the other textile companies do not, company A's products will rise in price and hence will run the risk of becoming noncompetitive. Eventually company A may be forced out of business. The competitive situation thus makes it unfair and, from an economic perspective, impossible for company A to do the morally appropriate thing. Only a rule that requires *all* textile companies to install pollution control devices will be fair and effective. It is often maintained that in situations paralleling this textile pollution case, government regulation is the only viable and appropriate answer.

Arrow argues, however, that the textile pollution case can potentially be adequately handled by an industry-wide code of ethics. He argues that at least some evidence exists that industry-wide codes can work; for not all moral problems of personal conflict in society are resolved in courts by law or by regulatory agencies. Some are suitably handled by society's general moral codes. Indeed, if moral codes were not widely efficacious, the legal and regulatory systems would be overwhelmed.

If self-regulation is to be judged effective, it would be useful if there were some way of measuring results—something like standard audit and accounting procedures for annual financial reports to stockholders. It has been suggested that the notion of an audit should be extended beyond the state of a corporation's financial health to the state of its moral health. The figures on pages 528–529 from the First National Bank of Minneapolis Social-Environmental Audit provide an example of a corporate social

1974 Internal Social-Environmental Audit

FIRST NATIONAL BANK OF MINNEAPOLIS

		1974 Performance Level	Net Percentage Performance Differential '73-'74 (2)	1974 Objectives (3)	1974 Social Performance Index (4)	1975 Objectives (5)
Housing 1 (1)	1. Number of residential mortgage loans originated in 1974 to families living in a.) Minneapolis b.) Suburbs & St. Paul	a.) 360 b.) 967	35%	+ / +	↑ / ↓	a.) 360 b.) 967
	2. Dollar amount of residential mortgage loans originated in 1974 to families in a.) Minneapolis b.) Suburbs & St. Paul	a.) $ 8,861,000 b.) $29,324,000		+ / +	↑ / ↑	a.) $ 8,861,000 b.) $29,324,000
	3. Number of outstanding home improvement loans made to families living in a.) Minneapolis b.) Suburbs & St. Paul	a.) 357 b.) 744				a.) 655 b.) 676
	4. Ratio originated residential mortgage loans to bank's total resources	1:50				1:50
	5. Foundation contribution	$10,000		$10,920	.92	$10,000
Education 2	1. Number of classes taken by employees paid by bank a.) internal b.) external	363 164 199	5%	+ / + / +	↓ / ↑ / ↓	
	2. Number of employees in bank college gift matching program	48		+	↑	55
	3. Employee community involvement man-hours per month	1,129		+	↑	1,241
	4. Foundation contribution to educational institutions	$51,750		$50,006	1.03	$55,000
Public Safety 3	1. Accidents on bank premises involving employees — 1974 (Does not include sports)	26	80%			26
	2. Accidents involving non-employees	14				14
Income 4	1. Clerical employees — monthly income related to area-wide averages	1:1.01				1:1
	2. Clerical employees — composite productivity relation to base 1973	1:1.06				1:1.10
Job Opportunities 5	1. Percent officers, managers and professionals (EEO defined) a.) women b.) racial minority	a.) 19.8 b.) 3.5	80%	+ / +	↑ / ↑	a.) 23.8 b.) 4.2
	2. Percent of job categories posted	77		75	1.03	77
Health 6	1. Estimated commitment to treatment of alcoholism a.) money b.) man-hours	a.) $5,460 b.) 222	50%	+ 50% +100%	.61 1.39	
	2. Number of days missed due to health problems per capita a.) women b.) men	a.) 3.43 b.) 1.65		a.) 5.0 b.) 2.3	a.) 1.7 b.) 4.3	a.) 3.43 b.) 1.65
	3. Prepaid health services (HMO) as employee health option a.) services offered b.) dollar c.) man-hours	a.) 0 b.) $1,000 c.) 141		+ / +	↓ / ↑	a.) 0 b.) $1,500 c.) 150
Transportation 7	1. Percent employees taking bus to work	61	50%	50	1.22	65
	2. Percent employees who come to work in car pools	17		30	.56	20
	3. Percent employees who drive to work alone	19		15	.79	15
Participation 8	1. Man-hours per month spent by employees in community activity a.) on bank time b.) non-bank time	4,632 585 4,047	50%	+ / 380 / +	1.54 / ↑	5,095 643 4,451
	2. Percent employees donating to United Way	83		+	↑	85
	3. Percent employees voting Nov. '74	75				

audit. When first discussed, the notion of a corporate social audit was received with some enthusiasm by the business community. Indeed, the Committee for Economic Development commissioned a study of the corporate social audit. That study, a portion of which is included in this chapter, explained the function of a corporate social audit and gave the concept some respectability in the business community. However, difficulties in implementation have muted the initial enthusiasm for the corporate social audit, and some observers predict its imminent demise.

The chief problem with the implementation of corporate social audits

1974 Internal Social-Environmental Audit

FIRST NATIONAL BANK OF MINNEAPOLIS

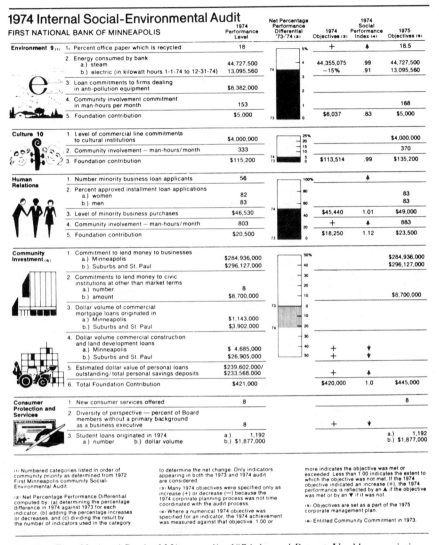

		1974 Performance Level	Net Percentage Performance Differential '73-'74 (2)	1974 Objectives (3)	1974 Social Performance Index (4)	1975 Objectives (5)
Environment 9 (1)	1. Percent office paper which is recycled	18		+	▲	18.5
	2. Energy consumed by bank					
	a.) steam	44,727,500		44,355,075	.99	44,727,500
	b.) electric (in kilowatt hours 1-1-74 to 12-31-74)	13,095,560		−15%	.91	13,095,560
	3. Loan commitments to firms dealing in anti-pollution equipment	$8,382,000				
	4. Community involvement commitment in man-hours per month	153				168
	5. Foundation contribution	$5,000		$6,037	.83	$5,000
Culture 10	1. Level of commercial line commitments to cultural institutions	$4,000,000				$4,000,000
	2. Community involvement — man-hours/month	333				370
	3. Foundation contribution	$115,200		$113,514	.99	$135,200
Human Relations	1. Number minority business loan applicants	56		▲		
	2. Percent approved installment loan applications					
	a.) women	82				83
	b.) men	83				83
	3. Level of minority business purchases	$46,530		$45,440	1.01	$49,000
	4. Community involvement — man-hours/month	803		+	▲	883
	5. Foundation contribution	$20,500		$18,250	1.12	$23,500
Community Investment (6)	1. Commitment to lend money to businesses					
	a.) Minneapolis	$284,936,000				$284,936,000
	b.) Suburbs and St. Paul	$296,127,000				$296,127,000
	2. Commitments to lend money to civic institutions at other than market terms					
	a.) number	8				
	b.) amount	$8,700,000				$8,700,000
	3. Dollar volume of commercial mortgage loans originated in					
	a.) Minneapolis	$1,143,000				
	b.) Suburbs and St. Paul	$3,902,000				
	4. Dollar volume commercial construction and land development loans					
	a.) Minneapolis	$ 4,685,000		+	▼	
	b.) Suburbs and St. Paul	$26,905,000		+	▼	
	5. Estimated dollar value of personal loans outstanding/total personal savings deposits	$239,602,000/ $233,568,000		+	▲	
	6. Total Foundation Contribution	$421,000		$420,000	1.0	$445,000
Consumer Protection and Services	1. New consumer services offered	8				8
	2. Diversity of perspective — percent of Board members without a primary background as a business executive	8		+	▼	
	3. Student loans originated in 1974 a.) number b.) dollar volume	a.) 1,192 b.) $1,877,000				a.) 1,192 b.) $1,877,000

(1) Numbered categories listed in order of community priority as determined from 1972 First Minneapolis community Social-Environmental Audit.

(2) Net Percentage Performance Differential computed by: (a) determining the percentage difference in 1974 against 1973 for each indicator, (b) adding the percentage increases or decreases, and (c) dividing the result by the number of indicators used in the category

to determine the net change. Only indicators appearing in both the 1973 and 1974 audit are considered.

(3) Many 1974 objectives were specified only as increase (+) or decrease (—) because the 1974 corporate planning process was not time coordinated with the audit process.

(4) Where a numerical 1974 objective was specified for an indicator, the 1974 achievement was measured against that objective. 1.00 or

more indicates the objective was met or exceeded. Less than 1.00 indicates the extent to which the objective was not met. If the 1974 objective indicated an increase (+), the 1974 performance is reflected by an ▲ if the objective was met or by an ▼ if it was not.

(5) Objectives are set as a part of the 1975 corporate management plan.

(6) Entitled Community Commitment in 1973.

Source: *First National Bank of Minneapolis. 1974 Annual Report.* Used by permission.

comes in knowing what to measure and how to make acceptable measurements. The notion of the corporate social audit has utilitarian roots, and problems of measurability that plague utilitarianism similarly constitute one of the chief stumbling blocks to the successful implementation of the corporate social audit. Further discussion of the measurability problems common to both self-regulation and government regulation is found in the concluding section of this chapter on regulating through cost-benefit analysis.

GOVERNMENT REGULATION

As social and economic systems in European and North American nations have grown more complex, there has been a correlative increase in the scope of government regulation of business (and of all economic activity). Sometimes the government intervenes for the purpose of shoring up the economic system itself, while at other times intervention is undertaken to support certain socially approved goals. Whatever the exact purpose, government regulation of business is now an enormous undertaking. Because this phenomenon has emerged so rapidly and amid such constant controversy, an historical survey of the setting and reasons for modern regulation of business in the United States will be helpful.

In the nineteenth and early twentieth centuries, an individualist philosophy prevailed in both government and business, according to which the success of business is due largely to individual effort, which the government restricts only at society's economic peril. The proper role of government relative to industry is thus that of encouraging the growth of unregulated business. Action in light of this philosophy led to a situation in which the corporation was privileged: tariffs intended to prevent foreign competition were erected, corporate taxes were kept at low levels, and the corporation enjoyed an advantaged status under law. Giant corporations quickly began to control the economy of the country. Before the turn of the twentieth century, the 200 largest corporations produced more of the GNP than the next 100,000 largest corporations combined. These monopolies stifled competition and inflated prices. While their corporate profits rapidly increased, wages were decreasing and the cost of living was soaring. At the same time, these corporations engaged in a number of ethically unacceptable practices, such as lowering product quality without warning, watering down the value of stock, etc.

In 1887, the Interstate Commerce Act was passed to protect farmers and small business persons from monopolistic practices, especially by the railroads. A federal regulatory agency, the Interstate Commerce Commission, was created to monitor the railroads, though it was given no real power to do so, and the act thus had little immediate effect. Only three years later, in 1890, the Sherman Antitrust Act was passed to protect small businesses from a wide variety of monopolistic practices. However, for many years thereafter, the courts continued to favor monopolistic interests, and not until Theodore Roosevelt's administration was a stricter interpretation placed on the Sherman Act. Finally, in 1914, both the Clayton Act and the Federal Trade Commission Act were enacted to control anticompetitive practices. The basic idea was to free the free enterprise system from monopoly and deceptive maneuvers.

Shortly thereafter, a World War I boom restored confidence in business, and not until the Depression was there renewed pressure for further regulation. However, from 1930 until the present, a broad range of federal legislation has been enacted to control those business activities believed to involve unfairnesses or inefficiencies analogous to those that earlier had resulted from unregulated industry. Thus, unfair advertising, deceptive trade, sluggish competition, powerful anticompetitive mergers, questionable investment practices, waste discharges, discrimination in hiring, etc., all gradually came under federal regulation. Many state and local government controls were also enacted. Consequently, federal regulation now affects virtually every business in the country. As the regulation has increased, so has the critical response.

Presumably, everyone would like to see the federal regulatory process achieve vital social ends without obstructing the productive capacity of the marketplace. We sometimes use shorthand to express this view by saying that we want business regulated "in the public interest." Yet what is the public interest, and do regulatory agencies now function so that this interest is best served? Virtually no one is satisfied with the current state of regulatory practices in the United States. Critics across a wide spectrum of political opinion accuse federal agencies of either too much, too little, or inefficient regulation.

This criticism reached its peak in the 1980 election, after which Ronald Reagan claimed a mandate to end unreasonable and burdensome government regulation. However, since government regulation serves many morally valuable functions, including some useful to the business community, it is important that only unreasonable and truly burdensome government regulation be ended.

But which regulations are reasonable and which ones are unreasonable? Some criteria are needed. In 1964, Lon Fuller published his important book *The Morality of Law* which provides eight criteria for evaluating good law and argues that extreme departures from those eight conditions threatens to undermine the legal system itself. In his article, Norman Bowie adapts Fuller's criteria for the special context of government regulation. It will be obvious that many government regulations fall short under the criteria he proposes.

There are also general limitations inherent in the nature of law which limit its effectiveness as a means of regulation. If the only means of ensuring moral conduct were the law, serious social repercussions would result. At best society would be burdened with an expensive enforcement apparatus; at the extreme, society would become either totalitarian or collapse in anarchy. The Internal Revenue Service, for example, admits that it would be powerless to prevent widespread cheating on income taxes, and if such cheating occurred the government could no longer use the income tax. In the article that concludes the Government Regulation section, Christopher Stone discusses some of the features of law which limit its effectiveness as a regulatory device.

MORAL REASONING AND COST-BENEFIT ANALYSIS

In recent years, especially in the regulative agencies of government, a particular method has been widely touted as a means of applying legal standards to the regulation of industry. This method is generally referred to as cost-benefit analysis, one segment of which is risk-benefit analysis. This method has also been employed by individual firms. For example, some corporate social audits are based on cost-benefit principles. The purpose is to provide a systematic method to facilitate tasks of decision making—whether decisions apply to the regulation of business or to the corporate management of a business. Since both management and the government have definite goals that fit the limits within which they operate (e.g., the firm strives to maximize profits), they are naturally interested in the most efficient means to those ends. It is here that cost-benefit reasoning plays a role, for this method is intended to show how one can bring about the desired result with the least possible expenditure.

The simple idea behind cost-benefit procedures is that one can *measure* costs and benefits by some acceptable device, at the same time identifying uncertainties and possible tradeoffs, in order to present policy makers or business persons with specific, relevant information on the basis of which a decision can be reached. Although such analysis usually proceeds by measuring different quantitative units—e.g., the number of worker accidents, statistical deaths, dollars expended, and number of workers fired—cost-benefit analysis (in the ideal) attempts in the end to convert and express these seemingly incommensurable units of measurement into a common one, usually a monetary unit. It is this ultimate reduction that gives the method its power in the minds of many, because judgments about tradeoffs can be made on the basis of perfectly comparable quantities. For example, it has been argued that among its other uses it can be employed to make financially explicit such tradeoffs (reached in government policy decisions) as those between environmental quality and factory productivity and between the quality of gasoline and the quality of the health of those who produce it.

Cost-benefit analysis has been widely criticized as a technique, especially when suggested for public policy purposes. First, the method has proved difficult to implement. Economists have been concerned largely with spelling out how such analyses can be carried out in *theory* rather than with providing practical and already quantified examples. The fact that many important variables are difficult to ascertain and reliably quantify—so difficult that we may never be very confident about the ending net sum—is a major reason why cost-benefit analysis has not been more widely used and has seemed to many a nonviable technique. This conclusion has been particularly drawn in the case of evaluating projects which would improve the quality of life, as opposed to considerations merely about the purchase of capital goods. A second and common objection to cost-benefit analysis is that we may not want it for *moral* reasons, and especially for reasons of (distributive) justice. It may be that some cost-benefit analyses will tell us that a particular device would be highly beneficial as compared to its costs, and yet provision of this benefit might function in an economy to deny more basic services to those who desperately need them. Perhaps instead, as a matter of justice, such needy persons ought to be subsidized, either in terms of services or financial awards, no matter what cost-benefit analyses reveal. When this problem is coupled with the generally acknowledged fact that the language of "costs" and "benefits" itself harbors implicit value judgments about positive and negative consequences, it appears that some fundamental moral thinking must be done, not only about whether to accept a *particular* cost-benefit model as decisive, but also about the acceptability of the *notions* of costs and benefits.

Vincent Vaccaro, a government employee, has participated in cost-benefit studies. His article, "Cost-Benefit Analysis and Public Policy Formation" is essentially a defense of the practice. However, his defense is tempered by the recognition that cost-benefit analyses are often improperly done and by the recognition that certain issues of distributive justice must be settled before the cost-benefit process. Vaccaro thus argues that cost-benefit analysis ought to be constrained by various social goals including moral ones. The critics of cost-benefit analysis remain unconvinced, however. Michael Baram argues that it is difficult to solve certain problems associated with actual cost-benefit studies, and John Byrne criticizes cost-benefit analysis on the grounds that its underlying decision procedure is inconsistent with democratic practice.

The federal government in the United States continues to push for both greater efficiency and decreased regulation in many areas. As it does, the role of cost-benefit analysis may substantially increase—a joy to its supporters and a source of irritation to its critics.

N.E.B.

INSTITUTIONALIZING ETHICS INTO THE CORPORATION

James Weber

> Beyond its responsibility to oversee management, strategic planning, and shareholder dividends, the board must monitor the integrity of all the corporation's actions—its social integrity, its community activities, its affirmative action programs. The board should satisfy itself that the corporation is being a responsible citizen in these matters. The pressure in the 1980's will be to perform this overview role.[1]

This challenge demonstrates the significance of the ethics issue to boards of directors. Major corporations are beginning to view ethical issues as a recognized part of doing business, thereby integrating or institutionalizing ethics into the corporate decision-making structure.

The term *institutionalizing ethics* is academic and may sound ponderous, but it has value. It simply means getting ethics formally and explicitly into daily business life, making it a regular and normal part of business. It

From *MSU Business Topics,* Spring 1981. Copyright © 1981 by Michigan State University Press. Reprinted by permission.

means putting ethics into company policy making at the board and top management levels and, through a formal code, integrating ethics into all daily decision making and work practices for all employees. . . .

A corporation may institutionalize ethics by three principal means: a company policy or code of ethics, a formally designated ethics committee on the board of directors, and a management development program that incorporates ethics into its curriculum. . . .

DEVELOPMENT OF A CODE

General Philosophy. The writers of the general policy statement should acknowledge, in the opening sentence, the difficulty of preparing a code and the need for constant review and revision. The policy statement should declare ethics a critical element of corporate concern and should define, as clearly and as simply as possible, the following terms: changing versus static values, business versus personal ethics, and illegal versus unethical actions.

A code also must consider ethical issues specific to the corporation.

The formulators of a code should be sensitive to the need to respond to the ethical dilemmas confronting the corporation. As the transnational Norton Company discovered, a universal code might need to be tempered due to differing local laws and customs. The observance abroad of U.S. laws (for example, the Foreign Corrupt Practices Act of 1977) by a U.S.-owned plant could result in a loss of sales and revenue to European competitors. The lost income must be weighed against the consequences of violating U.S. laws and the possibility of legal action. Solutions to these types of ethical dilemmas may not be reached easily, although projects such as the United Nations committee for developing a transnational code of ethics may help. Nonetheless, the framers of the corporate code must struggle with the attempt to resolve these matters.

Finally, the general policy statement of a code should promote ethics as a necessary value applicable throughout the corporate network, to every domestic and foreign plant and to every employee. To be institutionalized, ethics must be considered in daily business operations.

Areas of Concern. Following the general policy statement should be a section on matters of ethical concern for the corporation. Some possible areas are transnational responsibility, boycotts, government relations, community relations, environmental quality, energy conservation, labor disputes, antitrust compliance, interlocking directorates, false advertising, use of confidential information, product quality and safety, occupational safety and health, charitable contributions, political contributions, equal employment opportunity, gifts, favors, gratuities, bribes, personnel grievances, employee drug addiction, employee alcoholism, conflicts of interest, employee pilfering, accounting procedures, tax evasion, slush funds, company expense accounts, and embezzlement.

Drafters of the code should select areas germane to the company's daily operations and address the ethical component in these areas. The code should specify briefly how existing programs relate to the code, for example, affirmative action guidelines, occupational safety and health regulations, and environmental quality regulations. By including these, the corporation eliminates the potential problem of a conflict in responsibility between the ethics committee, which is the corporate enforcer of the company code, and the staff officer in charge of the specific program or regulation. The code should not and cannot be a substitute for existing programs. Rather, inclusion in the code would give greater emphasis to the programs, highlight their ethical nature, and avoid possible bureaucratic confusion.

Communication. The third major section of a code should be concerned with comprehensive communication. This could be achieved through periodic review of the code and through a general communiqué from the CEO to each employee. This communiqué should explain the code and request feedback. There should be a two-way flow of communication between the ethics committee, including the CEO, and middle management. A multilingual printing (especially for multinational corporations) and corporatewide distribution are essential. The firm should periodically review its code and corporate practices (probably annually), with participation of as many corporate levels as possible (especially middle management). The code should be distributed frequently to employees newly hired and acquired through mergers. Finally, a board-level ethics committee should be established, and communication of the code should be one of its primary functions.

Enforcement. The corporate code of ethics should give the ethics committee enforcement powers.

There should be a system of positive reinforcement. Incentives such as recognition, appreciation, commendation (already implemented in some firms), and possibly monetary rewards are examples. In cases of unethical behavior, there should be provision for the ethics committee to correct and punish. Within the limits of the law, the code should allow for investigation, judgment, and similar responses to violations.

In short, the code should be enforced through disciplinary measures delineated in a corporate policy statement *and* through positive rewards for ethical actions.

Ethics Committee Essential

Enforcement will be ineffective without a board-level ethics committee to further the involvement of *ethics* in daily corporate operations. It should provide the board of directors with a group of advisors well versed in the ethical issues of the company.

Composition. The committee should consist of a balance of internal and external directors. This balance is critical, as it has been recognized by the courts as desirable and beneficial to the corporate decision-making process.

In *Fogel* v. *Chesnutt,* a federal appeals court upheld a decision imposing liability on internal directors, but it observed that if they had reviewed their actions with external directors and secured the latter's advance approval, liability would have been unlikely. This case was heard under the

Investment Company Act, which requires that external directors be on the board. However, this practice would seem sensible whenever external directors are available. A mixture of internal and external directors provides for a sense of realism and is viewed favorably by the courts.

The knowledge of the company possessed by internal directors and the independence of external directors should lead to a more effective ethics committee. There should be a sensitivity to the vested interest each internal director has in the company and in his or her particular department. The balance within the committee should temper any prejudices and help overcome the weaknesses.

Another area of consideration for an ethics committee is the role of the company's CEO, who should have at least an *ex officio* role. The CEO should not simply be included because of his or her corporate position, but on the merit of personality, concern for ethics, and business skills. For example, Robert Cushman, CEO of the Norton Company, was found to be outstanding in all three areas by his board of directors and was asked to chair the firm's ethics committee.

In general, the size of the committee should be manageable (three to seven members); additional personnel may be invited to meetings to share their knowledge. Committee members should be selected by the board of directors on the basis of their concern for ethics, their ability to work with others having different opinions, and their expertise. Members should bring to the committee various abilities and approaches toward institutionalizing ethics in the corporation.

Resources. If a corporation is dedicated to institutionalizing ethics, the committee should be given adequate assistance, preferably through access to the regular staff or on an ad hoc basis. The primary function of the staff should be to assist the ethics committee in its activities—to communicate, investigate, and enforce the company code of ethics.

Functions. The ethics committee members should have eight primary functions: attend meetings to discuss ethical issues, probably semiannually; clarify the grey areas of ethics, as stipulated in the code; communicate the code to all corporate managers and employees; investigate possible violations; enforce the code through sanctions; reward or discipline code compliers or violators; review and revise the code based on annual corporate reviews by management and on the changing business climate; and report to the board of directors on all committee actions.

Areas of Concern. The ethics committee should be concerned primarily with those issues included in the corporate code of ethics. The committee also should work with the staff of existing programs related to the code. It would be beneficial for the ethics committee to develop a working agreement with each representative of the company's social/ethical programs, such as the coordinator of the affirmative action program, the antitrust compliance legal expert, and so forth. This agreement should entail an exchange of research expertise and cooperation in any investigation of unethical practices.

Sanctions. The sanctions the ethics committee can apply should be delineated in the code of ethics and should enable the committee to fulfill its eight primary functions. If additional or different powers are necessary, the committee should submit the appropriate recommendations for code changes to the board of directors.

Pitfalls. There are numerous pitfalls the corporate ethics committee must avoid. For example, integrating ethics into corporate decision making should not be viewed as a short-term consideration; nor should ethics be seen as the *sole* criterion for the firm's decisions. Corporations should recognize ethics as one criterion for daily business operations, including legal, financial, and marketing decisions.

A company should avoid the false comfort of merely formulating and adopting a code of ethics. A code needs continuous change and revision; it should not be written, approved, and then filed and forgotten.

A code should be observed, and a company should avoid the pitfall of creating a committee that is inoperable due to its lack of sanctions.

Finally, the corporation that has begun to institutionalize ethics should avoid the pitfall of seeking immediate, tangible results. The integration of ethics into corporate decision making is a slow and subtle process. The corporation should stand by its convictions and allow the institutionalization to occur.

DEVELOPMENT OF AN ETHICS MODULE

A corporation could further its efforts to institutionalize ethics by establishing an ethics training program within its management development program. Such a module need not be elaborate or expensive. The corporate ethics committee could determine the framework within which designated levels of managers would participate on a semi-annual or quarterly basis. A coordinator of these sessions may be called for.

Coordinator and Participants. The coordinator should be versed in basic ethical theory and in the ethical values pertinent to daily business operations. It may be profitable to recruit this individual from outside the firm to avoid any conflict of interest and to gain a fresh viewpoint. Participants could be selected by the corporate ethics committee from middle and lower management, with emphasis on those who appear to be moving up the organizational ladder.

Procedure. A procedure for these training sessions is outlined below. First, participants could describe ethical dilemmas they have confronted in their jobs. Second, these descriptions could be sent to the coordinator a few weeks before the group meets to allow time to evaluate them. Third, the group could meet for a roundtable discussion of the cases. The ethical values involved in these dilemmas, the ethical conflicts evident to the managers, and alternative actions could be discussed. Fourth, the session need not formulate specific solutions, but develop ethical guidelines for the managers to consider when confronted with similar issues.

Top management should follow up these sessions by requesting evaluations from participants, including recommendations for additions to or deletions from the corporate code of ethics.

Advantages. The advantages of the training module have already been mentioned, but to summarize: (1) An ethics module within the management development program could aid middle and lower management by reviewing the ethical content of the decisions they must make each day; (2) the module could assist managers in discovering new or better ways to deal with these decisions; (3) the module could benefit the corporate ethics committee by pointing out areas in the code that need review or revision; and (4) the module could further institutionalize ethics into the corporate decision-making structure.

SUMMARY

The business climate appears ripe for the institutionalization of ethics into each corporation's decision-making process. This can be done through the three principal means described in this article: a code of ethics, an ethics committee, and ethics training within the firm's management development program. While these methods have widespread application, each corporation is unique and should adapt these methods to its environment and size. This endeavor is essential if a firm is to become a responsible citizen. The 1980s will require this characteristic.

Note

1. Charles W. Battey, *Tempo,* a Touche Ross publication, 26, No. 2, 1980.

BUSINESS CODES AND ECONOMIC EFFICIENCY

Kenneth J. Arrow

This paper makes some observations on the widespread notion that the individual has some responsibility to others in the conduct of his economic affairs. It is held that there are a number of circumstances under which the economic agent should forgo profit or other benefits to himself in order to achieve some social goal, especially to avoid a disservice to other individuals. For the purpose of keeping the discussion within bounds, I shall confine my attention to the obligations that might be imposed on business firms. . . . Is it reasonable to expect that ethical codes will arise or be created? . . . This may seem to be a strange possibility for an economist to raise. But when there is a wide difference in knowledge between the two sides of the market, recognized ethical codes can be, as has already been suggested, a great contribution to economic efficiency. Actually we do have examples of this is our everyday lives, but in very limited areas. The case of medical ethics is the most striking. By its very nature there is a very

From "Social Responsibility and Economic Efficiency" by Kenneth J. Arrow, in *Public Policy,* vol. XXI, no. 3, Summer 1973. Copyright © 1973 by the President and Fellows of Harvard College. Reprinted by permission of John Wiley & Sons, Inc.

large difference in knowledge between the buyer and the seller. One is, in fact, buying precisely the service of someone with much more knowledge than you have. To make this relationship a viable one, ethical codes have grown up over the centuries, both to avoid the possibility of exploitation by the physician and to assure the buyer of medical services that he is not being exploited. I am not suggesting that these are universally obeyed, but there is a strong presumption that the doctor is going to perform to a large extent with your welfare in mind. Unnecessary medical expenses or other abuses are perceived as violations of ethics. There is a powerful ethical background against which we make this judgment. Behavior that we would regard as highly reprehensible in a physician is judged less harshly when found among businessmen. The medical profession is typical of professions in general. All professions involve a situation in which knowledge is unequal on two sides of the market by the very definition of the profession, and therefore there have grown up ethical principles that afford some protection to the client. Notice there is a mutual benefit in this. The fact is that if you had sufficient distrust of a doctor's services, you wouldn't buy them. Therefore the physician wants an ethical code to act as assurance to ehe buyer, and he certainly wants his competitors to obey this same code, partly because any violation may put him at a disadvantage but more especially because the violation will reflect on him, since the buyer of the medical services may not be able to distinguish one doctor from another. A close look reveals that a great deal of economic life depends for its viability on a certain limited degree of ethical commitment. Purely selfish behavior of individuals is really incompatible with any kind of settled economic life. There is almost invariably some element of trust and confidence. Much business is done on the basis of verbal assurance. It would be too elaborate to try to get written commitments on every possible point. Every contract depends for its observance on a mass of unspecified conditions which suggest that the performance will be carried out in good faith without insistence on sticking literally to its wording. To put the matter in its simplest form, in almost every economic transaction, in any exchange of goods for money, somebody gives up his valuable asset before he gets the other's; either the goods are given before the money or the money is given before the goods. Moreover there is a general confidence that there won't be any violation of the implicit agreement. Another example in daily life of this kind of ethics is the observance of queue discipline. People line up; there are people who try to break in ahead of you, but there is an ethic which holds that this is bad. It is clearly an ethic which is in everybody's interest to preserve; one waits at the end of the line this time, and one is protected against somebody's coming in ahead of him.

In the context of product safety, efficiency would be greatly enhanced by accepted ethical rules. Sometimes it may be enough to have an ethical compulsion to reveal all the information available and let the buyer choose. This is not necessarily always the best. It can be argued that under some circumstances setting minimum safety standards and simply not putting out products that do not meet them would be desirable and should be felt by the businessman to be an obligation.

Now I've said that ethical codes are desirable. It doesn't follow from that

that they will come about. An ethical code is useful only if it is widely accepted. Its implications for specific behavior must be moderately clear, and above all it must be clearly perceived that the acceptance of these ethical obligations by everybody does involve mutual gain. Ethical codes that lack the latter property are unlikely to be viable. How do such codes develop? They may develop as a consensus out of lengthy public discussion of obligations, discussion which will take place in legislatures, lecture halls, business journals, and other public forums. The codes are communicated by the very process of coming to an agreement. A more formal alternative would be to have some highly prestigious group discuss ethical codes for safety standards. In either case to become and to remain a part of the economic environment, the codes have to be accepted by the significant operating institutions and transmitted from one generation of executives to the next through standard operating procedures, through education in business schools, and through indoctrination of one kind or another. If we seriously expect such codes to develop and to be maintained, we might ask how the agreements develop and above all, how the codes remain stable. After all, an ethical code, however much it may be in the interest of all, is, as we remarked earlier, not in the interest of any one firm. The code may be of value to the running of the system as a whole, it may be of value to all firms if all firms maintain it, and yet it will be to the advantage of any one firm to cheat—in fact the more so, the more other firms are sticking to it. But there are some reasons for thinking that ethical codes can develop and be stable. These codes will not develop completely without institutional support. That is to say, there will be need for focal organizations, such as government agencies, trade associations, and consumer defense groups, or all combined to make the codes explicit, to iterate their doctrine and to make their presence felt. Given that help, I think the emergence of ethical codes on matters such as safety, at least, is possible. One positive factor here is something that is a negative factor in other contexts, namely that our economic organization is to such a large extent composed of large firms. The corporation is no longer a single individual; it is a social organization with internal social ties and internal pressures for acceptability and esteem. The individual members of the corporation are not only parts of the corporation but also members of a larger society whose esteem is desired. Power in a large corporation is necessarily diffused; not many individuals in such organizations feel so thoroughly identified with the corporation that other kinds of social pressures become irrelevant. Furthermore, in a large, complex firm where many people have to participate in any decision, there are likely to be some who are motivated to call attention to violations of the code. This kind of check has been conspicuous in government in recent years. The Pentagon Papers are an outstanding illustration of the fact that within the organization there are those who recognize moral guilt and take occasion to blow the whistle. I expect the same sort of behavior to occur in any large organization when there are well-defined ethical rules whose violation can be observed.

One can still ask if the codes are likely to be stable. Since it may well be possible and profitable for a minority to cheat, will it not be true that the whole system may break down? In fact, however, some of the pressures work in the other direction. It is clearly in the interest of those who are obeying the codes to enforce them, to call attention to violations, to use the ethical and social pressures of the society at large against their less scrupulous rivals. At the same time the value of maintaining the system may well be apparent to all, and no doubt ways will be found to use the assurance of quality generated by the system as a positive asset in attracting consumers and workers.

One must not expect miraculous transformations in human behavior. Ethical codes, if they are to be viable, should be limited in their scope. They are not a universal substitute for the weapons mentioned earlier, the institutions, taxes, regulations, and legal remedies. Further, we should expect the codes to apply in situations where the firm has superior knowledge of the situation. I would not want the firm to act in accordance with some ethical principles in regard to matters of which it has little knowledge. For example, with quality standards which consumers can observe, it may not be desirable that the firm decide for itself, at least on ethical grounds, because it is depriving the consumer of the freedom of choice between high-quality, high-cost and low-quality, low-cost products. It is in areas where someone is typically misinformed or imperfectly informed that ethical codes can contribute to economic efficiency.

THE LOGIC, SCOPE, AND FEASIBILITY OF THE CORPORATE SOCIAL AUDIT

John J. Corson and George A. Steiner in collaboration with Robert C. Meehan

The corporation, like the government, the hospital, the university, and the church, is being held accountable to its constituencies and to the general public in an unprecedented fashion today.

This demand is an inevitable consequence of the emergence of the compact society in which many more units—business firms, governments, hospitals, colleges, universities, and others—compete with one another in markedly limited living space to serve a people that expect a better quality of life than has previously been available to them. Each unit is being held accountable for contributing to making life safer, more secure, more healthful, more equitable, and more rewarding of honest effort, and to offering greater opportunity for every individual. These two trends (the increasing demand for accountability by the individual unit and the rising

From *Measuring Business's Social Performance: The Corporate Social Audit.* Copyright © 1974 by Committee for Economic Development, New York. Reprinted by permission of the publisher.

expectations as to the acceptable quality of life) underlie the development of the social audit. . . .

Historically, the primary *social* responsibility of the corporation has been to discover and develop goods and services that satisfy the needs of people. The accomplishment of that end—the production of an increasing abundance of steadily improving goods and services—has long been regarded as of such great value to the society as to warrant the earning of profits.[1]

As the basic wants for food, clothing, shelter, and health care of most members of American society have been satisfied, society's expectations have grown to include not only new and better goods and services but other things as well. For example: (1) services of clear social utility that were once provided by government and are now provided by corporations at a *profit;* such services include postsecondary education (e.g., the schools and educational services marketed by Bell and Howell Company) and providing food services for school programs and for aged and invalid persons in their homes; (2) a widening range of amenities, services, and information for employees, consumers, shareholders, and the community, without prospect of profit and at the cost of the corporation.

If the social audit is to catalogue all such activities, verify the costs entailed, and evaluate the benefits produced, it becomes an evaluation of everything a corporation is doing. When the scope is thus defined, it becomes impractical to accomplish a social audit and, indeed, the information it would present would likely be too massive to be useful.

If, on the other hand, the scope of the audit—that is, the activities to be catalogued, verified, and evaluated—is limited, it will not demonstrate to the constituencies the extent to which the corporation's social performance measures up to what the constituents expect. For example, the social audit will not perform this principal function if it is limited to (1) those activities for which a corporation's executives are particularly concerned about accomplishments and/or costs incurred; (2) those activities about which information is publicized to better the corporation's public image.

Therefore, the scope of the social audit (like the scope of the financial audit) is determined by the informational needs of those it is designed to serve—employees, consumers, concerned shareholders, the general public, and those who influence the shaping of public opinion. In the course of time those needs will undoubtedly change, but in the main they will include the need for information about: (1) statutorily required activities (e.g., the provision of equal employment opportunities for minority group members); (2) voluntary activities (e.g., the making of contributions to health, educational, and cultural agencies and the "adoption" of a local high school); and (3) socially useful activities undertaken for the making of profits (e.g., contracting to provide teaching services in the schools).

The key task for the corporation is to specify what activities are of concern to its constituencies at a particular time.[2] It is a difficult task, and new ways and means must be developed to accomplish it. . . .

Few social audits made today embrace the categories of activities that fall logically within its scope as suggested here. The scope of few if any of these audits is determined by the standard of social expectations that has been proposed. The failure to attain this ideal is to be expected at this early stage in the evolution of this form of appraisal. A methodology for identifying social expectations and appraising corporate social performance is still being developed. To indicate the point that has been reached, we will describe ways of determining what society expects of the corporation and examine existing yardsticks for measuring the corporation's performance of various social activities.

Society communicates its expectations in several ways. This is done through the crusading of reformers. It is also done by businessmen with social foresight who by taking advanced steps communicate the needs of society by example. Such examples have been set by Henry Ford when he established the $5 per-day wage in the automobile industry, by George Eastman and Marion B. Folsom when in the 1930s Eastman Kodak Company established its wage-dividend and pension policies, and by International Business Machines Corporation and Xerox Corporation more recently in granting leaves at full pay to employees who choose to engage in community activities.

Group pressures are another means by which society communicates its expectations. The National Consumers League in the 1930s and the United Farm Workers in 1972 communicated what they contended were the expectations of the society by mobilizing consumers to force employers to better conditions for their workers. Strikes, boycotts, sit-ins, and demonstrations have been used to convey other expectations to corporate leadership.

In theory, society communicates its expectations to corporate leadership through the voices of the corporation's stockholders. Many recent stockholders' meetings illustrate both the theoretical process as well as its ineffectiveness. A score of issues ranging from the corporation's efforts to curb pollution and employ women to changing its operations in South Africa have been presented by small, articulate minorities in the form of resolutions for stockholder approval which have been regularly voted down. The presentation of such resolutions by a few stockholders, despite their usual rejection, nevertheless forces corporate management to consider whether society expects it to perform the actions proposed.

Society conveys its expectations most clearly when they are finally enacted into law. Prior to 1935, a few employers provided pensions for employees who had spent much of their adult life in their employ. Unemployment and suffering among the aged during the depression of the 1930s attracted public concern and resulted in the enactment of the Social Security Act. By means of this law, society converted a growing public desire and the example of a few employers into an obligation for all employers. Other examples of such actions are apparent in the labeling requirements and product quality standards set by the Food and Drug Administration and the Federal Trade Commission, in the water quality standards established by the state governments, and in the financial reporting practices stipulated by the Securities and Exchange Commission.

Such channels of information provided the corporation executive with indications of society's expectations.[3] However, much of what is transmitted through these channels (other than actual legislation) is distorted by the opposing views of others in the society, is blurred by emotions, or is simply inaccurate. The executive is thus left with the task of weighing these messages and deciding what expectations have gained general acceptance among consumers, employers, stockholders, and citizens so strongly as to suggest, if not require, that the corporation take action. His problem is one of determining what social responsibilities are of such critical and continuing importance to the constituencies his firm serves as to warrant its acceptance of the associated costs and obligations.[4]

The methodology to make this determination has not been perfected but is now being developed. Staff members of the larger corporation usually have an understanding of the demands as well as threats made on the company at the present time and those that will be made in the future. What the corporation more often lacks is the capacity for objectively weighing its obligation to meet such demands. Yet some larger companies, General Electric Company, for instance, have made such assessments.[5] They have demonstrated that decisions can be made by staff, when guided by clear policy, about the relationship that the corporation strives to maintain to the society.[6] To ensure objectivity the corporation's staff and managers can be aided by market surveys and polls of constituent opinion that provide reliable indications of social expectations. From the results managers then can select those activities they think they should pursue to meet the most urgent needs of society. . . .

Presuming that the scope of a social audit can be determined, what yardsticks are available to measure the costs and accomplishments of activities included in the social audit? Without credible measures of business's social performance the social audit will make little progress. Many business executives hold views similar to that expressed by one respondent to [a] survey, who stated: "Most of the elements involved cannot be quantified in any meaningful way and . . . a balance sheet would result only in an oversimplified representation which might lend itself to puffery." Measures of accomplishment for many activities, as this respondent has accurately pointed out, do not yet exist, and the identification of costs is sometimes difficult. The problems involved in developing measures of accomplishment and in identifying relevant costs are substantial, yet the development of useful measures is progressing.

The financial auditor has numerous acceptable yardsticks for evaluating the financial operations of a business enterprise. They include unit production costs, the ratio of each category of costs to the sales dollar, the current ratio, inventory turnover, the aging of receivables, cash flow analyses, the ratio of net earnings to interest on debt, and others. The social auditor is at an early stage in forging similar yardsticks and faces formidable obstacles in perfecting measures for a number of social activities. . . .

The development of the social audit today is hobbled, as our survey indicates, by confusion as to purpose as well as by difficulties confronted in striving to measure costs and accomplishments. If the social audit is to inform insiders alone, one set of measures focusing on costs and efficiency of performance is needed. If the social audit is designed to meet the demands of outsiders for an assessment of social performance, a different set of measures is required.

If we assume that both needs must be served, the problem of measurement still remains. By definition an audit is a "methodical examination and review," but many businessmen view an audit as necessarily involving quantification, and, as we have stated, the quantification of costs and accomplishments is difficult, the latter more so than the former.

The costs involved in many social activities, although not all, are difficult to isolate. The benefits received by the company itself or those contributed to society are difficult to appraise. For example, what cost/benefit is involved in the maintenance by corporations of deposits in minority-owned and -operated banks? In increasing the proportion of blacks in the corporate work force? If the cost of building a plant in the inner city rather than moving it to the suburbs can be identified, how can the auditor measure the benefits produced for the company? For the community? What is the value to society of contributions to the support of black colleges and universities? Of the service of corporate employees on leave to teach in universities? Of the stimulation of interest in liturgical music?

The quantification that is involved in the financial audit (which conditions thinking as to the nature of a social audit) evolved over many years. Gradually accountants have found ways of quantifying concepts that at an earlier time were dealt with only or primarily as subjective judgments (e.g., cash flow). But even today some important concepts of costs and value are difficult to quantify and are treated in descriptive footnotes to corporate financial statements.

Methods for quantifying accomplishments of social activities are being developed. For those activities that are now required by government, some yardsticks that quantify what is expected have been established; for example, state and federal governments have established air quality and water quality standards. Yardsticks are evolving for some activities that are generally accepted by corporations as responsibilities they should bear, for example, the proportion of net income the corporation contributes to charitable, educational, religious, and welfare institutions. For many activities that corporations have undertaken, no yardsticks of accomplishment are yet available. To illustrate, there are no yardsticks to measure the performance of a company in helping society to improve its transportation systems or to preserve animal life or to recycle materials. . . . Gradually ways must and, hopefully, will be found to evaluate the worth as well as the cost of many activities that are now unmeasurable. . . .

One-half of the companies responding to our survey stated that they made the results of their audit of social activities available only to the company's executives and directors. Less than half the respondent companies made the results available to the stockholders and to the public. Do these practices constitute the kind of accountability being called for?

When one assesses the demands from constituents and the breadth of the social audits being made by the pioneering companies, the answer must be "No." Yet, an increasing number of corporations are now including statements in their annual and quarterly reports to stockholders describing what they have done in particular fields of social activity.[7] A few corporations use newspaper advertising to tell the general public about social activities they are engaged in,* and some others have prepared special reports describing rather comprehensively their activities and have made them generally available.

Examples of such special reports are those made in 1972, 1973, and 1974 by the General Motors Corporation entitled *Report on Progress in Areas of Public Concern*. These reports explain what General Motors did in these years to meet the problems of automobile pollution and automobile safety. They refine and make more generally known the corporation's policy relative to investments in South Africa, its policy and accomplishments in hiring members of minority groups, its efforts to assist minority group members to conduct their own businesses, and its efforts to seek the views of the consumers of its products and act upon their complaints.[8]

Notes

1. Criticisms of the "large corporation as a malevolent conscious force" ignore the central fact that "the large bureaucratized industrial enterprise is the principal tool that we have available for providing those resources which are needed to improve the quality of life." Joseph L. Bower, "On the Amoral Organization," in Marris, *The Corporate Society*, p. 178.
2. For a list of fourteen major constituencies likely to exert pressure that the corporation must consider in its strategic planning processes, see Ian H. Wilson, "Reforming the Strategic Planning Process: Integration of Social Responsibility and Business Needs," in Sethi, *The Unstable Ground*, pp. 245–255.
3. For views that have aided us in developing this analysis, see Dow Votaw, "Corporate Social Reform: An Educator's Viewpoint"; and George P. Hinckley and James E. Post, "The Performance Context of Corporate Responsibility," in Sethi, *The Unstable Ground*, pp. 14–23; 293–302.
4. For an ingenious method for making such determinations, see Allan D. Shocker and S. Prakash Sethi, "An Approach to Incorporating Social Preferences in Developing Corporate Action Strategies," in Sethi, *The Unstable Ground*, pp. 67–80.
5. For a discussion and evaluation of some ninety-seven demands made in this company, see Robert M. Estes, "Today's Demands on Business," in *The Changing Business Role in Modern Society*, ed. George A. Steiner (Los Angeles: University of California at Los Angeles, Graduate School of Management, 1974), pp. 160–178.
6. For an excellent example of such policy, see "What Should a Corporation Do?" *Roper Report*, no. 2 (October 1971), pp. 2–3. This contains an excerpt of the philosophy and goals of the Standard Oil Company (N.J.), now the Exxon Corporation.
7. Fry Consultants, *Social Responsibilities II* (Washington, D.C., 1971), p. 2.
8. Other companies that distribute similar reports for public consumption include the Bank of America, CNA Financial Corporation, Dayton Hudson Corporation, Eastern Gas and Fuel Associates, and Ford Motor Company.

---

* For example, the Chase Manhattan Bank advertised in a number of newspapers and journals that "We helped the Black magazine (*Black Enterprise*) that's helping Black businessmen."

CRITERIA FOR GOVERNMENT REGULATIONS

Norman Bowie

In a penetrating analysis of law (*The Morality of Law*), Lon Fuller identified eight conditions that any legal system must fulfill if it is to be considered a good legal system[1] These eight conditions include (1) laws must be general (laws are not made to apply to one individual), (2) laws must be publicized, (3) laws cannot be made retroactively, (4) laws must be understandable, (5) the set of laws should not contain rules that are contradictory, (6) laws must be within the power of citizens to obey them, (7) laws must maintain a certain stability through time, and (8) laws as announced must be in agreement with their actual administration.

Fuller's eight conditions for a good legal system have such a ring of self-evidence about them that explanatory comments can be kept to a minimum. However, in the course of supplying some explanatory comment, the extent to which government regulation violates these eight conditions for good law will become obvious. The condition of generality is clearly related to the analyses of justice and the universalizability required by Kant's categorical imperative. Rules are not directed toward a single person but rather are to apply to a class of persons. Relevantly similar persons are to be treated similarly. What is a reason in one case must be a reason in all similar cases.

Despite this requirement of generality, much regulatory law proceeds in an opposite direction. Fuller says,

> In recent history perhaps the most notable failure to achieve general rules has been that of certain of our regulatory agencies, particularly those charged with allocative functions. . . . [T]hey were embarked on their careers in the belief that by proceeding at first case by case they would gradually gain an insight which would enable them to develop general standards of decision. In some cases this hope has been almost completely disappointed; this is notably so in the case of the Civil Aeronautics Board and the Federal Communications Commission.[2]

If general rules are essential to good regulatory law as has been argued, then the case-by-case method is inadequate. If the government takes a position regarding water pollution from one of Bethlehem Steel's plants, the president of Bethlehem Steel should be able to conclude that the government will take a similar position on similar conditions at all Bethlehem's plants. Moreover, the president of Bethlehem Steel should be able to conclude that the same position will be taken when the same situation exists at other competing steel plants. If Fuller's description is right, the state of regulatory law is such that the president of Bethlehem Steel could *not* conclude that a similar position would be taken and hence much regulatory law is seriously deficient.

Adapted from Norman E. Bowie, *Business Ethics*, © 1982, pp. 118–124. Reprinted by permission of Prentice-Hall, Inc., Englewood Cliffs, N.J.

The second condition is that the laws be publicized. This condition goes hand in hand with the conditions of generality and stability. One cannot obey the law if one does not know what the law is. Regulatory law does conform—on the whole—to this condition. The regulations do appear in federal documents such as the *Federal Register.* However, any academic researcher who has worked with government documents knows that finding a rule or regulation is often no easy task. Large corporations have legal teams to assist them in knowing what the law is. However, as government regulations grow, the small business houses suffer a distinct handicap in their capability to know the law. To the extent the regulations change rapidly over time, the publicity requirement becomes harder and harder to meet.

Third, laws should not be made retroactively, and generally they are not. The reason for this requirement is clear. Laws are designed to guide behavior. A retroactive law violates the fundamental purpose of laws since it obviously cannot guide conduct. It punishes behavior that was legal at the time it was done. Business leaders complain that government regulators at least approach violating this condition when they threaten firms with penalties for environmental damage when there is no way for the firm to have known that some of its activities were causing environmental damage. A company should not be penalized for damage it caused to the earth's ozone layer when it produced fluorocarbons in the 1960s.

The fourth requirement of clarity is, to many business executives, the condition that government regulations most often violate. Loaded with jargon and bad grammar, these regulations often present a nightmare for highly trained corporate legal staffs and an impossible situation for small companies. An example to illustrate the point:

> 212.75 Crude Oil Produced and Sold from Unitized Properties.
> (b) Definitions. For purposes of this section—"Current unit cumulative deficiency" means (1) for months prior to June 1, 1979, the total number of barrels by which production and sale of crude oil from the unitized property was less than the unit base production control level subsequent to the first month (following the establishment of a unit base production control level for that unitized property) in which any crude oil produced and sold from that unit was eligible to be classified as actual new crude oil (without regard to whether the amount of actual new crude oil was exceeded by the amount of imputed new crude oil), minus the total number of barrels of domestic crude oil produced and sold in each prior month from that unitized property (following the establishment of a unit base production control level for that unitized property) which was in excess of the unit base production control level for that month, but which was not eligible to be classified as actual new crude oil because of this requirement to reduce the amount of actual new crude oil in each month by the amount of the current unit cumulative deficiency.[3]

Fifth, a system of laws that contains laws contradicting one another is inadequate because a situation covered by the contradictory laws requires the impossible. Fuller focuses on the federal Food, Drug, and Cosmetic Act.

> Section 704 of that act defines the conditions under which an inspector may enter a factory; one of these conditions is that he first obtain the permission of

the owner. Section 331 makes it a crime for the owner of the factory to refuse "to permit entry or inspection as authorized by section 704." The Act seems, then, to say that the inspector has a right to enter the factory but that the owner has a right to keep him out by refusing permission.[4]

Actually, the instances of contradiction cited by businesspersons are not so obvious as those in the case given. Most contradictions in laws governing business practice result from two sources: (1) from contradictory rules issued by independent agencies responsible for the same area and (2) from contradictory rules issued by independent agencies on separate matters but when applied in a specific case lead to contradiction.

To illustrate just how complex the issue of the contradictory nature of law can become, consider, for example, the recent Sears suit against a number of federal agencies or officers, including the attorney general, the secretary of Labor, the chairman of the Equal Opportunity Commission (EOC), and seven other cabinet officers and federal agencies. The issue of contention is antidiscrimination statutes. Employers like Sears are not to discriminate on the basis of race, sex, age, or physical and mental handicaps. Yet the employer is required to give preference to veterans. But since veterans are overwhelmingly male, the required preference for veterans is in contradiction with the requirement that no preference be given to sex. Preferences for veterans ipso facto give preference to males. It is reported that

> The Company [Sears] asked the court to grant an injunction requiring the defendants "to coordinate the employment of anti-discrimination statutes" and to issue uniform guidelines that would tell employers "how to resolve existing conflicts between affirmative-action requirements based on race and sex and those based on veterans' status, age, and physical or mental handicaps."[5]

Without judging either Sears' motives for the suit or its behavior with respect to nondiscrimination, the Sears request for consistency is warranted in point of logic and good regulation.

Sixth, laws requiring the impossible violate the fundamental purpose of law—the guidance of human conduct. This point seems so obvious that it hardly needs comment. Yet a tradition is growing in legal circles that clearly violates this principle. Strict liability holds a person or corporation liable for an act even when they are not responsible for it. Fuller points out the absurdity of allowing strict liability to expand so that it covers all activities.

> If strict liability were to attend, not certain specified forms of activity, but all activities, the conception of a causal connection between the act and the resulting injury would be lost. A poet writes a sad poem. A rejected lover reads it and is so depressed that he commits suicide. Who "caused" the loss of his life? Was it the poet, or the lady who jilted the deceased, or perhaps the teacher who aroused his interest in poetry? A man in a drunken rage shoots his wife. Who among those concerned with this event share the responsibility for its occurrence—the killer himself, the man who lent the gun to him, the liquor dealer who provided the gin, or was it perhaps the friend who dissuaded him from securing a divorce that would have ended an unhappy alliance?[6]

Hence, to conform to this requirement of good law, the government regulations of business must rest on an adequate theory that delineates a class of undesirable acts that can result from business activity and then assesses the extent to which business must be shown to be responsible for their acts before being held liable. It may well be, for example, that some activities (blasting) are so dangerous that strict liability should be invoked to discourage the activity in question. However, in many cases strict liability is not the appropriate legal category and business people are quite right in being concerned about its ever-growing application.

Another condition that seems constantly violated in the government regulation of business is Fuller's seventh requirement of constancy through time. Government regulations are in a constant state of flux. One political party replaces another in the White House and the rules of the game change. Let there be a change in the leadership of a major congressional committee and the rules change again.

During the early years of the environmental crisis, companies were forced or encouraged to abandon coal because it tended to be a highly polluting fuel. Now that the energy crisis is here, companies are being encouraged or forced to return to coal to save precious oil. The expenses involved in these transitions are staggering. Something must be done to control the anarchic flux so characteristic of the government regulation of business.

Finally, there should be agreement between the law and the way it is administered. It is one thing to discover what the law is. It is quite another to have the law enforced as written. Business people argue that the federal and state regulatory bureaucracies are filled with petty individuals whose only means of gaining self-respect is by blocking the legitimate plans or aims of business. The time and effort involved in fighting these people discourages the growth of small business and encourages large businesses to provide either a psychic or monetary bribe to clear the roadblocks. There has been much talk about protecting employee rights within the firm. Devices must also be found to protect the legitimate interests of individual businesses from the government bureaucracy.

To balance this criticism, the reader should know that Fuller's eight conditions for good law represent an ideal for a legal system. The reader should also realize that Fuller's ideal works best for statutes; it works somewhat less well for administrative decisions. No legal system can conform completely to Fuller's ideals. Take the condition that the law must be stable through time. Change, including change in the conditions that produced the law in the first place, requires changes in the law as well. Before OPEC and the oil crisis, cleaning up the atmosphere required regulations that discouraged the burning of coal. The oil embargo changed all that. Strategic considerations required encouragement for the use of coal. This shift in policy was expensive, but, given the changes in the world situation, the shift was necessary.

Fuller would agree here. Indeed, that is why he refers to his eight conditions as constituting a morality of the ideal rather than a morality of duty. However, Fuller is right in indicating that departures from these eight conditions do have costs, including the cost of undermining the law itself.

Others might argue that regulatory law is something of a misnomer. Regulatory "law" has less in common with law than it does with judicial decisions or executive decisions. What constitutes the disanalogy, Fuller's critics believe, is that judicial decisions or executive decisions are geared to specific situations and hence have less of the characteristic of generality than do statutes. Fuller might concede much of this point yet insist, correctly I believe, that his eight conditions still serve as an ideal for judicial and executive decisions as well. After all, Supreme Court *decisions* are viewed by everyone as establishing precedents. Perhaps the rule for the pricing of gas at the pumps need not be clear to everyone, but it should at least be clear to the oil companies, shouldn't it?

With these cautions in mind, Fuller's eight conditions for good law are fundamentally sound. Even when Fuller's eight conditions are recognized as an ideal, the fact that so much government regulatory policy stands in violation of them points out a serious inadequacy in the use of government regulation for achieving ethical corporate behavior. After all, government through its judicial system and through some regulation is, as we have seen, a requirement for a stable business environment. Both the law and business are rule-governed activities. When the rules that apply to business or that sustain and protect business violate the conditions for good law, business is harmed. Laws that are not stable do adversely affect incentives and efficiency. Laws that are not clear or that require the impossible, or that apply retroactively, or that are contradictory are unreasonable and unworkable. Both the business community and the public at large have every right to insist that the laws regulating business should conform to the criteria for good law.

Notes

1. Lon Fuller, *The Morality of Law,* rev. ed. (New Haven, Conn.: Yale University Press, 1964), p. 39.
2. *Ibid.,* p. 46.
3. *Federal Register,* Vol. 44, no. 69, April 9, 1979.
4. Fuller, *The Morality of Law,* p. 67.
5. "Sears Turns the Tables," *Newsweek,* February 5, 1979, pp. 86–87.
6. Fuller, *The Morality of Law,* p. 76.

WHY THE LAW CAN'T DO IT

Christopher D. Stone

Wherever the market is inadequate as a control, one can, of course, act to shore it up by law. . . . If the majority of the people believe the market and present laws inadequate to keep corporations within socially desirable bounds, the society can, through its democratic processes, make tougher laws. . . . But I am . . . suggesting that even if the corporation followed the law anyway, it would not be enough. The first set of reasons involves what I shall call the "time-lag problem"; the second concerns limitations connected with the making of law; the third concerns limitations connected with the mechanisms for implementing the law.

THE TIME-LAG PROBLEM

Even if we put aside the defects in the impact of the sanctions, there still remains the problem that the law is primarily a reactive institution. Lawmakers have to appreciate and respond to problems that corporate engineers, chemists, and financiers were anticipating (or could have anticipated) long before—that the drugs their corporations are about to produce can alter consciousness or damage the gene pool of the human race, that they are on the verge of multinational expansion that will endow them with the power to trigger worldwide financial crises in generally unforeseen ways, and so on. Even if laws could be passed to deal effectively with these dangers, until they are passed a great deal of damage—some perhaps irreversible—can be done. Thus, there is something grotesque—and socially dangerous—in encouraging corporate managers to believe that, until the law tells them otherwise, they have no responsibilities beyond the law and their impulses (whether their impulses spring from the id or from the balance sheet). We do not encourage human beings to suppose so. And the dangers to society seem all the more acute where corporations are concerned.

LIMITATIONS CONNECTED WITH THE MAKING OF LAW

To claim society's desires will be realized so long as the corporations "follow the edict of the populus" fails to take into account *the role of corporations in making the very law that we trust to bind them.* This is, incidentally, not an especially modern development or one peculiar to laws regulating corporations. The whole history of commercial law is one in which, by and large, the "legislation" has been little more than an acknowledgment of rules established by the commercial sector, unless there are the strongest and most evident reasons to the contrary. Thus, in many areas such as food, drug, and cosmetic regulation, and, more recently, with respect to the promulgation of safety rules by the Department of Transportation, the government effectively adopts the standards worked out with the industry. Such processes do not always bespeak, as is sometimes intimated, sinister sales of power. The real roots are more cumbersome, more bureaucratic, more "necessary," and therefore more difficult to remedy: The regulating body is considerably outstaffed and relatively uninformed; it knows that it has to "live with" the industry it is regulating; it does not want to set standards that it always will be having to fight to enforce. . . .

Even the specialized regulatory agencies, much less the Congress, cannot in their rule-making capacities keep technically abreast of the industry.

Are employees who work around asbestos being subjected to high risks of cancer? What psychological and physical dangers lurk in various forms of manufacturing processes? What are the dangers to field workers, consumers, and the environment of various forms of pesticides? Congress and the various regulatory bodies can barely begin to answer these questions. The companies most closely associated with the problems may not know the answers either; but they certainly have the more ready access to the most probative information. It is their doctors who treat the employees' injuries; it is their chemists who live with and test the new compounds; it is their health records that gather absentee data. Granted, there are practical problems of getting corporations to gather and come forward with the relevant data, . . . But at this juncture my point is only this: Here, too, it is a lame argument that working within traditional legal strategies, we can keep corporations in line.

In many cases lawmaking is an unsatisfactory way to deal with social problems not because of a lack of ''facts'' in the senses referred to above, but because we, as a society, *lack consensus as to the values we want to advance.* For example, people do not want corporations to deplete natural resources ''too fast,'' but desiring the luxuries that the resources can yield, differ on what ''too fast'' means. Then, too, we who live in the present do not know how to take into account the values that future generations might attach to the resources. Problems of this sort exist everywhere we look. Consider a drug that can benefit 99 percent of people who suffer from some disease, but could seriously injure 1 percent: Should it be banned from the market? People value inexpensive power. They also value a clean environment. These factors point toward construction of nuclear generating stations. But such stations put a risk on life. The problem ushered in is not merely a ''factual'' one in the narrow sense—for example, what is the probability over any time horizon of an accident that will cause such and such a magnitude of disaster. It is more complex still. For even if we could agree upon these ''facts,'' how can we agree upon and factor into our decision the various values involved—the value of human life, the value of a relatively clean environment, those ''fragile'' values so easily lost in the shuffle of a technological society with its computers geared for the consumption of hard, quantifiable facts?

A closely related difficulty involves our increasing *lack of confidence as to causes and effects.* Let me explain this by a contrast. Suppose A shoots B, intending to kill him, and B dies. We place A on trial for murder. Why A? No one who has reflected upon the matter would be so naïve as to suppose that A was the ''sole cause'' of B's death either in any valid scientific sense or from a broader social perspective. As the defense attorney might remind us, ''A was a product of a broken family, an intolerable social environment,'' and so on. What is more, by focusing on A as the legally responsible entity, we are overlooking the effect that a judgment of guilt will have on those other than A. His family will also be hurt by meting out ''justice'' to A. If he was a productive worker, the whole society will suffer to some degree. Thus, when we select A as the focus of legal responsibility, we are making simplifying judgments both on the causality side—supposing him to be the sole cause—and on the effect side—overlooking the effects on others. . . .

There are today, however, a whole host of major social problems that remain so for the reason that we cannot accept the simplified judgments as to causality and effect that traditional legal solutions demand. Take, as example of a major contemporary social dilemma, the problem of "inner-city blight." What entities can we single out for responsibility, either pragmatically or morally? The slum dwellers? Slum landlords? City employers who take their operations to other states? How complex, uncertain, and even counterintuitive are the implications of any particular remedy that we may try. Worse, our uncertainties seem only to increase the more we develop methods and machinery to take into account the variety of factors we are increasingly capable of seeing are involved. A sort of legislative paralysis results—or worse, a legislative panic.

Even in those instances when the relevant facts can be established, and the relevant values are matters of consent, we may be able to agree upon what to do only in the most general way, inadequately for translation into viable legal rules. As the earth gets more and more crowded, and life more complex, increasingly such problems arise. For example, while we can all agree that bad odors ought to be held to a tolerable level in residential or mixed residential areas, it is not easy to translate this decision into enforceable legal machinery. How does one spell out a rule so that those bound by it know how to orient their behavior. . . .

The vagueness problem has even more serious ramifications than appear on first glance. For one thing, the administration of justice in this country depends upon most litigation being settled out of court, and the more vague a statute, the more in doubt an outcome, and thus the more likely we are to find our court dockets crowded with cases that neither side is prepared to concede. A related point is that when standards are vague, the persons against whom they are turned are apt to feel personally and arbitrarily selected out for persecution, victims of men, rather than of the laws. When people—or corporations—feel themselves to have had no fair warning, increased friction between industry and government is likely to result, a development that has numerous regrettable ramifications. (The vagueness of the antitrust laws, real and imagined, is a common point of complaint among businessmen and serves as a justification for the short shrift they would like to give laws and "government interference" generally.) What is more, if the language really is vague, the law is that much less likely to be an effective force in the face of competing, more definite constraints on the organization, such as the "need" to return profits, increase price-earnings ratios, and the like.

One can, of course, try to obviate the vagueness by seeking more and more precision in the law's language. But in doing so we risk making matters considerably worse. There is the possibility that once we have unleashed the regulators to make finer and finer regulations, the regulations become an end in themselves, a cumbersome, frustrating, and pointless web for those they entangle. Second, what all too often happens when legislatures try to turn vague value sentiments into tangible, measurable legal terms is that the rules they come up with have lost touch with the values they were originally designed to advance. There is a fascinating example of this in the area of water pollution. In their study of the attempt to reduce pollution in the Delaware River area, Bruce Ackerman and James Sawyer have shown that the regulators have emphasized dissolved oxygen content (D.O.) as a critical standard—the amount of D.O. in the water being taken as an inverse measure of how badly the water is polluted. What Ackerman and Sawyer show, however, is that if one looks at the values that lie behind efforts to minimize water pollution—boating and swimming, potable water, support of fish life—actually over a broad range of D.O. content, D.O. is an inadequate measure of whether or not any of those values are being advanced. Thus, while D.O. has the attractiveness of being traditionally recognized among sanitary engineers (it is "hard" and computerizable), gearing laws to it makes limited sense, at best. . . .

LIMITATIONS CONNECTED WITH IMPLEMENTING THE LAW

When we do push ahead even in the face of our doubts as to values, our uncertainty as to facts, and the myriad difficulties of fashioning our wants into legal language, further problems lie ahead. Each of them raises its own doubts as to the virtue of a society in which the outer bounds of a corporation's responsibility are established by the limits we can set down through law.

The fact is that a combination of factors, including the increased expectations of today's citizens and the increasingly technical nature of the society, have left our traditional legal mechanisms unsatisfactory to cope with the problems that currently concern people. Consider, for example, the law of torts, the ordinary rules for recovering damages against someone who has injured you. A model tort case is one in which Smith, who is walking across the street, is accidentally but negligently driven into by Jones. Smith falls, suffering internal injuries, and sues for damages. Now, I call this "a model" case because certain of its features make it so well suited to traditional legal recovery. Note that (a) Smith knows *the fact* that he has been injured; (b) Smith knows *who* has caused the injury; (c) one can assess, fairly well, the *nature and extent* of his injuries; and (d) the *technical inquiry* involved in analyzing causality is not too extensive—that is, simple laws of physics are involved, not beyond commonsense experience.

But contrast that model case—a case in which the tort laws may be fairly adequate to make restitution—with the sort of case that is increasingly of concern in the society today. The food we will eat tonight (grown, handled, packaged, distributed by various corporations) may contain chemicals that are killing us, or at least reducing our life expectancy considerably. But (a) we cannot know with certainty the fact that we are being injured by any particular product; (b) it is difficult determining who might be injuring us—that is, even if we know that our bodies are suffering from a buildup of mercury, we are faced with an awesome task of pinning responsibility on any particular source of mercury; (c) we would have a difficult time proving the extent of our injuries (the more so proving the extent attributable to any particular source); and (d) the nature of the evidence that would have to be evaluated by the court is far more complex and technical than that in the "model" case above—perhaps too technical realistically to trust to courts or even agencies to handle. Thus, it seems inevitable that a certain percentage of harmful, even seriously harmful activity is not going to be contained by trusting to traditional legal mechanisms.

Then, too, at some point the costs of enforcing the law are going to transcend the benefits, and the law may not, on balance, be worth the effort. We can, for example, prohibit employers from discriminating on the basis of sex, and if we are using the law merely as a means of declaring social policy, it may make good sense to do so. But if we were to undertake serious systematic enforcement, the policing and prosecution costs (absent a strong sense by the employer that the law is right) would be questionably high. Some of the costs of falling back on law are obvious: administering court systems and staffing administrative agencies. . . . But there are other sorts of less direct "costs" hidden in such a system. There are various sorts of costs that arise from the attendant government-industry friction. A network of rules and regulations, backed by threats of litigation, breeds distrust, destruction of documents, and an attitude that "I won't do anything more than I am absolutely required to do."

The counterproductiveness of law can be extreme. I have already referred to the manner in which threatening directors and officers with legal liability impedes an ideal flow of information within the corporation, keeping potentially "tainting" knowledge away from those with most authority to step in and remedy the wrongdoing. But the law's bad effects on information are more pervasive still. To develop a system of total health care delivery demands not only a proper flow of information *within* pharmaceutical houses, but between the pharmaceutical houses and hospitals, doctors' offices, and coroners' laboratories. Information that doctors and hospital administrators should be regularly developing is, however, a potential source of medical malpractice liability. Because of the law, it may be best not to gather it and keep it on hand. . . .

Let me close by observing that in these and many criticisms of the federal agencies, I often find myself in strong agreement with the so-called "antis." But, in my mind, they fail to draw from their skepticism the correct implication for the corporate social-responsibility debate. If the agencies—or the other public control mechanisms—*were* effective, then it would be proper to brush aside the calls for corporate social responsibility by calling on the law to keep corporations in line. But the weaknesses of the agencies are simply a further argument that trust in our traditional legal machinery as a means of keeping corporations in bounds is misplaced—and that therefore something more is needed.

COST-BENEFIT ANALYSIS AND PUBLIC POLICY FORMULATION

Vincent Vaccaro

Unfortunately for many of us the mention of cost-benefit analysis conjures up a series of negative images: McNamara's whiz-kids and the Southeast Asia war, a Benthamic calculus in the hands of an uninspired bureaucrat or an analytical tool running roughshod over the analysts and the projects under review. Against such a hopelessly bleak backdrop, it almost seems ludicrous to ask whether cost-benefit analysis is adequate to serve as the basis for determining government policy.

Now having said this I shall attempt to discuss the role that cost-benefit analysis does and should play in determining government policy. At the very beginning, let it be clear that I do not believe that cost-benefit analysis alone is adequate as *the,* and I repeat *the,* (sole) basis for determining government policy. Certainly there are other factors and forms of analysis that are germane in determining what policy should prevail on one issue or another. However, cost-benefit analysis does provide " a conceptual structure and set of techniques for relating means to ends, for arranging the various costs associated with each course of action, and for describing, comparing, and assessing possible outcomes" and therefore warrants a central role in the formulation and execution of government policy. At this point, I hasten to add that the version of cost-benefit analysis that I shall be discussing is cost-benefit analysis as *practiced* within governmental agencies (primarily at the federal level) and not as a theoretical construct abstracted from its application within the political process. . . .

I

First, make no mistake about it, cost-benefit analysis is "a formal procedure for comparing the costs and benefits of alternative policies."[1] The words are clear—the purpose of the procedure is to compare only one aspect of alternative policies, not the policies themselves. For that reason, it is inappropriate to expect this analytical tool to serve as *the* basis for comparing alternative policies.

My next three points concern the interpretation of data. The second one is that, although cost-benefit analysis does require that the alternatives be displayed and compared in economic terms, it in no way ignores non-economic considerations, and, in fact, the analyst is *expected* to appeal to non-economic criteria and standards at numerous points in the analysis. Properly done, cost-benefit analyses begin with the definition of the objective, followed by a searching out of hypothetical alternatives for ac-

From V. Vaccaro, "Cost-Benefit Analysis and Public Policy Formulation" in *Ethical Issues in Government,* ed, Norman Bowie. Copyright © 1981 by Temple University Press. Reprinted by permission.

complishing the objectives and then formulation of the assumptions or "givens." . . . These steps precede (in theory at least) any attempts to determine, quantify, display, or compare costs and benefits. Although most discussions of alternatives and assumptions normally found in cost-benefit analyses are devoted to eliminating non-competing alternatives or are devoted to structuring the data that will be considered (that is, the economic data), a good cost-benefit analyst will always include discussions of alternatives or assumptions that cannot be assessed by cost-benefit procedures. The exclusion of such alternatives or factors, rather than eliminating them from consideration by the policy-maker, in fact, flags them as alternatives or factors that must be considered simply because they have not been adequately evaluated in the analysis. It is because cost-benefit theory is sensitive to identifying and clarifying critical non-economic issues that it is a valuable tool for those who must establish and implement our public policies and goals.

Third, the measurement of costs, but especially of benefits, involves interpretation of data in terms of economic theory. What constitutes a benefit? A cost? Whose benefit? Over what time scale? Such questions often depend for their answers upon a given theory or interpretation of economics. . . . Good cost-benefit analysts are extremely sensitive to the problems of "comparing apples and oranges" and have devised numerous methods and techniques that compare or at least measure (through cardinality as well as ordinality) apparent "incommensurables."[2] The important thing to note is that before employing any given cost-benefit technique—for example, option value or donor benefits[3]—a theoretical justification . . . must be presented and defended, and documentation of alternative measures or assumptions must be included. It is because of the requirement for more accurate measurement and complete documentation and justification that cost-benefit analyses are valuable to the policy-maker.

Fourth, the data available to the analyst may not be complete or the analyst may not be "satisfied" with what the data tells us. Here I am not talking about selecting data to prove a point. . . . There are times when a single figure may not accurately depict a given state of affairs or outcome of a course of action—economists will make the point in terms of single versus multiple indicies. Moreover, there may be a question about whether the data is somehow biased by the technique used in gathering or categorizing it—for example, for many public sector, regulatory issues, like urban transit systems, "comparisons of cost-related indicators have been impossible because of wide variations in accounting practices. Different procedures have been followed in assigning costs to different costs categories. Furthermore, estimates about the future or uncertainty about the appropriateness of a given measurement methodology may dictate that a range of values (based on various assumptions) be employed. In this way contingencies can be tested, various expected values for parameters displayed, and intuitive judgments introduced, using a technique called *a fortiori* analysis. Again, the analyst is expected to justify and document all such "interpretations." The introduction of such adjustments flags them as worthy of special consideration by the policy-maker. . . .

II

Certainly cost-benefit analysis has some serious shortcomings, especially when it comes to government policy. Here are some of the major drawbacks or limitations in cost-benefit analysis as it is now used in determining or evaluating policy alternatives.

The first is a conceptual point and in my opinion it represents the most serious to overcome. Cost-benefit analysis is a formal procedure for analyzing policy alternatives involving the use or allocation of the resources of our economy. Thus, its purpose is to assist policy-makers in their fundamentally economic (not political) task of allocating scarce resources among competing alternatives. In other words, the primary objective in cost-benefit analysis is the achievement of allocative efficiency, which means that there is an ''improvement'' in the allocation of economic resources. Most cost-benefit theorists base their definition of efficiency on the Pareto criterion, any change in the social state is desirable if at least one person judges himself or herself to be better off because of the change, while no one else is made worse off by the change.

But this still leaves the question of who should benefit from the distribution unresolved. I shall briefly discuss two issues—distributional equity and the normative force of rights or entitlements. First, to the question of distributional equity.

It is a generally accepted principle underlying the words, if not always the actions, of public officials that those less fortunate economically, physically, intellectually, and so on should benefit from the actions of those more fortunately endowed. Because both allocative efficiency and distributional equity appear to be equally intuitive and compelling in our society, attempts have been made to accommodate both within welfare economics and cost-benefit analysis—for example, by introducing a theory of compensation or by weighting the desired equity formula in some way and *then* applying the criteria of allocative efficiency. These ''shoe-horning'' efforts have not provided a conceptually sound principle of distributional equity needed to co-function with the principle of allocative efficiency. Without meeting this conceptual requirement, cost-benefit analysis alone can in principle never serve as *the* basis for determining government policy in this country.

The question of the normative force of rights or entitlements has recently been raised in discussions of cost-benefit analysis. Simply put, allocative efficiency and its related criterion of Pareto optimality focus upon what constitutes the most economically efficient distribution, but allocative efficiency in no way ensures that those who are entitled to benefit (either morally or legally) from the policy or program will actually be the ones who receive the benefit. Allocative efficiency fails to consider the normative force of rights and entitlements in its calculus and therefore fails to satisfy the minimum criterion for social justice.

Although determinations regarding public policy must respect the normative force of rights and entitlements, I do not see this issue presenting a problem to cost-benefit analysis. Cost-benefit analysis again is ''a conceptual structure and set of techniques for relating means to ends, for arranging the various costs associated with each course of action, and for describing, comparing, and assessing possible outcomes.'' Cost-benefit analysis is not conducted in a legal or moral vacuum. Questions or rights and entitlements and full consideration of their normative force can and should be considered as constraints and are generally introduced in steps 2 and 3 of the analysis. All too often, we tend to forget that cost-benefit analysis is an analytical tool that provides a map of how the policy will be *executed* should it be established, not simply what should be done, and for this reason cost-benefit analysis provides valuable information for the policy-maker (or legislator). Because moral and legal rights and entitlements are to be respected in the formulation of public policy (from the legislative, executive, and judicial viewpoints), their normative force is considered in evaluating costs and benefits of the various alternatives. Again, however, it is the decision-maker who decides, not the model; and the main focus of the public sector decision-maker is practical: will it work? . . .

How good are the studies being done? The quality of a study is directly related to three factors: the strength of the economic theory underlying cost-benefit analysis; the quality of the data available; and the quality of the analyst.

On the first point, as I have mentioned above, there are still many shortcomings and weaknesses of cost-benefit analysis, but the conceptual foundation and critical issues regarding the concept of cost and benefits, the measurement of benefits, estimating the worth of aesthetics and quality of life, cost-estimating methodologies, and the like are being debated and greatly improved. I have presented some of what is underway in section I.

On the second, the availability of data—especially regarding cost—is critical. Unlike the problem of measuring benefits, which is still enmeshed in conceptual difficulties, the primary problem with estimating costs is accessibility. Most cost figures in coke emissions, car emissions, carcinogenic effects, and the like belong to the industries being regulated or threatened with regulation. If the analyst must go to the industry to get the data, the question of its accuracy or completeness is always open. In cases such as the health effects of asbestos or benzine, the problem of projecting twenty or thirty years into the future or extracting data from the past rears its head.

On the third point, one of my pet concerns is: How good are the analysts? The entire gamut is covered, from exceptionally good to grossly incompetent. I think that it should be obvious by now that cost-benefit analysts must be innovative and creative thinkers who can deal effectively with economic and non-economic issues and not merely self-serving or obsequious, number-crunching drones. Some would suggest that outside consultants from highly respected research institutes would provide the safeguards needed (objectivity, professionalism, and perspective). And often they do. But I have come across an interesting example of how not to do a cost-benefit analysis. This study involved a proposed rapid transit system in a major U.S. city and was conducted by staff members of a major ''think tank.''[4] . . . My conclusion is simple: if we are going to use cost-benefit analysis as an effective tool in policy determination and formulation, we must attract and train intelligent and sensitive people to perform the analyses. The criteria used in selecting and developing analysts still leave a lot to be desired.

My last point is that all the work of the economic theorists, data gatherers, and cost-benefit analysts is useless if the policy-maker either cannot or does not take the time to read and understand the analysis. Many decision-makers, unfortunately, would like to see cost-benefit information expressed as a simple ratio on a one-page memo. The problem is that by themselves cost-benefit ratios do *not* provide sufficient guidance to enable one to pick out the best alternative. The proper way to view the cost-benefit ratio is in terms of the incremental ratio of costs to benefits of alternative policies. That is not a simple task by itself and does not include all the noneconomic issues "flagged" by the analyst, a point I raised in section I.

III

Several issues arise regarding the economic evaluation of public policy formulation that I shall now touch upon briefly. I shall not in this section attempt to do more than introduce some concerns and hope to provide a springboard for future discussions.

First, a need exists for determinations concerning those rights and principles that are fundamental to public policy formulation in the United States today. I have already discussed the issue of the adequacy of the Pareto criterion, the notion of distributional equity and the normative force of rights. In addition, there are a host of other issues that appear to be assuming the status of "informal" rights or principles, if I can coin a phrase: for example, the quality of the working environment, say, regarding benzine and coke emissions, the "no safe" principle regarding carcinogens in foods, esthetic integrity of rivers, forests, and the like, the quality of leisure or retirement, quality of life for the handicapped, and the "no benefit is too small or too costly" slogan regarding health care. Analysis of these concepts has barely begun. Likewise, it is about time that the United States formally establish certain national priorities, say, for air pollution abatement or minimum income, and require that these priorities be weighed in all regulatory or other cost-benefit analyses. Without some agreement about the meaning and relative importance of such issues, economic and other analytical methodologies will always produce "disputed" results. (National priorities are not that far removed from national needs, and "national needs" are defined in sixteen broad areas that provide a coherent and comprehensive basis for analyzing and understanding the U.S. budget for fiscal year 1980.)

The second regards the value of competing or supplemental (reinforcing) economic approaches, such as cost-effectiveness analysis, risk assessment, risk-benefit analysis, cost-benefit analysis, and to a limited extent inflationary impact assessment and regulatory analysis. Each approach has its own conceptual framework and evaluates policy alternatives in light of that framework. For example, cost-benefit analysis requires that decision-makers establish both societal goals and the means for achieving the goals as a basis for accomplishing cost-benefit comparisons. Cost-effectiveness analysis begins with the assumption that societal goals are established and reduces the *analytical* task to issues of cost and technical feasibility. Risk assessment, on the other hand, attempts to estimate how likely it is that some hazard will occur, how many people will be affected and in what way, and what steps can and to some extent should be taken to avert it. Its bottom line is an estimate of the extent to which the public fears or is willing to tolerate a particular risk (or is willing to tolerate lower levels of risk). Decisions must be made (presumably at the federal level) regarding what analytical technique or methodology is most appropriate for a given type of policy question.[5] Such (federal) decisions will also provide a basis for ensuring industry-wide, consistent collection of desired data.

A third issue deals with the need for non-economic and quasi-economic techniques or approaches. Here, one might include technology assessment, regulatory analysis, legal analysis, environmental impact assessment, policy evaluation, and political impact assessment. In addition, even ethical analyses are being proposed, and, in my opinion, such ethical analyses will provide needed insight into establishing national priorities and may possibly provide guidance in determining weights to be assigned in ordering the priorities. Through discussion of each type of analysis, the strengths and weaknesses of each, and clarification of the interrelationship between and compatibility with the various methodologies mentioned above, it may someday be possible to reach agreement concerning what constitutes an adequate analysis of a public policy issue.

The last issue is one of talent. As I mentioned in section II, the quality of the policy analysts of whatever type depends as much upon the insight and creative judgment of the analyst as it does on the analytical methodology or the data. For this reason, policy analysts must have perspective, interdisciplinary interests, and an ability not merely to analyze but to put parts back together into a coherent whole. Policy analysis is demanding, because it requires the analyst to clarify objectives, make assumptions, choose to include or exclude information, select the proper analytical technique, and consume, interpret, and in certain cases translate qualitative information in one field into quantitative data in another. The pressures on the analyst are great, and the professional demands are tremendous. Unfortunately, too many "analysts" (considering the widespread effects of policy analysis) fall short of the minimum level of competence we would hope for at the federal level. Simply put, we appear to be more worried about the methodological techniques than the analysts applying them. Considering the stakes, the establishment of government policy and the multi-million-dollar price tag, neither can be ignored.

Notes

1. Henry M. Peskin and Eugene P. Seskin, "Introduction and Overview," in Peskin and Seskin, *Cost Benefit Analysis,* p. 1. A similar definition is found in Peter G. Sassone and William A. Schaffer, *Cost-Benefit Analysis: A Handbook* (New York: Academic Press, 1978), p. 3: Cost-benefit analysis is "an *estimation* and *evaluation* of net benefits associated with alternatives for achieving defined public goals" (my emphasis).

2. For an interesting discussion of "measuring the incommensurable," see James Griffen, "Are There Incommensurable Values?" *Philosophy and Public Affairs* 7, no. 1 (Fall 1977): 39–59.
3. See the discussion of option value and donor benefits in Robert H. Haveman and Burton A. Weisbrod, "The Concept of Benefits in Cost-Benefit Analysis: With Emphasis on Water Pollution Control Activities," in Peskin and Seskin, eds., *Cost Benefit Analysis,* pp. 59–64.
4. I have not included any reference to the study or the institution, because I believe the quality of this particular study is the exception rather than the rule.
5. For instance, the cosmetics industry is vehemently opposed to the use of cost-benefit analysis as a basis for evaluating the industry's practices and policies. It believes that risk assessment is most appropriate and that prospective customers or users should be advised of health risks and then allowed to make their own choices (willingness to pay).

COST-BENEFIT ANALYSIS: AN INADEQUATE BASIS FOR HEALTH, SAFETY, AND ENVIRONMENTAL REGULATORY DECISIONMAKING

Michael S. Baram

INTRODUCTION

This Article critically reviews the methodological limitations of cost-benefit analysis, current agency uses of cost-benefit analysis under statutory requirements, the impact of recent Executive orders mandating economic balancing analyses for all major regulatory agency decisions, and agency efforts to structure their discretion in the use of cost-benefit analysis. The Article concludes that if the health, safety, and environmental regulators continue to use cost-benefit analysis, procedural reforms are needed to promote greater accountability and public participation in the decisionmaking process. Further, to the extent that economic factors are permissible considerations under enabling statutes, agencies should conduct cost-effectiveness analysis, which aids in determining the least costly means to designated goals, rather than cost-benefit analysis, which improperly determines regulatory ends as well as means. . . .

METHODOLOGICAL ISSUES IN REGULATORY USES OF COST-BENEFIT ANALYSIS

Inadequate Identification of Costs and Benefits of Proposed Action

. . . One of the first steps in cost-benefit analysis is identifying the implications of regulatory options. Forecasting techniques notoriously fail to identify the possible primary, secondary, and tertiary consequences of a proposed action—particularly if that action sets a standard with diffuse health or environmental consequences that extend geographically and temporally. For example, analysts have great difficulty estimating the specific social and economic costs and benefits of regulatory options for controlling carcinogens. Cost-benefit analysis "offers no protection against historically bad assumptions. . . .[F]oolproof techniques for forecasting unforeseen consequences are by definition nonexistent."

The problem of inadequate or impossible measurement of attributes is related to the deficiencies of forecasting techniques. For instance, the "skimpy science" of toxicity is an acknowledged problem for regulatory officials seeking to measure costs and benefits of possible regulatory options for the control of toxic substances. Without the knowledge, techniques, trained personnel, and funds to measure these factors adequately, gross error in estimation may result. Similarly, many environmental effects, such as changes in ecosystems, cannot be estimated with confidence because no acceptable method exists to measure these attributes.

Furthermore, characterization of attributes may be problematic. An attribute deemed a benefit by an agency official may pose the problem of beneficiaries who do not desire the benefit or who do not even consider the attribute to be a benefit. For example, "cheap energy" is normally characterized as a benefit in a proceeding considering the construction of an energy facility. It may, however, be immaterial to those who have enough energy, or may be viewed as a cost to proponents of resource conservation.

Even if costs and benefits are identified, they may not be included in subsequent analysis for pragmatic reasons. Attributes may be too costly or too complex to measure. Exclusion may be based on a tenuous causal connection between the planned action and the possible attribute, as with the predicted probabilities of secondary or tertiary effects of a proposed agency action. Identified attributes also may be excluded for self-serving reasons. For example, if consideration of a possible disastrous consequence of a regulatory decision would tilt the outcome of the analysis against a favored agency action, it might be omitted from the final balancing process.

Quantifying the Value of Human Life and Other Traditionally Unquantifiable Attributes

Cost-benefit analysis works best when (1) a socially accepted method, such as market pricing, is available to measure the costs and benefits, and (2) the measurement can be expressed in dollars or some other commensurable unit. Regulatory agencies using cost-benefit analysis face a critical problem when confronted with attributes that defy traditional economic valuation.

Analysts are well aware of these problems. Some refrain from placing their own values on immeasurable attributes and redirect their analyses. More typically, analysts recommend cautious use of cost-benefit analysis. Inconclusive analyses of valuation difficulties in cost-benefit literature reflect the hope that the problem will fade or be forgotten. For instance, although Stokey and Zeckhauser maintain that the complexity and importance of measuring intangible costs and benefits should not be underestimated, they ultimately conclude that perhaps quantification should be consciously postponed.

> In some cases, it may be best to avoid quantifying some intangibles as long as possible, carrying them along instead in the form of a written paragraph of description. Maybe we will find that the intangible considerations point toward the same decision as the more easily quantified attributes. Maybe one or a few of them can be adequately handled by a decision-maker without resort to quantification. We will find no escape from the numbers. . . . Ultimately the final decision will implicitly quantify a host of intangibles; there are no incommensurables when decisions are made in the real world.[1]

This use of cost-benefit analysis is morally and intellectually irresponsible.

Today, a number of agencies assign monetary values to human life. The Nuclear Regulatory Commission (NRC) uses a value of $1,000 per whole-body rem in its cost-benefit analysis. This figure, multiplied by the number of rems capable of producing different types of deaths, provides dollar values for human life. The Environmental Protection Agency's Office of Radiation Programs establishes its environmental radiation standards at levels that will not cost more than $500,000 for each life to be saved. The Consumer Product Safety Commission uses values ranging from $200,000 to $2,000,000 per life in its analyses.

But the fundamental issue is whether cost-benefit analysis is appropriate at all. Without an answer to this question from Congress or the courts, consideration turns to lesser issues: the proper method of valuation, the substantive basis for valuation (possibly relying on insurance statistics, jury awards, or potential lifetime earnings), and the extent agencies should articulate these issues and provide procedures for participation in the valuation process.

To date, agencies have expressed surprisingly little concern about these unresolved problems associated with cost-benefit analysis. Although officials deny valuing unquantifiable factors, these valuations are implicit in any cost-benefit based policy decision involving risks to human life. Responsible decisionmaking demands that implicit valuations be acknowledged and addressed explicitly. . . .

Improper Distribution of Costs and Benefits

Every regulatory decision on health, safety, or environmental problems results in costs and benefits that will be distributed in some pattern across different population sectors, and in many cases, over several generations. For example, a decision to allow the commercial distribution of a toxic substance may result in economic benefits to the industrial users, their shareholders and employees, and consumers. It may also result, however, in adverse health effects and property damage to plant employees and those living near the plant. In addition, future generations may suffer mutagenic health effects or the depletion or pollution of natural resources.

Analysts and decisionmakers using cost-benefit analysis recognize these implications. Nonetheless, in the absence of public policy directives, analysts frequently apply personal assumptions about the allocation of costs and benefits while calling for objective "fairness" in dealing with distributional problems. . . .

Such earnest analytical approaches to determining fair distributions of costs and benefits ignore constitutional precepts underlying public sector decisionmaking. Constitutional guarantees of due process, equal protection, property rights, and representative government should carry greater weight in solving the distributional problem than assumptions about fairness developed by economists and analysts.

Issues of temporal distribution, involving the allocation of costs and benefits for future generations, transcend even these constitutional values. Future generations possess neither present interests nor designated representatives to advance those interests. Our laws and values favor current benefits to those that accrue later. Cost-benefit analysis also reflects a preference for current benefits over future ones. Distribution over time, therefore, like the discount rate, is essentially an ethical issue for the nation. The assumptions that analysts must make about temporal distributions in using cost-benefit analysis are inadequate precisely because analysts, and not society, have made them.

Promoting Self-Interest and Other Analytical Temptations

Users of cost-benefit analysis can easily play a "numbers game" to arrive at decisions that promote or justify agency actions reached on other grounds. The purportedly objective framework of cost-benefit analysis can be used to promote rather than to analyze options by manipulating the discount rate, assigning arbitrary values to identified costs and benefits, excluding costs that would tilt the outcome against the preferred option, and using self-serving assumptions about distributional fairness. Indeed, the very use of cost-benefit analysis leads some observers to conclude that the action under consideration is scheduled for approval. Even self-corrective measures are suspect. For example, the use of safety factors ostensibly chosen to avoid certain effects may prove to be a facile solution that does not alter the preferred analytical result if these factors are determined only *after* completing a preliminary analysis. Furthermore, these factors are usually based on technical estimates and do not properly consider the value-laden aspects of large, irreversible risks.

In addition, the "technology-forcing function" of regulatory programs can be stifled by limited technical and economic information. Governmental officials must often rely on the regulated industry for news of recent technological developments. Industry information is likely to be unduly pessimistic about the costs, reliability, and availability of new techniques. Thus, cost-benefit analysis based upon industrial information may become a mechanism for economically convenient regulation that tends to perpetuate the technological status quo. This result is particularly predictable when regulatory agencies have not defined their objectives. If such objectives were established initially, they would "drive" the regulatory process and more readily force development of new technology.

Special Problems of Accountability

The use of cost-benefit analysis raises new issues in addition to the usual problems of ensuring agency accountability to the courts, Congress, the President, and the public. Certainly the jargon, presumably objective numbers, and analytical complexities of cost-benefit analysis obscure the subjective assumptions, uncertain data, and arbitrary distributions and valuations of the decisionmaking process, thereby preventing meaningful review of agency activity. Agency uses of cost-benefit analysis tend to promote the role of experts and diminish the participatory and review roles of nonexperts.

Senator Muskie has voiced his concern about agencies including ''questionable benefits'' that can make projects appear ''economically sound.''[2] He has called for evaluating projects at different stages of completion ''to find if the validity of benefits claimed at project authorization can be reaffirmed during and after construction.''[3] No governmental agency has adopted this approach despite its obvious value in improving subsequent uses of cost-benefit analysis.

In its cost-benefit analysis of nuclear reactor licensing decisions, NRC estimates the population that will live near the reactor site in the future. Yet neither NRC nor any other governmental body attempts to control actual population growth in the areas surrounding nuclear plants. Thus the estimated cost-benefit basis for approving a proposed activity is not used as a planning tool for maintaining predicted costs and benefits once the activity is undertaken. The actual costs and benefits consequently may vary considerably from those projected in the analysis.

Additionally, the combination of fragmented regulatory jurisdiction over pervasive problems and increased agency reliance on cost-benefit analysis ultimately leads to increased societal risk. For example, a trace metal such as mercury constitutes a health and environmental quality hazard. It is regulated by several agencies, including the Environmental Protection Agency (EPA), Occupational Safety and Health Administration (OSHA), Consumer Product Safety Commission (CPSC), and Food and Drug Administration (FDA). Each agency may permit some activity introducing an additional incremental amount of the pollutant into the environment because the minor amount of calculable human exposure or environmental harm in each instance is offset by a broad range of postulated societal benefits. Even though each agency may be making careful and objective decisions, without overall interagency accounting for the increasing risk to the general population and the environment from these many small decisions, the total societal risk will continue to aggregate.

The above taxonomy of methodological problems reveals the need for a ''best efforts'' approach, fostered by Congress and the President, and administered by the agencies and the courts, to exclude the use of cost-benefit analysis under certain conditions and to resolve rational and humanistic concerns. This best efforts approach should focus on: (1) improving the technical and objective quality of cost-benefit analysis; (2) establishing the limits and societal implications of cost-benefit analysis; (3) improving public participation; and (4) designing more effective measures for congressional and executive oversight of agency practices. . . .

Notes

1. E. Stokey & R. Zeckhauser, *A Primer for Policy Analysis,* (1978), p. 153.
2. Letter from Senator Edmund Muskie to Comptroller General Elmer Staats (August 5, 1977), reprinted in General Accounting Office, *Improved Formulation and Presentation of Water Resources Project Alternatives Provide a Basis for Better Management Decisions,* 18 (February 1, 1978), p. 19.
3. Id.

WHAT'S WRONG WITH BEING REASONABLE? : THE POLITICS OF COST-BENEFIT ANALYSIS*

John Byrne

The idea of governing under the constraint of a benefit-cost test of contemplated public actions is not a new one. Inspired by Jeremy Bentham's argument that, morally speaking, society's problem is the provision of the greatest happiness for the greatest number, it has been urged in one form or another in certain philosophic and economic circles for nearly two centuries. Until recently, however, government by "felicific calculus" had gone largely untried.

The central advantage claimed by advocates of cost-benefit government is that it would discipline public choice so that scarce public and private resources are rationally allocated to their highest valued uses. In this way, it is argued, contemporary social well-being is optimized and future happiness enhanced through resource conservation. To accomplish these ends, though, will require fundamental changes in the governmental decision-making process.

The tenability of this proposal rests upon the tenability of displacing politics with administrative forms in deciding issues of governance. Indeed, the advocacy of cost-benefit government represents an implicit, if not explicit, endorsement of the administrative state. My argument against the use of cost-benefit analysis in deciding questions of public policy is built here around the question of the normative "costs" of cost-benefit analysis and the displacement of politics that is essential to its effective use.

I. THE RULE OF REASON

Cost-benefit analysis is now an established tool of public policy making and evaluation. But while the uses of this mode of analysis are growing, they nonetheless continue to be confined to a limited number of decisions made in executive branch agencies. Legislative and judicial decisions are seldom if ever based on such logic.

Thus, advocates have directed their attention increasingly to the problem of expanding the use of cost-benefit analysis. Not surprisingly, much of the criticism as well as advocacy of cost-benefit analysis has been preoccupied with the appropriateness of this technique to certain classes of problems and to the value implications of its use in identifying solutions. Normative dilemmas, if they are recognized, are seen to derive from the nature of the problem to which the technique is applied, rather than from the implication for governance of its use. For advocates and many critics, the key questions have become: to what range of problems is cost-benefit analysis applicable; and under what conditions would its contribution be optimized. Responses to these questions can be separated into two groups: those which recognize social order as necessarily imperfect and treat cost-benefit analysis as an organizing rather than calculative framework for addressing social concerns, and those which see the use of this technique as part of an effort to establish formal rational criteria in government decision making. The first is characterized by a pragmatic understanding of social problems and deemphasizes the formal features of cost-benefit procedures in favor of the heuristic value of its general logic and perspective. The work of Alice Rivlin and Tom Beauchamp[1] is representative of this approach. The other, more formal approach stresses the precision and ethical superiority of cost-benefit decision making and calls for a decisive role to be played by such analysis. The arguments of E. J. Mishan and David Braybrooke and Peter Schotch[2] are indicative of this latter understanding.

For "informalists" like Beauchamp and Rivlin, the practical conditions of *Realpolitik* urge the use of cost-benefit analysis. The contemporary problem of governance is seen to be one of establishing rules of reason by which to decide issues of public concern in an otherwise untidy world of power and politics. While cost-benefit analysis cannot deliver the ultimate rules of governance, nonetheless this technique is seen as important and valuable for the opportunity it provides for arriving at a rational accommodation of the moral conflicts of an irrational world. In this respect, cost-benefit analysis represents an attractive answer to problems of modern governance offering the prospect of escape from total reliance on power and politics. Thus, for example, Beauchamp claims that cost-benefit analysis is a pragmatic necessity in "real" moral life where rights frequently conflict.

While recognizing that the value of cost-benefit analysis relates to its capacity to yield rational solutions of social problems, "formalists" see no means of using this technique within the contemporary world of politics. For these advocates, no minor modification of the world as it is will suffice. For example, Mishan argues that cost-benefit analysis is not arbitrarily based but draws its justification, as he demonstrates, from "propositions at the centre of welfare economics"[3] which are represented in the "virtual constitution"[4] of society. For precisely this reason, he argues that cost-benefit analysis represents and must be recognized as a constitutional device. As such, it cannot, nor should it be, constrained by the requirements of political concensus; as with all constitutional rules in a democracy, it antecedes consent.

Despite certain differences in the way advocates conceptualize the possibilities and limits of cost-benefit analysis, a common set of conditions for the optimal use of this technique is projected. The social world is generally approached as one in which problems occur or may be treated as occurring relatively independently of one another and are bounded in scope. In some versions, this independence condition is extended to the moral dimensions of social problems as well, with expectations that rights, needs, and preferences can be separately addressed without distorting the nature of the problem. To this condition about the nature of social problems, advocates add important conditions regarding the nature of their solution. The set of alternative solutions to a particular problem is treated, where such a set exists, as an analytically finite and commensurable one. This means that if solutions exist, there is always a superior one. Where no solutions are known,[5] no rational engagement of the problem is available and no public action can be justified. A third set of conditions concerns the issue of valuation. Thus, the costliness of a particular problem and the implementation of its solution as well as the worth of any advantages that might result (beyond the elimination of the particular social problem itself) are regarded as objectively knowable. Of special importance, these values are thought to be available to the analyst without recourse to individuals or communities who might be affected by the contemplated public action.

If these conditions can be met and much of the debate surrounding cost-benefit analysis is absorbed by this question, a distinct political opportunity emerges. Insofar as social problems can be treated as independent and bounded in scope, their solution regarded as a question of optimizing net benefit, and the availability of objective measures by which to evaluate competing solutions confidently assumed, government by right reason would seem to be within our grasp. Historic social conflicts such as those concerning the distribution of wealth and the public provision of basic rights and needs, as well as more recent ones like the protection of the environment, worker and product safety, and balanced economic growth, would all appear to reduce to discovering and implementing the best alternative and therefore to be resolvable through procedures of rational calculation. This is because, in a world made safe for cost-benefit analysis, conflict is the result not of irreconcilable substantive differences, as much of political theory has traditionally argued, but of the use of faulty "decisional premises." Correcting those premises that distort our understanding of the true costs of public services or that encourage suboptimal supply (either over- or under-) of such services should lead in a world fashioned from the postulates of cost-benefit analysis to the virtual elimination of social conflict. And indeed this is precisely what is envisioned by advocates with the advent of the widespread use of cost-benefit analysis.

II. What's Wrong With Being Reasonable

The worlds projected in formalist and informalist visions of cost-benefit government would require a profound transformation in the basis of governance. Fundamentally, these worlds call for the abandonment of rule by consent in favor of the rule of reason. The replacement of consent with reason as the foundation of governance is intended to dispense with the inefficiency and irrationality of politics, but in fact it dispenses with democracy in favor of the administrative state.

a. *Consumer Sovereignty and the Decline of the Citizen*

Government by cost-benefit analysis has no need of a participative citizenry. The processes of public decision making depend in such a model upon the identification of objective values. It is only with their identification that rational solutions can be found. To involve the citizenry in the process of identifying values could only result in contamination of the process, for all they can offer are subjective assessments of their idiosyncratic circumstances. To operate effectively, the world of cost-benefit analysis must be insulated from and pre-emptive of the participation of its citizens.

The arguments in a recent U.S. Supreme Court case covering the 1980 cotton dust standard set by the Occupational Safety and Health Administration (OSHA)[6] illustrate the tension between cost-benefit rule and democratic participation. At issue in the case was whether the OSHA standard could be challenged on the ground that it failed to pass a cost-benefit test. The 1970 enabling legislation mandated the promulgation of a standard which "most adequately assures, *to the extent feasible,* on the basis of the best available evidence, that no employee will suffer material impairment of health" from contact with cotton dust.[7] The American Textile Manufacturers Institute and the National Cotton Council of America, representing industry, argued that the "to the extent feasible" requirement should be interpreted to include the demonstration of net benefit. Not to do so, it was claimed, would extend to the Secretary of Labor and OSHA extraordinary discretion to interpret the requirement as mandating a workplace "utopia" free of risks and hazards based upon the unrealistic and irresponsible ideal of absolute safety.[8] Justice Rehnquist, in a minority opinion supporting the cotton industry position, was even more blunt: the cotton dust standard, he asserted, represents a choice of the balance to be observed between the statistical possibility of death or serious illness and the economic costs of avoiding death or illness; but Congress, by exacting the law without conducting a cost-benefit analysis or defining some other objective standard to determine this balance, abdicated its elected responsibility.[9] A majority of five justices with one abstaining concluded that a cost-benefit test of the cotton dust standard was not required because Congress, in establishing the need for the standard had chosen "to place preeminent value on assuring employees a safe and healthful working

environment limited only by the feasibility of achieving such an environment.''[10] Any further analysis of the standard's costs and benefits beyond
that implicitly performed by Congress when it passed the 1970 Act would
be, in the minds of the Court majority, an obstruction of legislative will.[11]

What this case illustrates is the constitutional upheaval threatened by
the installment of cost-benefit rule. If accepted, the industry argument and
Rehnquist dissent would have required the substitution of purported objective values[12] for democratic participation as the basis of legitimacy for
government policy. But if participation is precluded, what is left of the idea
of citizen? Little more than a glorified notion of consumer. In a world of
cost-benefit analysis, governance is a consumptive good. Citizens decide
whether and to what degree they are satisfied with the products of governance but they have no responsibility for the production of governance or
even overseeing its production. Indeed, the expectation is that citizens
have no substantial interest whatever in such matters beyond the desire for
objective government.

b. Freedom = Objectivity, Justice = Efficiency

Without an active citizenry, indeed with an active intolerance of democratic participation, can such a world be democratic? To characterize
the world of cost-benefit analysis in such a way would be to inflict much
violence on the term. The classic association of democracy and freedom
disappears in that world. For ''free'' in the new world refers neither to the
absence of constraints on choice or action nor positively to the pursuit of
collective goals such as the elevation of the intellectual and moral character
of society, the promotion of social equality, and the like. Instead, freedom
in the world of cost-benefit analysis refers to the appreciation of objective
existence. It is the knowledge that decisions about one's future are based
upon and limited to the facts that makes one free in this world. This is not
to say that the worlds projected by the advocates of cost-benefit government would not be populated by those sensitive to democratic ideals of
freedom. Rather, it is to argue that a world fashioned from the postulates of
cost-benefit analysis is indifferent to concerns with democratic freedom.

If cost-benefit rule is unconcerned with democratic freedoms, it likewise
shows little regard for the need to ground governance in principles of
justice.[13] Cannot such qualities either be monetized and included in rational calculations or treated as peremptory considerations? In one sense,
they can be and many writers have attempted to explain how they can be.[14]
But their suggestions appear to be negatively rather than positively
motivated as a response to the charge by critics that such matters cannot be
adequately incorporated. Little attention seems to have been given to the
question of the desirability of doing so.[15] Most important, the issue only
begins with the question of whether these dimensions can be incorporated
in the cost-benefit calculus. It must also be ascertained: with what relative
confidence can they be included, especially in comparison with what are
considered the non-normative dimensions of policy issues; and at what cost
to our understanding of the role and importance of these considerations
would this be done?

In a society governed by right reason, government is held accountable for the delivery of policies of maximum yield relative to the amount of resources used. Government has little to do with the goal of ensuring that public actions are moral, normatively preferred, fair. While such qualities may perhaps be deemed desirable, their "intuitive,"[16] more exactly, normative, foundations prevent them from being included as central commitments in the constitution of rational society.

c. Hypothetical Democracy

Might it not be argued in defense of cost-benefit tests of government policy that democratic attributes can be engrafted onto the decision-making process; that the above criticisms prove only the non-essentialness of democracy for cost-benefit rule, not its incompatibility; and that the real issue avoided by such criticisms is the prosperity of citizens under such rule? That is, are we not overlooking the fundamental importance of the *results* of government—whether the greatest happiness is provided for the greatest number—and that at the end of the day, cost-benefit rule delivers when democracy may not? Something like this defense lies at the center of much of modern utilitarianism.

First, caution should be observed in conceding the compatibility of the democratic graft. As Mishan has pointed out, accommodating democracy may be more costly than avoiding it:

> Decision-making through the political process, especially in a liberal democracy, is time-consuming. Even if the democratic process, alone and unaided, were somehow able to offer to each person the same opportunities and the same combination of goods that he already receives through the market, economists would have no difficulty in convincing people that the substitution of voting mechanisms for the pricing mechanism would take up an unconscionable amount of time and effort.[17]

Democracy's advocates should be equally reluctant to accept its compatibility with cost-benefit rule. Even if certain democratic mechanisms could somehow be warranted as positive and sizable, their function in a government where decisions are based on cost-benefit analysis would be seriously impoverished. For example, representational voting would in all probability remain in the world of cost-benefit analysis, for this mechanism conveniently solves a sticky problem for the new system of governance. As earlier noted, cost-benefit analysis is predicated on the assumption that if normative dilemmas exist, they exist as attributes of the problems engaged and not as attributes of social analysis itself. This being the case, though, how are the problems for analysis to be selected without bias under cost-benefit rule? Clearly, any selection must be normative, for it necessarily will favor one normative dilemma over another. To have some apparatus of analysis determine which problems are investigated and which are not would obviously undermine the very basis of authority on which rational society operates. But "democratic" voting removes at least the appearance of such a problem by transferring normative responsibility to the citizenry and its subjective proclivities. The insidious result is that a democratic mechanism is used to relieve the administrative state of democratic responsibility.

But the fundamental problem with this counterargument is that it is based on a misrepresentation of the nature of democracy. By challenging democracy to yield utilitarian results, it presumes the normative legitimacy of the criterion of net benefit while completely devaluing democratic results. It is as though the choice of democracy were an inherently utilitarian one. The possibility that decisions arrived at through democratic participation and consent could be valued in themselves independently of their economic implications is beyond the grasp of this counterargument. Such a thing simply makes no sense from this perspective. The fallacy of results is a basic one which Weinrib has captured in the following analogy:

> Assume that Jones loves playing golf and plays eighteen holes every Sunday morning. One particular Sunday Jones realizes that he cannot spare the time to play his usual game. Instead he goes out into his back yard, digs a hole, and drops the ball into it eighteen times. When questioned about his peculiar behaviour, he explains, ''Well, since it was impossible to play golf, I decided to mimic what happens when I actually play golf. Golf, as you know, is a game which results in a ball being repeatedly deposited into a hole in the ground. Of course, this is not the whole game, which includes the process by which this result is to be attained. But surely the result is the most significant part of the game, so that is the element which I reproduced. After all, what I was playing was not actual golf (that was impossible in the circumstances), but only hypothetical golf.'' It is unlikely that this explanation will persuade many golfers to try hypothetical golf when circumstances prevent the playing of actual golf . . . (And) a claim by Jones that his commitment to actual golf led him to try hypothetical golf would be regarded as incoherent, since the challenge which is integral to the former is completely lacking in the latter.[18]

To reap the promised benefits of cost-benefit rule, it will be necessary to forego democracy of the actual kind for a hypothetical variety, a bargain not without its costs.

The intolerance of the administrative state to participation and debate on questions of values is traceable directly to the distinctive attribute of this system of governance—its lodging of authority in reason rather than consent. There is no place in the workings of this system for majority votes and minority objections to interfere in, much less withhold legitimacy for, public actions dictated by rational analysis. Cost-benefit analysis and the system of governance it implies depend upon right reason to convince us of the sensibleness of policies selected by its use. In this respect, the achievement of a world in which the contributions of cost-benefit analysis to policy are optimized is the achievement of irresistibility for the decisions and actions of government. It is a world in which we must abandon political choice and participation to gain efficient and unassailable social order.

III. CONCLUSION

The problems of modern governance, moreover, are not mainly administrative and in need of rational definition. They are political, as they have always been, and require the exercise of political will and choice. While such solutions will necessarily be by some measures inefficient, temporary, and confused, this is a small price to pay compared with what has so far been offered as "non-political" alternatives. The rational utopia projected by advocates of cost-benefit analysis ultimately depends upon surrender to the irresistibility of right reason to garner converts. In this respect, the use of cost-benefit analysis to decide matters of governance is by no means a modest proposal that we "enjoy the advantages of the latest intellectual techniques."[19]

* I am indebted to Daniel Rich and Norman Bowie for their helpful comments and criticisms. Preparation of this paper was supported by the Center for the Study of Values, University of Delaware.

Notes

1. Alice Rivlin, *Systematic Thinking for Social Action* (Washington, D.C.: Brookings Institution, 1971); and Tom L. Beauchamp, "The Moral Adequacy of Cost-Benefit Analysis as the Basis for Government Regulation of Research," in Norman E. Bowie, ed., *Ethical Issues in Government,* Philosophical Monographs, Third Annual Series (Philadelphia: Temple University Press, 1981), pp. 163–175.
2. E. J. Mishan, *Cost-Benefit Analysis* (N.Y.: Praeger Books, 1976); and David Braybrooke and Peter K. Schotch, "Cost-Benefit Analysis Under the Constraint of Meeting Needs," in Bowie, *op cit.,* pp. 176–197.
3. Mishan, *op. cit.,* p. 382.
4. *Ibid.,* p. 385.
5. Actually, where the probability distribution of the solution set cannot be accurately estimated.
6. *American Textile Manufacturers Institute, Inc.,* et al. v. *Raymond J. Donovan, Secretary of Labor,* U. S. Department of Labor, et al., *U. S. Law Week,* 49 (June 16, 1981): 4720–4736.
7. *Ibid.,* 4720.
8. In Congressional debate of the bill, this was the principal objection of opponents. See, *ibid.,* 4727–4728.
9. *Ibid.,* 4735: "Congress simply abdicated its responsibility for the making of a fundamental and most difficult policy choice—whether and to what extent 'the statistical possibility of future deaths should . . . be disregarded in light of the economic costs of preventing those deaths.' . . . That is a 'quintessential legislative' choice and must be made by the elected representatives of the people. . . .' "
10. *Ibid.,* 4733.
11. An earlier U. S. Court of Appeals ruling concluded precisely this and its view was specifically affirmed in the Supreme Court majority opinion.
12. In an earlier paper, I argued that the claim of objectivity is unsupportable. See "A Critique of Beauchamp and Braybrooke-Schotch," in Bowie, *op. cit.,* pp. 198–217.
13. Indeed, one proponent of cost-benefit-type reasoning has argued that rights and justice should be administered so as to maximize their market value, thus substituting economic performance for justice as the primary aim of law. See Richard A. Posner, *Economic Analysis of Law* (Boston: Little, Brown, 1972), and also his "Utilitarianism, Economics and Legal Theory," *Journal of Legal Studies,* 8 (1979): 103–140.
14. James M. Buchanan and Gordon Tullock, *The Calculus of Consent* (Ann Arbor:

University of Michigan Press, 1962); Anthony Downs, *An Economic Theory of Democracy* (N.Y.: Harper & Row, 1957); and Posner, *op. cit.*

15. A prominent exception is the utopian writings of Milton Friedman. See his *Capitalism and Freedom* (Chicago: University of Chicago Press, 1962); and *Free to Choose: A Personal Statement,* with Rose Friedman (N.Y.: Harcourt, Brace and Jovanovich, 1979).

16. Braybrooke and Schotch, *op. cit.,* p. 189.

17. Mishan, *op. cit.,* p. 384.

18. Ernest J. Weinrib, "Utilitarianism, Economics and Legal Theory," *University of Toronto Law Journal,* 30 (1980): 321–322.

19. Braybrooke and Schotch, *op. cit.,* p. 196.

LICENSEE RESPONSIBILITY TO REVIEW RECORDS BEFORE THEIR BROADCAST

A number of complaints received by the Commission concerning the lyrics of records played on broadcasting stations relate to a subject of current and pressing concern: the use of language tending to promote or glorify the use of illegal drugs as marijuana, LSD, "speed," etc. This Notice points up the licensee's long-established responsibilities in this area.

Whether a particular record depicts the dangers of drug abuse, or, to the contrary, promotes such illegal drug usage is a question for the judgment of the licensee. The thrust of this Notice is simply that the licensee must make that judgment and cannot properly follow a policy of playing such records without someone in a responsible position (i.e., a management level executive at the station) knowing the content of the lyrics. Such a pattern of operation is clearly a violation of the basic principle of the licensee's responsibility for, and duty to exercise adequate control over, the broadcast material presented over his station. It raises serious questions as to whether continued operation of the station is in the public interest, just as in the case of a failure to exercise adequate control over foreign-language programs.

In short, we expect broadcast licensees to ascertain, before broadcast, the words or lyrics of recorded musical or spoken selections played on their stations. Just as in the case of the foreign-language broadcasts, this may also entail reasonable efforts to ascertain the meaning of words or phrases used in the lyrics. While this duty may be delegated by licensees to responsible employees, the licensee remains fully responsible for its fulfillment.

Thus, here as in so many other areas, it is a question of responsible, good faith action by the public trustee to whom the frequency has been licensed. No more, but certainly no less, is called for.

Action by the Commission February 24, 1971. Commissioners Burch (Chairman), Wells and Robert E. Lee with Commissioner Lee issuing a

Public Notice of March 5, 1971, 28 F.C.C. 2d 409. Commission decision with statements by Robert E. Lee and H. Rex Lee, Federal Communications Commission.

statement, Commissioners H. Rex Lee and Houser concurring and issuing statements, Commissioner Johnson dissenting and issuing a statement, and Commissioner Bartley abstaining from voting.

STATEMENT OF COMMISSIONER ROBERT E. LEE

I sincerely hope that the action of the Commission today in releasing a "Public Notice" with respect to *Licensee Responsibility to Review Records Before Their Broadcast* will discourage, if not eliminate the playing of records which tend to promote and/or glorify the use of illegal drugs.

We are all aware of the deep concern in our local communities with respect to the use of illegal drugs particularly among the younger segment of our population. Public officials, at all levels of government, as well as all interested citizens are attempting to cope with this problem.

It is in this context that I expect the Broadcast Industry to meet its responsibilities of reviewing records before they are played. Obviously, if such records promote the use of illegal drugs, the licensee will exercise appropriate judgment in determining whether the broadcasting of such records is in the public interest.

CONCURRING STATEMENT OF COMMISSIONER H. REX LEE

While the title of the notice seemingly applies to the licensee's responsibility to review all records before they are broadcast, the notice itself is directed solely at records which allegedly use "language tending to promote or glorify the use of illegal drugs. . . ."

Although I am concurring, I would have preferred it if the Commission had not decided to restrict today's notice to so-called "drug lyrics." The Commission may appear to many young people as not being so concerned with other pressing broadcasting problem areas. And to many of these young people (and not just to that segment who use illegal drugs) the Commission may appear as "an ominous government agency" merely out to clamp down on *their* music.

A preferable approach would have been to repeat, with an additional reference to drug abuse of all kinds, our *1960 Program Policy Statement* wherein we stated:

> Broadcasting licensees must assume responsibility for all material which is broadcast through their facilities. *This includes all programs and advertising material which they present to the public.* . . . This duty is personal to the licensee and may not be delegated. He is obligated to bring his positive responsibility affirmatively to bear upon all who have a hand in providing broadcast material for transmission through his facilities so as to assure the discharge of his duty to provide acceptable program schedule consonant with operating in the public interest in his community.[1] [Emphasis added.]

Because of the Commission's expressed concern with the drug problem, I would hope that we could initiate action with other appropriate Federal agencies to require a reassessment by pharmaceutical manufacturers, advertisers, and the media, looking toward the reform of advertising practices in the non-prescription drug industry. *Advertising Age* expressed its concern with the increased use of drugs—both the legal and illegal types—when it stated in an editorial:

> With an estimated $289,000,000 being spent annually on TV advertising of medicines, this serious question is being raised: Is the flood of advertising for such medicines so pervasive that it is convincing viewers that there is a medical panacea for any and all of their problems, medical and otherwise? Are we being so consistently bombarded with pills for this and pills for that and pills for the other thing that we have developed a sort of Pavlovian reaction which makes us reach for a pill everytime we are faced with an anxious moment, be it of physical or psychic origin?[2]

Drug abuse *is* a serious problem in the United States. It is found in every sector of the population, not merely among the young who listen to hard rock music.

I believe the broadcasting industry has made a good start in helping to discourage illegal drug abuse. Many local radio and television stations and the four networks have broadcast documentaries and specials, carried spot announcements, helped to raise funds for local drug abuse clinics and information centers, and have helped to establish "tie-lines" and "switch-boards" where all people can call for free medical and psychological help and guidance. These activities represent "communicating" in the best sense of the word.

My concurrence in this notice, therefore, should not be regarded as a reflection on the good start that I think most broadcasters have made in dealing with this problem. They must continue with even more determination and support from everyone.

Notes

1. *Report and Statement of Policy re: Commission En Banc Programming Inquiry,* FCC 60–970, 20 R.R. 1901, 1912–1913 (July 27, 1960).
2. *Advertising Age* (May 11, 1970), p. 24.

AMERICAN TEXTILE MANUFACTURERS INSTITUTE INC., v. RAYMOND J. DONOVAN, SECRETARY OF LABOR

Justice Brennan delivered the opinion of the Court.

Congress enacted the Occupational Safety and Health Act of 1970 (the Act) "to assure so far as possible every working man and woman in the Nation safe and healthful working conditions. . . ." 29 U. S. C. § 651 (b). The Act authorizes the Secretary of Labor to establish, after notice and op-

U.S. Reports 452 U.S. 490. Majority opinion by Justice Brennan, United States Supreme Court.

portunity to comment, mandatory nationwide standards governing health and safety in the workplace. 29 U. S. C. §§ 655 (a), (b). In 1978, the Secretary, acting through the Occupational Safety and Health Administration (OSHA), promulgated a standard limiting occupational exposure to cotton dust, an airborne particle byproduct of the preparation and manufacture of cotton products, exposure to which induces a "constellation of respiratory effects" known as "byssinosis." 43 Fed. Reg. 27352, col. 3 (1978). This disease was one of the expressly recognized health hazards that led to passage of the Occupational Safety and Health Act of 1970. S. Rep. No. 91–1282, 91st Cong., 2d Sess., 3 (1970), Legislative History of the Occupational Safety and Health Act of 1970, at 143 (1971) (Legis. Hist.).

Petitioners in these consolidated cases, representing the interests of the cotton industry challenged the validity of the "Cotton Dust Standard" in the Court of Appeals for the District of Columbia Circuit pursuant to § 6 (f) of the Act, 29 U. S. C. § 655 (f). They contend in this Court, as they did below, that the Act requires OSHA to demonstrate that its Standard reflects a reasonable relationship between the costs and benefits associated with the Standard. Respondents, the Secretary of Labor and two labor organizations, counter that Congress balanced the costs and benefits in the Act itself, and that the Act should therefore be construed not to require OSHA to do so. They interpret the Act as mandating that OSHA enact the most protective standard possible to eliminate a significant risk of material health impairment, subject to the constraints of economic and technological feasibility. The Court of Appeals held that the Act did not require OSHA to compare costs and benefits. . . .

I

. . . In enacting the Cotton Dust Standard, OSHA interpreted the Act to require adoption of the most stringent standard to protect against material health impairment, bounded only by technological and economic feasibility. *Id.*, at 27361, col. 3. OSHA therefore rejected the industry's alternative proposal for a PEL of 500 μg/m^2 in yarn manufacturing, a proposal which would produce a 25% prevalence of at least Grade ½ byssinosis. The agency expressly found the Standard to be both technologically and economically feasible based on the evidence in the record as a whole. Although recognizing that permitted levels of exposure to cotton dust would still cause some byssinosis, OSHA nevertheless rejected the union proposal for a 100 μg/m^2 PEL because it was not within the "technological capabilities of the industry." 43 Fed. Reg. 27359–27360. Similarly, OSHA set PELS for some segments of the cotton industry at 500 μg/m^2 in part because of limitations of technological feasibility. *Id.*, at 27361, col. 3. Finally, the Secretary found that "engineering dust controls in weaving may not be feasible even with massive expenditures by the industry," *id.*, at 27360, col. 2, and for that and other reasons adopted a less stringent PEL of 750 μg/m^2 for weaving and slashing.

The Court of Appeals upheld the Standard in all major respects. The court rejected the industry's claim that OSHA failed to consider its proposed alternative or give sufficient reasons for failing to adopt it. 617 F. 2d, at 652–654. The court also held that the Standard was "reasonably necessary and appropriate" within the meaning of § 3(8) of the Act, 29 U.S.C. § 652 (8), because of the risk of material health impairment caused by exposure to cotton dust. 617 F. 2d, at 654–655, 654, n. 83. Rejecting the industry position that OSHA must demonstrate that the benefits of the Standard are proportionate to its costs, the court instead agreed with OSHA's interpretation that the Standard must protect employees against material health impairment subject only to the limits of technological and economic feasibility. *Id.,* at 662–666. The court held that "Congress itself struck the balance between costs and benefits in the mandate to the agency" under § 6 (b) (5) of the Act, 29 U. S. C. § 655 (b) (5), and that OSHA is powerless to circumvent that judgment by adopting less than the most protective feasible standard. 617 F. 2d, at 663. Finally, the court held that the agency's determination of technological and economic feasibility was supported by substantial evidence in the record as a whole. *Id.,* at 655–662.

We affirm in part, and vacate in part.

II

The principal question presented in this case is whether the Occupational Safety and Health Act requires the Secretary, in promulgating a standard pursuant to § 6 (b) (5) of the Act, 29 U. S. C. § 655 (b) (5), to determine that the costs of the standard bear a reasonable relationship to its benefits. Relying on §§ 6 (b) (5), and 3(8) of the Act, 29 U. S. C. §§ 655 (b) (5), 652(8), petitioners urge not only that OSHA must show that a standard addresses a significant risk of material health impairment, see *Industrial Union Department* v. *American Petroleum Institute, supra,* slip op., at 29 (plurality opinion), but also that OSHA must demonstrate that the reduction in risk of material health impairment is significant in light of the costs of attaining that reduction. See Brief for Petitioners ATMI et al., at 38–41. Respondents on the other hand contend that the Act requires OSHA to promulgate standards that eliminate or reduce such risks "to the extent such protection is technologically and economically feasible." Brief for Respondent Secretary of Labor, at 38; Brief for Respondent Unions, at 26–27. To resolve this debate, we must turn to the language, structure, and legislative history of the Occupational Safety and Health Act. . . .

The legislative history of the Act, while concededly not crystal clear, provides general support for respondents' interpretation of the Act. The congressional reports and debates certainly confirm that Congress meant "feasible" and nothing else in using that term. Congress was concerned that the Act might be thought to require achievement of absolute safety, an impossible standard, and therefore insisted that health and safety goals be capable of economic and technological accomplishment. Perhaps most telling is the absence of any indication whatsoever that Congress intended OSHA to conduct its own cost-benefit analysis before promulgating a toxic material or harmful physical agent standard. The legislative history demonstrates conclusively that Congress was fully aware that the Act would impose real and substantial costs of compliance on industry, and believed that such costs were part of the cost of doing business. . . .

Not only does the legislative history confirm that Congress meant "feasible" rather than "cost-benefit" when it used the former term, but it also shows that Congress understood that the Act would create substantial costs for employers, yet intended to impose such costs when necessary to create a safe and healthful working environment. Congress viewed the costs of health and safety as a cost of doing business. Senator Yarborough, a cosponsor of the Williams bill, stated: "We know the costs would be put into consumer goods but that is the price we should pay for the 80 million workers in America." Legis. Hist. 444. He asked:

> "One may well ask too expensive for whom? Is it too expensive for the company who for lack of proper safety equipment loses the services of its skilled employees? Is it too expensive for the employee who loses his hand or leg or eyesight? Is it too expensive for the widow trying to raise her children on meager allowance under workmen's compensation and social security? And what about the man—a good hardworking man—tied to a wheel chair or hospital bed for the rest of his life? That is what we are dealing with when we talk about industrial safety. . . . We are talking about people's lives, not the indifference of some cost accountants." Legis. Hist. 510.

Senator Eagleton commented that "[t]he costs that will be incurred by employers in meeting the standards of health and safety to be established under this bill are, in my view, *reasonable and necessary costs of doing business.*" Legis. Hist. 1150–1151 (emphasis added).

Other Members of Congress voiced similar views. Nowhere is there any indication that Congress contemplated a different balancing by OSHA of the benefits of worker health and safety against the costs of achieving them. Indeed Congress thought that the *financial costs* of health and safety problems in the workplace were as large or larger than the *financial costs* of eliminating these problems. In its statement of findings and declaration of purpose encompassed in the Act itself, Congress announced that "personal injuries and illnesses arising out of work situations impose a substantial burden upon, and are a hindrance to, interstate commerce in terms of lost production, wage loss, medical expenses, and disability compensation payment." 29 U. S. C. § 651 (a). The Senate was well aware of the magnitude of these costs:

> "[T]he economic impact of industrial deaths and disability is staggering. Over $1.5 billion is wasted in lost wages, and the annual loss to the Gross National Product is estimated to be over $8 billion. Vast resources that could be available for productive use are siphoned off to pay workmen's compensation benefits and medical expenses." S. Rep. No. 91–1282, *supra,* at 2; Legis. Hist. 142.

. . .

V

When Congress passed the Occupational Safety and Health Act in 1970, it chose to place pre-eminent value on assuring employees a safe and healthful working environment, limited only by the feasibility of achieving such an environment. We must measure the validity of the Secretary's actions against the requirements of that Act. For "[t]he judical function does not extend to substantive revision of regulatory policy. That function lies elsewhere—in Congressional and Executive oversight or amendatory legislation." *Industrial Union Department* v. *American Petroleum Institute, supra,* slip op., at 2 (BURGER, C. J., concurring); see *Tennessee Valley Authority* v. *Hill,* 437 U. S. 153, 185, 187–188, 194–195 (1978).

Accordingly, the judgment of the Court of Appeals is affirmed in all respects except to the extent of its approval of the Secretary's application of the wage guarantee provision of the Cotton Dust Standard at 29 CFR § 1910.1043 (f) (2) (v). To that extent, the judgment of the Court of Appeals is vacated and the case remanded with directions to remand to the Secretary for further proceedings consistent with this opinion. . . .

case 1: The Advertising Code Case

The Advertising Code of American Business was part of a program of industry self-regulation announced September 28, 1971. This program arose in response to mounting public criticism of the advertising industry, to more aggressive action by federal regulatory agencies, and to fears of even greater government control in the future.

In announcing the new program of self-regulation, enforcement was emphasized. Complaints are received or initiated by the National Advertising Division (NAD) of the Council of Better Business Bureaus. During the first year, 337 complaints were placed on the table. Of these 337, investigations were completed on 184. Seventy-two of those complaints were upheld. In every case, the advertiser either agreed to withdraw the objectionable ad or to modify it. Six of the cases which were dismissed were appealed to a higher body, the National Advertising Review Board. Of the six cases, the NARB accepted the decision of the NAD in four cases, but agreed with two complaints. In these two cases, the challenged ads were withdrawn. All complaints were settled within several months. Supporters of the NAD applaud their time record for handling complaints as compared with frequent delays of several years in federal suits. *

The Advertising Code of American Business reads as follows:

1. *Truth.* Advertising shall tell the truth, and shall reveal significant facts, the concealment of which would mislead the public.
2. *Responsibility.* Advertising agencies and advertisers shall be willing to provide substantiation of claims made.

Adapted from "Advertising Code of American Business," 1971. Reprinted by permission of the American Advertising Federation and the author, Norman E. Bowie.

---

* These figures may be found in Howard H. Bell's "Self-Regulation by the Advertising Industry," in *The Unstable Ground: Corporate Social Policy in a Dynamic Society,* ed. S. Prakash Sethi (Los Angeles: Melville Publishing Company, 1974).

3. *Taste and Decency.* Advertising shall be free of statement, illustrations or implications which are offensive to good taste or public decency.
4. *Bait Advertising.* Advertising shall offer only merchandise or services which are readily available for purchase at the advertised price.
5. *Guarantees and Warranties.* Advertising of guarantees and warranties shall be explicit. Advertising of any guarantee or warranty shall clearly and conspicuously disclose its nature and extent, the manner in which the guarantor or warrantor will perform, and the identity of the guarantor or warrantor.
6. *Price Claims.* Advertising shall avoid price or savings claims which are false or misleading, or which do not offer provable bargains or savings.
7. *Unprovable Claims.* Advertising shall avoid the use of exaggerated or unprovable claims.
8. *Testimonials.* Advertising containing testimonials shall be limited to those of competent witnesses who are reflecting a real and honest choice.

Questions

1. How should rule 7 which forbids exaggerated claims be interpreted?
2. Is the set of rules comprehensive enough to forbid deceptive advertising?
3. Evaluate the described enforcement mechanism. Suggest improvements if you think any are needed.
4. Is the rule on "taste and decency" too broad and amorphous?

case 2: The Artificial Sweeteners Case

The potential for cyclamates as artificial sweeteners was discovered in the 1940s, and by the 1950s they were sold commercially to diabetics and obese persons who needed to limit their intake of sugar. Since cyclamates did not leave a bitter aftertaste as saccharin did, cyclamates became the preferred sweetener. During the 1960s producers of cyclamates promoted their use to a calorie-conscious public and soon cyclamates were used in many kinds of foods. Moreover, since cyclamates were far less expensive than sugar, there was an economic incentive to substitute cyclamates for sugar. Nearly all Americans ate food with cyclamates.

Gradually the safety of cyclamates came under question. The first doubts were raised as early as 1955. By 1962 the National Academy of Sciences-National Research Council (NAS-NRC) recommended that the use of cyclamates be restricted to special dietary foods, and by November 1968 the NAS-NRC indicated that the totally unrestricted use of cyclamates was not warranted. By 1969 there was evidence that feeding cyclamates to rats caused them to develop bladder cancer. Under the terms of the Delaney Clause of the Food Additives Amendment to the Federal Food, Drug, and Cosmetic Act,

This case was prepared by Norman E. Bowie. Reprinted by permission.

cyclamates were then banned from general use. The Delaney Clause stipulates "that no additive shall be deemed to be safe if it is found to induce cancer when ingested by man or animal, or if it is found, after tests which are appropriate for the evaluation of the safety of food additives, to induce cancer in man or animal." At first the ban was only partial, but legal proceedings forced a complete ban on August 14, 1970.

After the banning of cyclamates, the only available artificial sweetener was saccharin. However, as the 1970s progressed, similar doubts were raised about its safety. A Canadian study tipped the scales and in the summer of 1977 the FDA announced plans for the banning of saccharin. If the FDA program had gone into effect, almost all dietetic products would have been removed from the market. A public outcry ensued. Some challenged the adequacy of the tests on which the FDA had relied. Others, including many physicians, argued that the risks to health associated with obesity are greater than the risks from contracting cancer. If that were correct, it would be better on cost/benefit grounds to permit products containing artificial sweeteners on the market. As a result of the public outcry, products containing saccharin remain on the market.

Questions

1. Under the circumstances described in the case, should the government ban saccharin?
2. Suppose saccharin had no health benefits, but people liked the taste. Assuming the same risks, should saccharin be banned in that situation?
3. Is the Delaney clause too stringent as a principle for regulating potential carcinogens?
4. Should people be free to buy products, e.g., laetrile, which others find dangerous, so long as these people are informed of the risks and their use of the product will not harm others?

case 3: Flyover in Midland

On February 7, 1978, an aerial photography team commisioned by the EPA flew over and took detailed aerial photographs of the Midland, Michigan, plant of The Dow Chemical Co. The company had no knowledge that the flight was taking place. The flyover was apparently commissioned because of remarks made by an EPA chemical engineer to one of his subordinates.

Prior to February, 1978, the EPA had been conducting an investigation to determine whether to approve a consent order, issued by the State of Michigan, under the Clean Air Act. The order had to do with emissions from Dow power plants at its Midland location. The EPA later admitted that they had had "the

This case was adapted from an article by Edward M. Nussbaum and Garry L. Hamlin in *Chemical Engineering Progress,* April 1981. Case used by permission.

full cooperation of Dow, and Dow withheld nothing" that their inspectors had asked to see during their preliminary investigation in September of 1977. In addition, one month later when the EPA requested schematic drawings of the power plants, Dow voluntarily provided them.

In December, 1977, the EPA again requested access to the Midland plant, this time indicating that they intended to take pictures. In order to protect its trade secrets, it is Dow's policy not to allow cameras into its plants. After being informed of this policy, the chemical engineer, employed at the EPA's Region V office, apparently made comments which were interpreted by one of his subordinates to be an authorization for the flyover. Dow found out about the flyover a month after it occurred and promptly filed suit against the EPA in Federal Court.

Questions

1. Describe and comment on some of the ethical issues which arise when a government regulator takes matters into his/her own hands, e.g., authorizing a clandestine flyover rather than trying to obtain a court injunction forcing Dow to allow pictures.
2. If the EPA had gone to court to challenge Dow's policy not to allow cameras into its plants, what moral appeals could the lawyers for EPA and the lawyers for Dow make?
3. How high a priority should regulations protecting trade secrets have when such regulations conflict with other societal goals?
4. If a decision were to be made solely on moral grounds, how should a company's right to protect trade secrets be balanced against society's right to enforce environmental regulations?

Note

On April 19, 1982, the Eastern District of Michigan U.S. District Court ruled that the overflight violated the law.

case 4: Cost-Benefit Decision at Bluebird Smelter

Bluebird Smelter is owned by a large, national mining company and located in Bluebird, a town of 12,000 in western Montana. The smelter, which has been operating profitably for 35 years with 125 employees, processes copper ore arriving by railroad.

Bluebird Smelter is the only major industrial pollution source in the valley.

This case is extracted from a longer case by the same name. It was written by John F. Steiner for *Issues in Business and Society.* Our extracted case is used by permission of Random House, Inc.

On sunny days when the air is still and during periods of temperature inversion over the valley, the action of the sun on smelter emissions contributes to photochemical smog similar to that in urban areas. Auto emissions and agricultural activities are also sources of photochemical oxidants, but smelter emissions are far more important.

A group of economists from a prestigious research institute in another city picked the Bluebird Smelter as a test case for a research project on the health effects of pollution. The figures they produced led to debate among the various local groups involved in the controversy. The researchers looked at the operation of Bluebird Smelter in terms of costs and benefits to the community and to society. The following table shows their basic calculations.

The Earth Riders (a small local environmental group) seized upon the study, arguing that if total costs of smelter operation exceeded benefits, then a clear-cut case had been made for closing the plant. It was already operating at a loss; in this case a net social loss of $730,000. Thus, in the eyes of the environmentalists Bluebird Smelter was in social bankruptcy.

The smelter's managers and members of the Bluebird City Council, on the

TABLE 16.1
ANNUAL BENEFITS AND COSTS OF BLUEBIRD SMELTER

Benefits		Value
Payroll for 125 employees at an average of $15,000 each		$1,875,000
Benefits paid to workers and families at an average of $1,000 each		125,000
Income, other than wages and salaries, generated in the valley by the company		4,600,000
Local taxes and fees paid by the company		100,000
Social services to community and charitable contributions		20,000
	Total	$6,720,000
Costs		
Excess deaths of 5 persons at $1 million each *		$5,000,000
Other health and illness costs to exposed population		450,000
Crop and property damage from pollutants		1,000,000
Reduction of aesthetic value and quality of life		500,000
Lost revenues and taxes from tourism		500,000
	Total	$7,450,000

* Calculated on the basis of recent court decisions compensating victims of wrongful death in product liability cases in Western states. The figure reflects average compensation.

other hand, ridiculed the study for making unrealistic and overly simplistic assumptions. They questioned whether the costs were meaningful, citing estimates of the value of a human life that were much lower than $1 million, made by other economists. They argued that health risks posed by the smelter were less than those of smoking cigarettes, drinking, or riding motorcycles and that benefits to the community were great. They even suggested that important costs had been left out of the calculations such as sociological and psychological costs to workers who would be laid off if the plant closed.

Questions

1. Analyze the costs and benefits enumerated in Table 16.1. Are there items that belong on the list but aren't included? Are there items on the list that should be taken off?
2. When making public policy decisions, do you think a dollar value should be placed on human life? If your answer is no, how do you decide whether to spend an extra $100 million on highway safety? If your answer is yes, how do you decide how much a human life is worth?
3. Suppose it is true that the health risks posed by the smelter were less than those of smoking cigarettes. Does that mean that the smelter should not be closed down? that cigarettes should be banned?
4. Is the decision whether or not to close Bluebird Smelter the kind of decision that should be made by cost-benefit analysis?

SUGGESTED SUPPLEMENTARY READINGS

ACKERMAN, BRUCE A. and WILLIAM T. HASSLER. *Clean Coal, Dirty Air.* New London: Yale University Press, 1981.

BARKDOLL, GERALD L., "The Perils and Promise of Economic Analysis for Regulatory Decision-Making." *Food, Drug and Cosmetic Law Journal,* 34 (1979).

BATOR, FRANCIS M., "The Anatomy of Market Failure." *The Quarterly Journal of Economics* (August, 1958).

BAUER, RAYMOND A., and DAN H. FENN, JR. *The Corporate Social Audit.* New York: Russell Sage Foundation, 1972.

BELL, HOWARD H., "Self-Regulation by the Advertising Industry." *California Management Review,* 16 (Spring 1974).

BLAKE, DAVID H., WILLIAM C. FREDERICK, and MILDRED S. MYERS. *Social Auditing: Evaluating the Impact of Corporate Progress.* New York: Praeger Publishers, Inc., 1976.

CORTLE, DOUGLAS M. "Innovative Regulation." *Economic Impact,* 29 (1979).

EILBIRT, HENRY and I. R. PARKET. "The Corporate Responsibility Officer: A New Position on the Organizational Chart." *Business Horizons* (February 1973).

ESTES, RALPH. *Corporate Social Accounting.* New York: John Wiley and Sons, 1976.

GIBBONS, EDWARD F. "Making a Corporate Code of Ethics Work." In *Proceedings of the First National Conference on Business Ethics,* ed. W. Michael Hoffman. Waltham, Mass.: Center for Business Ethics at Bentley College, 1977.

GREEN, MARK and NORMAN WAITZMAN. *Business War On the Law: An Analysis of the Benefits of Federal Health/Safety Enforcement.* The Corporate Accountability Research Group, 1979.

HILL, IVAN. *The Ethical Basis of Economic Freedom.* Chapel Hill, N.C.: American Viewpoint, Inc., 1976.

LEWIS-BECK, MICHAEL S. and JOHN R. ALFORD. "Can Government Regulate Safety? The Coal Mine Example," *American Political Science Review* 74 (1980).

LINOWES, DAVID F. *The Corporate Conscience.* New York: Hawthorn Books, Inc., 1974.

NOVICK, DAVID. "Cost-Benefit Analysis and Social Responsibility." *Business Horizons,* 16 (October 1973).

OKRENT, DAVID. "Comment on Societal Risk." *Science,* 208 (April 25, 1980) pp. 372–375.

POSNER, RICHARD A. *Regulation of Advertising by the FTC.* Washington, D.C.: American Enterprise Institute for Public Policy Research, 1973.

PURCELL, THEODORE V., S.J. "Institutionalizing Ethics On Corporate Boards." *Review of Social Economy,* XXXVI #1 (April 1978) pp. 41–54.

———. "Electing an Angel's Advocate to the Board." *Management Review,* 65 (May 1976).

RHOADS, STEVEN E., ed., *Valuing Life: Public Policy Dilemmas.* Boulder, Colorado: Westview Press, 1980.

SCHUCK, PETER H. "Why Regulation Fails." *Harper's,* 251 (September 1975).

SETHI, S. PRAKASH. "Getting a Handle on the Social Audit." *Business and Society Review* (Winter 1972-73).

STONE, CHRISTOPHER D. *Where The Law Ends: The Social Control of Corporate Behavior.* New York: Harper & Row, Publishers, Inc., 1975.

WEAVER, PAUL H. "Regulations, Social Policy, and Class Conflict," *The Public Interest,* 50 (Winter 1978).

WERTHER, WILLIAM B., JR. "Government Control vs. Corporate Ingenuity." *Labor Law Journal* (June 1975).

WIEDENBAUM, MURRAY L. "The High Cost of Government Regulation." *Business Horizons,* 18 (August 1975).

CHAPTER 9

THEORIES OF ECONOMIC JUSTICE

INTRODUCTION

We have all noticed economic disparities between individuals and nations, and most of us have come to question some aspects of domestic and international systems for distributing wealth. We wonder whether tax burdens are unfairly distributed. For example, we may think that individuals are overtaxed and that wealthy corporations are undertaxed. We may wonder whether such wealthy corporations and their stockholders actually *deserve* their abundant profits, and whether their executives deserve the generous salaries that usually attend such positions. On the other hand, we may wonder whether it is fair that hard-earned corporate and individual incomes should be taxed in order to redistribute the money through social welfare. There are different answers to these questions, but underlying any sophisticated answer is a theory of economic justice, i.e., an answer to the problem of how economic goods and services are in general to be distributed.

This chapter deals with various problems and theories of economic justice, with emphasis on the major distinctions, principles, and methods of moral argument employed by influential writers on the subject. Each author attempts to answer the question, ''Which system of social and economic organization is most just?''

THE CONCEPTS OF JUSTICE AND DISTRIBUTIVE JUSTICE

It was observed in the Introduction to Chapter 1 that the notion of justice is kin to the notions of fairness and desert. It was also noted that the expression ''distributive justice'' refers to the proper distribution (or intentional nondistribution, as Robert Nozick suggests) of social benefits and burdens. Distributive justice pertains to the distribution of benefits and burdens through society's major and pervasive institutions, including branches of government, laws of property ownership, lending institutions, and systems of allocating benefits. Unjust distributions in the form of inequalities of income among different classes of persons and unfair tax burdens have been the dominant focus of recent discussions of distributive justice. One reason is that these issues of justice only arise in contexts of distributing *scarce* benefits, where there is some competition for resources. If there are plenty of salmon in a river so that everyone can have as many as he or she can catch, we do not establish patterns limiting fishermen or the fishing industry. It is only when we are worried that the fish supply will be exhausted or that future fishermen will be unfairly affected by present fishing that we set limits to the number of fish they may catch. The point is that there are no problems of distributive justice and no need of principles of distributive justice until some measure of scarcity exists.

THEORIES OF DISTRIBUTIVE JUSTICE

A few widely discussed, so-called material, principles of distributive justice were mentioned in Chapter 1 (pp. 40–44). Each principle states a relevant property on the basis of which burdens and benefits should be distributed. The list of candidates for the position of relevant properties includes rights, individual effort, societal contribution, and merit.

The diversity of these principles indicates that justice is an enormously broad normative concept. Consider the following example: A university professor hires three male students to help move the furniture in her house to a new location, promising each student the standard hourly wage for local professional movers. One student turns out to be capable of lifting large items by himself, and is both more efficient and more careful than either of the other students. The second, the professor learns during conversation, is desperately in need of money owing to a genuine and severe financial crisis that threatens the student's enrollment for the next semester. The third student carelessly breaks two vases and scars a table, but otherwise fulfills the conditions of the agreement, though in an undistinguished manner.

The first student deserves greater compensation on the basis of *merit or performance;* the second *needs* a larger share of the money to be divided among them, though for no reason related to performance; the third deserves less on the basis of performance, but deserves an *equal share* on the basis of the agreement (if one overlooks the unnegotiated problem of carelessly marred or broken items). The professor is therefore somewhat at a loss about what reward to offer each student at the end of the day. Suppose she tries to call on justice in general to tell her what ought to be done. It should be obvious by now that invoking our most general notion of justice will prove unsatisfactory, for the professor will have to accept one or more material principles of justice. She will perhaps wish for a general account of justice that will order this fragmented array of considerations, but if she is like most of us, no such account will be readily forthcoming. While we attach some weight to each of the possible material principles, none clearly outweighs the others.

Theories of distributive justice have been devised to handle not only such relatively minor situations, but also to give general guidelines for the entire scope of social justice. *Egalitarian* theories emphasize equal access to primary goods; *Marxist* theories emphasize need; *libertarian* theories emphasize rights to social and economic liberty; and *utilitarian* theories emphasize a mixed use of such criteria so that public and private utilities are maximized. The acceptability of any such theory of justice is determined by the quality of its moral argument that some one or more selected (material) principles ought to be given priority over the others.

The utilitarian theory follows from the explanation of utilitarianism in Chapter 1. Economic justice is viewed in this theory as merely one among a number of problems about how to maximize value in society. The ideal economic distribution, utilitarians argue, is *any* arrangement that would have this maximizing effect. According to Singer, this thesis leads directly to a position diametrically opposed to libertarianism: a heavy element of political and economic planning is said to be morally required in order that justice be done to individuals. Because utilitarianism as a general normative theory was thoroughly explored in Chapter 1 (pp. 21–31), it will not be explicated in detail in this Introduction. Detailed consideration will be given, however, to egalitarian, libertarian, and Marxist theories.

THE EGALITARIAN THEORY

The idea of equality in the distribution of social benefits and burdens has had an important place in most influential moral theories. For example, in utilitarianism different people are equal in the value accorded their wants, preferences, and happiness, and in Kantian theories all persons are considered equally deserving of respect as ends in themselves. Nonetheless, the question arises whether people may be considered equal for some moral purposes (e.g., in their basic moral rights and obligations), yet startlingly diverse and unequal for the purpose of justly distributing certain social burdens and benefits.

Radical and Qualified Egalitarianism

It is precisely this latter contention about inequalities that egalitarian theories closely scrutinize. In its radical form, egalitarianism is the thesis that individual differences are no more significant in an account of social justice than they are in other domains of morality. Accordingly, distributions of burdens and benefits in a society are just to the extent they are equal, and deviations from absolute equality in distribution can be determined to be unjust without consideration of the respects in which members of the society may differ. For example, the fact that roughly 20 percent of the wealth in the United States is owned by only 5 percent of the population, while the poorest 20 percent of the population controls only 5 percent of the wealth, would make American society unjust by this radical egalitarian standard, no matter how relatively deserving the people at both extremes might be (by a nonegalitarian standard of desert). For strict egalitarians, humanity alone is the respect in which people are to be compared in determining the justice of distributions, just as humanity alone is to be considered when determining who has basic political rights.

Most egalitarian accounts of justice, however, are qualified and more guardedly formulated than the radical version just characterized. Thus, mere membership in the human species might not entitle people to equal shares of *all* social benefits, even if such membership did entail the equal distribution of those goods necessary to satisfy fundamental human needs. Egalitarianism so construed points to a basic equality among individuals that takes priority over all their differences.

Rawls's Theory

In recent years an egalitarian book in the Kantian tradition has had great currency in deontological ethics. John Rawls's *A Theory of Justice* (1971) has as its central contention that we should distribute all economic goods and services equally except in those cases where an unequal distribution would actually work to everyone's advantage, or at least would benefit the worst off in society. Rawls presents this egalitarian theory as a direct challenge to utilitarianism on grounds of social justice. His objection to utilitarianism is that social distributions produced by maximizing utility could entail violations of basic individual liberties and rights expressive of human equality and deserving protection as a matter of social justice. Utilitarianism, being indifferent as to the *distribution* of satisfactions among individuals (but not of course to the *total* satisfaction in society) would, in Rawls's view, permit the infringement of some peoples' rights and liberties if the infringement genuinely promised to produce a proportionately greater utility for others.

Rawls therefore turns to a hypothetical social contract procedure strongly indebted to what he calls the "Kantian conception of equality." According to this account, valid principles of justice are those principles to which we would all agree if we could freely and impartially consider the social situation from a standpoint (the "original position") outside any actual society. Impartiality is guaranteed in this situation by a conceptual device Rawls calls the "veil of ignorance." This notion stipulates that in the original position, each person is (at least momentarily) ignorant of all his or her particular fortuitous characteristics. For example, the person's sex, race, IQ, family background, and special talents or handicaps are unrevealed in this hypothetical circumstance.

The veil of ignorance prevents people from promoting principles of justice that are biased toward their own combinations of fortuitous talents and characteristics—e.g., the various combinations of need, merit, experience, and sexual advantage that lead different parties to promote competing material principles. Rawls argues that under these conditions, people would unanimously agree on two fundamental principles of justice. The first requires that each person be permitted the maximum amount of equal basic liberty compatible with a similar liberty for others. The second stipulates that once this equal basic liberty is assured, inequalities in social primary goods (e.g., income, rights, and opportunities) are to be allowed only if they benefit everyone (so long as everyone has fair equality of opportunity). Rawls considers social institutions to be just if and only if they are in conformity with these two basic principles.

Rawls's theory makes equality a basic characteristic of the original position from which the social contract is forged. Equality is built into that hypothetical position in the form of a free and equal bargain among all parties, where there is equal ignorance of all individual characteristics and advantages that persons have or will have in their daily lives. Furthermore, people in such a position would choose to make the equal possession of a scheme of basic liberties the first commitment of their social institutions. Nevertheless, Rawls rejects radical egalitarianism, arguing that equal distribution cannot be justified as the sole moral principle. If there were inequalities rendering everyone better off by comparison to initial equality, these inequalities would be desirable (again, so long as they were consistent with equal liberty and fair opportunity). Rawls thus rejects radical egalitarianism in favor of his second principle of justice.

The first part of this second principle is called the *difference principle*. Rawls formulates this principle so that inequalities would be justifiable only if they maximally enhance the position of the "*representative* least advantaged" person—that is, a hypothetical individual particularly unfortunate in the distribution of fortuitous characteristics or social advantages. Formulated in this way, the difference principle could allow, for instance, extraordinary economic rewards to entrepreneurs if the resulting economic stimulation were to produce improved job opportunities and working conditions for the least advantaged members of society.

The difference principle rests on the view that because inequalities of birth, historical circumstance, and natural endowment are undeserved, persons in a cooperative society should correct them by making more equal the unequal situation of naturally disadvantaged members. This egalitarian demand had proved to be a controversial feature of Rawls's theory, and one directly challenged by libertarian theories.

THE LIBERTARIAN THEORY

In conformity with most recent work on distributive justice, libertarian theories of justice concentrate on individual rights to liberty as well as on economic justice. What makes such theories *libertarian* is their advocacy of distinctive processes, procedures, or mechanisms for ensuring that liberty rights are recognized in economic practice—typically the rules and procedures governing economic acquisition and exchange in capitalist or free market systems.

The Role of Individual Freedom

As Adam Smith classically described capitalist economic systems, people acting in an individually self-interested fashion exhibit behavior patterns that collectively further the interests of everyone in the larger society. (See Chapter 1, pp. 20–21.) Such a system presumes a model of economic behavior that attributes a substantial degree of economic freedom to individual agents. People are seen as freely entering and withdrawing from economic arrangements in accordance with a controlling perception of their own interest. A commitment to this model of individual freedom in economic activity accounts for the term "libertarianism." People choose to contribute in the ways they do to economic arrangements, and because contributions are freely chosen, they can be considered morally relevant bases on which to discriminate among individuals in distributing economic burdens and benefits.

In seeing free choice as central to an account of justice in economic distribution (more central than equality or utilitarian efficiency), libertarian writers often commit themselves to an individualist conception of economic production and value. These libertarians maintain that people should receive economic benefits in proportion as they freely contribute to their production, and this variant of the theory assumes that it is possible to recognize meaningful distinctions between individual contributions to production. The industrious and imaginative business executive, for instance, would from this perspective be contributing far more to his or her company's success than the similarly exemplary assembly-line worker or secretary, and the executive therefore deserves—on grounds of justice— the proportionately greater share of the profits.

Although the underlying assumption here corresponds closely to some economic presuppositions in Anglo-American society, many philosophers, including Rawls, would challenge it. They would maintain that, however great the differences between particular people's contributions initially appear to be, all individual contributions shrink to insignificance once the broader context of production is appreciated. On this egalitarian account, economic value is generated through an essentially communal process which renders differences between individual contributions morally negligible. Thus, the initiative and ideas of the business executive would be only one among a great many factors contributing to a corporation's success, a factor itself reflecting a diversity of formative influences including family background, education, and interaction with professional associates. Libertarian theorists, however, explicitly reject the conclusion that egalitarian patterns of distribution represent a normative ideal. People may be equal in a host of morally significant respects (e.g., entitled to equal treatment under the law and equally valued as ends in themselves), but for the libertarian, it would be a basic violation of justice to regard people as a priori deserving of equal economic returns. In particular, people are seen as having a fundamental right to own and dispense with the products of their labor as they choose, and this right must be respected even if its unrestricted exercise leads to great inequalities of wealth in society.

Nozick's Theory

The role of individual rights in a libertarian theory of justice is emphasized in this chapter in the article by Robert Nozick, who refers to the social philosophy presented in his book as an "entitlement theory" of justice. Nozick develops a detailed defense of the minimal or "night-watchman" state, a conception according to which government action is justified only when it *protects* the fundamental rights or entitlements of its citizens. He argues that a theory of justice should work to protect our rights not to be coerced and should not propound a thesis intended to "pattern" society through arrangements that redistribute economic benefits and burdens.

This theory of legitimate state power is meant as a challenge to many of the assumptions underlying political realities in contemporary industrial societies. It will therefore be helpful to keep those assumptions in mind while reading the selection by Nozick. In both socialist and (impure) capitalist countries, considerable government activity beyond mere protection of individual rights is usually allowed on grounds of social justice. Governments take pronounced steps to actively redistribute the wealth that has been acquired by individuals exercising their economic rights in accordance with free market laws. Thus, the wealthy are taxed at a progressively higher rate than those who are less wealthy, with the proceeds underwriting state support of the indigent through welfare payments and unemployment compensation. The goal of interference by the state is presumably the redistribution of the economic benefits that would accrue from the unchecked exercise of individual rights in the marketplace. Nozick's libertarian theory invites consideration of whether such common governmental activities are really what *justice* demands.

Nozick's entitlement theory presents social justice in terms of fundamental rights and three principles: those of *acquisition, transfer,* and *rectification.* On this libertarian account, it is a violation of justice to impose patterns of distribution which infringe upon individual economic rights, and thus his libertarian position is more accurately viewed as a rejection of *all* distributional patterns that might be imposed by material principles of justice. This feature of the theory suggests that the libertarian is committed to a form of *procedural* justice. That expression, however, has a variety of meanings (examined in Chapter 1, pp. 42–44), and these will have to be specified before the expression can be applied precisely. In Nozick's *pure* procedural justice, there must be no preplanned "pattern" of justice independent of the demands of a free market economy. With this type of justice, any outcome is just as long as it results from the consistent operation of the specified procedures. That is, for Nozick there is no pattern of just distribution independent of the procedures of acquisition, transfer, and rectification.

This claim has been at the center of philosophical controversy over the extreme libertarian account, and many of the most influential theories of justice can be seen as reactions against such a libertarian commitment to pure procedural justice and in favor of some independent substantive criterion or pattern. Consideration will now be given to the most revolutionary such theory and the one most squarely opposed to libertarianism: the Marxist approach.

THE MARXIST THEORY

Much of the discussion of business ethics in this text assumes a social and economic context. In the discussion of advertising ethics, for example, a competitive free market is taken as given. In this way the person discussing advertising ethics is in the same position as a judge sentencing a convicted criminal. Both operate from within a given social framework that establishes their roles and thereby their duties.

Some philosophers insist that the most important questions about ethics and business do not arise within capitalism, but instead arise as the result of *external criticisms* directed at the competitive market economy itself. Rather than discussing advertising ethics from within the capitalist framework, according to this viewpoint, we should assess the merits and demerits of the capitalist economic system. Perhaps the strongest and certainly the best-known challenge to capitalism comes from the political and social philosophy of Marxism. In this chapter the essay by Milton Fisk reflects this viewpoint, largely by criticizing operating assumptions in contemporary American business and society from the Marxist perspective.

Marx's Theory

Karl Marx's criticisms of capitalism focus on the notion of the voluntary exchange of private property—a notion fundamental to capitalist economic organization, as Nozick's theory clearly indicates. Exchange takes place when I surrender something of mine in return for something of yours that I want more. As industrial society develops, industries use the principle of the division of labor. As a result, men and women have little, if any, need for what they themselves produce. They produce only for their "share" of the money that their products represent. Since what they produce is simply a means toward something else, Marxists claim that workers are "alienated" from their product. A worker's creation of a product has no intrinsic value; one works simply in order to acquire products produced by others.

Under free market exchange, one's relations to other workers suffer as well, according to Marx. We view fellow workers and the fruits of their labor solely as a means for satisfying as yet unfulfilled wants. We are directly interested neither in our fellow workers nor in their products as objects of value in themselves. Rather, our interest in them is purely as a means to our end. Moreover, our *only* interest in others occurs when they produce something we value; otherwise they are valueless to us. In this way free market exchange based on private property corrupts a worker's relation both to his own product and to his fellow workers.

Marxist Critiques of the Free Market

Many of the most prominent Marxist critiques of free market theories similarly challenge the adequacy of any pure procedural account of justice. As Fisk points out, the Marxist critic finds both libertarians and egalitarians naive in their assumption that true freedom of choice in economic matters is compatible with systems of private property and capitalist exchange. The Marxist attack on this assumption naturally focuses on the relations between workers and the objects of their productive labor. Marxists thus argue that through the manipulation of language and technology, the dominant social class has successfully compromised the working class, which has come to desire the useless products of industry.

The inevitable frustration and alienation of the working class have been successfully redirected away from the ruling class into the abuse of some of the products of the consuming society, such as racing cars, guns, and power tools. This critique is a direct challenge to the notion of consumer sovereignty. The purchases of the affluent consumer society are not really *free* purchases at all, for the products of advanced capitalist society are antithetical to the true nature of free choice. (This Marxist challenge to the notion of consumer choice is mentioned in the discussion of advertising in Chapter 6.)

Defenders of the free market such as Nozick might respond to these Marxist arguments by maintaining that the justice of economic arrangements cannot be decided by assessing those arrangements at any one particular moment. Rather, it is necessary to take multiple historical details into account, for those details alone enable us to determine whether existing inequalities are *deserved.* An interesting example of this form of conflict occurred during the "ITT-Chile Affair" (1970–71). The Marxist candidate for President of Chile, Dr. Salvador Allende, proposed to nationalize ITT's $150 million investments in the Chile Telephone Company. Allende's view was that the company's exploitative history justified a government takeover. ITT, however, took the position that its property would be expropriated without compensation. ITT's central defense was an argument of justice: Allende's actions were unfair to the company and its stockholders (as well, they held, as a violation of the Chilean Constitution). Naturally Allende's rebuttal rested on the Marxist theory of justice.

Here again, however, the Marxist would not deny the contention that historical details figure prominently in an adequate account of justice in economic distribution. Indeed, Fisk makes many historical appeals and uses them to mount a further challenge to the justice of existing economic arrangements. In what sense, Marxists ask, did former Vice-President Nelson Rockefeller, as the descendant of the wealthy capitalist John D. Rockefeller, deserve his privileged social status and accompanying enhancement of economic choice? And how do the indigent workers' children employed by the Rockefeller estate deserve their correspondingly disadvantaged position? And how could one overlook the history of exploitation in Chile in assessing what ITT deserves?

Such considerations have led Marxists (and many non-Marxists as well) to reject all free-market conceptions of justice. In their place is substituted some material principle specifying need as the relevant respect in which people are to be compared for purposes of determining the justice of economic distributions. Of course, much turns on how the notion of a need is delineated. Generally, to say that someone has a need for something is to say that the person will be harmed or detrimentally affected if it is not obtained. For purposes of justice, a material principle of need would be least controversial if it were restricted to *fundamental* needs. If malnutrition, serious bodily injury, and the withholding of critical information involve fundamental harms, then presumably persons have a fundamental need for adequate nutrition, health care facilities, and education. According to theories based on this material principle, justice requires that the satisfaction of fundamental human needs be a higher social priority than the protection of economic freedoms or rights.

This broad construal of the material principle of need has provided an historically important alternative to the *pure* procedural theory of capitalist economic distribution, and Marxists have been quick to point out that all governments in "free-market" nations have adopted some version of this supplementary principle—though not of course for any reasons directly connected with Marxist theory.

CONCLUSION

Rawls, Nozick, and their utilitarian and Marxist opponents all capture many of our intuitive convictions about justice. Rawls's difference principle, for example, describes a widely shared belief about the role of fortuitous human characteristics (i.e., those determined by natural or historical contingency). But Nozick's theory also makes a strong appeal in the domains of taxation and property ownership; and utilitarianism is widely used in the development of public policy, while Marxist theory in some form dominates the sense of justice in many nations around the earth. Perhaps, then, there are several equally valid, or at least equally viable, theories of justice. Before this conclusion is accepted, however, attention should be addressed to the details of the arguments in the selections in this final chapter.

T.L.B.

AN EGALITARIAN THEORY OF JUSTICE

John Rawls

THE ROLE OF JUSTICE

Justice is the first virtue of social institutions, as truth is of systems of thought. A theory however elegant and economical must be rejected or revised if it is untrue; likewise laws and institutions no matter how efficient and well-arranged must be reformed or abolished if they are unjust. Each person possesses an inviolability founded on justice that even the welfare of society as a whole cannot override. For this reason justice denies that the loss of freedom for some is made right by a greater good shared by others. It does not allow that the sacrifices imposed on a few are outweighed by the larger sum of advantages enjoyed by many. Therefore in a just society the

John Rawls, *A Theory of Justice* (Cambridge, Mass.: Harvard University Press, 1971), pp. 3–4, 11–15, 18–19, 60–62, 64–65, 100–104, 274–277. Reprinted by permission.

liberties of equal citizenship are taken as settled; the rights secured by justice are not subject to political bargaining or to the calculus of social interests. The only thing that permits us to acquiesce in an erroneous theory is the lack of a better one; analogously, an injustice is tolerable only when it is necessary to avoid an even greater injustice. Being first virtues of human activities, truth and justice are uncompromising.

These propositions seem to express our intuitive conviction of the primacy of justice. No doubt they are expressed too strongly. In any event I wish to inquire whether these contentions or others similar to them are sound, and if so how they can be accounted for. To this end it is necessary to work out a theory of justice in the light of which these assertions can be interpreted and assessed. I shall begin by considering the role of the principles of justice. Let us assume, to fix ideas, that a society is a more or less self-sufficient association of persons who in their relations to one another recognize certain rules of conduct as binding and who for the most part act in accordance with them. Suppose further that these rules specify a system of cooperation designed to advance the good of those taking part in it. Then, although a society is a cooperative venture for mutual advantage, it is typically marked by a conflict as well as by an identity of interests. There is an identity of interests since social cooperation makes possible a better life for all than any would have if each were to live solely by his own efforts. There is a conflict of interests since persons are not indifferent as to how the greater benefits produced by their collaboration are distributed, for in order to pursue their ends they each prefer a larger to a lesser share. A set of principles is required for choosing among the various social arrangements which determine this division of advantages and for underwriting an agreement on the proper distributive shares. These principles are the principles of social justice: they provide a way of assigning rights and duties in the basic institutions of society and they define the appropriate distribution of the benefits and burdens of social cooperation. . . .

THE MAIN IDEA OF THE THEORY OF JUSTICE

My aim is to present a conception of justice which generalizes and carries to a higher level of abstraction the familiar theory of the social contract as found, say, in Locke, Rousseau, and Kant. In order to do this we are not to think of the original contract as one to enter a particular society or to set up a particular form of government. Rather, the guiding idea is that the principles of justice for the basic structure of society are the object of the original agreement. They are the principles that free and rational persons concerned to further their own interests would accept in an initial position of equality as defining the fundamental terms of their association. These principles are to regulate all further agreements; they specify the kinds of social cooperation that can be entered into and the forms of government that can be established. This way of regarding the principles of justice I shall call justice as fairness.

Thus we are to imagine that those who engage in social cooperation choose together, in one joint act, the principles which are to assign basic rights and duties and to determine the division of social benefits. Men are to decide in advance how they are to regulate their claims against one another and what is to be the foundation charter of their society. Just as each person must decide by rational reflection what constitutes his good, that is, the system of ends which it is rational for him to pursue, so a group of persons must decide once and for all what is to count among them as just and unjust. The choice which rational men would make in this hypothetical situation of equal liberty, assuming for the present that this choice problem has a solution, determines the principles of justice.

In justice as fairness the original position of equality corresponds to the state of nature in the traditional theory of the social contract. This original position is not, of course, thought of as an actual historical state of affairs, much less as a primitive condition of culture. It is understood as a purely hypothetical situation characterized so as to lead to a certain conception of justice. Among the essential features of this situation is that no one knows his place in society, his class position or social status, nor does any one know his fortune in the distribution of natural assets and abilities, his intelligence, strength, and the like. I shall even assume that the parties do not know their conceptions of the good or their special psychological propensities. The principles of justice are chosen behind a veil of ignorance. This ensures that no one is advantaged or disadvantaged in the choice of principles by the outcome of natural chance or the contingency of social circumstances. Since all are similarly situated and no one is able to design principles to favor his particular condition, the principles of justice are the result of a fair agreement or bargain. For given the circumstances of the original position, the symmetry of everyone's relations to each other, this initial situation is fair between individuals as moral persons, that is, as rational beings with their own ends and capable, I shall assume, of a sense of justice. The original position is, one might say, the appropriate initial status quo, and thus the fundamental agreements reached in it are fair. This explains the propriety of the name "justice as fairness": it conveys the idea that the principles of justice are agreed to in an initial situation that is fair. The name does not mean that the concepts of justice and fairness are the same, any more than the phrase "poetry as metaphor" means that the concepts of poetry and metaphor are the same.

Justice as fairness begins, as I have said, with one of the most general of all choices which persons might make together, namely, with the choice of the first principles of a conception of justice which is to regulate all subsequent criticism and reform of institutions. Then, having chosen a conception of justice, we can suppose that they are to choose a constitution and a legislature to enact laws, and so on, all in accordance with the principles of justice initially agreed upon. Our social situation is just if it is such that by this sequence of hypothetical agreements we would have contracted into the general system of rules which defines it.

. . . It may be observed, however, that once the principles of justice are thought of as arising from an original agreement in a situation of equality, it is an open question whether the principle of utility would be acknowledged. Offhand it hardly seems likely that persons who view themselves as equals, entitled to press their claims upon one another, would agree to a principle which may require lesser life prospects for some simply for the sake of a greater sum of advantages enjoyed by others. Since each desires to protect his interests, his capacity to advance his conception of the good, no one has a reason to acquiesce in an enduring loss for himself in order to bring about a greater net balance of satisfaction. In the absence of strong and lasting benevolent impulses, a rational man would not accept a basic structure merely because it maximized the algebraic sum of advantages irrespective of its permanent effects on his own basic rights and interests. Thus it seems that the principle of utility is incompatible with the conception of social cooperation among equals for mutual advantage. It appears to be inconsistent with the idea of reciprocity implicit in the notion of a well-ordered society. Or, at any rate, so I shall argue.

I shall maintain instead that the persons in the initial situation would choose two rather different principles: the first requires equality in the assignment of basic rights and duties, while the second holds that social and economic inequalities, for example inequalities of wealth and authority, are just only if they result in compensating benefits for everyone, and in particular for the least advantaged members of society. These principles rule out justifying institutions on the grounds that the hardships of some are offset by a greater good in the aggregate. It may be expedient but it is not just that some should have less in order that others may prosper. But there is no injustice in the greater benefits earned by a few provided that the situation of persons not so fortunate is thereby improved. The intuitive idea is that since everyone's well-being depends upon a scheme of cooperation without which no one could have a satisfactory life, the division of advantages should be such as to draw forth the willing cooperation of everyone taking part in it, including those less well situated. Yet this can be expected only if reasonable terms are proposed. The two principles mentioned seem to be a fair agreement on the basis of which those better endowed, or more fortunate in their social position, neither of which we can be said to deserve, could expect the willing cooperation of others when some workable scheme is a necessary condition of the welfare of all. Once we decide to look for a conception of justice that nullifies the accidents of natural endowment and the contingencies of social circumstance as counters in quest for political and economic advantage, we are led to these principles. They express the result of leaving aside those aspects of the social world that seem arbitrary from a moral point of view. . . .

THE ORIGINAL POSITION AND JUSTIFICATION

. . . The idea here is simply to make vivid to ourselves the restrictions that it seems reasonable to impose on arguments for principles of justice, and therefore on these principles themselves. Thus it seems reasonable and generally acceptable that no one should be advantaged or disadvantaged by natural fortune or social circumstances in the choice of principles. It also seems widely agreed that it should be impossible to tailor principles to the circumstances of one's own case. We should insure further that particular inclinations and aspirations, and persons' conceptions of their good, do not affect the principles adopted. The aim is to rule out those principles that it would be rational to propose for acceptance, however little the chance of success, only if one knew certain things that are irrelevant from the standpoint of justice. For example, if a man knew that he was wealthy, he might find it rational to advance the principle that various taxes for welfare measures be counted unjust; if he knew that he was poor, he would most likely propose the contrary principle. To represent the desired restrictions one imagines a situation in which everyone is deprived of this sort of information. One excludes the knowledge of those contingencies which sets men at odds and allows them to be guided by their prejudices. In this manner the veil of ignorance is arrived at in a natural way. . . .

Two Principles of Justice

I shall now state in a provisional form the two principles of justice that I believe would be chosen in the original position. . . .

The first statement of the two principles reads as follows.

First: each person is to have an equal right to the most extensive basic liberty compatible with a similar liberty for others.

Second: social and economic inequalities are to be arranged so that they are both (a) reasonably expected to be to everyone's advantage, and (b) attached to positions and offices open to all. . . . [The Difference Principle]

By way of general comment, these principles primarily apply, as I have said, to the basic structure of society. They are to govern the assignment of rights and duties and to regulate the distribution of social and economic advantages. As their formulation suggests, these principles presuppose that the social structure can be divided into two more or less distinct parts, the first principle applying to the one, the second to the other. They distinguish between those aspects of the social system that define and secure the equal liberties of citizenship and those that specify and establish social and economic inequalities. The basic liberties of citizens are, roughly speaking, political liberty (the right to vote and to be eligible for public office) together with freedom of speech and assembly; liberty of conscience and freedom of thought; freedom of the person along with the right to hold (personal) property; and freedom from arbitrary arrest and seizure as defined by the concept of the rule of law. These liberties are all required to be equal by the first principle, since citizens of a just society are to have the same basic rights.

The second principle applies, in the first approximation, to the distribution of income and wealth and to the design of organizations that make use of differences in authority and responsibility, or chains of command. While the distribution of wealth and income need not be equal, it must be to everyone's advantage, and at the same time, positions of authority and offices of command must be accessible to all. One applies the second principle by holding positions open, and then, subject to this constraint, arranges social and economic inequalities so that everyone benefits.

These principles are to be arranged in a serial order with the first principle prior to the second. This ordering means that a departure from the institutions of equal liberty required by the first principle cannot be justified, or compensated for, by greater social and economic advantages. The distribution of wealth and income, and the hierarchies of authority, must be consistent with both the liberties of equal citizenship and equality of opportunity.

It is clear that these principles are rather specific in their content, and their acceptance rests on certain assumptions that I must eventually try to explain and justify. A theory of justice depends upon a theory of society in ways that will become evident as we proceed. For the present, it should be observed that the two principles (and this holds for all formulations) are a special case of a more general conception of justice that can be expressed as follows.

> All social values—liberty and opportunity, income and wealth, and the bases of self-respect—are to be distributed equally unless an unequal distribution of any, or all, of these values is to everyone's advantage.

Injustice, then, is simply inequalities that are not to the benefit of all. Of course, this conception is extremely vague and requires interpretation.

As a first step, suppose that the basic structure of society distributes certain primary goods, that is, things that every rational man is presumed to want. These goods normally have a use whatever a person's rational plan of life. For simplicity, assume that the chief primary goods at the disposition of society are rights and liberties, powers and opportunities, income and wealth. These are the social primary goods. Other primary goods such as health and vigor, intelligence and imagination, are natural goods; although their possession is influenced by the basic structure, they are not so directly under its control. Imagine, then, a hypothetical initial arrangement in which all the social primary goods are equally distributed: everyone has similar rights and duties, and income and wealth are evenly shared. This state of affairs provides a benchmark for judging improvements. If certain inequalities of wealth and organizational powers would make everyone better off than in this hypothetical starting situation, then they accord with the general conception.

Now it is possible, at least theoretically, that by giving up some of their fundamental liberties men are sufficiently compensated by the resulting social and economic gains. The general conception of justice imposes no restrictions on what sort of inequalities are permissible; it only requires that everyone's position be improved. . . .

Now the second principle insists that each person benefit from permissible inequalities in the basic structure. This means that it must be reasonable for each relevant representative man defined by this structure, when he views it as a going concern, to prefer his prospects with the inequality to his prospects without it. One is not allowed to justify differences in income or organizational powers on the ground that the disadvantages of those in one position are outweighed by the greater advantages of those in another. Much less can infringements of liberty be counterbalanced in this way. Applied to the basic structure, the principle of utility would have us maximize the sum of expectations of representative men (weighted by the number of persons they represent, on the classical view); and this would permit us to compensate for the losses of some by the gains of others. Instead, the two principles require that everyone benefit from economic and social inequalities. . . .

THE TENDENCY TO EQUALITY

I wish to conclude this discussion of the two principles by explaining the sense in which they express an egalitarian conception of justice. Also I should like to forestall the objection to the principle of fair opportunity that it leads to a callous meritocratic society. In order to prepare the way for doing this, I note several aspects of the conception of justice that I have set out.

First we may observe that the difference principle gives some weight to the considerations singled out by the principle of redress. This is the principle that undeserved inequalities call for redress; and since inequalities of birth and natural endowment are undeserved, these inequalities are to be somehow compensated for. Thus the principle holds that in order to treat all persons equally, to provide genuine equality of opportunity, society must give more attention to those with fewer native assets and to those born into the less favorable social positions. The idea is to redress the bias of contingencies in the direction of equality. In pursuit of this principle greater resources might be spent on the education of the less rather than the more intelligent, at least over a certain time of life, say the earlier years of school.

Now the principle of redress has not to my knowledge been proposed as the sole criterion of justice, as the single aim of the social order. It is plausible as most such principles are only as a prima facie principle, one that is to be weighed in the balance with others. For example, we are to weigh it against the principle to improve the average standard of life, or to advance the common good. But whatever other principles we hold, the claims of redress are to be taken into account. It is thought to represent one of the elements in our conception of justice. Now the difference principle is not of course the principle of redress. It does not require society to try to even out handicaps as if all were expected to compete on a fair basis in the same race. But the difference principle would allocate resources in education, say, so as to improve the long-term expectation of the least favored. If this end is attained by giving more attention to the better endowed, it is permissible; otherwise not. And in making this decision, the value of education should not be assessed only in terms of economic efficiency and social welfare. Equally if not more important is the role of education in enabling a person to enjoy the culture of his society and to take part in its affairs, and in this way to provide for each individual a secure sense of his own worth.

Thus although the difference principle is not the same as that of redress, it does achieve some of the intent of the latter principle. It transforms the aims of the basic structure so that the total scheme of institutions no longer emphasizes social efficiency and technocratic values. . . .

. . . The natural distribution is neither just nor unjust; nor is it unjust that men are born into society at some particular position. These are simply natural facts. What is just and unjust is the way that institutions deal with these facts. Aristocratic and caste societies are unjust because they make these contingencies the ascriptive basis for belonging to more or less enclosed and privileged social classes. The basic structure of these societies incorporates the arbitrariness found in nature. But there is no necessity for men to resign themselves to these contingencies. The social system is not an unchangeable order beyond human control but a pattern of human action. In justice as fairness men agree to share one another's fate. In designing institutions they undertake to avail themselves of the accidents of nature and social circumstance only when doing so is for the common benefit. The two principles are a fair way of meeting the arbitrariness of fortune; and while no doubt imperfect in other ways, the institutions which satisfy these principles are just. . . .

There is a natural inclination to object that those better situated deserve their greater advantages whether or not they are to the benefit of others. At this point it is necessary to be clear about the notion of desert. It is perfectly true that given a just system of cooperation as a scheme of public rules and the expectations set up by it, those who, with the prospect of improving their condition, have done what the system announces that it will reward are entitled to their advantages. In this sense the more fortunate have a claim to their better situation; their claims are legitimate expectations established by social institutions, and the community is obligated to meet them. But this sense of desert presupposes the existence of the cooperative scheme; it is irrelevant to the question whether in the first place the scheme is to be designed in accordance with the difference principle or some other criterion.

Perhaps some will think that the person with greater natural endowments deserves those assets and the superior character that made their development possible. Because he is more worthy in this sense, he deserves the greater advantages that he could achieve with them. This view, however, is surely incorrect. It seems to be one of the fixed points of our considered judgments that no one deserves his place in the distribution of native endowments, any more than one deserves one's initial starting place in society. The assertion that a man deserves the superior character that enables him to make the effort to cultivate his abilities is equally problematic, for his character depends in large part upon fortunate family and social circumstances for which he can claim no credit. The notion of desert seems not to apply to these cases. Thus the more advantaged representative man cannot say that he deserves and therefore has a right to a scheme of cooperation in which he is permitted to acquire benefits in ways that do not contribute to the welfare of others. There is no basis for his making this claim. From the standpoint of common sense, then, the difference principle appears to be acceptable both to the more advantaged and to the less advantaged individual. . . .

BACKGROUND INSTITUTIONS FOR DISTRIBUTIVE JUSTICE

The main problem of distributive justice is the choice of a social system. The principles of justice apply to the basic structure and regulate how its major institutions are combined into one scheme. Now, as we have seen, the idea of justice as fairness is to use the notion of pure procedural justice to handle the contingencies of particular situations. The social system is to be designed so that the resulting distribution is just however things turn out. To achieve this end it is necessary to set the social and economic process within the surroundings of suitable political and legal institutions. Without an appropriate scheme of these background institutions the outcome of the distributive process will not be just. Background fairness is lacking. I shall give a brief description of these supporting institutions as they might exist in a properly organized democratic state that allows private ownership of capital and natural resources. . . .

In establishing these background institutions the government may be thought of as divided into four branches.[1] Each branch consists of various agencies, or activities thereof, charged with preserving certain social and economic conditions. These divisions do not overlap with the usual organization of government but are to be understood as different functions. The allocation branch, for example, is to keep the price system workably competitive and to prevent the formation of unreasonable market power. Such power does not exist as long as markets cannot be made more competitive consistent with the requirements of efficiency and the facts of geography and the preferences of households. The allocation branch is also charged with identifying and correcting, say by suitable taxes and subsidies and by changes in the definition of property rights, the more obvious departures from efficiency caused by the failure of prices to measure accurately social benefits and costs. To this end suitable taxes and subsidies may be used, or the scope and definition of property rights may be revised. The stabilization branch, on the other hand, strives to bring about reasonably full employment in the sense that those who want work can find it and the free choice of occupation and the deployment of finance are supported by strong effective demand. These two branches together are to maintain the efficiency of the market economy generally.

The social minimum is the responsibility of the transfer branch. . . . The essential idea is that the workings of this branch take needs into account and assign them an appropriate weight with respect to other claims. A competitive price system gives no consideration to needs and therefore it cannot be the sole device of distribution. There must be a division of labor between the parts of the social system in answering to the common sense precepts of justice. Different institutions meet different claims. Competitive markets properly regulated secure free choice of occupation and lead to an efficient use of resources and allocation of commodities to households. They set a weight on the conventional precepts associated with wages and earnings, whereas the transfer branch guarantees a certain level of well-being and honors the claims of need. . . .

It is clear that the justice of distributive shares depends on the background institutions and how they allocate total income, wages and other income plus transfers. There is with reason strong objection to the competitive determination of total income, since this ignores the claims of need and an appropriate standard of life. From the standpoint of the legislative stage it is rational to insure oneself and one's descendants against these contingencies of the market. Indeed, the difference principle presumably requires this. But once a suitable minimum is provided by transfers, it may be perfectly fair that the rest of total income be settled by the price system, assuming that it is moderately efficient and free from monopolistic restrictions, and unreasonable externalities have been eliminated. Moreover, this way of dealing with the claims of need would appear to be more effective than trying to regulate income by minimum wage standards, and the like. It is better to assign to each branch only such tasks as are compatible with one another. Since the market is not suited to answer the claims of need, these should be met by a separate arrangement. Whether the principles of justice are satisfied, then, turns on whether the total income of the least advantaged (wages plus transfers) is such as to maximize their long-run expectations (consistent with the constraints of equal liberty and fair equality of opportunity).

Finally, there is a distribution branch. Its task is to preserve an approximate justice in distributive shares by means of taxation and the necessary adjustments in the rights of property. Two aspects of this branch may be distinguished. First of all, it imposes a number of inheritance and gift taxes, and sets restrictions on the rights of bequest. The purpose of these levies and regulations is not to raise revenue (release resources to government) but gradually and continually to correct the distribution of wealth and to prevent concentrations of power detrimental to the fair value of political liberty and fair equality of opportunity. For example, the progressive principle might be applied at the beneficiary's end.[2] Doing this would encourage the wide dispersal of property which is a necessary condition, it seems, if the fair value of the equal liberties is to be maintained.

Notes

1. For the idea of branches of government, see R. A. Musgrave, *The Theory of Public Finance* (New York: McGraw-Hill, 1959), Ch. I.
2. See Meade, *Efficiency, Equality and the Ownership of Property,* pp. 56f.

THE ENTITLEMENT THEORY

Robert Nozick

The term "distributive justice" is not a neutral one. Hearing the term "distribution," most people presume that some thing or mechanism uses some principle or criterion to give out a supply of things. Into this process of distributing shares some error may have crept. So it is an open question, at least, whether *re*distribution should take place; whether we should do again what has already been done once, though poorly. However, we are not in the position of children who have been given portions of pie by someone who now makes last minute adjustments to rectify careless cutting. There is no *central* distribution, no person or group entitled to control all the resources, jointly deciding how they are to be doled out. What each person gets, he gets from others who give to him in exchange for something, or as a gift. In a free society, diverse persons control different resources, and new holdings arise out of the voluntary exchanges and actions of persons. . . .

The subject of justice in holdings consists of three major topics. The first is the *original acquisition of holdings,* the appropriation of unheld things. This includes the issues of how unheld things may come to be held, the process, or processes, by which unheld things may come to be held, the things that may come to be held by these processes, the extent of what comes to be held by a particular process, and so on. We shall refer to the complicated truth about this topic, which we shall not formulate here, as the principle of justice in acquisition. The second topic concerns the *transfer of holdings* from one person to another. By what processes may a person transfer holdings to another? How may a person acquire a holding from another who holds it? Under this topic come general descriptions of voluntary exchange, and gift and (on the other hand) fraud, as well as reference to particular conventional details fixed upon in a given society. The complicated truth about this subject (with placeholders for conventional details) we shall call the principle of justice in transfer. (And we shall suppose it also includes principles governing how a person may divest himself of a holding, passing it into an unheld state.)

If the world were wholly just, the following inductive definition would exhaustively cover the subject of justice in holdings.

1. A person who acquires a holding in accordance with the principle of justice in acquisition is entitled to that holding.
2. A person who acquires a holding in accordance with the principle of justice

From Robert Nozick, *Anarchy, State, and Utopia* (New York: Basic Books, Inc., Publishers, 1974), pp. 149-154, 156-157, 159-163, 168, 174-175, 178-179, 182. Copyright 1974 by Basic Books, Inc., Publishers, New York. Reprinted by permission of Basic Books, Inc., and Basil Blackwell Publisher.

in transfer, from someone else entitled to the holding, is entitled to the holding.

3. No one is entitled to a holding except by (repeated) applications of 1 and 2.

The complete principle of distributive justice would say simply that a distribution is just if everyone is entitled to the holdings they possess under the distribution. . . .

Not all actual situations are generated in accordance with the two principles of justice in holdings: the principle of justice in acquisition and the principle of justice in transfer. Some people steal from others, or defraud them, or enslave them, seizing their product and preventing them from living as they choose, or forcibly exclude others from competing in exchanges. None of these are permissible modes of transition from one situation to another. And some persons acquire holdings by means not sanctioned by the principle of justice in acquisition. The existence of past injustice (previous violations of the first two principles of justice in holdings) raises the third major topic under justice in holdings: the rectification of injustice in holdings. If past injustice has shaped present holdings in various ways, some identifiable and some not, what now, if anything, ought to be done to rectify these injustices? . . .

HISTORICAL PRINCIPLES AND END-RESULT PRINCIPLES

The general outlines of the entitlement theory illuminate the nature and defects of other conceptions of distributive justice. The entitlement theory of justice in distribution is *historical;* whether a distribution is just depends upon how it came about. In contrast, *current time-slice principles* of justice hold that the justice of a distribution is determined by how things are distributed (who has what) as judged by some *structural* principle(s) of just distribution. A utilitarian who judges between any two distributions by seeing which has the greater sum of utility and, if the sums tie, applies some fixed equality criterion to choose the more equal distribution, would hold a current time-slice principle of justice. As would someone who had a fixed schedule of trade-offs between the sum of happiness and equality. According to a current time-slice principle, all that needs to be looked at, in judging the justice of a distribution, is who ends up with what; in comparing any two distributions one need look only at the matrix presenting the distributions. No further information need be fed into a principle of justice. It is a consequence of such principles of justice that any two structurally identical distributions are equally just. . . .

Most persons do not accept current time-slice principles as constituting the whole story about distributive shares. They think it relevant in assessing the justice of a situation to consider not only the distribution it embodies, but also how that distribution came about. If some persons are in prison for murder or war crimes, we do not say that to assess the justice of the distribution in the society we must look only at what this person has, and that person has, and that person has, . . . at the current time. We think it relevant to ask whether someone did something so that he *deserved* to be punished, deserved to have a lower share. . . .

PATTERNING

. . . Almost every suggested principle of distributive justice is patterned: to each according to his moral merit, or needs, or marginal product, or how hard he tries, or the weighted sum of the foregoing, and so on. The principle of entitlement we have sketched is *not* patterned. There is no one natural dimension or weighted sum or combination of a small number of natural dimensions that yields the distributions generated in accordance with the principle of entitlement. The set of holdings that results when some persons receive their marginal products, others win at gambling, others receive a share of their mate's income, others receive gifts from foundations, others receive interest on loans, others receive gifts from admirers, others receive returns on investment, others make for themselves much of what they have, others find things, and so on, will not be patterned. . . .

To think that the task of a theory of distributive justice is to fill in the blank in "to each according to his _____" is to be predisposed to search for a pattern; and the separate treatment of "from each according to his _____" treats production and distribution as two separate and independent issues. On an entitlement view these are *not* two separate questions. Whoever makes something, having bought or contracted for all other held resources used in the process (transferring some of his holdings for these cooperating factors), is entitled to it. . . .

So entrenched are maxims of the usual form that perhaps we should present the entitlement conception as a competitor. Ignoring acquisition and rectification, we might say:

> From each according to what he chooses to do, to each according to what he makes for himself (perhaps with the contracted aid of others) and what others choose to do for him and choose to give him of what they've been given previously (under this maxim) and haven't yet expended or transferred.

This, the discerning reader will have noticed, has its defects as a slogan. So as a summary and great simplification (and not as a maxim with any independent meaning) we have:

> *From each as they choose, to each as they are chosen.*

HOW LIBERTY UPSETS PATTERNS

It is not clear how those holding alternative conceptions of distributive justice can reject the entitlement conception of justice in holdings. For suppose a distribution favored by one of these non-entitlement conceptions is realized. Let us suppose it is your favorite one and let us call this distribution D_1; perhaps everyone has an equal share, perhaps shares vary in accordance with some dimension you treasure. Now suppose that Wilt

Chamberlain is greatly in demand by basketball teams, being a great gate attraction. (Also suppose contracts run only for a year, with players being free agents.) He signs the following sort of contract with a team: In each home game, twenty-five cents from the price of each ticket of admission goes to him. (We ignore the question of whether he is "gouging" the owners, letting them look out for themselves.) The season starts, and people cheerfully attend his team's games; they buy their tickets, each time dropping a separate twenty-five cents of their admission price into a special box with Chamberlain's name on it. They are excited about seeing him play; it is worth the total admission price to them. Let us suppose that in one season one million persons attend his home games, and Wilt Chamberlain winds up with $250,000, a much larger sum than the average income and larger even than anyone else has. Is he entitled to this income? Is this new distribution D_2, unjust? If so, why? There is *no* question about whether each of the people was entitled to the control over the resources they held in D_1; because that was the distribution (your favorite) that (for the purposes of argument) we assumed was acceptable. Each of these persons *chose* to give twenty-five cents of their money to Chamberlain. They could have spent it on going to the movies, or on candy bars, or on copies of *Dissent* magazine, or of *Monthly Review*. But they all, at least one million of them, converged on giving it to Wilt Chamberlain in exchange for watching him play basketball. If D_1 was a just distribution, and people voluntarily moved from it to D_2, transferring parts of their shares they were given under D_1 (what was it for if not to do something with?), isn't D_2 also just? If the people were entitled to dispose of the resources to which they were entitled (under D_1), didn't this include their being entitled to give it to, or exchange it with, Wilt Chamberlain? Can anyone else complain on grounds of justice? Each other person already has his legitimate share under D_1. Under D_1, there is nothing that anyone has that anyone else has a claim of justice against. After someone transfers something to Wilt Chamberlain, third parties *still* have their legitimate shares; *their* shares are not changed. By what process could such a transfer among two persons give a rise to a legitimate claim of distributive justice on a portion of what was transferred, by a third party who had no claim of justice on any holding of the others *before* the transfer? To cut off objections irrelevant here, we might imagine the exchanges occurring in a socialist society, after hours. After playing whatever basketball he does in his daily work, or doing whatever other daily work he does, Wilt Chamberlain decides to put in *overtime* to earn additional money. (First his work quota is set; he works time over that.) Or imagine it is a skilled juggler people like to see, who puts on shows after hours. . . .

The general point illustrated by the Wilt Chamberlain example is that no end-state principle or distributional patterned principle of justice can be continuously realized without continuous interference with people's lives. Any favored pattern would be transformed into one unfavored by the principle, by people choosing to act in various ways; for example, by people exchanging goods and services with other people, or giving things to other people, things the transferrers are entitled to under the favored distributional patten. To maintain a pattern one must either continually interfere to stop people from transferring resources as they wish to, or continually (or periodically) interfere to take from some persons resources that others for some reason chose to transfer to them. . . .

Patterned principles of distributive justice necessitate *re*distributive activities. The likelihood is small that any actual freely-arrived-at set of holdings fits a given pattern; and the likelihood is nil that it will continue to fit the pattern as people exchange and give. From the point of view of an entitlement theory, redistribution is a serious matter indeed, involving, as it does, the violation of people's rights. (An exception is those takings that fall under the principle of the rectification of injustices.) . . .

LOCKE'S THEORY OF ACQUISITION

. . . [Let us] introduce an additional bit of complexity into the structure of the entitlement theory. This is best approached by considering Locke's attempt to specify a principle of justice in acquisition. Locke views property rights in an unowned object as originating through someone's mixing his labor with it. This gives rise to many questions. What are the boundaries of what labor is mixed with? If a private astronaut clears a place on Mars, has he mixed his labor with (so that he comes to own) the whole planet, the whole uninhabited universe, or just a particular plot? Which plot does an act bring under ownership? . . .

Locke's proviso that there be "enough and as good left in common for others" is meant to ensure that the situation of others is not worsened. . . .

. . . I assume that any adequate theory of justice in acquisition will contain a proviso similar to [Locke's]. . . .

I believe that the free operation of a market system will not actually run afoul of the Lockean proviso. . . . If this is correct, the proviso will not . . . provide a significant opportunity for future state action.

JUSTICE AND THE BUSINESS SOCIETY

Jan Narveson

"We're not in business for our health, Mister!" "Madam, at that price you're not asking for a bargain—you're asking for charity!" Remarks like these illustrate the basic facts—and raise the basic questions—about that realm of human activity known to us as "business." What is the "business world"? What are its main assumptions? The classic answers to these questions are well known and clear. Business transactions occur between free and independent persons presumed to be rationally seeking to promote their own advantage. The standard business relationship is between

Original essay written especially for this text. Reprinted with permission of the author.

people who are neither friends nor enemies, neither allies in a common cause nor hated competitors out to do each other dirt. It is almost impossible to overemphasize either of these facets. (1) On the one hand, business may be done between people who not only do not love each other but, indeed, don't even know each other. Such ties are entirely unnecessary— and might even get in the way. (One of the reasons why the supermarket has largely replaced the corner store is precisely because of its impersonal character. You don't feel compelled to discuss the weather, the latest poltical developments, or, worst of all, the goings-on of your new neighbors' children with the check-out person at the supermarket—who in any case is too busy for such things.) (2) On the other hand, there is no call for attributing malice even to the most avid competitors in the business world. A's loss is not identical with B's gain: A and B both want the business, but that's all they want. The satisfaction of one's own firm's getting the contract is due to getting the contract, not to the other fellow's not getting it.

Parties to any business transaction—from the lowliest purchase of an onion at the Farmer's Market to deals involving billions of dollars—may be as different as you like; yet business enables each party to benefit from the other. The free exchange of goods or services which is the essence of business is possible because each party has something which the other party values *more* than what he already has. If both possessed identical commodities, and especially if they were also in exactly the same circumstances, then mutually advantageous exchange could not readily happen. In business, our differences unite us. This is so, as economic analysis can readily demonstrate, even when our values are not only different but, in a rather important sense, incomparable. For profitable exchange, it is unnecessary for us to be able to say, "Aha—you are getting five units of Ultimate Value out of this, whereas I'm getting only three!" It is necessary merely that we consider what our options are, know which we prefer to which, and believe that what the other fellow has to offer is the best we can do in the circumstances. Given this, we are "ready to do business."

There is a great deal to be said for business transactions as the paradigm cases of human relationships. For consider the alternatives. On the one hand, imagine trying genuinely to live in accordance with Jesus Christ's injunction, "Love ye one another!" Any decently realistic view of the human situation will quickly reveal that this injunction is neither possible nor even desirable for the typical case. It is not *possible* because, in any but the most trivialized sense of the term "love," our capacity to love is wildly outstripped by the enormous number of people toward whom it might be directed. Anyone who thinks this is possible has probably never been in love, never really loved anyone, or has forgotten for the moment what loving involves. And even if it were *possible,* would it be *desirable*? Is it not far better to know a few people well, give them the kind of devoted attention and warmth of feeling which makes love so important and so fine an element in the good life, than to divide oneself a thousand and million ways, driving oneself crazy in the attempt to honor all those commitments?

On the other hand, consider how awful it would be, how intolerable and miserable, to regard all mankind as The Enemy. Quite apart from the fear, suspicion, and hatred inspired in us by the thought of someone who regards all of his fellows as evil and diabolical, do we not, on reflection, have the greatest pity for anyone like that? What could be a worse and more desperate frame of mind than to walk the streets in constant rage against the rest of mankind? This, of course, quite apart from the evils sure to be visited upon you if you take the actions appropriate to such paranoid beliefs.

No, neither of these alternatives will do. And then, isn't it inevitable that with regard to the greater part of mankind, either we simply have nothing to do with them at all, because they are much too far away, or we engage in relationships which are neither too onerously personal and involving nor dangerous and thoroughly unpleasant? And is there any better basis for such relationships than those of mutual profit and advantage? But that structure, in principle, is the world of business. Here we are not presumed to *owe* each other anything more than to leave each other in peace, to go about, as we say, his business; and if we do relate to each other, we do so on terms of mutual advantage. There is no expectation, no insistence that the other fellow will give me the shirt off his back. Rather, the assumption is that, apart from ordinary good manners, he will do something for me only if I reciprocally do something for him.

One of the ablest current writers[1] has coined an admirable phrase to characterize the ethics of what we might call Business Person. The phrase is "constrained maximization." The person operating on such a policy is one who is, indeed, out to get the best deal possible for himself; but he stops short in those cases where for all concerned to pursue such a policy would make each worse off. In such cases, he cooperates with the others involved, renouncing the policy of unlimited self-seeking and adhering instead to mutually satisfactory agreements.

It is possible to think that a world in which everyone adhered to the business orientation in his dealings with the world at large would be quite a good world, even, perhaps, the very best world we could humanly and reasonably expect. Yet there are plenty of people nowadays who are anything but convinced of that possibility. Why is this so?

The main reason has to do with a difference of view on the subject of Justice. Those who share the view that a Business World would be the best of all realistically possible worlds are apt to think of justice as the keeping of honestly made agreements and the avoidance of violence. On that general conception of justice, it will be noted, justice has no necessary connection with Equality. If we each make and reliably keep the best deals we can, there is no certainty, and indeed small probability, that the result, even in the long run, will be to yield approximately the same level of income, wealth, welfare, or happiness for everyone. Indeed, there is no limit to the discrepancies which could in principle arise as the result of successive just dealings, on this view of the matter.[2] But some—quite a few, evidently— want to insist that a just world is also an equal world. Usually such people have especially in mind the avoidance of poverty as the goal of justice;[3] but sometimes they proclaim the goal of real equality in the stronger sense, not merely that none will be in desperate want but also that the difference in wealth between the poorest and the richest would be negligible, which of course is to say that there would be no ''poor'' or ''rich.''[4]

Indeed, there are those who think that equality is so obviously a goal, or even *the* goal of justice that they accuse those who espouse the business world of ignoring or even opposing justice. But this accusation is unfair. Those who think that the world in which our typical relations with our fellows are those of free transactions for mutual advantage think that that *is* a just world. And they think that a world in which such transactions are substantially ''interfered with'' in the interests of equality is, on the contrary, an unjust world. For they think that to intervene forcibly in an activity carried on between mature people who have freely agreed to do what they do and who are not working for the detriment of anyone else is unjust.

It may at first seem that here is a ground-floor disagreement, one which it is scarcely possible to resolve. And this may be true, but we must not be too hasty. For the plot thickens when we consider more carefully the description which I have just produced of the business advocate's view of injustice. It is not so clear, in fact, that the advocate of equality must, or will, disagree that that description, just as it stands, is one of injustice. He may well agree that *if* an agreement between two normal and rational beings has been genuinely reached *freely,* and if indeed the resulting activity really does not work to the detriment of anyone else—*then* to interfere in this activity would be wrong or unjust, at least other things being more or less equal. But they will claim that this is not typically the case in the business world. They will insist that business agreements are not struck in perfect freedom, and that even if they were, they systematically work to disadvantage others. Is there any reason to think this is so?

First, why might it be felt that these agreements are not struck freely? In some cases, we may all agree, there is fraud, deception, or dishonesty involved. And in others, there is coercion or even violence. If I sell you what I have described as a can of peanuts, and upon opening it you find instead wood chips, then something has gone wrong and injustice may well be involved. Or if I give you your choice between paying me $10,000 and winding up in cement shoes at the bottom of the Welland Canal one fine evening, then again we do not have a ''free agreement.'' Injustice not only may well be, but certainly is, involved. But does the egalitarian think that either of these kinds of shortcomings is involved in typical business transactions?

He might. Along the former lines, he might, for instance, point to the use of advertising. He might claim that the customer in the contemporary world is typically bamboozled into buying, that the product is made to look alluring, and that in any case the ''need'' which the item allegedly satisfies is not a *real* need.[5] In turn, he may claim that in much of this world there are monopolies doing the supplying, so that the consumer has no real choice. Or in the case of labor contracts, he may say that the workman has no real choice either: he must either work or starve.

All these points are susceptible to cogent replies, however. The point about advertising simply doesn't establish what it needs to establish, for it is not claimed that typical ads are fraudulent. If they attempt to create an aura of attractiveness about the products being advertised, why shouldn't they? So does the New Testament, in its efforts to persuade us of the merits of the Christian religion. Does anyone think that it should be outlawed? And if advertisers insinuate that you will live a better life if you buy their products, why on earth *shouldn't* they do this? And if we are to have a centralized censor making decisions about what we should and shouldn't be told by sellers, or what we should or shouldn't buy, then how, please, is this argument going to be represented as that of a friend of "freedom"?

The other two arguments suffer from a different defect. They assume that it is the duty of the seller not only to offer the consumer the products he offers, but also to make sure that there are plenty of other sellers on the market with attractive alternatives! But if *that* is the argument, then there isn't genuinely an agreement about our original hypothesis that interference with freedom is on the face of it unjust. If I, the seller, had begun by forcibly depriving you of alternatives, in the manner of the mobster with his protection racket, then of course we would not have a situation of freedom between buyer and seller. But that is not what happens. The business person does not in general create the situation in which there is a potential market for his product. Rather, he discerns this situation, and he moves to supply it. *Not,* let us recall, out of motives of charity, but out of a desire for profit. And others are free to enter the market, too, if they've a mind to.

The business-world view of justice does, certainly, have its hard-nosed aspects. In that world, we do not *owe* each other even a minimum standard of living, let alone an equal one. I may be starving in the gutter and in rags: this still does not make it your obligation to feed and clothe me, even if you are exceedingly wealthy. Why not? Because there is no antecedent agreement, struck on terms of mutual self-interest, which requires me to do this. Had there been one, that would be another matter. But there may well not have. And if not, then what?

Well, one thing is that if I am in such desperate straits, I ought to be willing to accept any offer of employment which will get me out of them. And you, in turn, can make me a very favorable offer, from your point of view. The likelihood is that you will indeed make such an offer. After all, low labor costs are a main road to profit, are they not? Thus will industry move to depressed areas, provided that there are no minimum-wage laws standing in the way. Thus will our cotton shirts and our transistor radios come to be made in India or Hong Kong. It's good business—for *both* parties. The egalitarian, of course, will denounce this as Imperialism. Imperialism appears when you hire foreigners for 50 cents an hour—several times what they have ever earned before, quite likely!—when instead you could be hiring your fellow citizens for $6 an hour, plus time and a half, plus union featherbedding in the bargain. Obviously Justice will call upon us to leave the Indians, the Chinese, and the Mexicans to stay undernourished in their hovels in the interests of Equality for our fellow Americans or Canadians, right? And so our other fellow North Americans will pay 50 percent more for their shirts and their radios, thus making their fair sacrifice to equality too—even if they happen to be making less than $6 an hour themselves and do not belong to unions.

Is there a duty to our fellow man, as our fellow man, to attend to his health and welfare? To provide him with a tolerable diet if he doesn't already have one? To send him off to the public schools (whether he wants to go or not, of course!)? And to pay his way through a fine public university when he gets out of that public school? Or are we confusing the question of whether these would be *desirable* things to happen to him with the question of whether it is our duty, as a matter of justice, to provide him with them if we can afford to and he cannot? If we are, that might go far to explain the mixture of feelings we may well have when we consider these matters. For after all, how can any humane and decent person deny that it is *better* that people be healthy, well fed and clothed, and well educated than that they should be sick, starving, and ignorant? The fact that it is better, however, may not show that it is a matter of justice that those of us in a position to promote these ends *must* promote them.

What is the difference between these two, if they are different—between the desirable and the just? Between, to invoke two recent political slogans, the Good Society and the Just Society? Although these are difficult questions, with a long history of philosophical dispute behind them, I believe that a considerable part of the answer is not so difficult to come by. The difference I have in mind is the difference between what, as rational beings, we *should* do and what we *must* do. When we address ourselves to the former sort of questions, the assumption is that we are free to choose: we can make better or worse choices, and if we make a worse one we may come to regret it, and others may properly deplore the choice—but it remains that the choice is ours to make. In the latter case, however, the case of justice, things are different. Justice *requires* us to do some things and to refrain from others. More especially, others may properly not only upbraid us for failing to do what justice requires, but may even properly make us do it. Our freedom may properly be restricted, if it's a matter of justice; but not if it isn't. (Some theorists will want to have it that justice involves *rights,* whereas goodness and the desirable do not. But I believe that this formulation will be found to come to the same thing as what I have just said.)[6]

The question whether we have a duty in justice to part with some of our fairly gotten gains to help the unfortunate is, then, the question whether we may properly be *forced* to do so. If we may, then taxation, for instance, is in order—taxes being payments which we have no choice but to make, payments we must make whether we like it or not, and even whether we think the objects for which the money will be spent are desirable or not, whether the money is being spent wisely or foolishly. But if we may *not* be forced to do so, then taxation is out of order, even if the result is that some will be in want.

Do we think that this sort of thing is a matter of justice and duty? If it is so thought, then there is at least one problem to face: viz., why does it matter whether those in want are next door or in other countries, however far away? And how much of our incomes may we be required to part with in order to promote this end? These two questions cannot be tidily separated. For if justice requires that we help those less fortunate than ourselves, and if we could, literally, afford to help many more than only those in our own country before we began to be in desperation ourselves, then it is not obvious why justice should extend only to the borders of one's own country. And if, on the other hand, it *should* stop there, then it cannot be due to the sheer fact that others are in want and we can help that justice requires us to help them. It makes no sense to say, "X is a human right, and therefore we should see that everybody *who is subject to the same government we are* gets X." And this shows that we do not really believe that welfare *is* a human right.

But mightn't it still be a politically based right, that is, a right derived from common membership in the same political system? There will, again, be those who think so, perhaps on the ground that we all have the equal right to vote, and hence to whatever a democratic procedure provides in the way of welfare rights or whatever other kinds of rights there might be. But do we believe this, either? Do we not, on the contrary, think that genuine rights are beyond the reach of majorities? Such rights as free speech, assembly, religion, and so on are surely not rights which we think a majority can properly abrogate. Why should property rights, then, be an exception?

Among those who still think it should be an exception are, principally, people who take the view that inert nature, unlike the various bodies and minds which are around, does not intrinsically *belong* to anyone. Attempts, such as that of Locke, to get external nature into the sphere of private ownership by acts of appropriation of labor, for instance, are difficult to carry out satisfactorily for reasons which have lately been rather exquisitely set forth by Robert Nozick.[7] But while this may be so, it remains that there is likewise no obvious reason for saying that external nature belongs to *everyone*—to all of us equally or jointly or whatever.[8] And there is a strong reason for pointing out that the lion's share of what there is to own is manmade. If we add to this the inordinate difficulties of coherently articulating socialism in this area, we shall find it very hard to improve on property rights which are likewise strong enough to resist the blandishments of majority rule. When a person has acquired property or purchasing power through fair exchange and honest effort, it is not easy to resist the conclusion that to take some or all of it from him simply on the say-so of an obscure majority is as unjust as it would be to take some of his limbs, or some of his time. Indeed, it is tantamount to taking the latter, for if you take from me some important (to me) and replaceable thing, my only option is to expend some more of my precious time in replacing it.

These last arguments look uncomfortably like appeals to Natural Right. And such appeals have a notable potential for becoming dead ends. However, the situation may not be so bad as all that. I want to conclude this quick survey of a great deal of pertinent territory with two observations.

The first observation is that while the business conception of justice does not make it a duty to contribute to those in need, it does not preclude voluntary contributions to that end either. And if it is, as I have suggested above, so obvious that such contributions are a good thing, is it unbelievable that a system in which taxation was not resorted to in order to cater to needs would be able to cope sufficiently with them? Even in the current dispensation, after all, generosity is not unusual even among people of means and among business enterprises. The typical human breast is far from devoid of sympathy, and those who think that business society exterminates such sentiments have probably never served on fund-raising committees for charitable enterprises. And shouldn't we also ask why it is that motives of charity and humanity should make us resort to a sort of organized theft—which, after all, taxation appears to be equivalent to? There is also, of course, the question whether an unlimited free market would not do far better for problems of unemployment and the like; and who can doubt that full employment would be a far more efficient cure for poverty and its related ills than any amount either of tax-induced expenditure on welfare or of charitable contribution by the better-off? All in all, the upshot may be that the Just Society, if justice is measured by the business outlook, would also in fact be the Good Society! Perhaps, then, our predilection for governmental cures to problems is a function of two of the oldest enemies of mankind: fear and ignorance—fear of liberty ("dreadful freedom"!) and ignorance of economics.

The second observation is a more general theoretical cousin of the first. Those who defend the market economy, the business view of justice, on grounds of Natural Right cannot, of course, consistently base their defense of that society on such arguments as the above. But the rest of us can. And is it really believable that a society might be both perfectly just and perfectly miserable? Not readily, I think. But there is not, as has often been thought, a great gulf fixed between a theory of justice involving strong property rights and a theory based on general utility. Those who have supposed that there must be such a gulf have, I suspect, overlooked an important point about the terms of reference of a utilitarian outlook on these matters. For they suppose that the utilitarian must simply equate the just with what has maximal utility; and so, for instance, they suppose that if from the utilitarian point of view it would be preferable for A to have less and B to have more, then straightaway we must conclude that the just thing to do, on the utiliarian view, must be to bring it about, by whatever means, that A has less and B has more. Not so, however. For what must be evaluated is not simply the end result—A's level of material well-being versus B's, for instance—but *also* the means by which it is brought about that A and B each has what he has. For if we can bring about this result only by taking from A what he has acquired fairly through a highly natural and intuitive system of acquisition, and by giving it to B, who has not, then we have to evaluate the consequences of that *as well as* the distributive end result. And it is no longer so obvious that the arrangement of A having less and B more by virtue of A having been forcibly deprived of what B ends up with *is* going to be better on the whole—particularly if B, after all, was welcome to pursue his living on the same terms as A, if he was all that anxious to achieve what A has.

It is a very long way from the sort of society we in fact have to the sort of society envisaged by the proponent of the noninterventionist free market— a fact of considerable importance when we encounter the kind of diatribes against the latter currently fashionable in Western intellectual circles, since much of their complaint seems to be based on the assumption that current economic society is a good enough model of the free market to do. It is not very easy to say how things would be in a free market society; and further, so far as I can see, the theory of that kind of society is by no means complete. But we owe it to ourselves to take seriously the philosophical underpinnings of that view. This brief account is designed to suggest that those foundations are neither silly nor even inhumane.

Notes

1. David Gauthier, "Reason and Maximization," *Canadian Journal of Philosophy,* March 1975. Gauthier, I should note, does not coin this phrase especially to describe business society, but rather, to describe the normative stance of rational man. It fits and leads to the Business Society, however.
2. This is brought forcibly home in the brilliant exposition of this point of view by Robert Nozick, in *Anarchy, State and Utopia* (Basic Books, 1974). Cf. especially pp. 150–164.
3. For example, Nicholas Rescher's *Distributive Justice* (Bobbs-Merrill, 1966) advocates a "Utility Floor" (cf. Ch. 2, Sect. 2), and suggests a concept of "Effective Average" which tends in the direction of equality. The more recent *A Theory of Justice,* by John Rawls (Harvard, 1971), proposes principles of justice which favor the bottom classes of society rather strongly.
4. Many Marxists appear to embrace full equality, at least as an ultimate goal.
5. This point of view is urged, in rather delightful prose, by John Kenneth Galbraith in many places, e.g. *The New Industrial State* (Houghton Mifflin, 1967), especially Ch. xiii.
6. J. S. Mill's *Utilitarianism,* Chapter V ("On the Connection between Justice and Utility") in effect proposes a way to accomplish this. It is followed up in the author's *Morality and Utility* (Johns Hopkins, 1967), Chapter VI.
7. Nozick, *op cit.,* pp. 174–175 especially.
8. Nozick, again, p. 178. A good deal of the inspiration for this essay, I should say, comes from reading Nozick's stimulating book.

RICH AND POOR

Peter Singer

One way of making sense of the non-consequentialist view of responsibility is by basing it on a theory of rights of the kind proposed by John Locke or, more recently, Robert Nozick. If everyone has a right to life, and this right is a right *against* others who might threaten my life, but not a right *to* assistance from others when my life is in danger, then we can understand the feeling that we are responsible for acting to kill but not for omitting to save. The former violates the rights of others, the latter does not.

Should we accept such a theory of rights? If we build up our theory of

From Peter Singer, "Rich and Poor," in *Practical Ethics* (New York: Cambridge University Press, 1979), pp. 166, 168–179. Reprinted with permission.

rights by imagining, as Locke and Nozick do, individuals living independently from each other in a 'state of nature', it may seem natural to adopt a conception of rights in which as long as each leaves the other alone, no rights are violated. I might, on this view, quite properly have maintained my independent existence if I had wished to do so. So if I do not make you any worse off than you would have been if I had had nothing at all to do with you, how can I have violated your rights? But why start from such an unhistorical, abstract and ultimately inexplicable idea as an independent individual? We now know that our ancestors were social beings long before they were human beings, and could not have developed the abilities and capacities of human beings if they had not been social beings first. In any case we are not, now, isolated individuals. If we consider people living together in a community, it is less easy to assume that rights must be restricted to rights against interference. We might, instead, adopt the view that taking rights to life seriously is incompatible with standing by and watching people die when one could easily save them. . . .

The Obligation to Assist

The Argument for an Obligation to Assist

The path from the library at my university to the Humanities lecture theatre passes a shallow ornamental pond. Suppose that on my way to give a lecture I noticed that a small child has fallen in and is in danger of drowning. Would anyone deny that I ought to wade in and pull the child out? This will mean getting my clothes muddy, and either cancelling my lecture or delaying it until I can find something dry to change into; but compared with the avoidable death of a child this is insignificant.

A plausible principle that would support the judgment that I ought to pull the child out is this: if it is in our power to prevent something very bad happening, without thereby sacrificing anything of comparable moral significance, we ought to do it. This principle seems uncontroversial. It will obviously win the assent of consequentialists; but non-consequentialists should accept it too, because the injunction to prevent what is bad applies only when nothing comparably significant is at stake. Thus the principle cannot lead to the kinds of actions of which non-consequentialists strongly disapprove—serious violations of individual rights, injustice, broken promises, and so on. If a non-consequentialist regards any of these as comparable in moral significance to the bad thing that is to be prevented, he will automatically regard the principle as not applying in those cases in which the bad thing can only be prevented by violating rights, doing injustice, breaking promises, or whatever else is at stake. Most non-consequentialists hold that we ought to prevent what is bad and promote what is good. Their dispute with consequentialists lies in their insistence that this is not the sole ultimate ethical principle: that it is *an* ethical principle is not denied by any plausible ethical theory.

Nevertheless the uncontroversial appearance of the principle that we ought to prevent what is bad when we can do so without sacrificing anything of comparable moral significance is deceptive. If it were taken seriously and acted upon, our lives and our world would be fundamentally changed. For the principle applies, not just to rare situations in which one can save a child from a pond, but to the everyday situations in which we can assist those living in absolute poverty. In saying this I assume that absolute poverty, with its hunger and malnutrition, lack of shelter, illiteracy, disease, high infant mortality and low life expectancy, is a bad thing. And I assume that it is within the power of the affluent to reduce absolute poverty, without sacrificing anything of comparable moral significance. If these two assumptions and the principle we have been discussing are correct, we have an obligation to help those in absolute poverty which is no less strong than our obligation to rescue a drowning child from a pond. Not to help would be wrong, whether or not it is intrinsically equivalent to killing. Helping is not, as conventionally thought, a charitable act which it is praiseworthy to do, but not wrong to omit; it is something that everyone ought to do.

This is the argument for an obligation to assist. Set out more formally, it would look like this.

First premise:	If we can prevent something bad without sacrificing anything of comparable significance, we ought to do it.
Second premise:	Absolute poverty is bad.
Third premise:	There is some absolute poverty we can prevent without sacrificing anything of comparable moral significance.
Conclusion:	We ought to prevent some absolute poverty.

The first premise is the substantive moral premise on which the argument rests, and I have tried to show that it can be accepted by people who hold a variety of ethical positions.

The second premise is unlikely to be challenged. Absolute poverty is, as [Robert] McNamara put it, 'beneath any reasonable definition of human decency' and it would be hard to find a plausible ethical view which did not regard it as a bad thing.

The third premise is more controversial, even though it is cautiously framed. It claims only that some absolute poverty can be prevented without the sacrifice of anything of comparable moral significance. It thus avoids the objection that any aid I can give is just 'drops in the ocean' for the point is not whether my personal contribution will make any noticeable impression on world poverty as a whole (of course it won't) but whether it will prevent some poverty. This is all the argument needs to sustain its conclusion, since the second premise says that any absolute poverty is bad, and not merely the total amount of absolute poverty. If without sacrificing anything of comparable moral significance we can provide just one family with the means to raise itself out of absolute poverty, the third premise is vindicated.

I have left the notion of moral significance unexamined in order to show that the argument does not depend on any specific values or ethical principles. I think the third premise is true for most people living in industrialized nations, on any defensible view of what is morally significant. Our affluence means that we have income we can dispose of without giving up the basic necessities of life, and we can use this income to reduce absolute poverty. Just how much we will think ourselves obliged to give up will depend on what we consider to be of comparable moral significance to the poverty we could prevent: colour television, stylish clothes, expensive dinners, a sophisticated stereo system, overseas holidays, a (second?) car, a larger house, private schools for our children . . . For a utilitarian, none of these is likely to be of comparable significance to the reduction of absolute poverty; and those who are not utilitarians surely must, if they subscribe to the principle of universalizability, accept that at least *some* of these things are of far less moral significance than the absolute poverty that could be prevented by the money they cost. So the third premise seems to be true on any plausible ethical view—although the precise amount of absolute poverty that can be prevented before anything of moral significance is sacrificed will vary according to the ethical view one accepts.

Objections to the Argument

Taking care of our own. Anyone who has worked to increase overseas aid will have come across the argument that we should look after those near us, our families and then the poor in our own country, before we think about poverty in distant places.

No doubt we do instinctively prefer to help those who are close to us. Few could stand by and watch a child drown; many can ignore a famine in Africa. But the question is not what we usually do, but what we ought to do, and it is difficult to see any sound moral justification for the view that distance, or community membership, makes a crucial difference to our obligations.

Consider, for instance, racial affinities. Should whites help poor whites before helping poor blacks? Most of us would reject such a suggestion out of hand, [by appeal to] the principle of equal consideration of interests: people's need for food has nothing to do with their race, and if blacks need food more than whites, it would be a violation of the principle of equal consideration to give preference to whites.

The same point applies to citizenship or nationhood. Every affluent nation has some relatively poor citizens, but absolute poverty is limited largely to the poor nations. Those living on the streets of Calcutta, or in a drought-stricken region of the Sahel, are experiencing poverty unknown in the West. Under these circumstances it would be wrong to decide that only those fortunate enough to be citizens of our own community will share our abundance.

We feel obligations of kinship more strongly than those of citizenship. Which parents could give away their last bowl of rice if their own children were starving? To do so would seem unnatural, contrary to our nature as biologically evolved beings—although whether it would be wrong is another question altogether. In any case, we are not faced with that situation, but with one in which our own children are well-fed, well-clothed, well-educated, and would now like new bikes, a stereo set, or their own car. In these circumstances any special obligations we might have to our children have been fulfilled, and the needs of strangers make a stronger claim upon us.

The element of truth in the view that we should first take care of our own, lies in the advantage of a recognized system of responsibilities. When families and local communities look after their own poorer members, ties of affection and personal relationships achieve ends that would otherwise require a large, impersonal bureaucracy. Hence it would be absurd to propose that from now on we all regard ourselves as equally responsible for the welfare of everyone in the world; but the argument for an obligation to assist does not propose that. It applies only when some are in absolute poverty, and others can help without sacrificing anything of comparable moral significance. To allow one's own kin to sink into absolute poverty would be to sacrifice something of comparable significance; and before that point had been reached, the breakdown of the system of family and community responsibility would be a factor to weigh the balance in favour of a small degree of preference for family and community. This small degree of preference is, however, decisively outweighed by existing discrepancies in wealth and property.

Property rights. Do people have a right to private property, a right which contradicts the view that they are under an obligation to give some of their wealth away to those in absolute poverty? According to some theories of rights (for instance, Robert Nozick's) provided one has acquired one's property without the use of unjust means like force and fraud, one may be entitled to enormous wealth while others starve. This individualistic conception of rights is in contrast to other views, like the early Christian doctrine to be found in the works of Thomas Aquinas, which holds that since property exists for the satisfaction of human needs, 'whatever a man has in superabundance is owed, of natural right, to the poor for their sustenance'. A socialist would also, of course, see wealth as belonging to the community rather than the individual, while utilitarians, whether socialist or not, would be prepared to override property rights to prevent great evils.

Does the argument for an obligation to assist others therefore presuppose one of these other theories of property rights, and not an individualistic theory like Nozick's? Not necessarily. A theory of property rights can insist on our *right* to retain wealth without pronouncing on whether the rich *ought* to give to the poor. Nozick, for example, rejects the use of compulsory means like taxation to redistribute income, but suggests that we can achieve the ends we deem morally desirable by voluntary means. So Nozick would reject the claim that rich people have an 'obligation' to give to the poor, in so far as this implies that the poor have a right to our aid, but might accept that giving is something we ought to do and failing to give, though within one's rights, is wrong—for rights is not all there is to ethics.

The argument for an obligation to assist can survive, with only minor modifications, even if we accept an individualistic theory of property rights. In any case, however, I do not think we should accept such a theory. It leaves too much to chance to be an acceptable ethical view. For instance, those whose forefathers happened to inhabit some sandy wastes around the Persian Gulf are now fabulously wealthy, because oil lay under those sands; while those whose forefathers settled on better land south of the

Sahara live in absolute poverty, because of drought and bad harvests. Can this distribution be acceptable from an impartial point of view? If we imagine ourselves about to begin life as a citizen of either Kuwait or Chad—but we do not know which—would we accept the principle that citizens of Kuwait are under no obligation to assist people living in Chad?

Population and the ethics of triage. Perhaps the most serious objection to the argument that we have an obligation to assist is that since the major cause of absolute poverty is overpopulation, helping those now in poverty will only ensure that yet more people are born to live in poverty in the future.

In its most extreme form, this objection is taken to show that we should adopt a policy of 'triage'. The term comes from medical policies adopted in wartime. With too few doctors to cope with all the casualties, the wounded were divided into three categories: those who would probably survive without medical assistance, those who might survive if they received assistance, but otherwise probably would not, and those who even with medical assistance probably would not survive. Only those in the middle category were given medical assistance. The idea, of course, was to use limited medical resources as effectively as possible. For those in the first category, medical treatment was not strictly necessary; for those in the third category, it was likely to be useless. It has been suggested that we should apply the same policies to countries, according to their prospects of becoming self-sustaining. We would not aid countries which even without our help will soon be able to feed their populations. We would not aid countries which, even with our help, will not be able to limit their population to a level they can feed. We would aid those countries where our help might make the difference between success and failure in bringing food and population into balance.

Advocates of this theory are understandably reluctant to give a complete list of the countries they would place into the 'hopeless' category; but Bangladesh is often cited as an example. Adopting the policy of triage would, then, mean cutting off assistance to Bangladesh and allowing famine, disease and natural disasters to reduce the population of that country (now around 80 million) to the level at which it can provide adequately for all.

In support of this view Garrett Hardin has offered a metaphor: we in the rich nations are like the occupants of a crowded lifeboat adrift in a sea full of drowning people. If we try to save the drowning by bringing them aboard our boat will be overloaded and we shall all drown. Since it is better that some survive than none, we should leave the others to drown. In the world today, according to Hardin, 'lifeboat ethics' apply. The rich should leave the poor to starve, for otherwise the poor will drag the rich down with them. . . .

Anyone whose initial reaction to triage was not one of repugnance would be an unpleasant sort of person. Yet initial reactions based on strong feelings are not always reliable guides. Advocates of triage are rightly concerned with the long-term consequences of our actions. They say that helping the poor and starving now merely ensures more poor and starving in the future. When our capacity to help is finally unable to cope—as one day it must be—the suffering will be greater than it would be if we stopped helping now. If this is correct, there is nothing we can do to prevent absolute starvation and poverty, in the long run, and so we have no obligation to assist. Nor does it seem reasonable to hold that under these circumstances people have a right to our assistance. If we do accept such a right, irrespective of the consequences, we are saying that, in Hardin's metaphor, we would continue to haul the drowning into our lifeboat until the boat sank and we all drowned.

If triage is to be rejected it must be tackled on its own ground, within the framework of consequentialist ethics. Here it is vulnerable. Any consequentialist ethics must take probability of outcome into account. A course of action that will certainly produce some benefit is to be preferred to an alternative course that may lead to a slightly larger benefit, but is equally likely to result in no benefit at all. Only if the greater magnitude of the uncertain benefit outweighs its uncertainty should we choose it. Better one certain unit of benefit than a 10% chance of 5 units; but better a 50% chance of 3 units than a single certain unit. The same principle applies when we are trying to avoid evils.

The policy of triage involves a certain, very great evil: population control by famine and disease. Tens of millions would die slowly. Hundreds of millions would continue to live in absolute poverty, at the very margin of existence. Against this prospect, advocates of the policy place a possible evil which is greater still: the same process of famine and disease, taking place in, say, fifty years time, when the world's population may be three times its present level, and the number who will die from famine, or struggle on in absolute poverty, will be that much greater. The quesiton is: how probable is this forecast that continued assistance now will lead to greater disasters in the future?

Forecasts of population growth are notoriously fallible, and theories about the factors which affect it remain speculative. One theory, at least as plausible as any other, is that countries pass through a 'demographic transition' as their standard of living rises. When people are very poor and have no access to modern medicine their fertility is high, but population is kept in check by high death rates. The introduction of sanitation, modern medical techniques and other improvements reduces the death rate, but initially has little effect on the birth rate. Then population grows rapidly. Most poor countries are now in this phase. If standards of living continue to rise, however, couples begin to realize that to have the same number of children surviving to maturity as in the past, they do not need to give birth to as many children as their parents did. The need for children to provide economic support in old age diminishes. Improved education and the emancipation and employment of women also reduce the birthrate, and so population growth begins to level off. Most rich nations have reached this stage, and their populations are growing only very slowly.

If this theory is right, there is an alternative to the disasters accepted as inevitable by supporters of triage. We can assist poor countries to raise the living standards of the poorest members of their population. We can encourage the governments of these countries to enact land reform measures, improve education, and liberate women from a purely child-bearing role. We can also help other countries to make contraception and sterilization widely available. There is a fair chance that these measures will hasten the onset of the demographic transition and bring population growth down to a manageable level. Success cannot be guaranteed; but the evidence that improved economic security and education reduce population growth is strong enough to make triage ethically unacceptable. We cannot allow millions to die from starvation and disease when there is a reasonable probability that population can be brought under control without such horrors.

Population growth is therefore not a reason against giving overseas aid, although it should make us think about the kind of aid to give. Instead of food handouts, it may be better to give aid that hastens the demographic transition. This may mean agricultural assistance for the rural poor, or assistance with education, or the provision of contraceptive services. Whatever kind of aid proves most effective in specific circumstances, the obligation to assist is not reduced.

One awkward question remains. What should we do about a poor and already overpopulated country which, for religious or nationalistic reasons, restricts the use of contraceptives and refuses to slow its population growth? Should we nevertheless offer development assistance? Or should we make our offer conditional on effective steps being taken to reduce the birthrate? To the latter course, some would object that putting conditions on aid is an attempt to impose our own ideas on independent sovereign nations. So it is—but is this imposition unjustifiable? If the argument for an obligation to assist is sound, we have an obligation to reduce absolute poverty; but we have no obligation to make sacrifices that, to the best of our knowledge, have no prospect of reducing poverty in the long run. Hence we have no obligation to assist countries whose governments have policies which will make our aid ineffective. This could be very harsh on poor citizens of these countries—for they may have no say in the government's policies—but we will help more people in the long run by using our resources where they are most effective.

ECONOMIC JUSTICE

Milton Fisk

Defenders of the capitalist form of society do not defend a right to economic equality. Economic inequality is, they argue, to everyone's advantage. Yet some of these defenders of capitalism are also supporters of liberal democracy. They must then recognize limits to economic inequality

From Milton Fisk, *Ethics and Society* 1980, pp. 224–235. Reprinted by permission of The Harvester Press, Ltd. and New York University Press.

beyond which even capitalism should not go. Vast concentrations of economic wealth are sources of political power that strangle the basic liberties of a democratic society. But many defenders of capitalist society maintain that in the US at least these limits to economic inequality have not been reached.

The purpose of this [paper] is to show that the arguments justifying the existing high degree of economic inequality fall apart. To show this it will not be necessary to defend, or to reject, the right to complete economic equality. Nonetheless, this [paper] points in an egalitarian direction. For it shows also that the degree of economic inequality inevitable within even a reformed capitalist society cannot be justified from the perspective of working-class morality.

1 ECONOMIC INEQUALITY

According to many writers on US society, the stage of widespread affluence has been reached within the US. There is, on the one hand, a reduced level of economic inequality, and there is, on the other hand, an elimination of the lower classes as a majority in favour of a large and prosperous middle class. The misery and inequality that characterized nineteeth- and early twentieth-century capitalism have been redeemed with the arrival of the 'affluent society'. This picture, however, conceals the urgent problem of economic inequality within the US. As Gabriel Kolko notes in his pathbreaking dissenting work on income distribution, 'The predominantly middle-class society is only an image in the minds of isolated academicians.'[1]

First let us look at the distribution of before-tax personal, as opposed to corporate, income during the period 1910–70 to get some idea as to whether there has been a significant trend toward equality. To do this we can consider families as broken up into five groups of equal size, ranging from those with the highest to those with the lowest income. (People living in families make up roughly 90 per cent of the US population.) *In the sixty-year period considered, families in the highest fifth received between 40 and 45 per cent of all family income.* That is, they received at least two times more than they would have if every family received the same income. Despite variations from year to year, there is no overall trend in this period toward a significantly smaller share of the national income for the richest fifth. The middle fifth has received between 15 and 18 per cent of all family income. This means that it received over the entire sixty-year period less than it would have if income were egalitarian. For this group the trend, within these narrow limits, has been for a slight rise in its share of income, but after World War II that rise stopped completely. Finally, what about the families in the poorest quintile? That group has received between 4 and 6 per cent of the national personal income, which runs up to five times less than it would receive under equality. The overall trend has been for families in this bottom group to get proportionately the same during the sixty-year period. As regards income in the US, then, there is significant and continuing inequality.[2] The top fifth as a whole takes six to ten times more of the national family income than does the bottom fifth. (Data for non-family persons shows even greater inequality.)

Our data has so far been taken on before-tax income. Will not taxation make the picture one of greater equality? It does change the picture as regards equality but only in an insignificant way. Many taxes are regressive: they are a larger fraction of lower than of higher incomes. Social security taxes, property taxes, and sales taxes are all regressive. It cannot be expected that these would provide a shift toward equality. But even the federal income tax, which is progressive, has failed to do more than decrease by two per cent the share of national income of the top fifth. The increase in the share of the bottom fifth resulting from federal income taxes has remained a fraction of a per cent. Moreover, the percentage of all taxes coming from the non-owning classes has been rising steadily since World War II. Taxes have, then, failed to equalize income significantly.[3]

We are dealing with a society in which private ownership of the means of production is a fundamental feature. Some personal income comes from ownership, to be sure, but one cannot say exactly how wealth is distributed simply on the basis of knowing how income is distributed. For one thing, a significant but variable share of returns from ownership is invested in new means of production and does not appear as dividend income. Nonetheless, in a capitalist society we can predict that wealth, like income, is unevenly distributed. It is highly concentrated in the hands of a very few owners: they own the plants, the trucks, the warehouses, the mines, the office buildings, the large estates, and the objects of art. The poor are often net holders of 'negative wealth' because of their debts. *Between* 1810 *and* 1969, *the concentration of wealth has remained remarkably constant; the top one per cent as regards wealth has held between* 20 *and* 30 *per cent of all the wealth in the US.* In 1962 the poorest 20 per cent held less than one-half of one per cent of the nation's wealth.[4]

Nonetheless, some currency has been given to the view that corporate ownership has become widespread and that workers are now significant owners. Stock ownership is, indeed, more widespread, but this has not seriously affected the high degree of concentration of stock ownership in the hands of the wealthiest.

By 1962, the wealthiest one per cent of the population still held 72 per cent of the nation's corporate stock. In that year, the wealthiest one per cent also held 48 per cent of the nation's bonds, 24 per cent of the loans, and 16 per cent of the real estate.[5] Clearly then wealth is even less equitably distributed than income in the US, and the inequality has been one of long duration. Pensions for workers account for nearly ten per cent of corporate stock. This may provide workers with security after retirement, but it does not give them the power of wealth holders. The reason is that they have no control over these pension funds, which merely add power to the financial institutions that manage them. . . .

A large prosperous middle class has by no means replaced the struggling lower classes as the majority class. With more than half of the people living below the modest but adequate budget of the BLS, the underbelly of US capitalist society is a deprived majority, just as it was fifty years ago. 'In advanced capitalist societies, the costs of staying out of poverty (i.e. of satisfying invariant subsistence needs) grows as the economy grows. Consequently, there is no long-term tendency in advanced capitalist societies for the incidence of poverty to decrease significantly as the economy grows.'[6] The economic inequality of US society is not just relative inequality, for it is an inequality that means deprivation for a sizeable chunk of the society.

2 OWNERSHIP AND PRODUCTIVITY

There are several strategies used by spokespersons of the ruling class to defend the situation of inequality described above. The first defence rests on the rights of ownership. The second rests on the need for inequality in order to increase productivity. In the next section, a third strategy will be discussed: it rests on the notion of a fair wage.

According to the *first defence* of inequality, those who have put their hard-earned money into a business enterprise have the right to appropriate the fruits of that enterprise and divide them according to their own decisions. Thus the product that workers have made is controlled by owners and not by the workers. Owners are within their rights to divide the product in such a way that inequality is great and poverty widespread. An entire web of ideology has been woven on this basic frame of the rights of ownership. Part of that web is the system of law, backed by police force, entitling the owner to the fruits of the worker. From the perspective of members of the working class, there are several holes in this defence. These holes show that what is built on the frame of ownership rights is indeed only ideology.

On the one hand, if ownership rights lead to continued inequality and poverty, then from a working-class perspective there simply are no such rights. The attitude that ownership of the means of production is sacred merely protects the owners at the expense of those who suffer the resulting inequality. A right is more than such an attitude; it must be justified and indeed justified from a class standpoint. Economic inequality can be justified by ownership rights only if there are such rights. There may well be such rights from the perspective of the ruling class. Yet the continued inequality and poverty resulting from ownership are evidence favouring the view that relative to the working class owners have no legitimate right to the fruits of enterprise.

On the other hand, the basis given for the justification of the owner's right to the fruits of enterprise is not adequate. That basis was the hard work of the investor. Investment, however, is an on-going process in a viable firm. The initial investment is followed by many subsequent investments. Let us grant that the owner has worked hard—whether in the form of the honest toil of the self-employed person or in the form of the forcible plunder of the syndicated criminal—to accumulate the initial investment. But when the plant is rebuilt or expanded, the new investment will be possible only because of the hard work of the workers. Once new investment has been made, there is no longer the same basis for saying that the original owner has the right to control the entire product of the new investment. The logic of 'hard work' applies here too. If the owner worked hard to accumulate the initial investment, it is equally true that the workers worked hard to make the new investment possible. Thus, in a viable firm, the workers should, on the logic of hard work, have a right to appropriate an ever increasing share of the product. The capitalist's own logic backfires! . . .

According to the *second defence* of inequality, significant inequality with poverty at the bottom is a necessary condition for making the society as affluent as it is. In a widely published newspaper article entitled 'Morality and the Pursuit of Wealth' appearing in July 1974, the President of the US Chamber of Commerce, Arch Booth, said the realization of equality by the transfer of wealth from the haves to the have-nots would lessen the 'work incentive of the most productive members of society' and endanger 'the ability of the economic system to accumulate capital for new productive facilities'. Booth's solution is to let the rich keep on investing in productive facilities thereby increasing the share the poor get through better wages and higher employment.

There is one glaring fallacy in this argument. It is the logical fallacy of an 'incomplete disjunction'. The disjunction Booth offers us is that *either* we have a forced redistribution of income within capitalism *or* we let the income of the non-owners rise naturally by increasing investment. But the disjunction needs to be expanded to include at least one more alternative: beyond capitalism, it is possible to expand productive facilities through the investment of collective rather than of private capital. In one form of collective ownership, workers would manage the investment of collective capital in order to advance their interests. In this case, the inequality in both wealth and income needed for growth under private capitalism becomes unnecessary. Without significant inequality, private capitalism would lack the centres of economic power needed to put large amounts of labour to work in order to produce a surplus for growth. The model here for a system of collective ownership of the means of production is not that of nationalized industry run by a bunch of officials who are not controlled by workers. This would be the bureaucratic model found in places like the USSR which are no longer private capitalist societies. Rather, the model is that of a workers' democracy in which democracy extends down to the workplace and in which workplaces are coordinated by a council of representatives from each. This socialist alternative is sufficient to make Booth's disjunction incomplete. . . .

3 A Fair Wage

A *third strategy* for defending the inequality and the poverty that is to be found today in the US introduces the concept of compensation for work. The defence is that labour is sold on the free market and, on the whole, the free market determines a *just* price for things. Thus, since inequality and poverty are, in part, a result of the free market for labour, there is no *right* to economic equality or even to a 'modest budget'. A free market must not involve the use of power by those who exchange their goods and services within it to coerce those with whom they exchange.

This argument seems to leave open the possibility that wages should mount and thus that the worker should come closer to the owner in economic status. But in fact this possibility is not open. As pointed out in Section I, the range of inequality and the degree of poverty in the US have remained remarkably constant. The majority of the people are at or below the level of existence provided by the modest budget. Because of the greater power and organization of the owning class, the wages and salaries of workers remain at a level that allows them merely to perform their jobs well and to raise a new generation of workers. (Differences between the wages of, say, industrial and clerical workers need to be viewed against the background of a general pull toward this subsistence level.) To perform well and to reproduce themselves they have been forced to purchase the ever more elaborate and hence more expensive means of satisfying survival needs and the needs specific to their jobs. Short-term variations in the supply of and demand for labour are only part of this long-term pattern of compensating workers at a subsistence level. At this level, there is nothing much left over for savings and investments that might narrow the gap between them and the owning class. . . .

What, then, is a fair wage from the perspective of the working class? Suppose we are calves who face the prospect of going to slaughter as one-year olds. The farmers who send us to slaughter find that this is the age at which to realize a maximum profit on us. So one year is the 'fair' time, from the perspective of the farmers, for calves to enjoy themselves before slaughter. An inquisitive calf poses the question, 'What is the true "fair" time for cattle to live before slaughter? Is it two years, or even three?' A selfish calf who has no regard for the farmer and the future of cattle farming generally shouts, 'Stop quibbling; we should demand a moratorium on beef eating. An end to the slaughter of cattle!' Similarly, Marx said that the slogan, 'A fair day's wage for a fair day's work!' should be replaced by the slogan, 'An end to the wage system!'[7] Instead of the wage system, work should be done in such a way that the workers' compensation is not just a function of the greater power of a non-working ruling class.

The wage system is a system that in advanced industrial countries has been central to the domination of lower classes by a ruling class. Through that system people are set to work in order to preserve or increase the control of wealth by and, thus, the power of a minority class. They are thus given from what they produce only what is needed to reproduce their labour. When part of the product of workers is used in this way to perpetuate and strengthen the domination of a non-working class, workers are properly said to be 'exploited'. Acceptance of the wage system and plans to reform it from within do not face up to the key role wages play in domination. When workers themselves decide how they are to be compensated out of what they produce, the wage system has ceased to exist and along with it exploitation. . . .

The struggle for higher income begins the organization of people for the collective action that is needed to abolish the wage system itself. This long-term perspective has for some time been forgotten by trade unions everywhere. Their leaders advocate accommodation with the existing system of domination of working people. These leaders talk about a fair wage but they mean only the wages and benefits they think they can wheedle out of the owners. Their conception of fairness and of rights is no longer a class conception. A class conception makes overthrowing the wage system a right of working people.

4 A Just Distribution

Let us leave defences of present economic inequality and take up a proposal for limiting inequality. If capitalist arguments justifying present inequality fail, then where is the line to be drawn for an acceptable degree of inequality? Our problem is how to distribute a product that has come about through the combined efforts of people in different roles. Since isolated producers are the exception, we cannot start with the assumption that there is a product to which an individual producer is 'entitled' because he or she is 'responsible' for that product.[8] In deciding on a principle of just distribution there are two factors to be considered.

On the one hand, there is the average amount of goods per individual in the population, and, on the other hand, there is the degree of inequality with which goods are actually parceled out to individuals. Increasing the average amount of goods per individual might increase the inequality of distribution, whereas decreasing the inequality in distribution might decrease the average per individual. In capitalism we saw that inequality of wealth is a condition of economic growth. Also, inequality of income within the working class weakens solidarity, making possible a greater surplus and hence greater growth. If strict equality means poverty all around, we might recoil from strict equality and look for a balance between a large average amount and considerable equality. But so far we have no clue as to where to strike this balance.

John Rawls has recently proposed an interesting way of balancing a high average amount of goods with a low degree of inequality.[9] The idea is that we are to avoid demanding such a low degree of inequality that the worst off are penalized by getting less than they would with a higher degree of inequality. We are to avoid only those high degrees of inequality that are arrived at by preventing the worst off from getting the most they could get.

Rawls formulated this in his Principle of Difference which tells us to 'maximize the expectations of the least favoured position'. . . .

[But] Rawls talks about distribution without relating it to production. He assumes wrongly that the validity of his principle is absolute, rather than relative to circumstances within production. One thing is certain: in capitalist society there is not the least chance that the Rawlsian scheme could be put into practice. The reason is simply that the organization of production in a capitalist society centres around increasing productive facilities through the making of profits. The class of owners would not advance the interests characteristic of their class by agreeing to maximize the expectations of the least favoured. Given its power, this class would block the realization of the scheme.

Suppose, though, that some mode of production would allow for distribution in accordance with the Principle of Difference. Should not one simply choose to bring about such a mode of production? Certainly—if the Principle of Difference is valid. But its validity is relative to production in the following way. Validity in general is relative to classes, and classes are essential roles in a given mode of production. One should, then, choose to realize the principle only if it is valid relative to one's class. Nonetheless, that class might have to change the existing mode of production in order to realize the new distribution. Even though the capitalist mode of production excludes the application of the Principle of Difference, it may be a valid principle for one of the lower classes within capitalism.

A distributional plan is not just because it is elegant or intuitive but because it answers to needs arising in production. Not only the actual but also the just distribution is dependent on production.

Notes

1. Gabriel Kolko, *Wealth and Power in America* (Praeger, New York, 1962), p. 108.
2. These data are based on tables in Kolko, *Wealth and Power in America*, p. 14, and in Frank Ackerman and Andrew Zimbalist, "Capitalism and inequality in the United States," in *The Capitalist System*, 2nd ed., p. 298.
3. Kolko, *Wealth and Power in America*, Ch. II, and Ackerman and Zimbalist "Capitalism and inequality in the United States," in *The Capitalist System*, 2nd ed., p. 303. In Sweden, by contrast, taxes change the ratio of the bottom third to that of the top third from 38 to 48 percent.
4. Lititia Upton and Nancy Lyons, *Basic Facts: Distribution of Personal Income and Wealth in the United States* (Cambridge Institute, 1878 Massachusetts Ave., Cambridge, Mass., 1972), p. 6, and Ackerman and Zimbalist, "Capitalism and inequality in the United States," in *The Capitalist System*, 2nd ed., p. 301.
5. Upton and Lyons, *Basic Facts*, p. 31.
6. Bernard Gendron, "Capitalism and poverty," *Radical Philosophers' Newsjournal*, 4, January 1975, p. 13. This essay appears as Ch. XII of Gendron's *Technology and the Human Condition* (St. Martin's Press, New York, 1977).
7. Karl Marx, *Wages, Price, and Profit* (1865) (Foreign Language Press, Peking, 1970), Ch. XIV.
8. On entitlement, see Robert Nozick, *Anarchy, State, and Utopia* (Basic Books, New York, 1974), Ch. VII.
9. Rawls, *A Theory of Justice*, pp. 78–80.

case 1: Ashland Oil

President Carter shut off oil imports from Iran in November, 1979, in reaction to the taking of 52 American hostages in the American Embassy in Tehran. Only a few months prior to this, Iran had agreed to supply 25 percent of Ashland Oil Company's crude oil needs. That oil was crucial to Ashland, the largest independent refiner in the United States, since the company had begun selling off its own producing properties in 1978 and using the $1.2 billion of receipts for a diversification program.

Most refiners responded to the Iranian shutoff by purchasing their shortages of crude on the spot market at $40 per barrel. Ashland, on the other hand, went to the Department of Energy's Office of Hearings and Appeals (OHA) and threatened to shut down its 69,000 barrel-a-day refinery in St. Paul. This action posed the threat of inadequate heating for many residents during the coming winter. The OHA quickly ordered nine integrated companies to sell Ashland the needed crude, setting the price at $31.24 per barrel.

One of the companies ordered to sell to Ashland was Marathon, which had purchased much of Ashland's crude only the month before at a price of $37.15 a barrel. It was this same oil that Marathon was now ordered to resell to Ashland for $31.24 per barrel, creating a $3.5 million loss. Marathon complied with the order, but then sued the Department of Energy in federal court on the grounds that the order to sell was an unconstitutional taking of property.

A spokesman for Ashland had said prior to this incident that because the company was such a big factor in some local markets, "We're confident that we'll be able to purchase enough crude to service our capacity, and if we can't the government will step in and allocate."

Questions

1. What are the implications of this incident as they regard free market allocation versus governmental allocation of resources?
2. We often hear that businessmen prefer less government involvement in the allocation of resources. What does this incident indicate regarding this line of thought?
3. Was Marathon treated unjustly? If so, according to which theory of justice?
4. What action would the libertarian account of justice suggest in this case?

The facts for this case were found in the following article: Tom Alexander, "Day of Reckoning for Oil Refiners," *Fortune* (January 12, 1981), pp. 38–41. The case was prepared by Professor Charles W. Boyd of Southwest Missouri State University as a basis for class discussion rather than to illustrate either effective or ineffective handling of an administrative situation. Copyright 1981 by Charles W. Boyd, Ph.D., and reprinted with permission of the author.

case 2: Baseball Economics

On Wednesday, December 9, 1981 the Baltimore Orioles' great pitcher, Jim Palmer, gave a newspaper interview in Portland, Oregon. He was highly critical of the system of economic incentives in baseball. He argued that money now controlled almost all decisions by management and players alike, and many players, he said, "make a lot more money than they should." The salaries are often determined through "panic" on the part of management, he said, which plans at all cost against a situation in which star players leave and join other teams at increased salary levels. He noted that players now make $300,000–400,000 in their second year, and sign multi-year contracts. This kind of security, he argued, leads players to relax and lose their concentration on skilled performance.[1]

On the same day that Palmer gave his interview in Portland, Baseball Commissioner Bowie Kuhn was testifying before a Congressional Subcommittee on courts, civil liberties, and the administration of justice on issues surrounding cable television. Kuhn described the possible introduction of massive cable television broadcasts of baseball as economically intolerable for the sport. Both gate receipts and network television revenues would decline, he held, and this would be a disaster for a sport already "treading on financial quicksand." Kuhn supported this judgment with figures to show that only nine of baseball's twenty-six teams had made a profit in the previous year. He argued that the aggregate loss was $25 million. He further argued that cable television would bring competing sporting events into a city without the consent or agreement of anyone in baseball management.

Ted Turner, who owns both Turner Broadcasting System (cable television) and the Atlanta Braves baseball team, also testified at the same time as Kuhn. "If baseball is in trouble," he said, "it is because they are paying the baseball players a million and a half dollars a year." From Turner's perspective, "there isn't one single example of a proven economic harm from cable television. They just want total control to the detriment of the American public." Replied Kuhn, "We were prepared to negotiate with the cable people, but they had no interest."[2]

The National Basketball Association endorsed Kuhn's views in full.

Notes

1. See "Money Has Changed the Game," *Baltimore Sun* (Thursday, December 10, 1981), Sports Section, p. 1.
2. See "Kuhn Hits Cable T.V.," *The Washington Post* (Thursday, December 10, 1981), Sports Section, p. 1.

Questions

1. If Jim Palmer were claiming that players' high salaries constitute an injustice in the American economic system, would he be right? Would Nozick agree with your answer?
2. Do Bowie Kuhn's comments derive from a libertarian or utilitarian theory of justice? Does he stand opposed to a pure free-market conception of justice?
3. If Peter Singer's proposals were followed, what would be the obligations of major league baseball players to help the poor both within and outside of their own country? Is this a Marxist theory in disguise as utilitarianism?
4. Would it be unjust to place a baseball player making 1 1/2 million dollars per year in a 70 percent tax bracket? Would it be unjust to place anyone in business in a 70 percent bracket?

case 3: Libby, McNeil, & Libby on Cyclamates

In 1969 the Food and Drug Administration banned cyclamates, a sweetening agent, from the market. As with later controversies about saccharin, the evidence as to the dangers presented by cyclamates were much discussed at the time. What some persons regarded as telling animal studies were regarded by others as inconclusive. Nonetheless, by FDA criteria cyclamates presented an unacceptable level of risk. (For further analysis of the notion of acceptable and unacceptable risk, see Chapters 3 and 8 in this text.)

Over the next sixteen months, Libby, McNeil, & Libby sold approximately 300,000 cases of cyclamate-sweetened fruit to customers in West Germany, Spain, and other countries. James Nadler, Libby's vice-president for international business, was quoted by *The Wall Street Journal* as giving the following justification for the sales: "Fortunately the older civilizations of the world are more deliberate about judging momentary fads that are popular in the United States from time to time."[1] *The Wall Street Journal* article went on to note that such sales are commonly considered acceptable practice in American business. The *Journal* cited such products as Parke, Davis, & Co.'s Chloromycetin and Merck's Indocin, both of which are marketed abroad without the cumbersome warnings as to side effects that are required in the United States.

Elsewhere in this same *Journal* issue it was noted that this traffic is not simply unilateral from the United States. A number of drugs produced by Ciba-Geigy, Ltd., are banned in Sweden but marketed in the United States. Of course in all cases these drugs could not be marketed unless there were at least an implicit recognition and acceptance within the country into which they are imported.

In direct reply to vice-president Nadler's comment on cyclamates, Robert L. Heilbroner offered the following critical comment: "The momentary fad to which [Nadler] was referring was the upshot of nineteen years of increasingly alarming laboratory findings concerning the effects of cyclamates on chick embryos—effects that produced grotesque malformations similar to those induced by thalidomide."[2]

Notes

1. *The Wall Street Journal* (February 11, 1971).
2. Robert L. Heilbroner, "Controlling the Corporation," in *In the Name of Profit*, Robert L. Heilbroner, et al. (Garden City, N.Y.: Doubleday and Co., Inc., 1972). Heilbroner relies on evidence discussed in James Turner, *The Chemical Feast* (New York: 1970), p. 12.

Questions

1. Does Heilbroner seem to be accusing Libby of an injustice in marketing its product? If so, is it an implicit appeal to a utilitarian conception of justice?
2. Do you think Singer would agree with Heilbroner?
3. What might Nozick and Narveson say about Libby's actions in this case?
4. Should drug companies print the above-mentioned warnings when marketing their products abroad? If so, does justice demand that they do so?

case 4: AT&T Hiring and Promotion

In January of 1971, the Equal Employment Opportunity Commission (EEOC) brought charges of discrimination in hiring and promotion against AT&T. The EEOC filed a petition to block a rate increase of $385 million per year until the company ended its discriminatory practices. The petition alleged that job bias at AT&T kept rates from declining.

AT&T denied the charges, claiming that its record demonstrated equality of treatment for minorities and women. The company adduced statistics showing that (1) one-fourth of all employees hired from 1969 to 1971 were black, American Indian, oriental, or Hispanic; (2) while total employment since 1963 increased by 38 percent, the number of minority employees jumped by 265 percent; (3) 12.4 percent of the work force came from minority groups, a figure higher than the proportion of minorities in the United States population; (4) 55 percent of people on the payroll were women, and 33 percent of management positions were held by women. These statistics were marshaled to draw the conclusion that the company was in no respect guilty of the alleged injustices.

AT&T produced 100,000 pages of documents and statistics in support of these contentions, and the EEOC filed 30,000 pages of counterargument. The EEOC claimed that customers would pay lower phone rates if AT&T ended its discriminatory practices and that if AT&T had operated to minimize labor costs

This case was prepared originally by Sara Finnerty Kelly, and modified by Tom L. Beauchamp. Copyright 1982 by Applied Philosophy, Inc., and reprinted with permission.

(i.e., if it had employed workers at the lowest possible wage regardless of sex), the company would have employed more women in all job categories, for a total reduction in rates of 2 to 4 percent.

While the EEOC pursued its charges, divisions arose between leaders of the Communications Workers of America and female members of that union. Many of these women union members remained on strike against the instructions of union officials because they were displeased with the settlement between union and management. While that settlement called for a 31 percent increase in wages and benefits over three years, it did not ensure *equal* pay for women.[1] A government study gave support to the women's charges of economic discrimination.[2]

AT&T eventually settled with EEOC out of court. The main provision was that AT&T would rectify past unjust treatment by paying lump sums of money, totaling $15 million, to 13,000 of its female and 2,000 of its male employees, and would grant $23 million in pay increases to 36,000 workers who had suffered injustice through job discrimination. Management agreed to alter the patterns of hiring and to upgrade female and minority employees. The stipulations of the settlement were met by the company before an established 1979 deadline. Virtually all parties were doubtful, however, that justice had actually been achieved through this settlement.[3]

Notes

1. The female craft workers formerly earned 62 percent as much as the male craft workers, and the settlement proposed a reduction in that differential of only 3 percent. Women claimed that though 55 percent of the work force was female, the starting salaries for women were $30 per week less than for men in 96 percent of the cases.

2. This study (by the Federal Commerce Commission) indicated that (1) women lost $950 million annually in wages because discriminatory practices kept them in low-paying jobs; (2) blacks lost $225 million in wages in the nation as a whole because AT&T did not hire them in numbers proportionate to their percentage in the population; (3) Spanish-surnamed Americans lost $137 million for the same reasons. The EEOC argued that AT&T systematically channeled women into operator jobs and men into management positions. It showed that 99 percent of all operators were female, while only 1 percent of craft workers were female.

3. Sources for this case include the following: "AT&T Denies Job Discrimination Charges, Claims Firm Is Equal Employment Leader," *Wall Street Journal* (Dec. 14, 1970), p. 6; "AT&T Makes Reparation," *The Economist*, 246 (Jan. 27, 1973), p. 42; Byron Calame, "Liberating Ma Bell: Female Telephone Workers Hit Labor Pact, Say Men Still Get the Best Jobs, More Pay," *Wall Street Journal* (July 26, 1971), p. 22; "FCC Orders Hearing on Charge that AT&T Discriminates in Hiring." *Wall Street Journal* (Jan 22, 1971), p. 10; "Federal Agency Says AT&T Job Bias Keeps Rates From Declining," *Wall Street Journal* (Dec. 2, 1971), p. 21; Richard M. Hodgetts, "AT&T versus the Equal Employment Opportunity Commission," in his *The Business Enterprise: Social Challenge, Social Response* (Philadelphia: W. B. Saunders Company, 1977), pp. 176–182.

Questions

1. If this case presents a problem of justice, do the issues involve questions of economic justice about whole economic systems?
2. What might a Marxist observe about this case? Would the libertarian wholly disagree?
3. Is there any room in Nozick's libertarian system, or in Narveson's theory, for defending the EEOC regulatory actions?
4. Have the women and blacks mentioned in this case been unfairly treated? If so, is it because they have been unequally treated? Are they among the classes of persons Rawls has in mind in developing his second principle of justice? Does the "principle of redress" that he mentions apply to this case?
5. Is the eventual outcome in this case justifiable from a utilitarian point of view?

SUGGESTED SUPPLEMENTARY READINGS

Concepts and Principles of Justice

BENN, STANLEY I. "Justice," in Paul Edwards, ed., *The Encyclopedia of Philosophy.* New York: Macmillan Company and Free Press, 1967, vol. 4, pp. 298–302.

BOWIE, NORMAN E. *Towards a New Theory of Distributive Justice.* Amherst: University of Massachusetts Press, 1971.

———, and ROBERT L. SIMON. *The Individual and the Political Order.* Englewood Cliffs, N.J.: Prentice-Hall, 1977. Chapter 7.

FEINBERG, JOEL. "Justice and Personal Desert," in Carl J. Friedrich and John W. Chapman, eds., *Nomos 6: Justice.* New York: Atherton Press, 1963, pp. 68–97.

———. *Social Philosophy.* Englewood Cliffs, N.J.: Prentice-Hall, Inc., 1973, chap. 7.

FRANKENA, W. L. "Some Beliefs about Justice," in K. E. Goodpaster, ed., *Perspectives on Morality: Essays of William K. Frankena.* Notre Dame, Ind.: University of Notre Dame Press, 1976, pp. 93–106.

PERELMAN, CHARLES. *Justice.* New York: Random House, 1967.

PETTIT, PHILIP. *Judging Justice.* London: Routledge & Kegan Paul, 1980.

RESCHER, NICHOLAS. *Distributive Justice.* Indianapolis: Bobbs-Merrill Company, Inc., 1966.

STERBA, JAMES. *The Demands of Justice.* Notre Dame, Ind.: University of Notre Dame Press, 1980.

———, ed. *Justice: Alternative Political Perspectives.* Belmont, Calif.: Wadsworth Publishing Company, Inc., 1980.

Egalitarian Theories

BARRY, BRIAN. *The Liberal Theory of Justice, a Critical Examination of the Principal Doctrines in a Theory of Justice by John Rawls.* Oxford, England: Clarendon Press, 1973.

BLOCKER, H. GENE, and ELIZABETH SMITH, eds. *John Rawls' Theory of Social Justice: An Introduction.* Athens: Ohio University Press, 1980.

DANIELS, NORMAN, ed. *Reading Rawls: Critical Studies of a Theory of Justice.* New York: Basic Books, Inc., Publishers, 1975.

GAUTHIER, DAVID. "Justice and Natural Endowment: Toward a Critique of Rawls' Ideological Framework," *Social Theory and Practice, 3* (1974), 3–26.

LEKACHMAN, ROBERT. "Economic Justice in Hard Times," in A. L. Caplan and D. Callahan, eds. *Ethics in Hard Times.* New York: Plenum Press, 1981, pp. 91–116.

MACINTYRE, ALASDAIR. "Justice: A New Theory and Some Old Questions," *Boston University Law Review, 52* (1972): 330–334.

McCLOSKEY, HERBERT J. "Egalitarianism, Equality and Justice," *Australasian Journal of Philosophy, 44* (1966), 50–69.

NAGEL, THOMAS. "Equality," in *Mortal Questions.* Cambridge, England: Cambridge University Press, 1979.

RAWLS, JOHN. "Reply to Alexander and Musgrave," *Quarterly Journal of Economics*, **88** (1974), 633–655.

———. "Kantian Constructivism In Moral Theory: The Dewey Lectures 1980," *Journal of Philosophy*, **77** (1980), 515–572.

VLASTOS, GREGORY. "Justice and Equality," in Richard B. Brandt, ed., *Social Justice*. Englewood Cliffs, N.J.: Prentice-Hall, Inc., 1962.

Libertarian Theories

DWORKIN, GERALD, GORDON BERMANT, and PETER G. BROWN, eds. *Markets and Morals*. Washington: Hemisphere Publishing Corp., John Wiley, 1977.

FRIEDMAN, MILTON. *Capitalism and Freedom*. Chicago: University of Chicago Press, 1962.

HAYEK, FRIEDRICH. *Individualism and Economic Order*. Chicago: University of Chicago Press, 1948.

———. Law, Legislation, and Liberty. Vol. 2 in *The Mirage of Social Justice*. Chicago: University of Chicago Press, 1976.

HELD, VIRGINIA. "John Locke on Robert Nozick," *Social Research*, 43 (Spring 1976), pp. 169–195.

LOEVINSOHN, ERNEST. "Liberty and the Redistribution of Property," *Philosophy and Public Affairs*, 6 (1977), pp. 226–39.

LYONS, DAVID. "Rights Against Humanity," *Philosophical Review*, **85,** (1976), 208–215.

MACK, ERIC. "Liberty and Justice," in John Arthur and William Shaw, eds., *Justice and Economic Distribution*. Englewood Cliffs, N.J.: Prentice-Hall, Inc., 1978, pp. 83–93.

PAUL, JEFFREY, ed. *Reading Nozick: Essays on Anarchy, State, and Utopia*. Totowa, N.J.: Rowman & Littlefield, 1981.

SCANLON, THOMAS M. "Nozick on Rights, Liberty, and Property," *Philosophy and Public Affairs*, 6 (1976), pp. 3–25.

Utilitarian Theories

BECKER, EDWARD F. "Justice, Utility, and Interpersonal Comparison," *Theory and Decision*, **6** (1975), 471–484.

BRAYBROOKE, DAVID. "Utilitarianism with a Difference: Rawls' Position in Ethics," *Canadian Journal of Philosophy*, 3 (1973), 303–331.

BROCK, DAN W. "Contractualism, Utilitarianism, and Social Inequalities," *Social Theory and Practice*, 1 (1971), 33–44.

———. "Recent Work in Utilitarianism," *American Philosophical Quarterly*, 10 (1973), 241–276.

GOLDMAN, ALAN H. "Business Ethics: Profits, Utilities, and Moral Rights," *Philosophy and Public Affairs*, 9 (1980), pp. 260–86.

LYONS, DAVID. "Rawls versus Utilitarianism," *Journal of Philosophy*, **69** (1972), 535–545.

MILL, JOHN STUART. In A. D. Lindsay, ed., *Utilitarianism; On Liberty; Representative Government*. London: E. P. Dutton & Co., 1976.

SARTORIUS, ROLF. *Individual Conduct and Social Norms.* Encino, Calif: Dickenson Publishing Co., 1975, chap. 7.

SINGER, PETER. "The Right to Be Rich or Poor," *New York Review of Books,* 6 (March 1976), pp. 19–24.

———. "Famine, Affluence, and Morality," *Philosophy and Public Affairs,* 1 (1972).

TAYLOR, PAUL W. "Justice and Utility," *Canadian Journal of Philosophy,* 1 (1972), pp. 327–350.

Socialist and Marxist Theories

COHEN, G. A. "The Labor Theory of Value and the Concept of Exploitation," *Philosophy and Public Affairs,* 8 (1979), pp. 338–360.

DALTON, GEORGE. *Economic Systems and Society: Capitalism, Communism, and the Third World.* Baltimore: Penguin Books, 1974.

ENGELS, FRIEDRICH. "Socialism: Utopian and Scientific," reprinted in Arthur Mendel, ed., *Essential Works of Marxism.* New York: Bantam Books, Inc., 1961, pp. 45–82.

GALLIE, W. B. "Liberal Morality and Socialist Morality," in Peter Laslett, ed., *Philosophy, Politics, and Society.* Oxford, England: Blackwell Press, 1956, pp. 116–133.

HARRINGTON, MICHAEL. *Socialism.* New York: Bantam Books, Inc., 1973.

———. *The Twilight of Capitalism.* New York: Simon & Schuster, Inc., 1977.

MACPHERSON, C. B. *The Life and Times of Liberal Democrats.* New York: Oxford University Press, 1977.

MARX, KARL. *Economic and Philosophical Manuscripts,* in T. B. Bottomore, ed., *Karl Marx: Early Writings.* London: C. A. Watts & Co., Ltd., 1963.

MILBRAND, RALPH. *Marxism and Rights.* Oxford: Oxford University Press, 1977.

MILLER, DAVID. *Social Justice.* Oxford, England: Clarendon Press, 1976.

Some Applications

ACTON, H. B. *The Morals of Markets: An Ethical Exploration.* London: Longman Group Limited, 1971.

AIKEN, WILLIAM, and HUGH LaFOLLETTE. *World Hunger and Moral Obligation.* Englewood Cliffs, N.J.: Prentice-Hall, 1978.

ARTHUR, JOHN, and WILLIAM H. SHAW, eds. *Justice and Economic Distribution.* Englewood Cliffs, N.J.: Prentice-Hall, Inc., 1978.

BRANDT, R. B. "The Concept of Welfare," in *Talking About Welfare: Readings in Philosophy and Public Policy,* ed. Noel Timms and David Watson. London: Routledge and Kegan Paul, 1976.

CHAMBERLAIN, NEIL W. *The Place of Business in America's Future: A Study in Social Values.* New York: Basic Books, 1973.

DOBB, MAURICE. *Political Economy and Capitalism.* Westport, Conn.: Greenwood Press, 1972.

HAHN, FRANK, and MARTIN HOLLIS, eds. *Philosophy and Economic Theory.* Oxford: Oxford Unversity Press, 1979.

HELD, VIRGINIA, ed. *Property, Profits, and Economic Justice.* Belmont, Calif.: Wadsworth Publishing Company, Inc., 1980.

PHELPS, EDMUND S., ed. *Economic Justice.* Baltimore: Penguin Books, Inc., 1973.

Philosophical Forum, 10 (Nos. 2-4, 1978-1979). Special Issues on "Work."

THUROW, LESTER. *The Zero Sum Society.* New York: Basic Books, 1980.

SEN, AMARTYA. *On Economic Inequality.* Oxford: Clarendon Press, 1973.